Supervision

Third Edition

in Canada Today

Stephen P. ROBBINS

San Diego State University

David A. DE CENZO

Towson State University

Joan L. CONDIE

Sheridan College

Laurie KONDO

Sheridan College

Toronto

Canadian Cataloguing in Publication Data

Supervision in Canada today

3rd ed.
First ed. by Stephen P. Robbins, Joan L. Condie, Laurie C. Kondo.
Includes index.
ISBN 0-13-028642-7

1. Supervision of employees.   I. Robbins, Stephen P., 1943 -   .

HF5549.12.R62 2002   658.3'02   C00-933129-8

Copyright © 2002, 1998, 1995 Pearson Education Canada, a division of Pearson Canada Inc., Toronto, Ontario

Original edition published by Prentice-Hall, Inc., a division of Pearson Education, Upper Saddle River, NJ. Copyright © 2001 by Prentice Hall, Inc. This edition is authorized for sale in Canada only.

All Rights Reserved. This publication is protected by copyright, and permission should be obtained from the publisher prior to any prohibited reproduction, storage in a retrieval system, or transmission in any form or by any means, electronic, mechanical, photocopying, recording, or likewise. For information regarding permission, write to the Permissions Department.

0-13-028642-7

Vice President, Editorial Director: Michael Young
Acquisitions Editor: Samantha Scully
Marketing Manager: James Buchanan
Associate Editor: Susanne Marshall
Production Editor: Gillian Scobie
Copy Editor: Dianne Broad
Production Coordinator: Janette Lush
Page Layout: Prime Imaging and Typography
Permissions/Photo Research: Susan Wallace-Cox
Art Director: Mary Opper
Interior Design: Lisa LaPointe
Cover Image and Design: Lisa LaPointe

10 11 12 DPC 08 07 06

Printed and bound in Canada.

Photo Credits

No.	Source
Ch 1 opener	Tony Savino/The Image Works
1-1	Fatema Pirbhai
1-2	Brad Aie
1-3	Doug Bailey
1-7	Larry Clarke
1-8	Joan Condie
1-9	Joan Condie
1-10	Doug Bailey
1-11	Ron Mactavish
1-12	Pamela Gaspar
1-13	Brad Aie
1-16	Heather Barr
2-1	Fatema Pirbhai
2-2	Mathiesen & Hewitt Photographers Ltd.
Ch 3 opener	Michael Barley / Michael Barley Photography
3-1	Joan Condie
3-11	PhotoDisc, Inc.
3-14	Bob Daemmrich/Uniphoto Picture Agency
3-15	Fatema Pirbhai
3-16	Joan Condie
Ch 4 opener	Bob Daemmrich / Stock Boston Inc.
4-1	Pamela Gaspar
4-3	Harris Corporation
4-7	Churchill Falls Labrador Corporation
4-11	PhotoDisc, Inc.
4-14	Bettye Lanza/Photo Researchers Inc.
4-16	John Feingersh/Uniphoto Picture Agency
4-17	Gemma Di Giovanni
4-18	Gemma Di Giovanni
Ch 5 opener	R. Lord/The Image Works
5-1	Mathiesen & Hewitt Photographers Ltd.
5-2	Xerox
5-3	R. Lord/The Image Works
5-5	Gerry Gropp / Sipa
5-13	Pamela Gaspar
5-19	Mathiesen & Hewitt Photographers Ltd.
Ch 6 opener	Mike Surowiak/Tony Stone Images
6-1	Bob Daemmrich / Stock Boston Inc.
6-3	Robert Scott
6-4	Manpower Inc.
Ch 7 opener	James Schnepf
7-2	Jim Brown / The Stock Market
7-3	James Schnepf
7-8	Amanda Fisher
7-9	John Coletti/Stock Boston Inc.
7-10	Tim Defrisco/Allsport
Ch 8 opener	Courtesy The Lincoln Company
8-3	Sikorsky Aircraft
8-4	Mike Greenlar
8-6	Jon Riley/Tony Stone Images
Ch 9 opener	Gary Laufman Photography
9-7	Brad Aie
9-8	Joan Condie
9-9	Joan Condie
Ch 10 opener	Ralph Stayer / Steve Woit
10-2	Andy Sacks / Tony Stone Images
10-3	Joan Condie
10-9	Alicia Doyle
Ch 11 opener	Doug Plummer/Photo Researchers Inc.
11-1	Rhoda Sidney/ Stock Boston Inc.
11-3	M. Antman/ The Image Works
11-6	AP/ Wide World Photos
11-8	Brian Lemay/ Nelvana
Ch 12 opener	Charles Gupton/ The Stock Market
Ch 13 opener	David Stoecklein/ The Stock Market
13-3	Honda of America Mfg.
13-4	Churchill Falls Labrador Corporation
Ch 14 opener	Joe Sohm/ Uniphoto Picture Agency
Ch 15 opener	Bill Horsman/ Stock Boston Inc.
15-1	Churchill Falls Labrador Corporation
15-2	Brad Aie

BRIEF CONTENTS

PART ONE   INTRODUCTION   1

1   THE SUPERVISOR'S JOB AND CHALLENGES FOR THE 21ST CENTURY   2

PART TWO   PLANNING AND CONTROL   45

2   SUPERVISORY PLANNING AND TIME MANAGEMENT   46
3   DESIGNING AND IMPLEMENTING CONTROLS   80
4   PROBLEM SOLVING AND DECISION MAKING   122

PART THREE   ORGANIZING, STAFFING, AND EMPLOYEE DEVELOPMENT   171

5   ORGANIZING AN EFFECTIVE DEPARTMENT   172
6   ACQUIRING THE RIGHT PEOPLE   222
7   APPRAISING EMPLOYEE PERFORMANCE   262
8   DEVELOPING YOUR EMPLOYEES   306

PART FOUR   STIMULATING INDIVIDUAL AND GROUP PERFORMANCE   337

9   MOTIVATING YOUR EMPLOYEES   338
10   PROVIDING LEADERSHIP 376
11   COMMUNICATING EFFECTIVELY   414

PART FIVE   COPING WITH WORKPLACE DYNAMICS   453

12   MANAGING CONFLICT AND POLITICS   454
13   MANAGING CHANGE AND STRESS   492
14   DISCIPLINING EMPLOYEES   530
15   THE SUPERVISOR'S ROLE IN EMPLOYEE RELATIONS   558

ENDNOTES   A1
GLOSSARY   A5
INDEX   A13

CONTENTS

PART ONE INTRODUCTION 1

1 THE SUPERVISOR'S JOB AND CHALLENGES FOR THE 21ST CENTURY 2

PERFORMING EFFECTIVELY 4

SUPERVISORS AND THE MANAGEMENT PROCESS 5
Who Are Supervisors? 7 • What Is Management? 7 • What Do Managers Do? 8

THE TRANSITION FROM EMPLOYEE TO SUPERVISOR 8
Where Do Supervisors Come From? 10 • *Pop Quiz* 11 • Mastering a New Identity 12 • Do You Really Want to Be a Supervisor? 14 • *Something to Think About* 15

COMPETENCIES OF SUPERVISORS 17
Technical Competence 17 • Interpersonal Competence 17 • Conceptual Competence 18 • Political Competence 19 • Competencies and Managerial Level 19 • *Assessing Yourself: Do You Have What It Takes to Be Political?* 21

FROM CONCEPTS TO SKILLS 22
What Else Do I Need to Know about Supervising? 24

SUPERVISORY CHALLENGES FOR THE 21ST CENTURY 25
Changing Expectations of Supervisors 25 • *Pop Quiz* 27 • Changing the Size or the Structure of the Organization 28 • Managing Technology 34 • *Something to Think About* 30 • Managing Workforce Diversity 31 • *Supervision in Action: The Cultural Variables* 32 • Use of Contract Workers 34 • *Building a Supervisory Skill: Guidelines for Acting Ethically and Compassionately* 36 • *About the Skill* 36

UNDERSTANDING THE BASICS 38
Summary 38 • Key Terms and Concepts 39 • Reviewing Your Knowledge 39 • Answers to the Pop Quizzes 40

PERFORMING YOUR JOB 41
Case 1.A: The Stresses of Downsizing 41 • Case 1.B: From Dealing with Babies to Horses 42

PART TWO PLANNING AND CONTROL 45

2 SUPERVISORY PLANNING AND TIME MANAGEMENT 46

PERFORMING EFFECTIVELY 48

WHAT IS PLANNING? 49

PLANNING AND MANAGERIAL LEVEL 49
Planning Breadth 49 • *Something to Think About* 50 • Planning Time Frame 51 • Linking Managerial Levels 51

KEY PLANNING GUIDES 52
Standing Plans 52• Single-Use Plans 54 • *Pop Quiz* 59

SETTING GOALS 60
Characteristics of Effective Goals 61 • Management by Objectives 62

TIME MANAGEMENT 63
Time as a Scarce Resource 63 • Focusing on Discretionary Time 63 • How Do You Use Your Time? 64 • Five Steps to Better Time Management 64 • *Something to Think About* 66 • Some Additional Points to Ponder 66

FROM CONCEPTS TO SKILLS: GOAL SETTING 69
Assessing Yourself: Are You A Good Goal Setter? 69 • Skill Basics 70 • Applying Your Skills 72 • *Pop Quiz* 74

UNDERSTANDING THE BASICS 75
Summary 75 • Key Terms and Concepts 76 • Reviewing Your Knowledge 76 • Answers to the Pop Quizzes 77

PERFORMING YOUR JOB 78
Case 2.A: Is This the Beginning of the End? 78 • Case 2.B: MBO at A.C. & C.E 79

3 DESIGNING AND IMPLEMENTING CONTROLS 80

PERFORMING EFFECTIVELY 82

THE CONTROL PROCESS 83
Establish Performance Indicators and Determine Performance Standards 83 • Measure Actual Performance 84 • Compare Results with Standards 85 • Take Corrective Action 86 • Some Special Meaurement Tools 86 • *Pop Quiz* 91

TYPES OF CONTROL 91
Preventive Control 91 • Concurrent Control 92 • Corrective Control 93

FOCUS OF CONTROL 93
Costs 93 • Inventories 95 • Quality 96 • Safety 98 • Employee Performance 101 • *Something to Think About* 102

CHARACTERISTICS OF EFFECTIVE CONTROLS 103

POTENTIAL NEGATIVE OUTCOMES OF CONTROLS 105

Employee Resistance 105 • *Assessing Yourself: How Willing Are You to Encourage Self-Control?* 106 • Misdirection of Effort 108 • *Pop Quiz* 109 • Ethics and Control Devices 110

FROM CONCEPTS TO SKILLS: BUDGETING 111
Assessing Yourself: What Do You Know about Budgeting? 111 • Skill Basics 112 • Applying Your Skills 115

UNDERSTANDING THE BASICS 117
Summary 117 • Key Terms and Concepts 117 • Reviewing Your Knowledge 118 • Answers to the Pop Quizzes 118

PERFORMING YOUR JOB 119
Case 3.A: Practising What You Preach 119 • Case 3.B: The Business of Romance 119

4 PROBLEM SOLVING AND DECISION MAKING 122

PERFORMING EFFECTIVELY 124

THE DECISION-MAKING PROCESS 125
Identify the Problem 125 • Collect Relevant Information 126 • Develop Alternatives 127 • Evaluate Each Alternative 127 • Select the Best Alternative 128 • Implement the Decision 128 • Follow Up and Evaluate 129

DECISION TOOLS 129
Expected Value Analysis 129 • Decision Trees 130 • Marginal Analysis 132 • Risk Analysis 132 • Gap Analysis and the Five Whys 133 • Matrix Assessments 133 • Cause and Effect Diagrams 135 • Management Information Systems 136 • *Pop Quiz* 138

DECISION-MAKING STYLES 138
Assessing Yourself: What's Your Decision-Making Style? 140

ETHICS IN DECISION MAKING 143
Dealing with a Difficult Issue: Hiring a Friend 143 • Common Rationalizations 143 • Three Different Views on Ethics 144 • Some Ethical Decision Guides 147

GROUP DECISION MAKING 147
Advantages and Disadvantages 147 • A Guide to When to Use Group Decision Making 148 • Types of Group Decision Making 149 • *Building a Supervisory Skill: Conducting a Group Meeting* 152 • Techniques for Improving Group Decision Making 155 • *Pop Quiz* 158

FROM CONCEPTS TO SKILLS: CREATIVE PROBLEM SOLVING 159
Assessing Yourself: How Creative Are You? 159 • Skill Basics 163 • Applying Your Skills 165

UNDERSTANDING THE BASICS 166
Summary 166 • Key Terms and Concepts 167 • Reviewing Your Knowledge 167 • Answers to the Pop Quizzes 168

PERFORMING YOUR JOB 169
Case 4.A: Electronic Honesty 169 • Case 4.B: How Can You Make the Decision? 170

PART THREE ORGANIZING, STAFFING AND EMPLOYEE DEVELOPMENT 171

5 ORGANIZING AN EFFECTIVE DEPARTMENT 172

PERFORMING EFFECTIVELY 174

WHAT IS ORGANIZING? 175

BASIC ORGANIZING CONCEPTS 176
Division of Labour 176 • Span of Control 177 • Unity of Command 180 • Line, Staff and Functional Authority 180 • Equating Authority and Responsibility 182 • Centralized vs. Decentralized Authority 182 • *Pop Quiz* 184

GROUPING EMPLOYEES 184
Function 185 • Product 186 • Geography 186 • Customer 187 • Process 188 • Blending Function and Product: The Matrix 189 • *Dealing with a Difficult Issue: Do Matrix Structures Create Confused Employees?* 191 • Why Is There Movement to Simpler Employee Groupings? 192 • Are There Simple Structures for Larger Organizations? 193

ORGANIZING YOUR EMPLOYEES' JOBS 194
Identifying the Tasks to Be Done 195 • Combining Tasks into Jobs 196 • Creating Job Descriptions 196 • *Pop Quiz* 198

THE INCREASING USE OF TEAMS 198
Turning Groups into Teams 199 • Building Real Teams 200 • Overcoming the Obstacles 202 • *Something to Think About* 206 • *Pop Quiz* 207

FROM CONCEPTS TO SKILLS: EMPOWERING OTHERS THROUGH DELEGATION 208
Assessing Yourself: Are You Willing to Delegate? 208 • Skill Basics 209 • Applying Your Skills 213

UNDERSTANDING THE BASICS 216
Summary 216 • Key Terms and Concepts 217 • Reviewing Your Knowledge 217 • Answers to the Pop Quizzes 218

PERFORMING YOUR JOB 219
Case 5.A: Teams at NCR 219 • Case 5.B: Separating Team Members at Enbridge 220

6 ACQUIRING THE RIGHT PEOPLE 222

PERFORMING EFFECTIVELY 224

SUPERVISORS AND THE HUMAN RESOURCES DEPARTMENT 225

UNDERSTANDING EQUAL EMPLOYMENT OPPORTUNITY 225

Laws and Regulations 226 • Human Rights Legislation 227 • Your Role in Employment Equity 228 • EEO Goes Beyond Hiring 229 • *Pop Quiz* 230

DETERMINING STAFFING NEEDS 231
Current Assessment 231 • Future Assessment 231 • Developing a Future Program 232

FROM JOB DESCRIPTIONS TO JOB SPECIFICATIONS 232
Something to Think About 234

RECRUITING CANDIDATES 235
Internal Search 235 • Advertisements 235 • Employee Referrals 236 • Employment Agencies 237 • Schools, Colleges, and Universities 238 • Professional Organizations 239 • Casual or Unsolicited Applicants 239 • Unemployment Agencies and Centres 239 • Other Sources 240

EMPLOYEE SELECTION 240
Foundations of Selection 240 • Selection Devices 242 • *Something to Think About* 246 • *Building a Supervisory Skill: Behaviour-based Interviewing* 246

NEW-EMPLOYEE ORIENTATION 248
Supervision in Action: the Realistic Job Preview 251 • *Pop Quiz* 252

FROM CONCEPTS TO SKILLS: INTERVIEWING 253
Assessing Yourself: Do You Have Good Interviewing Skills? 253 • Skill Basics 253 • Applying Your Skills 255

UNDERSTANDING THE BASICS 256
Summary 256 • Key Terms and Concepts 257 • Reviewing Your Knowledge 257 • Answers to the Pop Quizzes 258

PERFORMING YOUR JOB 259
Case 6.A: The Recruiting and Selection Partnership: HR and Management 259 • Case 6.B: Hiring at Russell Food Equipment 259

7 APPRAISING EMPLOYEE PERFORMANCE 262

PERFORMING EFFECTIVELY 264
THE PURPOSE OF THE EMPLOYEE PERFORMANCE APPRAISAL 264
WHEN SHOULD APPRAISALS BE MADE? 265
THE SUPERVISOR'S ROLE IN PERFORMANCE APPRAISAL 265
Will You Be the Sole Appraiser? 266 • What Forms or Documentation Does the Organization Provide? 266 • Setting Performance Expectations 269 • Providing Performance Feedback 269

LEGAL ISSUES IN PERFORMANCE APPRAISALS 270
Pop Quiz 271

WHAT DO WE APPRAISE? 271
Individual Task Outcomes 272 • Behaviours 272 • Traits 272

GATHERING PERFORMANCE DATA 273
PERFORMANCE APPRAISAL METHODS 273
Absolute Standards 274 • Relative Standards 276 • *Something to Think About* 279 • Objectives 279

HURDLES IN THE WAY OF EFFECTIVE APPRAISALS 280
Leniency Error 280 • Halo Error 280 • Similarity Error 281 • Recency Error 281 • Central Tendency Error 281 • Inflationary Pressures 282

OVERCOMING THE HURDLES 282
Clarify Expectations 282 • Continually Document Employee Performance 283 • Use Behaviourally Based Measures 283 • Combine Absolute and Relative Standards 284 • Use Multiple Raters 285 • Rate Selectively 285 • Participate in Appraisal Training 286

WHAT ABOUT TEAM PERFORMANCE APPRAISALS? 286
Supervision in Action: Performance Appraisals in Contemporary Organizations 287

NOW WHAT? RESPONDING TO PERFORMANCE PROBLEMS 288
What Do You Need to Know about Counselling Employees? 288 • Is Your Action Ethical? 291 • *Pop Quiz* 292

FROM CONCEPTS TO SKILLS: CONDUCTING THE APPRAISAL REVIEW INTERVIEW 293
Assessing Yourself: Conducting the Appraisal Interview 293 • Skill Basics 294 • Applying Your Skills 298

UNDERSTANDING THE BASICS 300
Summary 300 • Key Terms and Concepts 301 • Reviewing Your Knowledge 301 • Answers to the Pop Quizzes 302

PERFORMING YOUR JOB 303
Case 7.A: Appraising Team Members— Refining the Process 303 • Case 7.B: Appraising the Remote Employee at NCR 304

8 DEVELOPING YOUR EMPLOYEES 306

PERFORMING EFFECTIVELY 308
EMPLOYEE TRAINING: WHAT IS IT AND WHY IS IT IMPORTANT? 308
NEEDS ASSESSMENT 309
ALLOCATING TRAINING RESPONSIBILITIES 309
DESIGNING THE PROPER TRAINING PROGRAM: UNDERSTANDING HOW PEOPLE LEARN 311
Learning Guidelines 312 • Designing Training Programs 314

TRAINING METHODS 314
On-the-Job Training 314 • *Building a Supervisory Skill: Asking Logical Consequence Questions as Part of Coaching* 317 • Off-the-

Job Training 319 • *Pop Quiz* 320

MATCHING TRAINING PROGRAMS TO OBJECTIVES 322

EVALUATING TRAINING EFFECTIVENESS 324

HOW IS EMPLOYEE DEVELOPMENT DIFFERENT FROM EMPLOYEE TRAINING? 324

CURRENT ISSUES IN TRAINING AND DEVELOPMENT 325
Diversity Training 325 • The Shift to Customer Orientation 326 • *Pop Quiz* 327

FROM CONCEPTS TO SKILLS: COACHING 328
Assessing Yourself: What is Effective Coaching? 328 • Skill Basics 328 • Applying Your Skills 330

UNDERSTANDING THE BASICS 332
Summary 332 • Key Terms and Concepts 333 • Reviewing Your Knowledge 333 • Answers to the Pop Quizzes 334

PERFORMING YOUR JOB 335
Case 8.A: Whose Job Is Employee Development? 335 • Case 8.B: Training on the Run 335

PART FOUR STIMULATING INDIVIDUAL AND GROUP PERFORMANCE 337

9 MOTIVATING YOUR EMPLOYEES 338

PERFORMING EFFECTIVELY 340

WHAT IS MOTIVATION? 341

UNDERSTANDING INDIVIDUAL DIFFERENCES 341
How Can an Understanding of Personality Help You Be a More Effective Supervisor? 343

EARLY APPROACHES TO MOTIVATION 343
Focus on Needs 343 • Focus on the Nature of People 345 • Focus on Satisfaction and Dissatisfaction 346 • *Pop Quiz* 348

CONTEMPORARY THEORIES OF MOTIVATION 348
Focus on Achievement 348 • Focus on Reinforcement 350 • Focus on Equity 351 • Focus on Goals 352 • Focus on Expectancies 352

APPLYING MOTIVATION CONCEPTS 354
Be Clear in Communicating What is Expected 354 • Recognize Individual Differences 354 • Match People to Jobs 355 • Set Challenging Goals 355 • Encourage Participation 355 • Individualize Rewards 356 • Give Recognition 356 • Link Rewards to Performance 357 • *Dealing with a Difficult Issue: Rewarding the Wrong Behaviour* 358 • Check for Equity 358 • Don't Ignore Money! 358

CHALLENGES FOR MOTIVATING TODAY'S EMPLOYEES 359
Motivating a Diversified Workforce 359 • *Supervision in Action: Motivating a Diverse Workforce* 360 • Motivating Low-Pay Service Workers 361 • Motivating Professionals 361 • Should Employees be Paid for Performance or Time on the Job? 362 • How Can Employee Stock Ownership Plans Affect Motivation? 363 • *Pop Quiz* 364

FROM CONCEPTS TO SKILLS: DESIGNING MOTIVATING JOBS 365
Assessing Yourself: Is Enrichment for You? 365 • Skill Basics 366 • Practising the Skill 367 • Applying Your Skills 369

UNDERSTANDING THE BASICS 371
Summary 371 • Key Terms and Concepts 372 • Reviewing Your Knowledge 372 • Answers to the Pop Quizzes 373

PERFORMING YOUR JOB 374
Case 9.A: Just Keep on Trucking 374 • Case 9.B: Finding the Pleasure in Number-Crunching 374

10 PROVIDING LEADERSHIP 376

PERFORMING EFFECTIVELY 378

WHAT IS LEADERSHIP? 378
Leaders and Supervisors 379 • Sometimes "No" Leader is Okay 379 • *Dealing with a Difficult Issue: Influencing without Power* 380 • Are you Born to Lead? 381 • Traits of Successful Leaders 382 • What is This Thing Called Charisma? 384

HOW DO YOU BECOME A LEADER? 385
Technical Skills 386 • Conceptual Skills 386 • Networking Skills 387 • Human Relations Skills 387

LEADERSHIP BEHAVIOURS AND STYLES 388
Task-Centred Behaviours 388 • People-Centred Behaviours 389 • What Behaviour Should You Exhibit? 390

EFFECTIVE LEADERSHIP 390
Pop Quiz 391 • Key Situational Models of Leadership 391 • Applying Situational Leadership 393

CONTEMPORARY LEADERSHIP ROLES 395
Credibility and Trust 395 • *Supervision in Action: National Culture Could Affect Your Leadership Style* 396 • Playing Favourites 397 • *Building a Supervisory Skill: Building Trust* 398 • Leading through Empowerment 399

LEADERSHIP ISSUES TODAY 400
Do Men and Women Lead Differently? 400 • *Something to Think About* 401 • Transactional and Transformational Leaders 401 • *Pop Quiz* 403

FROM CONCEPTS TO SKILLS: NETWORKING: HAVING CONVERSATIONS WITH PEOPLE YOU DO NOT KNOW WELL 404

Assessing Yourself: How Well Can You Connect With New People 404 • Skill Basics 405 • Applying Your Skills 407

UNDERSTANDING THE BASICS 408
Summary 408 • Key Terms and Concepts 409 • Reviewing Your Knowledge 409 • Answers to the Pop Quizzes 410

PERFORMING YOUR JOB 411
Case 10.A: This Boss Isn't Bossy 411 • Case 10.B: Leading a Virtual Team 412

11 COMMUNICATING EFFECTIVELY 414

PERFORMING EFFECTIVELY 416
WHAT IS COMMUNICATION? 417
METHODS OF COMMUNICATION 417
Oral Communication 417 • Written Communication 418 • Electronic Communication 418 • *Something to Think About* 419 • *Something to Think About* 420 • Nonverbal Communication 421 • The Grapevine 422

THE SUPERVISOR'S DAY-TO-DAY COMMUNICATION 423
BARRIERS TO EFFECTIVE COMMUNICATION 424
Language 425 • Poor Listening Habits 426 • Lack of Feedback 426 • Differences in Perception 426 • Role Requirements 427 • Choice of Information Medium 427 • Lack of Honesty 428 • *Dealing with a Difficult Issue: Should You Tell the Whole Truth?* 429 • Emotions 430

IMPROVING YOUR COMMUNICATION EFFECTIVENESS 430
Think First! 430 • Constrain Emotions 430 • Learn to Listen 431 • Tailor Language to the Receiver 431 • Match Words and Actions 431 • *Supervision in Action: Communication Differences in a Global Village* 433 • Utilize Feedback 433 • Participate in Assertiveness Training 434 • *Building a Supervisory Skill: Confronting* 435 • *Pop Quiz* 437

THE IMPORTANCE OF FEEDBACK SKILLS 438
What's the Difference Between Positive and Negative Feedback? 438 • How Do You Give Effective Feedback? 438

FROM CONCEPTS TO SKILLS: ACTIVE LISTENING 441
Assessing Yourself: Do You Listen Actively? 441 • Skill Basics 442 • Applying Your Skills 445 • *Pop Quiz* 447

UNDERSTANDING THE BASICS 448
Summary 448 • Key Terms and Concepts 449 • Reviewing Your Knowledge 449 • Answers to the Pop Quizzes 450

PERFORMING YOUR JOB 451
Case 11.A: Tricia Mah 451 • Case 11.B: Communicating Across the Miles 451

PART FIVE COPING WITH WORKPLACE DYNAMICS 453

12 MANAGING CONFLICT AND POLITICS 454

PERFORMING EFFECTIVELY 456
WHAT IS CONFLICT? 457
ARE ALL CONFLICTS BAD? 457
SOURCES OF CONFLICT 458
Communication Differences 458• Structural Differentiation 459 • Personal Differences 459

TECHNIQUES FOR MANAGING CONFLICT 459
Resolution Techniques 460 • *Building a Supervisory Skill: Handling Conflict Through a Role Reversal Technique* 462 • Which Conflicts Should You Tackle? 463 • Choosing the Appropriate Resolution Technique 463 • *Assessing Yourself: Your Preferred Conflict-Handling Style* 465 • Stimulation Techniques 467 • *Pop Quiz* 470

UNDERSTANDING ORGANIZATIONAL POLITICS 470
What Is Politics? 471 • Why Is There Politics in Organizations? 472

THE ETHICS OF "PLAYING POLITICS" 472
ASSESSING THE POLITICAL LANDSCAPE 473
Your Organization's Culture 473 • The Power of Others 474 • Your Power 475 • *Building a Supervisory Skill: Becoming Politically Smart* 475 • *Something to Think About* 478

FROM CONCEPTS TO SKILLS: NEGOTIATION 479
Assessing Yourself: Do You Understand What It Takes to Be an Effective Negotiator? 479 • Skill Basics 480 • Applying Your Skills 483 • *Pop Quiz* 486

UNDERSTANDING THE BASICS 487
Summary 487 • Key Terms and Concepts 488 • Reviewing Your Knowledge 488 • Answers to the Pop Quizzes 489

PERFORMING YOUR JOB 490
Case 12.A: Was the Knife a Joke? 490 • Case 12.B: Joe and Catalino Deal with Angry Clients 490

13 MANAGING CHANGE AND STRESS 492

PERFORMING EFFECTIVELY 494
FORCES FOR CHANGE 495
New Technologies 495 • Environmental Dynamics 495 • Internal Forces 495 • *Dealing with a Difficult Issue: Living with Equal Pay for Work of Equal Value* 496 • *Assessing Yourself:*

How Ready Are You for Coping with Work-Related Change? 497 • Can You Serve as a Change Agent? 501

CHANGING PERSPECTIVES ON CHANGE 501
The Old View of Change 501 • The Contemporary View of Change 502

RESISTANCE TO CHANGE 503
Habit 503 • Threat to Job or Income 504 • Fear of the Unknown 504 • Selective Perception 505 • Threat to Expertise 505 • Threat to Established Power Relationships 505 • Threat to Interpersonal Relationships 506 • *Pop Quiz* 506

REDUCING RESISTANCE TO CHANGE 507
Build Trust 507 • Open Channels of Communication 507 • Involve Employees 508 • Provide Incentives 508 • *Something to Think About* 509

WORK STRESS 509
What Is Stress? 510 • Sources of Work Stress 510 • *Assessing Yourself: How Much Stress in Your Life?* 513 • The Symptoms of Stress 515 • Companies Take Action on Stress 516

FROM CONCEPTS TO SKILLS: STRESS REDUCTION 517
Assessing Yourself: How Well Can You Identify Stressful Events? 517 • Skill Basics 518 • Applying Your Skills 521 • *Pop Quiz* 524

UNDERSTANDING THE BASICS 525
Summary 525 • Key Terms and Concepts 526 • Reviewing Your Knowledge 526 • Answers to the Pop Quizzes 527

PERFORMING YOUR JOB 528
Case 13.A: The Changes Never Stop 528 • Case 13.B: "New" is Exciting but Stressful 529

14 DISCIPLINING EMPLOYEES 530

PERFORMING EFFECTIVELY 532
WHAT IS DISCIPLINE? 532
TYPES OF DISCIPLINE PROBLEMS 534
Attendance 534 • On-the-Job Behaviours 534 • Dishonesty 534 • *Something to Think About* 535 • Outside Activities 536

DISCIPLINE ISN'T ALWAYS THE SOLUTION 536
BASIC TENETS OF DISCIPLINE 536
Lay the Groundwork 536• Make Discipline Progressive 537 • Follow the "Hot Stove" Rule 538 • *Pop Quiz* 540

FACTORS TO CONSIDER IN DISCIPLINING 540
DISCIPLINE AND THE LAW 542
Unionization 543 • *Pop Quiz* 544

FROM CONCEPTS TO SKILLS: DISCIPLINING 545
Assessing Yourself: Are You Effective at Disciplining? 545 • Skill Basics 546 • Applying Your Skills 549

UNDERSTANDING THE BASICS 553
Summary 553 • Key Terms and Concepts 554 • Reviewing Your Knowledge 554 • Answers to the Pop Quizzes 555

PERFORMING YOUR JOB 556
Case 14.A: Dealing with the Poor Performer Who Has Political Connections 556 • Case 14.B: Discipline in a Union Setting 556

15 THE SUPERVISOR'S ROLE IN EMPLOYEE RELATIONS 558

PERFORMING EFFECTIVELY 560
WHAT IS EMPLOYEE RELATIONS? 561
A BASIC QUESTION: WHY WOULD EMPLOYEES JOIN A UNION? 561
LABOUR LEGISLATION YOU NEED TO KNOW ABOUT 563
Federal and Provincial Labour Relations Acts 563 • The Charter of Rights and Freedoms 564

FROM CONFLICT TO COOPERATION 564
AN OVERVIEW OF THE COLLECTIVE BARGAINING PROCESS 564
Pop Quiz 565 • Organization and Certification 565 • OK, The Union Won—What Now? 567 • Preparation for Negotiation 567 • Negotiation 568 • Contract Administration 568

THE SUPERVISOR'S ROLE IN LABOUR MATTERS 568
Organizing Drives 568 • Negotiation 570 • Contract Administration 570 • Relations with the Union Steward 571 • When an Impasse is Reached 571

FROM CONCEPTS TO SKILLS: HANDLING GRIEVANCES 574
Assessing Yourself: Are You an Effective Grievance-Handler? 574 • Skill Basics 575 • Applying Your Skills 579 • *Pop Quiz* 581

UNDERSTANDING THE BASICS 582
Summary 582 • Key Terms and Concepts 583 • Reviewing Your Knowledge 583 • Answers to the Pop Quizzes 584

PERFORMING YOUR JOB 585
Case 15.A: Three Different Supervisory Views on Unions 585 • Case 15.B: Making a Union Unnecessary 586

ENDNOTES A1

GLOSSARY A5

INDEX A13

BOXED FEATURES

CHAPTER ONE

Pop Quiz 11 • Something to Think About 15 • Assessing Yourself: Do You Have What It Takes to Be Political? 21 • Pop Quiz 27 • Something to Think About 30 • Supervision in Action: The Cultural Variables 32 • Building a Supervisory Skill: Guidelines for Acting Ethically 36

CHAPTER TWO

Something to Think About 50 • Pop Quiz 59 • Something to Think About 66 • Assessing Yourself: Are You a Good Goal Setter? 69 • Pop Quiz 74

CHAPTER THREE

Pop Quiz 91 • Something to Think About 102 • Assessing Yourself: How Willing Are You to Encourage Self-Control? 106 • Pop Quiz 109 • Assessing Yourself: What Do You Know about Budgeting? 111

CHAPTER FOUR

Pop Quiz 138 • Assessing Yourself: What's Your Decision-Making Style? 140 • Dealing with a Difficult Issue: Hiring a Friend 143 • Building a Supervisory Skill: Conducting a Group Meeting 152 • Pop Quiz 158 • Assessing Yourself: How Creative Are You? 159

CHAPTER FIVE

Pop Quiz 184 • Dealing with a Difficult Issue: Do Matrix Structures Create Confused Employees? 191 • Pop Quiz 198 • Something to Think About 206 • Pop Quiz 207 • Assessing Yourself: Are You Willing to Delegate? 208

CHAPTER SIX

Pop Quiz 230 • Something to Think About 234 • Something to Think About 246 • Building a Supervisory Skill: Behaviour-based Interviewing 246 • Supervision in Action: The Realistic Job Preview 251 • Pop Quiz 252 • Assessing Yourself: Do You Have Good Interviewing Skills? 253

CHAPTER SEVEN

Pop Quiz 271 • Something to Think About 279 • Supervision in Action: Performance Appraisals in Contemporary Organizations 287 • Pop Quiz 292 • Assessing Yourself: Conducting the Appraisal Interview 293

CHAPTER EIGHT

Pop Quiz 320 • Pop Quiz 327 • Assessing Yourself: What is Effective Coaching? 328

CHAPTER NINE

Pop Quiz 348 • Dealing with a Difficult Issue: Rewarding the Wrong Behaviour 358 • Supervision in Action: Motivating a Diverse Workforce 360 • Pop Quiz 364 • Assessing Yourself: Is Enrichment for You? 365

CHAPTER TEN

Dealing with a Difficult Issue: Influencing without Power 380 • Pop Quiz 391 • Supervision in Action: National Culture Could Affect Your Leadership Style 396 • Building a Supervisory Skill: Building Trust 398 • Something to Think About 401 • Pop Quiz 403 • Assessing Yourself: How Well Can You Connect with New People? 404

CHAPTER ELEVEN

Something to Think About 419 • Something to Think About 420 • Dealing with a Difficult Issue: Should You Tell the Whole Truth? 429 • Supervision in Action: Communication Differences in a Global Village 433 • Building a Supervisory Skill: Confronting 435 • Pop Quiz 437 • Assessing Yourself: Do You Listen Actively? 441 • Pop Quiz 447

CHAPTER TWELVE

Building a Supervisory Skill: Handling Conflict Through a Role-Reversal Technique 462 • Assessing Yourself: Your Preferred Conflict-Handling Style 465 • Pop Quiz 470 • Building a Supervisory Skill: Becoming Politically Smart 475 • Something to Think About 478 • Assessing Yourself: Do You Understand What It Takes to Be an Effective Negotiator? 479 • Pop Quiz 486

CHAPTER THIRTEEN

Dealing with a Difficult Issue: Living with Equal Pay for Work of Equal Value 496 • Assessing Yourself: How Ready Are You for Coping with Work-Related Change? 497 • Pop Quiz 506 • Something to Think About 509 • Assessing Yourself: How Much Stress in Your Life? 513 • Assessing Yourself: How Well Can You Identify Stressful Events? 517 • Pop Quiz 524

CHAPTER FOURTEEN

Something to Think About 535 • Pop Quiz 540 • Pop Quiz 544 • Assessing Yourself: Are You Effective at Disciplining? 545

CHAPTER FIFTEEN

Pop Quiz 565 • Assessing Yourself: Are You an Effective Grievance-Handler? 574 • Pop Quiz 581

HOW TO USE THIS BOOK

The supervisor's job has changed dramatically in recent years. Supervisors now work with a more diverse workforce in terms of race, gender, and ethnic background. Supervisors' jobs are also being affected by technological changes, a more competitive marketplace, and corporate restructuring and workflow redesign. Despite all of these changes, supervisors still need to understand the traditional elements of directing the work of others and the specific skills they need: goal-setting, budgeting, scheduling, delegating, interviewing, negotiating, handling grievances, employee counselling, and evaluating employees' performance.

The ideal way to learn a task is to find out how it is done, watch it being done, and then complete the task yourself. *Supervision in Canada Today* takes you "on the job," presenting examples of how supervisors operate in real situations, and then placing you in the first-line position where you are making the decisions yourself.

Chapter Outline and Objectives—Each chapter begins with an outline and a list of learning objectives. This provides you a structure by which you can test whether you've learned the chapter's key concepts.

Performing Effectively—These chapter introductions demonstrate each new topic's relevance to your effective performance as a supervisor. You learn to think critically in typical work situations.

From Concepts to Skills—This section allows you to learn and practise relevant supervisory skills by combining your new knowledge and your natural talents. You assess your own progress.

Understanding the Basics—Closing each chapter is a summary of the important points and terms in the chapter, and review topics for discussion.

Performing Your Job—Each chapter concludes with two cases that allow you to apply your knowledge to solve real problems faced by real supervisors.

Margin Definitions and a Glossary—provide a quick reference to new terms.

SUPPLEMENTS TO LEARNING

Instructor's Manual with a lecture guide, transparency masters, video guides, and guidelines for evaluating case responses. This manual provides the latest guidance for teaching supervision in a dynamic way.

Test Item File with multiple choice, true/false, short answer, and short essay test questions. These questions are available to the instructor free with every adoption of the textbook.

Computerized Test Item File is an easy-to-access computer file. Generate your own tests or have the program select and print test questions at random. The software is free with every adoption of the textbook.

NEW IN THE THIRD EDITION

All of the cases, with the exception of one, have been replaced with new cases, all Canadian. The Performing Effectively chapter introductions have also been replaced. Several feature sections have been added, for example, discipline for improper e-mail use in Something to Think About (Chapter 14), asking logical consequence questions as part of coaching in Building a Supervisory Skill (Chapter 8), and rewarding the wrong behaviour in Dealing with a Difficult Issue (Chapter 9).

The major thrust of this new edition was tapping the voices of current excellent supervisors across Canada to reflect their reality. There was an enthusiastic response to requests for recommendations of excellent supervisors. As a result, you'll meet in these pages a wide variety of supervisors and managers from across Canada, working in all functions of their organizations, and from a spectrum of industries. The power of the research results and theoretical advice comes alive in the hands of the people who actually make it work.

We are always looking for examples of interesting supervisory challenges and exceptional supervisors and welcome your contact.

Joan Condie

joan.condie@sheridanc.on.ca

ACKNOWLEDGEMENTS

We would like to thank the following people for their generous help in the creation of this book, contributing toward making it a truly Canadian version. It was a privilege and a pleasure to speak with so many people who clearly care about their jobs and the people with whom they work.

Tammy Abel, *HRDC*
Gemma Ahn, *NRC*
Paula Aylward, *Cavendish Farms*
Susan Barr, *University of British Columbia*
Ray Berta, *Applied Consumer and Clinical Evaluation*
Larry Bowzeylo, *Suncor*
Ken Burfoot, *HRDC*
Susan Burton, *Ernst and Young*
Melanie Busby, *Grant McEwan Community College*
Mavis Campbell, *HRDC*
Bob Cartwright, *Suncor*
Fred Cassidy, *Larry's Sports*
Lana Clark, *University of Saskatchewan*
Brian Colbourne, *Robinson-Blackmore*
Heather Cook, *Children's Assessment and Treatment Centre*
Rita Cupitt, *Eagle's Flight*
Christina De Palo, *PROCOM*
Beth Dennis, *Human Resources Professionals Association of Ontario*
Rocco Di Giovanni, *Mohawk College*
Paul Dolan, *NRC*
Julia Donahue, *Ceridian*
Julie Dopko, *NRC*
Leigh Enlund, *Bank of Nova Scotia*
Zahid Fazal, *Ernst and Young*
Lee Fenwick, *CBC*
Paul Gallant, *HRDC*
Stacy Goodale, *Imperial Oil Ltd.*
Erin Gordon, *Prime Restaurants*
Rod Guild, *Highland Valley Copper*
Ingrid Hann, *Spar Aviation*
Krista Harris, *CBC*
Peggy Hebden, *The New VR*
Tom Heighway, *Ceridian*
Debbie Hoffman, *Data Business Forms*
Rob Horgan, *The Gap*
Dan Hughes, *Cavendish Farms*
Lenny Jackson, *CBC*
Kristina Jason
Bill Kaine, *Skyjack*
Rod Killough, *Highland Valley Copper*
Colin Kirby
Gisele Law, *HRDC*

Patrick Lee
Brian Lemay, *Sheridan College*
Ralph Liumes
Elizabeth Loweth, *Canadian Centre for Ethics and Corporate Policy*
Tricia Mah, *Royal Arch Masonic Home*
Rob Mastrotto, *Husky Injection Molding Systems*
Diane McArthur, *Ministry of Health, Ontario*
Bonnie Medeiros, *Husky Injection Molding Systems*
Susan Miller, *Enbridge Technology*
Suzana Milovanovic, *The Employer's Choice*
Catalino Misenas, *Russell Food Equipment Ltd.*
Susan Mocsan, *Brewers Retail*
Carolyn Moore, *NRC*
Anne Murphy, *City of Mississauga*
Colleen Murray, *City of Brampton*
Sue O'Hara, *Sprint Canada*
Edna Oleksiuk, *HRDC*
Sheila Otter, *Village Wedding Belles*
Susan Pander, *SaskTel*
Laura Park, *Fraser Milner*
Debbie Parsons, *Suncor*
Tina Payton, *Robinson-Blackmore*
Kerry Ann Provenzano, *OSF Inc.*
Joe Puiia, *HRDC*
Daniel Quondam, *Com Dev Wireless Group*
Kerri Reid, *Cedara*
John Ross, *Rio Algom Ltd.*
Marlene Roy, *HRDC*
Lynn Rutherford
Lynn Sachs, *Ernst and Young*
Rundell Seaman, *Seaman's Beverages*
Joe Sferrazza
Kim Sheppard, *Churchill Falls Labrador Corp.*
Cindy Sneddon, *Brewers Retail*
Chris Stott, *Smith Lyons*
Della Tardiff
Karol Traviss
Sheena Turnbull, *Cedara*
Graham Van Brunt, *Churchill Falls Labrador Corporation*
Chris Wentzell, *Com Dev Wireless Group*
Elizabeth Wright, *Hamilton-Wentworth Library Services*
Michelle Zapparoli, *Skyjack*

This edition is dedicated to Laura Condie and the late Jack Condie, who taught me that everyone's story is important.

PART ONE

INTRODUCTION

1. THE SUPERVISOR'S JOB AND CHALLENGES FOR THE 21ST CENTURY

1

THE SUPERVISOR'S JOB AND CHALLENGES FOR THE 21ST CENTURY

LEARNING OBJECTIVES

After reading this chapter, you should be able to:

1. Define supervisor.
2. Explain the difference between supervisors, middle managers, and top management.
3. Explain the pros and cons of being a supervisor.
4. Identify the four functions in the management process.
5. Describe the four essential management competencies.
6. Explain why the supervisor's job will be increasingly important and complex in the future.
7. Describe how the supervisor's role has changed from boss to coach.
8. Explain the impact that shrinking, growing, and changing the organization's structure can have on a supervisor.
9. Define what is meant by workforce diversity.
10. Explain how technology has affected the supervisor's job.

CHAPTER OUTLINE

PERFORMING EFFECTIVELY

SUPERVISORS AND THE MANAGEMENT PROCESS
Who Are Supervisors?
What Is Management?
What Do Managers Do?

THE TRANSITION FROM EMPLOYEE TO SUPERVISOR
Where Do Supervisors Come From?
Pop Quiz
Mastering a New Identity
Do You Really Want to Be a Supervisor?
Something to Think About

COMPETENCIES OF SUPERVISORS
Technical Competence
Interpersonal Competence
Conceptual Competence
Political Competence
Competencies and Managerial Level
Assessing Yourself: Do You Have What It Takes to Be Political?

FROM CONCEPTS TO SKILLS
What Else Do I Need to Know about Supervising?

SUPERVISORY CHALLENGES FOR THE 21st CENTURY
Changing Expectations of Supervisors
Pop Quiz
Changing the Size or the Structure of the Organization
Managing Technology
Something to Think About: The Off-Site Employee
Managing Workforce Diversity
Supervision in Action: The Cultural Variables

Building a Supervisory Skill: Guidelines for Acting Ethically and Compassionately

UNDERSTANDING THE BASICS
Summary
Key Terms and Concepts
Reviewing Your Knowledge
Answers to the Pop Quizzes

PERFORMING YOUR JOB
Case 1.A: The Stresses of Downsizing
Case 1.B: From Dealing with Babies to Horses

FIGURE 1-1

Zahid Fazal is a senior staff accountant with Ernst and Young in Montreal.

The six quotations in the left column come from a variety of supervisors from across Canada, who are listed in the right column. Guess who said what.

What was said

1. "You can never say anything too many times."

2. "You must have excellent inter-personal skills, and be able to lis-ten to others, while providing guidance without demeaning your subordinates."

3. "When there's a productivity issue, you want to address it in a way that does not seem confrontational, demeaning or controlling."

4. "You have to be able to handle stress. You can't fly off the handle."

5. "What are the "don'ts"? Lack of direction—especially when a job can be overwhelming. Giving unrealistic targets. And don't put employees in a position where they feel they must say OK even if they know they can't do it."

6. "Listen to your people as they have experience and ideas that you don't. Also, the simple act of listening to their input often ensures they become more inter-ested and involved in the job."

Who said it?

I. Tammy Abel, Coordinator of the Student Employment Centre in Winnipeg

II. Zahid Fazal, Senior Staff Accountant, Ernst & Young, Montreal

III. Diane McArthur, Director of Stakeholder Management and Operational Support, ServiceOntario, Toronto

IV. Tina Payton, Prepress Supervisor, Robinson-Blackmore, St. John's

V. Daniel Quondam, Operations Manager, Com Dev Wireless, Moncton

VI. Rod Guild, Senior Foreman, Highland Valley Copper mine, B.C. interior

It's tough to tell who said what, isn't it? And, in fact, when being interviewed by one of the Canadian authors, each one said something along the line of each of the six quotes. The point? Whether you are supervising employees at desks, computers, or machinery, the jobs are similar in many of the demands, challenges and skills needed.

By the way, the quotations are aligned with their originators (1 – I, 2 – II, etc.)

FIGURE 1-2

Rod Guild is a senior foreman with Highland Valley Copper mine in B.C.

FIGURE 1-3

Tina Payton is the prepress supervisor for Robinson-Blackmore, a printing firm in St. John's, Newfoundland.

This book is about supervisors. It assumes that you are reading it because you would like to be a supervisor and are preparing yourself for that event, or you are already a supervisor and are interested in developing your skills. In this book, you will learn about being an effective supervisor from actual supervisors and from the theorists who study them. The many supervisors described here were discovered through a process of approaching people and organizations across Canada and asking, "Is there an excellent supervisor at your organization whom you recommend I speak to when writing this book?" Perhaps you'll be among their number someday.

Nortel Networks
www.nortelnetworks.com

Victorian Order of Nurses
www.von.ca

**Grant McEwan
Community College**
www.gmcc.ab.ca

SUPERVISORS AND THE MANAGEMENT PROCESS

Let's start by looking at the role that supervisors play in the big picture. This means beginning with examining the concept of organizations since all supervisors work within an organizational setting.

An organization is a systematic grouping of people brought together to accomplish some specific purpose. Such groupings include businesses set up for profit such as Nortel, nonprofit organizations such as the Victorian Order of Nurses, educational institutions such as Grant McEwan Community College in Edmonton, churches, hospitals, and others. All organizations have three characteristics.

Organization
A systematic grouping of people brought together to accomplish some specific purpose.

First, every organization has a purpose—a distinct reason for being. Second, organizations require people to act in order to turn that purpose into reality. Third, all organizations develop a systematic structure that defines the roles of those people, and that often sets limits on their work behaviours. This could include writing job descriptions to clarify responsibilities, forming work teams, developing rules, regulations and procedures, and giving some people supervisory control over others.

In most traditional organizations, we can depict this structure as a pyramid with four general categories.

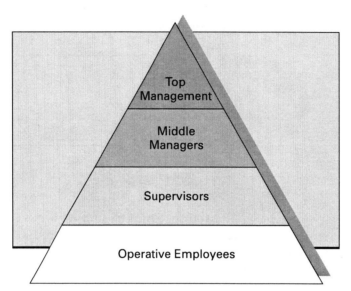

FIGURE 1-4

Levels in the organizational pyramid

Operative employees
Rank-and-file workers who physically produce an organization's goods and services.

Top management
The highest level of management. Those people responsible for establishing the organization's overall objectives and developing the policies to achieve those objectives.

Middle managers
All employees below the top-management level who manage other managers.

Operative employees form the base of the pyramid. These are the front-line workers who actually produce the organization's goods or provide its services. Such employees include the assembly-line worker at Ford, the postal carrier who delivers mail, and the salesperson at a Chapters store. It also includes many professional employees such as engineers, doctors, and computer specialists. What all operative employees have in common is that they do not manage or oversee the work of any other employees.

Moving from the base of the pyramid to the top of the pyramid, we find **top management**. These people are responsible for establishing the organization's overall objectives and developing the policies and strategies to accomplish these goals. Sample titles are CEO, vice president, museum director, and superintendent of schools.

Down one level, **middle managers** include all managers below the top management level who manage other managers. Titles could include sales director, division manager, area manager, or high school principal.

WHO ARE SUPERVISORS?

Returning to the organizational pyramid, the only level not yet described is **supervisors**. Like top and middle management, supervisors are part of management. However, they are unique in that they oversee operative employees. Supervisors, then, are the only managers who don't manage other managers. This is reflected in the term **first-level managers**. This means that, from the base of the pyramid moving up, supervisors represent the first level in the management hierarchy.

What kinds of titles are likely to indicate that someone is a supervisor? Assistant manager, coach, foreman, team leader, shift supervisor or department head are typical. Titles can be misleading, however. As you read about the various Canadian supervisors described and quoted in this book, you'll find one called a director because she directs a major project, but she is still the first-level manager. Another supervisor's title as coordinator may not sound impressive but she supervises staff at four different locations. So titles can be deceiving. What links all supervisors is the responsibility for operative employees.

An interesting aspect of supervisory positions is that many supervisors also engage in operative tasks like their employees. Zahid Fazal of Ernst & Young directs an audit team by planning and coordinating the audit process. He also joins in with the rest of the team in performing the planned procedures and reaching conclusions on an engagement. Catalino Misenas supervises a broad sales staff at Russell Food Equipment Ltd. in Vancouver but also handles some clients on his own. Anne Murphy is branch manager of the large, new Frank McKechnie Library in Mississauga. In addition to supervising 27 full- and part-time staff, Anne has scheduled time at the information desk and fills in when the library is shortstaffed. Finding time to accomplish the operative side of their job can be a challenge, given the heavy and often unpredictable load from the supervisory side.

A second interesting aspect of the supervisor's role is the link between operations and management. This can lead to each side demanding that the supervisor be their advocate, creating stress for some supervisors and confusion as to where their loyalties should lie.

WHAT IS MANAGEMENT?

The term **management** refers to the process of getting things done, effectively and efficiently, through and with other people. There are several components in this definition that warrant some discussion. These are the terms *process, effectively*, and *efficiently*.

The term **process** in the definition of management represents the primary activities supervisors perform. In management terms, we call these the *functions of management*. The next section will describe these functions.

Supervisors
First-level managers who oversee the work of operatives or nonmanagement employees.

Ernst and Young
www.ey.com

Russell Foods
www.russellfoods.com

Management
The process of getting things done, effectively and efficiently, through and with other people. *See also* Process; Efficiency; Effectiveness.

Process
The primary activities supervisors perform.

Efficiency
Doing a task right; also refers to the relationship between inputs and outputs.

Efficiency means doing the task right and refers to the relationship between inputs and outputs. If you get more output for a given input, you have increased efficiency. You also increase efficiency when you get the same output with fewer resources. Since supervisors deal with input resources that are scarce—money, people, equipment—they are concerned with the efficient use of these resources. Consequently, supervisors must be concerned with minimizing resource costs.

While minimizing resource costs is important, it isn't enough simply to be efficient. A supervisor must also be concerned with completing activities. We call this effectiveness. **Effectiveness** means doing the right task. In an organization, we call this *goal attainment*.

Effectiveness
Doing a task right; goal attainment.

The need for efficiency has a profound impact on the level of effectiveness. It's easier to be effective if you ignore efficiency. For instance, you could produce more sophisticated and higher-quality products if you disregarded labour and material input costs—yet that would almost certainly create problems. Consequently, being a good supervisor means being concerned with both attaining goals (effectiveness) and doing so as efficiently as possible.

WHAT DO MANAGERS DO?

Management functions
The four managerial functions of planning, organizing, leading, and controlling.

All managers engage in **management functions**. By that we mean they plan, organize, lead, and control. Since supervisors are part of management, we need to briefly review these four generic functions.

Imagine a boat with eight rowers, each rowing madly but each with a different direction in mind. The result is that they go nowhere and waste a lot of time and energy on the way. All members of a group need a common purpose and a common understanding of the means to get there. This is what **planning** is about. A plan sets out a common direction. In the planning function, managers must define objectives and develop a comprehensive set of plans to integrate and coordinate the activities necessary to achieve those objectives.

Planning
Defining objectives and the means of attaining them.

Organizing
Dividing work into manageable components and coordinating results to achieve objectives.

Change the rowboat to a large sailboat with several sails and a rudder. Not everyone can steer. It must be decided what tasks are to be done, when, and by whom. This refers to the **organizing** function. A manager must divide the work to be done into manageable components and coordinate the activities. Employees must understand what they are responsible for, how their work is grouped, where decisions are to be made, and who reports to whom.

Leading
Directing and coordinating people.

Sailing is fun on a brilliant sunny day with a brisk wind when everything is "shipshape," but what about the days when you are becalmed, or when you must face gale force winds? What about when you have to work with equipment that is in disrepair yet there is no money, time, or opportunity in sight? This is when the third management function of **leading** becomes particularly important. Subordinates need a leader to keep them going when times are tough, to resolve the unexpected difficulties, and to let them know how they are doing. When managers motivate employees, direct employees in their daily activities, communicate effectively, or resolve conflicts among team members, they are leading.

When a boat is "shipshape," it is due to the crew's effort to keep everything in top condition, ready to fulfill its function. This is part of the **controlling** function. To ensure that things are operating as they should, management must monitor activities and measure performance. Actual performance must be compared with the previously set objectives. If there are any significant deviations, it is management's responsibility to get things back on track. This process of measuring, comparing, and correcting is what we mean when we refer to the controlling function. This brings to mind the image of the captain checking position on a compass and ordering an adjustment to the person at the helm.

Controlling
Monitoring activities
to ensure that objectives are being met as
planned, and correcting any significant
deviations.

All managers perform the four functions of planning, organizing, leading, and controlling. The specifics of each function and the emphasis on each will vary with the level of management, however. For example, while we find top managers focusing on long-term, strategic planning such as what business the company should be in, supervisors emphasize short-term, tactical planning such as scheduling unit workloads for the upcoming week. Similarly, top management is concerned with designing the overall organization while supervisors focus on designing the jobs of individuals and groups.

While top managers spend most of their time organizing and planning, supervisors spend much of their time in activities related to the leading function (see Figure 1-5). Figure 1-6 lists the tasks identified by 650 supervisors as very important to performing their job successfully.[1]

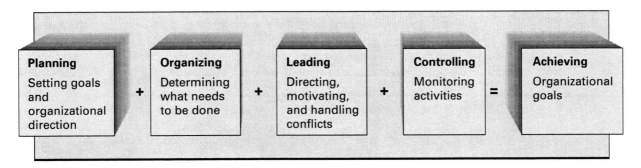

FIGURE 1-5

Management functions

- Motivate employees to change or improve their performance.

- Provide ongoing performance feedback to employees.

- Take action to resolve performance problems in your work group.

- Blend employees' goals with organization's work requirements.

- Identify ways of improving communications among employees.

- Inform employees about procedures and work assignments.

- Keep track of employees' training and special skills as they relate to job assignments to aid their growth and development.

FIGURE 1-6

Key supervisory tasks (based on a survey of more than 650 supervisors). (Based on Allen I. Kraut and others, "The Role of the Manager: What's Really Important in Different Management Jobs," *Academy of Management Executive*, November 1989, p.287.)

THE TRANSITION FROM EMPLOYEE TO SUPERVISOR

"For a year I was one of them. Then, all of a sudden I was in charge. Some didn't buy into it," explains Tammy Abel, coordinator of the Winnipeg Student Employment Centre.

"The micromanagement was a surprise for me when I first became a supervisor. I found a lot of employees turned to management to make decisions that they could make themselves," reported Daniel Quondam of Com Dev Wireless in Moncton.

Diane McArthur's "biggest concern about becoming a supervisor and having direct reports was performance management. What would I do about the employee who isn't performing?"

As you can see from these comments, the move from operative employee to supervisor can involve anxiety and surprises. In this section, we'll look at the primary routes people take to becoming supervisors and the challenges they face in mastering a new identity.

WHERE DO SUPERVISORS COME FROM?

Most supervisors are promoted from within the ranks of their own organization. For example, Larry Bowzeylo of Suncor in Fort McMurray started with the company in 1969 as an operator. He worked his way through all the operator positions (Suncor produces oil from material taken from the Athabasca Tar Sands). He was #1 operator, therefore holding a position of

Com Dev Wireless
www.comdev.ca

Are You Comprehending What You're Reading?

1. Which one of the following is not a characteristic of an organization?
   a. All organizations are made up of people.
   b. All organizations have structures.
   c. All organizations have goals.
   d. All organizations make a profit.
2. Organizational members who are responsible for establishing and meeting specific goals in a department are called top-level managers. True or false?
3. What is the difference between efficiency and effectiveness? All things being equal, which one of the two is the more important in today's organizations?
4. The management function that deals with determining what tasks are to be done and where decisions are made is the _____ function.
   a. planning
   b. organizing
   c. leading
   d. controlling

respect and prestige, before being promoted to shift supervisor in 1980. He held this until 1989 when he was promoted to middle management as an area manager. In 1995 he was assigned to a special project managing the building of a vacuum unit, which took several years. After that success he was assigned to another project. He is now the Operations Integration Manager for Plants 54 and 55 for Millennium Upgrading Operations, involved in managing the startup and commissioning and the implementation of a new hydrogen plant and three new Hydrotreaters. Interestingly, each time Larry was promoted, it was a lot more work than he thought it would be.

Employers tend to promote operative employees to first-line management jobs for several reasons. Operative employees know the job, understand the organization and typically know the people they'll be supervising. And the organization knows a lot about the candidate. When management promotes "one of their own," it minimizes risk. Finally, and importantly, promoting from within acts as an employee motivator; it provides an incentive for employees to work hard and excel.

Suncor
www.suncor.com

FIGURE 1-7

Larry Bowzeylo, like most supervisors, began work for his employer, Suncor, as an operative employee.

What criteria do management tend to use in deciding whom to promote to supervisor? Employees with good work records and an interest in management tend to be favoured. Ironically, good operative employees don't always make good supervisors. People with strong technical skills don't necessarily have the skills needed to manage others. Those organizations that successfully promote from within tend to select employees with adequate technical skills and then provide them with supervisory training early in their new positions.

The second source of supervisory personnel is new college or university graduates. But even here, it is unusual for the graduate to move directly into supervision. Typically the graduate must put in some time as an operative employee to learn and appreciate the tasks they will later be supervising.

A third source of supervisors is hiring people from other organizations who have relevant experience. This is more risky than hiring from within as the information the organization has about the candidate is limited and of questionable validity.

MASTERING A NEW IDENTITY

Moving from one middle-management job to another, or from a middle-management position to one in top management, rarely creates the anxiety that comes when one moves from being an employee to a supervisor. It's a lot like being a parent. If you already have three children, the addition of one more isn't too big a deal. Why? Because you already know quite a bit about parenting. The trauma lies in the transition from being childless to being a parent for the first time. The same applies in management. The trauma experienced when an employee moves into first-line management is unique, and unlike anything he or she will encounter later in climbing up the organizational ladder.

A study of what 19 new supervisors experienced in their first year on the job helps us to better understand what it's like to become a first-line manager.[2] The people in this study were 14 men and five women. All worked in sales or marketing. However, what they experienced would seem relevant to anyone making the employee-supervisor transition.

Even though these new supervisors had worked in their respective organizations as salespeople for an average of six years, their expectations of a manager's job were incomplete and simplistic. They didn't appreciate the full range of demands that would be made on them. Each had previously been a star salesperson. They were promoted, in large part, as a reward for their good performance. But "good performance" for a salesperson and "good performance" for a manager are very different— and few of these new supervisors understood that difference. Ironically, their previous successes in sales may actually have made their transition to management harder. Because of their strong technical expertise and high motivation, they had needed less support than the average salesperson. So when they became supervisors and suddenly had to deal with low-performing and unmotivated employees, they weren't prepared for it.

The 19 new supervisors actually encountered a number of surprises. We'll briefly summarize the major ones because they capture the essence of what many supervisors encounter as they attempt to master their new identity.

Their initial view of the manager as "boss" was incorrect. Before accepting their supervisory jobs, these managers-to-be discussed about the power they would have and about being in control. As one put it, "Now, I'll be the one calling the shots." After a month, however, they spoke of being a "trouble-shooter," "a juggler," and a "quick-change artist." All emphasized solving problems, making decisions, helping others, and providing resources as their primary responsibilities. They no longer perceived the manager's job as being "the boss."

They were unprepared for the demands and ambiguities they would face. In their first week, these supervisors were surprised by the unrelenting workload and pace of being a manager. On a typical day, they had to work on many problems simultaneously and were met with constant interruptions.

Technical expertise was no longer the primary determinant of success or failure. They were used to excelling by performing specific technical tasks and being individual contributors, not by acquiring managerial competence and getting things done through others. It took four to six months on the job for most to accept the fact they now would be judged by their ability to motivate others to high performance.

A supervisor's job comes with administrative duties. These supervisors found that routine communication activities such as paperwork and exchange of information were time-consuming and interfered with their autonomy.

They weren't prepared for the "people challenges" of their new job. The managers unanimously asserted that the most demanding skills they had to learn in their first year dealt with managing people. They said they were particularly uncomfortable in counselling employees and providing leadership. As one stated, "I hadn't realized... how hard it is to motivate people or develop them or deal with their personal problems."

Group leaders at Bend All Manufacturing Ltd in Ayr, Ontario are in an interesting position. They work for a rapidly growing organization that manufactures transmission lines for such clients as Chrysler and Mercedes Benz. They work somewhat as assistants to the supervisors, having no actual authority to make decisions but expected to facilitate production in many ways. However, as the organization is expanding quickly and they have been identified as potential supervisors, they are being given a series of workshops on supervisory skills such as delegating and disciplining to prepare them for the promotion. What scares them about moving up into a supervisory position?

Their fears fall in four main areas. One is moving up from former coworkers. "Will people respect me?" "Will others resent my new position?" "Will they still see me as a member of the team or as an outsider?"

Much of their fear revolves around discipline. "Can I discipline people I used to work beside?" "Can I discipline in a positive way?" "Will I be able to treat everyone fairly?" "It scares me to be responsible for an irresponsible employee."

Decision making also intimidates many of them. "The thought of being responsible for running the whole shop...!" "Can I make the right decisions?" "Will I be able to perform my duties as expected?" "Will production suffer when I become a supervisor?"

The fourth area of fear concerns the high expectations of anyone in management. "Can I keep a professional attitude?" "Can I control my emotions?" "I'm not comfortable with the idea of interacting with other managers."

Luckily, given the opportunity to prepare together for future supervisory roles and practise the skills in a "safe" environment, these group leaders realized that their fears were shared and therefore were not as frightening. As they practised the skills, they gained a sense of control and comfort.

Do You Really Want to Be a Supervisor?

The fact that you're learning about supervision indicates that you're interested in understanding how to supervise people. As in any job,

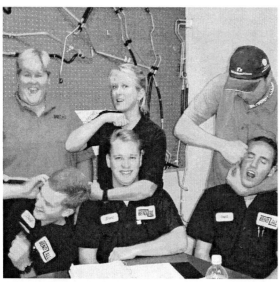
FIGURE 1-8

FIGURE 1-9

These group leaders at Bend All have been taking supervisory training in anticipation of promotion.

Becoming a supervisor is a challenging opportunity. Some individuals look forward to "taking the helm" of a crew of workers, while others are put into this situation with little advance notice—or training. As you consider going into a supervisory position—or making yourself a more effective supervisor than you are today—think about the following two areas.

1. List five reasons why you want to be a supervisor.

   _____

   _____

   _____

   _____

   _____

2. Identify five potential problems or difficulties that you may encounter when you become a supervisor.

   _____

   _____

   _____

   _____

   _____

though, the person who goes in with open eyes and realistic expectations is more likely to be successful and more likely to last. We'll cover the cons and then the pros of becoming a supervisor.

Supervisory positions are not easy. Even if you've been outstanding as an operative employee, there is no guarantee that you'll succeed as a supervisor. You know you're capable of doing excellent work, but there are other things to consider. One is that supervising may mean longer hours. Rob Mastrotto, team leader for the Inserts Finishing Team at Husky Injection Molding Systems in Bolton, Ontario, supervises about 45 people who work over three shifts. Rob typically arrives at work at 7 a.m. and stays until 6:30 p.m. to be in contact with all three shifts daily. He stays later when needed and sometimes comes in on weekends as well.

One of the reasons that Tina Payton came to Robinson-Blackmore printing company in St. John's, Newfoundland was the hours at her

**Husky Injection
Molding Systems**
www.husky.ca

FIGURE 1-10

As a supervisor at a daily newspaper, Tina was on call seven days a week, 24 hours a day.

Husky Injection Molding Systems
www.huskyims.com

Robinson-Blackmore
www.rb.nf.ca

Cedara
www.cedara.com

previous workplace, a daily newspaper. As a supervisor there she was on call seven days a week, 24 hours a day. She had to be accessible at all times, which meant that she couldn't even go far away on weekends. And, for printing a newspaper, the most critical hours are 11 p.m. to 4 a.m.—so this was when she was most likely to get the "We need you" emergency calls. Although both of these examples are at the extreme end, most supervisors do put in much more time than they are paid for.

These long hours are just one element of another issue for supervisors: stress. The increased responsibilities, accompanied by a limited amount of control, can be draining. Sheena Turnbull turned down a director-level position at her current employer, instead preferring to remain in her current position as manager of corporate staffing at Cedara. As she values the balance between work and her home life, she chose not to take a promotion.

Downsizing also causes stresses for many supervisors as it means releasing good employees and drastically increasing the workload for the remaining employees, who are understandably anxious about their own future. Joe Puiia's situation in dealing with "The Stresses of Downsizing" is described in Case 1.A at the end of the chapter.

You should also recognize that, as a supervisor, you may have a seemingly endless pile of paperwork to complete. This may include work schedules, production cost estimates, inventory documentation, budget or payroll matters, or performance appraisals for probationary and full-time staff.

Your pay as a supervisor also needs to be considered. As discussed above, it is unlikely that you will receive any overtime pay for all those extra hours. As a result, it is possible that operatives working fewer hours than you do may actually earn more because of overtime pay or commissions.

Another consideration focuses not on a negative but on a necessary shift in perspective. Your success as a supervisor will now typically come through other people's success. As an operative employee you were accustomed to tangible and immediate indication that you had performed your job well. As a supervisor, however, the feedback takes longer and is less closely tied to your own personal skills and efforts. This can be frustrating for some supervisors, leading them to keep their hand in more than they should on the operative side. This can overload you and cause resentment among the operative employees.

Despite the concerns expressed above, people still choose to move into management and then choose to stay in management. Why? Some of the positives include challenging yourself, learning new skills, getting the opportunity to work with a different group of people, making more money (yes, sometimes that happens), and having the opportunity to influence how things are done. "I enjoy working with the people, getting to know them, and I enjoy the challenge of making good quality product and getting it out the door by deadline", says Paula Aylward, a shift manager at a Cavendish Farms French fries plant in P.E.I. Diane McArthur of ServiceOntario says, "the most rewarding thing is to see someone who works for you succeed and move to the next level and know you had a little part in it."

Cavendish Farms
www.cavendishfarms.com

COMPETENCIES OF SUPERVISORS

What does it take to be an effective manager? Are the competencies or skills needed the same, regardless of a manager's level in the organization? These questions will be answered in this section.

Thirty years ago, Robert Katz identified three essential **management competencies**: technical, interpersonal, and conceptual.[3] They are as relevant today as when Katz originally described them. And they have been joined by a fourth general category of management skills: political competence.

FIGURE 1-11

Paula Aylward of Cavendish Farms in P.E.I. enjoys the challenge of her supervisory position.

TECHNICAL COMPETENCE

Top management is composed of generalists who don't need to be intimately familiar with the mechanics of the operative employee's job. Instead, top management activities—such as strategic planning, developing the organization's overall structure and culture, maintaining relationships with major customers, investors, and so on—are generic in nature. The technical demands on top managers tend to be related to knowledge of the industry and a general understanding of the organization's processes and products. But this is not true for managers at other levels.

Unlike top management, most other managers manage within areas of specialized knowledge: for example, *sales* manager, *call centre project* manager, *ATM production* manager, *student placement* coordinator, *finishing line* supervisor. These managers need **technical competence**—the ability to apply specialized knowledge or expertise. It's difficult, if not impossible, to effectively manage people with specialized skills if you lack understanding of their jobs. You will have little credibility with them and will be unable to fulfill the "troubleshooting" role so commonly expected of supervisors.

Management competencies
General categories of skills necessary to perform a managerial job.

Technical competence
The ability to apply specialized knowledge or expertise.

INTERPERSONAL COMPETENCE

A supervisor's job is working with and through other people. So **interpersonal competence** is critical—the ability to work with, understand, and motivate other people, both individually and in groups. Supervisors must listen well, speak well, and understand the needs of others. They need to give bad news and negative feedback, resolve conflicts, and confront

Interpersonal competence
The ability to work with, understand, and motivate other people, both individually and in groups.

unacceptable behaviour. They need to tune in to the varying motivations of people and act accordingly, yet still be viewed as fair.

This is a tall order and I suspect you have encountered a manager or two in your time who, although technically competent, failed in a leadership role because of inadequate interpersonal skills. "**Emotional intelligence**" is a concept now popularly used to describe a set of skills that correlate highly with effectiveness at work and in other realms. Goleman describes it as consisting of five basic emotional and social skills:[4]

Emotional intelligence
A set of skills including self-awareness, self-regulation, motivation, empathy and social skills that correlate highly with effectiveness at work.

Emotional Intelligence
www.eqi.org

- Self-awareness (a realistic assessment of one's abilities and shortcomings; use of awareness of one's feelings to guide actions appropriately)
- Self-regulation (conscientiousness, emotional control, the ability to delay gratification, self-discipline)
- Motivation (use of one's values and needs to take initiative; intent on improvement despite setbacks)
- Empathy (the ability to "tune in" to others' feelings and perspectives, to create rapport with diverse people)
- Social skills (smooth interaction with others, accurate reading of social situations and networks, and use of these skills to influence others, handle conflict, and promote cooperation)

The skills described above would certainly enhance any supervisor's ability to work with and through others. And they are skills, like technical competence, that can be consciously developed once one is aware of the need to develop them. One of the effective uses of 360-degree feedback, where a selection of employees who work with a supervisor all contribute their appraisals of his or her performance, is getting subordinates to anonymously give feedback to their supervisor on his or her skills. The feedback often most appreciated by supervisors, and often surprising to them, is the feedback on elements of their interpersonal competence.

CONCEPTUAL COMPETENCE

Conceptual competence
The mental ability to analyze and diagnose complex situations.

Managers must have the ability to analyze and diagnose complex situations. This is **conceptual competence**. Strong conceptual abilities allow a manager to see the "big picture" of the organization and its interrelated parts, and the bigger picture including the industry, community, and economy. On a more day-to-day level, these conceptual abilities allow a manager to anticipate events, plan more thoroughly, understand the priorities when faced with overwhelming demands, and make better decisions.

Stacy Goodale of Imperial Oil in Toronto notes, "I have to be a good analyst. To get things done, I not only have to articulate my ideas well, I have to know my audience and the context, know what is in my control, and know what is important. When should I be aggressive and push for my ideas in interfacing with senior management? What are they interested in?"

Imperial Oil
www.imperialoil.com

POLITICAL COMPETENCE

Supervisors also need to possess **political competence**. This refers to the supervisor's ability to enhance his or her power, build a power base, and establish the "right" connections in the organization. Politics is something supervisors engage in when they attempt to influence the advantages and disadvantages in a situation.[5] It is beyond normal work duties and their job description.

Susan Mocsan is manager of Human Resource Information System (HRIS) and Payroll at Brewers Retail Inc. in Ontario. She is working on a major project to develop and implement HRIS, a computer database of information about all employees, and works with both technicians and human resource staff in doing so. The HRIS must meet the needs of the organization, but this is a hard thing to pin down, seeming to change constantly as the company develops. People aren't rushing to her from the "business" side of the organization to inform her what she should be incorporating. So Susan has made it a point to get to know the various managers as individuals and "chat" with them regularly. She'll stop by an office and show an interest. "In five minutes with the VP of Logistics I've learned a lot about what's happening in that manager's area, built the relationship a bit, and ensured the doors are open."

Political competence
A supervisor's ability to enhance his or her power, build a power base, and establish the "right" connections in the organization.

FIGURE 1-12

Susan Mocsan of Brewers Retail Inc. uses her political skills to keep informed.

COMPETENCIES AND MANAGERIAL LEVEL

While managers need to possess all three competencies, the importance that each competency plays in the manager's job varies with the manager's level in the organization. Here are some general rules:

1. Technical competence declines in importance as managers rise in the organization.
2. Conceptual competencies increase in importance as managerial responsibility rises.
3. Interpersonal competencies are a constant to success, regardless of level in the organization.
4. Political competence grows in importance as managers rise in the organization.

Technical abilities have the greatest relevance for first-level managers. This is true for two reasons. First, many perform technical work as well as managerial work. In contrast to other levels of management, the distinction between individual contributor and first-line manager is often blurred. Second, supervisors spend more time on training and developing their employees than do other managers. This requires them to have a greater technical knowledge of their employees' jobs than that needed by middle- and top-level managers.

The importance of conceptual competence increases as managers move up in the organization because of the type of problems and

FIGURE 1-13

Rod Guild, senior fore-man at a B.C. copper mine, emphasizes the importance of inter-personal skills in his position.

Mining Technology
www.mining-technology.com/projects/highland/index.html

decisions that managers make at different levels. Generally speaking, the higher a manager rises in an organization, the more the problems he or she faces tend to be complex, ambiguous, and ill defined. This requires custom-made solutions. In contrast, first-level managers generally have more straightforward, familiar, and easily defined problems that lend themselves to more routine decision making. Ill-structured problems and custom-made solutions make greater conceptual demands on managers than do structured problems and routine decision making.

There is overwhelming evidence that interpersonal abilities are critical at all levels of management. This shouldn't come as a shock, because we know that managers get things done through other people. But supervisors are particularly in need of interpersonal competencies because they spend so much of their time in leading-function activities. For instance, Rod Guild, senior foreman at Highland Valley Copper Mine in British Columbia, emphasizes the importance of interpersonal skills: "Listen to your people as they have experience and ideas that you don't. Also, the simple act of listening to their input often ensures they become more interested and involved in the job. For example, we were building a road and needed good quality rock for it. Talking it over with the cat operator, who had run the cat longer than I had been alive, I suggested hauling rock in from an ore shovel with good material. His suggestion was to cut the rock from a bank immediately beside him. This saved 25 percent of the time to do the job and didn't interrupt ore flow to the crushers."

Regardless of what the company produces, it's people you work with as a manager. So the skills needed are the same anywhere. In talking with dozens of practising supervisors, the one common viewpoint we have heard is the importance of "people skills" to the successful achievement of their unit's objectives.

Finally, the higher one climbs in the organization's hierarchy, the more critical political competence becomes. Because resource allocation decisions are made at higher levels in an organization, middle and top managers are "fighting" for their piece of the organizational pie. Their need to develop alliances, support one project over another, or influence certain situations, involves higher-level political skills. But don't interpret this as implying that politics are less important for supervisors. Because so much of the supervisor's job is not well defined, he or she needs strong political skills to get the unit's work completed, and to survive (see Assessing Yourself)!

Assessing Yourself

DO YOU HAVE WHAT IT TAKES TO BE POLITICAL?

Are you an individual who likes to play politics? Is it something that you have the ability to do? Even if you prefer not to, can you "play" to protect yourself?

Undoubtedly, politics exist in every organization. Therefore, one of the first steps is understanding your political temperament. Listed below are several statements. Check True or False based on how you feel about the statement most of the time.

	True	False
1. I stay late just to impress my boss.	☐	☐
2. I do not tell others how I do things, so they don't know what I do.	☐	☐
3. I do not use gossip to my advantage.	☐	☐
4. I rarely express my opinion about my organization if my opinions are negative.	☐	☐
5. I go out of my way to make friends with powerful people.	☐	☐
6. I would not raise concerns about someone's ability to do a job, even if we were competing for a promotion.	☐	☐
7. I won't take credit for the work of someone else.	☐	☐
8. I'd tell my boss if a coworker was actively looking for a new job.	☐	☐
9. I would want my name on a group project, even though my effort was minimal.	☐	☐
10. I see nothing wrong in tooting my own horn.	☐	☐
11. I like having decorations all around my work area.	☐	☐
12. I take action only after I am sure it's ethical to do so.	☐	☐
13. I'd be foolish to publicly correct a mistake my boss made.	☐	☐
14. I'd purchase stock in my company even if it was a financial risk.	☐	☐
15. I would not be willing to play the "heavy" or the "big gun" who is brought in to fire people, even if it meant a promotion for me.	☐	☐
16. I want others to fear me more than like me.	☐	☐
17. I would not join in with coworkers making fun of the boss.	☐	☐
18. Getting ahead means promoting my self-interest.	☐	☐
19. I would not want to help a coworker who makes my performance look bad.	☐	☐
20. I think it's important to be friendly with everyone at work—especially those I don't like.	☐	☐

SCORING

Give yourself one point for each response that matches those given below.

1. True	6. False	11. False	16. True
2. True	7. False	12. False	17. True
3. False	8. True	13. True	18. True
4. True	9. True	14. True	19. True
5. True	10. True	15. False	20. True

MAKING SENSE OF THE ASSESSMENT

Your political score on this assessment indicates how likely you are to use politics to gain an advantage in a situation. Scores greater than 14 indicate you have an above-average willingness to use politics to get what you want. Scores from 10 to 13 indicate you use politics mainly to protect yourself - especially from your boss and those you perceive as having power. Scores from 6 to 9 indicate you have a true belief in others - that they are fair, honest, and not likely to mistreat you. Although noteworthy, this score may indicate you don't understand organizational politics, and you may be somewhat naive in assessing the effect politics may have on you. Finally, scores less than 5 indicate an absence of ability to play politics in an organization. Remember, politics isn't always destructive – there's a constructive component that you must use to your advantage.

Source: *Winning Office Politics* by Andrew Dubrin. Copyright © 1990. Reprinted with permission of Prentice Hall.

FROM CONCEPTS TO SKILLS

Supervision does come more easily to some than others. It helps if you've worked for a good manager so you have a role model to emulate. Or if you've grown up with parents, relatives or friends who were managers, you may have gained insights into the job and the skills needed. If your parents helped you set realistic goals, provided positive feedback, encouraged independence, communicated openly, and fostered the development of a strong self-concept in you, you have learned skills that will help you function as a manager. However, anyone can improve his or her supervisory abilities.

This book will help you to be an effective supervisor by focusing on both conceptual knowledge and practical skills. In the next chapter, for example, we'll discuss the importance of planning to a supervisor's success and show how setting goals is a key part of planning. Then we'll present specific techniques for helping employees set goals and provide you with an opportunity to practice and develop your goal-setting skills.

What exactly is a skill? **A skill** is the ability to demonstrate a system and sequence of behaviour that is functionally related to attaining a performance goal.[6] No single action constitutes a skill. For example, the ability to write clear communications is a skill. People who have this skill know the particular sequence of actions to be taken to propose a project or summarize a report. They can separate primary from secondary ideas. They can organize their thoughts in a logical manner. They can simplify convoluted ideas. But none of these actions is by itself a skill. A skill is a system of behaviour that can be applied in a wide range of situations.

What are the key skills related to supervisory effectiveness? While there is no unanimous agreement among teachers and trainers of supervision, certain skills have surfaced as being more important than others. Figure 1-14 lists those key supervisory skills organized as they'll be presented in this text. In aggregate, they form the competency base for effective supervision.

Skill
The ability to demonstrate a system and sequence of behaviour that is functionally related to attainment of a performance goal.

Related to Planning and Control
- Goal setting
- Budgeting
- Creative problem solving
- Developing control charts

Related to Organizing, Staffing, and Employee Development
- Empowering others
- Interviewing
- Providing feedback
- Coaching

Related to Stimulating Individual and Group Performance
- Designing motivating jobs
- Projecting charisma
- Listening
- Conducting a group meeting

Related to Coping with Workplace Dynamics
- Negotiation
- Stress reduction
- Counselling
- Disciplining
- Handling grievances

FIGURE 1-14

Key supervisory skills

What Else Do I Need to Know about Supervising?

If by now you're somewhat amazed at what a supervisor has to do and the skills he or she must have to succeed in an organization, there are nonetheless several other elements that you should consider. Specifically, what are the personal issues that you should address?

One of the first things you'll need to do is to recognize that as a supervisor, you are part of management. This means that you support the organization and the wishes of management above you. Although you might disagree with those wishes, you must, as a supervisor, be loyal to the organization. You must also develop a means of gaining respect from your employees, as well as from your peers and boss. In order to be effective as a supervisor, you'll need to develop their trust and build credibility with them. One means of doing this is to continually keep your skills and competencies up to date. You must continue your "education," not only because it helps you, but also because it sets an example for your employees. It communicates that learning matters.

Supervisors in various fields understand this need for continuing education. "Every time I turn around there's an upgrade. There's always new software coming out as well as new equipment. It's a constant challenge to keep up with it all and you have to take the initiative to keep up. We are currently reviewing new equipment to keep us on the leading edge of technology. We will be attending a huge graphic trade show in Chicago soon to research this equipment as well as checking out what else is new in the industry," says Tina Payton, prepress supervisor at Robinson-Blackmore, a printing company in St. John's. On the other hand, when Tricia Mah moved into her position as director of support services at an intermediate care residential home in Vancouver, she was in charge of food services, laundry, and housekeeping, knowing a great deal about food services but very little about the other areas. Since no courses were available to teach her the necessary information, she contacted colleagues in management at acute-care facilities and asked one friend to spend a day helping her to "learn the ropes." She also took a correspondence course in housekeeping methodology.

You'll also have to understand what legitimate power you have been given by the organization because you direct the activities of others. This legitimate power is your authority to act and to expect others to follow your directions. Yet, be aware that ruling with an iron fist may not work. You'll need to know when to assert your authority and how to get things done without resorting to "because I told you so." To get things done in the organization, you need to develop interpersonal skills that help you influence others. This is particularly true when dealing with organizational members whom you don't supervise.

Finally, you'll need to recognize that organizational members differ from one another—not only in their talents, but also as individuals. You'll need to be sensitive to their needs, tolerate and even celebrate their differences, and be empathetic to them as individuals. Success, in part, will begin with understanding the meaning of flexibility.

Throughout this text we'll address each of these areas.

SUPERVISORY CHALLENGES FOR THE 21ST CENTURY

The world of management has changed drastically because of the increasing use of computer technology, massive downsizings and restructurings to meet intense competition, and the diversity of today's workforce. In the remainder of the chapter, we will review some of the most significant forces now affecting supervisors.

CHANGING EXPECTATIONS OF SUPERVISORS

Forty years ago, if you asked a group of top executives what they thought a supervisor's or foreman's job was, you'd get a fairly standard answer. They'd describe a man (which it was likely to be back then) who made and enforced decisions, told employees what to do, closely watched over those employees to make sure they did as they were told, disciplined them when they broke the rules, and fired those who didn't "shape up." Supervisors were the bosses on the "operating floor" and their job was to keep the employees in line and get the work done.

If you asked top executives that same question today, you'd find a few who still hold to the supervisor-as-boss perspective. But you'd be far more likely to hear executives describe today's supervisor with terms such as "trainer," "adviser," "mentor," "facilitator," or "coach." In this section, we will look at how top management, the public, and even operative employees have developed changing expectations of supervisory managers.

ROLE AMBIGUITY

The supervisor's job—unique in that it bridges both the management and operative ranks—has long had an ambiguous role. For example, each of the following offers a different perspective of the supervisor's role:[7]

Key person. Supervisors serve as the critical communication link in the organization's chain of authority. They are like the hub of a wheel around which all operating activities revolve.

Person in the middle. Because they are "neither fish nor fowl," supervisors must interact and reconcile the opposing forces and competing expectations from higher management and workers. If unresolved, this ambiguous status can create frustration and stress for supervisors.

Just another worker.   To some, particularly among upper-level managers, supervisors are often viewed as "just another worker" rather than as management. This is reinforced when their decision-making authority is limited, when they're excluded from participating in upper-level decisions, and when they perform operating tasks alongside the people they supervise.

Behavioural specialist.   Consistent with the belief that one of the most important abilities needed by supervisors is strong interpersonal skills, we can view them as behavioural specialists. To succeed in their jobs, supervisors must be able to understand the varied needs of their staff; and be able to listen, motivate, and lead.

While each of these four role descriptions has some truth to it, each also offers a slanted view of the supervisor's job. Our point is that different people hold different perceptions of this job, which can create ambiguity and conflicts for today's supervisor.

INCREASED IMPORTANCE

Despite differing perceptions of the supervisor's role, the job has always been important and complex. It will likely become even more so in the future for at least three reasons.[8]

First, organizations are implementing significant change programs to cut costs and increase productivity. Examples include quality improvement, the use of teams, group bonus plans, and stress-reduction programs. These programs tend to focus on the work activities of operative employees. Supervisors are, therefore, important because they are the ones typically responsible for implementing these change efforts on the operating floor.

Second, many organizations have imposed extensive cutbacks in their numbers of employees. Middle management and support-staff personnel have been particularly thinned out. Because there are fewer middle managers, supervisors tend to have more people reporting to them: a span of control of 50 employees per supervisor is not uncommon today yet was unheard of not long ago. Many of the tasks previously performed by support personnel are now moving to supervisors; for example, scheduling and quality control.

Finally, employee training is increasing in importance as organizations seek to improve productivity. New employees, many of whom lack literacy or numeracy skills, and some immigrants with limited English, require basic training in reading and writing. Current employees typically need occasional but ongoing training to keep their skills up-to-date. Supervisors carry the primary burden of identifying skill deficiencies, and sometimes also design and deliver the training.

Are You Comprehending
What You're Reading?

5. Interpersonal skills are relatively unimportant for supervisors but become increasingly important as one moves up in management. True or false?

6. Interpersonal competence involves:
   a. the ability to enhance one's power base.
   b. the ability to analyze and diagnose complex situations.
   c. the ability to motivate, negotiate with, and delegate to others.
   d. the ability to apply specialized knowledge.

7. Why do technical abilities frequently have greater relevance for supervisors than for middle or top managers?

8. Which of the following is true of the supervisory role today?
   a. Supervisors are expected to play a much tougher role today, coming down hard on people who don't perform, in order to improve productivity.
   b. Supervisors have ambiguous roles.
   c. Supervisors are becoming much less involved with training because specialists are now assuming that function.
   d. Supervisors do no planning today; middle management performs that function while supervisors then put those plans into action.

FROM BOSS TO COACH

Marlene Roy is supervisor of the Labour Market Information Unit of HRDC in Winnipeg, but she is also formally referred to as the team leader. Rob Mastrotto supervises over 40 people at Husky Injection Molding Systems but his official title is Inserts Finishing Team Leader.

These titles are significant. The focus for supervisors now in most companies is not on being a boss but rather on "coaching" a team. The analogy with a sports team can be expanded even further. Today's supervisor is expected to identify and develop skills, as well as support and motivate individuals. The supervisor ensures that each employee learns to play his or her part, but also facilitates employees' movement towards a cohesive, synergistic whole. Supervisors are also expected to make tough decisions when things are going badly.

Note that the skills of a coach include the technical, conceptual, and political skills noted earlier. But a major emphasis for a coach must be on his or her interpersonal skills. People obey a boss because they have to "or else." People go along with a coach because they consider it to be in their best interest, they respect the coach, and they want to contribute to the team.

CHANGING THE SIZE OR THE STRUCTURE OF THE ORGANIZATION

DOWNSIZING

Many Canadian organizations have attempted to become "lean and mean" by reducing their workforce, or **downsizing**. The goal in each case was to create greater efficiency and cut costs. Many activities were outsourced and there has been increased use of contract workers to give the organization greater flexibility.

Downsizing can have various effects on supervisors. Employees who are laid off and those left behind, feeling insecure and overloaded with work, may become angry. Despite not being the one to make the downsizing decision, the supervisor may take the brunt of employees' resentment. The supervisor may also have had the excruciating responsibility of helping to decide which employees were to be let go. Many supervisors feel that the worst thing they have ever had to do in their position was to lay off an excellent performer and loyal employee simply because that person had less seniority than others.

An important challenge for supervisors is to motivate the remaining staff, who may feel resentful, less committed, stressed, and disloyal. Downsizing may also cause increased competition among the employees, trying to outdo each other to protect their position. They may be less likely to help each other. In such a situation the idea of a team seems ridiculous.

Along with the loss of staff through downsizing, it is unlikely that the demand on the department's productivity will become any less. Work systems and procedures may need to be altered drastically, and this will likely be the supervisor's responsibility. Workloads for all, including the supervisor, will be heavier. Productivity and/or quality may suffer, and the supervisor must answer for this.

GROWTH

To be a supervisor in an organization that is healthy and growing may seem ideal; however, such a situation brings its own problems. Production demands are high. New employees must be recruited, hired, given the appropriate orientation and training, and integrated into the workflow. But, due to production demands, they may be thrown on the floor without adequate preparation and then cause quality problems. The supervisor must train employees, deal with the quality problems, push production, and interview new staff while his or her own workload is incredibly high. It's a challenging and stimulating endeavour but it can also be extremely draining for the individuals involved.

Downsizing
A reduction in the workforce and reshaping of operations to create "lean and mean" organizations. The goals of organizational downsizing are greater efficiency and reduced costs.

RESTRUCTURING

Organizations may change their organizational structure for a variety of reasons, for example, in an attempt to streamline activities, make them more responsive to customer demands, or save money. For example, an organization may move from a traditional functional structure to one that is more responsive to customers. In a traditional structure, employees are grouped by function—marketing people are grouped together, production staff are grouped, finance people are grouped, and so on. This can focus employee attention and loyalty on their unit rather than on the organization and the customer. As a result, many companies have now moved to a customer base structure where a department may consist of a selection of people from all those functions who are grouped to meet the needs of one particular customer to whom they are assigned. The supervisory role in these two structures is very different—moving from one of technical specialist and troubleshooter to coordinator.

Another example of restructuring involves moving to a team structure. Paul Dolan, as ATM production manager at NCR in Waterloo, Ontario, is directly responsible for over 90 people. This is only possible because employees are divided into three self-directed teams. Each team takes on such tasks as interteam rotation of staff, quality, deciding vacation schedules, and health and safety. As a result, Paul is freed to concentrate on planning and problem-solving (long-term improvements) and do less day-to-day decision-making of a routine nature. His job is very different from that of a line supervisor where employees are not involved in routine decision-making. Paul's situation will be discussed much more in Chapter 5.

NCR
www.ncr.com

Managing Technology

Carolyn Moore supervises employees in England, the United States, Australia and Germany from her office at NCR in Waterloo, and she only meets most of them once a year face to face. How does she do it? Through conference calls, individual phone conversations, and a ton of e-mail. Carolyn leads a team in developing NCR's international HRTT (Human Resource Technology Team). The system itself will be high-tech personified and Carolyn's team members perform their work using those high-tech methods to communicate and share information (to be described in greater detail in Chapter 11).

Few jobs today are unaffected by technology. As he drives around the large mine site in his truck, Rod Guild of Highland Valley Copper in British Columbia uses a digital handheld voice recorder and a handheld computer notebook to note his observations. He regularly consults these notes when he is in a position to act on his observations. He has no office.

Undoubtedly, technology has had a positive effect on internal operations within organizations. How, specifically, has it changed the supervisor's job? To answer that question we need only to look at the way the typical office is set up. Organizations today have become integrated communications centres. By linking computers, telephones, fax machines, copiers, printers, and the like, supervisors can get more complete information more quickly than ever before. With that information, they can better formulate plans, make faster decisions, more clearly define the jobs that workers need to perform, and monitor work activities on an "as-they-happen" basis. In essence, technology today has enhanced supervisors' ability to more effectively and efficiently perform their jobs!

Technology is also changing where a supervisor's work is performed. Historically in organizations, the supervisor's work site was located close to the operations site. As a result, employees were in close proximity to their bosses. A supervisor could observe how the work was being done, as well as easily communicate with employees face-to-face. Through technological advancements, supervisors are now able to supervise employees in remote locations (see Something to Think About, below). Face-to-face interaction has decreased dramatically. Work, for many, occurs where their computers are. Telecommuting capabilities—linkage of a remote worker's computer and modem with coworkers and management at an office—have made it possible for employees to be located anywhere in the global village. Communicating effectively with individuals in remote locations, and ensuring that their performance objectives are being met, are some of the supervisor's new challenges.

SOMETHING TO THINK ABOUT
•AND TO PROMOTE CLASS DISCUSSION•

THE OFF-SITE EMPLOYEE

If you were to go back some 150 years in Canadian history, you'd find that it was not uncommon for most workers to be performing their jobs at home. Most goods were not mass-produced. Individuals produced a finished product and then took it to market to sell. Then along came the Industrial Revolution, which changed how work was done. Now we may be coming full circle—once again working at home. It is estimated that off-site employees comprise about one-quarter of the Canadian workforce today, and that number is expected to rise. Most of these workers are in such professions as sales, medicine, law, accounting, and a wide range of service occupations.[9]

What benefits do you see for organizations that have work done off site? What benefits do you believe exist for employees who work at home? What are the potential problems a supervisor may face in supervising off-site workers?

The primary implications for supervisors of advances in computer technology relate to training, overcoming resistance to change, and dealing with a vastly greater amount of communication than previously. Many supervisors deal with literally dozens of e-mail and voice-mail messages daily.

Managing Workforce Diversity

Canada's workforce reflects its society and, particularly in urban areas, that workforce is multicultural. As well as increasing in cultural diversification, the Canadian workforce is composed of a greater percentage of women than it used to be, is better educated, and also comes with an almost endless variety of "family" systems to return home to. See Figure 1-15 for a summary of how the Canadian workforce has changed.

The implications of **workforce diversity** for management are widespread. Employees don't set aside their cultural values and lifestyle preferences when they come to work. As a result, management must be accommodating and flexible enough to meet the needs of valued workers. For example, this may mean more flexible work schedules to allow those responsible for children, the elderly, or others needing special care to work, or benefit programs may need to be redesigned to reflect employees' varied needs.

On a day-to-day level, supervisors must set an example of tolerating and embracing differences. A supervisor must be careful not to use inappropriate words or use humour that may be offensive. Inappropriate words or actions by subordinates indicating discrimination or lack of respect must be confronted. A supervisor may need to give extra support to an employee having difficulties outside of work that are affecting his or her performance at work. A supervisor may also need to strive to build a relationship with an employee whose culture includes extreme deference to authority. That person may be extremely reluctant to ask for help or make suggestions.

In addition to the diversity brought about by such factors as lifestyle, gender, nationality, and race, supervisors must be aware of the age differences they'll encounter. Today, there are three distinct age groupings.[12] Studies have shown that their views of each other vary widely and are often negative. First, there is the mature worker, those born prior to 1946. This group of workers, born shortly after the Great Depression, is security-oriented and has a committed work ethic. While mature workers have until recently been viewed as the foundation of the workforce, they may be regarded by other generational groups as having obsolete skills and being inflexible in their ways. The baby boomers, born in the late 1940s to early 1960s, are the largest group in the workforce. They are regarded as the career climbers—at the right place at the right time. Their careers advanced rapidly during their initial years of employment, because organizational growth at that time was unsurpassed. Yet, the view of them by mature workers is that they are unrealistic in their views and tend to be workaholics. Finally, there are the Generation Xers, those born between 1964 and 1975. These "twentysomething baby-busters" are bringing a new perspective to the workforce—less committed, less rule-bound, more concerned with their own gratification, and intolerant of the baby boomers and their attitudes.[13] As a result, they are viewed by the other two groups as being selfish and unwilling to play by the rules.

Workforce diversity
The increasing heterogeneity of organizations with the inclusion of different groups.

Supervision in *Action*

The Cultural Variables

To date, the framework most valuable in helping managers better understand differences between national cultures is one developed by Geert Hofstede.[10] He surveyed over 116 000 IBM employees in 40 countries, and found that supervisors and employees vary in four dimensions of national culture:

1. individualism versus collectivism
2. power distance
3. uncertainty avoidance
4. quantity versus quality of life[11]

Individualism refers to a loosely knit social framework in which people are expected to look after their own interests and those of their immediate family. This is made possible because of the large amount of freedom that such a society allows individuals. Its opposite is *collectivism*, which is characterized by a tight social framework. People expect others in groups to which they belong (such as a family or an organization) to look after them and protect them when they are in trouble. In exchange for this, they feel they owe absolute allegiance to the group.

Power distance is a measure of the extent to which a society accepts the fact that power in institutions and organizations is distributed unequally. A high power-distance society accepts wide differences in power within organizations. Employees show a great deal of respect for those in authority. Titles, rank, and status carry a lot of weight. In contrast, a low power-distance society plays down inequalities as much as possible. Supervisors still have authority, but employees are not fearful or in awe of the boss.

A society that is high in *uncertainty avoidance* is characterized by an increased level of anxiety among its people, which manifests itself in greater nervousness, stress, and aggressiveness. Because people feel threatened by uncertainty and ambiguity in these societies, mechanisms are created to provide security and reduce risk. Their organizations are likely to have more formal rules, there will be less tolerance for deviant ideas and behaviours, and members will strive to believe in absolute truths. Not surprisingly, in organizations in countries with high uncertainty avoidance, employees demonstrate relatively low job mobility, and lifetime employment is widely practised.

Quantity versus quality of life, like individualism and collectivism, represents a dichotomy. Some cultures emphasize the quantity of life, and value things such as assertiveness and the acquisition of money and material goods. Other cultures emphasize the quality of life, placing importance on relationships and showing sensitivity and concern for the welfare of others.

Where do Canadian supervisors fit within this framework? Which cultures would be likely to involve the biggest adjustment problems for Canadian supervisors? To answer these questions, we must identify those countries that are most and least like Canada on the four dimensions. Canada is strongly individualistic, but low on power distance. This same pattern is exhibited by Great Britain, Australia, the United States, the Netherlands, and New Zealand. Those least similar to Canada on these dimensions are Venezuela, Colombia, Pakistan, Singapore, and the Philippines.

Canada scored low on uncertainty avoidance and high on quantity of life. This same pattern was shown by Ireland, Great Britain, the United States, New Zealand, Australia, India, and South Africa. Those least similar to Canada on these dimensions are Chile and Portugal.

The study supports what many suspected—that the Canadian supervisor who transfers to London, New York, Melbourne, or a similar "Anglo" city has the fewest adjustments to make. The study further identifies the countries in which "culture shock" is likely to be the greatest, suggesting a need to radically modify the Canadian supervisory style.

Supervisors will need to learn how to blend these three age groups in order to be effective. That is, supervisors will need to be trained to effectively deal with each group, and to respect the diversity of views that each offers.[14] Companies such as the Travelers and the Hartford Insurance companies go to great lengths to train younger supervisors in how to deal with older employees. Likewise, more mature supervisors are made aware of the different work attitudes that younger workers may bring to the job. Inasmuch as work attitude conflict is natural between these groups, these companies have been successful in keeping problems to a minimum by helping the various groups learn about one another.[15]

Unfortunately, supervisors may even need to deal with others in the organization who discriminate against them. For example, Paula Aylward of Cavendish Farms says, "I need to have more [guts] than anything.

If I don't, the fight is twice as hard." Paula is a shift manager of a production plant, one of only eight women in management. When she first moved into management, some of the men she supervised would question her decisions, uncomfortable with a woman directing them. Even in dealing with upper management, Paula believes that her gender has affected how she is treated.

Characteristic	1950s	Today
Gender	Predominantly male	Male and Female
Race	Caucasian	Caucasian, Asian-Canadian, African-Canadian
Ethnic Origin	European descent	European descent, Asian, Middle Eastern, African
Age	20 to 65	16 to 80+ (with a higher average age)
Family Status	Single or married with children	Single, married with children, married with no children, cohabitating, dependent elders, dual-career couple, commuter relationship
Sexual Orientation	Heterosexual	Heterosexual, gay, lesbian, bisexual
Physical Abilities	Physically able	Physically able and physically challenged
Education Level	High school	About half with post-secondary education.

FIGURE 1-15

The diversification of the Canadian workforce

USE OF CONTRACT WORKERS

Organizations are now much more likely than previously to hire temporary help through the use of contract workers. This allows them to get the job done by people with exactly the skills needed without incurring the additional costs of extensive training, benefits, and employment insurance. Organizations can then terminate their relationship with contract workers when the demand for them no longer exists. How does this affect the supervisor who likely supervises a mixed staff of full-time and contract workers? With work being done by a series of contract workers rather than full-time workers, supervisors must do more hiring and training. The team's structure is upset somewhat every time personnel change. The contract worker may know the job but cause difficulties because he or she doesn't understand the culture, the "way things are done here" and the supervisor ends up working with the employee to overcome that, and working to put out the fires created.

Stacy Goodale has had several contract workers on her project and explains, "It can be a challenge building their credibility to others in the organization so they can get their job done. And sometimes I feel like a football blocker because a contract worker is criticized for putting his nose in where it doesn't belong. I need to deflect the comments so it doesn't become an issue—for the contract worker, the team, or the project."

Perhaps the biggest challenge for supervisors is handling change. The challenges noted above all combine together and do not have a distinct finish line. All supervisors must deal with never-ending change, both planned and unplanned. Trish Mah, who works at an intermediate care home in Vancouver, saw the home suddenly expand from 90 beds to over 150. "All the systems had to change. And change is hard for everyone." Daniel Quondam at Com Dev Wireless in Moncton explains that there is such demand for his product, components for cellular phones, that customers keep changing their orders, yet still expect them to be ready as soon as possible. As a result, it is extremely difficult to forecast sales and plan production accurately. Daniel becomes mired in trying to meet planned production, plus squeezing in the extra demands.

In the midst of all this change, supervisors need to use those emotional intelligence skills to keep themselves calm and motivated, and work with others to accept the changes and then implement them. It's a challenge, but never boring, and supervisors will be kept alert and developing. More specifics on managing change will be discussed in Chapter 13.

GUIDELINES FOR ACTING ETHICALLY AND COMPASSIONATELY

About the Skill

Making decisions can be difficult for supervisors when there seems to be an **ethical dilemma**. Yes, you must follow the law and you are supposed to follow the organization's rules and regulations. But do you want to discipline someone for leaving a little early from their shift when you know it's because they are going for cancer treatments? Should you recognize someone for an excellent report when you know they asked someone else to do most of the work even though you can't prove it?

As a supervisor you will face a lot of "grey" areas where you don't like what is happening but it isn't clear what you should do, if anything. For example, Marlene Roy at Winnipeg's Labour Market Information Unit of Human Resources Development Canada speaks of private consultants coming in to get specialized information from her office free of charge. What really irks her and her staff is that they know some of the consultants then go back to their clients and charge a lot of money for that information. Meanwhile, the client could have got the information for free if they had known. Her office therefore doesn't like dealing with those particular consultants. But do they have a choice, as a government information service?

Rob Mastrotto of Husky Injection Molding Systems says, "As bad as my day may be, it's sad to see how much personal misery some people have to endure outside of the workplace yet come into work in a high-pressure environment." If Rob knows these personal circumstances, can he allow this knowledge to affect the way he treats one employee compared to another?

Here are some guidelines for choosing what to do.

1. **Know your organization's policy on ethics.** Company policies on ethics, if they exist, describe what the organization perceives as ethical behaviour and what it expects you to do. This policy will help you clarify what is permissible for you to do—the managerial discretion you have. It will become your code of ethics to follow.

2. **Understand the ethics policy.** Just having the policy in your hand does not guarantee that it will achieve what it is intended to do. You need to fully understand it. Ethical behaviour is rarely a "cut and dried" process. With the help of the policy as a guiding light, you will have a basis from which to resolve ethical questions in the organization. Even if a policy doesn't exist, there are several steps you can take when confronted with a difficult situation.

Ethical dilemmas
Situations requiring one to define right and wrong conduct.

Human Resources Development Canada
www.hrdc-drhc.gc.ca

3. **Think before you act.** Ask yourself, why are you doing what you're about to do? What led up to the problem? What is your true intention in taking some action? Is it for a valid reason, or are there ulterior motives behind it—such as demonstrating organizational loyalty? Will your action injure someone? Can you disclose to your manager or your family what you're going to do? Remember, it's your behaviour that will be seen in your actions. You need to make sure that you are not doing something that will jeopardize your role as a manager, your organization, or your reputation.

4. **Ask yourself "what if" questions.** When you think ahead about why you're doing something, you should also be asking yourself "what if" questions. For example, the following questions may help you shape your actions: What if you make the wrong decision—what will happen to you? To your job? What if your actions were described, in detail, on your local TV news or in the newspaper? Would it bother or embarrass you or those around you? What if you get caught doing something unethical? Are you prepared to deal with the consequences?

5. **Seek opinions from others.** If it is something major that you must do, and you're uncertain about it, ask for advice from other managers. Maybe they've been in a similar situation and can give you the benefit of their experiences. If not, maybe they can just listen and act as a sounding board for you.

6. **Do what you truly believe is right.** You have a conscience and you are responsible for your behaviour. Whatever you do, if you truly believe it is the right action to take, then what others say (or what the proverbial "Monday morning quarterbacks" say) is immaterial. You need to be true to your own ethical standards. Ask yourself: Can you live with what you've done?

SUMMARY

This summary is organized by the Learning Objectives.

1. A supervisor is a first-level manager who oversees the work of operative or nonmanagement employees.
2. While supervisors, middle managers, and top management are all part of the managerial ranks, they differ by their level in the organization. Supervisors are first-level managers—they manage operative employees. Middle management includes all managers from those who manage supervisors up to those in the vice presidential ranks. Top management is composed of the highest-level managers—responsible for establishing the organization's overall objectives and developing the policies to achieve those objectives.
3. Being a supervisor offers challenge, the development of new skills, stimulating and ever-changing demands, and, often, more money and recognition to match the increased responsibility. However, supervisory responsibilities may be accompanied by greater stress, longer hours (and no overtime pay), the loss of immediate and tangible results from one's work, and paperwork demands.
4. The four functions of planning, organizing, leading, and controlling comprise the management process.
5. The four essential management competencies are technical, interpersonal, conceptual, and political competencies.
6. The supervisor's job will be increasingly important and complex in the future because of programs that focus on the work activities of operating employees, middle-management cutbacks (which have increased supervisory responsibilities), and the increased focus on training employees, which will be substantially implemented at the supervisory level.
7. Supervisors are now expected to coach a team of employees, treating them with respect and motivating them to reach their potential. They are no longer expected to "tell" employees what to do, but rather to explain what is needed and facilitate their achievement.
8. A shrinking staff sees the supervisor dealing with surviving employees who are frightened of their own security and may be overwhelmed with work demands. A growing company forces the supervisor to deal with high production demands while hiring and training new workers. Restructuring the organization can change the number of subordinates, the type of subordinates, and the demands on a supervisor.

9. Workforce diversity seeks to increase the heterogeneity of organizations with the inclusion of different groups. This includes, but is not limited to, women, members of racial minority groups, immigrants, and people with disabilities.
10. Technology has changed the equipment with which workers produce the company's product and service and introduced computers to many aspects of work. Supervisors use computers in their daily work (for example, creating reports or communicating via e-mail) and need to work with increased skill demands placed on workers by the newer technologies.

KEY TERMS AND CONCEPTS

Conceptual competence
Controlling
Downsizing
Effectiveness
Efficiency
Emotional intelligence
Ethical dilemmas
First-line managers
Interpersonal competence
Leading
Management
Management competencies
Management functions
Management process
Middle managers
Operative employees
Organizing
Planning
Political competence
Process
Skill
Supervisors
Technical competence
Top management
Workforce diversity

REVIEWING YOUR KNOWLEDGE

1. What differentiates supervisory positions from all other levels of management?
2. Is the owner-manager of a small store, with three employees, an operative, supervisor, or top manager? Explain.
3. What specific tasks are common to all managers?
4. Contrast time spent on management functions by supervisors versus time spent by top management.
5. "The best rank-and-file employees should be promoted to supervisors." Do you agree or disagree with this statement? Explain.

6. Why is conceptual competence more important for top managers than for first-level supervisors?

7. How can a supervisor be a "key person" and "just another worker"?

8. Based on your past work experience, describe two ethical dilemmas you faced on your job. How did you handle them?

9. What challenges does workforce diversity create for first-level managers?

10. What, if anything, can organizations do to help managers and employees alike learn to thrive on constant change?

ANSWERS TO THE POP QUIZZES

1. **d. All organizations make a profit.** While almost all organizations need to make money to survive, making a profit is not a characteristic of an organization.

2. **False.** Organizational members who are responsible for establishing and meeting specific goals in a department are called middle-level managers.

3. Efficiency involves a relationship between inputs and outputs. It focuses on doing things right. Effectiveness implies goal attainment. It focuses on doing the right things. If all things are equal, effectiveness is more important because it supports reaching the goals of the organization. [Note: Don't interpret this to mean that efficiency doesn't matter. It does!]

4. **b. Organizing.** The question addresses part of the definition of the organizing function.

5. **False.** Interpersonal skills are critical for all levels of management.

6. **c. The ability to motivate, negotiate with, and delegate to others.** The question addresses the definition of interpersonal competence.

7. Technical abilities frequently have greater relevance for supervisors because, unlike higher-level managers, many supervisors perform technical work as well as managerial work. Also, supervisors spend more time training and developing their employees, work that requires greater technical knowledge of their employees' jobs.

8. **b. Supervisors have ambiguous roles.** Supervisors are seen in different ways by different people in different circumstances.

CASE 1.A

The Stresses of Downsizing

Joe Puiia is acting supervisor of the Human Resources Development Canada (HRDC) office in Summerside, Prince Edward Island. His office handles pensions, child benefits, employment benefits and other government services for the area.

"We're surviving right now because we have committed soldiers who are still serving clients, despite the difficulties. We had 48 employees; now we have 22, but just as many clients.

"The employees are highly trained and a great group of people, and they know that they're not delivering their potential or what clients need. Time management courses won't work. Today I worked my backside off, solved a crisis, and did many important things, but none of the things on my plan for today.

"What's my role? I have no authority to really make the day better other than being a human being. I let them know how desperately I appreciate them. In meetings and privately, I say I know they go far beyond what I could even imagine. In management meetings, I speak up about conditions. So does my manager. I try to accommodate workers for personal time they need. I let someone leave early if they've been working extra hard. I'm honest in terms of my capacity to change things. I respect their efforts. Sometimes I'll e-mail them a thank-you. People get sick because they can't handle the load.

"Day to day, I'm the 'go-to' person. There's always ambiguity and I'm the person to bring it to. There are different interpretations of policies—grey areas. I deal with angry clients and employees having a spat. I deal with MP and MLA office inquiries, explaining why one of their constituents was refused something (e.g., entry into a skills development program)."

Joe has been the acting supervisor for three years. Why? "I'm getting supervisory pay but the government won't solidify people in their posi-tions. My counterpart in Charlottetown was just made supervisor after being acting supervisor for five years."

What has happened? "Downsizing, rightsizing, flatsizing. Whatever you call it, it's difficult. We have two counsellors dealing with 400 to 500 clients. Voicemails are filled every day. I'm so proud of the people in this building despite their inability to deliver the best service. They're not allowed to. They try and they care. But the political agenda to restrict costs seems paramount right now."

"When I leave at the end of the day, I silently wish the best for our workers and the clients they serve. I leave my work at the office and do my own maintenance. Family is big to me (wife and four children); sports and community involvement keep me fresh and energized. When I get back to the office on Monday, there will be much to deal with and I will pick it up and move forward. Despite the issues at hand I am fully aware that I must stay positive and professional in my approach to have any impact. My goal is to commit myself to do so."

RESPONDING TO THIS CASE

1. Why does it matter whether Joe is "acting supervisor" or "supervisor"? He is still doing the job and getting a supervisor's pay.
2. Assess Joe's apparent interpersonal competence or emotional intelligence.
3. Refer to the Role Ambiguity viewpoints discussed earlier in the chapter and apply them here as appropriate.
4. The way to manage stress will be discussed later in Chapter 13. Without knowing more about stress management yet, how do you think Joe effectively deals with his feelings and continues on in this seemingly impossible position?
5. Would you like to have Joe as your supervisor? Why or why not?

CASE 1.B

From Dealing with Babies to Horses

The Veterinary Teaching Hospital at the University of Saskatchewan is the only place in Western Canada that provides training for veterinary students. Its new director, Lana Clark, is a former nurse who worked in the Saskatoon Health Service for many years as a senior administrator. Lana is not a veterinarian and has never worked in a veterinary hospital. But the university recognized her skills as highly transferable and she obviously has an interest in animals (since she operates a horse farm and cattle business).

Lana is responsible for running the hospital as a business. This means ensuring that students have a sufficient caseload, that all staffing and equipment needs are met, and that appropriate funding is secured for the hospital. Five unit supervisors report to Lana, ranging from human resources to materials management. And, like anyone moving into a new supervisory position, Lana must also build credibility with her new staff. "People will look at how I make decisions and how I react to things. They'll make up their mind about me based on what I do." Lana also has to get to know the staff and understand their work. To accomplish this, Lana has spent much time in her first month on the job on the work units, helping out wherever she could, watching and asking questions. "If I understand the work, then I can explain it better to others and this is especially important when I go to lobby and get funds for the hospital."

As Lana does her best to fulfill the expectations and hopes of her new colleagues and subordinates, her actions will reflect the experience and skills she gained working in a health service focused on humans rather than animals. This posed many challenges for Lana. One challenge involved merging obstetrical services from two locations into one. Although it was not her decision, nor that of her subordinates, they were responsible for executing it. "I told the staff that there was no choice about what the future

would be, but we could help shape the future." The merger affected 150 staff and, in line with her decision-making philosophy, they were involved as much as possible in the change. Committees were formed to deal with the renovations and the actual movement of people, among other things. Lana believes that the "worst you can do is make a decision on your own without involving the people that work in the area affected. If you let them participate, then they know what they're getting into and they share a common vision." To learn whether the merger negatively affected service quality and access to obstetrical services, an outcome evaluation was planned. A baseline survey was conducted before the merger, followed up two and a half years later by another survey. This second survey indicated that results were as good as or better than the results before the merger. Lana felt it was important for all the staff to know how well they had managed the merger.

Another challenge Lana has had to deal with in her administrative past is laying off employees. She has been through several downsizings and has had to lay off people—from individuals on a one-on-one basis to sitting down with a group of up to 50 people to inform them of the bad news. "I try to help them understand the rationale of why it is happening, why their area is affected, that it has nothing to do with their performance, nothing to do with them personally. But some people do take it personally. It's much harder to lay off people due to a reorganization, not a downsizing, because the decision seems so much more subjective. I listen to them, hear them out, and offer whatever assistance I can to help them move forward."

What challenges will Lana face on this new job? "One major one is the fact that many of our employees are very long-term—more than 20 years. They are very specialized and very experienced with knowledge of the equipment and the building that others don't have. We have to make sure people are developed and ready to fill in their shoes when those long-term people leave. A second challenge is financial. We have major equipment capital needs. We can't make enough money ourselves to pay for the expensive equipment so we need ongoing funding for replacing equipment as needed. Planning can also be a challenge. We can basically plan what we should need in future but, if something breaks down unexpectedly or if there's a big medical advancement, we can't predict that and the equipment can be very expensive. So the department heads, the vets, and I need to keep up with research advances so we can budget for them.

"This veterinary hospital, like the health services before, is challenging in that both places deliver a 24-hour-a-day service. Running the business but still giving people their needed time off can be tough. Being flexible with time off can be important in satisfying employees (who can't always plan exactly when they will need time off). But the hospital still needs to be staffed.

"Another organizational challenge is looking at new ways to do work. Money doesn't always solve the problem. For example, sometimes you need changes to the physical environment or the schedule so that activity peaks are handled more smoothly and people feel less overloaded.

"What have I liked about being in management positions? Lots of challenges. I'm never bored—never sure of what my day will be like. I like the challenge of solving a problem, getting everyone to buy in. And I love working with people."

FIGURE 1-16

Lana Clark at home in Saskatchewan.

RESPONDING TO THIS CASE

1. Why would someone moving into a senior management position feel the need to prove themselves as if they were moving into supervision for the first time?
2. Note any evidence you can find for Lana having each of the four competencies.
3. Describe how the distribution of time Lana spends on the different management functions seems to have changed over her career as she moved up in different managerial positions.
4. Predict how well you think Lana will do in her new position. Justify.

PART TWO

PLANNING AND CONTROL

2. SUPERVISORY PLANNING AND TIME MANAGEMENT

3. DESIGNING AND IMPLEMENTING CONTROLS

4. PROBLEM SOLVING AND DECISION MAKING

2

SUPERVISORY PLANNING AND TIME MANAGEMENT

LEARNING OBJECTIVES

After reading this chapter, you should be able to:

1. Contrast formal and informal planning.
2. Describe how plans should link from the top to the bottom of an organization.
3. Contrast policies and rules.
4. Explain why managers create single-use plans.
5. Describe the Gantt chart.
6. Explain the information needed to create a PERT chart.
7. Describe the characteristics of effective goals.
8. Contrast response time and discretionary time.
9. List the five steps to better time management.

CHAPTER OUTLINE

PERFORMING EFFECTIVELY

WHAT IS PLANNING?

PLANNING AND MANAGERIAL LEVEL
   Something to Think About
   Planning Breadth
   Planning Time Frame
   Linking Managerial Levels

KEY PLANNING GUIDES
   Standing Plans
   Single-Use Plans
   Pop Quiz

SETTING GOALS
   Characteristics of Effective Goals
   Management by Objectives

TIME MANAGEMENT
   Time as a Scarce Resource
   Focusing on Discretionary Time
   How Do You Use Your Time?
   Five Steps to Better Time Management
   Something to Think About
   Some Additional Points to Ponder

FROM CONCEPTS TO SKILLS: GOAL SETTING
   Assessing Yourself: Are You a Good Goal Setter?
   Skill Basics
   Applying Your Skills
   Pop Quiz

UNDERSTANDING THE BASICS
   Summary
   Key Terms and Concepts
   Reviewing Your Knowledge
   Answers to the Pop Quizzes

PERFORMING YOUR JOB
   Case 2.A: Is This the Beginning of the End?
   Case 2.B: MBO at A.C. & C.E

FIGURE 2-1

Zahid Fazal, senior
staff accountant at
Ernst and Young's
Montreal office

Ernst & Young
www.ey.com

"The key to successful auditing begins with careful planning. Once established, the plan should be thoroughly communicated to all team members," says Zahid Fazal, a senior staff accountant at Ernst and Young LLP's Montreal office. An important tool used by the audit team is a local area network allowing each member to work individually while being connected to a paperless file. Access to this network is allowed through individual laptops provided to each staff accountant. Zahid is in charge of this network. His responsibilities as a senior on the audit also include selecting and supervising staff, reaching conclusions, and preparing summaries for manager and partner review. His personal dedication to each audit is demonstrated through his daily presence on the field along with his staff. Once an audit is completed, the team dissolves. Each member then works with other clients from various industries, creating a new audit group.

Much of Zahid's work is done upfront in the planning stage. When planning an audit, there is always a similar structure but it must be modified based on the client's business, prior history, and the audit risks involved. "We have to carefully plan our audit strategy in order to maximize efficiency and obtain the necessary conclusions. I have to make a budget, the audit program, and allocate procedures to staff team members. Every job is different. These guidelines are especially important if the audit mandate involves working for a client in different locations. The key is to maximize efficiency and avoid redundant and unnecessary work.

"Before we go out to the client's, the team has an internal meeting where we explain to new members the industry, the audit plan, particular issues and their roles on the engagement. I have a chart with the names and responsibilities of team members, including the manager and partner. Each accountant gets the chart and also gets an operating agreement. In talking to them, I set out the ground rules, one of which is to ask any questions."

Zahid needs to keep all information from the various clients well organized as he works on various engagements with various partners and managers at the same time.

WHAT IS PLANNING?

As discussed in Chapter 1, planning encompasses defining an organization's objectives or goals, establishing the overall strategy for achieving those goals, and developing a comprehensive hierarchy of plans to integrate and coordinate activities. And for our purposes, we'll treat the terms objectives and goals as interchangeable. Each is meant to convey some desired outcome that an organization, department, work group, or individual seeks to achieve.

Does planning require that goals, strategies, and plans be written down? Ideally they should be, but they often aren't. In formal planning, specific goals are formulated, committed to writing, and made available to other organization members. Additionally, specific action programs will exist in formal planning to define the path for achieving these goals.

But many managers engage in informal planning. They have plans in their heads, but nothing is written down and there is little or no sharing of these plans with others. This probably most often occurs in small businesses where the owner-manager has a vision of where he or she wants to go and how to get there. In this chapter, when we use the term *planning* we'll be implying the formal variety. It is this formal planning that is most often required for an organization to be productive (see Something to Think About).

PLANNING AND MANAGERIAL LEVEL

All managers should plan, but the type of planning they do tends to vary with their level in the organization.

PLANNING BREADTH

A common way to describe planning is to distinguish strategic from tactical or operational planning. Susan Miller, vice president of Enbridge Technology, an international consulting company that is part of Enbridge Corporation, is involved in **strategic planning**. The corporation owns and operates oil and gas pipelines, terminals, storage facilities, and natural-gas distribution systems both in North America and internationally. This means Susan must focus on the entire organization, establishing goals and positioning the organization's products or services against the competition. For example, she makes the final decision on what projects the company should bid on based not only on what will earn money, but also on what will enhance Enbridge's profile and reputation, thereby leading to desirable future projects. On the other hand, at a tactical level, her consultants must create a specific plan to fulfill the mandate of a specific consulting job for a

FIGURE 2-2

Susan Miller, VP of Enbridge Technology

Enbridge Corporation
www.enbridge.com

Strategic planning Covering the entire organization, it establishes overall goals and positions the organization's products or services against the competition.

Formalized planning became very popular in the 1960s, and, for the most part, it's still popular today. It makes sense to establish some direction. But recently, critics have begun to challenge some of the basic assumptions underlying planning.

Canadian management expert Henry Mintzberg believes that plans may create rigidity.[1] Formal planning efforts can lock organizational members into specific goals to be achieved within specific timetables. When these objectives are set, assumptions may be made that the "outside world" won't change during the period that the objectives cover. This may be a faulty assumption. Nevertheless, rather than remaining flexible—and possibly scrapping the plan—some supervisors may continue to fulfill the actions required to achieve the originally set objectives.

Other experts believe that formal plans can't replace intuition and creativity.[2] Formal planning efforts typically follow a specific methodology—making it a routine event. That can spell disaster for an organization. For instance, the rapid rise of Apple Computer Inc. between the late 1970s and the late 1980s was attributed, in part, to the creativity and anti-corporate attitudes of its cofounder, Steve Jobs. However, as the company grew, Jobs felt a need for more formalized management—a style he was personally uncomfortable with. He hired a CEO (Chief Executive Officer), who ultimately ousted Jobs from his own company. With Jobs' departure came increased organizational formality—the very thing Jobs despised so much because it hampered creativity. By 1996, this one-time industry leader had lost much of its creativity, and was struggling for survival. (Eventually, Jobs was brought back on board to try to revive Apple's fortunes.)[3]

Finally, there's a perception that while formal planning may reinforce success, it may also lead to failure.[4] We have been taught that success breeds success. That's been a North American "tradition." After all, if it's not broken, don't fix it—right? Well, maybe not! Success may, in fact, breed failure in the changing world of work. It's tough to change or discard successful plans—leaving the comfort of what works for the anxiety of the unknown. Formal plans may provide a false sense of security, generating more confidence than is warranted. Consequently, supervisors often won't deliberately face that unknown until forced to do so by changes in the environment. Unfortunately, by then it may be too late!

So, given these facts, should we still plan formally? Is it worth it? What do you think?

Why is it that, as a company grows in size, it is much more likely to engage in formal planning?

client. Their operational or **tactical planning** provides specific details on how to attain certain goals The two viewpoints, strategic and tactical, can come into conflict. "Sometimes I have to pry their fingers off a project when we realize that it is not worth pursuing." says Susan.

Tactical planning
Specific plans on how overall goals are to be achieved.

For the most part, strategic planning tends to be done by top-level managers; a supervisor's time tends to be devoted to tactical planning. Both types of planning are important for an organization's success, but they are different in that one focuses on the big picture, while the other emphasizes the specifics within that big picture. Zahid Fazal's role in running an audit, as described above, is considered to be tactical planning.

PLANNING TIME FRAME

Planning often occurs in three time frames—short term, intermediate term, and long term.

Short-term plans
Plans that are less than one year in length.

Short-term plans are less than one year in length. **Long-term plans** cover a period of five years or more. Plans of one to five years are **intermediate-term plans**. A supervisor's planning horizon tends to emphasize the short term: preparing plans for the next month, week or day. Zahid Fazal's planning for specific client audits falls under short-term planning. Employees in middle-management jobs, such as Susan Miller, typically focus on one- to three-year plans. Long-term plans tend to be performed by top executives.

Long-term plans
Plans covering more than five years.

Intermediate-term plans
Plans that cover from one to five years.

LINKING MANAGERIAL LEVELS

It's important to keep in mind that effective planning is integrated and coordinated throughout the organization. Long-term strategic planning sets the direction for all other planning. That is, once top management has defined the organization's overall strategy and goals and the general plan for getting there, then, in descending order, the other levels of the organization develop plans.

Figure 2-3 illustrates this linking of plans from the top to the bottom of an organization. The president, vice president, and other senior executives define the organization's overall strategy. Then upper-middle managers, such as regional sales directors, formulate their plans. And so on down to first-level managers. Ideally, these plans will be coordinated through joint participation. In the case of Figure 2-3, for instance, the Vancouver territory manager would participate with other territory managers by providing information and ideas to the B.C. district manager as she formulates plans for her entire district. If planning is properly linked, then the successful achievement of all the territory managers' goals should result in the B.C. district manager achieving her goals. If all the district managers meet their goals, this should lead to the successful attainment of the regional sales manager's goals, and so on up each level in the organization.

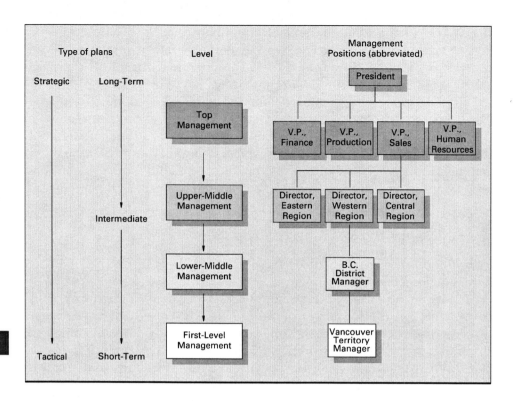

FIGURE 2-3

Planning and
managerial levels

KEY PLANNING GUIDES

Standing plans
Plans used over and
over again for recur-
ring activities.

Single-use plans
Detailed courses of
action used once or
only occasionally.

Once an organization's strategy and overall goals are in place, management will design additional plans to help guide decision makers. Some
of these plans will be **standing plans**. Once designed, they can be used
repeatedly by managers faced with recurring activities. Others will be
single-use plans, which are detailed courses of action used once or only
occasionally to deal with problems that don't occur repeatedly.

In this section we'll review the popular types of each plan.

STANDING PLANS

Standing plans allow managers to save time by handling similar situations in a predetermined and consistent manner. For example, when a
supervisor has an employee who consistently fails to show up for
work, it can be handled more efficiently and consistently if a discipline
procedure has been established in advance. In this section, we'll
review the three major types of standing plans: policies, procedures,
and rules.

POLICIES

"We promote from within wherever possible." "Do whatever it takes to
satisfy the customer." "Our employees should be paid competitive

wages." These three statements are examples of **policies**. That is, they're broad guidelines for managerial action. Typically established by top management, they define the limits within which managers must stay as they make decisions.

Policies
Broad guidelines for managerial action.

Supervisors rarely make policies. Rather, they interpret and apply them. Within the parameters that policies set, supervisors must use their judgment. For instance, the company policy that "our employees should be paid competitive wages" doesn't tell a supervisor what to pay a new employee. However, if the going rate in the community for this specific job is in the range of $8.20 to $9.50 an hour, the company policy would clarify that neither a starting hourly rate of $7.75 or $10.00 is acceptable.

PROCEDURES

A **procedure** is a series of steps for responding to a recurring problem. And a procedure can be a good friend to a supervisor who must deal with a problem employee. For example, Paula Aylward, a shift manager at Cavendish Farms' New Annan French-fries plant, explains, "You never fire anyone; they do it themselves. If I follow the steps in a disciplinary procedure for someone who, for example, is late consistently, I give them the appropriate verbal and written warnings. They know the consequences if they repeat the offence. They can't argue when they are fired. The union has never contested a firing I've been involved in."

Procedure
A series of steps for responding to a recurring problem.

Where procedures exist, managers only have to identify the problem. Once the problem is clear, so is the procedure to handle it. Other examples of procedures include hiring, completing purchasing requisitions with the right information and signatures, and handling overtime payment.

Procedures are more specific than policies. But, as with policies, procedures provide consistency. By defining the steps to be taken and the order in which they should be carried out, procedures provide a standardized way of responding to situations. As a result, the supervisor using these procedures appears fair.

Supervisors follow procedures set by higher levels of management and also create their own procedures for staff to follow. As conditions change and new problems surface that tend to be recurring, supervisors will develop standardized procedures for handling them. For example, Rita Cupitt, the Manager of Human Resources at Eagle's Flight in Guelph, Ontario, developed a hiring manual for team leaders outlining their "preflight checklist" of all the steps to follow. This was done because, without a clear and consistent hiring process and the requirement to get specific approvals from Finance and the CEO, crucial steps were being overlooked and the organization's recruiting goals were not being met. Another example of a created procedure is the appeals procedure developed by Paul Dolan, the ATM Production Manager at NCR in Waterloo, Ontario. He created the appeals procedure to cover situations where people felt their performance appraisal was unfair. The interesting angle to this is that the performance appraisal was being done by 5 coworkers who were chosen by the self-directed team to appraise all members of the team for a year.

RULES

Rule
An explicit statement that tells a manager what he or she ought or ought not to do.

A **rule** is an explicit statement that tells an employee about specific behaviour that is either required (e.g., all staff must wear safety boots in this area) or prohibited (e.g., no smoking). Similar to policies and procedures, rules ensure consistency. For example, if the rule says that no jewellery may be worn in the machine shop, the supervisor should ensure that all employees are aware of this rule and comply with it.

The main issue that arises with respect to rules is inconsistent enforcement. Nothing makes it more difficult for a supervisor to enforce a rule (e.g., employees are only allowed 15-minute breaks) than his or her subordinates knowing that their colleagues in another area are allowed to break the rule without consequence. In recent years, one of the most common areas of inconsistency concerns "smoke breaks." If some supervisors allow smokers to take extra breaks (beyond the normal breaks allowed to everyone else), this leads to the nonsmokers feeling cheated and the other supervisors being challenged on their attempts to enforce the strict adherence to break times. What can a supervisor do? This is an issue that should be addressed at a supervisors' meeting or through their common manager. The only way a rule can be enforced is if it is enforced by a united front.

SINGLE-USE PLANS

In contrast to the previous discussions of standing plans, single-use plans are designed for a specific activity or time period. The most popular types of these plans are programs, budgets, and schedules.

PROGRAMS

In January 1998, an ice storm hit parts of Quebec and Ontario, causing terrible damage and knocking out power to large regions for several weeks. Businesses were especially badly affected. At a major Canadian financial institution, Lynn Rutherford, a specialist in employment standards, was part of the Business Recovery Planning Team at head office whose role was to advise the regions on how to handle the crisis. The team met daily to see how the situation was unfolding and what needed to be done. Among the issues they looked at were how to get information to management groups in the different areas (with no phones, faxes, or e-mail); what to do about employees working in potentially dangerous conditions; whether transportation and food needed to be provided to employees; which of the many branches should be opened first; how to help employees get loans for home repairs and temporary accommodation; whether trauma teams were needed to help employees cope; and how to ensure that no computers were restarted until conditions were appropriate. Lynn was on the team on behalf of HR at the bank to represent the staff and ensure their safety. What she developed with the team was a program—a single-use set of plans for a specific major undertaking within the organization's overall goals.

All managers develop **programs**. A major program—such as building a new manufacturing plant or merging two companies and consolidating their headquarters' staff—will tend to be designed and overseen by top management, can extend over several years, and may even require its own set of policies and procedures. But supervisors frequently must create programs for their departments. Examples include the creation of a comprehensive ad campaign for a new client by an account manager of an advertising firm, and the development of a unique training program by the regional sales supervisor for Hallmark to help her people learn the intricacies of the company's new phone-activated, computerized inventory system. Note the common thread through all these examples: These are nonrecurring undertakings that require a set of integrated plans to accomplish their objectives.

Program
A single-use set of plans for a specific major undertaking.

BUDGETS

Budgets are numerical plans. They typically express anticipated results in dollar terms for a specific time period. For example, a department may budget $8000 this year for travel. But budgets can also be calculated in nondollar terms, such as employee hours, capacity utilization, or units of production. And budgets can cover daily, weekly, monthly, quarterly, semi-annual, or annual periods.

Budgets
Numerical plans.

Budgets are certainly important planning guides as they give direction. However, they also serve other functions. One such function is coordination, forcing the person creating the budget to seek pertinent information from the other parts of the business that influence it, and to focus on the goals of the unit and the organization.

Budgets also enforce communication. Through the allocation of funds, budgets clearly identify the important activities to others. They also place the creator in the position of justifying the specific details of the budget, thereby communicating the underlying plans and priorities to others.

Third, budgets act as a control device. They typically set out standards for comparison with actual performance (e.g., Were expenses beyond what was set out? Were hours within reason of the budgeted number? Are we on target for material costs?). Budgeting is discussed in more detail in the From Concepts to Skills section at the end of the next chapter on Designing and Implementing Controls.

A fourth function of budgets is performance evaluation. Whether a unit performed within budget is often an important aspect of a supervisor or manager's performance evaluation, addressing both their ability as planners and as doers.

If there is one type of plan in which most supervisors become involved, it is a budget. For instance, supervisors typically prepare their department's expense budget and submit it to the manager at the next higher level for review and approval (see Figure 2-4). Once approved by higher management, these budgets set specific standards for supervisors and their unit staff to achieve.

SCHEDULES

If you were to observe a group of supervisors or department managers for a few days, you'd see them regularly detailing what activities have to be done, the order they are to be done in, who is to do each, and when they are to be completed. These managers are **scheduling**.

Two popular scheduling techniques that can help you prioritize activities and complete work on time are the Gantt chart and the PERT chart. In the rest of this section, we'll describe each.

The **Gantt chart** was developed early in this century by an industrial engineer named Henry Gantt. The idea was inherently simple but has proved extremely helpful in scheduling work activities. The Gantt chart is essentially a bar graph with time on the horizontal axis and activities to be scheduled on the vertical axis. The bars show output, both planned and actual, over a period of time. The Gantt chart visually shows when tasks are supposed to be done and compares that to the actual progress on each. As we stated, it is a simple but important device that allows managers to detail easily what has yet to be done to complete a job or project and to assess whether it is ahead, behind, or on schedule.

Figure 2-5 depicts a simplified Gantt chart that was developed for producing a book by a manager in a publishing firm. Time is expressed in

Scheduling
Determining what activities have to be done, the order they are to be done in, who is to do each, and when they are to be completed.

Gantt chart
A bar graph, with time on the horizontal axis and activities to be scheduled on the vertical axis, that shows planned and actual activities.

Department Expense Budget
Calendar Year 2001

ITEM	QUARTER			
	1ST	2ND	3RD	4TH
Salaries/Fixed	$23 600	$23 600	$23 600	$23 600
Salaries/Variable	3 000	5 000	3 000	10 000
Performance Bonuses				12 000
Office Supplies	800	800	800	800
Photocopying	1 000	1 000	1 000	1 000
Telephone	2 500	2 500	2 500	2 500
Mail	800	800	800	800
Travel	2 500	1 000	1 000	1 000
Employee Development	600	600	600	600
Total Quarterly Expenses	$34 800	$35 300	$33 300	$52 300

FIGURE 2-4

An example of a budget that could be used as a planning guide months across the top of the chart. The major activities are listed down the left side. The planning comes in deciding what activities must be done to get the book finished, the order in which they need to be done, and the time that should be allocated to each activity. Where a box sits within a time frame reflects its planned sequence. The shading represents actual progress. The chart becomes a control device when the manager looks for deviations from the plan.

Gantt charts are helpful as long as the activities being scheduled are few in number and independent of each other. But what if a supervisor has to plan a large project such as a departmental reorganization, the launching of a cost-reduction campaign, or the installation of a major piece of new equipment that requires the coordination of inputs from a number of different sources? Such projects often require the coordination of hundreds of activities, some of which must be done simultaneously and some of which cannot begin until earlier activities have been completed. If you're constructing a building, for example, you obviously can't start erecting walls until the foundation is laid. How, then, can you schedule such a complex project? You could use a Program Evaluation and Review Technique (PERT) chart.

The PERT chart was originally developed in the late 1950s for coordinating the more than 3000 contractors and agencies working on the Polaris submarine weapon system.[5] This project was incredibly complicated, with

Sample PERT and Gantt charts
http://www.sonic.net/
~webclass/BusWeb/
pert_gant.shtml

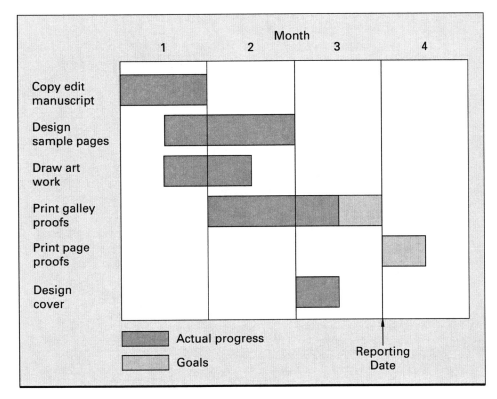

FIGURE 2-5

A Gantt chart

hundreds of thousands of activities that had to be coordinated. PERT is reported to have cut two years off the completion date for the Polaris project. A PERT chart can be a valuable tool in the hands of a supervisor.

A **PERT chart** is a diagram that depicts the sequence of activities needed to complete a project and the time or costs associated with each activity. With a PERT chart, a supervisor must think through what must be done, determine which events depend on one another, and identify potential trouble spots. A PERT chart makes it easy to compare what effect alternative actions will have on scheduling and costs. Thus PERT allows supervisors to monitor a project's progress, identify possible bottlenecks, and shift resources as necessary to keep the project on schedule.

To understand how to construct a PERT chart, you need to know three terms: *events, activities,* and *critical path*. Let's define these terms, outline the steps in the PERT process, and then work through an example.

Events are end points that represent the completion of major activities. **Activities** represent the time or resources required to progress from one event to another. The **critical path** is the longest or most time-consuming sequence of events and activities in a PERT chart.

Developing a PERT chart requires the supervisor to identify all key activities needed to complete a project, rank them in order of dependence, and estimate each activity's completion time. This can be translated into five specific steps as in Figure 2-6:

PERT chart
A technique for scheduling complex projects.

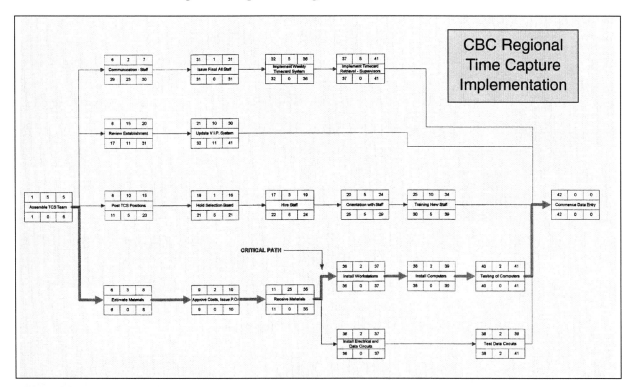

FIGURE 2-6 PERT used by CBC to plan implementation of new time card system. Provided by Lenny Jackson, Halifax CBC. Numbers in boxes refer to early start date, duration, early finish date (on top line); late start date, slack, late finish date (bottom line).

Are You Comprehending
What You're Reading?

1. Explain both the pros and cons of formal planning.
2. A supervisor develops plans to establish specific details about departmental objectives, which must be fulfilled to achieve overall organizational goals. Such plans are called:
   a. strategic plans
   b. tactical plans
   c. long-term plans
   d. detailed plans
3. Describe policies, procedures, and rules. Give an example of each.
4. A bar graph showing time on the horizontal axis and activities to be completed on the vertical axis is a Gantt chart. True or false?

1. Identify every significant activity that must be achieved for a project to be completed. The accomplishment of each activity results in a set of events or outcomes.

2. Ascertain the order in which these events must be completed.

3. Diagram the flow of activities from start to finish, identifying each activity and its relationship to all other activities. Use circles to indicate events and arrows to represent activities. This results in the diagram that we call the PERT chart.

4. Compute a time estimate for completing each activity.

5. Finally, using a PERT chart that contains time estimates for each activity, the supervisor can determine a schedule for the start and finish dates of each activity and for the entire project. Any delays that occur along the critical path require the most attention because they delay the entire project. That is, the critical path has no slack in it; therefore any delay along that path immediately translates into a delay in the final deadline for the completed project.

SETTING GOALS

"If you don't give people targets, they don't know what to strive for. If you do, they will care more, they will flag problems, and the goal will become a personal goal, not a company goal," explains Daniel Quondam, operations manager for Com Dev Wireless in Moncton, thereby highlighting the importance of giving employees specific targets to accomplish.

Daniel's description of the motivational importance of goals or objectives differs from the traditional use of goals for control purposes. Historically, goals were imposed by top management who then told the next level of management what they had to accomplish, who then told the next layer, and so on, down to operative employees. This one-way process assumed that top management knew best because only top managers could accurately see the "big picture." The current use of goal setting is much more likely to be participative, allowing the employees who must achieve the goals to help determine the goals themselves. This makes it much more likely that the goals will be realistic and that the employees will "buy in" to the goals.

City of Brampton
www.city.brampton.on.ca

Colleen Murray, director of marketing and sales for Parks and Recreation at the City of Brampton in Ontario, agrees with Daniel Quondam's emphasis on goals. Colleen supervises 17 marketing coordinators who provide marketing for the many recreational programs and facilities offered by the City. When she meets with them for their mid-year and end-of-year performance reviews, employees know they are expected to bring specific information on their goals for discussion at that meeting. What training will they be undertaking? What is their business plan? What is their marketing plan? Specifically, how do they plan to achieve their participation numbers? (The City's main objective is to achieve 50 percent participation in leisure activities through direct programming such as swim lessons at the aquatic centres and indirect programming such as minor sports leagues.) And, finally, what is their financial goal for their area? Colleen has had great feedback on her new approach. After the first mid-year review, every coordinator had achieved at least 50 percent of his or her year's objectives and they all said it was simple because, for the first time, expectations were clear. Interestingly, it was the coordinators who actually created the clear expectations, although Colleen had insisted that they do so.

Colleen uses this emphasis on goals not just for long-term planning but also for short-term planning. For example, at the start of each departmental meeting, she will identify the focus of the meeting. "What are we trying to achieve? What specific objectives do we have for this meeting?" In fact, an agenda forms the objectives for many meetings. And, for those who have attended a meeting without an agenda, you'll appreciate the direction and focus provided by an agenda.

CHARACTERISTICS OF EFFECTIVE GOALS

The characteristics of effective goals are often summarized under the acronym **SMART**. Good goals are:

Specific—they can be described in terms of exact behaviours or outcomes

Measurable—because they are specific, they can be quantified; this way there will be much less dispute than if the results are subjectively evaluated

Accepted—participation in setting the goals will greatly increase their acceptability to subordinates but, as long as they are viewed as reasonable and the logic supporting them is valid, employees may be willing to go along with goals set for them by others

Reasonable—part of this is that the circumstances surrounding the achievement of the goal are under the control of the employee; if reaching the goal depends partly on coworkers and their cooperation, it is not fair to make one person responsible for its success

Time-bound—there should be a deadline; as you probably know from personal experience, if there is no deadline, there is not much motivation to complete a goal

Tom Heighway, sales manager of Ceridian Canada's Atlantic region, believes in **SMART** goals and uses them regularly with his staff. Each of Tom's salespeople created three **SMART** goals, which he then framed to sit on the employee's desk and focus employees daily on what is important.

Ceridian Canada
www.ceridian.ca

Being SMART is what makes goals effective. But what are they then effective at doing? Goals certainly offer clarity and direction, thereby fulfilling a planning role. The request to set specific goals forces someone to think carefully through what they want to happen and how they can achieve it. Goals can also increase motivation, involvement, and commitment, which may result from participation in setting the goals. Such commitment can also result from the feedback that is naturally generated when specific measurable goals are set and a procedure is set up to monitor progress. Another benefit from goals is their occasional use to create fair, objective criteria for performance appraisal and for allocating rewards. Finally, the use of goal setting as a process involving both supervisor and subordinate can improve the relationship between the two levels of employees. Unlike the many circumstances where a supervisor seems to have little real understanding of a subordinate's position and little concern for the frustrations in it, when a supervisor must work with a subordinate on jointly setting goals, the supervisor must understand the employee's position. The supervisor must also commit him- or herself to supporting the employee in those goals because the supervisor agrees that they are reasonable. The resulting communication and sharing of information likely brings the two parties to a closer and common understanding of each other's expectations.

MANAGEMENT BY OBJECTIVES

Management by objectives (MBO)
A system in which subordinates jointly determine specific performance objectives with their superiors, progress toward objectives is periodically reviewed, and rewards are allocated on the basis of this progress.

Sasktel
www.sasktel.com

Some organizations formalize the goal-setting process into a regular activity undertaken by all in the organization, and integrated so that all goals work together. This is referred to as **management by objectives (MBO)**. In MBO, objectives cascade down through the organization, set at first at the top. But this does not mean the objectives are imposed. Rather, each supervisor or manager works with each employee to create a set of objectives for that particular employee. While doing this, the manager will, of course, be keeping in mind the objectives he or she has committed to in his or her own position. So the employees' objectives must ultimately help the manager achieve his or her objectives. This is exactly the point of MBO—coordinating everyone's activities to work towards the corporate good.

A form of MBO is being used at SaskTel in Saskatchewan. Their performance management process (called Partnership in Excellence) expects that each manager work with each employee on developing appropriate objectives. This is done after there has been a full discussion of corporate vision and values, and the direction in which the division is heading. The discussion leads to how the employee can contribute to the corporate goals within their own role, what specific objectives would be appropriate, what standards are set, how performance would be measured, identifying development needs, and how the manager can support the employee. It is expected that this process will involve ongoing feedback and communication rather than a once-a-year performance review.

MBO has not been successful in all its applications, however. Some employees find the paperwork too overwhelming. Others find that upper managers exempt themselves from the process, which destroys the mandate of the program and allows others to take it less seriously. Also, goals cannot be applied to certain jobs. Applying goals to a repetitive job where the work is controlled by the machine or the customer rather than the employee means that goal setting doesn't work. Furthermore, not all work has easily measured outcomes or behaviours. For example, how do you measure how effective someone is as a teacher in inspiring a love for the material or an interest in the area? How do you measure the quality of a consultant's handling of a project if it has never been done before, there are no comparisons, and it was difficult to forecast what a "good" outcome would look like as compared to a "bad" one?

TIME MANAGEMENT

"I'm always on the go, dealing with machines, people, quality, safety. I rarely have a moment to myself. I'm usually juggling 10 balls at a time." (Paula Aylward, shift manager, Cavendish Farms, P.E.I.).

"I work from 8:30 to 5:30 but I'm on call 24 hours a day. When I come in in the morning, I do a walkabout to take care of concerns, and gravitate to areas where I'm needed. I just have to go with the flow." (Trish Mah, director of support services, Royal Arch Home, Vancouver)

"I work from 7 a.m. to about 6:30 p.m. and I occasionally come in on weekends. It's definitely not a 9 to 5 job. I'm never out of something to do." (Catalino Misenas, sales manager, Russell Food Equipment, Vancouver)

"The biggest challenge for me is creating the time to lead people, to let people know I'm there for them. I can get very caught up in the administrative work. And it can be difficult to make the time to coach people, even though my typical work day starts at 7 and ends at 6." (Susan Pander, manager of human resources, SaskTel, Regina)

The most effective supervisors have learned to manage their time. Like Catalino and Susan, many put in long hours. Others put in a more normal workday but it is a day crammed with pressures to do an incredible amount. In this section, we'll discuss how **time management** is actually a personal form of scheduling. Supervisors who use their time effectively know what they want to accomplish and when.

> **Time management**
> A personal form of scheduling; maximizing the allocation of the use of time.

TIME AS A SCARCE RESOURCE

Time is a unique resource in that, if it's wasted, it can never be replaced. While people talk about saving time, the fact is that time can never actually be saved. It can't be stockpiled for use in some future period. If wasted, it can't be retrieved. When a minute is gone, it's gone forever.

The positive side of this resource is that all supervisors have it in equal abundance. While money, personnel, and other resources are distributed unequally in organizations, thus putting some supervisors at a disadvantage, every supervisor is allotted 24 hours every day and seven days every week. Some just use their allotments better than others.

> **Response time**
> Responding to requests, demands, and problems initiated by others.

FOCUSING ON DISCRETIONARY TIME

Supervisors can't control all their time. They are routinely interrupted and have to respond to unexpected crises. It's necessary, therefore, to differentiate between **response time** and **discretionary time**.

> **Discretionary time**
> The portion of a supervisor's time that is under his or her control.

Most of a supervisor's time is spent responding to requests, demands, and problems initiated by others. We call this response time and treat it as uncontrollable. The portion that is under a supervisor's control is called discretionary time. Most of the suggestions offered to improve time management apply to its discretionary component. Why? Because only this part is manageable!

Sometimes this lack of discretionary time, accompanied by the expectation of accomplishing tasks that require blocks of thinking time, means that supervisors take work home with them. For example, Rob Mastrotto, the inserts finishing team leader at Husky Injection Molding Systems in Bolton, Ontario, takes performance appraisal forms home. He is expected to do annual performance reviews on all 45 people he supervises. Yet he works in a "fishbowl" office that he shares with another team leader and his duties mean he is almost never in the office, always moving around handling things on the plant floor. Rob spends evenings for weeks each fall working at home on the reviews to prepare for the review meetings that must be held with each employee by the end of October. The meetings themselves take about an hour per employee, indicating the depth in which Rob prepares for the meeting and the extent of information sharing. "I remember feeling bitter about my own reviews in the past because I would work hard for a year and then my boss would give me a one-liner on an evaluation that would tell me nothing," he explains.

How Do You Use Your Time?

How can supervisors, or anyone for that matter, determine how well they use their time? The answer is to keep a log or diary of daily activities for a short period of time, then evaluate the data you record.

The best log is a daily diary or calendar broken down into 15-minute intervals. To get enough information from which to generalize, you need about two weeks of entries.

When your diary is complete, you will have a detailed time and activity log. Then you can analyze how effectively you use your time. Rate each activity in terms of its importance and urgency (see Figure 2-7). If you find that many activities received Cs or Ds, you'll find the next sections valuable. They provide detailed guidelines for better time management.

Five Steps to Better Time Management

The essence of time management is to use your time effectively. This requires that you know the objectives you want to accomplish, the activities that will lead to their accomplishment, and the importance and urgency of each activity. We've translated this into a five-step process.

Rate Each Activity for:

Importance

    A. Very important: must be done

    B. Important: should be done

    C. Not so important: may be useful, but is not necessary

    D. Unimportant: doesn't accomplish anything

Urgency

    A. Very urgent: must be done now

    B. Urgent: should be done now

    C. Not urgent: can be done some time later

    D. Time not a factor

FIGURE 2-7

Analyzing activities for importance and urgency

1. **Make a list of your objectives.** What do you want to accomplish? You're familiar with this from having created "to do" lists.
2. **Rank the objectives according to their importance.** You are setting priorities because time is limited and you should get the important things done first.
3. **List the activities necessary to achieve your objectives.** To really know where your time is going, you need to consider *all* the things you must do in order to accomplish an objective. Sometimes we overload ourselves because we commit to too much, having underestimated the time that activities will take. Remember how meetings get postponed, information is not always available when it should be, and computers go down so that work is delayed.
4. **Assign priorities to the various activities required to reach each objective.** Assign priorities to the various activities required to reach each objective. This imposes a second set of priorities. Here, you need to emphasize both importance and urgency. Decide what you *must* do, what you *should* do, what you will do *when you can*, and what you can *delegate to others*.
5. **Schedule your activities according to the priorities you've set.** At the beginning of each day or last thing before you leave work for the day, list the five or so most important things you want to do for the day. Then set priorities on these.

Below are listed many of the typical factors that supervisors cite as time wasters. Check all those that apply to you in both Column A and Column B.

Column A	Column B
____ Interruptions	____ Procrastinations
____ Attending meetings	____ Too much work to do
____ Drop-in visitors	____ Complete easy tasks first
____ Telephone calls	____ Messy desk
____ Red tape	____ Unnecessary mail
____ Unclear expectations	____ Can't say no
____ Lack of clear goals	____ Failure to listen
____ Lack of help	____ Waiting for others
____ Unrealistic time estimates	____ Lack of self-discipline
____ Too many bosses	____ Visual distractions
____ Lack of motivation	____ Misplaced items

After you've checked those that apply, study your time wasters. Do they have anything in common?

Irrespective of what you checked, did you see any relationship between the items in the two columns? If you observed closely, you probably found that Column A includes those things that waste your time but are not in your direct control. In Column B are time wasters we bring on ourselves. However, time management isn't that simple. Contrary to what most of us want to believe, every item in each column is within our control. Many of those things in Column A that we shrug off as impossible to deal with can in fact be addressed. That's the purpose of good time management.

How will you address your time wasters? How will you face these issues? What will you do to correct your time management "problems"?

SOME ADDITIONAL POINTS TO PONDER

FOLLOW THE 10-90 PRINCIPLE

Ten per cent of most supervisors' time produces 90 per cent of their results. It's easy for supervisors to get caught up in the activity trap and confuse actions with accomplishments. Those who use their time well make sure that the critical 10 per cent receives highest priority.

KNOW YOUR PRODUCTIVITY CYCLE

Each of us has a daily cycle. Some of us are morning people, while others are late-afternoon or evening people. Supervisors who know their cycle and schedule their work accordingly can significantly increase their effectiveness. They handle their most demanding problems during the high part of their cycle, when they are most alert and productive. They relegate their routine and undemanding tasks to their low periods.

REMEMBER PARKINSON'S LAW

Parkinson's Law says that work expands to fill the time available. The implication for time management is that you can schedule too much time for a task. If you give yourself an excess amount of time to perform an activity, you're likely to pace yourself so that you use up the entire time allotted.

GROUP LESS IMPORTANT ACTIVITIES TOGETHER

Set aside a regular time period each day to make phone calls, do follow-ups, and perform other kinds of busywork. Ideally, this should be during your low cycle. This avoids duplication, waste, and redundancy; it also prevents trivia from intruding on high-priority tasks.

MINIMIZE DISRUPTIONS

When possible, try to minimize disruptions by setting aside a part of the day when you are most productive as a block of discretionary time. Then, try to insulate yourself. During this time—which may only be 20 or 30 minutes—limit access to your work area and avoid interruptions. Refuse phone calls or visits during this period. You can set aside other blocks of time each day to be accessible, and to initiate or return all your calls.

KNOW YOUR POLYCHRONICITY

People differ in terms of their preference for doing one thing at a time rather than doing two or more things simultaneously. People range from being highly monochronic (focusing entirely on doing one thing at a time) to highly **polychronic** (having no difficulty writing a report, talking on the phone, eating a snack, and watching a television program simultaneously). In terms of time management, highly polychronic types are more flexible in their schedules. They're less likely to be precise in scheduling completion times for tasks; have little trouble in grouping certain tasks together to be performed during the same time period; and are

Polychronicity
The degree to which a person prefers doing two or more things simultaneously.

more likely to add, delete, and alter their priorities as the day proceeds. Maybe most interestingly, the highly polychronic person is much better at responding to unscheduled events. An unplanned phone call, for instance, typically has little effect on the highly polychronic type's work schedule, while it is a distinct distraction and likely to interrupt the monochronic's scheduled activities.

LEARN TO SAY NO

Some supervisors become overloaded because they accept everything they are asked to do. Sometimes it's appropriate to say no. For example, if your manager asks you to undertake a big task that will make it difficult to complete what you're already committed to doing, don't just work a lot of unpaid overtime to complete both tasks. Instead, ask your manager which task has the higher priority because you can't accomplish both in the time allowed. Put the decision back on your manager. If subordinates ask you what to do in a particular situation, it may not be best to simply give the answer. If you ask them instead what they think they should do or could do, you are helping them problem-solve in a way that may get them solving the problem on their own next time instead of coming back to you.

Susan Pander of SaskTel emphasizes that sometimes it is important to limit work commitments and to recognize the need to balance work and home life. Susan tries not to take work home with her, concentrating instead on home life when she is there. As she explains, "Family comes first." Although she still works a 50- to 55-hour week and sometimes takes her laptop home with her, she has a comfortable balance and feels she is focusing her energy where she is needed.

GOAL SETTING

Now we turn to skill development and application. In this section, we introduce a skill in three parts.

1. You complete a self-assessment "Check Yourself" exercise relating to a specific supervisory skill.

2. We present some basic skill information.

3. We present a skill application on which you can practise.

For this chapter, the skill is goal setting. Each of the remaining chapters of this book will conclude with a section entitled From Concepts to Skills, which will introduce a supervisory skill using the same three-part approach.

ASSESSING YOURSELF: ARE YOU A GOOD GOAL SETTER?

For each of the following questions, check the answer that best describes your relationship with subordinates. Remember to respond as you have behaved or would behave, not as you think you should behave. If you have no supervisory experience, answer the questions assuming you are a supervisor.

THE PEOPLE WHO WORK FOR ME HAVE:

	Usually	Sometimes	Seldom
1. Specific and clear goals.	❑	❑	❑
2. Goals for all key areas relating to their job performance.	❑	❑	❑
3. Challenging but reasonable goals (neither too hard nor too easy).	❑	❑	❑
4. The opportunity to participate in setting their goals.	❑	❑	❑
5. A say in deciding how to implement their goals	❑	❑	❑
6. Deadlines for accomplishing their goals.	❑	❑	❑
7. Sufficient skills and training to achieve their goals.	❑	❑	❑
8. Sufficient resources (i.e., time, money, equipment) to achieve their goals.	❑	❑	❑

9. Feedback on how well they are
   progressing toward their goals. ❏   ❏   ❏

10. Rewards (i.e., pay, promotions) allocated to them
    according to how well they reach their goals. ❏   ❏   ❏

SCORING KEY AND INTERPRETATION

For all questions, give yourself 3 points for "Usually," 2 points for "Sometimes," and 1 point for "Seldom."

Total up your points. Scores of 26 or higher demonstrate a strong use or understanding of goal-setting techniques. A score of 21 to 25 indicates you can improve your goal-setting skills. Scores of 20 or less suggest that you have significant room for improvement.

SKILL BASICS

We presented management by objectives earlier in this chapter. Now we will take the basic concepts of MBO and turn them into specific goal-setting skills that you can apply on the job.

Let's begin by summarizing the five basic rules that should guide you in defining and setting goals.

1. **Make your goals specific.** Goals are only meaningful when they're specific enough to be verified and measured.

2. **Make your goals challenging.** Goals should be set so as to require employees to stretch in order to reach them. If they're too easy, they offer no challenge. If set unrealistically high, they create frustration and are likely to be abandoned.

3. **Impose specific time limits for accomplishment of the goals.** Open-ended goals are likely to be neglected because no sense of urgency is associated with them.

4. **Goals should be jointly determined by the supervisor and the employee.** Participation increases an employee's goal-aspiration level. Additionally, jointly set goals are often more readily accepted, and accepted goals are more likely to be achieved.

5. **Provide feedback on performance.** Feedback lets people know if their level of effort is sufficient or needs to be increased. It can also induce them to raise their goal level after attaining a previous goal and can inform them of ways in which they can improve their performance.

Effective goal-setting skills can be condensed to eight specific behaviours. When you follow all eight you will have mastered the skill of goal setting.

1. **Identify an employee's key job tasks.** Goal setting begins by defining what it is that you want your employees to accomplish. The best source for this information is each employee's job description, if one is available. It details what task an employee is expected to perform, how these tasks are to be done, what outcomes the employee is responsible for achieving, and the like.

2. **Establish specific and challenging goals for each task.** This is self-explanatory. We should add that, if possible, these goals should be made public. When a person's goals are made public—announced in a group or posted for others to see—the individual seems to be more highly committed to them.

3. **Specify deadlines for each goal.** Again, as previously discussed, goals should include a specific time limit for accomplishment.

4. **Allow the subordinate to actively participate.** Employees are less likely to question or resist a process in which they actively participate than one that is imposed upon them from above.

5. **Prioritize goals.** When someone is given more than one goal, it is important to rank the goals in order of importance. The purpose of this step is to encourage the employee to take action and expend effort on each goal in proportion to its importance.

6. **Rate goals for difficulty and importance.** Goal setting should not encourage people to choose easy goals in order to ensure success. So goal setting should take into account the difficulty of the goals selected and whether individuals are emphasizing the right goals. When these ratings are combined with the actual level of goal achievement, you will have a more comprehensive assessment of overall goal performance. This procedure gives credit to individuals for attempting difficult goals even if they don't fully achieve them.

7. **Build in feedback mechanisms to assess goal progress.** Ideally, feedback on goal progress should be self-generated rather than provided externally. When an employee is able to monitor his or her own progress, the feedback is less threatening and less likely to be perceived as part of a management control system.

8. **Make rewards contingent on goal attainment.** Offering money, promotions, recognition, time off, or similar rewards to employees

contingent on goal achievement is a powerful means to increase goal commitment. When the going gets tough on the road toward meeting a goal, people are prone to ask themselves, "What's in it for me?" Linking rewards to the achievement of goals helps employees to answer this question.

Applying Your Skills

PART A

For each of the following goals, identify what is wrong with it and rewrite it to be more effective.

Increase your sales by 10 percent.

Improve your relationship with your coworkers.

Manage your time better.

Tidy up your work area.

Put together a comprehensive report on how to cut costs by 25 percent in this department.

Eliminate the stress in your life.

Improve production output by 50 percent without incurring greater costs or sacrificing quality.

Get a major newspaper to publish an article on the success of our change efforts.

Improve quality.

Get those two people who are thinking of quitting to stay.

PART B—SETTING GOALS TOGETHER

This is a role-play exercise. Break into groups of three or four students. One student in each group will assume the role of Kelly and one will assume the role of Brad. The other students will serve as observers and evaluators.

Kelly has finally hired someone to take on part of her workload. The 80-hour weeks she was putting in running her new specialty bookstore were beginning to take the thrill out of entrepreneurship. She will continue to do all the buying but will spend less time on the shop floor. Brad, her new employee, will work full-time selling the computer books and magazines. Kelly wants to reduce her hours overall and to spend more time keeping up with the new publications, especially since she is now writing a regular book review for a computer magazine.

Kelly wants to start off well with Brad. She knows he is experienced in sales and something of a computer hacker on the side. But since much of her business's future will depend on how well Brad handles himself, she has decided that they should work together to create a set of goals for him. Kelly has set up a meeting to begin this goal-setting process.

The object of this exercise is to end up with a set of goals for Brad. They might address issues such as prompt and polite attention to customer needs, handling sales appropriately (e.g., credit), maintaining store appearance, preventing shoplifting and dealing with it when it occurs, dealing with telephone inquiries, and keeping up to date with new publications.

This exercise should take no more than 15 minutes. When completed, the observers from each group should discuss with the role players how their goal-setting session went. Focus specifically on the skill behaviours presented in this section and any problems that surfaced.

5. When would a **PERT** chart *not* provide much help?
   a. when sequencing is important
   b. for complicated jobs
   c. for unconnected projects
   d. for jobs with many steps involved
6. How does **MBO** assist in answering the question "What's in it for me?"
7. Effective goals are **SMART**, which means:
   a. specific, measurable, accepted, realistic, and time-bound.
   b. short, moderate, ability-related, and tested.
   c. sensitive to conditions, mixed, apt, rooted in organizational support, tended.
   d. sensible, moderate, appropriate, reliable, and tested.
8. Goal setting always provides tangible rewards when goals are reached. True or false?

SUMMARY

This summary is organized by the Learning Objectives.

1. In formal planning, specific goals are formulated, committed to writing, and made available to other organization members. Specific-action programs will define the path for the achievement of these goals. In informal planning, plans are kept in the manager's head. Nothing is written down and there is little or no sharing of these plans with others.
2. Plans link the organization from top to bottom. Long-term strategic plans are set by top management. Then each succeeding level down the organization develops its plans. Plans at each level should help to accomplish plans for the level above and give direction for the level below.
3. Policies and rules are both standing plans. Policies are broad and leave room for managerial discretion, while rules are explicit statements that allow no discretion.
4. Managers create single-use plans to cover specific activities or time periods. They provide detailed courses of action to handle unique or nonrecurring activities.
5. The Gantt chart is a simple scheduling device. It is a bar graph with time on the horizontal axis and activities on the vertical axis. It shows planned and actual activities, and allows managers to easily identify the status of a job or project.
6. To compute a PERT chart, you need to identify all key activities needed to complete a project, their order of dependence, and an estimate of each activity's completion time.
7. Effective goals are SMART. That is, they are specific, measurable, accepted by the person who must implement them, realistic, and time-bound with a specific deadline.
8. Response time is uncontrollable and encompasses the time one spends responding to actions initiated by others. Discretionary time is controllable and within the discretion of the individual.
9. A five-step process to better time management includes making a list of your objectives, ranking the objectives according to their importance, listing the activities necessary to achieve the objectives, assigning priorities to the various activities required to reach each objective, and scheduling your activities according to their importance and urgency.

UNDERSTANDING THE BASICS

KEY TERMS AND CONCEPTS

Activities

Budgets

Critical path

Discretionary time

Events

Gantt chart

Intermediate-term plans

Long-term plans

Management by objectives

PERT chart

Policies

Polychronicity

Procedures

Programs

Response time

Rules

Scheduling

Short-term plans

Single-use plans

Standing plans

Strategic planning

Tactical planning

Time management

REVIEWING YOUR KNOWLEDGE

1. Contrast the planning top managers do with that done by first-level managers.
2. Explain how budgets are both a planning and a control device.
3. How might you use a Gantt chart to schedule a group term paper for a college class?
4. What are the implications of the critical path for PERT analysis?
5. Contrast MBO with traditional objective setting.
6. Why is goal setting effective in some jobs and ineffective in others?
7. What specific things can you do, that you're not currently doing, to make you better at managing your time?
8. Why are highly polychronic people likely to be more flexible in their schedules?

ANSWERS TO THE POP QUIZZES

1. Pros: **common focus, integration of efforts, preparation**
   Cons: **rigidity, dampens use of creativity**
2. **b. tactical plans.** This is the definition of tactical plans and the distinction between strategic and tactical plans.
3. Policies are broad guidelines for managerial action. Typically established by top management, they define the limits within which managers must stay as they make decisions. For example, a policy might state that a supervisor can "sign off" on purchases under $6500. A procedure defines the steps that are to be taken and the order in which they are to be done. They provide a standardized way of responding to repetitive problems. An example of a procedure would be the steps that supervisors are expected to follow when establishing, completing, and submitting their unit's budget for the coming year. A rule is an explicit statement that tells a supervisor what he or she ought or ought not to do. An example of a rule would be an organization's statements about not permitting scrap materials to be taken home by employees.
4. **True.** This is the definition of a Gantt chart.
5. **c. for unconnected projects.** For a PERT chart to be effective, there must be interdependency, or relatedness of activities. If the activities are independent of each other, no relationship exists among them. Accordingly, a PERT chart would not help in this situation.
6. MBO assists in answering the question "What's in it for me?" by showing the linkage of goal achievement and rewards. That is, money, promotions, recognition, time off, or similar rewards an employee receives are dependent on his or her meeting established work expectations.
7. **a. specific, measurable, accepted, realistic, and time-bound.**
8. **False.** Rewards may follow successful goal achievement but are not necessary.

CASE 2.A

Is This the Beginning of the End?*

Deanna watches Peter pass by the office window. He doesn't look happy these days. There are rumours that he is looking for another position. Such a move would be disastrous for the company. As production manager, Peter is the person who keeps everything together at this place. And Peter is so good he should have no problems finding another job. But if Peter goes, several other managers will also probably go. Everyone is fed up. If Peter goes, maybe Deanna will also leave.

Deanna is the human resources manager at a food processing company in southeast Ontario. It began about 15 years ago as a small operation but has grown amazingly in the last few years, expanding its product line and becoming the main supplier to two very large companies. But the growing pains are becoming debilitating. The owner/president of the company has turned most of the company management over to a handpicked successor, the vice president, while the owner concentrates on sales. But he still sticks his nose in every once in a while and dictates what should happen. The vice president doesn't dare refuse him. Both the owner and the vice president know the older staff intimately and give them special treatment. It has frustrated Deanna that she has worked hard with management to create a set of policies, rules, and guidelines for staff yet they are constantly undermined. The supervisors really wanted clear policies and rules so they knew what they could and couldn't do and had some firm guidance in confronting problem behaviour. But the rules and procedures have not had the desired impact because the senior employees who don't like a rule just go to the owner or vice president who then give them permission to ignore the rule.

Deanna arrived two years ago to create a human resources function in the company of 250 people that had no such function. She set about creating job descriptions so everyone knew their responsibilities, and lines of authority were clear. That project remains unfinished since the assistant assigned to work with Deanna was pulled to work on other matters closer to production. Deanna still shares three support people with Production but knows that her demands are lower priority and can be shoved aside at a moment's notice. Most of Deanna's time is spent on recruiting. The company has a very high turnover rate. The jobs are not exciting, the pay is not particularly high, there are few benefits (e.g., they are not paid any sick days), and the employees without seniority must work the afternoon or evening shift since only the long-term employees get to work the more desirable day shift. Deanna shudders at the thought of staffing the new plant that is planned for construction next year out of province.

Peter is the production manager and a friend of Deanna's. He began as an operative employee and worked his way up, proving himself in each position to be competent and able. But he finds his job very difficult. Like Deanna, he has no budget to work with. The company has always simply spent money as needed and tried to keep costs as low as possible. He is now expected to keep up production while half the machines are being moved into a newly expanded plant space. That was supposed to happen during the summer downtime but then they discovered at the last minute that the new end of the plant had not been supplied with sufficient electrical power to handle the machines so it needed to be rewired. And now the move is happening in the fall, their busiest time of the year. Peter also has to deal with catastrophes like the recent debacle with a major customer because it made a huge error on a shipment. This did not happen because production failed but because there was a miscommunication to production and a critical adjustment to the machine settings was not implemented, thereby allowing a whole lot of useless product to be churned out. It was only when the customer received a batch of food that did not meet their specifications that the mistake was realized.

Peter has not decided definitely to leave the company but he is feeling more and more like that each day. The company has great potential and he feels almost like he would be abandoning family members, but the working situation has become too stressful and he feels he can't make a difference. Deanna and other managers know that Peter is the one link pin holding things together. This is why Deanna feels that, if Peter goes, she'll also need to leave.

RESPONDING TO THIS CASE

1. Explain all the ways in which this company appears to be ignoring planning advice. Then attempt to explain why the company does not follow typical planning guidelines and how it has managed to be successful despite this.
2. Explain the impact that the lack of planning has had on employees, on management, and on the success of the company as a whole.
3. Explain how this case demonstrates the link between planning and time management.

* This case is based on a real situation. The names and certain details have been changed to disguise the identity of the individuals and organization.

CASE 2.B

MBO at A.C. & C.E.

Shama has just been hired as the new office manager for Applied Consumer and Clinical Evaluation of Mississauga, a company mainly involved in consumer testing for packaged goods manufacturers. The woman Shama is replacing had been with the firm since its inception as a three-person enterprise, was seen as highly competent, and only left because of family demands. This is rather intimidating to Shama, despite the fact that she herself has experience as office manager at two other companies and was recognized as highly capable in those positions.

Another factor intimidating Shama about this position is that Ray Berta, the owner of the firm, uses MBO throughout the operation. Shama has never worked in an MBO environment and she knows that not only will she have to set objectives for herself, but she will also have to work with the people she supervises on their goal setting. Shama's impression is that Ray is a caring individual as well as a clever businessman, and that he wants a harmonious and happy staff as well as a profitable company. That's why she was willing to take the job. But knowing this still doesn't ease her qualms about MBO. Ray has set up a meeting for next week when he and Shama can discuss the MBO process and begin work on her own plan for the upcoming six months.

RESPONDING TO THIS CASE

1. Discuss what it is about MBO that intimidates some people.
2. Outline the specific steps Ray should follow with Shama to ensure the MBO process works well.
3. Should he share with Shama the goals and plans of the prior office manager to help her get a feel for the job?
4. What can Shama expect to happen during the meeting and afterwards?

3

DESIGNING AND IMPLEMENTING CONTROLS

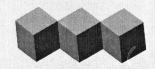

LEARNING OBJECTIVES

After reading this chapter, you should be able to:

1. Describe the control process.
2. Contrast two types of corrective action.
3. Compare preventive, concurrent, and corrective control.
4. Explain how a supervisor can reduce costs.
5. Describe what a supervisor can do to control employee behaviour.
6. List the characteristics of an effective control system.
7. Explain potential negative outcomes that controls can create.

CHAPTER OUTLINE

PERFORMING EFFECTIVELY

THE CONTROL PROCESS
Establish Performance Indicators and Determine Performance Standards
Measure Actual Performance
Compare Results with Standards
Take Corrective Action
Some Special Meaurement Tools
Pop Quiz

TYPES OF CONTROL
Preventive Control
Concurrent Control
Corrective Control

FOCUS OF CONTROL
Costs
Inventories
Quality
Safety
Employee Performance
Something to Think About

CHARACTERISTICS OF EFFECTIVE CONTROLS

POTENTIAL NEGATIVE OUTCOMES OF CONTROLS
Employee Resistance
Assessing Yourself: How Willing Are You to Encourage Self-Control?
Misdirection of Effort
Pop Quiz
Ethics and Control Devices

FROM CONCEPTS TO SKILLS: BUDGETING
Assessing Yourself: What Do You Know about Budgeting?
Skill Basics
Applying Your Skills

UNDERSTANDING THE BASICS
Summary
Key Terms and Concepts
Reviewing Your Knowledge
Answers to the Pop Quizzes

PERFORMING YOUR JOB
Case 3.A: Practising What You Preach
Case 3.B: The Business of Romance

City of Brampton
www.city.brampton.on.ca

Colleen Murray, manager of sales and marketing for the parks and recreation unit of the City of Brampton, Ontario, maintains a file on each of her subordinates. "I sat down with each one of them and said I have this file and I want you to know what's in this file so there are no surprises. Here's where I keep it and who helps me maintain it. Feed the file so it's accurate. Give me good news. Give me reasons to say why you're brilliant."

There are three components to each staff member's file. One is e-mails. Colleen keeps a print copy of all e-mail communications with an employee. This is where she wants staff members to send her information regarding successes or positive feedback from clients. If there is a problem, Colleen deals with it in person but then documents it in an e-mail form for the employee involved. If the problem is corrected, she removes it from the file and destroys it. If it is not corrected, however, the documentation remains on file.

The second component of each file contains the employee's written performance objectives. Although individual objectives may vary, the same areas are covered: mandatory educational training, submitting a business plan by a certain date, submitting their marketing plan by a certain date, explaining how they will increase their participation numbers (i.e., number of community members who use the recreational facility or program that the employee works with), and their financial goal.

The final component contains their budgets. Each marketing coordinator who reports to Colleen must perform a cost-analysis report and provide sessional reports on whether budgets are being met.

Through these files, both Colleen and her subordinates clearly understand the performance standards. Although Colleen meets with employees individually at mid-term and at the end of the year for formal discussions of performance, the files themselves are works in progress. Colleen also holds monthly staff meetings to discuss progress. Her staff work fairly independently but she is always there for help if needed. With the emphasis on the importance of the information in the files and on keeping Colleen up-to-date through e-mail communication, Colleen finds she is in touch with what is going on despite the independence of her staff. She also finds the new office design helpful. The open office design allows her to see who is in and who isn't, to stop in for occasional updating chats, and to be visible herself.

Despite Colleen's large and busy staff (over 20 employees, and all involved in different activities), Colleen knows what they are accomplishing. And her staff is extremely productive, accomplishing what they are expected to do. Without appearing to be highly controlling, Colleen has created a setup that gives her the information she needs and keeps her employees right "on track" doing what they should be doing.

The greatest plans still depend on execution to realize their potential. And how does a supervisor know if the plan is being achieved? The supervisor won't know, unless he or she has developed controls.

As described in Chapter 1, controlling is the management function concerned with monitoring activities to ensure that activities are being accomplished as planned, and with correcting any significant deviations. In this chapter, we will show you how effective supervisors perform the controlling function. Specifically, we'll detail the controlling process, discuss the timing of controls, identify the major areas where supervisors concentrate their control activities, describe the characteristics of effective controls, and discuss some of the potentially undesirable side effects of controls that supervisors need to guard against.

THE CONTROL PROCESS

The **control process** consists of five steps:

1. Establish performance indicators.
2. Determine performance standards.
3. Measure actual performance.
4. Compare actual performance with planned performance.
5. Take corrective action.

Control process
Establishing performance indicators, establishing performance standards, measuring actual performance, comparing actual performance with planned performance, and taking corrective action where needed.

Establish Performance Indicators and Determine Performance Standards

The supervisor may have the performance indicators and standards set for him or her and then be in the position of simply communicating them to subordinates (e.g., "We've been told that our department must generate this much in sales over the next quarter." "Tonight we not only have to complete the regular production quota but we've been given two special orders to squeeze in as well.").

However, the supervisor is often in the position of working with employees on what aspects of performance are to be emphasized (for example, not only specific quantity but also quality as indicated by certain measures). And, whereas the supervisor may be given group goals, specific performance expectations for individual employees are often decided by the supervisor and the employee.

As we'll discuss later in the chapter under preventive controls, the information value of clear performance expectations is tremendous. It has great power to "control" behaviour in employees.

MEASURE ACTUAL PERFORMANCE

We need information to determine whether performance is actually occurring as planned. So measurement is a critical aspect of control. We will consider both *how* we measure and *what* we measure (see Figure 3-1).

HOW WE MEASURE

Colleen Murray uses all of the four common sources of information in working with her subordinates. She asks them to provide *written* reports, which sometimes also include *statistics*. Subordinates also provide *oral* reports. And Colleen uses *personal observation*. Colleen's emphasis on written reports is common because those reports are comprehensive and concise, provide documentation, and are easy to catalogue and reference. Oral reports are also valuable, though, in that a spoken report at a meeting or a brief conversation is fast, conveys rich information through voice and body language as well as content, and allows for immediate feedback. Colleen's use of personal observation is probably the most widely used way in which supervisors assess actual performance. It has even acquired a label—Management by Walking Around (MBWA). It allows the supervisor to pick up minor as well as major performance activities, and observe relationships and atmosphere.

FIGURE 3-1

How supervisors can measure performance

WHAT WE MEASURE

What we measure is more critical than how we measure. This is only partly because measuring the wrong thing gives us useless information. The act of measurement itself also has an impact on performance. Employees will focus on activities and behaviours that are measured rather than those that are not measured. This sounds obvious and appropriate; however, if employees are measured, for example, solely on sales and not on customer service (which the company just assumes comes along with effective salesmanship), what happens? No one wants to do inventory, clean the sales area, handle a customer with a return, or help a customer with a small sale when there is another customer around offering the potential of a big sale. Customer service, and other aspects of the sales job, end up suffering because only one aspect of performance is measured, and, often, the only one rewarded. And the company also loses. The emphasis created by specific performance measures applies to all jobs, not only sales.

Given the above discussion, we see that not only is it important that the criteria measured are important and accurate measures of performance, but also that they include *all* of the important activities. Among those criteria, all supervisors would likely be able to use information on employee satisfaction, on the costs of activities, and on rates of absenteeism. But other specific performance measures will vary depending on the job and the goals of the department. For instance, Paula Aylward at the Cavendish Farms' French-fries plant in New Annan, P.E.I., is interested in kilograms of fries produced per hour, quality of fries sampled every half hour, water usage, and oil usage. On the other hand, in dealing with his salespeople at Russell Food Equipment Ltd. in Vancouver, Catalino Misenas is interested in sales made, number of sales calls, number of converts to his company from another, and timeliness of shipments.

COMPARE RESULTS WITH STANDARDS

This step involves comparing what actually happened to what was planned. Some variation in performance can be expected in all activities. Therefore, it is critical to determine the acceptable **range of variation**. Deviations beyond this acceptable range are deemed unacceptable and are "scrapped" or given further attention and correction.

Range of variation
The degree of acceptable variation between actual performance and the standard.

Paula Aylward's information on the criteria noted above comes from regular measurement using monitoring equipment set up for that purpose. Catalino Misenas expects daily sales reports from all salespeople so that he receives the information he needs. When Paula and Catalino use this information to compare what was planned with what is actually happening, they can then decide whether they need to undertake the next step in the controlling process, which is taking corrective action.

TAKE CORRECTIVE ACTION

Realizing that performance is not meeting expectations, a supervisor has several choices. He or she can try to adjust actual performance. For example, Paula can examine machine settings and change them or reinforce the importance of employees taking specific steps in their normal procedures. Or Catalino can coach his salespeople. Another choice is altering standards, or expectations. For instance, if a shipment of potatoes received does not meet quality standards, Paula will have to adjust production goals until an adequate supply can be received. Catalino may decide that the sales goal for a specific individual should be adjusted as the employee has had substantial absenteeism lately due to illness. The third choice is a combination of adjusting standards and attempting to improve performance.

SOME SPECIAL MEASUREMENT TOOLS

Any discussion of how you measure would be incomplete without a discussion of the basic statistical techniques used to control variability. In this section, we'll describe the more popular statistical process control techniques.

Cause-effect diagrams
Diagrams used to depict the causes of a problem and to group them according to common categories such as machinery, methods, personnel, finances, or management.

Cause and Effect Diagrams. **Cause-effect diagrams** (also sometimes called fish-bone diagrams) are used to depict the causes of a certain problem and to group the causes according to common categories such as machinery, materials, methods, personnel, finances, or management.

As shown in Figure 3-2, these diagrams look somewhat like a fish skeleton, with the problem—the effect—as the "head." On the "bones," growing out of the "spine," are the possible causes of production problems. They're listed in order of possible occurrence. Cause-effect diagrams provide guidance for analyzing the influence that alternative courses of action will have on a given problem.

Flow charts
Visual representations of the sequence of events for a particular process that clarify how things are being done, so that efficiencies can be identified and the process improved.

Flow Charts. **Flow charts** (or process mapping) are visual representations of the sequence of events for a particular process. They clarify exactly how things are done so that inefficiencies can be identified and the process improved. Figure 3-3 provides an illustration (also showing some of the standard symbols used: a rectangle signifies an activity or action taken in the process; a diamond represents a decision point in the process; oval identifies inputs or outputs; an arrow identifies main flow from one activity to another).

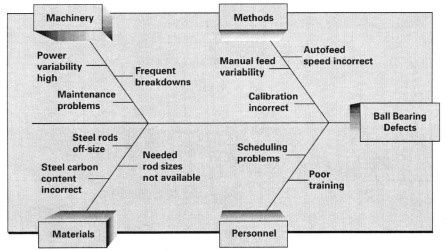

FIGURE 3-2

Example of a fish-bone diagram.

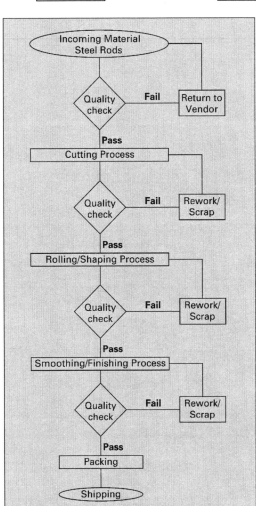

FIGURE 3-3

Example of a flow chart. (Reprinted with permission of the publisher. From *Putting Total Quality Management to Work*, p. 177, copyright © 1993 by Marshall Sashkin and Kenneth J. Kiser, Berrett-Koehler Publishers, Inc., San Francisco, CA. All rights reserved.)

Process mapping can also be altered to follow the *people* involved in each step of a process, identifying the flow of activity through the individuals in an organization to determine its apparent efficiency. Lenny Jackson, a manager at CBC Halifax television, has been involved in several work-flow assessments. In one, he and a Vancouver manager interviewed 65 people involved in program production at a major production centre. They examined the production work-flow process from program approval through to the completion of production. The resultant flow chart showing the people connections was so jammed with processes that it had to be constructed with an overlay so that others could understand the issues. The duplication spelled out what appeared to be a less-than-efficient process. This chart provided the basis for a focused redesign of the process, streamlining it to reduce redundancy and make the process more efficient and effective. Lenny has also been involved in process-mapping a national news group and the current affairs group at a Toronto production centre. In process-mapping a 60-minute dinner show, the process mapping involved many measures, including how many minutes to produce an item and the cost per item. Figure 3-4 shows the process map of the resources coordination for production of an in-house television program at the CBC Toronto Production Centre.

Scatter diagrams
Diagrams that illustrate the relationship between two variables by visually depicting correlations and possible cause-and-effect.

Scatter Diagrams. **Scatter diagrams** illustrate the relationship between two variables such as height and weight, or the hardness of a ball bearing and its diameter (see Figure 3-6). These diagrams visually depict correlations and possible cause-and-effect. So, for instance, a scatter diagram could reveal that the percentage of rejects increases as the size of production runs increase. This, in turn, might suggest the need to reduce production runs or re-evaluate the process in order to improve quality.

Control charts
Run charts of sample averages with statistically determined upper and lower limits.

Control Charts. **Control charts** are the most sophisticated of the statistical techniques we'll describe. They are used to reflect variation in a system. Control charts reflect measurements of sample products averaged with statistically determined upper and lower limits. For instance, Coca Cola samples its one-litre bottles after they are filled to determine their exact quantity. These data are then plotted on a control chart, which tells management when the filling equipment needs adjustment. As long as the process variables fall within the acceptable range, the system is said to be "in control" (see Figure 3-5). When a point falls outside the limits set, then the variation is unacceptable. Improvements in quality should, over time, result in a narrowing of the range between the upper and lower limits through elimination of common causes.

FIGURE 3-4

This process map illustrates the resources coordination for the production of an in-house CBC television program at the Toronto Production Centre.

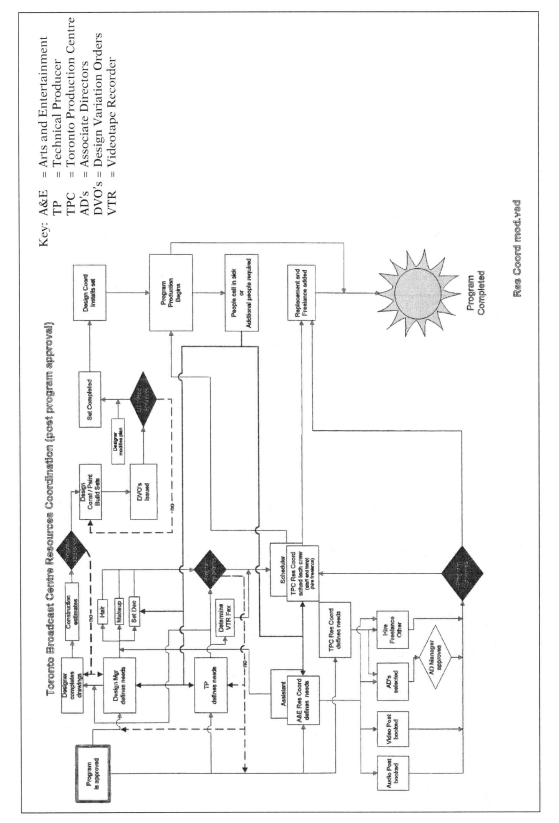

Key: A&E = Arts and Entertainment
TP = Technical Producer
TPC = Toronto Production Centre
AD's = Associate Directors
DVO's = Design Variation Orders
VTR = Videotape Recorder

Toronto Broadcast Centre Resources Coordination (post program approval)

Res Coord mod.vsd

FIGURE 3-5

Example of a control chart. (Reprinted with permission of the publisher. From *Putting Total Quality Management to Work,* p. 170, copyright © 1993 by Marshall Sashkin and Kenneth J. Kiser, Berrett-Koehler Publishers, Inc., San Francisco, CA. All rights reserved.)

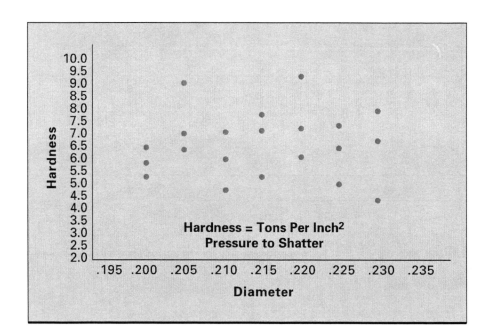

Hardness = Tons Per Inch² Pressure to Shatter

Total Quality Management

www-mmd.eng.cam.ac.uk/people/ahr/dstools/represent/tqm.htm

FIGURE 3-6

Example of a scatter diagram. (Reprinted with permission of the publisher. From *Putting Total Quality Management to Work,* p. 176, copyright © 1993 by Marshall Sashkin and Kenneth J. Kiser, Berrett-Koehler Publishers, Inc., San Francisco, CA. All rights reserved.)

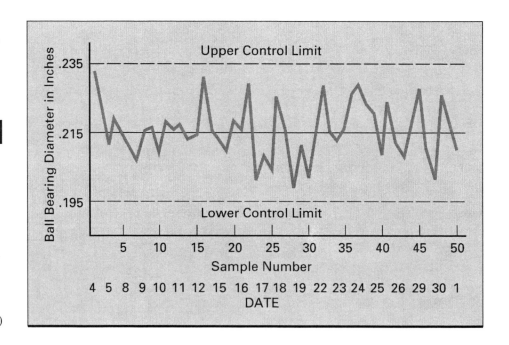

1. The ultimate aim of any control system is:
   a. cost savings
   b. greater productivity
   c. higher profits
   d. achieving goals
2. Explain why planning must come before the control process.
3. Personal observation as a method for measuring performance is one of the most widely used means by which supervisors assess actual performance. True or false?
4. If a supervisor performs the job of an employee who has called in sick that day, the supervisor is:
   a. performing immediate corrective action
   b. illustrating the role of an effective supervisor
   c. performing basic corrective action
   d. none of the above

TYPES OF CONTROL

Where in the process should controls be applied? Supervisors can implement controls before an activity commences, while the activity is going on, or after the fact. The first type is called preventive control, the second is concurrent control, and the last is corrective control (see Figure 3-7).

PREVENTIVE CONTROL

There's an old saying: An ounce of prevention is worth a pound of cure. Its message is that the best way to handle a deviation from standard is to ensure that it doesn't occur. Managers understand that the most desirable type of control is **preventive control** because it anticipates and prevents undesirable outcomes.

Preventive control
Controls that anticipate and prevent undesirable outcomes.

What are some examples of preventive controls? Companies such as Spar Aerospace, McDonald's, General Motors, and Air Canada spend millions of dollars each year on preventive maintenance programs for their equipment with the sole purpose of avoiding breakdowns during operations. Sport Canada requires that all federally funded coaches be certified to at least Level 4 of the National Coaching Certification Program's five levels, which requires successful completion of a long applied-training program and approval from the relevant National Sport Organization. Other examples of preventive controls include hiring and training people in anticipation of new business, inspection of raw materials, practising fire drills, and providing employees with company "code of ethics" cards to carry in their wallets.

Setting performance standards and communicating clear expectations of what and how performance is to be achieved are also preventive controls (to be discussed further in Chapter 5). These are particularly important in circumstances where a subordinate operates at a distance from the supervisor who cannot monitor and correct activity and where feedback after the fact may be too late to correct problems.

Quality systems introduced to a company, such as total quality management or ISO 9000-series certification, are expensive and time-consuming initiatives deemed worthwhile by many organizations because they prevent quality problems and promote greater quality (discussed later in this chapter).

CONCURRENT CONTROL

Concurrent controls
Controls that are enacted while an activity is in progress.

As the name implies, **concurrent control** occurs while an activity is in progress. When control is enacted while the work is being done, management can correct problems before they get out of hand or become too costly. This reminds us of the old saying, "A stitch in time saves nine."

Much of a supervisor's day-to-day activities involve concurrent control. When he or she directly oversees the actions of an employee, monitoring the employee's work and correcting problems as they occur, concurrent control is taking place. While there is obviously some delay between the action and the supervisor's corrective response, the delay is essentially minimal. You'll find other examples of concurrent control on factory machinery and computers. Temperature, pressure, and similar gauges that are checked regularly during a production process, and which automatically send a signal to an operator if there is a problem, are examples of concurrent controls. So, too, are programs on computers that provide operators with an immediate response when an error is made. If the operator inputs the wrong command, the program will reject it and may even provide the correct command.

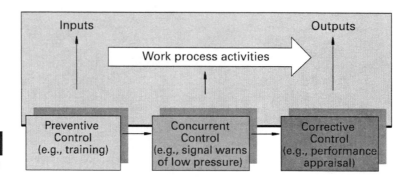

FIGURE 3-7

Three types of controls

CORRECTIVE CONTROL

Corrective control provides feedback after an activity is finished, in order to prevent any future deviations.

Examples of corrective control include final inspection of finished goods, annual employee performance appraisals, financial audits, quarterly budget reports, and the like. The obvious shortcoming of corrective control is that, by the time a supervisor has the information, it's too late to do anything about what has already happened. The damage or mistakes have already occurred. For instance, where information controls are weak, a department head may only learn for the first time in August that her employees have already spent 110 percent of the department's annual photocopying budget. Nothing she can do in August can correct the overexpenditure. What corrective control does do is alert her that there is a problem. Then she can determine what went wrong and initiate basic corrective action.

Corrective control
Provides feedback after an activity is finished, to prevent any future deviations.

FOCUS OF CONTROL

What do supervisors control? Most of their control efforts are directed at one of five areas (see Figure 3-8):

- costs
- inventories
- quality
- safety
- employee performance

COSTS

Supervisors are regularly under pressure to keep their costs in line. Let's look at those cost categories and present a general program for cost reduction.

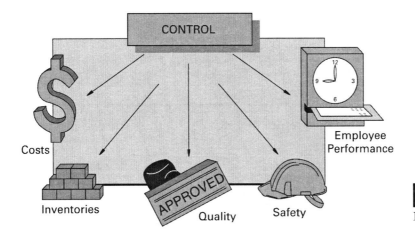

FIGURE 3-8

Focus of control

MAJOR COST CATEGORIES

The following list presents the major cost categories that a supervisor will come in contact with and which need to be monitored.

- **Direct labour costs**. Expenditures for labour that are directly applied in the creation or delivery of the product or service. Examples: Machine operators in a factory or teachers in a school.
- **Indirect labour costs**. Expenditures for labour that are not directly applied in the creation or delivery of the product or service. Examples: Cost accountants, human resource recruiters, public relations specialists.
- **Raw material costs**. Expenditures for materials that go directly into the creation of a product or service. Examples: Sheet steel at a Mazda plant or hamburger buns at a McDonald's.
- **Supportive supplies costs**. Expenditures for necessary items that do not become part of the finished product or service. Examples: Cleaning compounds at the Mazda plant or photocopying costs at Sun Life.
- **Utility costs**. Expenditures for electricity, gas, water, and similar utilities. Example: Monthly electric bill for a regional office.
- **Maintenance costs**. Material and labour expenditures incurred to repair and maintain equipment and facilities. Examples: Repair parts for equipment or jet-engine maintenance technicians at Canadian Airlines.
- **Waste costs**. Expenditures for products, parts, or services that cannot be reused. Examples: Unsold French fries at McDonald's or scrap metal at a Camco plant.

Typically, supervisors will have a budget for each major cost category. Then, by monitoring expenditures, costs can be kept within their budget plans. (See the skill module on budgeting at the end of this chapter.)

COST-REDUCTION PROGRAMS

When costs are too high, managers will implement a cost reduction program. Beginning in the late 1980s, Canadian corporations began a massive effort to reduce costs and improve their competitive position in relation to their global competitors. Much of this cost-cutting had a direct effect on supervisors. For instance, direct labour costs have been cut by automating jobs and redesigning work around teams that are more productive than individuals; and indirect labour costs have been slashed by laying off tens of thousands of support personnel in research, finance, human resources, and clerical functions. Budgets for training, travel, telephone calls, photocopying, computer software, office supplies, and similar expenditures have undergone significant cuts.

The following outlines a six-step program that can guide you in reducing costs in your department.[1]

1. **Improve methods**. Eliminate any unnecessary activities and introduce new work methods that can increase efficiency.

2. **Level the work flow.** Peaks and valleys in a work flow imply inefficiencies. By levelling the work flow, you can manage with fewer employees and reduce overtime.
3. **Minimize waste.** Burning lights in unused areas, misuse of office supplies, underemployed workers, underutilization of equipment, and wasteful use of raw materials add considerably to a supervisor's departmental costs.
4. **Install modern equipment.** Budget for new equipment to replace obsolete and worn-out machinery, computers, and the like.
5. **Invest in employee training.** People, like machines, can become obsolete in that their skills become dated.
6. **Make cuts selectively.** Avoid across-the-board cuts. Some people and groups contribute significantly more than others. Make cuts where they will generate the greatest efficiencies.

INVENTORIES

Supervisors are routinely responsible for ensuring that adequate inventories of materials and supplies are available for activities under their jurisdiction. For a shift supervisor at Burger King, that would include paper products, buns, burger patties, French fries, condiments, cooking utensils, cleaning supplies, and even proper change for the cash register. For a nursing supervisor at a hospital, it might mean supplies such as pharmaceuticals, gloves, hypodermic needles, and bed linen.

The challenge in monitoring inventory costs is balancing the costs of maintaining inventories against the cost of running out of inventory. If excessive inventory is carried, money is needlessly tied up and unnecessary storage costs are incurred. Excessive inventory also adds to insurance premiums and taxes. And, of course, there are potential obsolescence costs—unused inventory may remain unused because products change. If inventories drop too low, operations can be disrupted and sales lost. A stock-out of paper can bring a publisher's printing to a halt. And if a Tim Horton's supervisor fails to monitor the inventory of milk, there may be some very disgruntled coffee customers.

The **just-in-time (JIT) inventory** system is a popular inventory system that attempts to balance the trade-offs between costs of having too much or too little inventory. In this system, inventory items arrive from suppliers as they are needed in the production process rather than being stored in stock. Despite its apparently ideal setup, JIT is not used by all organizations as it requires a great deal of planning. Backup plans to cover the inevitable occasion when parts are not delivered on time must be created. What if the received inventory does not meet quality requirements and must be returned? A strong relationship with suppliers, including excellent and complete communication of quality, quantity, and delivery needs, is required.

When JIT works as designed, it results in a number of positive benefits for a manufacturer: reduced inventories, reduced setup time, better

Just-in-Time (JIT) Inventory System
A system in which inventory items arrive when they are needed in the production process instead of being stored in stock.

Materials Requirements Planning
www-mmd.eng.cam.ac.uk/people/ahr/dstools/process/mrp.htm

work flow, shorter manufacturing time, less space consumption, and even higher quality. Of course, suppliers who can be depended on to deliver quality materials on time must be found. Because there are no inventories, there is no slack in the system to absorb defective materials or delays in shipments.

Materials requirement planning (MRP) is another inventory control tool used in some organizations. This system uses a bill of materials, which is essentially a recipe for the product specifying what is needed and in what order. The bill of materials is used to instruct the computer program that controls inventory and schedules production. MRP is similar to JIT in that it tries to ensure that the right raw materials and parts arrive at the right time in the right place.

Gantt and PERT charts, described in the last chapter as planning tools, also provide scheduling control in the production process.

QUALITY

With the possible exception of controlling costs, achieving high quality has become a primary focus of today's organizations. Many North American products were criticized as being shoddy in quality compared to their Japanese and German counterparts. On the other hand, companies such as Bombardier have thrived in the past decade by focusing on quality products or services. With this new emphasis has come increased demand on supervisors to engage in quality control.

Quality control refers to monitoring quality (weight, strength, consistency, colour, taste, reliability, and so on) to ensure that it meets preestablished standards. It is needed at multiple points in a process. It begins with the receipt of inputs. Are the raw materials satisfactory? Do new employees have the proper skills and abilities? It continues with work in process and in all steps up to the completion of the final product or service. Assessments at intermediate stages of the transformation process are typically part of quality control. Early detection of a defective part or process can save the cost of further work on the item.

A comprehensive quality control program would encompass preventive, concurrent, and corrective controls. For example, controls would inspect incoming raw materials, monitor operations while they are in progress, and include final inspection and rejection of unsatisfactory outputs. Of course, this same comprehensive program could be applied to services. For instance, a claims supervisor for Dominion Insurance could hire and train her people to ensure that they fully understand their jobs, monitor their daily work flow to ensure it is done properly and on time, review completed claims for accuracy and thoroughness, and follow up with customers to determine their degree of satisfaction with the way their claims were handled.

Total quality management (TQM) A philosophy of management that is driven by the attainment of customer satisfaction through the continuous improvement of all organizational processes.

Quality has taken on a meaning larger than quality control in the expanded perspective of **total quality management (TQM)**, a program that has been adopted by many Canadian companies. TQM is based on the ideas of W. Edwards Deming, an American whose ideas found an interested audience in postwar Japan (see Figure 3-9) before they were accepted in North America. Among his ideas was the use of statistics to analyze variability in production processes. A well-managed organization, according to Deming, was one in which statistical control reduced variability and resulted in uniform quality and predictable quantity of output. TQM's management philosophy sees customers as everyone who interacts with the organization's product or service, internally or externally, thereby including employees and suppliers as well as clients who purchase the organization's output. The objective is to create an organization committed to continuous improvement. There is never enough quality. Quality improvement is an ongoing, never-ending process.

If a supervisor works in an organization focused on TQM, that supervisor must be familiar with statistical control processes but also comfortable working closely with subordinates on quality. TQM is based on the participation of the people closest to the work. Employees are respected for their ideas on continuous improvement and a supervisor is expected to support and seek their input.

ISO 9000
www.iso.ch/
welcome.html

ISO registration is another quality initiative used by many companies that influences work procedures and, therefore, the supervisor's job. It is often part of a company's TQM strategy.

---

1. **Focus on the customer.** The customer includes not only outsiders who buy the organization's products or services, but also internal customers (such as shipping or accounts payable personnel) who interact with and serve others in the organization.

2. **Continuous improvement.** TQM is a commitment to never being satisfied. "Very good" is not enough. Quality can always be improved.

3. **Improvement of the quality of everything the organization does.** TQM uses a very broad definition of quality. It relates not only to the final product, but also to the way the organization handles deliveries, how rapidly it responds to complaints, how politely the phones are answered, and the like.

4. **Accurate measurement.** TQM uses statistical techniques to measure every critical variable in the organization's operations. These are compared against standards or benchmarks to identify problems, trace them to their roots, and eliminate their causes.

5. **Involvement of employees.** TQM involves the people on the line in the improvement process. Teams are widely used in TQM programs for finding and solving problems.

FIGURE 3-9

The foundations
of TQM

The International Standards Organization developed the ISO 9000 series of standards. To be certified as meeting these standards, thereby proving that certain quality assurance procedures and documentation are in place, a company must be audited both when it applies for registration and then on a regular, ongoing basis. Elements of the ISO guidelines refer to management responsibility, control of customer-supplied product, document and data control, design control, process control, inspection and testing, handling, packaging, storage, preservation and delivery, training and control of quality records, among others.

Tina Payton, prepress supervisor at Robinson-Blackmore printing company in St. John's, Newfoundland, says that her company's ISO 9002 registration significantly affects her job. "There are very strict policies and procedures to follow. It reduces errors so it is beneficial. The downside is that it takes a lot of time, for example, on preventative maintenance on equipment. And there's more paperwork, for example, signing off that a disk coming in from a client is not damaged, doing weekly calibrations on equipment, and recording the results. The controls created are time-consuming but important, improving productivity in the long run. One aspect that has improved is that not as much time is wasted tracking down information needed to carry out a job. Sales representatives would not fill out all the areas of the job docket, which would cause unnecessary downtime trying to collect information needed. With these policies in place, these problems have decreased significantly."

SAFETY

Paula Aylward at Cavendish Farms of P.E.I. knows that, of all her priorities, safety is at the top. At Suncor's oil production facility in Fort McMurray, Alberta, Larry Bowzeylo agrees. "You must make the work as safe as possible. You can't replace people."

Safety is a concern to any supervisor but particularly to those in a production facility where the equipment or chemicals used could have very dangerous consequences. In a manufacturing facility, a supervisor will always be on the lookout for potential sources of accidents. For example, the supervisor may inspect the floor for loose tiles or grease, the ladders or scaffolding for signs of stress, anything clogging aisles and walkways, employees not following safety rules (like wearing safety glasses). Accident prevention involves both preventive and corrective control. The supervisor does it to maintain productivity (accidents result in downtime and can cost the company a lot of money) but, primarily, for the benefit of the employees who work there and deserve the security of knowing that all precautions have been taken to protect them.

OCCUPATIONAL HEALTH AND SAFETY LEGISLATION

Canadian legislation in occupational health and safety is based on an "internal responsibility" system. This system recognizes that workers, supervisors, and employers share a common goal of preventing work-related injury or illness, and that they are all in a position to identify and prevent circumstances leading to injury or illness in the workplace. The legislation identifies rules for this joint accountability in the form of legally enacted duties, rights, and responsibilities.

For organizations under federal jurisdiction (for example, banks, airlines, post offices), the regulations governing health and safety fall under the Canada Labour Code. Health and safety matters for organizations not covered by federal jurisdiction are regulated by the province or territory in which the organization is located (see Figure 3-10).

The supervisor's role is an important one with respect to ensuring that health and safety regulations are followed. In fact, in Ontario, the Occupational Health and Safety Act specifies that an employer is required

Jurisdiction	Main body of health & safety law	Department
Canada	*Canada Labour Code*	Labour
Alberta	*Occupational Health and Safety Act*	Environment
British Columbia	*Workers' Compensation Act* *Workplace Act*	WCB* Labour
Manitoba	*Workplace Safety and Health Act*	Labour - Workplace Safety and Support Services
New Brunswick	*Occupational Health and Safety Commission Act* *Occupational Health and Safety Act*	New Brunswick Occupational Health & Safety Commission
Newfoundland	*Occupational Health and Safety Act*	Labour
Nova Scotia	*Occupational Health and Safety Act* *Workers' Compensation Act*	Health WCB
Ontario	*Occupational Health and Safety Act* *Workplace Safety and Insurance Act*	Labour Workplace Safety and Insurance Board
Prince Edward Is.	*Occupational Health & Safety Act* *Workers' Compensation Act*	Fisheries and Labour WCB
Quebec	*An Act respecting occupational health and safety* *An Act respecting industrial accidents and occupational disease*	Occupational Health and Safety Commission
Saskatchewan	*Occupational Health and Safety Act*	Human Resources, Labour & Employment

* Workers' Compensation Board

FIGURE 3-10

Federal and provincial Health and Safety Acts

to appoint "competent persons" as supervisors. A "competent person" under the Act is one who

(a) is qualified because of knowledge, training, and experience to organize the work and its performance
(b) is familiar with this Act and the regulations that apply to the work
(c) has knowledge of any potential or actual danger to health or safety in the workplace

(Occupational Health and Safety Act, sections 1 and 25)

The supervisor is also expected to apply this knowledge by advising workers of hazards; giving specific instructions, procedures, and equipment to provide appropriate protection; and taking "every precaution reasonable in the circumstances for the protection of a worker."

A supervisor who fails to comply may be liable for a fine or imprisonment. Let's look at an example: On February 28, 1994, Raglan Industries Inc. of Oshawa, a company director, and a supervisor were all convicted under the Ontario Occupational Health and Safety Act. They had failed to ensure suitable lighting in a confined space during a paint-spraying application despite a concern being raised by a worker. In a subsequent explosion, the worker received burns to almost 90 per cent of his body, head wounds, a fractured back, and a partially amputated hand. The supervisor's part of the conviction involved a $5000 fine.

ACCIDENT PREVENTION

What can you do to prevent accidents? A number of things. Here are some actions you might consider..

1. **Match people and jobs.** Factors such as visual skills and experience have been found to be related to increased accident rates on certain types of jobs. Moreover, when employees are undergoing personal problems or other sources of stress, their potential for accidents increases on some jobs. Rotating a person temporarily to a lower-risk job, for instance, should be considered if you think their personal problems might increase accident-proneness. Or you can restrict the activities of an employee who is temporarily accident-prone.

2. **Engineer the job and equipment.** The proper design of job activities, work devices, protective gear, and equipment can reduce accidents and injuries. Office workers, for instance, are less likely to suffer back problems if their desk and chair arrangement is designed to their specific work activities and body movements.

3. **Educate and train employees.** Make sure your employees know the safety rules and incorporate accident prevention into training programs. Create safety awareness by posting highly visible signs that proclaim the importance of safety, use safety committees to identify and correct potential problems, and publicize safety statistics.

4. **Enforce safety standards**. The best rules and regulations will be ineffective in reducing accidents if they are not enforced. Make regular visits to the work floor and visually check to make sure safety standards are being maintained.

5. **Reward employees for safe performance**. Make sure employee safety is viewed as important and worthwhile. Provide incentives and awards for safe performance.

EMPLOYEE PERFORMANCE

Supervisors accomplish things through other people. They need and depend on subordinates to achieve their unit goals. It is, therefore, important for them to get their employees to perform in ways they consider desirable. But how do supervisors ensure that employees are performing as they are supposed to? How do you, for example, minimize employee lateness, absenteeism, and accidents? How do you control the quantity and quality of employee effort? Obvious means include direct supervision and performance appraisals (see Figure 3-11).

An employee typically behaves with the best intentions in mind. So, if there is a problem with performance, it can often be traced to the employee not understanding fully what expectations the supervisor had in mind, for example, concerning quality, or documentation or safety procedures. It is essential that the supervisor ensure that each employee is informed about the organization's expectations toward that employee. As you'll see in Something to Think About, a supervisor's perception of what a subordinate's job role includes often differs from the subordinate's perception—and it does so in the same way in several countries.

On a day-to-day basis, supervisors oversee employees' work and correct problems as they occur. The supervisor who notices an employee

FIGURE 3-11

Giving performance appraisals is a significant part of a supervisor's controls function.

Researchers examined the job expectations of bank tellers working for the same large multinational bank in the United States, Australia, Japan, and Hong Kong, and compared these with the expectations of their supervisors. It was discovered that, in all countries, supervisors had broader definitions of the teller job role than did their subordinates. It appears that, within the teller role, supervisors include any actions that could reasonably be taken by the subordinate to improve efficiency and effectiveness. The subordinate is less likely to have such a wide-open perception of the job, instead focusing on specific expected duties.[2]

1. What could be the consequences of these differing perceptions?

_____

_____

_____

_____

_____

2. How could these differences in perception be reduced?

_____

_____

_____

_____

_____

taking an unnecessary risk when operating his or her machine can point out the correct way to perform the task and tell the employee to do it the correct way in the future.

Supervisors assess the work of their employees in a more formal way by means of systematic performance appraisals. An employee's recent performance is evaluated. If performance is positive, the employee's behaviour can be reinforced with a reward such as a pay increase. If performance is below standard, the supervisor will seek to correct it or, depending on the nature of the deviation, discipline the employee.

As Figure 3-12 demonstrates, supervisors have at their disposal a considerably larger menu of behavioural control devices. In actual practice, supervisors use almost all of the options described in the figure to increase the likelihood that employees will perform as desired.

- **Selection.** Identify and hire people whose values, attitudes, and personality fit with what the supervisor desires.
- **Goals.** When employees accept specific goals, the goals then direct and limit behaviour.
- **Job design.** The way jobs are designed determines, to a large degree, the tasks that a person does, the work pace, the people he or she interacts with, and similar behaviours.
- **Orientation.** New-employee orientation defines what behaviours are acceptable and what aren't.
- **Direct supervision.** The physical presence of supervisors acts to shape employee behaviour and allows for rapid detection of undersirable behaviour.
- **Training.** Formal training programs teach employees desired work practices.
- **Regulations.** Formal rules, policies, job descriptions, and other regulations define acceptable practices and constrain undesirable behaviour.
- **Performance appraisals.** Employees will behave so as to look good on the criteria by which they will be appraised.
- **Rewards.** Pay raises, recognition, desired job assignments, and similar rewards act as reinforcers to encourage desired behaviours and to extinguish undesirable ones.

FIGURE 3-12

Behavioural control devices

CHARACTERISTICS OF EFFECTIVE CONTROLS

Effective control systems tend to have certain qualities in common (these qualities are summarized in Figure 3-13). The importance of these characteristics varies with the situation, but the following can provide guidance to supervisors in designing their unit's control system.

TIMELINESS

Controls should alert the supervisor to a problem as soon as possible. The best information has little value if it is dated. Therefore, an effective control system must provide timely information.

ECONOMY

A control system must be economically reasonable to operate. Any system of control has to justify the benefits that it gives in relation to the costs it incurs. To minimize costs, supervisors should try to impose the least amount of control necessary to produce the desired results. The widespread use of computers is due to a large extent to their ability to provide timely and accurate information in a highly efficient manner.

1. **Timeliness** ensures quick response.

2. **Economy** ensures that the benefits of control exceed the cost.

3. **Flexibility** provides the ability to adjust to change.

4. **Understandability** increases the likelihood that controls will be used.

5. **Reasonable criteria** ensure that controls will not act as demotivators.

6. **Critical placement** recognizes that controls can't be imposed on everything and, therefore, need to be located where there is the greatest potential for harm.

7. **Emphasis on the exception** lessens the chance that a manager will be overwhelmed with information on variations from standard.

FIGURE 3-13

Characteristics of effective controls

FLEXIBILITY

Effective controls must be flexible enough to adjust to adverse change or to take advantage of new opportunities. In today's dynamic and rapidly changing world, supervisors should design control systems that can adjust to the changing nature of departmental objectives, work assignments, and job tasks..

UNDERSTANDABILITY

Controls that cannot be understood by those who must use them are of little value. It is sometimes necessary, therefore, to substitute less complex controls for sophisticated devices. A control system that is difficult to understand can cause unnecessary mistakes, frustrates employees, and is eventually ignored.

REASONABLE CRITERIA

Consistent with our discussion of goals in the previous chapter, control standards must be reasonable and attainable. If they are too high or unreasonable, they no longer motivate. Since most employees don't want to risk being labelled as incompetent for telling their bosses that they ask too much, employees may resort to unethical or illegal shortcuts. Controls should, therefore, enforce standards that are reasonable; they should challenge and stretch people to reach higher performance levels without being demotivating or encouraging deception.

CRITICAL PLACEMENT

Supervisors can't control everything that occurs within their department. Even if they could, the benefits couldn't justify the costs. As a result, they should place controls on those factors that are critical to their unit's performance goals. Controls should cover the critical activities, operations, and events within their unit. That is, they should focus on where variations from standard are most likely to occur or where a variation would do the greatest harm. In a department where labour costs are $20 000 a month and postage costs are $50 a month, a 5 per cent overrun in the former is more critical than a 20 per cent overrun in the latter. Hence, we should establish controls for labour and a critical dollar allocation, whereas postage expenses would not appear to be critical.

EMPHASIS ON THE EXCEPTION

Since supervisors can't control all activities, they should place their strategic control devices where they can call attention only to the exceptions. A **control by exception** system ensures that a manager is not overwhelmed by information on variations from standard. For instance, the accounts receivable supervisor at a Sears store instructs her people to only inform her when an account is 15 days past due. The fact that 90 per cent of the store's customers pay their bills on time or no more than two weeks late means she can devote her attention to the 10 per cent exceptions.

Control by exception
Strategic control devices should call attention only to exceptions from standard.

POTENTIAL NEGATIVE OUTCOMES OF CONTROLS

Controls can create their own problems. The introduction of controls comes with potential negatives that you will need to guard against. These include employee resistance, misdirection of employee effort, and ethical dilemmas for supervisors concerning control devices. Let's take a brief look at each.

EMPLOYEE RESISTANCE

Many people don't like to be told what to do or to know that they're being "checked up on." When work performance is deficient, few people enjoy being criticized or corrected. The result is that employees often resist controls. They view their supervisor, daily production reports, performance appraisals, and similar control devices as evidence that their employer doesn't trust them.

Reality tells us that controls are a way of organizational life because management has a responsibility to ensure that activities are going as planned. So what can you, as a supervisor, do to lessen this resistance?

First, wherever possible, encourage employee self-control (see Assessing Yourself). Once employees know their goals, give them the benefit of the doubt and leave them alone. Let them monitor and correct their own performance. Supplement this with regular communication so they can let you know what problems they've encountered and how they've solved them. The assumption with self-control is that employees are responsible, trustworthy, and capable of personally correcting any significant deviation from their goals. Only if this assumption proves incorrect do you need to introduce more formalized external control mechanisms.

When external controls are needed, here are a few suggestions to minimize employee resistance.

- Have employees participate in setting the standards. This lessens the likelihood that they'll view them as unrealistic or too demanding.
- Explain to employees how they will be evaluated. Surprisingly, the problem is often not the controls themselves creating resistance but the lack of understanding of how information will be gathered and how it will be used.
- Provide employees with regular feedback. Ambiguity causes stress and resistance, so it makes sense to let people know how they're doing.
- Finally, treat controls as a device for helping employees improve rather than for punishing them. Most people want the satisfaction that comes from doing their work better and want to avoid the pain and embarrassment that comes with discipline.

Assessing Yourself

HOW WILLING ARE YOU TO ENCOURAGE SELF-CONTROL?

For each of the following eighteen statements, rate each on a scale of 1 to 5, where 5 = strongly agree, 4 = agree somewhat, 3 = neither agree nor disagree, 2 = disagree somewhat, and 1 = strongly disagree.

	Strongly Agree				Strongly Disagree
1. I'd let others do more, but it appears the jobs never seem to get done the way I want them to be done.	5	4	3	2	1
2. I don't feel I have the time to explain to others what to do.	5	4	3	2	1

3. I carefully check on others' work without letting them know I'm doing it, so I can correct their mistakes if necessary, before they cause too many problems. 5 4 3 2 1

4. I let others control the whole job—giving them the opportunity to complete it without any of my involvement. Then I review the result. 5 4 3 2 1

5. When I have given clear instructions and the task isn't done right, I get upset. 5 4 3 2 1

6. I feel that others may lack the commitment I have. Any task I ask them to do won't get done as well as I'd do it. 5 4 3 2 1

7. I'd let others control things more, but I feel I can do the job better than the person I might have given the job to. 5 4 3 2 1

8. I'd let others control more, but if the individual I give this responsibility to does an incompetent job, I'll be severely criticized. 5 4 3 2 1

9. If I were to give up control, my job wouldn't be nearly as much fun. 5 4 3 2 1

10. When I give up control, I often find that the outcome is such that I end up doing the task over again myself. 5 4 3 2 1

11. I have not really found that giving up control saves any time. 5 4 3 2 1

12. I tell others exactly how something should be accomplished. 5 4 3 2 1

13. I can't give up control as much as I'd like to because others lack the necessary experience. 5 4 3 2 1

14. I feel that when I give up control, I lose control. 5 4 3 2 1

15. I would give up control more, but I'm pretty much a perfectionist. 5 4 3 2 1

16. I work longer hours than I should. 5 4 3 2 1

17. I can give others the routine tasks, but I feel I must do nonroutine tasks myself. 5 4 3 2 1

18. My own boss expects me to keep very close to all details of my job. 5 4 3 2 1

SCORING

Total your score by adding the circled numbers for the eighteen statements.

WHAT THE INSTRUMENT MEANS

How much control you're willing to give up or share is directly related to how willing you are to assign this "authority" to others. Depending on your total score, the following interpretations can be made:

> 72–90 points = ineffective assignment of self-control
> 54–71 points = assigning self-control habits needs substantial improvement
> 36–53 points = assigning self-control habits are positive, but some improvement needed
> 18–35 points = superior assignment of self-control

Source: Reprinted by permission of the publisher from *Management Review*, May 1982 ©1982, American Management Association, New York. All rights reserved.

MISDIRECTION OF EFFORT

Three managers at a General Motors plant installed a secret control box in a supervisor's office to override the control panel that governed the speed of the assembly line.[3] The device allowed the managers to speed up the assembly line—a serious violation of GM's contract with the United Auto Workers. When caught, the managers explained that, while they knew what they had done was wrong, the pressure from higher-ups to meet unrealistic production goals was so great that they felt the secret control panel was the only way they could meet their targets. As described by one manager, senior GM executives would say (regarding the high production goals), "I don't care how you do it—just do it."

Have you ever been frustrated by the "service" you receive when trying to get some information, fill out a form, or solve a problem?

Some employees can be so fixated on ensuring that every rule is followed that they lose sight of the fact that their job is to serve the public, not hassle them! This tendency illustrates another potential problem with controls: People may misdirect their efforts in order to look good on the control criteria.

Because any control system has imperfections, problems occur when individuals or organizational units attempt to look good exclusively in

Are You Comprehending
What You're Reading?

5. Because a supervisor cannot control all activities, controls should be placed on _____ activities.
   a. risky   c. critical
   b. risk-free   d. complex
6. Explain what is meant by just-in-time inventory systems.
7. In some jurisdictions a supervisor can be held personally liable when health and safety regulations are not followed in the workplace. True or false?
8. An annual employee performance appraisal is an example of a _____ control.
   a. preventive
   b. concurrent
   c. corrective

FIGURE 3-14

Employees in government offices often become so fixated on following every rule that they lose sight of what is really important.

terms of the control devices while in actuality, the result is dysfunctional in terms of the organization's goals. More often than not, this situation is caused by incomplete measures of performance. If the control system evaluates only the quantity of output, people will ignore quality. Similarly, if the system measures activities rather than results, people will spend their time attempting to look good on the activity measures.

What can you, as a supervisor, do to minimize this problem? Two things. First, make sure that control standards are reasonable. Very importantly, this should not merely be your perception. The employees must believe the standards are fair and within their capability. Second, you should select and evaluate criteria that are directly related to achievement of employee job goals. If the licensing supervisor in the motor vehicle office evaluates her people on how well they follow rules rather than on how effectively they serve the needs of clients, then her employees will not give much attention to satisfying clients. Finding the right criteria will often mean using a multiple set of standards. For instance, the goal of "serving clients" might require the licensing supervisor to evaluate her clerks on criteria such as "greets all clients with a smile and friendly greeting," "answers all client questions without seeking outside assistance," and "solves the client's problems in one visit." In addition, the supervisor might set up a client comment box in her licensing department where individual employees could be praised or criticized on their service, and then use this feedback as one measure of how well employees were doing their jobs.

ETHICS AND CONTROL DEVICES

Just because a supervisor *can* monitor the most minute details of an employee's work day doesn't mean he or she *should*. This has become a particularly sensitive issue in recent years as sophisticated communication systems and computer software make it possible for a supervisor's control capability to potentially interfere with an employee's right to privacy.

Supervisors at General Electric's Answering Centre record and review employees' handling of customer telephone inquiries. At Vantreight's huge flower farm in Saanichton, British Columbia, supervisors use handheld computers to track each picker's output. The technology now exists for "big brother" to directly and indirectly monitor employees. But is it ethical?

We have no absolute answer. It can be argued that this type of computer performance monitoring helps people do their jobs better. It enables supervisors to review employee performance and provide feedback that can improve the quality of the employees' work. But employees certainly should be aware that this monitoring is going on. Even then, studies have shown that stress-related complaints increase when employees know that somebody may be listening in on their phone calls.[4] This suggests that great care needs to be taken by supervisors as advanced technology expands their control capability

BUDGETING

Assessing Yourself: What Do You Know about Budgeting?

For each of the following statements, record your response by circling the corresponding number.

WHEN DESIGNING AND CONTROLLING A BUDGET, I WOULD:

		Strongly Agree	Agree	Neutral	Disagree	Strongly Disagree
1.	Begin the budget process by focusing on my department's goals.	1	2	3	4	5
2.	Delegate responsibility for developing my budget to a team of employees.	1	2	3	4	5
3.	Use last period's budget as a guide for developing this period's budget, especially in times of significant departmental change.	1	2	3	4	5
4.	Use the budget process as a way to convey to upper management new programs and responsibilities that my department might pursue.	5	4	3	2	1
5.	Focus on controlling costs because expense budgets are the most frequently used supervisory budgets.	5	4	3	2	1
6.	Try to underspend my current budget because that typically results in a larger budget in the next budget period.	1	2	3	4	5

SCORING KEY AND INTERPRETATION

Add up your score. The higher your total, the better your understanding of budgeting. Individuals with scores below 20, in particular, should find the following coverage of budgeting valuable.

Skill Basics

An organization needs to forecast its financial needs in order to be able to meet them adequately at the right time. A budget is essentially a forecast of financial needs. It then operates also as a control tool to keep expenses in check with the forecast and to avoid shortfalls and unexpected debt.

A company will typically prepare a long-term capital budget to forecast expenses that will occur over a long time, for example, predicting when equipment will need to be replaced or hardware and software upgraded or a new plant built. A supervisor will have some input into this capital budget in that the supervisor has information to contribute to that forecast (such as incidence of breakdown, leading to forecasts of equipment replacement).

But the supervisor is much more likely to get involved with short-term operational budgets, forecasting financial needs over the next year, breaking that down typically into quarters. Because the supervisor is so close to where the work is accomplished, he or she is best qualified to make the most accurate judgement of what expenses will be incurred in the near future. Given that the creation of this short-term expense budget is a common expectation for supervisors, we'll use the expense budget as the focus for our discussion.

INCREMENTAL vs. ZERO-BASE BUDGETS

Incremental budget
A budget that develops out of the previous budget.

The traditional budget is incremental in nature. It develops out of the previous budget. In the **incremental budget**, each period's budget begins by using the last period as a reference point. Then adjustments are made to individual items within the budget. The major problems with the incremental approach are that it tends to hide inefficiencies and waste, encourages continual increases, and hinders change. Inefficiencies tend to grow because, in the typical incremental budget, nothing ever gets cut. Each budget begins with the funds allocated for the last period—to which are added a percentage for inflation and requests for new or expanded activities. So, unfortunately, this approach to budgeting often provides money for activities long after the need is gone. And because incrementalism builds on the past, this type of budget also tends to constrain bold or radical changes.

Zero-base budget
A budget that makes no reference to previous appropriations; all items must be justified.

An option that deals directly with the incremental budget's limitations is the **zero-base budget** (ZBB). With the ZBB, the entire budget begins from scratch and each budget item must be justified. No reference is made to previous appropriations. The major advantage to the ZBB is that all programs, projects, and activities taking place within every department in the organization are reassessed in terms of benefits and costs. The primary drawbacks of ZBB include increased paperwork and preparation time, the tendency for managers to exaggerate the benefits of activities they want funded, and the negative effect on intermediate and long-term planning. On this last point, when departmental budgets have to be completely justified every year, the potential for dramatic ups and downs in funding can create chaos for managers and make intermediate and long-term planning almost impossible.

While most organizations rely on incremental budgeting, the zero-base approach continues to have its advocates. We suggest that when organizations are developing new strategies, making major shifts in the products and services they offer, undertaking a significant reorganization, or introducing similar organization-wide change programs, managers should at least temporarily utilize zero-base budgeting. This approach will lessen the likelihood that outdated or less important activities will continue to receive their prior level of funding.

TOP-DOWN vs. BOTTOM-UP BUDGETING

Another decision that must be made about budgeting is where the budget will initially be prepared. **Top-down budgeting** originates at the upper levels of the organization. Budgets are initiated, controlled, and directed by top management. This approach assumes top management is best able to allocate resources among alternative uses within the organization. These budgets are then given to middle-level and lower-level managers, who are responsible for carrying them out. This method has the advantage of simplifying the budgeting process and focusing attention on the organization's overall strategy and goals. However, the top-down approach has some huge disadvantages. It assumes that top management has comprehensive data on all activities within the organization. This assumption is rarely valid, especially in relatively large organizations. Since operating personnel and lower-level managers have no input, the top-down approach also does nothing to build support for and commitment to budgets.

Top-down budgeting
Budgets that are initiated, controlled, and directed by top management.

Most organizations today have moved to **bottom-up budgeting**, where the initial budget requests are prepared by those who must implement them. These requests are then sent up for approval to higher levels of management where modifications may be suggested. When differences occur, they are negotiated. The process is followed upward until an organization-wide budget is developed. The bottom-up approach to budgeting essential-

Bottom-up budgeting
Budget requests are prepared by those who implement them and then sent to higher levels of management for approval.

ly has the opposite advantages and disadvantages to those of budgets initiated from the top. Because supervisors and other lower-level managers are more knowledgeable about their needs than are managers at the top, they are less likely to overlook important funding requirements. And very importantly, lower-level managers are also much more likely to enthusiastically accept and try to meet budgets they had a hand in shaping.

THE BUDGETING PROCESS

You're a new supervisor who has been asked to submit your first budget. What do you do? The following steps will provide you with some guidance:

1. **Review the organization's overall strategy and goals.** Understanding your organization's strategy and goals will help you focus on where the overall organization is going and your department's role in that plan.

2. **Determine your department's goals and the means to attain them.** What activities will allow you to reach your departmental goals and help the organization achieve its overall goals? What resources will you require to achieve these goals? Think in terms of factors such as staffing requirements, workloads, and the materials and equipment you'll need. This is also your opportunity to formulate new programs and propose new responsibilities for your department.

3. **Gather cost information.** You'll need accurate cost estimates of those resources you identified in step 2. Old budgets may be of some help. But you'll also want to talk with your immediate manager, other superiors, colleagues in similar positions, key subordinates, and use other contacts you have developed both inside and outside your organization.

4. **Share your goals and cost estimates with superiors.** Your immediate manager will need to approve your budget, so his or her support is necessary. Discuss your goals, cost estimates, and other ideas with your immediate manager and key superiors before you include them in your budget. This will ensure that they align with upper management's vision of your department's role and will build consensus for your proposed submission.

5. **Draw up your proposed budget.** Once your goals and costs are in place, constructing the actual budget is fairly simple. But be sure to show the linkage between your budget items and your depart-

mental goals. You need to justify your requests. And be prepared to explain and sell your budget to your immediate manager and upper management. Remember that there will almost certainly be other managers competing for some of the same resources that you want.

6. **Be prepared to negotiate.** It's unlikely that your budget will be approved exactly as you submitted it. Be prepared to negotiate changes that upper management suggests and to revise your original budget. Recognize the politics in the budget process and negotiate from the perspective of building credits for future budgets. If certain projects aren't approved this time, use this point in the budget process to get some assurance that they will be reconsidered next time.

7. **Monitor your budget.** Once approved and implemented, you'll be judged on how well you carry out your budget. Manage by exception. Set variance targets that include both percentages and dollars. For instance, you could set a decision rule that says you'll investigate all monthly variances of 15 per cent or larger where the actual dollar variance is $200 or more.

8. **Keep superiors informed of your progress.** Keep your immediate manager and other relevant parties advised on how you're doing in terms of meeting your budget. This is likely to help protect you if you exceed your budget for reasons beyond your control. Also, don't expect to be rewarded for underspending your budget. In incremental budgets, underspending will only mean you'll be allocated fewer funds in the next budget period!

Applying Your Skills

You wish to attend a three-day training course in Halifax. To get approval, you need to submit a cost estimate to your supervisor. This estimate will also serve as your budget for the trip.

1. Describe how you would approach this cost estimate. For example, what information will you need and where will you get it? Remember to apply the appropriate steps of the budgeting process.

2. Create a proposed budget using cost estimates for all items. Then look at your completed budget and decide which items are negotiable and why.

3. Now take the role of the *manager* who will be receiving the above request.

    a) Assuming you approve the trip, would you prefer to cover the costs of the trip in advance or reimburse afterwards? Explain why. What are the implications for control?

    b) You want to encourage employee development, yet at the same time keep costs down. What kinds of expenses on the submitted budget might you decide to declare as personal expenses that the company will not cover? Which expenses should the company accept and why?

    c) What "controls" might your company apply to ensure that all such travel and training expenses are both legitimate and within reason?

SUMMARY

This summary is organized by the Learning Objectives.

1. The control process consists of five separate and distinct steps: 1. measure actual performance; 2. compare results with standards; and 3. take corrective action; 4. establish the performance indicators; and 5. determine the performance standards.
2. There are two types of corrective action: immediate and basic. Immediate deals predominantly with symptoms. Basic corrective action looks for the cause of the deviation and seeks to permanently adjust the differences.
3. Preventive control is implemented before an activity begins. It anticipates and prevents undesirable outcomes. Concurrent control takes place while an activity is in progress. Corrective control is implemented after an activity is finished, and facilitates prevention of future deviations.
4. Supervisors can reduce costs in their departments by improving work methods, levelling the work flow, reducing waste, installing more modern equipment, investing in employee training, and making selective cuts that will generate the greatest efficiencies.
5. To control employee behaviour, supervisors can select employees who will fit well in the department, provide specific goals, control the design of jobs, use new-employee orientation to convey acceptable behaviour, engage in direct supervision, provide formal training, impose formal regulations, use performance appraisals, and reward desirable behaviour.
6. An effective control system should be timely, economical, flexible, and understandable; have reasonable standards and strategically placed controls; and emphasize the exception.
7. Some potential negative outcomes from controls include employee resistance, employees directing their efforts to the wrong activities, and ethical dilemmas created by advances in control technology.

KEY TERMS AND CONCEPTS

Bottom-up budgeting
Cause-effect diagrams
Concurrent control
Control by exception
Control charts
Control process
Corrective control
Flow charts

Incremental budget
Just-in-time inventory
Materials requirement planning
Preventive control
Range of variation
Scatter diagrams
Top-down budgeting
Total quality management
Zero-base budget

REVIEWING YOUR KNOWLEDGE

1. Why is it that what we measure may be more critical to the control process than how we measure it?
2. What constitutes an acceptable range of variation?
3. Which type of control is preferable—preventive, concurrent, or corrective? Why? What type do you think is most widely used in practice?
4. What is the challenge of monitoring inventory costs?
5. In terms of characteristics of an effective control system, where do you think most control systems fail? Why?
6. Why should a supervisor control "by exception"?
7. How can a supervisor lessen employee resistance to controls?
8. How can a supervisor minimize the problem of people trying to look good on control criteria?
9. Contrast incremental and zero-base budgets. Which is best for facilitating change? Why?
10. Why do most organizations use bottom-up budgeting?

ANSWERS TO THE POP QUIZZES

1. **d. achieving goals.** This is a basic premise of control systems. They should be designed to ensure that goals are achieved.
2. Control means examining activities to determine whether performance is acceptable. You must first have established standards of what is to be considered acceptable. Therefore you must figure out what it is you want before determining whether you have got it.
3. **True.** Personal observation is one of the most widely used means by which supervisors assess actual performance. It enables a supervisor to pick up verbal omissions, facial expressions, and tones of voice that may be missed by other methods.
4. **a. performing immediate corrective action.** This is the definition of immediate corrective action.
5. **c. critical.** Placing controls on critical activities is one of the elements of effective controls. It also enables a supervisor to focus on the variations from standards that are most likely to occur or where a variation would do the greatest harm.
6. Just-in-time inventory systems involve having inventory items arrive when they are needed in the production process instead of being kept in stock.
7. **True.** The text cites a specific incident at Raglan Industries in Ontario, where a supervisor was fined $5000 after a worker was badly injured.
8. **c. Corrective.** The employee appraisal provides feedback on past performance, with the intention of thereby improving future performance.

CASE 3.A

Practising What You Preach

At the beginning of Chapter 2, on planning, you read about Zahid Fazal, a senior staff accountant at Ernst & Young LLP in Montreal. Zahid emphasized the importance of planning in leading to a successful audit at a client's company. But Zahid must then follow up and actually execute the audit successfully, working on site with the staff accountants on that audit team. The objective of an audit is to conclude whether a financial statement is free of material misstatements and to provide an independent "audit report" to the users. The audit team expects that the client will have all the relevant information complete and accessible to them. For its own credibility and the credibility of the team's conclusions, it is essential that the audit team itself know exactly the objectives of the current procedures. So Zahid has a great deal of pressure on him to ensure the audit goes as planned. He does this in a number of ways.

The audit program described at the beginning of Chapter 2 comes in as a control device. It describes exactly the steps in the audit process and what a team member should do at each step (for example, when doing cash, make sure you get a bank statement). When a step is completed, the staff accountant must sign off to indicate that all appropriate actions were taken at that step. Accountants refer to the previous year's audit file on the company but, if assistance is needed, the audit program—as well as Zahid himself—is available to provide guidance.

FIGURE 3-15
Zahid Fazal

Zahid works with the other accountants doing his own section of the audit but also communicates any issues and acts as a resource for the others. Before going on the audit, he has described to the team the client's business, the timeline, and individual responsibilities. When the audit is closed off, Zahid reviews the entire audit file once again to ensure that standard procedures were applied. Then the file goes to his manager to review and Zahid must deal with any queries the manager has. An Ernst & Young partner does the final review.

RESPONDING TO THIS CASE

1. Using both the description above and the one at the beginning of Chapter 2, identify all the preventive, concurrent, and corrective controls at work for the audit team.

2. Which of the five control areas (costs, inventories, quality, safety, and employee performance) are the main focus of control and why? What other kinds of businesses would have the same emphasis? Generate examples of organizations whose control emphasis would be different. Explain why.

CASE 3.B

The Business of Romance

PART A

"Brides come in all shapes, sizes, and personalities. But they all come in here insecure about their bodies and anxious about what they see as the most important dress purchase in their life." Sheila Otter is the owner/manager of Village Wedding Belles in Waterdown, Ontario. "Why is my shop so successful? I've got an extensive selection of dresses, I'm up on the trends—what brides are looking for—I market well, and my dresses are affordably priced. Location is not so important because brides will drive a long way for the right dress. But warm, nonthreatening, attentive, and honest service is critical.

We understand our clients' needs, know what's important to them on a personal level, validate their feelings that this is an important decision for them, validate their need for detail, and then deliver what they want in exactly the way they want."

A bride will typically make three visits before purchasing a gown: first just scouting, then returning for a closer look, and finally to get approval from her mother or a friend. Each visit can last a couple of hours. And the work is not over after the purchase—Sheila's staff must order the dress and accessories, tailor it to an exact fit, and have everything ready and in perfect condition for the big day.

Within Sheila's small shop are hundreds of dresses and extensive paperwork on the order for each client, so no detail is missed. It could easily fall into chaos. This would mean the end of the business. So Sheila has designed extensive controls to ensure everything is done correctly.

Sheila has special procedures and checking systems for unpacking and for ordering, and clearly outlines to staff the problems that are created when procedures aren't followed. She hires very carefully; trains new staff for months by having them work with her or with other experienced staff; gives constant feedback; and clearly outlines her expectations and standards. Both praise and suggestions for improvement are given in private, to avoid humiliation or envy on the part of others. All staff are on straight salary because commission would create competition, destroying the team effort required when a customer makes several visits and is helped by different staff members before she actually makes a decision to purchase.

Sheila herself phones in all the orders to suppliers so she can check over everything,

because once a dress is ordered, it cannot be returned. She keeps an eye on seamstresses when they do customer fittings to ensure both quality work and good customer relations. She also monitors all selling activities, giving suggestions, reminders, feedback, and praise on the service provided to a customer.

Retail does not pay well, so staff turnover can be high. But it takes about eight months for Sheila's staff to come up to speed on all aspects of the store, and excellent customer service is essential to her business. So Sheila needs a strongly motivated staff that's going to stay. Besides the daily feedback, Sheila has performance reviews every four months during which staff are encouraged to express their concerns. There are regular staff meetings to share information. Sheila says it's important for her to share the "fun" part of her job, too, so whenever she's visiting a Toronto supplier she takes one of her staff (on a rotating basis) to see the new stock, express opinions, and have a paid day out with dinner included. If suppliers are visiting the shop to show Sheila their new designs, Sheila invites all the staff to see the designs and express their preferences for the shop's new line. She also gives occasional prizes to staff who most accurately predict what will be the hot-selling items.

Sheila also makes sure staff are aware of the "big picture"—how the store is doing, and what kind of money is needed for advertising, expanding inventory, and making renovations on the shop. The staff understand the reality of the business, so there's no resentment that Sheila doesn't pay higher wages. And Sheila balances this with flexibility the staff would not find in many other places. She schedules around their preferred work times and accommodates their need for time off for children's sickness or activities or days off school.

And there's a family atmosphere in the shop, with all staff being treated with kindness and respect. Because customers must be treated with kindness, warmth and honesty, it's important that staff feel comfortable in their work environment and support each other. Tensions can run high as the bride's wedding day approaches and staff must remain patient and courteous.

Sheila says a bridal shop would be a great setting for a sitcom, with all the mini-dramas that occur. Her job is to ensure that it's not only an interesting place to work but also a profitable one.

FIGURE 3-16

Even a bridal shop needs extensive controls to keep on top (see Case 3.B).

RESPONDING TO THIS CASE

1. a. List the controls Sheila has in place.

   b. Which type of control is most prevalent? Why?

   c. Which of the characteristics of effective controls apply to Sheila's controls?

2. Explain the control issues Sheila likely faces regarding:

   a. cost categories

   b. inventory

   c. quality control

3. Look at the list of behavioural control devices and select those that Sheila appears to use.

4. Explain how Sheila has avoided the problems that are sometimes created by controls.

5. If Sheila decided to open up a second shop in another location, what effect would this have on her controls?

PART B

Sheila's second store, Victoria's Bridal and Formal Wear, opened in Hamilton almost one year ago. As Sheila expected, it is taking time to make a profit but she feels it is gaining attention in the market and doing well.

As Sheila is a "hands on" manager, who keeps an eye on everything to make sure operations are running smoothly, how does she manage to split herself between locations a half hour's drive apart? In fact, Sheila spends very little time at the new location, leaving the running of the store to Judy, an employee who has been with Sheila for four years. Judy impressed Sheila in the Waterdown store, proving herself to be trustworthy and thorough, excellent at marketing and thinking on her feet. Sheila duplicated the systems she had already developed to the new store (codes, accounting systems, procedures). Judy was trained in these systems and is comfortable with them. Sheila and Judy hired the initial staff together and now, as the need for new staff members arises, Sheila is backing off and letting Judy make many of the decisions. Sheila set up a financial incentive for Judy, essentially a profit-sharing plan, so Judy is motivated even more to make the store work (and less tempted to leave and set up independently). Judy now speaks of the store as "her" store. She continues to be excited by the responsibility and opportunity, even a year later.

The two stores act as sister stores, complementing each other. Although they carry some similar lines, Victoria's caters to a more budget-oriented market, tending to have all the sales merchandise (samples or any slow-moving gowns). Judy and Sheila buy the lines together. Between the stores, they want to offer an excellent range of dresses so they ensure different lines between the stores as well as some similar ones. This means that they can send customers to each other. Brochures at each store tell all clients about the "sister" store.

There are further differences between the stores. Victoria's is not a full-service store as there are no seamstresses. Instead, clients receive a referral list of bridal seamstresses. This is in contrast to the Village store, where Sheila spends every Tuesday evening from February to September attending fittings where seamstresses pin and tuck. Sheila oversees the process and deals with the need for headpieces, veils, gloves, shoes, and jewellery. Because Victoria's does not offer this service, they do not need as many staff members or as knowledgeable staff. Another difference is that Judy does no bill paying or accounting. She faxes all invoices to the Waterdown store and everything is paid from that location.

RESPONDING TO THIS CASE

1. Despite choosing to stay in the background in the running of the new store, it is still Sheila's money invested in all the merchandise and the overhead costs. What controls does Sheila have in place that allow her to sleep at night, knowing that she does not have to be there?

4

PROBLEM SOLVING AND DECISION MAKING

LEARNING OBJECTIVES

After reading this chapter, you should be able to:

1. List the seven steps in the decision-making process.
2. Describe expected value analysis.
3. Explain the value of decision trees.
4. Contrast data with information.
5. Describe the four types of decision styles.
6. Explain three different ethical viewpoints.
7. Compare and contrast group and individual decision making.
8. List four techniques for improving group decision making.

CHAPTER OUTLINE

PERFORMING EFFECTIVELY

THE DECISION-MAKING PROCESS
  Identify the Problem
  Collect Relevant Information
  Develop Alternatives
  Evaluate Each Alternative
  Select the Best Alternative
  Implement the Decision
  Follow Up and Evaluate

DECISION TOOLS
  Expected Value Analysis
  Decision Trees
  Marginal Analysis
  Risk Analysis
  Gap Analysis and the Five Why's
  Matrix Assessments
  Cause-and-Effect Diagrams
  Management Information
    Systems
  Pop Quiz

DECISION-MAKING STYLES
  Assessing Yourself: What's Your
  Decision-Making Style?

ETHICS IN DECISION MAKING
  Dealing with a Difficult Issue:
  Hiring a Friend
  Common Rationalizations
  Three Different Views on Ethics
  Some Ethical Decision Guides

GROUP DECISION MAKING
  Advantages and Disadvantages
  A Guide to When to Use Group
    Decision Making
  Types of Group Decision
    Making
  Building a Supervisory Skill:
  Conducting a Group Meeting
  Techniques for Improving
    Group Decision Making
  Pop Quiz

FROM CONCEPTS TO SKILLS:
CREATIVE PROBLEM SOLVING
  Assessing Yourself: How
    Creative Are You?
  Skill Basics
  Applying Your Skills

UNDERSTANDING THE BASICS
  Summary
  Key Terms and Concepts
  Reviewing Your Knowledge
  Answers to the Pop Quizzes

PERFORMING YOUR JOB
  Case 4.A: Electronic
    Honesty
  Case 4.B: How Can You
    Make the Decision?

FIGURE 4-1

Susan Mocsan makes a variety of decisions as the manager of HRIS and payroll at Ontario's Brewer's Retail.

Susan Mocsan is the manager for human resources information system (HRIS) and payroll at Ontario's Brewer's Retail. The payroll part of her job is an ongoing and established function. As such, the decisions to be made are fairly routine with extensive past practice to refer to. But the HRIS part of her job is much more complex and presents greater challenges in terms of problem solving and decision making. Brewer's Retail has not had a computerized employee databank before (they went from a mainframe to the new system) and brought in Susan to be the project manager supervising the ongoing design and the implementation of the HRIS. She works with both technical specialists and human resources people on the team to accomplish this task. As the HRIS had to be designed to meet the needs of this specific company (e.g., easily and quickly generating the kind of information they will need), an "off-the-shelf" package wouldn't do. Susan and her team, in deciding how to most effectively use all of their system's components, conducted major research and work with the other parts of the organization. Susan spends time with the business side of the company to find out, for example, what retail needs and what logistics is doing or changing. She drops in for brief chats with other business sections on a regular basis to keep up to date on events so she can be alerted to a possible impact on the HRIS. None of this "networking" is in her job description, but she knows it will help her accomplish her job.

At her previous position heading up the HRIS project for the Ontario Ministry of Transportation, Susan supervised both technical and functional specialists as part of the team. Here, at Brewer's Retail, the technical (computer) specialists report to a technical manager although most of their work is for her project. So, Susan works hard to build the technical/functional relationship and ensure that both sides understand the other's perspective when it comes to making decisions about the HRIS. She holds biweekly meetings with all people working on the project—and invites the technical specialists' manager—where she ensures all issues are on the table, whether it is a particular technical problem or a newly introduced process that is not working. Susan made sure her HR people were adequately trained in Peoplesoft, the program on which their HRIS is based. And Susan herself undertakes regular professional development, whether it is Peoplesoft conferences and seminars, or workshops on how the human resources function is changing in other ways, particularly due to technical advances.

Susan's job reflects the position that many supervisors find themselves in. Many of her decisions are routine. But she is also responsible for dealing with problems that had not been anticipated and have no easy answers. She is responsible for decisions where she cannot get all the information she would ideally like to have and there's an element of time pressure. It's stressful but it is also stimulating and, to many supervisors, a really enjoyable part of the job.

What kinds of decisions will you have to make? The range is wide. For instance, suppose one of your employees has been coming to work late recently and the quality of his work has fallen off—what do you do? Or you've got a vacancy in your department and your company's human resource manager has sent you six candidates to select from—which one do you choose? Or several of your salespeople have told you that they're losing business to an innovative new product line introduced by one of your competitors—how do you respond?

Supervisors are regularly confronted with problems that require decisions. But how do supervisors learn to make good decisions? Are they born with some intuitive talent? No! There are some who because of their intelligence, knowledge, and experience are able subconsciously to analyze problems; and that can result, over time, in an impressive trail of decisions. But there are decision-making techniques that anyone can learn to help make him or her a more effective decision maker. We'll review a number of these techniques in this chapter.

THE DECISION-MAKING PROCESS

Let's begin by describing a rational and analytical way of looking at decisions. We call this approach the decision-making process. It's composed of seven steps (see Figure 4-2).

1. Identify the problem.
2. Collect relevant information.
3. Develop alternatives.
4. Evaluate each alternative.
5. Select the best alternative.
6. Implement the decision.
7. Follow up and evaluate.

To help illustrate this process, we'll work through a problem faced by Peggy Hebden, program director for The New VR television station in Barrie, Ontario.

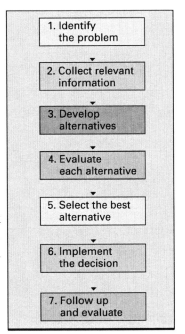

The NewVR
www.chumcity.com/newvr/

FIGURE 4-2

The decision-making process

IDENTIFY THE PROBLEM

The decision-making process begins with the existence of a **problem**, or an opportunity, as Peggy prefers to see it. For Peggy, it's having two half-hour program availabilities for Canadian programming in the next six months. She's looking for creative programming suggestions.

Problem
A discrepancy between an existing and a desired state of affairs.

FIGURE 4-3

Peggy Hebden of the New VR is faced with many
tough programming decisions.

In the real world, problems don't come with neon signs identifying
them as such. Many of the problems supervisors will confront aren't as
obvious as Peggy's programming need. One of the most difficult tasks at
this stage, then, is separating symptoms from problems. Is a five per cent
decline in sales a problem? Or are declining sales merely a symptom of
another problem, such as product obsolescence or an inadequate advertising budget? To use a medical analogy, aspirin doesn't deal with the
problem of stress on the job—it merely relieves the headache symptom.

COLLECT RELEVANT INFORMATION

Once you have identified the problem, you need to gather the relevant
facts and information. Why has the problem occurred now? How is it
affecting productivity in my department? What organizational policies, if
any, are relevant for dealing with this problem? What time limitations
exist for solving it? What costs are involved?

Peggy Hebden received a number of program pitches. She must consider which of these would not only serve her programming mandate

(sports and recreation) but also fulfill the sales department's needs. Some programs are pitched as coproduction opportunities, some as straight cash sales, and others as barter (airtime in exchange for some commercial time in the program).

DEVELOP ALTERNATIVES

Now all possible alternatives need to be identified. It is at this step in the decision process that you demonstrate your creativity. What alternatives exist beyond the obvious or those that may have been used previously?

Keep in mind that this step requires only that you *identify* alternatives. So no alternative—no matter how unusual—should be discarded at this stage. If an alternative isn't viable, you'll find out at the next stage. Also avoid the tendency to stop searching for alternatives after only a couple have been identified. If you see only two or three choices, you probably haven't thought hard enough. Remember that, generally speaking, the more alternatives you can generate, the better your final solution will be. Why? Because your final choice can only be as good as the best alternative you've generated.

In our example, several independent producers have been anxiously pitching their program concepts and want to have their programs broadcast on The New VR. Peggy contacts the producers and asks them to send her as much information as possible on their concepts. A full presentation and business plan are acceptable. However, a "pilot" or sample of the video is preferred.

EVALUATE EACH ALTERNATIVE

Now all the strengths and weaknesses of each alternative need to be evaluated. For example, what will each cost? How long will each take to implement? What's the most favourable outcome I could expect from each? Most unfavourable outcome?

In this step in particular, it's important to guard against biases. Undoubtedly some alternatives will look more attractive when initially identified. Others, at first glance, may seem unrealistic or exceedingly risky. As a result, you may have a tendency to prematurely favour some outcomes over others and then bias your analysis accordingly. Try to put your initial prejudices on hold and evaluate each alternative as objectively as you can. Of course, no one is perfectly rational. But you can improve the final outcome if you acknowledge your biases and overtly attempt to control them.

Figure 4-4 summarizes the highlights from Peggy's evaluations of her five alternatives. By formally writing down key considerations, it is often easier for decision makers to compare alternatives.

Alternative	Strengths	Weaknesses
1. *Gardening Show*	Growing interest in gardening; this is a barter pitch, so would save money; currently have gardening shows on our station that could be of better quality; know and trust producers; unique approach to the subject; works well with our recreational mandate.	Risk to attract ad dollars to support genre; doesn't fit sports mandate.
2. *Video Road Show*	Very good presentation tape; targets young, 18–34 audience; great guests; barter.	Inexperienced producer; cannot do as a local production due to budget constraints; risk.
3. *Cooking Show*	Interesting concept (three young guys cooking).	Doesn't fit sports and rec theme
4. *Martial Arts Show*	Good genre; not a lot of martial arts shows available.	Risk to attract advertising
5. *Personal Watercraft Show*	Great pilot; perfect fit for sports and rec; professional pitch	None

FIGURE 4-4

Evaluating alternatives

SELECT THE BEST ALTERNATIVE

After analyzing the pros and cons for each alternative, it is time to select the best alternative. Of course, what's "best" will reflect any limitations or biases that you bring to the decision process. It depends on things such as the comprehensiveness and accuracy of the information gathered in step 2, your ingenuity in developing alternatives in step 3, the degree of risk that you're willing to take, and the quality of your analysis in step 4.

Peggy's main objectives are to attract an audience, attract advertisers, and meet her sports and recreation mandate. After analyzing her needs, and much discussion internally on which alternatives best fit current needs, Peggy chooses the Video Road Show and the Personal Watercraft Show.

IMPLEMENT THE DECISION

Even if you've made the proper choice, the decision may still fail if it is not implemented properly. This means you need to convey the decision to those affected and get their commitment to it. You'll specifically want to assign responsibilities, allocate necessary resources, and clarify any deadlines.

Peggy's main challenge is to ensure the Video Road Show's success despite the producer's inexperience. Peggy feels that he has a good deal of talent and the show will attract the desired 18- to 34-year-old audience, so it's well worth taking the risk. To reduce this risk, the New VR station agrees to provide a mentoring role for the producer to help him learn in some of the areas where he is weak.

Follow Up and Evaluate

The last phase in the decision process is to follow up and evaluate the outcomes of the decision. Did the choice accomplish the desired result? Did it correct the problem that was originally identified in step 1?

Peggy can fairly easily evaluate the working relationship and mentoring roles by the way the finished program fits the program flow and by how it looks. However, it will take at least one month to see whether the show will gain an audience. If the audience watches, the sales department will be able to sell the program to advertisers and The New VR will be in a solid position to decide whether to extend the relationship or to return to the drawing board.

If the follow-up and evaluation indicate that the sought-after results weren't achieved, you'll want to review the decision process to see where you went wrong. In that case, you essentially have a brand-new problem and you should go through the decision process again with a new perspective.

DECISION TOOLS

A number of tools and techniques have been developed over the years to help supervisors improve their decision-making capabilities. In this section, we'll present several of them.

Expected Value Analysis

Fred Cassidy, the co-owner and manager of Larry's Sports in Hamilton, Ontario, is looking at several brands of hockey skates. Given his space and budget limitations, he can only purchase one of these brands to add to his department. Which one should he choose?

Expected value analysis could help with this decision. It permits decision makers to place a monetary value on the various consequences likely to result from the selection of a particular course of action. The procedure is simple. You calculate the expected value of a particular alternative by weighting its possible outcomes by the probability (0 to 1.0, with 1.0 representing absolute certainty) of achieving the alternative, then summing up the totals derived from the weighting process.

Expected value analysis Calculating the expected value of a particular alternative. This is achieved by weighting its possible outcomes according to the probability of achieving the alternative, then summing up the totals derived from the weighting process.

FIGURE 4-5

Alternative	Possible Outcome	Probability	Expected Value
Bauer	$ 12 000	0.2	$ 2 400
	10 000	0.6	6 000
	6 000	0.2	1 200
			$ 9 600
CCM	$ 10 000	0.4	$ 4 000
	6 000	0.5	3 000
	2 000	0.1	200
			$ 7 200
Graf	$ 9 000	0.2	$ 1 800
	6 000	0.6	3 600
	4 000	0.2	800
			$ 6 200

Payoff table for hockey skate decision

Let's say Fred is looking at three lines of skates: Bauer, CCM, and Graf. He's constructed the payoff table in Figure 4-5 to summarize his analysis. Based on his past experience and personal judgement, he's calculated the potential yearly profit from each alternative and the probability of achieving that profit. The expected value of each alternative ranged from $6200 to $9600. Based on this analysis, the supervisor could anticipate the highest expected value that could be reached by purchasing the Bauer line of skates.

DECISION TREES

Decision trees
A diagrammatic technique for analyzing decisions by assigning probabilities to various outcomes and calculating payoffs for each outcome.

Decision trees are a useful way to analyze hiring, marketing, investment, equipment purchases, pricing, and similar decisions that involve a progression of decisions. They're called decision trees because, when diagrammed, they resemble a tree and its branches. Typical decision trees encompass expected value analysis by assigning probabilities to each possible outcome and calculating payoffs for each decision path.

Figure 4-6 illustrates a decision facing Mike Rosen, the eastern region site-selection manager for a large bookstore chain. Mike supervises a small group of specialists who analyze potential locations and make store-site recommendations to the eastern region's manager. The lease on the company's store in Moncton, New Brunswick, is expiring and the landlord has decided not to renew it. So Mike and his group must make a relocation recommendation to the regional manager.

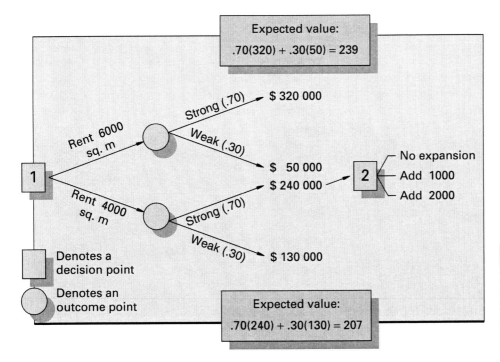

Expected value:

.70(320) + .30(50) = 239

Rent 6000 sq. m

Strong (.70) → $ 320 000

Weak (.30) → $ 50 000

$ 240 000 → 2 — No expansion
— Add 1000
— Add 2000

Rent 4000 sq. m

Strong (.70)

Weak (.30) → $ 130 000

☐ Denotes a decision point

○ Denotes an outcome point

Expected value:

.70(240) + .30(130) = 207

FIGURE 4-6

Decision tree and expected values for renting a large or small retail space

Mike's group has identified an excellent site in a nearby shopping mall. The mall owner has offered him two comparable locations: one with 4000 square metres (the same as he has now) and the other a larger 6000-square-metre space. Mike has an initial decision to make about whether to recommend renting the larger or smaller location. If he chooses the larger space and the economy is strong, he estimates the store will make $320 000 profit. However, if the economy is poor, the high operating costs of the larger store will mean only $50 000 in profit will be made. With the smaller store, he estimates the profit at $240 000 with a good economy and $130 000 with a poor one.

As you can see from Figure 4-6, the expected value for the larger store is $239 000 [(.70 × 320 000) + (.30 × 50 000)]. The expected value for the smaller store is $207 000 [(.70 × 240 000) + (.30 × 130 000)]. Given these results, Mike is planning to recommend the rental of the larger store space.

But what if Mike wants to consider the implications of initially renting the smaller space and then possibly expanding if the economy picks up? He can extend the decision tree to include this second decision point. He has calculated three options: no expansion, adding 1000 square metres, and adding 2000 square metres. Following the approach used for Decision Point 1, he could calculate the profit potential by extending the branches on the tree and calculating expected values for the various options.

MARGINAL ANALYSIS

Marginal analysis
Analyzing decisions in terms of their incremental costs

The concept of marginal, or incremental, analysis helps decision makers to optimize returns or minimize costs. **Marginal analysis** deals with the additional cost in a particular decision, rather than the average cost. For example, the operations supervisor for a large commercial dry cleaner wonders whether she should take on a new customer. She should consider not the total revenue and the total cost that would result after the order was taken, but rather what additional revenue would be generated by this particular order and what additional costs incurred. If the incremental revenues exceed the incremental costs, total profits would be increased by accepting the order.

RISK ANALYSIS

Risk analysis
Analyzing decisions in terms of their relative risk.

FIGURE 4-7

Graham van Brunt uses risk analysis to target high priorities in his decision making.

Risk Analysis
www-mmd.eng.cam.ac.uk/people/ahr/dstools/simulation/costbe.htm

Another way of approaching a decision situation uses **risk analysis** as opposed to expected value analysis. Either the decision tree or expected value analysis formats described above could be used, replacing value with risk. Graham Van Brunt, the director of Plant Operations and Maintenance at Churchill Falls Labrador Corporation's hydro power plant, knows that his 25-year-old equipment will soon need replacing. But he cannot afford the huge expense of replacing everything at once. The old way of doing maintenance was essentially accomplished by following manufacturer's recommended procedures for refurbishment, repair and/or replacement. But this starts to get very expensive as a plant ages (it could, for example, recommend simultaneous replacement of similar parts). Instead, Graham and his team assess the risk involved in not replacing a piece of equipment. For some old equipment, failure to work would have dire consequences. For others, the consequences would be minor. Graham provides the analogy of landing gear on a 747 jet not working versus the sink in one of its many washrooms. Because of risk analysis, Graham is able to target money into replacing the high-priority items.

Diane McArthur found a risk/benefit analysis useful for her work as well. She is the director of a project for the Province of Ontario, attempting to house all the routine services (e.g., motor vehicle licenses, address changes) for citizens under one roof rather than forcing citizens to go to different ministries for the various services. When she began the project, she was given a very defined strategic model to work with. As she and her team got to the 3/4 mark of completing the model for the new operation, they realized there was no way they could make it work with an appropriate risk/control balance. So the management team presented their risk analysis to the committee of deputy ministries in charge of overseeing the project. They agreed that the risks could be managed under the current model but only with a great deal of time and cost. It wasn't worth it. They, therefore, got permission to start from scratch with a new model that she and her team could generate based on achieving the objectives but without the constraint of having to do it a certain way. For example, now they could consider the possibility of best using private sector expertise to improve the business processes.

GAP ANALYSIS AND THE FIVE WHYS

Gap analysis involves defining the difference between what is actually happening and what you would like to have happen. You can then use backward-chaining logical sequences of actions to identify the root cause of the gap and what needs to be done to get to the desired state. This is the "5 whys." The process involves starting with a problem or gap (e.g., our customer satisfaction rate is lower than we wish) and asking yourself "why" this is the case until you can determine the apparent root cause. This often takes four or five or more whys. For example, one reason for customer dissatisfaction relates to errors made on shipments. Why? We have many new people in the customer service centre and they have been making errors when completing the order forms. Why? They have a very short training period and the procedural manual is outdated. Why? We are so short-staffed that we need new employees on the floor immediately and no one has time to update the manual. Why? Turnover is high. Why? The job is very stressful and doesn't pay well. Why? The company does not think the skills needed are worth much and basically sets employees up for failure by not training them well and not giving them the tools to do the job well (such as an up-to-date manual). Why? The company seems to believe that anyone can do a customer service job, and that it is low skill and low priority.

Gap analysis
Gap analysis involves defining the difference between what is actually happening and what you would like to have happening.

At the end of this analysis, you get some immediate ideas for correcting the problem. One of the interesting aspects of this technique is that, as you do the gap analysis and "whys" for different issues in the organization, you often find that certain themes or basic root causes emerge. The problems often arise out of very few basic concerns (such as a company treating its customer service people as low-priority, low-skill employees).

MATRIX ASSESSMENTS

When there are a number of alternative actions being considered and you, or you and your team, want to assess them in a clearly logical way,

Matrix assessment
Sets up a comparison
between alternatives
based on weighted
criteria.

you may choose to use a **matrix assessment**. There are many types of matrices, but basically you want to judge the alternatives on the important criteria and conclude with a priority ranking of those alternatives. You can set up whatever comparisons you want.

Two examples are provided below. Figure 4-8 looks at how to choose among candidates for a position, having decided on what the hiring criteria should be and weighted them according to importance. Note that, as in most hiring situations, there are some strong candidates and others who are not as strong. The criteria end up being important in separating the top one from the two close behind.

The other matrix, Figure 4-9, looks at a ranking of continuous improvement initiatives, using predetermined criteria choosing, this time, not to weight the criteria to reflect their importance. Note that, although the structure provided by the matrix promotes a focus on the most important factors, it does not eliminate subjectivity. The actual scores of the choices on the criteria are still subjective judgements by the decision maker(s).

Hiring Criterion	Weighting of Criterion (1 low to 10 high)	Candidate 1 Sam	Candidate 2 Lorenzo	Candidate 3 Satwinder	Candidate 4 Reg	Candidate 5 Petra
Knowledge of SAP software (1 low to 10 high)	7	Score 1 X7 =7	Score 8 X7 =56	Score 10 X7 =49	Score 4 X7 =28	Score 6 X7 =42
Experience (two or more years) in related business (1 low to 10 high)	9	Score 3 X9 =27	Score 9 X9 =81	Score 10 X9 =90	Score 6 X9 =54	Score 7 X9 =63
"Fit" with team (1 low to 10 high)	10	Score 9 X10 =90	Score 6 X10 =60	Score 6 X10 =60	Score 3 X10 =30	Score 10 X10 =100
Degree None = 1 Bach=5 Masters = 10	3	Score 10 X3 =30	Score 5 X3 =15	Score 1 X3 =3	Score 5 X3 =15	Score 5 X3 =15
Willingness to travel and work unusual hours (1 low to 10 high)	10	Score 10 X10 =100	Score 9 X10 =90	Score 10 X10 =100	Score 7 X10 =70	Score 8 X10 =80
Total		254	302	302	197	310
Summary		4	2 (tied)	2 (tied)	5	1

FIGURE 4-8

Hiring decision matrix — the decision makers have determined the pertinent criteria and their weighting beforehand, then rate the candidates on each criterion, and combine the scores in the matrix to see who has the top score; that person should be the one recommended for the hire.

	Alternative Continuous Improvement Ideas			
	Train supervisors on supervisory skills	Top management holds monthly town hall meeting with employees	Redesign order form	Post weekly production results
Criterion				
Ease of doing (1 difficult to 10 easy)	5	8	7	9
Cost of doing (1 expensive to 10 inexpensie)	2	9	9	10
Assists in meeting department quality goal (1 low to 10 high)	5	1	2	3
Assists in achieving customer service goal (1 low to 10 high)	3	1	6	1
Improves team work (1 low to 10 high)	6	2	1	3
Total	**21**	**21**	**25**	**26**
Summary	**3 (tied)**	**3 (tied)**	**2**	**1**

FIGURE 4-9

Decision-making matrix to select continuous improvement initiatives (once ideas are generated, they are assessed regarding their relative ease and cost as well as their contributing to departmental goals).

CAUSE-AND-EFFECT DIAGRAMS (FISHBONE DIAGRAMS)

In Chapter 3 on controlling, you read about using a **cause-and-effect diagram** to assist you in looking at the myriad of potential causes of a problem. This diagram (see Figure 4-10) can be used in a different way to determine what the effects of an action *will* be by reversing the setup of the fishbone—having the head to the left and the bones or arrows leading to the right and recording possible consequences of a planned action. By laying out these ideas, encouraging participants to look at many different subsets of consequences, it is more likely that the action's impact will be thoroughly explored.

Cause-and-effect diagrams
Used to speculate on potential effects of taking an action, grouping the effects according to common categories.

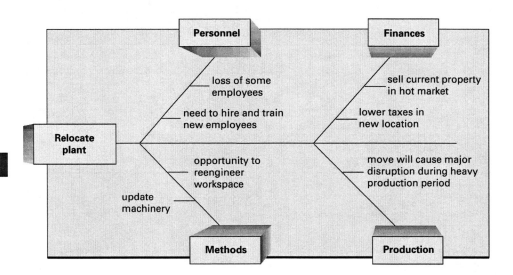

FIGURE 4-10

Sample cause-and-effect diagram. Start with proposed decision, then generate potential consequences to consider.

MANAGEMENT INFORMATION SYSTEMS

How can supervisors improve their ability to collect the information needed for assessing problems and for accurately evaluating alternatives? The answer is to learn to effectively use their organization's management information system.

A **management information system** (MIS) is a mechanism to provide managers with needed and accurate information on a regular and timely basis. It can be manual or computer-based, although recently almost all discussion of MIS focuses on computer-supported applications.

The term "system" in MIS implies order, arrangement, and purpose. Further, an MIS focuses specifically on providing management with information, not merely data. These two points are important and require elaboration.

A library provides a good analogy. Although it can contain millions of volumes, a library doesn't do users much good if they can't quickly find what they want. That's why libraries spend a lot of time cataloguing their collections and ensuring that volumes are returned to their proper locations. Organizations today are like well-stocked libraries. There is no scarcity of data. The limitation is in the ability to process it so that the right information is available to the right person when he or she needs it. An MIS has data organized in some meaningful way so you can access the information in a reasonable amount of time. Data are raw, unanalyzed facts such as names, numbers, or quantities. As data, these facts are relatively useless to managers. When data are analyzed and processed, they become information. An MIS collects data and turns them into relevant information for managers to use. The Human Resources Information

Management information system (MIS) A mechanism to provide managers with needed and accurate information on a regular and timely basis.

System (HRIS) that Susan Mocsan is implementing at Brewer's Retail, described at the beginning of the chapter, is an example of an MIS.

Fifteen or twenty years ago, supervisors essentially had two choices for getting the information they needed to make decisions. They could get it themselves through crude methods such as looking in files, making telephone calls, asking questions in meetings. Or, if they worked anywhere but the smallest organization, they could rely on reports generated by the organization's data processing specialist or centralized data processing department. Today, management information systems have become decentralized; that is, decisions and control of the systems have been pushed down to the users (see Figure 4-11). With decentralization has come a major change—supervisors can now take responsibility for information control. They have become end-users. They can access the data they need and analyze that data on their personal computers. As a result, today's supervisors need to be knowledgeable about their information needs and accept responsibility for their systems' operations.

The good news is that sophisticated management information systems dramatically improve the quantity and quality of information available to supervisors, as well as the speed with which it can be obtained. Gone are the long delays between the appearance of a serious discrepancy and a supervisor's ability to find out about it. On-line, real-time systems allow supervisors to identify problems almost as they occur. Database management programs allow supervisors to look things up or get to the facts without either going to other people or digging through piles of paper. This reduces a supervisor's dependence on others for data and makes fact gathering far more efficient. Today's supervisor can identify alternatives quickly, evaluate those alternatives by using a spreadsheet program, pose a series of what-if questions, and finally select the best alternative on the basis of answers to those questions.

FIGURE 4-11

Fifteen or twenty years ago, large mainframe computers drove an organization's MIS. Today, supervisors are end-users.

1. When an Air Canada ticketing supervisor observed that business was declining because more passengers were travelling with Canada 3000 on the route from Toronto to Orlando, Florida, she was:
    a. recognizing a problem by comparison with another unit in the organization
    b. analyzing alternatives
    c. recognizing a problem by comparison with past performance
    d. identifying relevant information
2. Explain how decision making is related to the planning process.
3. Solving the wrong problem perfectly is better than coming up with a wrong solution to a problem. True or false?
4. After implementation has been accomplished
    a. the decision-making process is complete.
    b. the control function of management becomes important.
    c. the alternatives are ranked.
    d. the supervisor must complete written evaluation forms.

DECISION-MAKING STYLES

Each of you brings your own unique personality and experiences to the decisions you make. For instance, if you're someone who is basically conservative and uncomfortable with uncertainty, you're likely to value decision alternatives differently from someone else who enjoys uncertainty and risk taking. These facts have led to research that has sought to identify individual decision styles.[1] To make the following discussion more personal, take 10 minutes to complete the Assessing Yourself questionnaire.

The basic foundation for a decision-style model is the recognition that people differ along two dimensions. The first is their way of thinking. Some people are logical and rational, and process information serially. In contrast, some people are intuitive and creative, and perceive things as a whole. The other dimension addresses a person's tolerance for ambiguity. Some people have a high need to structure information in ways that minimize ambiguity, while others are able to process many thoughts at the same time. When these two dimensions are diagrammed, they form four styles of decision making (see Figure 4-12). These are directive, analytic, conceptual, and behavioural.

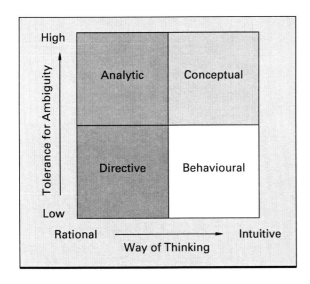

FIGURE 4-12

Decision-style model

DIRECTIVE STYLE

People using the directive style have low tolerance for ambiguity and seek rationality. They are efficient and logical. But their efficiency concerns result in their making decisions with minimal information and after assessing few alternatives. Directive types make decisions fast and they focus on the short run.

ANALYTIC STYLE

The analytic type has a much greater tolerance for ambiguity than does a directive manager. This leads to the desire for more information and consideration of more alternatives than is true for directives. Analytic managers would be best characterized as careful decision makers with the ability to adapt or cope with new situations.

CONCEPTUAL STYLE

Individuals with a conceptual style tend to be very broad in their outlook and consider many alternatives. Their focus is long range and they are very good at finding creative solutions to problems.

BEHAVIOURAL STYLE

The final category—the behavioural style—characterizes decision makers who work well with others. They're concerned with the achievement of subordinates. They're receptive to suggestions from others and rely heavily on meetings for communicating. This type of supervisor tries to avoid conflict and seeks acceptance.

SUMMARY

Although these four categories are distinct, most supervisors have characteristics that fall into more than one. So it's probably best to think in terms of a manager's dominant style and his or her backup styles. While some supervisors rely almost exclusively on their dominant style, more flexible supervisors can make shifts depending on the situation. Referring to the Assessing Yourself results, the box with the highest score reflects your dominant style. The closer a person is to a score of 75 in each category, the greater flexibility he or she shows.

Business students, supervisors, and top executives tend to score highest in the analytic style. That's not surprising, given the emphasis that formal education, particularly business education, gives to developing rational decision-making skills. For instance, courses in accounting, statistics, and finance all stress analytical thinking.

Focusing on decision styles can be useful in helping you understand how two intelligent people, with access to the same information, can differ in the ways they approach decisions and in the final choices they make. It can also explain conflicts between supervisors and their subordinates. For example, the directive supervisor expects work to be performed rapidly and gets frustrated by the slowness and deliberate actions of a conceptual or analytic subordinate. At the same time, the analytic supervisor might criticize a decisive subordinate for incomplete work or acting too hastily. And the analytic supervisor will have great difficulty with his or her behavioural counterpart because of lack of understanding of why feelings rather than logic have been used as the basis for a decision.

Assessing Yourself

WHAT'S YOUR DECISION-MAKING STYLE?

INSTRUCTIONS

1. Use the following numbers to answer each question:
   8: when the question is *most* like you.
   4: when the question is *moderately* like you.
   2: when the question is *slightly* like you.
   1: when the question is *least* like you.

2. Each of the numbers must be inserted in the box following the answers to each question.

3. *Do not* repeat any number on a given line.

4. For example, the numbers you might use to answer a given question could look as follows: 8 2 1 4

5. Notice that each number has been used only once in the answers for a given question.

6. In answering the questions, think of how you *normally* act in your work situation.

7. Use the first thing that comes to your mind when answering the question.

8. There is no time limit in answering the questions and there are no right or wrong answers.

9. Your responses reflect how you feel about the questions and what you prefer to do, not what you think might be the *right* thing to do.

Score the following questions based on the instructions given. Your score reflects how you see yourself, not what you believe is correct or desirable, as related to your work situation. It covers typical decisions that you make in your work environment.

		I	II	III	IV
1.	My prime objective is to:	Have a position with status ☐	Be the best in my field ☐	Achieve recognition for my work ☐	Feel secure in my job ☐
2.	I enjoy jobs that:	Are technical & well defined ☐	Have a considerable variety ☐	Allow independent action ☐	Involve people ☐
3.	I expect people working for me to be:	Productive and fast ☐	Highly capable ☐	Committed and responsive ☐	Receptive to suggestions ☐
4.	In my job, I look for:	Practical results ☐	The best solutions ☐	New approaches or ideas ☐	Good working environment ☐
5.	I communicate best with others:	In a direct one-to-one basis ☐	In writing ☐	By having a group discussion ☐	In a formal meeting ☐
6.	In my planning I emphasize:	Current problems ☐	Meeting objectives ☐	Future goals ☐	Developing people's careers ☐
7.	When faced with solving a problem, I:	Rely on proven approaches ☐	Apply careful analysis ☐	Look for creative approaches ☐	Rely on my feelings ☐
8.	When using information I prefer:	Specific facts ☐	Accurate and complete data ☐	Broad coverage of many options ☐	Limited data which is easily understood ☐
9.	When I am not sure about what to do, I:	Rely on intuition ☐	Search for facts ☐	Look for a possible compromise ☐	Wait before making a decision ☐
10.	Whenever possible I avoid:	Long debates ☐	Incomplete work ☐	Using numbers or formulas ☐	Conflict with others ☐

	I		II		III		IV	
11. I am especially good at:	Remembering dates & facts	☐	Solving difficult problems	☐	Seeing many possibilities	☐	Interacting with others	☐
12. When time is important, I:	Decide and act quickly	☐	Follow plans and priorities	☐	Refuse to be pressured	☐	Seek guidance or support	☐
13. In social settings I generally:	Speak with others	☐	Think about what is being said	☐	Observe what is going on	☐	Listen to the conversation	☐
14. I am good at remembering:	People's names	☐	Places we met	☐	People's faces	☐	People's personalities	☐
15. The work I do provides me:	The power to influence others	☐	Challenging assignments	☐	Achieving my personal goals	☐	Acceptance by the group	☐
16. I work well with those who are:	Energetic and ambitious	☐	Self-confident	☐	Open-minded	☐	Polite and trusting	☐
17. When under stress, I:	Become anxious	☐	Concentrate on the problem	☐	Become frustrated	☐	Am forgetful	☐
18. Others consider me:	Aggressive	☐	Disciplined	☐	Imaginative	☐	Supportive	☐
19. My decisions typically are:	Realistic and direct	☐	Systematic or abstract	☐	Broad & flexible	☐	Sensitive to the needs of others	☐
20. I dislike:	Losing control	☐	Boring work	☐	Following rules	☐	Being rejected	☐

SCORING THE DECISION-STYLE INVENTORY

1. Add the points in each of the four columns—I, II, III, IV.
2. The sum of the four columns should be 300 points. If your sum does not equal 300 points, check your addition and your answers.
3. Place your scores in the appropriate box—I, II, III, IV.

Analytic II	Conceptual III
Directive I	Behavioural IV

Source: A. J. Rowe, R. Mason, and K. Dickel, *Strategic Management and Business Policy*. Reading, MA: Addison-Wesley, 1982, p. 217. Reproduced by permission of Alan J. Rowe.

ETHICS IN DECISION MAKING

Decision making is a prime instance of an occasion when supervisors have to confront ethical concerns (see Dealing with a Difficult Issue). For instance, one alternative may generate a considerably higher financial return than the others but might be ethically questionable because it compromises employee safety.

Ethics
www.mapnp.org/library/
ethics/ethics.htm

Dealing with a Difficult Issue

HIRING A FRIEND

In making hiring decisions, supervisors often face difficult issues. Take the following situation:

Your company is advertising for a new employee to work in your department. The person in this position will be important because the work directly affects the quality and quantity of your performance. One of your friends needs a job and you think he is qualified for the position. But you feel you *could* find better qualified and more experienced candidates if you keep looking.

What would you do? What might influence your decision? Would you tell your friend? How do you handle this sensitive situation?

COMMON RATIONALIZATIONS

Through the ages, people have developed some common rationalizations to justify questionable conduct.[2] These rationalizations provide some insights into why supervisors might make poor ethical choices.

"It's not really illegal or immoral." Where is the line between being smart and being shady? Between an ingenious decision and an immoral one? Because this line is often ambiguous, people can rationalize that what they've done is not really wrong. If you put enough people in an ill-defined situation, some will conclude that whatever hasn't specifically been labelled as wrong must be acceptable, especially if there are rich rewards for attaining certain goals and the organization's appraisal

system doesn't look too carefully at how those goals are achieved. The practice of profiting on a stock tip through insider information seems often to fall in this category.

"It's in my (or the organization's) best interest." The belief that unethical conduct is in a person's or an organization's best interests nearly always results from a narrow view of what those interests are. For instance, supervisors can come to believe that it's acceptable to bribe officials if the bribe results in the organization's getting a contract, or to falsify financial records if this improves their unit's performance record.

"No one will find out." This rationalization accepts the wrongdoing but assumes that it will never be uncovered. It is often stimulated by inadequate controls, strong pressures to perform, the appraisal of performance results while ignoring the means by which they're achieved, the allocation of big salary increases and promotions to those who achieve these results, and the absence of punishment for those who get caught.

"Since it helps the organization, the organization will condone it and protect me." This response represents loyalty gone berserk. Managers come to believe that not only do the organization's interests override the laws and values of society, but also that the organization expects its employees to exhibit unqualified loyalty. Such managers believe that, even if he or she is caught, the organization will support and reward him or her for showing loyalty. Managers who use this rationalization to justify unethical practices place the organization's good name in jeopardy. This rationalization has motivated some supervisors for defence contractors to justify labour mischarges, cost duplications, product substitutions, and other contract abuses. While managers should be expected to be loyal to the organization against competitors and detractors, that loyalty should not put the organization above the law, common morality, or society itself.

THREE DIFFERENT VIEWS ON ETHICS

In this section we will present three different ethical positions. They can help us to see how individuals can make different decisions by using different ethical criteria (see Figure 4-13).

THE UTILITARIAN VIEW

Utilitarian view of ethics
Decisions are based solely on the basis of their outcomes; the goal is to provide the greatest good for the greatest number.

The first position is the **utilitarian view of ethics**, in which decisions are made solely on the basis of their outcomes or consequences. The goal of utilitarianism is to provide the greatest good for the greatest number. This view tends to dominate business decision making because it's consistent with the goals of efficiency, productivity, and high profits. By maximizing profits, for instance, a manager can argue that he or she is securing the greatest good for the greatest number.

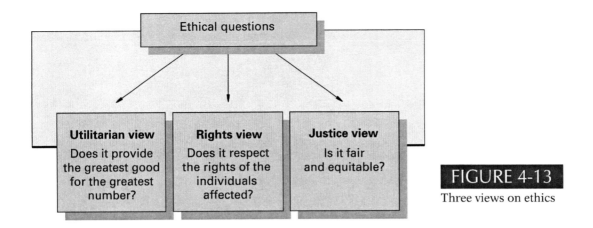

FIGURE 4-13

Three views on ethics

THE RIGHTS VIEW

Another ethical perspective is the **rights view of ethics**. This calls upon individuals to make decisions consistent with fundamental liberties and privileges as set forth in documents such as the Charter of Rights and Freedoms. The rights view of ethics is concerned with respecting and protecting the basic rights of individuals; for example, the right to privacy, free speech, and due process. This position would protect employees who report unethical or illegal practices by their organization to the press or government agencies on the grounds of their right to free speech.

Rights view of ethics
Decisions emphasize respecting and protecting the basic rights of individuals.

THE JUSTICE VIEW

The final perspective is the **justice view of ethics**. This requires individuals to impose and enforce rules fairly and impartially so there is an equitable distribution of benefits and costs. Union members typically favour this view. It justifies paying people the same wage for a given job, regardless of performance differences, and it uses seniority as the criterion in making layoff decisions (see Figure 4-14).

Justice view of ethics
Decisions seek fair and impartial distribution of benefits and costs.

DISCUSSION OF THE THREE VIEWS

The same decision can be judged very differently in terms of its ethics, depending on which of the three views is the basis of the judgement. For example, you may catch an employee going through the papers on another employee's desk after hours. Your reaction may be that it is an invasion of privacy, and therefore unethical (rights view). The employee may justify the action based on either of the other two views. For example, "Hey, she has locks on her desk and her filing cabinet. It's an open office area and she knows to lock anything away that is sensitive" (justice view). Or,

FIGURE 4-14

Affirmative efforts to hire and promote women and minorities represent an application of the justice view of ethics.

"Look, here's the information I've been looking for. It's been holding me up and now I can get my report done, which is good for the whole department, right?" (utilitarian view).

Each of these three perspectives has advantages and liabilities. The utilitarian view promotes efficiency and productivity, but it can result in the rights of some individuals—particularly those with minority representation in the organization—being ignored. The rights perspective protects individuals from injury and is consistent with freedom and privacy, but it can create an overly legalistic work environment that hinders productivity and efficiency. The justice perspective protects the interests of the underrepresented and less powerful, but it can encourage a sense of entitlement that reduces risk taking, innovation, and productivity.

Even though each of these perspectives has its individual strengths and weaknesses, as we noted, managers in business tend to focus on utilitarianism. But times are changing and so too must supervisors and other managers. New trends toward individual rights and social justice mean that supervisors need ethical standards based on nonutilitarian criteria. This is a solid challenge to today's supervisor because making decisions using criteria such as individual rights and social justice involves far more ambiguities than using utilitarian criteria such as effects on efficiency and profits.

SOME ETHICAL DECISION GUIDES

There is no simple credo that we can provide to ensure that you won't err in your ethical judgements. What we can offer are some questions that you can—and should—ask yourself when making important decisions, or decisions with obvious ethical implications.[3]

1. How did this problem occur in the first place?
2. Would you define the problem differently if you stood on the other side of the fence?
3. To whom and to what do you give your loyalty as a person and as a member of your organization?
4. What is your intention in making this decision?
5. What is the potential for your intentions to be misunderstood by others in the organization?
6. How does your intention compare with the probable result?
7. Whom could your decision injure?
8. Can you discuss the problem with the affected parties before you make the decision?
9. Are you confident that your position will be as valid over a long period of time as it seems now?
10. Could you disclose your decision to your boss or your immediate family?
11. How would you feel if your decision was described, in detail, on the front page of your local newspaper?

GROUP DECISION MAKING

Decisions in organizations are increasingly being made by groups rather than by individuals. There seem to be at least two primary reasons for this. First is the desire to develop more and better alternatives. The adage "two heads are better than one" translates into groups being able to generate a greater number, and potentially a more creative set, of decision alternatives. Second, organizations are relying less on the historical idea that departments and other organizational units should be separate and independent decision units. To get the best ideas and to improve their implementation, organizations are increasingly turning over their decision making to teams that cut across traditional departmental lines. This choice requires group decision-making techniques (see Figure 4-15).

Group Decision Making
www.duke.edu/~rnau/
readlist.htm

http://interneg.carleton.ca/

ADVANTAGES AND DISADVANTAGES

Individual and group decisions each have their own set of strengths. Neither is ideal for all situations. Let's begin by reviewing the advantages that group decisions have over an individual decision maker.

1. **Provides more complete information.** A group will bring a diversity of experience and perspective to the decision process that an individual, acting alone, cannot.
2. **Generates more alternatives.** Because groups have a greater quantity and diversity of information, they can identify more alternatives than can an individual.
3. **Increases acceptance of a solution.** Many decisions fail after the final choice has been made because people do not accept the solution. If the people who will be affected by a certain solution and who will help implement it get to participate in the decision making itself, they will be more likely to accept the decision and to encourage others to accept it.
4. **Increases legitimacy.** The group decision-making process is consistent with democratic ideals and therefore may be perceived as more legitimate than decisions made by a single person.

If groups are so good, how did the phrase "A camel is a racehorse put together by a committee" become so popular? The answer, of course, is that group decisions are not without their drawbacks. The major disadvantages of group decision making are as follows

1. **Time consuming.** It takes time to assemble a group. Additionally, the interaction that takes place once the group is in place is frequently inefficient. The result is that groups almost always take more time to reach a solution than an individual making the decision alone.
2. **Minority domination.** Members of a group are never perfectly equal. They may differ in terms of rank in the organization, experience, knowledge about the problem, influence with other members, verbal skills, assertiveness, and the like. This creates the opportunity for one or more members to use their advantages to dominate others in the group and impose undue influence on the final decision.
3. **Pressures to conform.** There are social pressures in groups. The desire of group members to be accepted and considered assets to the group can quash any overt disagreement and encourage conformity among viewpoints. The withholding by group members of different views in order to appear in agreement is called **groupthink**.
4. **Ambiguous responsibility.** Group members share responsibility, but who is actually responsible for the final outcome? In an individual decision, it is clear who is responsible, but in a group decision the responsibility of any single member is watered down. Conscious of this, group members may not give their full effort or think through the issue as thoroughly as they would on their own.

Groupthink
Group members withhold different views in order to appear to be in agreement.

A GUIDE TO WHEN TO USE GROUP DECISION MAKING

When are groups better than individuals and vice versa? That depends on what you mean by better. Let's look at four criteria frequently associated with "better" decisions: accuracy, speed, creativity, and acceptance.

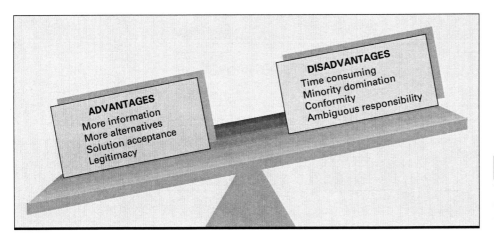

FIGURE 4-15

The advantages and disadvantages of group decision-making

Group decisions tend to be more accurate. The evidence indicates that, on the average, groups make more accurate decisions than individuals. This doesn't mean, of course, that all groups outperform every individual. Rather, group decisions have been found to be more effective than those that would have been reached by the average individual in the group. However, groups are seldom as good as the best individual.

If *better* is defined in terms of decision speed, individuals are superior. Group decision processes are characterized by give and take, a process that is often time-consuming.

Decision quality can also be assessed in terms of the degree to which a solution demonstrates creativity. If creativity is important, groups tend to do better than individuals. This requires, however, minimizing the forces that foster groupthink—pressure to repress doubts about the group's shared views or the validity of favoured arguments, excessive desire by the group to give an appearance of consensus, and the assumption that silence or abstention by members is a "yes" vote.

As noted previously, because group decisions have input from more people, they are likely to result in solutions that will have a higher degree of acceptance.

TYPES OF GROUP DECISION MAKING

The process used by a group to make a decision will influence the effectiveness of the decision. There is no single best process, though. The way the group should make its decision depends on the needs of the group as well as on the situation and on how much time is available.

The most commonly used method is **majority vote**. It offers the appeal of a democratic process and is as quick as it takes to get 51 percent of the members to agree. It can leave a powerful minority very dissatisfied, however. This can harm the implementation of the decision.

Majority vote
Agreement to a decision by at least 51 percent of a group's members.

Majority vote is fine if the decision is not a critical one and not worth spending a lot of time on. For instance, Larry Bowzeylo at Suncor in Fort McMurray believes in involving his people in decisions that affect them. They needed new Control Room chairs and he brought them three to try and recommend. From the 25 guys, he got three different recommendations out but one chair got 90% acceptance so they went with that one.

Consensus
Agreement to support a decision by all members of a group.

Deciding by **consensus** is highly desirable. If there is sufficient time, it provides the best decisions and the most commitment to the decision. And, in practice, reaching a consensus does not mean everyone agrees absolutely but that all members are willing to support the decision, knowing that everyone has been heard and the issues have been thoroughly addressed. This decision-making method is not often used, however. Not only does it take time but it takes effort and skill, particularly on the part of the chair, to keep the discussion progressing in a constructive way. Each morning Rod Guild, the senior shift supervisor at Highland Valley Copper mine in B.C., tours the two mine pits in a crew cab with engineers and the mine superintendent. The engineers have already created a mine plan for the day but the final decision is a joint decision of the five or six people in the truck. Rod's field experience is as respected as the engineers' theoretical knowledge. The final plan for mining is agreed upon by all of them by the end of the morning tour.

Decision by expert
Decision delegated to a person with special skill or knowledge in a particular field.

Decision by minority vote
Decision-making power held by a subgroup of a larger group.

Sometimes a group uses its power to turn the decision-making authority over to someone else. The group may choose someone deemed an **expert** to make the decision. That choice itself could be made via consensus or majority vote. A second form of decision referral is the use of minority vote. In its legitimate form, this involves assigning a decision to a committee made up of a few members of the larger group. Its illegitimate form occurs when a subgroup railroads a decision through, quickly forcing a decision before real debate can occur. In either expert decision or minority vote, the advantages include putting the decision in the hands of potentially more qualified people and at the same time freeing up time for the remainder of the group. An example of decisions being made by a minority comes in the self-directed teams at NCR in Waterloo, Ontario. Within the ATM (Automatic Teller Machine) production area, there are three self-directed teams. Within each team, many decisions are allocated to committees made up of people voted to those positions on a temporary basis. The small teams (within the larger team) make decisions on vacation schedule, recognition, health and safety audits, and rotation from one product line to another.

Decision by authority after discussion
Decision-making by a group leader after weighing group members' opinions.

A final method of group decision making is **authority after discussion**. In this, the supervisor holds a full discussion with the whole group to hear their ideas and issues. Then the supervisor makes the final decision, which may or may not reflect the wishes of the group. In practice, this method is often similar to consensus because a group trend becomes apparent and the supervisor simply applies official approval. However, the supervisor may choose not to follow the group if the group's goals are not in the best interests of the organization. Krista Harris, regional director of CBC Radio for the Maritimes, uses participative decision making the vast majority of the time. For example, she passes on regional objectives to the individual radio stations for input and works with them to identify their objectives. Regional programming is discussed and decided at joint meetings. Sometimes, however, Krista tells them what they must do. For example, she asked that each station create two "remotes" for each show this year (broadcasting from the community). She is always open for discussion but sometimes, as for any manager, there are critical objectives that must be met by the organization and are not negotiable.

Basically, it is a good idea to involve people in group decision making whenever there is time and the decision is pertinent to them. Group decision making as seen in Figure 4-16 can make the group more cohesive, can be an important forum for learning and sharing, and can improve motivation.

Whichever decision technique is used, it is likely that the context will often be a meeting conducted by you. And running a good meeting is a challenge, as you've probably discovered by attending meetings that were a waste of time. See "Building a Supervisory Skill: Conducting a Group Meeting" for guidance running meetings.

FIGURE 4-16

Meetings are a widely used, excellent vehicle for implementing decisions.

CONDUCTING A GROUP MEETING

ABOUT THE SKILL

Many supervisors report that they spend 10 hours or more a week in meetings. Many of these are called and run by others.

When it's your responsibility to conduct a meeting, do you know what to do? Experts say one-third of the time spent in meetings is a waste. What can you do to cut out that waste and make your meetings both efficient and effective? We'll provide you with the answers in this section.

STEPS IN PRACTISING THE SKILL

The following summarizes the key actions you should take as a leader to increase the likelihood that the meetings you conduct are run efficiently and effectively.

1. **Prepare a meeting agenda.** An agenda defines what you hope to accomplish at the meeting. It should state the meeting's purpose. Is the purpose only to exchange information or is it to make decisions? Will all relevant parties in the organization be included or merely their representatives? And if decisions are to be made, how are they to be arrived at? Will consensus be sought? If decisions are to be made by voting, what constitutes approval: a simple majority, a two-thirds majority? These issues should be clarified ahead of time in the agenda. The agenda should also identify who will be in attendance; what, if any, preparation is required of each participant; a detailed list of items to be covered; the specific time and location of the meeting; and a specific finishing time.

2. **Distribute the agenda in advance.** If you want specific people to attend your meeting, and particularly if participants need to do some homework beforehand, get your agenda out well in advance of the meeting. What's an adequate lead time? That depends on such factors as the amount of preparation necessary, the importance of the meeting, and whether the meeting will be recurring or is being called once to deal with an issue that has arisen and will be repeated only under similar circumstances.

3. **Consult with participants before the meeting.** An unprepared participant can't contribute to his or her full potential. It is your responsibility to ensure that members are prepared. What data will they need ahead of time? Do they have that data? If not, what can you do to help them get it?

4. **Prepare your "stage."** Check the meeting location beforehand to ensure it is suited to the purpose and everything you need is there and in working order (e.g., overhead projector, room not too hot or cold, extension cord). Consider whether you want to alter the seating arrangement, where it would be best for you and others to sit, and whether any refreshments should be available.

5. **Establish specific time parameters.** Meetings should begin on time and have a specific time for completion. It is your responsibility to specify these time parameters and to hold to them.

6. **Maintain focused discussion.** As chairperson, it is your responsibility to give direction to the discussion; to keep it focused on the issues; and to minimize interruptions, disruptions, and irrelevant comments. If participants begin to stray from the issue under consideration, intercede quickly to redirect the discussion. Similarly, one or a few members cannot be allowed to monopolize the discussion or to dominate others. Appropriate preventive action can range from a subtle stare, a raised eyebrow, or other nonverbal communication, on up to an authoritative command such as ruling someone "out of order" or withdrawing someone's right to continue speaking.

7. **Encourage and support participation by all members.** Participants were not selected randomly. Each is there for a purpose. To maximize the effectiveness of problem-oriented meetings, each participant must be encouraged to contribute. Quiet or reserved personalities must be drawn out so their ideas can be heard.

8. **Maintain a balanced style.** You need to exert the appropriate level of control. The style of leadership can range from authoritative domination to laissez-faire. The effective group leader pushes when necessary and is passive when need be.

9. **Encourage the clash of ideas.** You need to encourage different points of view, critical thinking, and constructive disagreement. Your goals should be to stimulate participants' creativity and to counter the group members' desire to reach an early consensus.

10. **Discourage the clash of personalities.** An effective meeting is characterized by the critical assessment of ideas, not attacks on people. When running a meeting, you must quickly intercede to stop personal attacks or other forms of verbal insult.

11. **Exhibit effective listening skills.** If your group meeting is to achieve its objectives, you need to listen actively rather than passively. Do whatever is necessary to get the full intended meaning from a speaker's comments. Effective listening reduces misunderstandings, improves the focus of discussion, and encourages the critical

assessment of ideas. Even if other group members don't exhibit good listening skills, you can keep the discussion focused on the issues and facilitate critical thinking if you listen well.

12. **Bring proper closure.** Close a meeting by summarizing the group's accomplishments; clarifying what actions, if any, need to follow the meeting; and allocating follow-up assignments. If any decisions have been made, you also need to determine who will be responsible for communicating and implementing them.

Suggestions for Overcoming Obstacles at a Meeting

The Talker. If the person's points are on topic, tactfully interrupt, summarize the person's point, and ask for others to comment on it. If the person is discussing an issue off-topic, interrupt, make a positive comment on what the person was discussing, for example, "I wish we had time to discuss that right now but we have to…", and steer the discussion back to the proper focus.

Chit-Chat on the Sidelines. If the private conversation continues for more than a short time and seems to be distracting others, call one of the people by name, asking for their contribution on the point being discussed, or confront him or her tactfully on whether there is something you have missed that they wish to bring to your attention. Or, you may think it most suitable to make a joke about their conversation, for example, "Hey, you two, we know you haven't seen each other in two weeks since your offices were moved but we'd like to get in on the reunion, too."

The Silent Meeting Member. Ask that person specifically for their input, remembering to word it as an open question rather than closed so they cannot respond with a one-word answer. You may refer to something you know the person has done or said pertinent to the topic and draw him or her into the discussion in that way.

The Critic. If someone makes non-productive comments, you may discourage further comments by simply ignoring them. If that doesn't work, ask the person for a positive suggestion or specific proof for their criticism. For example, "You say that won't work. We've discussed specific situations where it has worked in the past. I'd like to hear about specific negative instances so I can understand your pessimism." Or, "Yes, you're right, that would cost a lot the way we have been picturing it. Do you see a way to achieve the same objective without it costing so much?"

TECHNIQUES FOR IMPROVING GROUP DECISION MAKING

When group members physically confront and interact with one another, they create the potential for groupthink. They can censor themselves and pressure other group members into agreement. There are four techniques that you might want to consider as ways to stimulate creativity in group decision making.

BRAINSTORMING

Brainstorming is a relatively simple technique for overcoming pressures for conformity that can retard the development of creative alternatives. It achieves this by using an idea-generating process that actively encourages any and all alternatives while withholding any criticism of those alternatives.

In a typical brainstorming session, group members sit around a table. The group leader states the problem in a clear manner so it is understood by all participants. Members then "freewheel" as many alternatives as they can in a given time. No criticism is allowed, and all the alternatives are recorded for later discussion and analysis.

Brainstorming, however, is merely a process for generating ideas, not for choosing among them. The next three techniques go further by offering ways to arrive at a preferred solution.

> **Brainstorming**
> An idea-generation process that specifically encourages any and all alternatives while withholding any criticism of those alternatives.

NOMINAL GROUP TECHNIQUE

The nominal group restricts discussion during the decision-making process, hence the term **nominal group technique**. Group members are all physically present, as in a traditional committee meeting, but the members are required to operate independently. Specifically, the following steps take place:

1. Members meet as a group; however, before any discussion takes place, each member independently writes down his or her ideas on the problem.
2. This silent period is followed by each member presenting one idea to the group. Each member takes his or her turn, going around the table, presenting one idea at a time until all ideas have been presented and recorded (typically on a flip chart or chalkboard). No discussion takes place until all ideas have been recorded.
3. The group now discusses the ideas for clarity and evaluates them.
4. Each group member silently and independently assigns a rank to the ideas. The final decision is determined by choosing the idea with the highest aggregate ranking.

> **Nominal group technique**
> A group decision technique where all members are present but operate independently.

DELPHI TECHNIQUE

Delphi technique
A group decision technique where members act independently but need not be physically present for discussion.

A more complex and time-consuming alternative is the **Delphi technique**, which is similar to the nominal group technique except that it doesn't require the physical presence of group members. This is because the Delphi technique never allows the group members to meet face to face. The following steps characterize the Delphi technique:

1. The problem is identified, and members are asked to provide potential solutions through a series of carefully designed questionnaires.
2. Each member anonymously and independently completes the first questionnaire.
3. Results of the first questionnaire are compiled at a central location, transcribed, and reproduced.
4. Each member receives a copy of the results.
5. After reviewing the results, members are again asked for their solutions. The results typically trigger new solutions or cause changes in the original position.
6. Steps 4 and 5 are repeated as often as necessary until consensus is reached.

ELECTRONIC MEETINGS

Electronic meeting
A group of individuals make decisions by communicating anonymously on computer terminals.

The most recent approach to group decision making blends the nominal group technique with sophisticated computer technology (see Figure 4-17). It's called the **electronic meeting**. It has been used with great success by Royal Trust, Sears Canada, Ontario Hydro, and Met Life.

The major advantages to electronic meetings are anonymity, honesty, and speed. Participants can anonymously type any message they want and it flashes on the screen for all to see at the push of a key. It also allows people to be brutally honest with no penalty. And it's fast because chit-chat is eliminated, discussions don't digress, and many participants can "talk" at once without stepping on others' toes. Electronic meetings offer an excellent means for supervisors and members of their department to efficiently exchange information and make decisions that affect their work group.

Experts claim that electronic meetings are as much as 55 percent faster than traditional face-to-face meetings.[4] At Mohawk College's Procor Decision Support Centre in Hamilton, many organizations have found the facility useful for electronic meetings. The RCMP spent two intensive days developing competencies for their investigators. Their best investigators, normally spread across Canada to do their work, could be brought together and questioned intensively about how they do their work in order to look for commonalities among them and identify competencies that should be selected or developed in future investigators. The RCMP were so impressed with the value of the electronic meeting method that they plan to return to use it in the investigation of a telephone fraud campaign. Twelve of the victims of the campaign will be interviewed through the electronic-meeting format and the RCMP will look for common themes in their stories. Stelco and a major Ontario educational institution are two organizations that have used the Procor Centre for strategic planning. For more on Mohawk College's electronic facility, see Case 4.A.

Mohawk College
www.mohawkc.on.ca/
b&i/#help

However, there are drawbacks to electronic meetings. Those who can type quickly can outshine those who may be verbally eloquent but are lousy typists; those with the best ideas don't get credit for them. This technology is currently only in its infancy. The future of group decision making is likely to include extensive usage of electronic meetings.

FIGURE 4-17

Procor uses electronic meetings to bring together people in the company from diverse backgrounds. Many companies have taken part in these meetings.

5. A conceptual style of decision making reflects an individual who:
   a. thinks intuitively and has a low tolerance for ambiguity
   b. thinks rationally and has a high tolerance for ambiguity
   c. thinks intuitively and has a high tolerance for ambiguity
   d. thinks rationally and has a low tolerance for ambiguity
6. What is groupthink? What are its implications for decision making?
7. The justice view of ethics is concerned with respecting and protecting the basic freedoms of individuals, such as free speech and due process. True or false?
8. Group decisions will usually be superior to individual decisions except when:
   a. speed is a concern
   b. accuracy is critical
   c. widespread acceptance of the solution is essential
   d. flexibility is needed

CREATIVE PROBLEM SOLVING

ASSESSING YOURSELF: HOW CREATIVE ARE YOU?

How creative are you? The following test helps determine if you have the personality traits, attitudes, values, motivations, and interests that comprise creativity. It is based on several years' study of attributes possessed by men and women in a variety of fields and occupations who think and act creatively.

INSTRUCTIONS

For each statement, write in the appropriate letter:

      A = Agree
      B = Undecided or Don't Know
      C = Disagree

Be as frank as possible. Try not to second-guess how a creative person might respond.

____ 1. I always work with a great deal of certainty that I am following the correct procedure for solving a particular problem.

____ 2. It would be a waste of time for me to ask questions if I had no hope of obtaining answers.

____ 3. I concentrate harder on whatever interests me than do most people.

____ 4. I feel that a logical step-by-step method is best for solving problems.

____ 5. In groups I occasionally voice opinions that seem to turn some people off.

____ 6. I spend a great deal of time thinking about what others think of me.

____ 7. It is more important for me to do what I believe to be right than to try to win the approval of others.

____ 8. People who seem uncertain about things lose my respect.

___ 9. More than other people, I need to have things interesting and exciting.

___ 10. I know how to keep my inner impulses in check.

___ 11. I am able to stick with difficult problems over extended periods of time.

___ 12. On occasion I get overly enthusiastic.

___ 13. I often get my best ideas when doing nothing in particular.

___ 14. I rely on intuitive hunches and the feeling of "rightness" or "wrongness" when moving toward the solution of a problem.

___ 15. When problem solving, I work faster when analyzing the problem and slower when synthesizing the information I have gathered.

___ 16. I sometimes get a kick out of breaking the rules and doing things I am not supposed to do.

___ 17. I like hobbies that involve collecting things.

___ 18. Daydreaming has provided the impetus for many of my more important projects.

___ 19. I like people who are objective and rational.

___ 20. If I had to choose from two occupations other than the one I now have, I would rather be a physician than an explorer.

___ 21. I can get along more easily with people if they belong to about the same social and business class as myself.

___ 22. I have a high degree of aesthetic sensitivity.

___ 23. I am driven to achieve high status and power in life.

___ 24. I like people who are most sure of their conclusions.

___ 25. Inspiration has nothing to do with the successful solution of problems.

___ 26. When I am in an argument, my greatest pleasure would be for the person who disagrees with me to become a friend, even at the price of sacrificing my point of view.

___ 27. I am much more interested in coming up with new ideas than in trying to sell them to others.

___ 28. I would enjoy spending an entire day alone, just "chewing the mental cud."

___ 29. I tend to avoid situations in which I might feel inferior.

___ 30. In evaluating information, the source is more important to me than the content.

___ 31. I resent things being uncertain and unpredictable.

___ 32. I like people who follow the rule, "business before pleasure."

___ 33. Self-respect is much more important than the respect of others.

___ 34. I feel that people who strive for perfection are unwise.

___ 35. I prefer to work with others in a team effort rather than solo.

___ 36. I like work in which I must influence others.

___ 37. Many problems that I encounter in life cannot be resolved in terms of right or wrong solutions.

___ 38. It is important for me to have a place for everything and everything in its place.

___ 39. Writers who use strange and unusual words merely want to show off.

Below is a list of terms that describe people. Choose ten words that best characterize you.

❏ energetic	❏ alert
❏ persuasive	❏ curious
❏ observant	❏ organized
❏ fashionable	❏ unemotional
❏ self-confident	❏ clear-thinking
❏ persevering	❏ understanding
❏ original	❏ dynamic
❏ cautious	❏ self-demanding
❏ habit-bound	❏ polished
❏ resourceful	❏ courageous
❏ egotistical	❏ efficient
❏ independent	❏ helpful
❏ stern	❏ perceptive
❏ predictable	❏ quick
❏ formal	❏ good-natured
❏ informal	❏ thorough

❏ dedicated	❏ impulsive	
❏ forward-looking	❏ determined	
❏ factual	❏ realistic	
❏ open-minded	❏ modest	
❏ tactful	❏ involved	
❏ inhibited	❏ absent-minded	
❏ enthusiastic	❏ flexible	
❏ innovative	❏ sociable	
❏ poised	❏ well liked	
❏ acquisitive	❏ restless	
❏ practical	❏ retiring	

Source: Eugene Raudsepp, President, Princeton Creative Research, Inc.

SCORING DIRECTIONS

To compute your score, circle and add up the values assigned to each item. The values are as follows:

	A Agree	B Undecided or Don't Know	C Disagree		A Agree	B Undecided or Don't Know	C Disagree
1.	0	1	2	**21.**	0	1	2
2.	0	1	2	**22.**	3	0	-1
3.	4	1	0	**23.**	0	1	2
4.	-2	0	3	**24.**	-1	0	2
5.	2	1	0	**25.**	0	1	3
6.	-1	0	3	**26.**	-1	0	2
7.	3	0	-1	**27.**	2	1	0
8.	0	1	2	**28.**	2	0	-1
9.	3	0	-1	**29.**	0	1	2
10.	1	0	3	**30.**	-2	0	3
11.	4	1	0	**31.**	0	1	2
12.	3	0	-1	**32.**	0	1	2
13.	2	1	0	**33.**	3	0	-1
14.	4	0	-2	**34.**	-1	0	2
15.	-1	0	2	**35.**	0	1	2
16.	2	1	0	**36.**	1	2	3
17.	0	1	2	**37.**	2	1	0
18.	3	0	-1	**38.**	0	1	2
19.	0	1	2	**39.**	-1	0	2
20.	0	1	2				

40. The following have values of 2:

energetic	dynamic	perceptive	dedicated
resourceful	flexible	innovative	courageous
original	observant	self-demanding	curious
enthusiastic	independent	persevering	involved

The following have values of 1:

self-confident	determined	informal	forward-looking
thorough	restless	alert	open-minded

The rest have values of 0.

TOTAL SCORE

95–116	Exceptionally creative		20–39	Average
65–94	Very creative		10–19	Below average
40–64	Above average		Below 10	Noncreative

SKILL BASICS

There's good news on the creativity front! Most of us have unleashed creative potential, but we get into psychological ruts. In this skill module, we want to show you how you can unleash your creative problem-solving talent.

CHARACTERISTICS OF THE EXCEPTIONALLY CREATIVE PERSON

Let's begin with the obvious. People differ in their inherent creativity. Einstein, Picasso, and Mozart were individuals of exceptional creativity. What personality characteristics do the exceptionally creative share? Generally they are independent, risk-taking, persistent, and highly motivated. They're also nonconformists who can be hard to get along with. Additionally, highly creative individuals prefer complex and unstructured tasks. Disorder doesn't make them anxious.

How widespread is exceptional creativity? Not very! A study of lifetime creativity of 461 men and women found that fewer than one per cent were exceptionally creative.[5] But 10 percent were highly creative and about 60 percent were somewhat creative. As you'll see, even if you didn't score in the exceptionally creative category on the self-assessment exercise, there are ways to improve your potential.

THE ORGANIZATION MATTERS

Your creative potential is also influenced by characteristics of the organization in which you work. For instance, rigidly structured organizations that inhibit communication between departments tend to limit creativity.

Every organization has a culture. This organizational culture represents a shared perception of the organization's values. It's sort of an organizational equivalent of an individual's personality. That is, just as some people are open, or aggressive, or controlling, so too are organizations. The difference is that in organizational culture, all members of the organization tend to share a common understanding about the organization, how things are done in it, and the way members are supposed to behave. Certain organizational cultures can restrict creativity. Specifically, these are cultures that punish risk-taking and failure, and reward excessive loyalty and conformity.

STIMULATING YOUR CREATIVITY

Creativity is the ability to combine ideas in a unique way to make unusual associations between them. Each of us has the ability to be creative, yet some use their creativity more than others. Although creative people are sometimes referred to as "artsy," and their precise characteristics are difficult to describe, there are certain steps you can take in becoming more creative.[6]

1. **Think of yourself as creative.** Although it's a simple suggestion, research shows that if you think you can't be creative, you won't be. Just as the little train in the children's fable says, "I think I can," if we believe in ourselves, we can become more creative.

2. **Pay attention to your intuition.** Everyone has a subconscious mind that works well. Sometimes answers come when we least expect them. For example, when you are about to go to sleep, your relaxed mind sometimes comes up with solutions to problems you face. You need to listen to this intuition. In fact, many creative people keep a note pad near their bed and write down those "great" ideas when they come to them. That way, they are not forgotten.

3. **Move away from your comfort zone.** Every individual has a comfort zone in which certainty exists. But creativity and the known often don't mix. To be creative, we need to move away from the status quo, and focus on something new.

4. **Engage in activities that put you outside your comfort zone.** Not only must we think differently, we need to do things differently. By engaging in activities that are different to us, we challenge ourselves. For example, learning to play a musical instrument or learning a foreign language opens the mind up and allows it to be challenged.

5. **Seek a change of scenery.** As humans, we are creatures of habit. Creative people force themselves out of their habits by changing their scenery. Going into a quiet and serene area where you can be alone with your thoughts is a good way to enhance creativity.

6. **Find several right answers.** Just as we set boundaries in rationality, we often seek solutions that are only good enough. Being creative means continuing to look for other solutions, even when you think you have solved the problem. A better, more creative solution just might be found.

7. **Play your own devil's advocate.** Challenging yourself to defend your solutions helps you develop confidence in your creative efforts. Second guessing may also help you find more correct answers.

8. **Believe in finding a workable solution.** Like believing in yourself, you also need to believe in your ideas. If you don't think you can find a solution, one won't be found. Having a positive mental attitude, however, may become a self-fulfilling prophecy.

9. **Brainstorm with others.** Creativity is not an isolated activity. By bouncing ideas off others, a synergistic effect occurs.

10. **Turn creative ideas into action.** Coming up with ideas is only half of the process. Once the ideas are generated, they must be implemented. Great ideas that remain in someone's mind, or on papers that no one reads, do little to expand one's creative abilities.

APPLYING YOUR SKILLS

Form groups of four or five. You are a committee of employees at the student centre on campus. The centre has several fast-food franchises and a pub. The centre is doing well but analysis of the statistics reveals that much of that success is due to strong liquor and beer sales in the pub. This concerns the committee because the student mix on campus is changing. There are now many more mature students, who don't spend nearly as much on liquor and beer as the younger students. In fact, the mature students are much less likely to spend time in the student centre.

You have 30 minutes for your committee to develop a list of ideas for how the student centre can attract more of the older students, both to "hang out" and mix with the other students, and to spend their money there. Be prepared to discuss a) your top three recommendations, and b) what your committee believes to be its most creative option.

SUMMARY

This summary is organized by the Learning Objectives.

1. The seven steps in the decision-making process are: 1. identify the problem; 2. collect relevant information; 3. develop alternatives; 4. evaluate each alternative; 5. select the best alternative; 6. implement the decision; 7. follow up and evaluate.

2. Expected value analysis calculates the expected value of a particular alternative by weighting its possible outcomes by the probability of achieving the alternative, then summing up the totals derived from the weighting process.

3. Decision trees are a device for analyzing decisions that involve a progression of decisions. They help decision makers visualize key decision points and outcomes.

4. Data are raw, unanalyzed facts. Data become information when they are analyzed and processed. It is information that is most relevant for making informed decisions.

5. There are four types of decision styles. The directive type is efficient and logical. The analytic type is careful, with the ability to adapt or cope with new situations. The conceptual type considers many alternatives and is good at coming up with creative solutions. The behavioural type emphasizes suggestions from others and conflict avoidance.

6. The utilitarian view of ethics makes decisions based on the greatest good for the greatest number. The rights view of ethics makes decisions consistent with fundamental liberties and privileges. The justice view of ethics seeks fairness and impartiality.

7. Group decisions are based on more complete information, more alternatives, increased acceptance of a solution, and increased legitimacy. Individual decisions take less time, have clear accountability and are not subject to pressures to conform.

8. Techniques for improving group decision making include brainstorming, nominal group technique, Delphi technique, and electronic meetings.

UNDERSTANDING THE BASICS

KEY TERMS AND CONCEPTS

Brainstorming
Cause-and-effect diagram
Consensus
Decision by authority
    after discussion
Decision by expert
Decision by minority vote
Decision trees
Delphi technique
Electronic meeting
Expected value analysis
Gap analysis

Groupthink
Justice view of ethics
Majority vote
Management information system
Marginal analysis
Matrix assessment
Nominal group technique
Problem
Risk analysis
Rights view of ethics
Utilitarian view of ethics

REVIEWING YOUR KNOWLEDGE

1. Contrast symptoms with problems. Give three examples.
2. In which step of the decision-making process do you think creativity would be most helpful? In which step would quantitative analysis tools be most helpful?
3. Calculate your estimated grade average this term using expected value analysis.
4. What is meant by the expression "supervisors are increasingly becoming end-users in MIS"?
5. How might certain decision styles fit better with specific jobs? Give examples.
6. What rationalizations do people use to justify questionable conduct?
7. Which view of ethics dominates in business firms? Why?
8. When should managers use groups for decision making? When should they use individuals?
9. Contrast the nominal group technique, Delphi technique, and electronic meeting.

ANSWERS TO THE POP QUIZZES

1. **c. recognizing a problem by comparison with past performance.** This question reinforces the importance of properly defining a problem. That is, a problem is a discrepancy between an existing and a desired state of affairs. Past performance sets standards against which current performance is compared.

2. Planning sets the standards against which a supervisor can compare actual performance. A significant variation from the plan represents a problem—which then requires a decision about how to correct it.

3. **False.** Solving the wrong problem is a waste of time. The first step in problem solving is to identify what the problem is. Solving the wrong problem can actually make the situation worse by creating new problems.

4. **b. the control function of management becomes important.** Follow-up and evaluation involves determining whether the problem has been corrected. This means that actual progress is again compared to the "standard." This is the fundamental activity of control.

5. **c. thinks intuitively and has a high tolerance for ambiguity.** This is the definition of conceptual decision-making style.

6. Groupthink is a term used to reflect the withholding by group members of different views in order to appear in agreement. It affects decision making by manifesting as pressure on group members to keep doubts about the group's shared views to themselves; this silence is taken to mean a "yes" vote. Because of this pressure, poorer decisions may result.

7. **False.** This is the definition of the rights view of ethics. The justice view of ethics seeks fairness and impartiality.

8. **a. speed is a concern.** Responses *b*, *c*, and *d* are advantages of group decision making. Where speed is concerned, individuals perform better. Therefore, response *a* is the exception to the advantages of group decision making.

CASE 4.A

Electronic Honesty

Rocco Di Giovanni is the manager of Mohawk College's Procor Decision Support Centre, which is an electronic-meeting facility using GroupSystems.com software. He also acts as a facilitator within many of the meetings. This means that he sits at the "leader station" located at the front of the room, guiding up to 15 people seated at their own terminals. Their terminals are recessed, guaranteeing anonymity but also allowing participants to have a normal face-to-face meeting without the obstruction of computers. Rocco will start the process with a trigger question, which participants answer electronically. Within minutes, the answers are scrolled onto a screen at the front of the room. Typically, this is followed by electronic voting and a display of the collective ranking. Discussion follows as various perceptions and ideas are explored. The greatest value often comes from the exposure of internal problems. Unlike in the normal work environment where individuals fail to be honest for fear of repercussions, in electronic meetings people can be brutally honest.

This brutal honesty led to an interesting situation for Rocco. In facilitating an electronic meeting with one organization, the issue that was to be discussed was trust. When the trigger question asked for points within the organization where trust is an issue, the answers that scrolled onto the screen for everyone to see pointed clearly to one person in the organization whom the others did not trust. That person was present at the meeting: the president of the company. At this point, Rocco suggested that the group take a break. Then he spoke privately with the president, saying, "Do you want to pursue this? This is how I would tackle it if you did. I would ask for participants to report specific incidents illustrating their concern. What do you think?" The president was open enough to continue with the process. Rocco then asked the participants to provide specific incidents where breach of trust had occurred, they were reported (anonymously), and the president then addressed and explained each incident. As the meeting progressed, it was clear that a major barrier had been broken.

Rocco explains that this example demonstrates what commonly happens: electronic meetings allow issues to be identified and then it becomes much easier to tackle them. Although these issues may be embarrassing, no individual person needs to be embarrassed. For example, in one meeting where participants were discussing the marketing strategy electronically, it became clear that some people did not understand the marketing plan even though it was expected that they should. This lack of understanding could be addressed without any fingerpointing.

As indicated above, in actuality, electronic meetings are a combination of confidential reporting, questioning and voting, combined with normal face-to-face discussion. They are not the cool, distant interaction of nameless fingers on keyboards. This is why Rocco does not foresee the type of electronic meeting he facilitates being replaced by electronic meetings where participants simply "conference call" on their computers from separate locations. The face-to-face interaction still has great value.

FIGURE 4-18
Rocco Di Giovanni at Procor Decision Support Centre

RESPONDING TO THIS CASE

1. Sometimes Rocco is asked to entirely run an organization's electronic meeting. At other times he is simply a technician, running the software. He prefers to have a meeting where he plays a role in between the two, working with one or more organizational members to plan and run the meeting. What do you see to be the advantages and disadvantages of each of these three formats (Rocco runs it, the organization's facilitator runs it, the two jointly handle the meeting)?

2. Explain how planning an electronic meeting would be different from planning a normal meeting.

3. Explain why the "obstacles" at a meeting noted earlier (e.g., the critic, the silent meeting member) would likely not be obstacles in an electronic meeting. Can you anticipate other kinds of obstacles emerging?

4. Explain how electronic meetings overcome the disadvantages of group decision making noted earlier in the chapter.

CASE 4.B

How Can You Make the Decision?

You have just moved to Mississauga from Fredericton for your spouse to accept a new position. In response to a newspaper ad, you applied for a position running a storefront business centre that supplies photocopying, printing, and other business services for local businesses. It is a very busy place, staffed by four people. The owner has been managing the business until hiring you to take over. He has decided to concentrate on two other businesses he is running. Although you have never run a business exactly like this one, you have been an office manager as well as a retail manager in a computer store, and you are familiar with all the services offered in this business. You are very familiar with typical business software and your supervisory skills are strong.

You decide to spend your first week learning as much as possible about the state of this business and figuring out what is needed. At the end of this time, your list of observations includes the following:

The scheduling of staff did not cover the peak customer times adequately.

Two of the four staff seem to know their customers very well, having strong and friendly relationships; one seems to be knowledgeable but is much quieter, not chatting with either customers or other staff; the fourth staff person seems to find anything to do that involves working on her own and avoiding both staff and customers; there appears to be tension between that person and the two outgoing staff members.

The good customer relationships seem to be in spite of an apparent problem in getting work orders done on time; staff appear to make unrealistic promises.

Equipment seems to be needing replacement, judging by the amount of downtime and the recent repair costs you have found in examining the books.

You find the organization of inventory inappropriate; it is difficult to find some things, items that relate are not shelved together, some stock is split into two storage areas, making it difficult to ascertain inventory levels.

The staff members turn to you for approval for many of their actions; this puzzles you as they obviously have more experience in this environment and many of the approvals seem a silly waste of time; you guess that the owner demanded to check everything and they expect you to do the same.

You know a lot needs to be done in the store.

RESPONDING TO THIS CASE

1. What decisions need to be made?
2. What decision-making methods and/ or tools from the chapter would be appropriate?
3. What decision-making methods or tools from the chapter would not be appropriate?
4. As a new manager, what do you want to achieve in the next few months in addition to getting the store into better shape? How do these aims influence your choice of how to approach decision making?

PART THREE

ORGANIZING, STAFFING, AND EMPLOYEE DEVELOPMENT

5. ORGANIZING AN EFFECTIVE DEPARTMENT

6. ACQUIRING THE RIGHT PEOPLE

7. APPRAISING EMPLOYEE PERFORMANCE

8. DEVELOPING YOUR EMPLOYEES

5

ORGANIZING AN EFFECTIVE DEPARTMENT

LEARNING OBJECTIVES

After reading this chapter, you should be able to:

1. Define organizing.
2. Describe why division of labour should increase economic efficiency.
3. Explain how the span of control affects an organization's structure.
4. Contrast line and staff authority.
5. Explain why organizations are increasingly becoming decentralized.
6. Describe functional departmentalization.
7. Identify the strengths and weaknesses of the matrix.
8. Explain the value of job descriptions.
9. Identify the four-step process of delegation.

CHAPTER OUTLINE

PERFORMING EFFECTIVELY

WHAT IS ORGANIZING?

BASIC ORGANIZING CONCEPTS
   Division of Labour
   Span of Control
   Unity of Command
   Line, Staff and Functional
      Authority
   Equating Authority and
      Responsibility
   Centralized vs. Decentralized
      Authority
   Pop Quiz

GROUPING EMPLOYEES
   Function
   Product
   Geography
   Customer
   Process
   Blending Function and Product:
      The Matrix
   Dealing with a Difficult Issue:
      Do Matrix Structures Create
      Confused Employees?
   Why Is There Movement to
      Simpler Employee
      Groupings?
   Are There Simple Structures for
      Larger Organizations?

ORGANIZING YOUR
EMPLOYEES' JOBS
   Identifying the Tasks to Be
      Done
   Combining Tasks into Jobs
   Creating Job Descriptions
   Pop Quiz

THE INCREASING USE OF TEAMS
   Turning Groups into Teams
   Building Real Teams
   Overcoming the Obstacles
   Something to Think About
   Pop Quiz

FROM CONCEPTS TO SKILLS:
EMPOWERING OTHERS
THROUGH DELEGATION
   Assessing Yourself: Are You
      Willing to Delegate?
   Skill Basics
   Applying Your Skills

UNDERSTANDING THE BASICS
   Summary
   Key Terms and Concepts
   Reviewing Your Knowledge
   Answers to the Pop Quizzes

PERFORMING YOUR JOB
   Case 5.A: Teams at NCR
   Case 5.B: Separating Team
      Members at Enbridge

FIGURE 5-1

Susan Miller, VP of
Enbridge Technology,
Edmonton

Susan Miller is the vice president of Enbridge Technology, an international engineering consulting firm. The firm is headquartered in Edmonton with Enbridge Pipelines, but has staff working all over the world. There are 14 full-time employees in the organization but up to 50 contract people can also be working at any given time. Shortly after Susan's move to Enbridge Technology, she reported to her boss that it looked like it was imploding, in that parts of the company were working against each other. Despite the fact that all employees were supposed to be working together for the success of the company, Susan found that they were actually divided into three silos (training, advising, and engineering) that communicated poorly and failed to cooperate. For example, despite its high-tech business, the company lacked a Web site because the three areas could not agree on which department would be responsible for paying for it. Susan believed that this internal competition was hurting the company and she undertook a reorganization to create a team. As a result, there was turnover. Most people moved to Enbridge's operating divisions, and some were laid off. The new "green" team started with a team focus. All individual performance indicators were removed from performance appraisals. Instead, the focus became corporate goals and team achievement.

As you can see, the way in which people are grouped has an impact on the organization. It creates loyalties, lines of communication and cooperation, and barriers, too. Often, the supervisor has no choice as to the grouping or structure. The supervisor of a unit must work within the opportunities and restrictions created by that structure. The structure itself can influence the unit's activity and effectiveness, as Susan observed at Enbridge Technology. A supervisor can, however, sometimes affect the organization of his or her subordinates through, for example, an influence on job descriptions, or through exerting effort to turn the work group into a team.

When we examine the impact of structure, many questions arise. How many people can one person supervise effectively? When does the supervisor have authority to make a decision? What tasks can a supervisor delegate? These are all dependent on the organization of the company. This chapter examines the basics of organization within a company and within a department, and looks at ways in which organizational structures are changing.

In the 1920s and 1930s, as organizations got bigger and more formal, supervisors felt a need to provide more coordination of activities and tighter control over operations. Early business researchers argued that formal bureaucracies would best serve the company—and that was true many years ago. These bureaucratic structures flourished. By the 1980s, the world began to change drastically. The global marketplace, rapid technological advancements, diversity in the workforce, and socioeconomic conditions made these formal bureaucracies inefficient for many businesses. As a result, since the late 1980s many organizations have restructured to be more customer- and market-oriented, and to increase productivity.

FIGURE 5-2

This department at Xerox is organized with procedures, rules, and policies that guide employee activities.

It is critical today for an organization to have the right structure. Although setting up the organization's structure is typically done by top management in an organization (or the owner in a small business), it is important for all organizational members to understand how these structures work. Why? Because you'll understand your job better if you know why you're "arranged" as you are. For example, how many people can you effectively supervise? When do you have authority to make a decision and when is it merely advice that you're providing? What tasks can you delegate to others? Will you supervise employees who produce a specific product? Will your department exist to serve a particular customer, a geographic region, or some combination of these? You'll see how to find the answers to questions like these in this chapter. We'll look at the traditional components that go into developing an organization's structure, discuss the various ways that employees may be grouped, and look at how organizational structures change over time.

Xerox Canada
www.xerox.ca

WHAT IS ORGANIZING?

Organizing is arranging and grouping jobs, allocating resources, and assigning work in a department so that activities can be accomplished as planned. The top management team in an organization typically establishes the overall organization structure. They'll determine, for instance, how many layers there will be in the organizational chart (e.g., number of management levels). They will also decide the extent to

Organizing
Arranging and grouping jobs, allocating resources, and assigning work in a department so that activities can be accomplished as planned.

which lower-level managers will have to follow formal rules and procedures in carrying out their jobs. In large corporations, it's not unusual for there to be five to eight levels from top to bottom; hundreds of departments; and dozens of manuals (for example, purchasing, human resources, accounting, engineering, maintenance, sales) that define procedures, rules, and policies within departments. Once the overall structure is in place, individual supervisors will need to organize their departments. In this chapter, we'll show you how to do that.

Keep in mind that our discussion here is with the formal arrangement of jobs and groups of jobs. These are defined by management. In addition, individuals and groups will develop informal alliances that are neither formally structured nor organizationally determined. Almost all employees in all organizations develop these informal arrangements to meet their needs for social contact. We'll discuss informal groups later in the book.

BASIC ORGANIZING CONCEPTS

The early writers on management developed a number of basic organizing principles that today's supervisors often use as they organize their departments.

DIVISION OF LABOUR

Division of labour
The breakdown of jobs into narrow, repetitive tasks.

Division of labour (also known as work specialization) means that an entire job is broken down into a number of steps, each step being completed by a different individual. In essence, individuals specialize in doing part of an activity rather than the entire activity. Assembly-line production, in which each worker does the same standardized task over and over again, is an example of division of labour.

Until very recently, designers of organizations have felt that greater economic gains are achieved by breaking jobs down into smaller steps. In most organizations, some tasks require highly developed skills; others can be performed by the untrained. If all workers were engaged in each step of, say, an organization's manufacturing process, all would require the skills necessary to perform the most demanding and the least demanding jobs. The result would be that, except when performing the most highly skilled or highly sophisticated tasks, employees would be working below their skill level. Since skilled workers are paid more than unskilled workers and their wages tend to reflect their highest level of skill, it is not economical to pay highly skilled workers to do easy tasks.

Today, supervisors understand that while division of labour provides economic efficiencies, it is not an unending source of increased productivity. There is a point at which the human costs of division of labour—boredom, fatigue, stress, low productivity, poor quality, increased absenteeism, and high turnover—exceed the economic advantages. Contemporary supervisors utilize the division-of-labour concept in designing jobs but also recognize that, in an expanding number of situations, productivity, quality, and employee motivation can be increased by giving employees a variety of activities to perform, allowing employees to do a whole and complete piece of work, and joining employees together in teams.

SPAN OF CONTROL

It's not very efficient for a supervisor to direct only one or two subordinates. Conversely, it's pretty obvious that even the best of supervisors would be overwhelmed if he or she had to directly oversee several hundred

FIGURE 5-3

The advantages of division of labour are evident on an assembly line, such as the one at this frozen food plant. Each worker performs a narrow and standardized operation. This requires a limited range of skills and allows for increased efficiency.

people. This, then, begs the **span of control** question: How many subordinates can a supervisor effectively direct?

There is, unfortunately, no universal answer. For most supervisors, the optimum number is probably somewhere between five and thirty. Where, within that range, the exact span should be depends on a number of factors.

- How experienced and competent is the supervisor? The greater his or her abilities, the larger the number of subordinates that can be handled.
- What level of training and experience do subordinates have? The higher their abilities, the fewer demands they'll make on their supervisor and the more subordinates that supervisor can directly oversee.
- How complex are the subordinates' activities? The more difficult the employees' jobs, the narrower the span of control.
- How many different types of jobs are under the supervisor's direction? The more varied the jobs, the narrower the span.
- How extensive are the department's formal rules and regulations? Supervisors can direct more people when employees can find solutions to their problems in organizational manuals rather than having to go to their immediate manager.

An important trend currently taking place in organizations is for spans of control to be almost universally expanded (see Figure 5-4). It is a way for management to reduce costs. By doubling the span size, the number of supervisors you need is cut in half. Of course, this move to wider spans couldn't be effectively carried out without modifications in work assignments and improvements in skill levels. So, in order to make wider spans work, organizations are spending more on supervisory and employee training, as well as redesigning jobs around teams so individuals can help each other solve problems without needing to go to their manager. For instance, NCR in Waterloo organizes much of its work around teams. Paul Dolan, the ATM (Automatic Teller Machine) production manager, has over 90 people reporting to him. How can he handle that responsibility? Because his employees are organized into teams that undertake a lot of the decisions typically handled by supervisors in other organizations.

Something else important is taking place in organizations that involves a supervisor's span of control. This is the increased use of telecommuting. **Telecommuting** allows employees to do their work at home on a computer that is linked to their office (see Figure 5-5). The big advantage of telecommuting is that it gives employees more flexibility. It frees them from the constraints of commuting and fixed hours, and increases opportunities for meeting family responsibilities. For supervisors, telecommuting means managing people they rarely see. Where it is used, supervisors usually have a fairly wide span of control. This is because telecommuters tend to be skilled professionals and clerical employees—computer programmers, marketing specialists, financial analysts, and administrative support personnel—who make minimal demands on their supervisors. Additionally, because the supervisor's computer and the employee's computer are typically networked so they can interact with each other, supervisors often are able to communicate as well or better with telecommuters than with employees who are physically in their office.

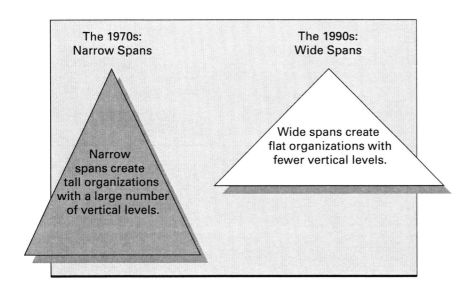

FIGURE 5-4

Contrasting spans of control

FIGURE 5-5

Pacific Bell's Steve Caulter supervises about twenty employees, most of them telecommuters. Steve himself does much of his work from home

UNITY OF COMMAND

Unity of command
The principle that a subordinate should have one and only one superior to whom he or she is directly responsible.

The **unity of command** principle states that a subordinate should have one and only one superior to whom he or she is directly responsible. No person should report to two or more managers. Otherwise, a subordinate might have to cope with conflicting demands or priorities from several people at once. If this happens, employees are placed in a no-win situation. Whatever they do, they're going to upset someone.

There are occasional times when management will specifically break the unity of command. This might be necessary, for instance, when a project team is created to work on a specific problem or when a sales representative must report to both her immediate district supervisor and a marketing specialist at head office who is coordinating the introduction of a new product. Nevertheless, these are exceptions to the rule. For the most part, when allocating tasks to individuals or grouping assignments in your department, you should ensure that each employee has one manager, and only one manager, to whom he or she directly reports.

LINE, STAFF AND FUNCTIONAL AUTHORITY

Authority
The managerial right to give orders and expect the orders to be obeyed.

Authority refers to the managerial right to give orders and expect the orders to be obeyed. Each supervisory position has specific rights that are acquired from the position's rank or title. Authority, therefore, relates to one's position within an organization and ignores the personal characteristics of the individual supervisor. Employees obey individuals in authority not because they like or respect them but because of the rights inherent in their position.

There are three different types of authority relations: line, staff, and functional (see Figure 5-6). The most straightforward and easiest to understand is **line authority**. This is the authority that gives the supervisor the right to direct the work of his or her employees and make certain decisions without consulting others.

Line authority
The authority that entitles a supervisor to direct the work of his or her employees, and to make certain decisions without consulting others.

Staff authority supports line authority by advising, servicing, and assisting, but it is typically limited. For instance, the assistant to the department head has staff authority. She acts as an extension of the department head and can give advice and suggestions, but they needn't be obeyed. However, the assistant may be given the authority to act for the department head. In such cases, she gives directives under the line authority of her boss. For instance, she might issue a memo and sign it "Joan Wilson for R.L. Dalton." In this instance, Wilson is only acting as an extension of Dalton. Staff authority allows Dalton to get more things done by having an assistant who can act on his behalf.

Staff authority
A limited authority that supports line authority by advising, servicing, and assisting.

Functional authority
Rights over individuals outside one's own direct areas of responsibility.

A third type of authority, **functional authority**, represents rights over individuals outside one's own direct areas of responsibility. For example, it is not unusual for a supervisor in a manufacturing plant to find that his

FIGURE 5-6

Organization chart depicting line, staff, and functional authority relationships

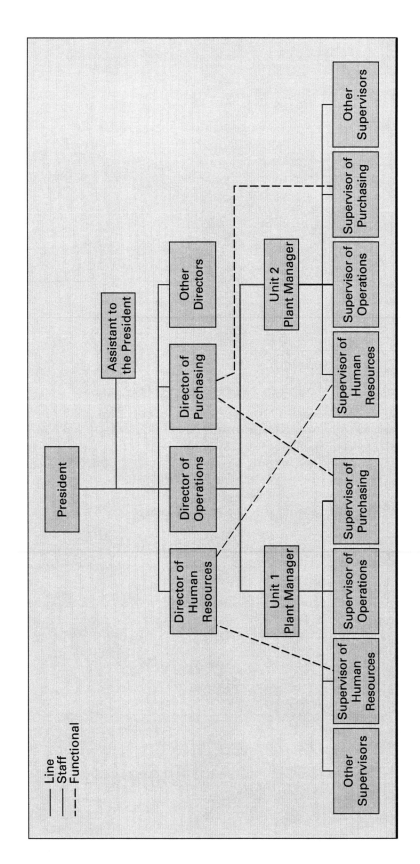

immediate boss has line authority over him but that someone in corporate headquarters has functional authority over some of his activities and decisions. The supervisor in charge of a plant purchasing department is responsible to that plant's manager and the corporate director of purchasing at the company's head office.

Why, you might wonder, would the organization create positions of functional authority? After all, it breaks the unity of command principle by having people report to two bosses. The answer is that it can create efficiencies by permitting specialization of skills and improved coordination. Its major problem is overlapping relationships. This is typically resolved by clearly designating to an individual the activities over which his or her line boss has authority and those that fall under the direction of someone else with functional authority. To follow up our purchasing example, the director might have functional authority to specify corporation-wide purchasing policies on forms to be used and common procedures to be followed. All other aspects of the purchasing supervisor's job would fall under the authority of the plant manager.

EQUATING AUTHORITY AND RESPONSIBILITY

Supervisory jobs come with authority. They also come with obligations. Supervisors are obliged to achieve their unit's goals, keep costs within budget, follow organizational policies, and motivate their subordinates. We call these obligations **responsibility**.

Responsibility
An obligation to perform assigned activities.

Authority without responsibility creates opportunities for abuse. For instance, a supervisor who isn't held responsible for his or her actions may become inclined to make excessive demands on an employee, resulting in that employee being injured on the job. Conversely, responsibility without authority creates frustration and the feeling of powerlessness. If you're held responsible for your territory's sales performance, you should have the authority to hire, reward, discipline, and fire the salespeople who work for you.

When top management creates organizational units such as divisions, regions, territories, and departments—and allocates managers with specific goals to achieve and other responsibilities to fulfill—it must also give the managers enough authority to successfully carry out those responsibilities. The more ambitious and far-reaching the goals that a supervisor undertakes, the more authority he or she needs to be given.

CENTRALIZED VS. DECENTRALIZED AUTHORITY

Centralized authority
Decision making is done by top management.

Where does decision making lie? The design of any organization requires top management to answer this question. If the answer is "with top management," you have **centralized authority**. With centralization, problems "flow up" to senior executives, who then choose the appropriate solution.

Where top management pushes decision making down to lower levels, you have **decentralized authority**.

Decentralized authority
Top management pushes decision making down to lower levels of organization.

Twenty-five years ago, centralization ruled in most organizations. Why? Top management typically had the necessary critical information and the expertise to make most key decisions. Additionally, time was not a problem. If it took a couple of months for top management to get around to making a decision, there were minimal negative consequences. That's no longer true. As jobs have become more complex, it's become nearly impossible for top managers to keep current and knowledgeable on everything going on in their organization. Moreover, the dynamics of competition make it increasingly necessary for organizations to make decisions fast. Because speedy decision making and centralization don't usually go together, top management has in recent years been forced to decentralize decision making.

Today, more than any time in recent years, supervisors and employees are being actively included in the decision-making process. As organizations have cut costs and streamlined their organizational design to respond better to customer needs, they have pushed decision-making authority down to the lowest levels in the organization and empowered employees. In this way, those people most familiar with a problem are able to quickly size it up and solve it. We'll present specific delegation skills later in this chapter, which will show you how to effectively push decision-making authority downward. Note that decentralization also is sometimes chosen because of its link to acceptance of change and perceived fairness. As we will see in a later chapter, employees who are involved in the decision making of a change are much more likely to accept the change and less likely to resist it. Also, involving employees in decision making can motivate them (see Chapter 9) and lead them to believe the decisions made are fair.

1. The principle that jobs should be broken down into the simplest of steps, with one step generally assigned to each individual, is known as:
   a. span of control
   b. line authority
   c. chain of command
   d. none of the above
2. Describe the advantages and disadvantages of the division of labour.
3. Early business experts believed top managers should have a larger span of control. True or false?
4. The main problem to be expected when the unity of command principle is ignored is that:
   a. Employees potentially have trouble coping with conflicting priorities and demands.
   b. Supervisors cannot keep abreast of what all their employees are doing.
   c. Decision making is slow.
   d. There is not enough flexibility.

GROUPING EMPLOYEES

Early business experts argued that activities in the organization should be specialized and grouped into departments. Work specialization creates specialists who need coordination. This coordination is facilitated by putting specialists together in departments under the direction of a supervisor. Creation of these departments is typically based on the work functions being performed, the product or service being offered, the target customer or client, the geographic territory being covered, or the process being used to turn inputs into outputs. This process of grouping departments is called **departmentalization**. No single method of departmentalization was advocated by the early experts. The method or methods used should reflect the grouping that would best contribute to the attainment of the organization's objectives and the goals of individual units.

Departmentalization Grouping jobs according to work functions, product or service, target customer or client, geographic territory, or the process used to turn inputs into outputs.

Specialization is found throughout organizations. For instance, when a company appoints vice presidents for marketing, finance, production, and research, it is dividing up organizational activities by specialization. While major decisions—such as what departments an organization will have and how they will interrelate—are typically made by top management, supervisors still make organizing decisions. These decisions are confined to activities within their own areas of responsibility. As a result, supervisors need to understand various options for organizing their departments and for grouping activities. These are, incidentally, the same options available to top managers when they make decisions about the organization's overall structure. Thus, as a supervisor, you can departmentalize on the basis of work function, product or service, geographic territory, target customer or client, or the process being used to turn inputs into outputs.

FUNCTION

One of the most popular ways to group activities is by functions performed—**functional departmentalization**. When you see a company that separates engineering, accounting, manufacturing, human resources, and purchasing specialists into common departments, you have an example of departmentalizing by function (see Figure 5-7). Similarly, hospitals use this approach when they create departments devoted to research, patient care, accounting, and so forth.

Functional departmentalization Grouping activities by functions performed.

Why is the functional department so popular? Because it most directly takes advantage of occupational specialization. By placing together jobs that are performed by people with the same kinds of training and experience, it is easier for people within the department to communicate with each other. It also makes it easier for the supervisor to coordinate activities, because he or she will be overseeing activities that have a somewhat common component.

Heartland Livestock Services
www.hls.ca

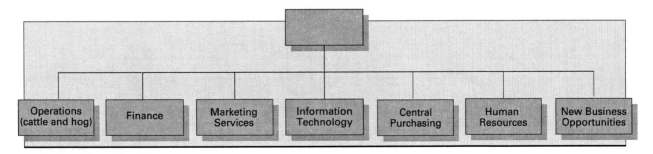

FIGURE 5-7

Functional Departmentalization at Heartland Livestock Services

One downside of functional specialization is that it can encourage greater loyalty to one's functional area, such as marketing, than to the organization as a whole, and can create competition between different functional areas. Companies want all of their employees on the same side, not vying with each other.

PRODUCT

Product departmentalization Grouping activities by product line.

Canadian Utilities Inc.
www.cul.ca

Another way to departmentalize is by product. This means that each major product area in the organization is under the authority of a manager who is a specialist in, and responsible for, everything to do with his or her product line.

In contrast to functional departments, **product departmentalization** creates relatively independent units. Any problem or issue that surfaces related to a product will fall under the responsibilities of that product's manager. Thus a major advantage of organizing around products is that it places ultimate responsibility for everything concerning a specific product with one manager, thus eliminating the potential for "passing the buck."

Canadian Utilities' organizational chart demonstrates a product-based departmentalization. See Figure 5-8.

GEOGRAPHY

Geographic departmentalization Grouping activities on the basis of territory.

Another way to departmentalize is on the basis of geography or territory—**geographic departmentalization**. For instance, the Canadian Forestry Service has five regional centres reporting to an assistant deputy minister (see Figure 5-9).

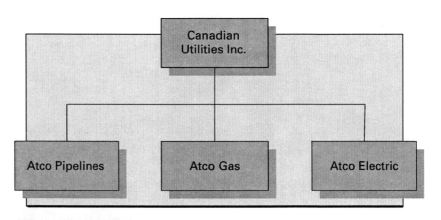

FIGURE 5-8
Product departmentalization at Canadian Utilities

What's the advantage to this form of departmentalization? It puts decision-making authority close to where the work is being done. If activities are physically dispersed and different locations face different types of problems, management will want to ensure that the people who make the decisions understand those differences. For instance, Denison Hydraulics has Western Canada, Eastern Canada, and Quebec sales and distribution centres. The Ontario Provincial Police have major operational units to cover northeastern Ontario, northwestern, central, western, eastern Ontario, and the Greater Toronto Area.

Denison Hydraulics
www.denisonhydraulics.com

Ontario Provincial Police
www.gov.on.ca/opp

CUSTOMER

The fastest-growing form of departmentalizing is by customer. Why? Because companies are learning that success requires staying close to the customer. Organizations that lose touch with the changing needs of their diverse customer base aren't likely to be around for too long. The primary force that has driven the growth of many current companies has been careful listening to and response to the needs of their customers.

Where an organization has a diverse set of customers that can be grouped around common interests, concerns, or needs, then a customer form of departmentalization makes sense. For instance, most provincial governments organize departments to service different customers. The Attorney General's office is divided into criminal court, family court, and small claims court. Provincial tax offices are organized according to customer needs into commercial taxes, employer health taxes, tax grants for seniors, and retail sales tax (see Figure 5-10). The ReMax real estate organization is subdivided to serve both residential and commercial customers. The Bank of Montreal separates its Personal and Commercial Client Group from its Corporate Services.

Customer departmentalization Grouping activities on the basis of common customers.

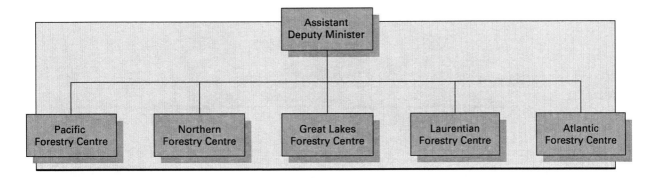

FIGURE 5-9

Geographic departmentalization at the Canadian Forestry Service

Bank of Montreal
www.bmo.ca

Remax Canada
www.remax.ca

PROCESS

The final pure form of departmentalization is by process. Figure 5-11 depicts the various production departments in Hilton Works in Hamilton, part of Stelco. The metal is melted in huge blast furnaces and poured into castings; the castings are then sent to the hot roll mill, where the metal is rolled into scaly coils of steel; next, the pickling process cleans the scale; the coils then go to the cold roll mill where they are rolled again but to a much more accurate tolerance since the surface is clean; after cold rolling the metal is annealed to remove the stress in the metal from the cold rolling operation; then the metal goes to a galvanize line to be coated against rust; and the metal is then ready for shipping. Since each process requires different skills and specialized equipment, this method offers a basis for the categorizing of activities.

Process departmentalization can be used for processing customers as well as products. If you have ever arrived at a major airport after an international flight, you probably went through several departments

Process departmentalization
Grouping activities on the basis of product or customer flow.

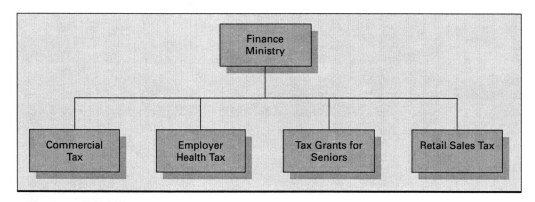

FIGURE 5-10

Customer departmentalization

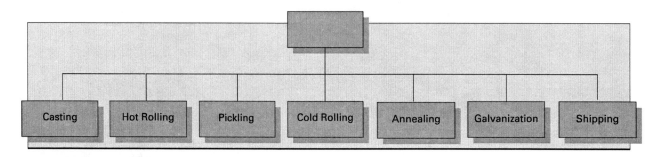

FIGURE 5-11

Process departmentalization in steel production at Stelco

between leaving the plane and heading for home. Immigration verifies your eligibility to enter Canada, you pick up your luggage at the arrivals carousel, and the customs department verifies your purchases for import.

BLENDING FUNCTION AND PRODUCT: THE MATRIX

The functional department offers the advantages of specialization. The product department has a greater focus on results but suffers from duplication of activities and resources. If the organization were completely organized around products—that is, if each product the company produced had its own supporting functional structure—the focus on results would again be high. Each product could have a product manager responsible for all activities related to that product. This, too, would result in redundancy, however, because each product would require its own set of functional specialists. Does any form combine the advantages of functional specialization with the focus and accountability that product departmentalization provides? The answer is yes, and it's called the **matrix**.

The matrix structure creates a dual chain of command. It explicitly breaks the principle of unity of command. Functional departmentalization is used to gain the economies of specialization. But overlaying the functional departments is a set of supervisors who are responsible for specific *products*, *projects*, or *programs* within the organization. (We'll use the terms products, projects, and programs interchangeably, since matrix structures can use any of the three).

Figure 5-12 illustrates the matrix structure of an aerospace firm. Notice that along the top of the figure are the familiar functions of engineering, accounting, human resources, and so forth. Along the vertical dimension, however, have been added the various projects that the aerospace firm is currently working on. Each project is directed by a supervisor who staffs his or her project with people from the functional departments. The addition of the vertical dimension to the traditional functional departments in effect weaves together elements of functional and product departmentalization—hence the term *matrix*.

How does the matrix work? Employees in the matrix report to two managers—their functional departmental supervisor and their product or project supervisor (see Dealing with a Difficult Issue). The project supervisors have authority over the functional members who are part of that supervisor's project team. For instance, the purchasing specialists who work on the Gamma project are responsible to both the supervisor of purchasing and the Gamma project supervisor. Authority is shared between the two supervisors. Typically, this is done by giving the project supervisor authority over project employees relative to the project's goals, while decisions such as promotions, salary recommendations, and annual reviews remain the functional supervisor's responsibility. To work effectively, project and functional supervisors must communicate regularly and coordinate the demands upon their common employees.

Matrix
A structural design that assigns specialists from functional departments to work on one or more projects that are led by a project manager.

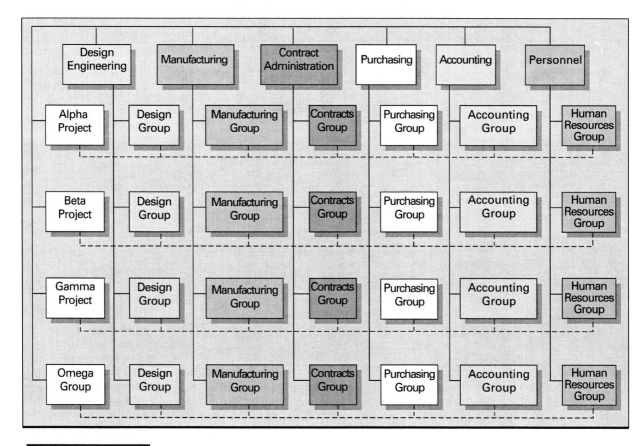

FIGURE 5-12

A matrix structure in an aerospace firm

FIGURE 5-13

Susan Mocsan at Brewers Retail in Ontario runs a project where some of the project staff are her direct reports and others report to a technical manager not involved in her project.

Susan Mocsan of Brewers Retail in Ontario finds herself in a matrix structure. As the manager of HRIS and payroll, she finds herself working with technical staff who are allocated to her project (the developing Human Resource Information System) but are under the actual supervision of a technical specialist. The technical staff must approach both Susan and their technical supervisor to approve vacation time. Susan provides input to their appraisal but does not create it. Susan has biweekly meetings with all her project staff, both technical and functional, and invites the technical supervisor to these meetings. If something unusual surfaces that requires a technical person's time elsewhere, the technical supervisor never pulls that person away from Susan without first checking with her. The matrix arrangement is workable because both managers communicate well, keep each other informed, and respect each other's needs.

The matrix creates a structure that possesses the strengths of both functional and product departmentalization, while avoiding the weaknesses of both. That is, the strength of the functional form lies in putting like specialists together, minimizing the numbers, and allowing for the pooling and sharing of specialized resources across products. Its primary drawback is the difficulty in coordinating the tasks of the specialists so that their activities are completed on time and within budget. The product form, on the other hand, has exactly the opposite benefits and disadvantages. It facilitates the coordination among specialists to achieve on-time completion and meet budget targets, and furthermore provides clear responsibility for all activities related to a product or project. But no one is responsible for the long-run technical development of the specialists, and this results in duplication of costs.

Dealing with a Difficult Issue

DO MATRIX STRUCTURES CREATE CONFUSED EMPLOYEES?

Workers in matrix structures face a difficult issue that never arose in traditional organizational structures. That is, they have at least two bosses. They are responsible to their functional supervisor, who has the responsibility to evaluate their performance and make salary increase determinations. Concurrently, these employees are responsible to their project leader for specific project tasks.

In this situation, whose authority takes precedence? Do employees give their functional supervisor's requests priority because, after all, it is this individual who handles the administrative and personnel-related paperwork? Or is it the project leader—who is more involved with the employees on a day-to-day basis—who gets the "top-billing"? Failure to complete the required tasks on the project could result in being removed from the project team—a decision that may place an employee's job in jeopardy. Are both supervisors given equal priority? Should employees simply accept that they have to serve "two masters"? What do you think?

WHY IS THERE MOVEMENT TO SIMPLER EMPLOYEE GROUPINGS?

Many of the departmentalizations mentioned above are highly complex and formalized, and decisions are made in a centralized fashion—resulting in rigid, often massive, multilevelled structures. Although they were designed to promote efficiency, they do not easily adjust to the dynamic world around them. As a result, more emphasis today has been given to organizations that focus on simplicity. As discussed in Chapter 1, changing organizational structures is one of the challenges facing many supervisors today. Let's look at what we mean by a simple structure.

If "bureaucracy" is the term that best describes most large organizations, "simple structure" is the one that best characterizes most small ones. A **simple structure** is defined more by what it is not than by what it is. It is not an elaborate structure.[1] If you see an organization that appears to have almost no structure, it is probably of the simple variety. By that we mean that it is low in complexity, has little formalization, and has its authority centralized in a single person. The simple structure is a "flat" organization; it usually has only two or three levels, employees who perform a variety of tasks, and one individual who makes most of the decisions.

The simple structure is most widely practised in small businesses in which the manager and the owner are one and the same. This is illustrated in Figure 5-14—an organization chart for a men's clothing retail store. Jack Singleton owns and manages this store. Although Jack employs five full-time salespeople, a cashier, and part-time weekend help, he "runs the show."

The strengths of the simple structure should be obvious. Communications are efficient, accountability is clear, and it has flexibility to respond to the changing environment. One major weakness is that, in the past, it was viewed as effective only in small organizations. It became

Simple structure
A non-elaborate structure low in complexity, with little formalization, and with authority centralized in a single person; a "flat" organization with only two or three levels.

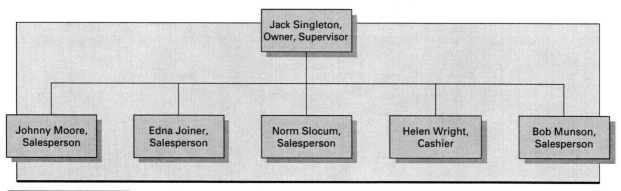

FIGURE 5-14

Jack Singleton's structure

increasingly inadequate as an organization grew, because the low degree of formalization and high degree of centralization resulted in information overloads at the top. As size increased, decision making became slower and eventually came to a standstill as the single person in charge tried to continue making all the decisions. This often proved to be the undoing of many small businesses. The simple structure's other weakness is that it is risky: everything depends on one person. One heart attack, or a fatal auto accident on the way to work, can literally destroy the organization—for the only one who held the critical information is now gone. However, these weaknesses were not necessarily the fault of the simple structure. Rather, those in charge just couldn't give up the control that they had so enjoyed.

ARE THERE SIMPLE STRUCTURES FOR LARGER ORGANIZATIONS?

If yesterday's organizations had one feature in common, it was the rigid boundaries that separated employees from other members of the organization. Employees were often segregated by the jobs they did and rarely interacted with others in different parts of the business. A select few "ran the show." That setup may no longer provide the best advantage in organizations. Some of those boundaries are being broken down, giving employees more interaction with others whom they count on for getting jobs done. In business today, we call this arrangement the horizontal structure.

THE HORIZONTAL STRUCTURE

Before we begin this discussion, let's set the record straight. A horizontal structure is really nothing new. **Horizontal structures** are simply very flat structures—basically the same as what we called simple structures. What's new about them, however, is that they are being used not only in small businesses, but in giant companies such as AT&T, Du Pont, General Electric, and Motorola. Horizontal organizations, as the term implies, means job-related activities cut across all parts of the organization. Rather than having employees perform specialized jobs and work in departments with people who do similar tasks, they are grouped with other employees who have different skills—forming a work team. These individuals come together to work toward a common objective. They are given the authority to make the necessary decisions to do the work, and are held accountable for measurable outcomes.[2] Their jobs encompass the entire work to be completed, from beginning to end—rather than focusing on individualized job tasks.[3] In a horizontal structure, control shifts from those in management to supervisors and workers.

Working in a horizontal organization brings about other changes for supervisors. For instance, supervisors reward employees for mastering multiple skills, rather than just a few specialized skills. The more jobs

Horizontal structures Very flat structures used in small businesses as well in as giant companies in which job-related activities cut across all parts of the organization.

employees can do, the more valuable they are. Additionally, rather than being evaluated on the work one individual does, the rewards are based on how the team performs. In a horizontal organization, the supervisor's evaluations are no longer the only ones. Instead, employees are likely to be evaluated by anyone who has knowledge of their work. This could include a selection of subordinates, coworkers, and customers, as well as the supervisor. Known as 360-degree evaluation or multisource evaluation, it is being increasingly used in organizations, both for developmental information and evaluative feedback.

FITTING EMPLOYEE GROUPING TO THE SITUATION

Although the movement toward simple structures brings with it many strengths and may provide an exciting work atmosphere, keep one thing in mind. Simple structures must be used only where appropriate. The question then arises: When does each of the different groupings work best? For example, in industries where efficiency of mass production is warranted, grouping employees by the jobs they perform may better serve the organization. The answer will depend on the environment in which you work.

Organizations group employees in a given way for a particular reason. They don't implement structures haphazardly for the fun of it. It's too expensive, and very difficult, to make these changes. When an organization does make such a change, you should learn from it. Recognize what the structure is telling you as a supervisor. If grouping employees by the job performed appears to be the norm, then your organization has made the decision that efficiency matters most. Therefore, to be successful in this element of your supervisory job, you need to focus on being efficient and continue refining your current skills. That may mean emphasizing work specialization for your employees—and yourself, too. In such an arrangement, you'll also be given clues on how best to make some of your decisions. You'll want to give greater weight to the alternatives that are most cost effective or provide greater output for a given input. Play to the strength of the employee grouping—that's usually what you'll be rewarded for.

Similar guidelines can be found in other employee groupings. For example, grouping by the product produced means that the "bigger" picture is most important. That is, achieving organizational goals is a "must," and the company is willing to use resources to do it.

ORGANIZING YOUR EMPLOYEES' JOBS

Once your departmental structure is in place, you need to organize the specific jobs of each of your employees. How do you do that? By identifying the tasks to be done, combining them into jobs, and then formalizing the process by creating job descriptions. This process may be coordinated by the human resources department but will never be totally completed by them. The closer to the tasks and jobs that the people analyzing them are, the more accurate they will be. The supervisor, therefore, is always involved in identifying tasks and creating job descriptions to some extent.

IDENTIFYING THE TASKS TO BE DONE

Begin by making a list of all the specific tasks with which your department has been charged. These are the tasks that, when effectively accomplished, result in your department successfully achieving its goals. Figure 5-15 illustrates a partial list drawn up by a production supervisor in a large book publishing company.

- Attend initial planning meeting with acquisition editor to launch a new book

- Contact with acquisition editors

- Contact with authors

- Contact with marketing personnel

- Contact with advertising group

- Contact with manufacturing buyers

- Develop production schedules for each book

- Design the internal layout of books and develop sample pages

- Draw up detailed design specifications for the computer, to be used for creating pages

- Have figures and tables drawn

- Design book covers

- Organize and direct weekly coordination meetings for each book

- Proof galleys and pages

FIGURE 5-15

Partial list of tasks in a book production department

COMBINING TASKS INTO JOBS

It is unlikely that one person can do all the tasks that need to be accomplished. So the tasks need to be combined into individual jobs.

The supervisor will create jobs by separating specialized tasks, allowing each employee to become more proficient at his or her special job.

So the book production supervisor will create specific jobs such as copy editor, proofreader, photo editor, production coordinator, and designer.

In addition to grouping similar tasks together, supervisors need to be sure that workloads within the department are balanced. Employee morale and productivity will suffer if some employees' jobs are significantly more difficult or time-consuming than others. The supervisor should take into consideration the physical, mental, and time demands that the various tasks require, and use this information to help balance the workloads among department employees. Skills required will also be a natural basis for grouping tasks.

CREATING JOB DESCRIPTIONS

Job description
A written statement of what a jobholder does, how the job is done, and why it is done.

A **job description** is a written statement of what a jobholder does, how the job is done, and why it is done. It typically portrays job duties, working conditions, and operating responsibilities. Figure 5-16 illustrates a job description for a production editor in a publishing company. Note each of its elements. It lists the job title, to whom the position reports, and the department to which the position is assigned. It notes wage category (exempt meaning exempted from overtime payments). There is a brief description of the job followed by a more specific list of duties, all of which are phrased using action verbs. This list must be comprehensive and accurate. There are omissions from this particular job description, however, that could lead to potential problems for a supervisor. It does not say who created the description or when. Without this, the supervisor does not know whether the description is up-to-date and accurate. It also does not include job qualifications—the skills needed to do the job effectively. This is important information for anyone needing to make hiring decisions. A supervisor may not necessarily know the skills required, especially if the supervisor lacks experience in that position.

Why do supervisors need to write job descriptions for each job in their department? For two reasons. First, the job description provides the supervisor with a formal document describing what the employee is supposed to be doing. It acts as a standard against which the supervisor can determine how well the employee is performing. This, in turn, can be used to make performance appraisal, feedback, wage adjustment, and training decisions. Second, the job description helps employees learn their job duties and clarifies the results that management expects them to achieve.

Note that supervisors are not totally on their own in developing job descriptions. If no template has been created by a human resources

Job Title: Project Production Editor

Department: College Book Editorial Production

Wage Category: Exempt

Reports to: Business Team Production Supervisor

Job Class: 7-12B

Job Statement:
 Performs and oversees editing work in the areas of book specifications, design, composition, printing, and binding. May carry a number of books at the same time. Works under general supervision. Incumbent exercises initiative and independent judgment in the performance of assigned tasks.

Job Duties:

1. Identifies activities to be completed, determines sequencing, and prepares a schedule for the ten-month process.

2. Performs or contracts out copy editing of book manuscript.

3. Coordinates specification (size, colour, paper, covers) and design (typefaces, art) with assigned designer. Coordinates preparation of galleys and pages with manufacturing buyers and compositor.

4. Distributes scheduling-status reports to acquisition editors and others as needed.

5. Acts as liaison with authors on all production issues.

6. Checks all permissions for completeness and accuracy.

7. Responsible for maintaining in-stock date set at initial launch meeting.

8. Performs related duties as assigned by team supervisor.

FIGURE 5-16

A job description for a production editor in a publishing company

division, information is available elsewhere. For instance, HRDC (Human Resource Development Canada) provides labour market profiles for many occupations (see **www.on.hrdc-drhc.gc.ca/english/lmi/eaid/occ.info/ojp/occupr_e.html**). Various guides are also available through the Internet (e.g., **www.farmshow.net/oahrc/handbook/book22.html**, and **http://ttg.sba.dal.ca/sba/profs/jduffy/jobdes/JobDes.html**)

www.on.hrdc-drhc.gc.ca/english/lmi/eaid/occ.info/ojp/occupr_e.html
HRDC site with occupational profiles for 157 occupations

www.farmshow.net/oahrc/handbook/book22.html
Job description information from the Ontario Agricultural HR Committee

http://ttg.sba.dal.ca/sba/profs/jduffy/jobdes/JobDes.html
Job Description advice from Dr. John Duffy at Dalhousie University

5. When a leather manufacturer groups some employees under a supervisor to dye the leather, and another group with a different supervisor to cut the leather, _____ is being demonstrated.
   a. functional departmentalization
   b. geographic departmentalization
   c. process departmentalization
   d. product departmentalization
6. Identify the five different ways in which you can departmentalize, or group, your employees.
7. A strength of the matrix structure is that it capitalizes on the accountability of product departmentalization and the efficiency of work specialization. True or false?
8. Which one of the following is not reflective of the term *job description?*
   a. A job description is a written statement of what a jobholder does.
   b. A job description involves allocation of duties, assignment of authority, responsibility, and accountability.
   c. A job description defines how and why a job is done.
   d. A job description typically portrays job duties and working conditions.

THE INCREASING USE OF TEAMS

Team
Members are committed to a common purpose, have a set of specific performance goals, and hold themselves mutually accountable for the team's results.

Teams are increasingly becoming the prime vehicle around which work is being designed. Why? Because teams typically outperform individuals when the tasks being done require multiple skills, judgement, and experience. As organizations restructure themselves to compete more effectively and efficiently, they are turning to teams as a way to better utilize employees' talents. Organizations are finding that teams are more flexible and responsive to changing events than are departments or other forms of permanent groupings. They can be quickly assembled, deployed, refocused, and disbanded.

Teams fall into one of three categories, depending on their objectives. Some organizations use teams to provide advice. For instance, they create temporary task forces to recommend ways to cut costs, improve quality, or select a site for a new plant. Some organizations use teams to manage. They introduce management teams at various levels in the organization to run things. However, supervisors are most likely to be involved with teams that are created to make or do things. They include production teams, design teams, and office teams that handle administrative work.

Companies such as Pratt and Whitney Canada, Honeywell, Motorola, Dofasco, and Imperial Oil are making work teams the centrepiece in creating new work units. For instance, the Imperial Oil refinery in Dartmouth, Nova Scotia, threatened with closure just a few years ago, is now an industry leader thanks to its organizational redesign based on teams.

In organizations reorganizing work around teams, supervisors are learning to effectively coordinate team activity. In many cases, management's emphasis has been on creating self-managed teams. As we'll see, this is redefining the supervisor's managerial role.

TURNING GROUPS INTO TEAMS

Groups and teams are not necessarily the same thing. Many formal work groups are merely individuals who sporadically interact, but who have no collective commitment that requires joint effort. That is, the group's total performance is merely the sum of the individual group members' performance.

What differentiates a team is that members are committed to a common purpose, have a set of specific performance goals, and hold themselves mutually accountable for the team's results. Teams, in other words, are something greater than the sum of their parts. Figure 5-17 illustrates how a work group evolves into a real team. The primary force that moves a work group toward a real high-performing team is its emphasis on performance.

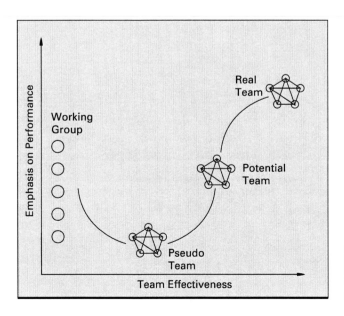

FIGURE 5-17

Comparing groups and teams

A working group is a group of individuals who interact primarily to share information and to make decisions, in order to help each other perform within a given area of responsibility. Members of such a group have no need or opportunity to engage in collective work that requires joint effort, so their performance is merely the sum of each group member's individual contribution. There is no positive synergy to create an overall level of performance that is greater than the sum of the inputs.

A *pseudoteam* is the product of negative synergy. The performance or output of the whole is less than the potential of the individual parts, because of factors such as poor communication, antagonistic conflicts, and avoidance of responsibilities. Even though members may call themselves a team, they're not. Because it doesn't focus on collective performance and because members have no interest in shaping a common purpose, a pseudoteam actually underperforms a working group.

"Going in the right direction but not there yet" is the best way to describe a *potential team*. It recognizes the need for, and is really trying hard to achieve, higher performance, but some roadblocks are in the way. Its purpose and goals may need greater clarity or the team may need better coordination. The result is that it has not yet established a sense of collective accountability.

The ultimate goal is to become a real team. This is a unit with a set of common characteristics that lead to consistently high performance.

BUILDING REAL TEAMS

Studies of effective teams have found that they contain a small number of people with complementary skills who are equally committed to a common purpose, goals, and working approach for which they hold themselves mutually accountable.[4] This section describes the six characteristics of real teams.

SMALL SIZE

The best teams tend to be small. When they have more than about 10 members, it becomes difficult for them to get much done. They have trouble interacting constructively and reaching agreement. Large numbers of people usually cannot develop the common purpose, goals, approach, and mutual accountability of a real team. They tend merely to go through the motions. So in designing effective teams, keep them to 10 people or fewer. If the natural working unit is larger, and you want a team effort, break the group into subteams. Federal Express, for instance, has divided the 1000 clerical workers at its headquarters into teams of five to ten members each.

COMPLEMENTARY SKILLS

To perform effectively, a team requires three types of skills. First, it needs people with *technical expertise*. Second, it needs people with the *problem-solving and decision-making skills* to identify problems, generate alternatives, evaluate those alternatives, and make competent choices. Finally, teams need people with good *interpersonal skills* (listening, feedback, conflict resolution).

No team can achieve its performance potential without developing all three types of skills. The right mix is crucial. Too much of one at the expense of others will result in lower team performance.

Teams don't need to have all the complementary skills at the beginning. Where team members value personal growth and development, one or more members often take responsibility to learn the skills in which the group is deficient, as long as the skill potential exists. Additionally, personal compatibility among members is not critical to the team's success if the technical, decision-making, and interpersonal skills are in place.

COMMON PURPOSE

Does the team have a meaningful purpose that all members aspire to? This purpose is a vision. It's broader than any specific goals. High-performing teams have a common and meaningful purpose that provides direction, momentum, and commitment for members.

For example, the development team at Apple Computer that designed the Macintosh was almost religiously committed to creating a user-friendly machine that would revolutionize the way people used computers. Production teams at Saturn are united by the common purpose of building a North American automobile that can successfully compete in terms of quality and price with the best of Japanese cars.

Members of successful teams put a tremendous amount of time and effort into discussing, shaping, and agreeing upon a purpose that belongs to them collectively and individually. This common purpose, when accepted by the team, becomes the equivalent of what celestial navigation is to a ship captain—it provides direction and guidance under any and all conditions.

SPECIFIC GOALS

Successful teams translate their common purpose into specific, measurable, and realistic performance goals. Just as goals lead individuals to higher performance (see Chapter 2), they also energize teams. Specific goals facilitate clear communication and help teams maintain their focus on getting results. Examples of specific team goals might be responding to all customers within 24 hours, cutting production-cycle time by 30 per cent over the next six months, or maintaining equipment at a level of zero downtime every month.

COMMON APPROACH, SHARED "MENTAL MODELS"

Goals are the ends a team strives to attain. Defining and agreeing upon a common approach assures that the team is unified on the *means* for achieving those ends.

Recent research suggests that sharing "mental models" greatly enhances a team's effectiveness.[5] This means that the more alike team members are in terms of their understanding, the more quickly they can cooperate to cope with difficult and changing conditions. To adapt effectively, team members need to be able to predict what their coworkers will do and what they will need to do it. Common understanding will greatly enhance this adaptability. This means common understanding of the technology and equipment—functioning, limitations, likely problems; the job itself—procedures, likely scenarios, task strategies; team interaction—who is responsible for what, how communication and information flow; and the team members—individual strengths and weaknesses, attitudes, and preferences.

MUTUAL ACCOUNTABILITY

The final characteristic of high-performing teams is accountability at both the individual and group level.

Successful teams make members individually and jointly accountable for the team's purpose, goals, and approach. Members understand what they are individually responsible for and what they are jointly responsible for.

Social loafing
The tendency of group members to do less than they are capable of individually when their individual contribution is not measured.

Studies have shown that when teams focus only on group-level performance targets, and ignore individual contributions and responsibilities, team members often engage in **social loafing**.[6] They reduce their efforts because their individual contributions can't be identified. In effect, they become "free riders" and coast on the group's effort. The result is that the team's overall performance suffers. This reaffirms the importance of measuring both individual contributions to the team as well as the team's overall performance. And successful teams have members who collectively feel responsible for their team's performance (see Figure 5-18).

OVERCOMING THE OBSTACLES

Critical obstacles that can prevent a team from becoming high performers include a weak sense of direction, infighting, shirking of responsibilities, lack of trust, critical skill gaps, and lack of external support.

There are a number of things supervisors can do to overcome the obstacles mentioned and help teams to reach their full potential.

CREATE A CLEAR PURPOSE AND GOALS

High-performance teams have both a clear understanding of their goals and a belief that the goals embody a worthwhile or important result.

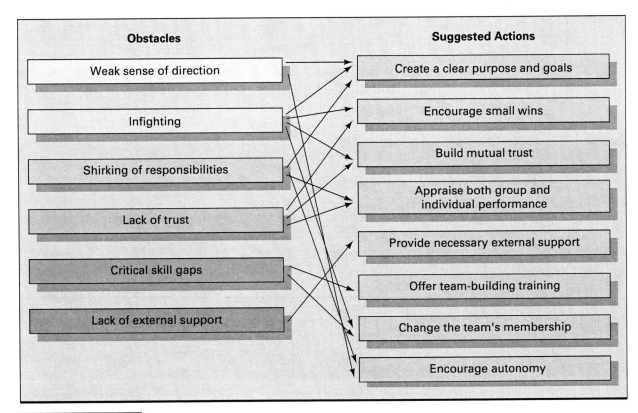

Obstacles	Suggested Actions
Weak sense of direction	Create a clear purpose and goals
Infighting	Encourage small wins
Shirking of responsibilities	Build mutual trust
Lack of trust	Appraise both group and individual performance
Critical skill gaps	Provide necessary external support
Lack of external support	Offer team-building training
	Change the team's membership
	Encourage autonomy

FIGURE 5-18

Creating effective teams

Moreover, the importance of these goals encourages individuals to subli-
mate personal concerns to the team goals. In effective teams, members
are committed to the team's goals, know what they are expected to
accomplish, and understand how they will work together to achieve
these goals.

As a supervisor, your job is to ensure that teams under your leadership have a clear purpose and goals. Whether you participate in setting
them or delegate this task to the team itself, it's your responsibility to
make sure that it is accomplished. Make the goals "front-of-mind" by
posting them, mentioning them at meetings, giving frequent feedback
regarding their accomplishment, and questioning decisions and proposals in terms of those goals.

ENCOURAGE TEAMS TO GO FOR SMALL WINS

The building of real teams takes time. Team members have to learn to
think and work as a team. New teams can't be expected to hit home runs,
right at the beginning, every time they come to bat. So encourage the
team to begin by trying to hit singles.

Help the team identify and set attainable goals. The eventual goal of cutting overall costs by 30 percent, for instance, can be dissected into five or ten smaller and more easily attainable goals. As the smaller goals are attained, the team's success is reinforced. Cohesiveness is increased and morale improves. Confidence builds. Success breeds success, but it's a lot easier for young teams to reach their goals if they start with small wins.

BUILD MUTUAL TRUST

Trust is fragile. It takes a long time to build and can be easily destroyed. However, there are things a supervisor can do to create a climate of mutual trust.[7]

Keep team members informed by explaining upper-management decisions and policies and by providing accurate feedback. Create a climate of openness where employees are free to discuss problems without fear of retaliation. Be candid about your own problems and limitations. Make sure you're available and approachable when employees need support. Be respectful and listen to team members' ideas. Develop a reputation for being fair, objective, and impartial in your treatment of team members. Show consistency in your actions, and avoid erratic and unpredictable behaviour. Finally, be dependable and honest. Make sure you follow through on all explicit and implied promises.

Interestingly, the way trust appears to work within a work group is that high trust translates into group effort, whereas low trust translates into individual effort.[8] Lack of trust, therefore, does not destroy performance, but it does redirect the effort to behaviour which the individual can control. As a result, performance that depends on coordination and cooperation is much more likely to suffer.

APPRAISE BOTH GROUP AND INDIVIDUAL PERFORMANCE

Team members should all share in the glory when their team succeeds, and they should share in the blame when it fails. So a large measure of each member's performance appraisal should be based on the overall team's performance. But members need to know that they can't ride on the backs of others. Therefore, each member's individual contribution should also be identified and made a part of his or her overall performance appraisal.

PROVIDE THE NECESSARY EXTERNAL SUPPORT

You're the link between the teams and upper management. As such, it's your responsibility to make sure that teams have the necessary organizational resources to accomplish their goals. That means you should be prepared to make the case to your boss and other key decision makers in the organization for tools, equipment, training, personnel, physical space, or other resources the teams may require.

OFFER TEAM-BUILDING TRAINING

Teams, especially in their early stages of formation, will need training to build their skills. Typically, these skills include problem solving, communication, negotiation, conflict resolution, and group process. If you can't personally provide this kind of skill training for your team members, look to specialists in your organization who can, or secure the funds to bring in outside facilitators who specialize in this kind of training.

CHANGE THE TEAM'S MEMBERSHIP

When teams get bogged down in their own inertia or internal fighting, allow them to rotate members. You might want to manage this change by considering how certain personalities will mesh, and reforming teams in ways that will better combine skills. If lack of leadership is the problem, use your knowledge of the people involved to create teams in which there will be a high probability that a leader will emerge.

ENCOURAGE AUTONOMY

The supervisor can refuse to make decisions or solve problems until the team has attempted to deal with it. Paul Dolan, the ATM production manager at NCR with over 90 people organized into self-directed teams reporting to him, supports this concept wholeheartedly. When an individual comes to him about an issue, he will first ask, "What have you done about it?" Once the individual has tried to work within the team to solve a problem, Paul is then willing to come in as a conciliator or adjudicator. The attempt must be made first within the team, however. For example, there was some grumbling over perceived unfairness when two pregnant employees were given light duties. Paul refused to step in. Subsequently, the whole team discussed the issue and resolved it. As a result, their problem-solving skills had grown and they felt they had accomplished something as a team.

A study of over 100 construction and road crews in the northeastern United States[9] investigated the effect of performance barriers on the work crews' effectiveness, which crews were more successful in overcoming those barriers, and why. To no one's surprise, performance constraints, such as machine breakdowns, had a negative impact on performance. However, some groups were more likely than others to take action to prevent these problems or minimize their impact. What was distinctive about those groups that were much more effective in their problem management strategies? They were more likely to be self-managing—already given the responsibility for making decisions for the team. They also had strong teamwork processes in that they were confident in approaching their tasks, their experience had led them to a common understanding of what might go wrong and what to do about it, and there was excellent communication and coordination among the team members. Their managers were also distinctive in that they tended to encourage self-management and autonomy. For example, forepeople encouraged their crews to plan activities, set performance goals, encourage each other, and monitor their performance and work processes. County managers linked with these crews provided the crews some discretion in decision making, recognized crews regularly, and provided resource support.

What do you see as the potential difficulties in giving work crews more power? Could the above scenario be possible in a unionized environment? What are the challenges for a supervisor of a self-managed team? What in the road crews' task and environment might help them pull together as a team? Are these conditions present in most jobs?

Are You Comprehending
What You're Reading?

9. Describe the six characteristics of teams.

10. Personal compatibility among members is not critical to the team's success if the complementary skills are in place. True or false?

11. Which of the following is an obstacle to creating an effective team?
    a. a weak sense of direction
    b. lack of external support
    c. shirking of responsibilities
    d. all of the above

12. "Encourage teams to go for small wins" means:
    a. Help the team identify and set major goals so they will work together towards significant accomplishments.
    b. Allow them to rotate and replace members until they achieve an effective meshing of individuals.
    c. Involve them in team-building activities aimed at creating a lot of fun and a supportive atmosphere.
    d. Break down overall goals into smaller ones that are easier to achieve.

EMPOWERING OTHERS
THROUGH DELEGATION

Contemporary supervisors need to learn to empower others. Empowerment means increasing your employees' involvement in their work through making decisions and taking responsibility for work outcomes. Two ways to empower people are to delegate authority to them and to redesign their jobs. In this section, we'll address delegation. In Chapter 9, we'll show you how to empower people through job design.

ASSESSING YOURSELF: ARE YOU WILLING TO DELEGATE?

Think of times when you have been in charge of a group - this could be a full-time or part-time work situation, a student work group, or similar experience. Complete the following questionnaire by recording how you feel about each statement according to this scale. Remember to be honest in your answers.[10]

> 5 = Strongly disagree
>
> 4 = Disagree
>
> 3 = Neutral
>
> 2 = Agree
>
> 1 = Strongly agree

When in charge of a group I find:

___ 1. Most of the time other people are too inexperienced to do things, so I prefer to do them myself.

___ 2. It often takes more time to explain things to others than to just do them myself.

___ 3. Mistakes made by others are costly, so I don't assign much work to them.

___ 4. Some things simply should not be delegated to others.

___ 5. I often get quicker action by doing a job myself.

_____ 6. Many people are good only at very specific tasks, and thus can't be assigned additional responsibilities.

_____ 7. Many people are too busy to take on additional work.

_____ 8. Most people just aren't ready to handle additional responsibility.

_____ 9. In my position, I should be entitled to make my own decisions.

SCORING KEY AND INTERPRETATION

This questionnaire gives you an idea of your willingness to empower others through delegation. Add up your score on the nine items. Possible total scores range from 9 to 45. The higher your score, the more willing you appear to be to delegate to others. A score of 36 or higher indicates a strong willingness to allow others to assume workplace responsibilities and exercise self-control in their work. Scores in the 25-35 range imply serious reluctance to give up authority and control. Scores below 25 suggest considerable room for improvement in this area.

SKILL BASICS

There is no question that effective supervisors need to be able to delegate. But supervisors tell us that it's hard for them. Why? They're typically afraid to give up control. Tammy Abel of the Winnipeg Student Employment Centre says, "One of the hardest things to do is delegate. I'm new in my position and I like to know exactly what is happening. It is hard to let go and let someone else do something even when I know I should because I don't have time or because it would be a great opportunity to develop staff." Tammy is learning, however. This year she was approached by a Quebec HRDC office asking whether her centre would compete in a national résumé contest. At first Tammy declined, due to her workload, but then realized she did not have to do it herself and delegated it to one of her staff. Another situation arose in which one of her senior staff members approached her about an idea. There was a new morning variety show on local television called The Big Breakfast. The show suggested that the employment centre participate in a regular slot on the show advertising their services and the job opportunities currently available for students. Previously, Tammy had been in charge of media relations and had enjoyed her experiences. She was also aware of the need to be careful in presenting the right image. However, she knew she needed to take a backseat role in this situation. Tammy delegated the entire project to the senior staff member, coaching him, but letting him do all the preparation and the actual "on air" episodes for 10 weeks during the summer. He loved doing it and did a good job.

In this section, we will show that delegation increases a supervisor's effectiveness and that, when done properly, still provides supervisory control.

WHAT IS DELEGATION?

Delegation is frequently depicted as a four-step process: 1. allocation of duties; 2. delegation of authority; 3. assignment of responsibility; and 4. creation of accountability.

Delegation
A four-step process of allocating duties, delegating authority, assigning responsibility, and creating accountability.

1. **Allocation of duties.** Duties are the tasks and activities that a manager desires to have someone else do. Before you can delegate authority, you must allocate to a subordinate the duties over which the authority extends. You must explain to the person exactly what you wish him or her to do.

2. **Delegation of authority.** The essence of the delegation process is empowering the subordinate to act for you. It is passing to the subordinate the formal rights to act on your behalf. Ask yourself: Did I give my subordinate enough authority to get the materials, the equipment, and the support from others necessary to get the job done?

3. **Assignment of responsibility.** When authority is delegated, you must assign responsibility. That is, when you give someone "rights," you must also assign to that person a corresponding "obligation" to perform. This means clarifying not only the duties but also the standards and the deadlines.

Accountability
Holding a person to performing an assignment in a satisfactory manner.

4. **Creation of accountability.** To complete the delegation process, you must create **accountability**; that is, you must hold your subordinate answerable for properly carrying out his or her duties. So while responsibility means a subordinate is obliged to carry out assigned duties, accountability means the subordinate must perform the assignment in a satisfactory manner. Subordinates are responsible for the completion of tasks assigned to them, and are accountable to you for the satisfactory performance of that work. If you establish follow-up checkpoints, they will keep their accountability in mind.

DELEGATION IS NOT ABDICATION

If you dump tasks on a subordinate without clarifying exactly what is to be done, the range of the subordinate's freedom, the expected level of performance, when the tasks are to be completed, and similar concerns, you are abdicating responsibility and inviting trouble. But don't fall into the trap of assuming that, in order to avoid the appearance of abdicating, you should minimize delegation. Unfortunately, this is the approach taken by many new and inexperienced supervisors. Lacking confidence in their subordinates, or fearful that they will be criticized for their subordinates' mistakes, they try to do everything themselves.

It may very well be true that you're capable of doing the tasks you delegate to your subordinates better, faster, or with fewer mistakes. The catch is that your time and energy are scarce resources. It's not possible for you to do everything yourself. So you need to learn to delegate if you're going to be effective in your job. This suggests two important points. First, you should expect and accept some mistakes by your subordinates. It's part of delegation. Mistakes are often good learning experiences for your subordinates, as long as their costs are not excessive. Second, to ensure that the costs of mistakes don't exceed the value of the learning, you need to put adequate controls in place. As we'll show, delegation without proper feedback controls that let you know when there are serious problems is abdication.

DELEGATION SKILLS

A number of actions differentiate the effective from the ineffective delegator. The following summarizes those actions.

1. **Clarify the assignment.** Begin by determining what is to be delegated and to whom. You need to identify the person best capable of doing the task, then determine if he or she has the time and motivation to do the job.

   Assuming you have a willing and able subordinate, it is your responsibility to provide clear information on what is being delegated, the results you expect, and any time or performance expectations you hold.

   Unless there is an overriding need to adhere to specific methods, you should delegate only the end results. That is, get agreement on what is to be done and the end results expected, but let the subordinate decide on the means. By focusing on goals and allowing the employee the freedom to use his or her own judgement as to how those goals are to be achieved, you increase trust between you and the employee, improve the employee's motivation, and enhance accountability for the results. Diane McArthur at ServiceOntario works with subordinates who need to produce important reports. Even though she is an excellent writer herself, she cannot do all the reports, so they must be delegated. Diane thinks carefully, however, about the feedback she gives her subordinates after reports, keeping her focus on the position being expressed in the paper—was the right concept described, capturing the full breadth of the pertinent information? Diane tries not to make editorial comments about the writing itself because everyone expresses him- or herself differently and she needs to give her subordinates that freedom.

2. **Specify the subordinate's range of discretion.** Every act of delegation comes with constraints. You're delegating authority to act, but not unlimited authority. What you're delegating is authority to act on certain issues and, on those issues, within certain guidelines. You need to specify all guidelines so subordinates know, in no uncertain terms, the range of their discretion. When this has been successfully communicated, both you and the subordinate will have the same idea of the limits to the latter's authority and how far he or she can go without checking further with you.

   How much authority do you give a subordinate? In other words, how tightly do you draw the guidelines? The best answer is that you should allocate enough authority to allow the subordinate to successfully complete the task. Your level of confidence in the employee's ability should help establish appropriate guidelines.

3. **Allow the subordinate to participate.** If you allow employees to participate in determining what is delegated, how much authority is needed to get the job done, and the standards by which they'll be judged, you increase employee motivation, satisfaction, and accountability for performance.

   Be aware, however, that participation can present its own set of potential problems. For example, some subordinates are personally motivated to expand their authority beyond what they need and beyond what they are capable of handling. Allowing such people too much participation in deciding the tasks they should take on and the level of authority they must have can undermine the effectiveness of the delegation process.

4. **Inform others that delegation has occurred.** Delegation should not take place in a vacuum. The supervisor, the employee, and anyone else who may be affected by the delegation act all need to be informed. This includes people outside the organization as well as inside. If you fail to follow through on this step, your subordinate's authority will probably be called into question. Failure to inform others makes conflicts likely and decreases the chances

that your subordinate will be able to accomplish the delegated task efficiently.

5. **Establish feedback controls.** There is always the possibility that a subordinate will misuse the discretion that he or she has been delegated. The establishment of controls to monitor the subordinate's progress increases the likelihood that important problems will be identified early and that the task will be completed on time and to the desired specifications.

   Ideally, controls should be determined at the time of the initial assignment. Agree on a specific time for completion of the task, and then set progress dates when the subordinate will report back on how well he or she is doing and any major problems that have surfaced. This can be supplemented with periodic spot checks to ensure that authority guidelines are not being abused, organization policies are being followed, and proper procedures are being met. But too much of a good thing can be harmful. If the controls are too constraining, the subordinate will be deprived of the opportunity to build self-confidence. A well-designed control system permits your subordinate to make small mistakes, but quickly alerts you when big mistakes are imminent.

6. **When problems surface, insist on recommendations from the subordinate.** Many supervisors fall into the trap of letting subordinates reverse the delegation process: the subordinate runs into a problem and then comes back to the supervisor for advice or a solution. Avoid being sucked into reverse delegation by insisting from the beginning that when subordinates want to discuss a problem with you, they come prepared with a recommendation. When you delegate downward, the subordinate's job includes making necessary decisions. Don't allow the subordinate to push decisions back upward to you.

APPLYING YOUR SKILLS

This is a role-playing exercise. Break into groups of four to six students. One student in each group will assume the role of Chris Hall and one the role of Dale Morgan. The other students will serve as observers and evaluators.

Students playing the roles of Chris and Dale should read the Situation and his or her respective role *only*. Observers should read the Situation and *both* roles, and record observations on their Observer's Sheet.

SITUATION

CHRIS HALL is Director of Research and Development for a small pharmaceutical manufacturer. Chris has six direct subordinates: Sue Traynor (Chris's secretary), DALE MORGAN (the laboratory supervisor), Todd Connor (quality standards supervisor), Linda Peters (patent coordination supervisor), Ruben Gomez (market coordination supervisor), and Marjorie England (senior project supervisor). Dale is the most senior of the five supervisors, and is generally acknowledged as the chief candidate to replace Chris when Chris is promoted.

CHRIS HALL'S ROLE

You have received your annual instructions from the CEO to develop next year's budget for your area. The task is relatively routine but takes quite a bit of time. In the past, you've always done the annual budget yourself. But this year, because your workload is exceptionally heavy, you've decided to try something different. You're going to assign budget preparation to one of your supervisors. The obvious choice is Dale Morgan. Dale has been with the company longest, is highly dependable, and, as your probable successor, is most likely to gain from the experience. The budget is due on your boss's desk in eight weeks. Last year it took you about 30 to 35 hours to complete. However, you had done a budget many times before. For a novice, it might take double that amount of time.

The budget process is generally straightforward. You start with last year's budget and modify it to reflect inflation and changes in departmental objectives. All the data that Dale will need are in your files or can be obtained from your other supervisors.

You have decided to walk over to Dale's office and inform him or her of your decision.

DALE MORGAN'S ROLE

You like Chris Hall. You think Chris is a first-rate manager and you've learned a lot from him or her. You also consider yourself Chris's heir apparent. To better prepare yourself to take Chris's job, you'd like to take on more of Chris's responsibilities.

Running the lab is a demanding job. You regularly come in around 7:00 a.m. and it's unusual for you to leave before 7:00 p.m. Four of the last five weekends, you've even come in on Saturday mornings to get your work done. But, within reasonable limits, you'd try to find the time to take on some of Chris's responsibilities.

As you sit behind your desk reviewing a lab report, Chris walks into your office.

SKILL APPLICATION—OBSERVER'S SHEET

INSTRUCTIONS

This exercise should take no more than 10 to 15 minutes. When completed, representatives from each group should discuss with the entire class how their delegation exercise went. Focus specifically on the skill behaviours presented in the previous section and any problems that surfaced.

	1 Poor	2	3 Good	4	5 Excellent
1. Chris was clear in defining the assignment—expected results, deadlines	☐	☐	☐	☐	☐
2. Chris specified the range of discretion—guidelines and authority	☐	☐	☐	☐	☐
3. Chris allowed Dale to participate in the delegation process	☐	☐	☐	☐	☐
4. Chris discussed informing others of Dale's involvement	☐	☐	☐	☐	☐
5. Chris established feedback controls—times, sessions	☐	☐	☐	☐	☐

SUMMARY

This summary is organized by the Learning Objectives.

1. Organizing is arranging jobs and groups of jobs in a department so that activities can be accomplished as planned.
2. Division of labour increases economic efficiency by allocating the most difficult and complex tasks to those employees with the highest skill level and paying other people less to do the less difficult and less skilled tasks.
3. The narrower the span of control, the more management levels are necessary to directly oversee activities. Wider spans create fewer managerial levels and flatter organization structures.
4. Line authority refers to the right to direct the work of subordinates. Supervisors with staff authority, on the other hand, advise, and assist line supervisors in accomplishing their job. So only line authority allows individuals to make decisions independently and without consulting others.
5. Organizations are becoming increasingly decentralized in order to meet competitive challenges through knowledgeable and rapid decision making.
6. Functional departmentalization means that group activities are organized around functions performed—for example, accounting, engineering, manufacturing, personnel, and purchasing.
7. The strength of the matrix is that it provides the economies of functional specialization with the accountability of product departmentalization. Its major weakness is that, because the principle of unity of command is broken, it is difficult to coordinate tasks of people who have more than one manager.
8. Job descriptions 1. provide supervisors with a formal document describing what the employee is supposed to be doing, 2. help employees learn their job duties, and 3. clarify the results that management expects.
9. Delegation consists of 1. allocation of duties, 2. delegation of authority, 3. assignment, and 4. creation of accountability.

UNDERSTANDING THE BASICS

KEY TERMS AND CONCEPTS

Accountability	Line authority
Authority	Matrix
Centralized authority	Organizing
Customer departmentalization	Process departmentalization
Decentralized authority	Product departmentalization
Delegation	Responsibility
Departmentalization	Simple structure
Division of labour	Social Loafing
Empowerment	Span of control
Functional authority	Staff authority
Functional departmentalization	Team
Geographic departmentalization	Telecommuting
Horizontal structures	Unity of command
Job description	

REVIEWING YOUR KNOWLEDGE

1. What are the limitations, if any, to division of labour?
2. How might wider spans of control lead to cost reductions for an organization?
3. What is functional authority? When is it useful to an organization?
4. What happens when authority and responsibility are out of balance?
5. What are the advantages of a) product, b) geographic, c) customer, and d) process departmentalization?
6. Why would an organization use a matrix structure?
7. Describe the four-step delegation process.
8. Is delegation synonymous with abdication? Discuss.

ANSWERS TO THE POP QUIZZES

1. **d. none of the above.** The idea that jobs should be broken down into the simplest of steps with one step generally assigned to each individual is known as **work specialization** or **division of labour**.

2. The advantages of division of labour relate to economic efficiencies. Skills are developed through repetition, less time is wasted, and training is easier and less costly. The disadvantages of division of labour are potential boredom, fatigue, stress, low productivity, poor quality, increased absenteeism and high turnover.

3. **False.** Early business experts believed top managers should have a smaller span of control.

4. **a. employees potentially have trouble coping with conflicting priorities and demands.** This is one element that early experts wanted to avoid when they identified chain of command. Conflicting priorities and demands create potential problems that can easily be avoided by having unity of command.

5. **c. process departmentalization.** This question focuses on grouping employees by the stage in the processing of the leather.

6. You can group your employees on the basis of function (work being done), product (product or service being generated) customer (group served), geography (location of operations), or process (work flow).

7. **True.** This statement identifies the strengths of the matrix structure, which includes combining the strengths of functional departmentalization (work specialization) and product departmentalization (accountability).

8. **b. A job description involves allocation of duties, assignment of authority, responsibility, and accountability.** Response b) actually describes the process of delegation, and has little to do with defining the term job description.

9. Teams tend to be small; require complementary skills (within the team are needed technical expertise, interpersonal skills, and problem-solving and decision-making skills); must have a common purpose and translate this into specific, measurable and realistic performance goals; agree upon a common approach; and hold members individually and jointly responsible for performance.

10. **True.** People do not need to be friends to work effectively together. Good interpersonal skills will ensure that indifference or dislike towards each other doesn't get in the way of successfully using their technical and problem-solving skills.

11. **d. all of the above**

12. **d. break down overall goals into smaller ones that are easier to achieve.**

CASE 5.A

Teams at NCR

You've been introduced previously to Paul Dolan, the ATM (Automatic Teller Machine) production manager at NCR in Waterloo, Ontario. Although there are more than 80 production employees, Paul is the first line of management above them. Paul manages to oversee production effectively yet still work a 40-hour week. He can do this, on the one hand, because the jobs assembling the ATMs are not highly complex, but also because the production employees are organized into three large self-directed teams that undertake extensive decision making and problem solving. They make these decisions through their participation on the following committees:

- Cycle time team—records how long it takes to build the ATM units
- Cycle audit team—regularly counts stock on an ongoing, weekly basis
- Rotation team—working with Paul, decides who should be moved and trained; because of changing production demands, employees sometimes need to be rotated between lines
- Payroll and production team—compiles weekly time for individuals and fills out appropriate forms; uses the information regarding hours and production for the week to determine productivity
- Vacation and recognition team—creates vacation schedule; determines which employees should be rewarded through special recognition program
- Health and safety team—regularly tours production area and monitors practices for safety
- Quality team (one for each line)—works with the process improvement support staff to create opportunities for greater efficiency

These committees meet on varying schedules depending on the demands of their role. However, each large team meets every morning for about 15 minutes to discuss any issues.

Employees are actively involved in each other's performance reviews. New hires receive team feedback at the three- and six-month points. Everyone's performance review is based partially on the entire ATM division's success in reaching shared objectives, partly on their team's effectiveness (as assessed by the team itself and by Paul), and partly on their own individual effectiveness, as assessed by other team members.

Paul says one aspect critical to the teams succeeding is management of the escalation process. By this he means that it is important to contain conflicts and get them dealt with at the team level so he does not have to handle them. Therefore, he screens all concerns brought to him by first making sure there has already been an attempt to deal with them at the team level.

RESPONDING TO THIS CASE

1. Production demands are increasing. Paul says that, although most people are on day shift right now, there will soon be two more full shifts. What difficulties will this cause? How can the current three teams anticipate and deal with these?

2. What is different about being a fairly low-skilled employee in this manufacturing environment as compared to working in a more traditional plant? For example, how do you think these employees see their work and themselves differently?

3. Earlier in the chapter, you read that, ideally, teams are no larger than 10. Why do you think NCR has managed to see success from much larger teams?

4. NCR's Waterloo production facility is not unionized. However, their Dundee, Scotland facility is unionized. Paul says that the democratic team process used in Waterloo would not succeed in Dundee, where he formally worked, because of the "culture of dependency" and the adversarial relationship between management and employees. What does he mean?

CASE 5.B

Separating Team Members at Enbridge

At the beginning of this chapter, you read about Susan Miller, the VP of Enbridge Technology, an international engineering consulting firm. When she took over the helm, she discovered a lot of internal strife, which worked against the organization's success. Susan, therefore, reorganized them into a group functioning as one team, focused on corporate objectives rather than functional ones, and assessed on team performance rather than individual performance.

Susan made another, more unusual move, however. She physically separated many of the employees from their supervisors, placing some in Edmonton and some in Calgary. Why? "I planned this because people at Enbridge have to be outstanding communicators. This separation develops their communication skills even further." Because of the separation, employees and supervisors are forced to use the phone and, mostly, computers, to communicate. Also, they are forced to think about the channel they need to go through to get something approved or to discuss an issue. They can't depend on convenience—Susan may be down the hall from an employee but she is their boss's boss and will remind them who they need to speak to. Through Lotus Notes, being continually connected to the Internet, and through an on-line chatroom, communication is instant and frequent. Susan still sees this as helping build the team, despite its dispersion. For example, lack of knowledge can be much more alienating than physical distance, making someone feel disconnected if he or she is "out of the loop." Therefore, all employees are kept updated on all projects. Susan finds that employees are enjoying the whole idea that, even though there are activities they are not directly involved in, they can find out about them, contribute ideas if they wish, or simply be "in-the-know." It sounds as if this might mean overload of information, but Susan says that if it is good information and clearly labelled FYI (for your interest) so there is no responsibility involved, people can put it in another compartment in their mind.

RESPONDING TO THIS CASE

1. What do you think of Susan's deliberately separating people who need to work together in order to force them to improve their communication skills? How well would you do in this work situation? What difficulties might it create?

2. What was the problem with focusing on functional objectives in the previous format? The functions were training, advising, and engineering.

3. This new organization will create some interesting control concerns for Susan. Using ideas from Chapter 3, how could Susan determine whether the organization she has created is effective or not? How can she find out if communication skills are actually improving and if that advantage outweighs difficulties created by the dispersion of the team?

FIGURE 5-19
Susan Miller

6

ACQUIRING THE RIGHT PEOPLE

LEARNING OBJECTIVES

CHAPTER OUTLINE

After reading this chapter, you should be able to:

1. Identify key laws and regulations affecting human resource practices.
2. Define the three steps in human resource planning.
3. Explain the purpose of the job specification.
4. List the primary sources for job candidates.
5. Discuss the different problems created by accept errors and reject errors.
6. Identify the strengths and weaknesses of the best-known selection devices.

PERFORMING EFFECTIVELY

SUPERVISORS AND THE HUMAN RESOURCES DEPARTMENT

UNDERSTANDING EQUAL EMPLOYMENT OPPORTUNITY
    Laws and Regulations
    Human Rights Legislation
    Your Role in Employment Equity
    EEO Goes Beyond Hiring
    Pop Quiz

DETERMINING STAFFING NEEDS
    Current Assessment
    Future Assessment
    Developing a Future Program

FROM JOB DESCRIPTIONS TO JOB SPECIFICATIONS
    Something to Think About

RECRUITING CANDIDATES
    Internal Search
    Advertisements
    Employee Referrals
    Employment Agencies
    Schools, Colleges, and Universities
    Professional Organizations
    Casual or Unsolicited Applicants
    Unemployment Agencies and Centres
    Other Sources

EMPLOYEE SELECTION
    Foundations of Selection
    Selection Devices
    Something to Think About
    Building a Supervisory Skill

NEW-EMPLOYEE ORIENTATION
    Supervision in Action: The Realistic Job Preview
    Pop Quiz

FROM CONCEPTS TO SKILLS: INTERVIEWING
    Assessing Yourself: Do You Have Good Interviewing Skills?
    Skill Basics
    Applying Your Skills

UNDERSTANDING THE BASICS
    Summary
    Key Terms and Concepts
    Reviewing Your Knowledge
    Answers to the Pop Quizzes

PERFORMING YOUR JOB
    Case 6.A: The Recruiting and Selection Partnership: HR and Management
    Case 6.B: Hiring at Russell Food Equipment

Cedara
www.cedara.com

As corporate staffing manager for Cedara, Sheena Turnbull has a tough job. Cedara creates state-of-the-art medical imaging software, such as software for fetal ultrasound imaging, CT scans, and MIR. Therefore, the company is highly dependent on the skills of its top-notch engineering, software, and medical people. "This is an interesting business. It's a constant challenge. There's a limited supply of software development people with specialized skills and we're competing with all industries now as opposed to ten years ago when mostly hi-tech software companies hired these people. Because they are in such high demand, we have to be more creative in marketing our positions to our targeted audience. We have had to become very sophisticated in international recruiting. And, when we target university grads, we're competing with the likes of Microsoft and Nortel—we can't always compete with their perquisites. However, we do have a great, friendly culture and wonderful products. Our products truly contribute to society, for example, a surgical tool to perform brain and back surgery. And we focus more on our people than a big company normally does.

Cedara's Mississauga building has its design and colours based on "feng shui," the Chinese concept that states if a building is positioned appropriately, it will be in greater harmony with its surroundings and there will be a smoother flow of "ch'i" energy or the life force. The company is very cosmopolitan and multicultural. Conference rooms are named after places from which employees come, for example, France, Austria, and Israel. Employees are encouraged to remain with the company through training opportunities, for example, English classes at work for those who wish to improve their English skills, and technical training for anyone who wants to upgrade their skills.

Flexibility is also important—software employees are allowed to work any hours and wear what they want. Employees are very dedicated but may not arrive at work until 11 a.m., wearing flip-flop sandals and Bermuda shorts. But they may then stay half the night. As long as they're meeting their deadlines, management is flexible.

"Recruiting for this company is very dynamic. You need a sense of urgency to do this job well. But I get an adrenaline rush when I find a fabulous candidate."

With a healthy Canadian economy, many organizations are faced with Sheena's challenge. Today it is often difficult to find the people you need to fill your positions and then convince them to join your organization. Staffing your organization means getting people with the right skills and knowledge, the right attitudes, and the right "fit" with your culture and team and the demands of the position. As Sheena says, this can be very tough. However, it is in every supervisor's interest to focus on the importance of recruiting.

Supervisors, by definition, oversee the work of other people. If supervisors have employees who lack the necessary skills, experience, or motivation, their unit is sure to be underperforming. So supervisors want qualified, high-performing people working for them. But how do they find such people? When they have a vacancy to fill, what can they do to increase the probability that they'll hire a high-performing candidate from among the applicant pool?

In this chapter, we'll address a number of key human resources issues including employee recruitment and selection. Let's start, however, by considering the role of the human resources department in staffing decisions.

SUPERVISORS AND THE HUMAN RESOURCES DEPARTMENT

Some readers may be thinking, "Sure, human resources decisions such as recruitment and selection are important, but aren't they made by specialists in the human resources department? These aren't decisions that supervisors get involved in!"

It's true that large organizations have human resources departments. But the people in these departments rarely make specific staffing decisions. Rather, as staff specialists, they help supervisors by writing and placing employment ads, screening applicants, and providing legal advice on various issues. The final decision, typically, is the supervisor's. Moreover, many small organizations don't have human resources departments. In such cases, supervisors typically have sole responsibility for hiring.

Every supervisor will be involved in staffing decisions. So, regardless of the size of your organization or the presence of a human resources department staffed with specialists, there will be certain activities you need to understand. These include, at a minimum, human resources planning, how to conduct employment interviews, and techniques for new-employee orientation. Also, very importantly, every supervisor must have a fundamental understanding of the current laws and regulations governing equal employment opportunity (EEO).

UNDERSTANDING EQUAL EMPLOYMENT OPPORTUNITY

Ron Gelber had worked in the lumber business for more than 20 years, but he'd never held a management position before. About five months ago he was hired as a supervisor in the finishing department at a small lumber mill. When he recently had an opening in his department, he interviewed four candidates sent to him by the firm's human resources department. During an interview with one of the applicants, a woman who was not made a job offer, he asked her a number of questions. Two of them were "Are you married?" and "Do you have any children at home?" He didn't, however, ask those questions of the male candidates he interviewed. Ron learned today, from his boss, that this applicant has filed a discrimination suit against him and the company. When Ron's boss asked if it was true that he had asked the woman about her marital status and whether she had children, Ron responded, "Sure. I was concerned she might miss work because of family responsibilities." Ron's boss was shocked. "Let me tell you something, Ron. Regardless of your intentions, you've just gotten yourself and this company into a heck of a mess!"

Ron Gelber broke the law by asking questions of women job candidates that he didn't ask of men, questions that in fact may not even have been job-relevant. In so doing, he made himself and his employer potentially liable for damages.

This example illustrates the importance of every supervisor understanding the law and its effect on human resource practices. For supervisors in large organizations, your organization will undoubtedly provide you with specific guidelines to help ensure that you don't discriminate. You'll also probably have someone in the human resources department to turn to for advice when you face an uncertain situation. For supervisors in small organizations, where there are no formal guidelines or specialists to turn to, you must keep abreast of current laws and make sure your hiring practices are in compliance. When in doubt, you should use outside lawyers or human resource consultants for advice. As we briefly review equal employment opportunity, remember that engaging in discrimination not only exposes you and your organization to potential liability, but also deprives you of hiring the applicant who is most qualified.

Laws and Regulations

In Canada, human rights legislation guarantees each person's right to equal opportunity for employment. Depending on your place of employment, your rights to equal treatment at work are protected by either the Federal Human Rights Act or one of the provincial acts. Although the acts vary in the categories they specify for protection, their basic intent is to prevent discrimination on the basis of race, colour, gender, religion, marital status, age, or handicap (see Figure 6-1). Additionally, each jurisdiction can specify additional "protected groups." The fundamental intent of all the acts is to protect equal opportunity.

FIGURE 6-1

All provinces prohibit age discrimination but the parameters differ slightly, e.g., British Columbia and Newfoundland ages 19 to 65; Saskatchewan 18 to 64; and Ontario 18 to 65. Employees in these provinces must fall within these age ranges.

HUMAN RIGHTS LEGISLATION

Human rights legislation protects job applicants from possible discriminating practices by prohibiting various questions. The following guidelines from the B.C. Human Rights Commission, similar to those offered in other provinces, indicate which questions are allowed and not allowed to ask when recruiting.

Age
Questions employers may ask:
- "Have you reached BC's legal working age?"
- After hiring, an applicant's age may be asked for benefit and insurance plans.

Questions to avoid:
- Asking about age in general, or about birth certificates.

Race, Colour, Ancestry, Place of Origin
Questions employers may ask:
- "Are you legally entitled to work in Canada?"
  All those legally entitled to work in Canada must be given equal employment opportunity unless there is a legal restriction stating otherwise.

Questions to avoid:
- Asking about birthplace or nationality, including nationality of relatives or spouse.

Criminal or Summary Conviction
Questions employers may ask:
- Inquiries about criminal or summary convictions are discouraged unless directly related to job duties.
- If bonding is required, ask applicants if they are eligible to be bonded.

Questions to avoid:
- Asking for statements of criminal and/or arrest record, unless job involves working with children.

BC Human Rights Legislation
www.bchumanrights.org

B.C. Human Rights Legislation guidelines used with permission of the B.C. Human Rights Commission.

Education

Questions employers may ask:

- Any educational requirements should be related to job duties.

Mental or Physical Disability

Questions employers may ask:

- Applicants may be asked job-related questions concerning ability to do the essential components of the job.
- An applicant's disability is relevant to the job only if it prevents that person from effectively carrying out the essential components of the job.

Questions to avoid

- Asking for a general statement of disabilities, limitations, or health problems.

Political Belief

Questions to avoid

- Asking for statements of political beliefs and philosophy.

Religious Belief

Questions employers may ask:

- Applicants may be asked job-related questions such as whether they are available for the required work time.
- Employers must be responsible in accommodating the religious needs of employees.

Questions to avoid:

- Asking for statements concerning religious affiliation, religious beliefs, and church membership.

Canadian Human Rights Commission
www.chrc-ccdp.ca/
publications/prohibit-
motifs.asp?1=e

Ontario Human Rights Commission
http://www.ohrc.on.ca/
english/publications/
emp_app_forms_eng.htm

Sex, Sexual Orientation, Marital/Family Status

Questions employers may ask:

- If job mobility is required, ask the applicants if they are willing to travel or be transferred.
- Information regarding spouse, children and/or dependants required for benefit and pension plans can be obtained after hiring.

Questions to avoid:

- Asking about an applicant's sex or sexual orientation.
- Asking for information regarding pregnancy, childcare arrangements, or child-bearing plans.
- Asking whether the applicant is single, married, divorced, engaged, separated, widowed or living common-law.

From The Employers' Guide, B.C. Human Rights Commission. Used with permission of the B.C. Human Rights Commission.

YOUR ROLE IN EMPLOYMENT EQUITY

Employment Equity: A Guide for Employers
http://info.load-otea.
hrdc-drhc.gc.ca/
~weeweb/homeen.shtml

Some employers will institute employment equity programs, with specific goals, to increase the number of women and minorities in their organization. As a supervisor, you may be asked to actively pursue female and minority candidates and make a good-faith effort to get them into the applicant pool.

Does this mean you must hire an unqualified applicant in order to meet employment equity goals? No! As we'll discuss shortly, before you begin looking to fill a position in your department, you need to know the skills, knowledge, and ability requirements of the job. If candidates meet these criteria, they are qualified. But the law doesn't require you to hire unqualified employees. So you should extend your search for female and minority applicants far and wide—for example, possibly placing ads in papers that are specifically targetted at multicultural groups or sending a notice of your job opening to the local disabled training centre—but you are not forced to hire any individual under this process. The objective of employment equity is to eliminate discrimination, not ensure the hiring of individuals from certain groups.

EEO GOES BEYOND HIRING

Equal employment opportunity goes beyond recruitment and selection of employees. It also addresses issues such as training, promotion, and eliminating discriminatorily abusive work environments.

TRAINING OPPORTUNITIES

Are you making sure *all* of your employees have equal access to training?

Do your employees need special training to learn to understand and work more effectively with individuals who are different from them? As the workforce becomes more culturally diverse, you will want to ensure that women, racial and ethnic minorities, gay employees, and members of any other group who may be perceived as "different" are not treated prejudicially by others. This may require your employees to participate in awareness and sensitivity workshops to help them better understand and work with people who are unlike themselves.

ELIMINATING SEXUAL HARASSMENT

Few workplace topics have received more attention in recent years than that of sexual harassment.

Sexual harassment generally encompasses sexually suggestive remarks, unwanted touching and sexual advances, requests for sexual favours, and other verbal and physical conduct of a sexual nature. It is considered illegal; it is a violation of the human rights legislation.

Courts have widened the test for sexual harassment to whether a comment or behaviour in a work environment "would reasonably be perceived, and is perceived, as hostile or abusive." In so doing, employees need not show they have been psychologically damaged to prove sexual harassment in the workplace, merely that they are working in a hostile or abusive environment.

Sexual harassment
Sexually suggestive remarks, unwanted touching and sexual advances, requests for sexual favours, and other verbal and physical conduct of a sexual nature.

From a supervisor's standpoint, sexual harassment is a growing concern because it intimidates employees, interferes with job performance, and exposes the organization to liability. To ensure that you do not have a hostile or abusive environment, you must establish a clear and strong position against sexual harassment. If higher management doesn't have a sexual harassment policy, then you need to establish one for your department. The policy should be reinforced by regular discussion sessions in which employees are reminded of the rule and carefully instructed that even the slightest sexual overture to another employee will not be tolerated. In some companies, employees have been specifically advised that they can be fired for making repeated unwelcome sexual advances, using sexually degrading words to describe someone, or displaying sexually offensive pictures or objects at work.

POP QUIZ

Are You Comprehending What You're Reading?

1. Sexual harassment:
   a. involves only physical conduct between male and female organizational members
   b. does not interfere with job performance
   c. holds the organization liable for the conduct of the supervisor
   d. is relevant only in large organizations
2. The objective of employment equity is to ensure the hiring of individuals from certain groups. True or false?
3. Specific staffing decions:
   a. are typically made by the human resources department
   b. are usually made by the supervisor
   c. are made as a result of multiple employee input
   d. do not have to be concerned about compliance with laws and regulations concerning hiring
4. List some questions that are prohibited in the hiring process because of their potential use for discrimination.

DETERMINING STAFFING NEEDS

You've organized your department. You've identified the tasks that need to be done and grouped them into jobs. Now you must ensure that you'll have the right number and kinds of people to achieve your department's goals. We call this **human resource planning** and it can be condensed into three steps:

1. assessing current human resources
2. assessing future human resource needs
3. developing a program to meet future human resource needs

> **Human resource planning** Ensuring that a department has the right personnel, who are capable of completing those tasks that help the department reach its objectives.

CURRENT ASSESSMENT

Begin your assessment by reviewing your current human resource status. Your goal is to create a departmental human resource inventory.

To build this inventory, your employees will complete forms for the human resources department. Increasingly, these files can be accessed by computer. This departmental inventory will typically include a list of your employees' names, education, training, prior employment, languages spoken, capabilities, and specialized skills. When completed, this inventory allows you to assess what talents and skills are available within your department. It lets you know what your individual employees can do. Make sure the files are updated periodically so the information is current.

FUTURE ASSESSMENT

Future human resource needs are determined by the organization's overall objectives and your departmental goals.

The organization's demand for human resources is directly related to the demand for the organization's products or services. From its estimate of total revenue, top management can attempt to establish the number and mix of human resources needed to reach these revenues. In some cases, the situation may be reversed. Revenues may be determined by human resources if the particular skills are in scarce supply, and are not available in the labour market. In recent years, this has been the case for Microsoft. This designer of computer software has more business opportunities than it can handle. Its primary limiting factor in building revenues has been its ability to locate and hire designers and programmers with the qualifications to write new software. In most cases, however, the overall organizational goals and the revenue forecast provide the major input determining the organization's human resource demand requirements.

Based on forecasts provided by upper management, you can calculate their implications for your department's operations. What will be the increase or decrease in workload? What new or changing skills will be called for?

DEVELOPING A FUTURE PROGRAM

After you've assessed both current capabilities and future needs, you'll be able to estimate shortages—both in number and kind—and to highlight areas in which your department will be overstaffed. Additionally, of course, your departmental projections will need to be combined with forecasts made by other supervisors in your organization and coordinated with the human resources department. This is important because it ensures that you can identify individuals with skills and capabilities that cut across departmental lines.

In addition, as we move to a global economy, supervisors need to consider the possibility of contracting out work to foreign countries. Assigning programming jobs to "software parks" in developing countries is a growing practice in Canada, especially when foreign export laws can result in significant savings.

FROM JOB DESCRIPTIONS TO JOB SPECIFICATIONS

You'll remember from the previous chapter that once your departmental structure is in place, you then create job descriptions. These job descriptions tell employees what they're supposed to do. Another document, closely tied to the job description and often included as part of it, is needed before you're ready to begin efforts at recruitment and selection. This document is the job specification.

Job specification
The minimum acceptable qualifications an employee must possess to perform a given job successfully.

The **job specification** states the minimum acceptable qualifications an employee must possess to perform a given job successfully. It identifies the knowledge, skills, and abilities needed to do the job effectively. In large organizations, job specifications are written by specialists in the human resources department. In smaller organizations, you may develop these yourself. An example of a job specification for a book production editor is shown in Figure 6-2.

Competency research has generated another way of developing a job specification. By researching what distinguishes the top performers in a

```
Job Title: Project Production Editor

Department: College Book Editorial Production

Job Class: 7-12B

Education:
    Graduation from an accredited college or university with a
      specialization in creative writing, English, journalism, or equal.

Knowledge:
    No prior knowledge of book production necessary.

Abilities and skills:
    Ability to copy edit manuscripts; ability to organize and
    coordinate multiple projects simultaneously; ability to
    secure good working relationships with outside vendors;
    ability to meet deadlines; ability to express ideas clearly
    and concisely, orally and in writing; strong interpersonal
    skills; and skill in the use of Macintosh computers.
```

FIGURE 6-2

Sample job specification

position from the average performers, one can generate a picture of competencies or skills that go beyond simply being able to do the job. This can take a lot of work, for example, through interviewing the top and mediocre performers or their managers and coworkers, but if there is a huge difference in performance between the two groups, as in sales, the resulting information is worth the effort.[1]

Why is the job specification important? It's the standard against which job applicants will be compared. It keeps your attention focused on the specific necessary and preferred qualifications for an individual to do a job effectively, and it assists you in determining whether candidates are qualified. The criteria to use as a basis for hiring may even include personality characteristics, which adds more complexity to the situation (see "Something to Think About").

Once you've identified a vacancy in your department and have a job specification for that position, you can begin the search for the right candidate to fill that vacancy.

Predicting group performance is tricky. We've all seen groups that have not performed exceptionally well despite having exceptional talent. And we've seen groups with mediocre talent pull together and beat the odds. Obviously group potential is more than simply adding up the skill levels of individual members.

One recent study that supports this points to personality as an influential factor. Neuman and Wright examined the work performance of 316 full-time human resource (HR) representatives who work in teams of four at local stores across the United States in a large wholesale department store organization.[2] When they were hired, all 316 employees completed commercial tests of personality, cognitive ability, and job-related skills. The scores were *not* used in the hiring decisions. Three years later, each representative's work performance was evaluated by their peers on six dimensions. Each four-person team's performance was measured on the same six dimensions by three department supervisors who work in the same store as the HR team. The supervisors were not aware of the original scores, which prevented bias in their evaluations. Two more measures were taken: work completed—meaning the number of days for one year that team tasks were completed within schedule; and work accuracy—the percentage of forms processed by the team without error in the year.

The results showed that scores on two personality traits predicted peer ratings of individual performance beyond measures of job-specific skills and general cognitive ability. The same two personality measures predicted supervisor ratings of team performance and objective measures of work team accuracy and work completed. These two important personality variables are agreeableness and conscientiousness. Individuals high on these characteristics were more likely to be evaluated as strong performers by their peers, and teams high on these characteristics were more likely to have their work completed accurately and on time, and to be seen as effective teams by supervisors.

Agreeableness refers to the extent to which someone tends to trust others; be straightforward, altruistic, cooperative in conflict situations, and modest; and be able to express sympathy and empathy. Conscientiousness describes a combination of thinking carefully before acting, working hard to achieve goals, following up on commitments, adhering to ethical and moral obligations, and maintaining self-discipline.

How would these personality characteristics influence the team so that its performance is enhanced? Would it be fair to test applicants on these personality traits and use their scores to screen their suitability for a position? Consider how conscientiousness and agreeableness could be explored using behaviour-based questions, described later in this chapter, when hiring someone to work as part of a team.

RECRUITING CANDIDATES

If you have a departmental vacancy, where do you look to find potential candidates to fill it? In this section, we'll review the primary sources for job candidates.

INTERNAL SEARCH

Most organizations give preference to current employees for new openings. Employees like this practice because it gives them an advantage over outsiders in applying for lateral transfers and promotions. Managers prefer internal candidates because they are more likely to be able to get detailed and accurate information on how the candidate did on prior jobs within the organization. While outside references are often vague and noncommittal, other managers within your organization can typically provide you with the full history of an internal employee's performance record. In addition, internal candidates are already familiar with the organization. They should therefore take less time to adjust to a new job.

When looking for people to staff her brand new library branch, Anne Murphy of the Frank McKechnie library in Mississauga presented a workshop at the library system's staff conference, encouraging people to apply for transfer to the new branch.

There are several drawbacks to relying on an internal search. First, it provides a limited set of candidates. You wouldn't want to hire a second-rate employee merely because he or she was there, when excellent candidates are available outside the organization. Second, excessive reliance on internal search tends to perpetuate "inbreeding." Internal candidates are less likely to bring new ideas and fresh perspectives to the job. Third, if past hiring decisions were discriminatory, internal hiring will continue to fail the "equal opportunity" test.

ADVERTISEMENTS

The sign outside the plant reads: "Now Hiring—Experienced Machinists." The newspaper advertisement reads: "Speech Pathologist. Large urban hospital is looking for a speech pathologist to join our rehabilitation group. Accredited licence required. Minimum of four years' experience necessary. Salary to $40 000. Call Ms. Resnick at 579-5060."

Most of us have seen both types of advertisements. When an organization seeks to communicate to the public that it has a vacancy, advertisements are one of the most popular methods.

The higher the position in the organization, or the more specialized the skills sought, the more widely dispersed the advertisement is likely to be. While advertisements for blue-collar jobs are usually confined to the local daily newspaper or regional trade journals, the search for individuals with highly specialized technical skills might include advertisements in a national periodical.

Advertisements are an excellent means of informing a wide audience of a vacancy. Also, by careful selection of the medium for the ad, you can target specific minority groups or individuals with similar interests. The major drawback of advertisements is that, unless ads are very carefully worded, they tend to attract many unqualified candidates. Cost must also be considered.

Employee Referrals

One of the best sources of individuals who will perform effectively on the job is a recommendation from a current employee.[3] The reasons are fairly obvious. Employees will rarely recommend someone unless they believe that the referral will perform adequately. Such a recommendation reflects on the recommender and, when someone's reputation is at stake, we can expect the recommendation to be based on relatively strong beliefs. Employee referrals may also have acquired more accurate information about their potential jobs. The recommender often gives the applicant more realistic information about the job than could be conveyed through employment agencies or newspaper advertisements (see Figure 6-3). This information reduces unrealistic expectations. As a result of these pre-selection factors, employee referrals tend to be more acceptable applicants, to have a greater probability of accepting an offer if one is made, and, once employed, to have a higher job-survival rate. Some organizations encourage employee referrals by giving "finder's fees" (for example, $500) to employees who recommend someone who is later hired.

There are, of course, some potentially negative features of employee referrals. For one thing, recommenders may confuse friendship with job-performance competence. Individuals often like to have their friends join them at their place of employment for social and even economic reasons. For example, they may be able to share rides to and from work. As a result, a current employee may recommend a friend for a position without giving unbiased consideration to the friend's job-related competence.

Employee referrals may also lead to nepotism; that is, hiring individuals who are related to persons already employed by the organization. The hiring of relatives is particularly widespread in family-owned organizations. While such actions do not necessarily meet the objective of hiring the most qualified applicant, interest in the organization and loyalty to it may be long-term advantages.

Finally, employee referrals may not help the organization in actively seeking minority and women candidates. Employees often refer someone who shares something with them—religion, demographics, race, etc. Accordingly, an organization that wants to increase the presence of protected groups must guard against over-reliance on employee referrals from members of nonprotected groups.

EMPLOYMENT AGENCIES

Employment agencies can be divided into three categories: full-service agencies, temporary help services, and executive search firms. Since the last type has little relevance to supervisors—they specialize in placing middle-level and top-level executives—we'll focus on the other two.

Manpower Global Home Page
http://www.manpower.com/

The typical full-service agency charges for its services. Their fees can be paid by the employer, the applicant, or on a shared basis. These agencies provide a complete line of services. They advertise the position, screen applicants against the criteria specified by the employer, and usually provide a guarantee covering six months or a year as protection to the employer, in case the applicant does not perform satisfactorily.

An increasingly popular type of employment agency is the one that specializes in temporary employees. Organizations such as Kelly and Manpower can be excellent sources of employees to fill part-time or short-term staffing needs (see Figure 6-4). As employers look for ways to increase their staffing flexibility and at the same time keep benefit costs down, the use of contingent workers hired through temporary help services is seen as a highly attractive alternative.

FIGURE 6-3

"I don't run ads for vacancies," says Robert Scott of Southwest Doors. "When I have an opening, one or more of our people will have connections around town. They'll find good people and bring them in."

FIGURE 6-4

Manpower, the world's largest temporary help firm, tests applicants in order to match their skills to employer needs.

SCHOOLS, COLLEGES, AND UNIVERSITIES

Educational institutions at all levels offer opportunities for recruiting recent graduates. Most educational institutions operate placement services where prospective employers can review credentials and interview graduates; and many offer internship and co-op programs where you can find students who are looking for opportunities to practise on the job what they're learning. Whether the educational qualification required for the job is a high school diploma, specific vocational training, or a university background with a bachelor's, master's, or doctoral degree, educational institutions are an excellent source of potential employees for entry-level positions in organizations.

High schools or vocational-technical schools can provide blue-collar applicants; business or secretarial schools can provide white-collar staff; and colleges and universities can provide technical and professional personnel.

While educational institutions are usually viewed as sources of young, inexperienced entrants to the workforce, it is not uncommon to find individuals with considerable work experience using an educational institution's placement service. They may be workers who have recently returned to school to upgrade their skills, or alumni using their former school's placement centre.

PROFESSIONAL ORGANIZATIONS

Many professional organizations, including labour unions, operate place-ment services for the benefit of their members and employers. The pro-fessional organizations include such varied occupations as accountants, industrial engineers, training specialists, and seafarers.

These organizations publish rosters of job vacancies and distribute these lists to members. It is also common practice to provide place-ment facilities at regional and national meetings where those looking for employment and companies looking for employees can find each other.

CASUAL OR UNSOLICITED APPLICANTS

"Walk-ins," whether they reach an employer by letter, telephone, or in person, can be a major source of applicants. Although the qualification level of unsolicited applicants can depend on economic conditions, the organization's image, and the job seeker's perception of the types of jobs that might be available, this source does provide an excellent supply of stockpiled applicants. Even if there are no particular openings when the applicant makes contact with the organization, the application can be kept on file for later needs.

Applications from individuals who are already employed can be referred to many months later and can provide applicants who 1. are interested in considering other employment opportunities and 2. regard the organization as a possible employer.

Unsolicited applications made by unemployed individuals, however, generally have a short life. Those individuals who have adequate skills will usually find employment with some other organization that does have an opening. But in tough economic times, excellent prospects are often unable to locate the type of job they desire and may stay actively looking in the job market for some time.

UNEMPLOYMENT AGENCIES AND CENTRES

Provincial unemployment agencies are another source of available workers. These agencies will provide the service of posting vacancies, matching applicants, and prescreening for job openings. Increasingly, computerized files are simplifying the process of matching available workers to the skills required in available jobs.

OTHER SOURCES

Organizations that are focused on hiring particular types of applicants can use non-traditional sources such as Work Able in Hamilton, Ontario, which helps to place people with disabilities, and other associations that represent older workers. Such associations can be a source of highly motivated workers.

When you want to reach out and expand the diversity among applicants, sources might include local religious organizations, minority-oriented media, schools in low-income neighbourhoods, multicultural organizations, and agencies dealing with ex-prisoners.

EMPLOYEE SELECTION

You've developed a pool of applicants. Now you need some method for screening the applicants and for identifying the most appropriate candidate. That screening method is the selection process.

FOUNDATIONS OF SELECTION

Selection is a prediction exercise. It seeks to predict which applicants will be successful if hired. "Successful" in this case means performing well on the criteria the organization uses to evaluate employees. In filling a sales position, for example, the selection process should be able to predict which applicants will generate a high volume of sales for the company.

PREDICTION

Consider, for a moment, that any selection decision can result in four possible outcomes. As shown in Figure 6-5, two of these outcomes would indicate correct decisions, but two would indicate errors.

A decision is correct when the applicant was predicted to be successful and later proved to be successful on the job, or when the applicant was predicted to be unsuccessful and would perform accordingly if hired. In the first case, we have successfully accepted; in the second case, we have successfully rejected. Thus the purpose of selection activities is to develop the outcomes shown as "correct decision" in Figure 6-5.

In selection, a supervisor is open to two different mistakes: reject errors and accept errors.

Reject errors Rejecting candidates who would later perform successfully on the job.

Reject errors occur when a supervisor eliminates a candidate who would have performed well on the job. The cost of reject errors might be additional recruitment and selection expenses. More significant, and potentially harmful, are the possible claims of discrimination.

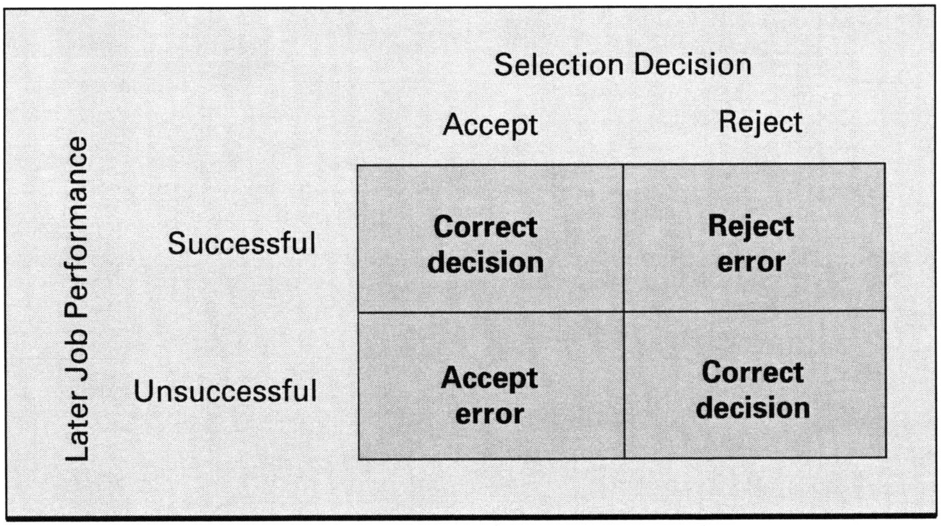

FIGURE 6-5

Selection decision outcomes

Accept errors occur when a supervisor selects a candidate who is unable to perform the job successfully. Here, the costs of a poor decision include extra training, productivity losses, possible severance costs, and ultimately additional recruitment and selection costs. The major thrust of any selection activity is therefore to reduce the probability of making reject errors or accept errors, while increasing the probability of making correct decisions.

Accept errors
Accepting those candidates who subsequently perform poorly on the job.

VALIDITY

Any selection device that a supervisor uses—such as application forms, tests, and interviews—must demonstrate **validity**. That is, there must be a proven relationship between the selection device and some relevant criterion. For example, the law prohibits management from using a test score as a selection device unless there is clear evidence that individuals with high scores on this test outperform, on the job, individuals with low test scores.

Validity
The proven relationship that exists between a selection device and some relevant criterion.

The burden is on management to show that any selection device it uses to differentiate applicants is related to job performance. For instance, while management can give applicants an intelligence test and use the results to help make selection decisions, it must be prepared to demonstrate, if challenged, that this intelligence test is a valid measure; that is, that scores on the test are positively related to later job performance.

RELIABILITY

In addition to being valid, a selection device must demonstrate reliability. **Reliability** indicates whether the device measures the same thing consistently. For example, if a test is reliable, any single individual's score

Reliability
The ability of a selection device to measure the same thing consistently.

should remain fairly stable over time, assuming that the characteristics it is measuring are also stable.

The importance of reliability should be evident. No selection device can be effective if it is low in reliability. That is equivalent to weighing yourself everyday on an erratic scale. If the scale is unreliable—randomly fluctuating, say, five to ten kilograms every time you step on it—the results will not mean much. The same applies to selection devices. To be effective predictors, they must possess an acceptable level of consistency.

SELECTION DEVICES

Supervisors can use a number of selection devices to reduce accept and reject errors. The best-known devices include an analysis of the prospect's completed application form, written and performance-simulation tests, interviews, background investigations, and in some cases a physical examination. Let's take a look at each of these devices, noting their respective strengths and weaknesses.

THE APPLICATION FORM

Almost all organizations require candidates to fill out an application (see Figure 6-6). The form might ask a prospect to give his or her name, address, and telephone number. At the other extreme, it might be a comprehensive personal history profile, detailing the applicant's activities, skills, and accomplishments. Are these forms valid?

Hard and relevant biographical data that can be verified—for example, rank in graduating class—have been shown to be valid measures of performance for some jobs.[4] Additionally, when application-form items have been appropriately weighted to reflect job relatedness—that is, points are allocated to variables such as education and experience—the device has proven a valid predictor for such varied groups as sales clerks, engineers, factory workers, clerical employees, and technicians. But typically, only a couple of items on the application prove to be valid predictors, and then only for a specific job. Supervisors are encouraged to use weighted applications for selection purposes, but it is critical that application items be validated for each job and that the items be continually reviewed and updated to reflect changes in weights over time.

WRITTEN TESTS

Typical written tests include tests of intelligence, aptitude, ability, and interest. Historically, these written tests were popular selection devices, but there has been a marked decline in their use over the past quarter-century. Why? The reason is that these tests have frequently been characterized as discriminatory, and many organizations have been unable to demonstrate that they're job related. In other words, their validity is low.

Job Application

Date: _____

Name: _____
               Last   First   Middle Init.

Address: _____
             Street   City/Town   Prov.   Postal Code

Phone: ( ) _____

Employment History: Last 3 Jobs

1. Employer: _____
   Address: _____
   Phone: ( ) _____
   Position: _____ Salary/Rate _____

2. Employer: _____
   Address: _____
   Phone: ( ) _____
   Position: _____ Salary/Rate _____

3. Employer: _____
   Address: _____
   Phone: ( ) _____
   Position: _____ Salary/Rate _____

Education: Post-Secondary
1. School: _____ Degree earned _____
   Address: _____

2. School: _____ Degree earned _____
   Address: _____

Education: Secondary   Degree earned _____

Additional information: _____
_____
_____
_____

FIGURE 6-6

Sample application form

Tests in intellectual ability, spatial and mechanical ability, perceptual accuracy, and motor ability have shown to be moderately valid predictors for many semiskilled and unskilled operative jobs in industrial organizations.[5] However, remember the burden is on management to demonstrate that any test used is job-related. Since many of these tests examine characteristics that are considerably removed from the actual performance of the job itself, getting high validity scores has often been difficult across a wide spectrum of jobs. The result has been a decreased use of traditional written tests and increased interest in performance simulation tests.

PERFORMANCE SIMULATION TESTS

What better way to find out whether an applicant can do a job successfully than by having him or her do it? The logic of this question has resulted in increased usage of performance simulation tests. Undoubtedly, the enthusiasm for these tests lies in the fact that they are based on actual job behaviours rather than on surrogates. The best-known performance simulation test is called **work sampling** and is designed for routine jobs.

Work sampling
A selection device in which job applicants are presented with a miniature replica of a job and are asked to perform tasks central to that job.

Work sampling involves presenting applicants with a miniature replica of a job and letting them perform a task or set of tasks that are central to the job. Applicants demonstrate that they possess the necessary talents by actually doing the tasks. By carefully devising work samples, supervisors can determine the knowledge, skills, and abilities needed for each job. Each work-sample element is then matched with a corresponding job-performance element. For instance, for a job that involves computations on a calculator, a work sample would require applicants to make similar computations.

The results from work-sample experiments have generally been impressive.[6] They have almost always yielded validity scores that are superior to those of written aptitude, personality, or intelligence tests.

INTERVIEWS

The interview, along with the application form, is an almost universal selection device. Not many of us have ever been hired for a job without one or more interviews. Unfortunately, interviews are typically poorly conducted and result in distorted findings.[7] This doesn't mean that interviews can't provide valid and reliable selection information, but rather that untrained interviewers tend to make common mistakes. For example, interviewers often hold a stereotype of what represents a "good" applicant; they often tend to favour applicants who share the interviewer's own attitudes; the order in which applicants are interviewed often influences evaluations, as does the order in which information is elicited; negative information is given unduly high weight; and interviewers forget much of the interview's content within minutes of its conclusion. See "Something to Think About" regarding the questions often used in interviews.

BACKGROUND INVESTIGATIONS

Background investigations are of two types: verification of application data and reference checks. The first type has proven to be a valuable source of selection information, whereas the latter is essentially worthless. Let's briefly review each.

Verifying the "facts" given on an application form pays dividends. The reason is that a significant percentage of job applicants—studies indicate upwards of 15 percent—exaggerate or misrepresent dates of employment, job titles, past salaries, or reasons for leaving a prior position.[8] Confirmation of hard data on the application with prior employers is therefore a worthwhile endeavour.

The reference check is used by many organizations but is extremely difficult to justify. Whether they are work-related or personal, references provide little valid information for the selection decision. Employers are frequently reluctant to give candid evaluations of a former employee's job performance for fear of legal repercussions. In fact, one survey found that only 55 percent of human resource executives would "always" provide accurate references to a prospective employer. Seven percent said they would never give an accurate reference![9] Personal references should also be given little weight. Who among us doesn't have three or four friends who will speak in glowing terms about our integrity, work habits, positive attitudes, knowledge, and skills? There just isn't enough variation among personal references for them to provide supervisors with any meaningful selection information.

PHYSICAL EXAMINATIONS

For jobs that require certain physical requirements—for example, police officers, airline pilots, train engineers—the physical examination has some validity. In most cases, nowadays, the physical examination is done for insurance purposes only. Management wants to eliminate insurance claims for injuries or illnesses contracted prior to being hired.

Great care must be taken to ensure that physical requirements are job-related and do not discriminate. Some physical requirements may exclude persons with disabilities, when, in fact, such requirements do not affect job performance. Similarly, the use of height and weight requirements may discriminate against female and some ethnic minority applicants.

What do you think are good interview questions? List three of them below.

_____

_____

_____

Share your questions and then discuss how you could "fake out" the interviewer on these questions, by giving impressive answers that may have nothing to do with your actual suitability for the job.

What are your comments on the following questions?

> Do you have any experience in this area?
>
> What do you see yourself doing five years from now?
>
> What are your strengths and weaknesses?

Interviews are widely used and, additionally, tend to be given considerable weight in the final selection decision. As a result, supervisors need to perfect their interviewing skills. In From Concepts to Skills at the end of this chapter, we'll present some guidelines to help you conduct effective employment interviews. More immediately, the "Building a Supervisory Skill" section describes a specific interviewing approach called behaviour-based interviewing, which has been highly successful.

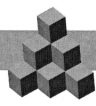

Building a Supervisory Skill

BEHAVIOUR-BASED INTERVIEWING

ABOUT THE SKILL

The best predictor of future behaviour is past behaviour. This is why we are so interested in résumés as a job-selection device. Do we get the whole story from résumés, however?

An increasingly popular form of interviewing that focuses on effectively eliciting specific information about past behaviour is called behaviour-based interviewing, also known as behaviour description interviewing or behavioural event interviewing. It asks candidates to tell a series of true "stories" about themselves, detailing accounts of specific events from their past. It has much higher predictive power than traditional interviews.[10]

STEPS IN PRACTISING THE SKILL

www.staffingworld.com/hrlinks.htm#interviewing

Determine what you are looking for in the candidate. As described earlier, use job descriptions and job specifications to develop a picture of the ideal candidate.

Develop a series of questions based on those desired skills. These will be asked of all job candidates. Each question seeks detailed information on past behaviour. For example, if you were hiring for a retail clerk, you may ask: "Tell me about the last time you handled a slow time in your job." "People are not always easy to deal with. Think about a time you had a challenging customer to deal with. What happened?" "We're a busy workplace. Tell me about a specific time when your workload was very fast-paced and may have seemed overwhelming. Describe it. How did you handle it?"

Prepare the candidate by describing this approach before launching into the questions. Candidates may never have been faced with this type of question before and may find it difficult. Before asking the questions, explain what you will be doing. For example, you may say, "I'm going to be asking you to describe in detail some experiences you've been through in your past work. This way I'll get a much clearer picture of your experience. When I ask a question like this, feel free to take time to think about your answer. You may not have had to describe your work in this way before."

Give the person time to think after asking a behaviour-based question. Don't rush the person or feel you need to fill the silence. If they answer that they cannot think of an appropriate situation, consider changing the question slightly or giving some sample situations to describe events that might fit this question.

After the person's initial answer to a behaviour-based question, follow up with probes. For instance, you may ask who was involved, what were you thinking at the time, what did you learn from this, what happened as a result, and what specifically did you say. Persist until you get a clear and complete picture of each event and the candidate's role in it. You may spend five or ten minutes discussing one event. This is considered superior to hypothetical questions, such as "What would you do if..." because people can make up anything for a hypothetical question. You may be thinking that applicants also do that for past events. However, evidence suggests that this is unlikely to happen. By probing a situation fully, you will get a sense of how genuine it is.

Take notes throughout. Recording the answers allows you to refer to them later when making decisions. It also allows you to follow up when doing a reference check to confirm whether a specific event described by the candidate actually happened.

NEW-EMPLOYEE ORIENTATION

Orientation
The introduction of a new employee into his or her job and the organization.

Once a job candidate has been selected, he or she needs to be introduced to the job and the organization. This introduction is called **orientation**.

Have you ever had the experience of being "dumped" into a position the first day on the job without any preparation, explanation, or introductions? Many people have and know that it does not set them up to be successful or happy in their job. All employees should receive an orientation. The major objectives of orientation are to reduce the initial anxiety all new employees feel as they begin a new job; to familiarize new employees with the job, the work unit, and the organization as a whole; and to facilitate the outsider-insider transition. Job orientation expands on the information the employee received during the recruitment and selection stages. The new employee's specific duties and responsibilities are clarified, as is the way his or her performance will be evaluated. This is also the time to rectify any unrealistic expectations new employees might hold about the job (see Supervision in Action). Work-unit orientation familiarizes the employee with the goals of the work unit, clarifies how his or her job contributes to the unit's goals, and includes introduction to coworkers. Organization orientation informs the new employee about the organization's objectives, history, philosophy, procedures, and rules. This should include relevant human resource policies and benefits such as work hours, pay procedures, overtime requirements, and fringe benefits. A tour of the organization's physical facilities is often part of the organization orientation. Figure 6-7 illustrates what an orientation program can include to meet its goals.

Many organizations have formal orientation programs. Such a program might include a tour of the offices or plant, a video describing the

Employee Question	Employer Response	Orientation Goal
Will I like workng here?	Set a warm, welcoming tone.	1. Inspire confidence and acceptance.
What exactly will I be doing?	Specify procedures for work, equipment, and safety.	2. Encourage expertise through knowledge.
Who else works here and how do I fit in?	Introduce to all people with whom this employee will interact.	3. Motivate by establishing a sense of community.
Who/where do I go for information?	Introduce the immediate supervisor and provide an employee handbook or handout with pertinent information.	4. Activate the lines of authority.

FIGURE 6-7

Orientation from the Ontario Agricultural Human Resource Committee Employer's Handbook guidelines. With permission from Ralph Liumes.

Eagle's Flight
www.eaglesflight.com

history of the organization, and a short discussion with a representative from the human resources department, who describes the organization's benefit programs. Eagle's Flight of Guelph, Ontario, puts all new employees through an extensive orientation including having all employees go through the programs that Eagle's Flight sells (experiential training programs for the business community). This way, everyone working for the company in any position is intimately familiar with what Eagle's Flight represents, what it sells and what they, as employees, can be proud of. The formal orientation is also augmented by the written expectation that all supervisors will ensure that all appropriate supports are in place for the new employee when the employee arrives. For example, when requesting a specific hire, supervisors must also complete a form requesting new or changing services, such as a desk, new office equipment, a phone, and an IT user account with specific software access.

Other organizations utilize an informal orientation program in which, for instance, the supervisor assigns the new employee to a senior member of the work unit, who introduces the new employee to immediate coworkers and shows him or her the locations of the rest rooms, cafeteria, coffee machine, and the like.

Supervisors will want to make the integration of the new employee into the organization and department as smooth and as free of anxiety as possible. Successful orientation results in an outsider-insider transition that makes the new member feel comfortable and fairly well adjusted, lowers the likelihood of poor work performance, and reduces the probability of a surprise resignation by the new employee only a week or two into the job.

FIGURE 6-8

Guidelines for the introduction to the workplace from the Ontario Agricultural Human Resource Committee and Ralph Liumes, with permission. Available from Ontario Ministry of Agriculture as "Employee Handbook for Agriculture and Horticulture," Order #AF0009/99, AGDEX#810.

TASK	EFFICIENCY TIPS
1. Tour the work area.	Organize the work area exactly as the employee is expected to keep it. Explain standards of cleanliness and tidiness.
2. Show tools and equipment.	Explain the function/purpose of equipment and demonstrate storage, care and maintenance requirements.
3. Explain the job duties.	Encourage questions to determine the employee's skill level. Emphasize why the duties are important.
4. Present one task at a time.	Proceed step by step, pausing frequently to check for understanding. Don't rush!
5. Supervise first efforts.	Correct errors and reinforce success. Adopt a supportive attitude to reduce employee stress. Continue to supervise the employee until performance standards are met.
6. Let the employee fly solo.	If problems occur, work with the employee to find solutions. Continue to provide encouragement.
7. Maintain a progress record.	Tell the employee when competency has been attained and keep a progress record in the employee's file.

Supervision in *Action*

The Realistic Job Preview

Supervisors who treat the recruiting and hiring of employees as if the applicants must be sold on the job and exposed only to an organization's positive characteristics set themselves up to have a dissatisfied workforce that is prone to high turnover.[11]

Every job applicant acquires, during the hiring process, a set of expectations about the company and about the job for which he or she is being interviewed. When the information an applicant receives is inflated, a number of things happen that have potentially negative effects on the company. First, mismatched applicants who would probably become dissatisfied with the job and quit soon would be less likely to withdraw from the search process. Second, the absence of accurate information builds unrealistic expectations. Consequently the new employees are likely to become quickly dissatisfied—again leading to premature resignations. Third, new hires are prone to become disillusioned and less committed to the organization when they face the "harsh" realities of the job. In many cases, these individuals feel that they were duped or misled during the hiring process and, therefore, may become problem employees.

To increase job satisfaction among employees and reduce turnover, supervisors should provide a **realistic job preview (RJP)**. An RJP includes both positive and negative information about the job and the company. For example, in addition to the positive comments typically expressed in the interview, the candidate would be told of the downside of joining the company. He or she might be told that there are limited opportunities to talk to coworkers during work hours, that promotional advancement is slim, or that work hours fluctuate so erratically that employees may be required to work during typically off hours (nights and weekends). Applicants who have been given a more realistic job preview hold lower and more realistic job expectations for the jobs they'll be performing and are better able to cope with the job and its frustrating elements. The result is fewer unexpected resignations by new employees.

For supervisors, realistic job previews offer a major insight into the selection process. That is, retaining good people is as important as hiring them in the first place. Presenting only the positive aspects of a job to an applicant may initially entice him or her to join the organization, but it may be an affiliation that both parties quickly regret.

5. A human resource inventory is:
   a. a statement of what a current jobholder does, how it is to be done, and the accountabilities of the job
   b. a statement indicating employees' education, capabilities, and specialized skills
   c. a statement of the minimum qualifications required for job candidates to be successful on the job
   d. none of the above
6. What is the difference between reliability and validity? Is reliability alone sufficient for the selection process?
7. Negative information is frequently given more weight in an interview. True or false?
8. Name five of the primary sources for recruiting job candidates.

INTERVIEWING

ASSESSING YOURSELF: DO YOU HAVE GOOD INTERVIEWING SKILLS?

Are the following questions true (T) or false (F)? Circle what you believe is the right answer.

1. On an application form, it's illegal to ask an applicant what foreign languages he or she can read, write, or speak fluently.	T	F
2. It's illegal to ask an applicant about his or her past work experience.	T	F
3. It's illegal to ask the full names of an applicant's dependants.	T	F
4. It is better for the interviewer to examine the candidate's resume after the interview rather than before, so that the interviewer is open and lacks preconceived ideas about the candidate.	T	F
5. It's a good idea to tape record or takes notes during an interview.	T	F
6. A good interviewer takes control of an interview and does most of the talking.	T	F
7. An interviewer should avoid asking questions that can be answered with a simple yes or no.	T	F
8. Early in the interview, you should provide the applicant with as much detail about the job being interviewed for as possible.	T	F

SCORING INSTRUCTIONS

Questions 3, 4, 5, and 7 are true. Questions 1, 2, 6, and 8 are false. If you got seven or eight correct, you already have some understanding of how to conduct an effective selection interview.

SKILL BASICS

In conducting an employment interview, you're trying to get answers to three questions:

1. Can the applicant do the job?

2. Is the applicant motivated to do the job?

3. Will the applicant fit into your work group and organization? Everything you do regarding the interview—from preparation to closure—should help you to answer these three questions.

Interviewing is difficult because it is, in effect, an art. Developing the art of the interview is learning what to do and how to do it. Then it's a matter of practice to ensure your interviewing skills don't become stale from lack of use.

STEPS IN PRACTISING THE SKILL

This list summarizes the key actions in preparing for and conducting an interview.

1. **Review job description and job specification.** Reviewing pertinent information about the job provides valuable information about what you'll assess the candidate on. Furthermore, relevant job requirements help to eliminate interview bias.

2. **Prepare a structured set of questions to ask all applicants for the job.** By having a set of prepared questions, you ensure that the information you wish to elicit is attainable. Furthermore, by asking similar questions, you are able to better compare all candidates' answers to a common base.

3. **Prior to meeting a candidate, review his or her application form and résumé.** This helps you create a complete picture of the candidate in terms of what is represented on the résumé/application and what the job requires. You will also begin to identify areas to explore in the interview. Areas not clearly defined on the résumé/application that are essential for your job should become a focal point in your discussion with the candidate.

4. **Open the interview by putting the applicant at ease and providing a brief preview of the topics to be discussed.** Interviews are stressful for job candidates. By opening with small talk (e.g., the weather or the traffic) you give the candidate time to adjust to the interview setting. By providing a preview of topics to come, you are giving the candidate an "agenda." This helps the candidate to begin framing what he or she will say in response to your questions.

5. **Ask your questions and listen carefully to the applicant's answers.** Select follow-up questions that naturally flow from the answers given. Focus on the responses as they relate to information

you need to ensure that the candidate meets your job requirements. Any uncertainty you may have requires a follow-up question to further probe for the information.

6. **Close the interview by telling the applicant what's going to happen next.** Applicants are anxious about the status of your hiring decision. Be upfront with the candidate regarding others who will be interviewed and the remaining steps in the hiring process. If you plan to make a decision in two weeks or so, let the candidate know. Additionally, tell the applicant how you will respond to him or her about your decision.

7. **Write your evaluation of the applicant while the interview is still fresh in your mind.** Don't wait until the end of your day, after interviewing several candidates, to write your analysis of a candidate. Memory can fail you! The sooner after an interview you complete your write-up, the better chance you have of accurately recording what occurred in the interview.

APPLYING YOUR SKILLS

1. Break into groups of three.

2. Spend up to 10 minutes writing up to five challenging job-interview questions that you think would be relevant in the hiring of new college graduates for a sales-management training program at Procter & Gamble. Each hiree will spend 18 to 24 months as a sales representative calling on retail grocers. After this training period, successful candidates can be expected to be promoted to the position of district sales supervisor.

3. Exchange your five questions with another group.

4. Each group should allocate one of the following roles to their three members: interviewer, applicant, and observer. The person playing the applicant should rough out a brief résumé of his or her background and experience, then give it to the interviewer.

5. Role-play a job interview. The interviewer should include, but not be limited to, the questions provided by the other group.

6. When completed, the observer should evaluate the interviewer's behaviours in terms of the skills presented in this section.

SUMMARY

This summary is organized by the Learning Objectives.

1. All employees in Canada are protected by either federal or provincial human rights legislation. Depending on the jurisdiction, different acts specify "protected groups" with the intention of guaranteeing equal employment opportunity.

2. The three steps in human resource planning are assessing current human resources, assessing future human-resource needs, and developing a program to meet future human-resource needs.

3. The job specification, which states the minimum acceptable qualifications that an applicant needs for a job, guides supervisors in recruitment and selection by establishing the standard against which job applicants can be compared.

4. The primary sources for job candidates are an internal search; advertisements; employee referrals; employment agencies; schools, colleges, and universities; professional organizations; casual or unsolicited applicants; and nontraditional sources such as disabled and women's organizations.

5. Accept errors increase the costs to employers in the following areas: training, lost productivity, possible severance, and the recruiting and selection costs to find a replacement. Reject errors increase the number of candidates that must be screened. Additionally, they can subject the organization to charges of discrimination if members from protected groups are systematically rejected from jobs for which they are actually qualified.

6. Hard and relevant data on an application form have been shown to provide valid information, but care must be taken not to ask for information that isn't job-relevant. Some written tests demonstrate moderate validity, but they place a burden on management to support job-relatedness. Work samplings are expensive but tend to yield high validity scores. Interviews are widely used and people have confidence in them, but they are typically poorly conducted and result in distorted findings. Verification of facts on an application form is a worthwhile endeavour but reference checks provide little valid information. Physical exams as selection tools are relevant for only a small portion of jobs and care must be taken not to discriminate on the basis of physical requirements.

UNDERSTANDING THE BASICS

KEY TERMS AND CONCEPTS

Accept errors
Human resource planning
Job specification
Orientation
Reject errors

Reliability
Sexual harassment
Validity
Work sampling

REVIEWING YOUR KNOWLEDGE

1. Why do supervisors need to know the basics of employee recruitment and selection?
2. Contrast job specifications with job descriptions.
3. Why might advertisements be effective as a recruitment source?
4. Why are employee referrals called "one of the best sources" for job applicants?
5. Explain the importance of validity in a selection device.
6. Explain the importance of reliability in a selection device.
7. Why are work samples more likely to be valid than written tests as selection devices?
8. Why should a supervisor spend time orienting a new employee?

ANSWERS TO THE POP QUIZZES

1. **c. holds the organization liable for the conduct of the supervisor.** Anything of a sexual nature, where it is a condition of employment, has an employment consequence, or creates an offensive or hostile environment, is sexual harassment. Sexual harassment conduct by supervisors toward their employees can make the organization liable for their actions.

2. **False.** The objective of employment equity is to eliminate discrimination. It wishes to ensure fair treatment of all individuals.

3. **b. are usually made by the supervisor.** Although the human resources department may help by writing and placing ads and screening applicants, the final decision, typically, is the supervisor's.

4. How old are you? Are you married? Do you have children? How old are they? Your religion? Any health problems?

5. **b. a statement indicating employees' education, capabilities, and specialized skills.** This response reflects the definition of a human resource inventory.

6. Reliability reflects consistency. Validity reflects job relatedness. While a selection device can be consistently applied, it is risky if it doesn't measure something that is directly related to successful job performance.

7. **True.** Giving negative information undue weight in an interview is one of the problems that can lead to a distortion of interview findings.

8. Primary sources for recruiting job candidates include current employees, advertisements, employee referrals, employment agencies, colleges and universities, professional organizations, and employment centres.

CASE 6.A

The Recruiting and Selection Partnership: Human Resources and Management

At the beginning of the chapter, you read about Sheena Turnbull, corporate staffing manager at Cedara. Finding people with the right skills and bringing them to Cedara is a challenge, given the great demand for software people internationally and the limited supply of qualified people. Sheena and the other HR staff do not do this job on their own, however. They work as joint partners with managers through all steps of the hiring process. Like HR staff in many other companies, they have found that many managers don't understand the process. Also, some managers don't want to be bothered, preferring to leave the hiring to HR, or procrastinating until the candidate has been lost anyway.

As a result, the Cedara HR staff have developed a highly successful full-day presentation to educate managers on the importance and "how-to's" of hiring. They present this every few months, inviting anyone who is involved in the hiring process.

The presentation has two parts. The morning is spent looking at the big picture, that is, the importance of hiring to the company. For example, they go over the costs of hiring and of turnover, and how much it saves the company to get the right person and keep him or her. They also discuss how slow decision making in a tight market leads to lost opportunities. Also covered are who they are hiring these days: the younger people who have values and attitudes that may not match their older coworkers, and international employees who bring excellent skills but will need help fitting into a new culture as well as a new job. The legal side of hiring is also examined, demonstrating the cost of misrepresenting the company or handling the hiring process unfairly. Specific cases are cited to the audience from outside legal cases.

The afternoon of the training session focuses on the practical side of hiring. It starts by addressing job profiles and the importance of job descriptions, screening résumés, and preparing for the interview. Then participants are shown how to take the competencies from a job profile and create behavioural questions. Interviewing is also covered—the importance of making the applicant comfortable, for example, by offering him or her something to drink.

Sheena says the feedback has been positive. Managers are much more comfortable with the process now and also trust it more. They feel that it's more "scientific," reassured that the hiring decision is based on assessment of ability rather than "gut feel."

RESPONDING TO THIS CASE

1. Why do you think some supervisors and managers consider hiring to be extraneous to their "real" job?
2. Consider why it is important for the employee's future supervisor to be involved in the hiring process and decision, rather than leaving it up to the HR person. Answer this from the point of view of:
   a. the company
   b. the HR recruiter
   c. the future supervisor
   d. the future employee

CASE 6.B

Hiring at Russell Food Equipment

As the sales manager at Russell Food Equipment, Catalino Misenas supervises the work of five inside sales and 10 outside sales representatives who sell over 8000 items to B.C. restaurants. Strong sales of any kind demands not only good products to sell but also sales representatives who can work effectively with customers. A good salesperson cannot be easily replaced. Losing that salesperson also means losing a set of relationships that the person established with ongoing customers.

Catalino, an excellent salesperson himself who still works with some clients, recognizes the importance and the challenges of hiring good salespeople. This is made more difficult by the fact that most applicants don't have much sales experience. And his sales reps encounter some very demanding people.

How does Catalino hire? Candidates for a sales rep position are interviewed at least three times, individually by himself and two other managers, and sometimes also as a group. All interviewers must agree on a hire. Within the interview, Catalino likes to pose situational questions—how would you handle the following situation...? He always checks references from past jobs and follows a set of guidelines. For example, he asks previous employers how long the person was at a past job. He also inquires about the applicant's lateness record, absenteeism, work habits, ability, cooperation, dependability, industriousness, memory, relationships with others, and whether the previous employer would rehire the applicant. Catalino probes any negative information that surfaces, and focuses on any

service aspect of a past job since so many applicants have little sales experience.

Catalino also uses testing for basic literacy and numeracy, for example, to see whether applicants can convert from imperial to metric measurement and can read numbers accurately.

Sales departments are notorious for high turnover but that is not the case in Russell Food Equipment. Catalino's management of sales staff, including hiring, coaching, and ongoing training, has resulted in a productive sales staff that stays with the company.

RESPONDING TO THIS CASE

1. Compare Catalino's use of hypothetical questions , for example, "How would you handle...?", with the behaviour-based interviewing described in the chapter.
2. Comment on Catalino's reference-check questions and their usefulness.
3. Why would Catalino have potential salespeople interviewed by managers other than himself and insist that they all agree on a hiring decision?
4. If you were Catalino and know there are few people with experience selling food equipment for restaurants, where would you look as a potential source of applicants for sales positions? How would you reach those potential candidates?

7

APPRAISING EMPLOYEE PERFORMANCE

LEARNING OBJECTIVES

After reading this chapter, you should be able to:

1. Contrast the three purposes of the performance appraisal.
2. Differentiate formal and informal performance appraisals.
3. Describe key legal concerns in performance appraisals.
4. Identify the three most popular sets of criteria that supervisors appraise.
5. Contrast absolute and relative standards.
6. Describe the graphic rating scale.
7. Explain the recent interest in behaviourally anchored rating scales.
8. List human errors that can distort performance appraisal ratings.
9. Identify the three variables that most often result in employee performance deficiencies.

CHAPTER OUTLINE

PERFORMING EFFECTIVELY

THE PURPOSE OF THE EMPLOYEE PERFORMANCE APPRAISAL

WHEN SHOULD APPRAISALS BE MADE?

THE SUPERVISOR'S ROLE IN PERFORMANCE APPRAISAL
  Will You Be the Sole Appraiser?
  What Forms or Documentation Does the Organization Provide?
  Setting Performance Expectations
  Providing Performance Feedback

LEGAL ISSUES IN PERFORMANCE APPRAISALS
  Pop Quiz

WHAT DO WE APPRAISE?
  Individual Task Outcomes
  Behaviours
  Traits

GATHERING PERFORMANCE DATA

PERFORMANCE APPRAISAL METHODS
  Absolute Standards
  Relative Standards
  Something to Think About
  Objectives

HURDLES IN THE WAY OF EFFECTIVE APPRAISALS
  Leniency Error
  Halo Error
  Similarity Error
  Recency Error
  Central Tendency Error
  Inflationary Pressures

OVERCOMING THE HURDLES
  Clarify Expectations

Continually Document Employee Performance
Use Behaviourally Based Measures
Combine Absolute and Relative Standards
Use Multiple Raters
Rate Selectively
Participate in Appraisal Training

WHAT ABOUT TEAM PERFORMANCE APPRAISALS?
  Supervision in Action: Performance Appraisals in Contemporary Organizations

NOW WHAT? RESPONDING TO PERFORMANCE PROBLEMS
  What Do You Need to Know about Counselling Employees?
  Is Your Action Ethical?
  Pop Quiz

FROM CONCEPTS TO SKILLS: CONDUCTING THE APPRAISAL REVIEW INTERVIEW
  Assessing Yourself: Conducting the Appraisal Interview
  Skill Basics
  Applying Your Skills

UNDERSTANDING THE BASICS
  Summary
  Key Terms and Concepts
  Reviewing Your Knowledge
  Answers to the Pop Quizzes

PERFORMING YOUR JOB
  Case 7.A: Appraising Team Members—Refining the Process
  Case 7.B: Appraising the Remote Employee at NCR

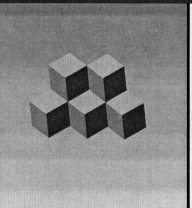

In 1997, Watson Wyatt Worldwide surveyed over 2000 Canadian workers about performance appraisals. Given your own work experience and those of others you've spoken with, predict what you think the survey results were on the following dimensions.

What percentage of employees:
1. understood the measures used by their employer to evaluate their performance?
2. thought their performance was rated fairly?
3. said their managers clearly expressed goals and assignments?
4. reported that their performance review was helpful in improving their on-the-job performance?

The actual numbers are discouragingly low—60%, 57%, 47%, and 39% respectively.[1] Yet, performance appraisals are used for determining rewards and promotions, for setting goals, and for supposedly motivating employees. Something somewhere has gone very wrong.

Generally, employees dislike being appraised, finding it a stressful experience. Supervisors find it equally distasteful, feeling like they are expected to play "judge" yet are unequipped to do so. Interestingly, supervisors do not become more comfortable in doing this as they age, as they gain experience, or with more time knowing an employee.[2]

In this chapter, we'll review the performance appraisal and provide you with some techniques that can make the appraisal and performance review a less traumatic experience for both the supervisor and employee.

THE PURPOSE OF THE EMPLOYEE PERFORMANCE APPRAISAL

Twenty-five years ago, the typical supervisor would sit down annually with his or her employees, individually, and critique their job performance. The purpose was to review how well they did toward achieving their work goals. Those employees who failed to achieve their goals found the performance appraisal to result in little more than their supervisor documenting a list of their shortcomings. And, of course, since the performance appraisal is a key determinant in pay adjustments and promotion decisions, anything to do with appraising job performance struck fear into the hearts of employees. Not surprisingly, in such a climate supervisors often wanted to avoid the whole appraisal process.

Today, effective supervisors treat the **performance appraisal** as both an evaluation tool and a development tool. It reviews *past* performance—emphasizing positive accomplishments as well as deficiencies. In addition, supervisors use the performance appraisal as a means of helping employees improve *future* performance. If deficiencies are found, the supervisor can help employees draft a detailed plan to correct the situation. With emphasis on the future as well as the past, employees are less likely to respond defensively to performance feedback, and the appraisal process is more likely to motivate employees to correct their performance deficiencies. Finally, the performance appraisal functions as an important legal document. Taking action against an employee for poor performance can create a problem if the problem is not well documented, and the performance evaluation serves a vital purpose in providing the documentation necessary for any personnel action that is taken.

Performance appraisal
An evaluation and development tool. Reviewing past performance to identify accomplishments and deficiencies and creating detailed plans to improve future performance.

**Ethics Connection –
The Case of the
Performance Appraisal**
www.scu.edu/SCU/
Centers/Ethics/

WHEN SHOULD APPRAISALS BE MADE?

The performance appraisal is both a formal and an informal activity. *Formal performance reviews* should be conducted at least once a year. Twice a year is better. Just as students don't like to have their entire course grade hanging on the results of one final exam, neither do employees appreciate having their careers depend on an annual review. Two formal reviews a year means less "performance" will be appraised at each review, and lessens the tension employees often associate with the formal review.

The *informal performance appraisal* refers to the day-to-day assessment a supervisor makes of an employee's performance, and the ongoing feedback the supervisor gives to the employee. The effective supervisor continually provides informal information to employees—commenting on the positive aspects of their work and pointing out any problems that surface. So while formal reviews may occur only once or twice a year, informal reviews should be taking place all the time. Moreover, when the informal feedback has been open and honest, the formal reviews will be less threatening to the employee and won't present any surprises.

THE SUPERVISOR'S ROLE IN PERFORMANCE APPRAISAL

How much latitude do supervisors have in the appraisal process? The larger the organization, the more likely there will be standardized forms and procedures to follow. But, as you'll see in the next section, even small companies will tend to standardize some appraisal procedures in order to ensure that equal employment opportunity requirements are met.

WILL YOU BE THE SOLE APPRAISER?

Historically, the supervisor was the only performance evaluator of his or her employees. In fact, about 95 per cent of all employee performance appraisals are conducted by supervisors.[3] But supervisors aren't always the sole source of pertinent performance information about employees. Employees themselves often have valuable insights to provide. So, too, do their peers. Hence, in recent years, some organizations have added self-evaluations and peer evaluations to those made by the supervisor.

Self-evaluations get high marks from employees themselves, tend to lessen employees' defensiveness about the appraisal process, and make excellent vehicles for stimulating job performance discussions between employees and their supervisors. Self-assessment should be treated as enhancing the supervisor's evaluation rather than replacing it. The use of self-evaluations, however, is fully consistent with the view of performance appraisal as a developmental rather than a purely evaluative tool.

For some elements of an employee's job, peers are better at judging performance than is the employee's supervisor. In some jobs, for instance, supervisors don't regularly observe their employee's work because their span of control is quite large or because of physical separation. If work is done in teams, the team members are often better at evaluating each other than any supervisor because they have a more comprehensive view of each member's job performance. In such instances, supplementing supervisory appraisals with peer evaluations can increase the accuracy of the appraisal process

WHAT FORMS OR DOCUMENTATION DOES THE ORGANIZATION PROVIDE?

Most organizations require supervisors to use a standardized form to guide them in doing their performance appraisals. In some cases, top management or the human resources department will provide an abbreviated form and allow you considerable freedom in identifying and assessing job performance factors. At the other extreme, some organizations provide detailed forms and instructions that all supervisors and managers must follow (see, for example, Figure 7-1).

Our point is that supervisors rarely have complete discretion in evaluating the people who report to them. So begin by reviewing any standard forms that your organization uses for appraisals. Familiarize yourself with the information you'll be expected to provide and make sure all the people reporting to you—especially new employees—understand how and on what criteria they will be evaluated.

PERFORMANCE APPRAISAL

EMPLOYEE NAME: TITLE:

REVIEW PERIOD: _____ _____
             Month/Year   Month/Year

SUPERVISOR'S NAME: TITLE:

Writing the Appraisal
Performance Ratings

E Exceptional — Consistently exceeds expectations in major areas of responsibility.

C Commendable — Performs the job as it is defined and exceeds expectations in some of the major areas of responsibility.

I Improvement Recommended — Meets minimum requirements in most areas, but needs improvement in select areas of responsibility.

U Unsatisfactory — Does not meet minimum performance requirements. Must improve if present position is to be maintained.

PERFORMANCE FACTORS

Rate employee in each performance category. Include supporting examples for each performance factor.

E = EXCEPTIONAL
C = COMMENDABLE
I = IMPROVEMENT RECOMMENDED
U = UNSATISFACTORY

Performance Factors	E	C	I	U	Comments and Supporting Examples
Quality — Consider accuracy, comprehensiveness and orderliness of work.					
Quantity — Consider speed and volume of work produced					
Initiative — Consider the ability to think independently with minimal direction and apply new concepts and techniques					
Job Knowledge — Consider the understanding of the job and the ability to apply knowledge and skills effectively					
Problem Solving/ Decision Making — Consider the ability to identify, analyze and solve problems, suggest viable alternatives and analyze impact of decisions before executing them					
Judgment — Consider the ability to make logical and sound decisions and to know when to act independently or to seek assistance					

Performance Factors	E	C	I	U	Comments and Supporting Examples
Punctuality — Consider adherence to the work schedule and promptness in notifying supervisor of absence					
Planning and Organizational Skills — Consider the ability to establish priorities, maintain schedules and manage time effectively					
Communication — Consider the ability to express oneself clearly, both verbally and in writing, and to listen well					
Interpersonal Skills — Consider the ability to interact diplomatically and tactfully with internal and external contacts					
Dependability — Consider adherence to the work schedule, the ability to maintain confidentiality, complete work under deadlines, follow through on assignments, and be reliable and flexible					
Job Skills — Consider skills in areas such as typing/word processing, computer, telephone, etc.					

OVERALL PERFORMANCE RATING

___ Exceptional   ___ Commendable   ___ Improvement Recommended   ___ Unsatisfactory

FIGURE 7-1

Sample employee appraisal form—*continues*

PERFORMANCE SUMMARY

I. Performance vs. Goals for Past Year:

Describe how the employee met stated goals for past year and met additional goals if applicable.

II. Goals for Upcoming Year:

List quantifiable goals with timetables for completion.

PERFORMANCE SUMMARY

III. Strengths

Identify employee unique strengths in relation to performance factors previously listed.

IV. Areas for Improvement

Identify areas in which employee can focus to achieve improved performance.

PERFORMANCE SUMMARY

V. Personal Growth and Development

Describe activities to be undertaken that will maximize the employee's career development. These may include educational programs, counseling, on-the-job training, etc.

_____   _____
Supervisor's Signature   Date

EMPLOYEE'S COMMENTS
Your comments are beneficial to the performance appraisal process. Additional comments may be attached on a separate page if desired.

THE EVALUATION AND COMMENTS WERE DISCUSSED WITH THE EMPLOYEE

Employee's Signature and date

Supervisor's Signature and date   Title

FIGURE 7-1
continued

PART 3   ORGANIZING, STAFFING, AND EMPLOYEE DEVELOPMENT

268

SETTING PERFORMANCE EXPECTATIONS

Every supervisor should be involved in determining performance standards for their employees. This principle ties back to our discussion of goal setting in Chapter 2 and setting performance standards in Chapter 3.

Ideally, a supervisor and subordinate should jointly review the subordinate's job, identify the processes and results needed, and then determine performance standards that will define how well the results are being accomplished. Remember, before an employee's performance can be appraised, some standard must exist against which the appraisals can be made. Supervisors must ensure that performance expectations have been defined for every employee and that employees fully understand these expectations.

PROVIDING PERFORMANCE FEEDBACK

Employees can receive performance feedback in one of two forms: it can be provided intrinsically by the work itself, or given extrinsically by a supervisor or some other external source.

In some jobs, employees regularly receive feedback on how well they're doing, because the feedback is built into the job. For example, a factory worker who assembles a CD player and tests it to determine if it operates properly gets self-generated feedback on her work. Similarly, a freight clerk in a shipping department at a trucking company keeps an ongoing tally of the number of boxes he packs and the weight of each. At the end of the day, he totals the numbers and compares them to his daily goals. These calculations provide him with self-generated or **intrinsic feedback** on how he did that day.

Extrinsic feedback is provided to an employee by an outside source. If the previously mentioned factory worker routes the completed CD player on to a quality control inspector, who tests it for proper operation and makes needed adjustments, her performance feedback is extrinsic. If the freight clerk's shipping totals are calculated each day by his supervisor and posted on the department's bulletin board, his performance feedback is also extrinsic.

Every supervisor should provide his or her employees with ongoing extrinsic feedback, even if their jobs are rich in the intrinsic variety. This aim can be accomplished through informal performance reviews—ongoing comments that let an employee know how he or she is doing—and through formal performance reviews on a semiannual or annual basis.

Intrinsic feedback Self-generated feedback on performance provided by the work itself.

Extrinsic feedback Performance feedback provided by an outside source.

FIGURE 7-2

These shipping employees at a chemical plant record their data, which will be tallied by their supervisor and posted the next day for extrinsic feedback.

LEGAL ISSUES IN PERFORMANCE APPRAISALS

A great many lawsuits have arisen because supervisors said or did something that their employees believed adversely affected them. For instance, a supervisor told an employee that he had downgraded the employee's evaluation because he had taken time off work for religious holidays; another employee argued that her supervisor's appraisals were arbitrary and based on subjective judgements; and a third employee was awarded damages because his supervisor failed to follow the company's performance appraisal policies and procedures.

Maybe the two most important legal facts you need to keep in mind concerning performance appraisals are:

1. Performance appraisal policies and procedures, as set forth in organizational handbooks, are being increasingly construed by the courts as binding unilateral contracts; and
2. You must do everything possible to avoid prejudice and discrimination.

Does your company have a published handbook that describes its performance appraisal procedures? If so, the courts in most provinces consider it a binding contract. The organization can be held accountable if those procedures are not followed or are followed improperly. If the handbook states, for instance, that appraisals must be performed annually or that supervisors will counsel employees to correct deficiencies, then you are obliged to fulfill these commitments. On the other hand, the courts have generally supported giving supervisors a wide range of discretion when their organizations have no published performance appraisal policies, as long as fairness and equity are not compromised. So, if your organization has a published handbook that covers its policies on performance appraisal, make sure you fully understand its contents.

The second point above reminds us that human rights laws require that all human resource practices be bias-free—including employee performance appraisals. The appraisal criteria, methods, and documentation must be designed to ensure that they are job-related. They must not create an unfair impact on any protected group. For instance, appraisal judgements must be neutral regarding an employee's race, colour, religion, age, sex, or national origin. An increasing number of organizations are providing supervisory training in the mechanics of performance appraisal specifically to minimize the likelihood that discrimination might occur in the appraisal process.

Another issue that supervisors need to be aware of is the potential charge of defamation of character. Under the law, "qualified privilege" allows you as a supervisor to point out performance problems. In law, it is your duty to honestly, without malicious intent, inform employees of unsatisfactory performance. Your duty may also be extended to other company supervisors who are considering promotions or transfers of employees who are not fulfilling their job requirements.

POP QUIZ

Are You Comprehending
What You're Reading?

1. A performance appraisal can be used:
   a. as a criterion against which the effectiveness of a selection device can be evaluated
   b. to determine if employees are in need of training
   c. to demonstrate compliance with equal employment opportunity regulations
   d. all of the above
2. What is the difference between intrinsic and extrinsic feedback?
3. You and each employee should jointly review the employee's job, identify what needs to be done, and establish performance standards that will define how well the results are accomplished. True or false?
4. Which one of the following statements is correct regarding the legal implications of performance evaluations?
   a. Supervisors are concerned with documenting performance appraisals because the courts are more closely examining policies and procedures.
   b. Supervisors are concerned with documenting performance appraisals because documentation can demonstrate that the process was proper and bias-free.
   c. Supervisors are concerned with documenting performance appraisals because they want to ensure that performance is evaluated on job-related criteria.
   d. All of the above

WHAT DO WE APPRAISE?

As noted in Chapter 3, the criteria that supervisors choose to appraise when evaluating employee performance will have a major influence on what employees do. Consider what happened in an employment agency that served workers seeking employment and employers seeking workers. Employment interviewers were appraised by the number of interviews they conducted. Consistent with the idea that the evaluation criteria influence behaviour, the interviewers tended to focus on the number of interviews they conducted rather than the placement of clients in jobs.[4]

Packing in the interviews is not the same as actually placing clients, and only the latter makes money for the organization.

The preceding example demonstrates the importance of criteria in performance appraisal. This, of course, begs the question: What should supervisors appraise? The three most popular sets of criteria are individual task outcomes, behaviours, and traits.

INDIVIDUAL TASK OUTCOMES

If the ends count, rather than the means, then supervisors should evaluate an employee's task outcomes. If task outcomes were used, a carpet cleaner might be judged on the number of square metres he was able to clean per day. A salesperson could be assessed on overall sales volume in her territory, dollar increase in sales, and number of new accounts established.

BEHAVIOURS

Evaluating employees on behaviour requires the opportunity to observe employees or devise a system for reporting to you on specific behaviour criteria. Using the previous examples, behaviours of a carpet cleaner that could be used for performance appraisal purposes might include promptness in reporting to work sites or thoroughness in cleaning equipment at the end of the work day. Pertinent behaviours for the salesperson could be average number of contact calls made per day or sick days used per year.

In many cases, it is difficult to identify specific outcomes that can be directly attributable to an employee's actions. This is particularly true of people in staff positions and individuals whose work assignments are intrinsically part of a group effort. In the latter case, the group's performance may be readily evaluated, but the contribution of each group member may be difficult or impossible to identify clearly. In such instances, it is not unusual to appraise the employee's behaviour rather than outcomes.

TRAITS

When you rate people on the degree to which they are dependable, confident, aggressive, loyal, cooperative, and the like, you are judging traits. Experts seem to agree that traits are inferior to both task outcomes and behaviours as appraisal criteria.[5] The reason is that traits refer to potential *predictors* of performance, not performance itself. So the link between traits and job performance is often weak. Additionally, traits typically have a strong subjective component. What, for instance, does *aggressive* mean? Is the meaning "pushy," "dominating," or "assertive"? Your evaluation of someone on this trait is largely determined by what the term means to you. Despite the drawbacks of traits, they are still widely used in organizations for appraising employee performance.

GATHERING PERFORMANCE DATA

Once performance standards have been set, expectations communicated, and appraisal criteria defined, you need to gather performance data. This is an activity every supervisor can and should do.

The best approach is to gather performance data on a continuous basis. Don't wait until a week or so before the appraisal interview. You should keep an ongoing journal for each of your employees, in which you record actual incidents (behaviours and/or outcomes) that affect his or her job success or failure. Such documentation reduces the potential for errors caused by relying on your memory of recent events, and provides supportive evidence to substantiate your eventual ratings. Remember that the more opportunities you have to observe your employee's behaviour firsthand, the more accurate your performance appraisals are likely to be.

PERFORMANCE APPRAISAL METHODS

Once you have your data, you can begin your actual performance appraisals, using either the forms provided by the organization or your own rating forms (see Figure 7-3). The object is to replace the "global impression" that each of us creates about someone else's overall performance with a systematic procedure for assessing performance. This systematic procedure increases the accuracy and consistency of results.

There are three different approaches for performing appraisals. Employees can be appraised against 1. absolute standards, 2. relative standards, or 3. objectives. No single approach is always best; each has its strengths and weaknesses. However, keep in mind that your choice may be affected by the human resource policies and procedures in your organization.

FIGURE 7-3

Many organizations still place a high importance on traits such as effort and dependability in their appraisal system.

ABSOLUTE STANDARDS

The use of absolute standards means that employees are not compared against any other person. Rather, employees are evaluated within the context of the behaviour expected of them. Included in this approach are the following methods: the written essay, critical incidents, the checklist, graphic rating scales, and behaviourally anchored rating scales.

WRITTEN ESSAYS

Written essay
A performance appraisal technique in which an evaluator writes out a description of an employee's strengths, weaknesses, past performance, and potential, and then makes suggestions for improvement.

Probably the simplest method of appraisal is to write a narrative describing an employee's strengths, weaknesses, past performance, potential, and suggestions for improvement. The **written essay** requires no complex forms or extensive training to complete. But the results often reflect the ability of the writer to express him- or herself well, the writer's opinion of what is notable, and a totally subjective assessment of those notable events. Comparing an employee's appraisal from one year to the next may be difficult, as will be comparing one employee to another.

CRITICAL INCIDENTS

Critical incidents
A performance appraisal technique in which an evaluator lists key behaviours that separate effective from ineffective job performance.

Critical incidents focus attention on those employee behaviours that are crucial in ensuring that a job is executed effectively. The supervisor writes down examples that describe what the employee did that was especially effective or ineffective. The key here is that only specific behaviours, not vaguely defined personality traits, are cited. A list of critical incidents provides a rich set of examples from which the employee can be shown those behaviours that are desirable and those that call for improvement.

CHECKLISTS

Checklist
A performance appraisal technique in which an evaluator uses a list of behavioural descriptions and checks off those behaviours that apply to the employee.

With a **checklist**, a supervisor uses a list of behavioural descriptions and checks off those behaviours that apply to the employee. As Figure 7-4 illustrates, you merely go down the list and check off yes or no to each question.

A major drawback to checklists is the cost. Where an organization has a number of job categories, checklist items must be developed for each category.

GRAPHIC RATING SCALES

Graphic rating scale
A performance appraisal technique in which an evaluator rates a set of performance factors on an incremental scale.

One of the oldest and most popular methods of appraisal is the **graphic rating scale**. An example of some graphic rating scale items is shown in Figure 7-5.

Graphic rating scales can be used to assess factors such as quantity and quality of work, job knowledge, cooperation, loyalty, dependability, attendance, honesty, integrity, attitudes, and initiative. However, this method is most valid when subjective traits such as loyalty or integrity are avoided, unless they can be defined in specific behavioural terms.

	Yes	No
1. Are supervisor's orders usually followed?	____	____
2. Does the individual approach customers promptly?	____	____
3. Does the individual suggest additional merchandise to customers?	____	____
4. Does the individual keep busy when not servicing a customer?	____	____
5. Does the individual lose his or her temper in public?	____	____
6. Does the individual volunteer to help other employees?	____	____

FIGURE 7-4

Sample of items from a checklist

Performance Factor	Performance Rating				
Quality of work is the accuracy, skill, and completeness of work.	**1** Consistently unsatisfactory	**2** Occasionally unsatisfactory	**3** Consistently satisfactory	**4** Sometimes superior	**5** Consistently superior
Quantity of work is the volume of work done in a normal workday.	**1** Consistently unsatisfactory	**2** Occasionally unsatisfactory	**3** Consistently satisfactory	**4** Sometimes superior	**5** Consistently superior
Job knowledge is information pertinent to the job that an individual should have for satisfactory job performance.	**1** Poorly informed about work duties	**2** Occasionally unsatisfactory	**3** Can answer most questions about the job	**4** Understands all phases of the job	**5** Has complete mastery of all phases of the job
Dependability is following directions and company policies without supervision.	**1** Requires constant supervision	**2** Requires occasional follow-up	**3** Usually can be counted on	**4** Requires very little supervision	**5** Requires absolute minimum of supervision

FIGURE 7-5

Example of graphic rating scale items

With the graphic rating scale, you go down the list of factors and note that point along the scale or continuum that best describes the employee. There are typically 3 to 10 points on the continuum. In the design of the graphic scales, the challenge is to ensure that both the factors evaluated and the scale points are clearly understood by the supervisor doing the rating.

Why are graphic rating scales so popular? Though they don't provide the depth of information that essays or critical incidents do, they are less time-consuming to develop and administer; they allow for easy numerical tallying and comparison and, in contrast to the checklist, there is greater standardization of items, so that comparison with other employees in diverse job categories is possible.

BEHAVIOURALLY ANCHORED RATING SCALES

Behaviourally anchored rating scales (BARS) have received a great deal of attention in recent years. These scales combine major elements from the critical incident and graphic rating scale approaches: Supervisors rate their employees based on items along a continuum, but the points are examples of actual behaviour on the given job rather than general descriptions or traits.

Behaviourally anchored rating scales specify definite, observable, and measurable job behaviours. Examples of job-related behaviours and performance dimensions are found by obtaining specific illustrations of effective and ineffective behaviour for each performance dimension. These behavioural examples are then translated into a set of performance dimensions, each dimension having varying levels of performance. The results of this process are behavioural descriptions, such as *anticipates, plans, executes, solves immediate problems, carries out orders,* and *handles emergency situations.* Figure 7-6 provides an example of a BARS.

Studies conducted on the use of BARS indicate that this method of appraisal tends to reduce rating errors. But its biggest advantage may stem from the dimensions BARS generates rather than from any particular superiority of behaviour anchors over trait anchors. The process of developing the behavioural scales is valuable in and of itself for clarifying to both the employee and supervisor which behaviours reflect good performance and which bad.

However, BARS is not without its drawbacks. It, too, suffers from the distortions inherent in most rating methods. BARS is also costly and time-consuming to develop and to maintain.[6]

RELATIVE STANDARDS

In the second category of performance appraisals—relative standards –employees' performance is evaluated by comparing it against other employees' performance. We'll discuss two relative methods: group order ranking and individual ranking.

Behaviourally anchored rating scales (BARS)
A performance appraisal technique in which an evaluator rates employees on specific job behaviours derived from performance dimensions.

Performance dimension scale development under BARS for the dimension "Ability to Absorb and Interpret Policies for an Employee Relations Specialist."

This employee relations specialist

	9	could be expected to serve as an information source concerning new and changed policies for others in the organization
could be expected to be aware quickly of program changes and explain these to employees	8	
	7	could be expected to reconcile conflicting policies and procedures correctly to meet HRM goals
could be expected to recognize the need for additional information to gain a better understanding of policy changes	6	
	5	could be expected to complete various HRM forms correctly after receiving instruction on them
could be expected to require some help and practice in mastering new policies and procedures	4	
	3	could be expected to know that there is always a problem, but go down many blind alleys before realizing they are wrong
could be expected to incorrectly interpret guidelines, creating problems for line managers	2	
	1	could be expected to be unable to learn new procedures even after repeated explanations

FIGURE 7-6

Sample BARS for an employee relations specialist (*Source:* Reprinted from *Business Horizons*, August 1976. Copyright 1976 by the Foundation for the School of Business at Indiana University.)

GROUP ORDER RANKING

Group order ranking requires supervisors to place their employees into particular classifications, such as "top one-fifth" or "second one-fifth." So if you have 20 employees and you're using the group-order ranking method, only four of your people can be in the top fifth, and, of course, four also must be relegated to the bottom fifth (see Figure 7-7).

The advantage of this group ordering method is that it prevents supervisors from inflating their evaluations so everyone looks good, or homogenizing the evaluations so everyone is rated near the average—outcomes that are not unusual with the graphic rating scale. The predominant disadvantages surface when the number of employees being compared is small. At the extreme, if you are assessing only four

Group order ranking A performance appraisal approach that groups employees into ordered classifications.

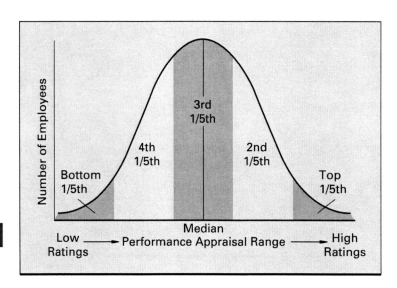

FIGURE 7-7

Group order ranking
distribution

employees, all of whom may actually be excellent, you are forced to rank them into top quarter, second quarter, third quarter, and bottom quarter! Of course, as the sample size increases, the validity of relative scores as an accurate measure also increases.

Another disadvantage, which plagues all relative measures, is the zero-sum consideration. This means that any change must add up to zero. For example, if there are 12 employees in your department performing at different levels of effectiveness, then by definition three are in the top quarter (sometimes called *quartile*), three in the second quarter, and so forth. The sixth-best employee, for instance, would be in the second quarter. But if two of the workers in the third or fourth quarters were to leave the department and not be replaced, then the sixth-best employee would drop into the third quarter. Because comparisons are relative, an employee who is mediocre may score high only because he or she is the "best of the worst"; in contrast, an excellent performer who is matched against tough competition may be evaluated poorly, when in absolute terms his or her performance is outstanding.

Individual ranking
A performance appraisal approach that ranks employees in order from highest to lowest.

INDIVIDUAL RANKING

The **individual ranking** method requires supervisors to list all their employees in order from the highest to lowest performer. In this method, only one can be "best." This method also assumes that differences between people are uniform. That is, in appraising 30 employees, it is assumed that the difference between the first and second employee is the same as that between the twenty-first and twenty-second. This method allows for no ties—this can be an advantage because it forces supervisors

SOMETHING TO THINK ABOUT
•AND TO PROMOTE CLASS DISCUSSION•

Nearly everything you've been reading so far in this chapter can be directly applied to your classroom. Every day you come to class, every quiz or test you take, and any assignments you turn in are evaluated in some form. You're being appraised—even if you hadn't thought about it that way.

Let's look at how you are evaluated. More than likely, your instructor has laid out his or her grading policy in the course outline. Is it based on absolute standards, relative standards, objectives—or a combination of all of these? For example, on an exam based on 100 points, your grade on that exam is being rated against an absolute standard. If your instructor curves the exam, some relative standards are appearing. Maybe the final grade in the course is determined by how well you met certain goals (objectives). Of course, the list could go on.

Consider how you are evaluated. Do you believe it meets the three purposes of evaluations—feedback, development, and documentation? If you had the opportunity to redesign the evaluation component of your class, what would you recommend? (Of course, you realize that "no evaluation" is not acceptable!)

to confront differences in performance levels. But its major drawback is that, in those situations where differences are small or nonexistent, this method magnifies and overemphasizes differences.

OBJECTIVES

The final method for appraising performance is the use of objectives, as was discussed in Chapter 2.

With this method, you and your employee will set standards to assess performance by agreeing on measurable goals that encompass key results for achievement. At the end of the objective-setting period—which might be monthly, quarterly, semiannually, or annually—you and your employee can sit down and appraise how well he or she performed. If the goals were carefully chosen to capture the essential performance dimensions in the employee's job, and written so they could be readily measured, they should provide you with a fairly accurate appraisal of the employee's overall job performance.

HURDLES IN THE WAY OF EFFECTIVE APPRAISALS

While you and your employer may seek to make the performance appraisal process free from personal biases, prejudices, and idiosyncrasies, a number of potential problems can creep into the process. As a supervisor, you can try to avoid distorted performance appraisals by recognizing the following errors.

LENIENCY ERROR

Leniency error
The tendency to appraise a set of employees too high (positive) or too low (negative).

Every appraiser has his or her own value system that acts as a standard against which appraisals are made. Relative to the true or actual performance an individual exhibits, some appraisers mark high and others low. The former is referred to as positive **leniency error**, and the latter as negative leniency error. When appraisers are positively lenient in their evaluations, an employee's performance is rated higher than it actually should be. Conversely, a negative leniency error underrates performance, giving the individual a lower appraisal than deserved.

If all employees in an organization were appraised by the same person, there would be no problem. Although there would be an error factor, it would be applied equally to everyone. The difficulty arises when we have different raters with different leniency errors. For example, assume that Jones and Smith are performing the same job for different supervisors, but they have absolutely identical job performance. If Jones's supervisor tends to err toward positive leniency, while Smith's supervisor errs toward negative leniency, we might be confronted with two dramatically different performance appraisals. Smith may end up feeling angry and cheated because the same performance level has resulted in dramatically different bonuses or promotion opportunities.

HALO ERROR

Halo error
A tendency to rate an individual high or low on all factors due to the impression of a high or low rating on some specific factor.

The **halo error** is a tendency to rate an individual high or low on *all* factors as a result of the impression of a high or low rating on *one* specific factor. For example, if an employee tends to be dependable, you might become biased toward that individual and rate him or her high on many desirable traits. The halo effect is more likely to arise if a supervisor has limited exposure to the employee. For instance, if the supervisor only sees the employee in meetings, and the employee is a very confident and imaginative contributor, the supervisor may assume, incorrectly, that everything else the employee does is just as impressive. Conversely, if the employee is shy and a reluctant meeting participant, the supervisor may assume, again incorrectly, that the employee fades into the background in all aspects of work.

The halo effect confronts the people who design teaching appraisal forms for college students to fill out in order to evaluate the effectiveness of their instructors. Students tend to rate a faculty member as outstanding on all criteria when they are particularly appreciative of a few things he or she does in the classroom. Similarly, a few bad habits—showing up late for lectures, being slow in returning papers, or assigning an extremely demanding reading assignment—might result in students evaluating the instructor negatively across the board.

SIMILARITY ERROR

When appraisers rate other people giving special consideration to those qualities they perceive in themselves, they are making a **similarity error**. For example, the supervisor who perceives himself as aggressive may evaluate others by looking for aggressiveness. Those who demonstrate this characteristic tend to benefit, while others are penalized.

Similarity errors hurt an organization if the rated quality does not further the organization's success.

Similarity error
Giving special consideration when rating others to those qualities that the evaluator perceives in himself or herself.

RECENCY ERROR

Most of us can remember more vividly what happened yesterday than what happened six months ago. This creates the potential for the **recency error** to surface in performance appraisals.

The recency error results in evaluators recalling, and then giving greater importance to, employee job behaviours that have occurred near the end of the performance-measuring period. So if supervisors have to complete an appraisal form on each of their employees every June 1, those accomplishments and mistakes that took place in May tend to be remembered while those behaviours exhibited the previous November tend to be forgotten. Given the reality that we all have good days and bad days—even good and bad months—and that they don't occur at the same time for all employees, a semiannual or annual review may be significantly biased by employee behaviours just prior to their supervisor's review. Employees are aware of this, as indicated by the "best behaviour" they show as appraisal time nears.

Recency error
The tendency for evaluators to recall and give greater importance to employee job behaviours that have occurred near the end of the performance-measuring period.

CENTRAL TENDENCY ERROR

It's possible that, regardless of who the appraiser evaluates and what characteristics are used, the pattern of evaluation will remain the same. It is also possible that a supervisor's ability to appraise objectively and accurately will be impeded by a failure to use the extremes of the appraising scale. This reluctance to assign extreme ratings, in either direction, is the **central tendency error**.

Raters who are prone to the central tendency error avoid the "excellent" category as well as the "unacceptable" category, and assign all

Central tendency error
A reluctance by an evaluator to use the extremes of the appraising scale.

ratings around the "average" or midpoint range. By failing to use the extreme ratings, the pattern of evaluation becomes the same for all employees. For example, if a supervisor rates all subordinates as 3, on a 1 to 5 scale, then no differentiation among the subordinates exists. And by suppressing differences, employees' work performances appear considerably more homogeneous than they really are.

Inflationary Pressures

Inflationary Pressures Tendency to minimize performance differences and be positively lenient as well so all appraisals are inflated.

A clerical employee at a large insurance company was disappointed by the small salary increase she received following her recent performance review. After all, her supervisor had given her an 86 overall rating. And she knew that the company's appraisal system defined "outstanding performance" as 90 and above, "good" as 80 to 89, "average" as 70 to 79, and "inadequate performance" as anything below 70. This employee was really bewildered when she heard from some friends at work that her pay increase was below the company average. You can imagine her surprise when, after meeting with the assistant director for human resources, she learned that the "average" rating of clerical personnel in the company was 92!

This example illustrates a potential problem in appraisals—inflationary pressures. This problem arises when supervisors both minimize differences among their subordinates *and* push all evaluations into the upper range of the rating scale.

Inflationary pressures have always existed, but they have become more of a problem over the past three decades. As equality has grown in importance, and fear of retribution from disgruntled employees who fail to achieve excellent appraisals has increased, there has been a tendency for evaluators to be less rigorous and to reduce the negative repercussions from the appraisal process by generally inflating or upgrading evaluations.

OVERCOMING THE HURDLES

Just because there are potential hurdles to effective appraisals, supervisors shouldn't give up on the process. There are several things you can do to help overcome these hurdles.

Clarify Expectations

Make no assumptions that an employee knows exactly what you expect. Discuss your expectations with each subordinate. As you read earlier in Chapter 3, Colleen Murray, sales and marketing manager for the parks and recreation department at the City of Brampton, believes strongly in communicating expectations so there are no surprises. Colleen jointly sets objectives with her staff and she makes it very clear what they will be measured on through a face-to-face meeting long before the performance appraisal.

According to Susan Pander, HR manager at SaskTel, all managers are expected to work with all employees to ensure that they understand the corporate vision and direction, and where their division is going. Then managers are expected to work with them to set individual objectives within their job description so employees can contribute to the division and the corporation.

CONTINUALLY DOCUMENT EMPLOYEE PERFORMANCE

Keep a file for each of your employees and continually enter notes describing specific instances of accomplishments and behaviours, as in Figure 7-9. Include dates and details. When the time comes for you to conduct formal employee appraisals, you'll have a comprehensive history of each employee's performance record during the appraisal period. This will minimize the recency error, increase the accuracy of your ratings, and provide you with specific documentation to support your assessments. You will be much more credible to the employee.

Rod Guild, senior foreman at Highland Valley Copper in BC, uses a digital handheld voice-recorder to make notes as he drives around the site and later records them in a small computer notebook. Rob Mastrotto, team leader of the Inserts Finishing team at Husky Injection Molding Systems in Bolton, Ontario, carries his black notebook with him constantly. "I write down what happens as I go along. I document all verbal warnings I give. I'm trying to concentrate on also recording more of the good things I observe."

USE BEHAVIOURALLY BASED MEASURES

As we've noted previously, behaviourally based measures are superior to those developed around traits. Many traits often considered to be related to good performance may, in fact, have little or no performance relationship. Traits such as loyalty, initiative, courage, and reliability are intuitively

FIGURE 7-8

Susan Pander of SaskTel

FIGURE 7-9

The effective supervisor regularly documents information on her employees' performance.

appealing as desirable characteristics in employees. But the relevant question is: Are employees who are evaluated as high on these traits higher performers than those who rate low? We can't answer that question. We know that there are employees who rate high on these characteristics and are poor performers. And we can find others who are excellent performers but don't score well on traits such as these. Our conclusion is that traits such as loyalty and initiative may be prized by organizations, but there is no evidence to support the view that certain traits will be adequate substitutes for performance in a large cross-section of jobs. Additionally, as we noted previously, traits suffer from weak agreement among multiple raters. What you consider "loyalty," I may not.

Behaviourally based measures can deal with both of these objections. Because they deal with specific examples of performance—both good and bad—you avoid the problem of using inappropriate substitutes. Moreover, because you're evaluating specific behaviours, you increase the likelihood that two or more evaluators will see the same thing. You might consider a given employee as "friendly" while I rate her "standoffish." But when asked to rate her in terms of specific behaviours, we might both agree that she "frequently says 'good morning' to customers," "rarely gives advice or assistance to coworkers," and "almost always avoids idle chatter with coworkers."

In one company of over 200 employees, the introduction of a new performance appraisal system that was much more acceptable than the old one meant a significant increase in employee trust of management. The new performance appraisal added a self-appraisal component and focused on specific behaviours and outcomes expected of the employee. Presumably, because they believed that the system was fairer and more accurate, employees felt they could better trust management decisions based on that appraisal.[7]

Combine Absolute and Relative Standards

A major drawback to absolute standards is that they tend to be biased by inflationary pressures—evaluators lean toward packing their subjects into the high part of the rankings. On the other hand, relative standards suffer when there is little actual variability among the subjects.

The obvious solution is to consider using appraisal methods that combine absolute and relative standards. For example, you might want to use the graphic rating scale and the individual ranking method. It's much more meaningful to compare two employees' performance records when you know that Supervisor A gave Bob Carter an overall rating of 86, which ranked fourth in a department of 17; while Supervisor B gave Tina Blackstone the same overall rating—an 86—but ranked her twelfth in a department of 14. It's possible that Supervisor B has higher-performing employees than Supervisor A. But Supervisor B's ratings may also suffer from inflationary pressures. By providing both absolute and relative assessments, it is easier to more accurately compare employees across departments.

USE MULTIPLE RATERS

As the number of evaluators increases, the probability of attaining more accurate information increases. If rater error tends to follow a normal curve, an increase in the number of appraisers will tend to find the majority congregating about the middle. You see this approach being used in athletic competitions in such sports as diving, gymnastics, and figure skating (see Figure 7-10). A set of evaluators judges a performance, the highest and lowest scores are dropped, and the final performance appraisal is made up from the cumulative scores of those remaining. The logic of multiple raters applies to organizations as well (hence the increasing popularity of an approach known as 360-degree feedback).

If an employee has had 10 supervisors, nine having rated her excellent and one poor, the one poor appraisal takes on less importance. Multiple raters, therefore, increase the reliability of results by tending to lessen the importance of rater biases - leniency, similarity, and central tendency errors.

FIGURE 7-10

Figure skating performances are judged by multiple raters in order to increase accuracy

RATE SELECTIVELY

As an employee's direct supervisor, you are not always in a position to comprehensively appraise all the key aspects of that employee's job. You should only rate in those areas where you have significant job knowledge and have been able to observe, first-hand, the employee's job performance. If you appraise only those dimensions that you are in a good position to rate, you make the performance appraisal a more valid process.

If there are important parts of an employee's job in which you aren't able to make accurate judgements, you should supplement your appraisal with self-appraisals, peer evaluations, or even customer appraisals, if that's more appropriate. For instance, a number of sales supervisors use customer input as part of their evaluation of sales representatives. And in cases where supervisors must be away from their work areas frequently, thus limiting their opportunities to observe their employees' job behaviour, the use of peer reviews can improve the validity of the appraisal process.

One study demonstrated that peer ratings were more strongly influenced by interpersonal facilitation skills whereas supervisory ratings were more influenced by technical/administrative task performance, probably due to differing opportunities to observe. Therefore, the inclusion of both types of appraisals towards an overall performance rating probably creates a fuller and more accurate appraisal.[8]

PARTICIPATE IN APPRAISAL TRAINING

Good appraisers aren't necessarily born. If your appraisal skills are deficient, you should participate in performance-appraisal training because there is evidence that training can make you a more accurate rater.

Common problems such as leniency and halo errors have been minimized or eliminated in workshops where supervisors practise observing and rating behaviours. These workshops typically run from one to three days, but allocating many hours to training may not always be necessary. For instance, one case has been cited where both halo and leniency errors were decreased immediately after exposing evaluators to explanatory training sessions lasting only five minutes.[9] But the effects of training appear to diminish over time, which suggests the need for regular refresher sessions.

PricewaterhouseCoopers uses an interesting training exercise to impress upon managers the impact of performance appraisals. They are asked to sit opposite another manager and form a first impression of that person. Then they are told that they will be reporting that first impression to the person in a few minutes. When the time has expired, they are relieved to find out that, in fact, they won't be asked to share their impressions after all, or receive an appraisal from someone else. However, they have had the experience of knowing how fearfully most people approach being appraised, and the uncomfortable feelings they get when they are asked to appraise someone else.[10] Even when performance appraisals are improved to be more behaviour-based, there are still mental barriers to overcome.

WHAT ABOUT TEAM PERFORMANCE APPRAISALS?

Performance appraisal concepts have been almost exclusively developed with the individual employee as the focus point. This reflects the historic belief that individuals are the core building block around which organizations are built. But as we've noted a number of times in this book, more and more organizations are restructuring themselves around teams: self-managed teams, cross-functional teams, task forces, and the like (see Supervision in Action)

In team-based departments, job performance is a function of each individual's contribution to the team, and of his or her ability to be a good team player. Both these performance dimensions are often better assessed by the team's members than by the team's supervisor. We suggest, therefore, that supervisors include peer evaluations from team members in the performance appraisals of those whose jobs are inherently designed around teamwork. This enhances the autonomy of the team, reinforces the importance of cooperation, and increases the validity of the

Supervision in *Action*

Performance Appraisals in Contemporary Organizations

The foundation of the performance appraisal process is the concept that performance standards are clearly identified.[11] This fundamental fact implies that for workers to perform effectively, they must know and understand what is expected of them. This concept, however, applies only where clear job descriptions and specifications exist, and where variations to the job are minimal. In other words, conventional performance appraisals were designed to fit the needs of the traditional organization. But what happens when the organization is far from traditional? Let's consider some possibilities.

First, setting goals for an employee could become a thing of the past. Your workers may go from project to project, with the demands and requirements of their work rapidly changing. No formalized performance appraisal system may be able to capture the complexities of the jobs being done. Second, employees will likely have several bosses, not just you. Who, then, will have the responsibility for the performance appraisal? It is more likely to be the team members themselves—setting their own goals and evaluating each other's performance. One can even speculate that this will take the format of an ongoing informal process, rather than some formal "ritual" held every 12 months. All in all, while we surmise a drastic change in the performance appraisal process, it should not be interpreted that you will become less concerned with evaluating employee performance. On the contrary, individual performance will still matter most. The major difference is that employee performance information is likely to be collected from a number of sources—from anyone who's familiar with the employee's work.

appraisal process. Additionally, supervisors should consider the benefits of downplaying individual contributions by substituting group performance measures. Where teams have clear responsibilities for achieving specific objectives, it makes more sense to appraise the team's overall performance than to focus on its individual members.

One of the issues that comes up with peer appraisals in a team is the willingness to be totally honest. Particularly if important consequences are attached to the ratings, such as bonuses or reprimands, team members may be reluctant to "tattle" on peers who are likely friends as well. Anne Murphy, branch manager at Frank McKechnie library in Mississauga, encourages honesty in several ways. She chooses five or six people to appraise an individual. Each person must sign his or her name to the appraisal, encouraging accountability, but the feedback is passed on anonymously to the individual being appraised. The peer appraisals are not done annually because they are so time-consuming and the staff is large. People want to make it meaningful and tend to "agonize over the wording." So Anne performs appraisals for new employees, if someone requests it, or when she needs the backing of other staff members to note that improvement is needed. Other than that, she will arrange appraisals for individuals about every two years.

NOW WHAT? RESPONDING TO PERFORMANCE PROBLEMS

Employee counselling
An emphasis on encouraging training and development efforts in a situation where an employee is unwilling or unable to perform his or her job satisfactorily.

You've completed your employees' performance appraisals. What if you've identified a significant performance deficiency? What are your options? You can provide personal coaching, attempt to increase employee motivation, provide skill training, reassess the employees, or try to eliminate external performance barriers. Which option you select depends on the reason why performance is lacking.[12]

If you realize the performance problem is ability-related, your emphasis becomes one of encouraging training and development efforts. However, when the performance problem is desire-related, whether the unwillingness to correct the problem is voluntary or involuntary, **employee counselling** is the next logical approach.[13]

What Do You Need to Know about Counselling Employees?

Although employee counselling processes differ, some fundamental steps should be followed when counselling an employee (see Figure 7-11).

LISTEN TO WHAT THE EMPLOYEE HAS TO SAY

You can't effectively counsel others unless you listen to what they have to say.[14] Your actions should be tailored to the needs, demands, and personality of your employee. These factors can't be accurately assessed without active listening.

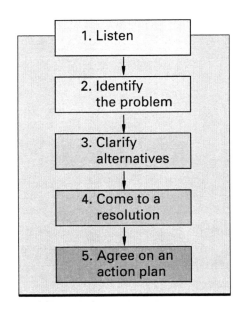

1. Listen

2. Identify
the problem

3. Clarify
alternatives

4. Come to a
resolution

5. Agree on an
action plan

FIGURE 7-11

The counselling
process

When you sit down with your employee, demonstrate your willingness and desire to be helpful. Then, listen to what he or she has to say.
Also, listen to what is not being said. How is the employee framing the
problem? Who does the employee think is to blame? Are his or her emotions driving out rational thinking? Don't make judgements too quickly.
Try to grasp the employee's perception of the situation without agreeing
or disagreeing with that perception. At this point, it's not as important to
determine whether the employee is right or wrong as it is to try to fully
understand the problem from his or her point of view.

IDENTIFY THE PROBLEM

After you've listened to your employee's initial assessment of the situation, begin the search to identify the problem and its causes. What does
the employee think is the problem? Who or what is the cause? How is this
problem affecting the employee? What, if any, responsibility is your
employee taking for the problem? You must remember, though, you're
attacking some behaviour, not the employee!

CLARIFY ALTERNATIVES, BUT DON'T GIVE ADVICE
ON PERSONAL ISSUES

Problems come with options. In most cases a number of alternative
actions can correct the problem. These actions need to be explored and
clarified. At this step, a participative approach can be particularly valuable because you may see and know things that escape the employee. As a
result, the merging of both your insights and those of the employee can
result in a larger number of quality options.

Once alternatives are identified, they need to be evaluated. What are the strengths and weaknesses of each? Again, two heads are better than one. Your goal should be to have the employee weigh the pluses and minuses of each course of action.

Avoid giving advice. Identify the options and give information, but don't tell the person what he or she *should* do. Why? If the advice works, the employee may become dependent on you for future advice and less likely to solve problems independently. If the advice does not work, you may be blamed and will lose credibility. The employee may then be reluctant to discuss concerns in the future. Whether advice is good or bad, the simple act of giving advice, especially on a personal matter, can offend some people, making them defiant.

Let's look at an example. An employee's productivity has been suffering and she has been chronically late recently. In discussing this issue with her, you discover that she is dealing with a very sick parent. You can describe possible options such as taking vacation time, going to half-time temporarily, taking a leave of absence, accessing help through community resources, or utilizing the company's Employee Assistance Program. Feel free to discuss the pros and cons of the various options—she'll probably appreciate the support and another perspective on the situation—but don't recommend a particular course of action. She is responsible for her own actions.

COME TO A RESOLUTION

What's the best option for the employee? Remember, the best option for one employee is not necessarily the best option for another. The solution should reflect the unique characteristics of the employee. And ideally, both you and the employee will agree on the solution. You want to be sure the employee buys into the final choice, whether that final choice was made by you, the employee, or jointly. A terrific solution that's not accepted by the employee is unlikely to result in any meaningful change in the problem. Obviously, here we're discussing a work issue rather than an employee's personal issue. For example, an employee is not performing well in a new role. Your discussion with him reveals that he does not enjoy this role because of its isolation from other people and he would prefer to work in a more social setting. Together you can discuss his options, such as altering the current job so it is less isolated, remaining with the job and improving performance until another opening comes up, returning to the old job, or transferring to another position. However, business circumstances may restrict the choices so you may inform him that there is no option but to stay until another opening arises and, therefore, his performance must improve, despite his feelings. If he understood the restrictions, was clear on expectations and consequences, and felt you were being fair, he would likely accept your explanation.

AGREE ON AN ACTION PLAN

Finally, the employee needs to develop a concrete plan of action for implementing the solution. What, specifically, is the employee going to do? When will he or she do it? What resources, if any, will be needed?

It's usually a good idea to end a counselling session with the employee summarizing what has taken place and the specific actions he or she plans on taking. You should establish a follow-up point at some specific date in the future for reassessing the employee's progress. If a formal meeting isn't needed, request a short memo from the employee updating you on his or her progress. This can be effective as a reminder to the employee that progress is expected, and as a control device for you to assess the employee's progress.

Is Your Action Ethical?

What business do you have delving into an employee's personal life? That's a valid question, and it requires us to look at the ethics of counselling.

Employees bring a multitude of problems and frustrations from their personal lives to their jobs. They have difficulty finding quality day care for infants. A teenage child is expelled from high school. They have fights with their spouses. A family member suffers a nervous breakdown. They get behind in their bills and they're harassed by creditors. A close friend is seriously hurt in an automobile accident. A parent is diagnosed with Alzheimer's disease.

It may seem wise to keep your nose out of your employees' personal lives, but that is often unreasonable. Why? Because there is no clear demarcation that separates personal and work lives. Consider the following scenario involving one of your employees, Denise. Denise's son was arrested last night for drug possession. She spent most of the night with police and lawyers. Today, at work, she is tired and psychologically distant. She has trouble concentrating. Her mind is not on her job. It's naive to believe that employees can somehow leave their personal baggage at the door when they come to work each morning. Colleen Murray, sales manager of the parks and recreation department, at the City of Brampton, is acutely aware of the impact of the aging population and the "sandwich" generation. She has an employee whose mother is dealing with cancer, another whose son has a brain tumour, and one who took time off to help her 80-year-old father through surgery and recovery.

Employees have a right to privacy. However, when personal problems interfere with work performance, you should not consider it beyond your jurisdiction to inquire about the problem, offer yourself as an open ear, and genuinely seek to help with the problem. If your offer is rejected, don't push. If the employee understands how his or her personal problem

5. As a supervisor, you evaluated two of your employees. Employee A received an evaluation of 90; employee B, an evaluation of 92. Which of the following statements is the best interpretation of these results?
   a. Employee B is superior to Employee A.
   b. You give inflated performance evaluations.
   c. There is probably no significant difference between the two employees.
   d. Both employees are ready for promotion.
6. Identify six means by which you can help reduce the barriers to effective performance appraisals.
7. Evaluating employee performance in terms of traits is often a weak predictor of performance. True or false?
8. The process designed to help employees overcome performance-related problems when the problem is related to unwillingness to do the job is called:
   a. performance appraisal
   b. employee counselling
   c. employee assistance
   d. team appraisals

is affecting work performance, and you make clear what the consequences will be if the work performance doesn't improve, you've reached the ethical limit of your involvement. If the employee is protective of the privacy of his or her personal life, your rights as a supervisor don't extend to helping solve his or her personal problems. However, you do have the right and the obligation to make sure employees understand that if personal problems interfere with their work, they need to solve those personal problems—and you're there to help, if asked.

CONDUCTING THE APPRAISAL REVIEW INTERVIEW

ASSESSING YOURSELF: CONDUCTING THE APPRAISAL INTERVIEW

For each of the following questions, check the answer that best describes your relationship with subordinates. Remember to respond as you have behaved or would behave, not as you think you should behave. If you have no supervisory experience, answer the questions assuming you are a supervisor.

WHEN CONDUCTING AN EMPLOYEE'S PERFORMANCE APPRAISAL REVIEW, I:

	Usually	Sometimes	Seldom
1. Try to put the employee at ease.	❏	❏	❏
2. Make sure I fully understand the employee's job duties and responsibilities.	❏	❏	❏
3. Encourage the employee to engage in self-evaluation.	❏	❏	❏
4. Do most of the talking.	❏	❏	❏
5. Avoid criticism.	❏	❏	❏
6. Focus discussion on the employee's behaviour rather than on his or her personal characteristics.	❏	❏	❏
7. Use specific examples to support my judgments.	❏	❏	❏
8. Try to get the appraisal over with as quickly as possible.	❏	❏	❏

For questions 1, 2, 3, 6, and 7, give yourself 3 points for "Usually," 2 points for "Sometimes," and 1 point for "Seldom." For questions 4, 5, and 8, give yourself 3 points for "Seldom," 2 points for "Sometimes," and 1 point for "Usually."

Add up your points. A score of 21 or higher indicates excellent performance appraisal skills. Scores in the 16–20 range imply some deficiencies in this skill. Scores below 16 denote that you have considerable room for improvement.

Skill Basics

There are three basic approaches to conducting the performance review: 1. tell and sell, 2. tell and listen, and 3. problem solve.[15] With *tell and sell*, the supervisor acts as a judge. That is, the supervisor tells the employee how well he or she is doing and then persuades the employee to change in the way the supervisor desires. The *tell and listen* approach is similar, except that the supervisor conveys assessments of the strengths and weaknesses in the employee's performance and then lets the employee respond to these statements. The supervisor tries to understand the employee's feelings by being a good listener and by displaying empathy. The *problem-solving* approach takes a very different tack. In this approach, the supervisor acts as a partner and works jointly with the subordinate to develop the employee's performance. It requires the supervisor to practise both joint goal setting and effective listening.

Most contemporary discussions of the performance review advocate the problem-solving approach. We acknowledge our debt to this approach in developing many of the following guidelines

1. **Schedule the formal appraisal review in advance and be prepared.** Many supervisors treat the entire performance appraisal as a lark. They put neither time nor thought into it.

   If a performance review is to be effective, planning must precede it. Review the employee's job description. Go over your rating sheet. Have you carefully considered the employee's strengths as well as weaknesses? Can you substantiate, with specific examples, all points of praise and criticism? Given your past experiences with the employee, what problems, if any, do you anticipate cropping up in the review? How do you plan to react to these problems?

   Once you have worked out these kinds of issues, you should schedule a specific time and place for the review and give the employee ample advance notice. You should also do whatever is necessary—close your office door, have your phone calls held, and the like—to ensure there are no outside interruptions once the review begins.

2. **Put the employee at ease.** Regardless of your personal feelings about performance reviews—and many supervisors feel uncomfortable judging others, or fear that being honest will create resentment among their employees—you are responsible for creating a supportive climate for the employee. The performance review can

be a traumatic experience for the best of employees. People don't like to hear their work criticized. On the other hand, many employees have little confidence that the organization's performance-appraisal system will accurately assess their contribution. Add the fact that people tend to overrate themselves (approximately 60 percent place their own performance in the top 10 percent[16]) and you have the ingredients for tension and confrontation. Recognize that the employee is probably uptight, so be supportive and understanding.

3. **Be sure that the employee understands the purpose of the appraisal review.** What's the purpose of the review? Is it to be used for personnel decisions or to promote the employee's growth and development? The former purpose warrants focusing on the past, while the latter points to the future. In the problem-solving approach, the review is seen as an opportunity to provide recognition for those things the employee is doing well and to discuss any job-related problems that the employee may be experiencing. Regardless of the purpose, however, you should clarify at the start any uncertainty the employee may have about what will transpire during the review and the resulting consequences.

4. **Minimize threats.** You will want to create a helpful and constructive climate. The review should not be an inquisition. Try to maximize encouragement and support, while minimizing threats.

5. **Obtain employee participation.** Effective performance reviews are characterized by high employee participation. Let the employee do the majority of the talking. The evidence indicates the more the employee talks, the more satisfied he or she will be with the appraisal.[17]

6. **Have the employee engage in self-evaluation.** Consistent with high participation, encourage the employee to evaluate his or her own performance. If the climate is supportive, the employee may well openly acknowledge performance problems thus eliminating your need to raise them. Further, the employee may offer viable solutions to these problems. By encouraging self-evaluation and being a good listener, you become a partner who is helping the employee perform better, rather than a "boss" who is looking for negatives to criticize. The employee might be the best person to identify a training plan or program that will improve his or her own performance.

Starting the review by asking the person for his or her perspective on how things have gone is often an effective beginning. Most employees appreciate this opportunity and, if you prove to be an effective listener, are very open with their comments. This means that the employee is often the first to address the topic of performance problems or particular performance challenges. This takes the supervisor off the hook for mentioning such issues and may even put you in the position of being the one to focus on the employee's positives. Often employees are too hard on themselves.

7. **Criticize performance but not the person.** If you need to criticize, direct the criticism at specific job-related behaviours that negatively affect the employee's performance. Never criticize the employee. It's the person's performance that is unsatisfactory, not the person.

8. **Soften the tone when criticizing, but not the message.** Many of us find it difficult to criticize others. If you believe criticism is necessary, don't water down the message, don't dance around the issue, and certainly don't avoid discussing a problem in the hope that it'll just go away. State your criticism thoughtfully and show concern for the employee's feelings, but don't soften the message. Criticism is criticism, even if it's constructive. When you try to sell it as something else, you're liable to create ambiguity and misunderstanding.

9. **Don't exaggerate**. Many of us tend to make extreme statements in order to make our point. Don't stretch the facts. If an employee has been late for four out of five recent meetings, don't say, "You're always late for meetings." Whenever possible, avoid absolutes such as "always" or "never." Such terms encourage defensiveness and undermine your credibility. An employee only has to introduce one exception to your "always" or "never" statement to destroy the entire statement's validity. Instead, list the four occasions on which the employee was late for the meeting.

   Another example of exaggeration that is likely to cause repercussions is a statement like "You've got a bad attitude." This comment attacks the person, and generalizes to all circumstances. Rather than noting a "bad attitude," be more specific in your feedback. For example, you might say, "There have been three customer complaints about you in the last six months. All focused on apparent unwillingness to help, and resentment about taking you away from another task."

10. **Use specific examples to support your ratings.** Document your employee's performance ratings with specific examples. This adds credibility to your ratings and helps employees to better understand what you mean by "good" and "bad" performance. If you use critical instances to record specific actions in each employee's file, it will be easier to support your rating.

11. **Give positive as well as negative feedback.** No matter how poorly an employee is performing, he or she will have exhibited some strengths worthy of recognition. State what was done well and why it deserves recognition. What you want to avoid is turning the performance review into a totally negative feedback session. Interestingly, research indicates that those areas of job performance that are most criticized are least likely to show an improvement.[18] Of course, you want to avoid the other extreme, too, of unjustified blanket praise. If blanket praise is given, the employee is reinforced for mediocre as well as excellent behaviour.

12. **Have the employee sum up the appraisal review.** As the review nears its conclusion, encourage the employee to summarize the discussion that has taken place. This gives your subordinate an opportunity to put the entire review into perspective. It will also tell you whether you have succeeded in clearly communicating your evaluation. How do you do this? For example, you may say, "I want to make sure I've been clear and that we've covered everything. So I'd appreciate your recapping what you believe we've discussed."

13. **Detail a future plan of action.** Where there are serious performance deficiencies, the final part of the review should be devoted to helping the employee draft a detailed, step-by-step plan to correct the situation. Your role should be supportive: "What can I do to provide assistance?" Do you need to make yourself more available to answer questions? Do you need to give the employee more freedom or responsibility? Would securing funds to send the employee to professional meetings, workshops, or training programs help? The object is to demonstrate your support for the employee by asking him or her where you can provide assistance and then committing to provide that assistance. In effect, you fulfill your partnership role by helping employees clear the obstacles on the road toward their goals. Remember, outstanding employees also need to know future plans for their own advancement.

Applying Your Skills

PART A—WHAT'S WRONG WITH THIS PERFORMANCE APPRAISAL?

Read the following script and "appraise the appraisal". Better yet, ask two class members to act out the roles. Use the following observer's sheet to assess Sarah. At the end, discuss what was not done well. How should it have been done?

Characters: Sarah, the supervisor, and Mike, the subordinate

> *(Mike knocks on Sarah's door)*

Mike: "Hi, Sarah, I'm here for the appraisal meeting."

Sarah: "Oh, dear, was that today?"

Mike: "Well, that's what you e-mailed me."

Sarah *(waving him to a seat, pulling open a drawer and removing a file):* "Well, I guess you're right then. Have a seat. So, tell me how you think I should rate you."

Mike: "Well, that's kind of hard. What are you rating me on?"

Sarah: "Everything that's important in your job, of course. So tell me what's important and then how you've done." *(phone rings)* "Hold on a minute. I'd better take this."

(Sarah takes the call and mumbles quietly for two or three minutes. Mike looks increasingly uncomfortable. Sarah hangs up the phone and starts to speak again:) "Mike, how long is it since we've looked at that project of yours anyway? It must have been a couple of weeks, eh?"

Mike: "Actually, it's been two months."

Sarah: "Boy, time flies in this business. Well, let's start by looking at your punctuality. You know, I can recall several instances recently where you were late. Not good."

Mike: "When was that? I don't remember anyone saying anything to me about lateness."

Sarah: "Look, I don't memorize everything around here so I can't give you the exact dates. But punctuality is important. Let's move on to the next item—unit productivity. I have written here that the goal was an increase of five percent. Have you reached that?"

Mike: "Uh, I think so."

Sarah: "Great. Now, what else should we look at... Oh, I remember, I'm going to have to put a note in your file about not contributing to that meeting on future project management in the division. You should have been there."

Mike: "I wasn't even invited to that meeting."

Sarah: "Mike, you've got to show some initiative." *(phone rings again, Sarah answers it briefly and says, "OK, I'll be there right away", then hangs up and turns to Mike)* "Look, Mike, something's come up and I'm going to have to leave. Don't worry, you're a great employee and I see no real issues. You'll get a good appraisal. I'll chat to you soon."

(Sarah stands and reaches out to shake Mike's hand)

Mike *(looking unhappy)*:

"Okay. See you."

As the role-play proceeds, record Sarah's skill in the performance appraisal.

		1 not used	2	3	4 used very well
1.	Put employee at ease	❑	❑	❑	❑
2.	Clearly set out the purpose of the interview	❑	❑	❑	❑
3.	Obtain employee participation	❑	❑	❑	❑
4.	Ask for self-evaluation	❑	❑	❑	❑
5.	Criticize performance, not the person	❑	❑	❑	❑
6.	Soften the tone, not the message, when criticizing	❑	❑	❑	❑
7.	Don't exaggerate	❑	❑	❑	❑
8.	Use specific examples	❑	❑	❑	❑
9.	Give positive feedback	❑	❑	❑	❑
10.	Detail a future plan	❑	❑	❑	❑

UNDERSTANDING THE BASICS

SUMMARY

This summary is organized by the Learning Objectives.

1. Performance appraisal is both an evaluation/development tool and a legal document. It reviews past performance to identify accomplishments and deficiencies; it offers a detailed plan to improve future performance through training and development. It also becomes a legal document that can be used to justify or support personnel actions.

2. Formal performance appraisals are regular, planned meetings where the supervisor and employee discuss and review the latter's work performance. Informal performance appraisal is the day-to-day assessment a supervisor makes of an employee's performance and the ongoing feedback the supervisor gives to the employee about that performance.

3. To minimize legal problems, supervisors should ensure that they carefully follow all performance appraisal policies and procedures set forth in the organization's handbooks (if any), and make every effort to avoid prejudice and discrimination.

4. The three most popular sets of criteria used by supervisors in appraisals are individual task outcomes, behaviours, and traits. The first two are almost always preferable to the third.

5. Absolute standards compare the employee's performance against specific traits or behaviours rather than against other people. In contrast, relative standards compare employees against other employees.

6. The graphic rating scale lists a set of factors—traits or behaviours—that are related to job performance. The rater then uses a 3- to-10-point scale to rate the employee on each of these factors.

7. Behaviourally anchored rating scales have received increased interest because they focus on job-related behaviours specific to a given job. This tends to reduce rating error and increase the validity of findings.

8. Common human errors that can distort appraisals include leniency, halo, similarity, recency, central tendency, and inflationary pressures.

9. The three variables that most often result in employee performance deficiencies are inadequate skills, low levels of effort, and unfavourable external conditions.

UNDERSTANDING THE BASICS

KEY TERMS AND CONCEPTS

Behaviourally anchored
   rating scales (BARS)
Central tendency error
Checklist
Critical incidents
Employee counselling
Extrinsic feedback
Graphic rating scale
Group order ranking

Halo error
Individual ranking
Intrinsic feedback
Leniency error
Performance appraisal
Recency error
Similarity error
Written essay

REVIEWING YOUR KNOWLEDGE

1. Why do many supervisors dislike and even avoid giving employees performance feedback?
2. Contrast the advantages of supervisor-conducted appraisals, self-evaluations, and peer appraisals.
3. What is the relationship between goal setting and performance appraisal?
4. Contrast intrinsic and extrinsic feedback.
5. If appraising behaviours is superior to appraising traits, why do you think so many organizations evaluate their employees on criteria such as effort, loyalty, and dependability?
6. Do formal performance appraisals replace informal ones? Discuss.
7. Compare written essay appraisals with BARS.
8. Would human errors in the appraisal process be eliminated in small organizations where one person does all the appraisals?
9. What can a supervisor do to minimize distortions in the appraisal process?

ANSWERS TO THE POP QUIZZES

1. **b. to determine if employees are in need of training.** One dimension of performance appraisals is to recognize weaknesses and use that information for employee training and development.

2. Intrinsic feedback involves getting information on performance on a daily basis simply by doing the job. It is built into the job in terms of numbers produced, daily goals, and the like. Extrinsic feedback is provided to an employee by an outside source—such as a supervisor, a quality inspector, or a customer.

3. **True.** This is one of the guiding principles of performance evaluations. It involves you and the employee establishing standards that, when accomplished, will lead to successful performance and departmental goal attainment.

4. **d. All of the above.** Each response deals with a particular documentation concern. Having performance appraisal policies that are consistent and able to withstand review by external agencies; having bias-free processes; and demonstrating that what is appraised and evaluated is job-related.

5. **c. There is probably no significant difference between the two employees.** Although a 92 is higher than a 90, the difference is relatively small. Accordingly, there is probably no significant difference between the two employees.

6. The six ways to reduce the barriers to effective performance appraisals are: 1. continually documenting employee performance; 2. using behaviourally based measures; 3. combining absolute and relative standards; 4. using multiple raters; 5. rating selectively; and 6. participating in appraisal training.

7. **True.** This is one of the difficulties with using only traits. The reason is that traits refer to potential predictors of performance, not performance itself. Additionally, traits typically have a strong subjective component. They may mean different things to different people.

8. **b. employee counselling.** This question and response reflects the definition of employee counselling.

CASE 7.A

Appraising Team Members— Refining the Process

Paul Dolan, ATM production manager at NCR in Waterloo, Ontario, is responsible for the appraisals of the many plant people within his area. However, his subordinates operate in three self-directed teams so he is not in a position to appraise their individual performance. And, because they operate in teams, their appraisals should focus on their contributions to the team's success.

Consequently, an interesting review process

has developed, one that is still undergoing revision. Last year, the review process was composed of three elements: 60 percent was based on the unit's success in achieving its shared objectives; 20 percent was based on the team's score on a team continuum evaluation; and 20 percent was based on team feedback about the individual's contributions. This individual feedback was based on the assessments of three to five partners who were chosen by the employee at the beginning of the year to provide ongoing feedback on individual feedback forms. The team continuum feedback is a multi-point scale on performance criteria for the self-directed work team. It is evaluated by both Paul and the team itself. See Figure 7-12 for an example.

	Goals	Group 1	Group 2	Group 3	Paul (1-4)	Area of Weakness/ Scope for Improvement
1	Customer Satisfaction	Yes	Yes	3	3	
2	Human Resource Planning	Yes	Yes	4	3	
3	Decision Making	Yes	Yes	4	3	
4	Administration	Yes	Yes	4	2	Process for consumable re-ordering
5	Flexibility	Yes	Yes	4	4	
6	Health & Safety	Yes	Yes	3	3	
7.	Performance Management	Yes	Yes	4	2	Smaller teams with own performance measurements
8	Communication	Yes	Yes	4	2	Improved format for monthly meetings. Monthly performance summaries
9	Conflict Resolution	No	No	2	1	Ongoing training with smaller teams
10	Continuous Improvement	Yes	No	3	1	Smaller teams with facilitation by support team members
11	Team Conduct	No	Yes	3	1	As per 10
12	Sharing Best Practices with other Teams	Yes	Yes	4	2	As per 8
	Conclusion	Far Exc.	Far Exc.	Far Exc.	Exc.	

FIGURE 7-12 ATM Team Continuum Ratings at NCR, Waterloo; Conclusions refer to the following: meets expectations if achieves goals 1 through 6, exceeds expectations if achieves goals 1 through 7 plus any other 2, far exceeds expectations if achieves goals 1 through 7 plus any other 3.

Paul has decided to alter the weighting of the review components for next year. He believes that last year's process did not adequately differentiate between individuals. So this year 40 percent of the review will be based on shared objectives for the entire ATM production unit, 30 percent will come from the team continuum ratings, and 30 percent will be feedback on the individual from the team. However, this year the feedback will be done differently. The team must choose five people who will review all team members. Another change is that the feedback form will be more specifically related to production.

RESPONDING TO THIS CASE

1. Explain why you think the first review process described was designed as it was. How did it attempt to be fair and accurate in appraising performance, measure the "right" criteria, and still be faithful to the self-directed team concept?
2. Explain why you think the review process is being changed in the ways Paul describes. What is it further achieving?
3. Describe the challenges facing Paul in both doing the assessments and in discussing them with the team members.

CASE 7.B

Appraising the Remote Employee at NCR

Carolyn Moore is the HRTT (Human Resource Technology Team) user support team leader for Global Human Resources at NCR. Although she is based in Waterloo, Ontario, her four subordinates are all located outside of Canada. The person in London, England, supports all the NCR human resource information system users in the United Kingdom and in the Scandinavian countries. Central and eastern Europe, including Germany, France, Italy, Poland, and Switzerland are covered by the team member in Germany. Another person based in Sydney, Australia, serves NCR in the Asia Pacific region, including Japan, Malaysia and Australia. The last team member resides in Dayton, Ohio, and serves NCR Human Resource Managers in the Caribbean and Latin America.

Carolyn is responsible for the performance appraisals of these four members of her "virtual team," yet she rarely sees them doing their work or otherwise. A meeting at the beginning of each year brings together both Carolyn's team and the technical people to discuss the requirements for the upcoming year, what will be needed, and how they will collect the necessary information. At other times of the year, all contact is through phone and computer.

How, then, does Carolyn appraise individual performance? Not only are her team members in a variety of countries and time zones, but they are all independent in their jobs, supporting many different internal "customers," and involved in diverse activities.

All of Carolyn's team members set measurable objectives for the year. Objectives are set around training users, support of existing HR technology for the countries they are assigned as well as defining requirements for new functionality as part of the current year's project. The achievement of objectives is relatively straightforward to measure. Measuring the service provided to internal customers is much more difficult, however. Here, Carolyn turns to the customers for information, asking for specific details on what was requested from the individual and how well it was done. For example, Carolyn herself supports HR managers in Canada and the UK and was asked, for her own review, to solicit feedback partners from among them.

Those solicited for performance appraisal feedback include: members of the HR community who use Carolyn's team's services; and the technical people who work with Carolyn's team to implement HR technology. Carolyn wants to know whether they received what they needed from her team in order to do their job.

RESPONDING TO THIS CASE

1. List the challenges of doing performance appraisals on an employee who works at a distance from the supervisor. This would include telecommuters as well as employees, like Carolyn's, who serve different regions.

2. What elements of the performance appraisal process are particularly important in doing performance appraisals with employees who are physically distant?

3. Which "errors" might someone in a position like Carolyn's be more likely to include in performance appraisals? Why?

4. If performance issues are determined to be due to factors other than ability and employee counselling is needed, how should Carolyn carry it out?

8

DEVELOPING YOUR EMPLOYEES

LEARNING OBJECTIVES

After reading this chapter, you should be able to:

1. Define training.
2. Identify signs that suggest employee training may be necessary.
3. Describe the role of reinforcement in learning.
4. Explain the learning curve.
5. Describe four on-the-job training methods.
6. Describe four off-the-job training methods.
7. List three skill deficiency categories.
8. Explain the importance of evaluating training effectiveness.
9. Explain diversity training.
10. Explain how asking questions can be a powerful part of the coaching process.

CHAPTER OUTLINE

PERFORMING EFFECTIVELY

EMPLOYEE TRAINING: WHAT IS IT AND WHY IS IT IMPORTANT?

NEEDS ASSESSMENT

ALLOCATING TRAINING RESPONSIBILITIES

DESIGNING THE PROPER TRAINING PROGRAM: UNDERSTANDING HOW PEOPLE LEARN
    Learning Guidelines
    Designing Training Programs

TRAINING METHODS
    On-the-Job Training
    Building a Supervisory Skill
    Off-the-Job Training
    Pop Quiz

MATCHING TRAINING PROGRAMS TO OBJECTIVES

EVALUATING TRAINING EFFECTIVENESS

HOW IS EMPLOYEE DEVELOPMENT DIFFERENT FROM EMPLOYEE TRAINING?

CURRENT ISSUES IN TRAINING AND DEVELOPMENT
    Diversity Training
    The Shift to Customer Orientation
    Pop Quiz

FROM CONCEPTS TO SKILLS: COACHING
    Assessing Yourself: What is Effective Coaching?
    Skill Basics
    Applying Your Skills

UNDERSTANDING THE BASICS
    Summary
    Key Terms and Concepts
    Reviewing Your Knowledge
    Answers to the Pop Quizzes

PERFORMING YOUR JOB
    Case 8.A: Whose Job Is Employee Development?
    Case 8.B: Training on the Run

Russell Food Equipment sells over 8000 items to restaurants throughout BC and Catalino Misenas, the Sales Manager, must ensure that the company's sales representatives are familiar with all of them. This means that a major part of Catalino's job is training. New outside sales reps take up to 18 months to become thoroughly knowledgeable and, even at that, the training does not stop. Every second week, Catalino holds a sales meeting with all inside and outside sales reps. Several new products are presented in each one, sometimes by a manufacturer's rep, often by Catalino. "The more senses you use, the more the information will stick. I show them the item, for example a glass or some china, pass it around so they can handle it, they hear about its features and benefits, they read a handout. There is a question and answer time. At the next meeting, I may ask them to draw a sketch of an item from the previous week so I know they can describe it to a client. Sometimes I ask them to recap the highlights so I know they absorbed the information.

"Bringing in new items to show clients helps keep the reps motivated. And I can never train too much. I have to keep reminding them that salespeople can get in reaction mode and forget that their primary purpose is to sell and not take orders."

As for the salespeople at Russell Food Equipment, training today is a major focus for new employees but also an ongoing focus to keep employees up-to-date.

EMPLOYEE TRAINING: WHAT IS IT AND WHY IS IT IMPORTANT?

As we'll show in this chapter, employee training and development is more important today than ever. It's relevant to big companies and small ones, and for businesses and nonprofit organizations alike. Additionally, organizations are increasingly looking to supervisors to identify employee training needs, recommend programs, and even conduct training sessions.

Training
Learning experience that results in a relatively permanent change in an individual that improves his or her ability to perform on the job.

Employee **training** refers to a learning experience that results in a relatively permanent change in an individual that improves his or her ability to perform on the job. It can involve changing skills, knowledge, attitudes, or behaviour. It includes obvious development of technical skills such as operating sophisticated equipment or using new software programs. But it also includes learning other, more subtle behaviours, such as developing teamwork skills.

In today's fast-changing world, victory increasingly goes to the company whose entire workforce can solve problems and make good decisions. That means investing in training. As companies seek continuous process improvements, employees must be trained to use control charts and other statistical tools. And as technology rapidly transforms the workplace, employees must upgrade or alter their skills to allow new technologies to realize their full potential in increasing productivity.

Training is becoming an integral part of most jobs. The goals of high productivity and avoidance of obsolescence require that employees be in a constant state of learning and adapting. In this chapter, we want to present the fundamental aspects of training and the supervisor's role in these efforts.

NEEDS ASSESSMENT

As a supervisor, how do you tell whether an employee could benefit from training? Begin by assuming that *every* new employee needs orientation training. Joining a new organization and settling into a new job is typically an uncomfortable experience. There are new people to meet and new policies to learn—the "right way" to do a job in one company is not necessarily the "right way" in another company or even in a different department at the same company. Provide initial orientation training to new members in order to reduce their anxiety and to allow them to become comfortable in their new surroundings.

Beyond orientation training, look for signals that suggest employee training may be necessary. What are some of these signals?

1. The introduction of new equipment or processes that may affect an employee's job
2. An increase in the number of errors
3. An increase in the number of questions that employees ask you or their colleagues
4. An increase in complaints by customers or coworkers
5. A rise in the number of accidents
6. A drop in individual or group productivity

If you see any of these signs, you cannot automatically assume the solution is increased training. As we noted in the previous chapter, training is not the only response to performance problems. If the problem is lack of motivation, a poorly designed job, or external conditions, training is not likely to offer much help. For example, training is not likely to be the answer if a performance deficiency is caused by low salaries, inadequate benefits, a poorly designed work layout, or the trauma of layoffs associated with corporate downsizing.

Information from AMX International Inc. on Conducting a Training Needs Assessment
www.amx_mi30.htm

Identifying Internet Training Needs
www.imr.on.ca/needsassess.pdf

Management Training and Development Needs Analysis from the U.S. Dept. of Energy
www.t2ed.com/cgi-bin/descriptions.pl?docID=13

Example of completed training needs assessment for community of King's County, Nova Scotia
www.ns.hrdc-drhc.gc.ca/English/kentvill/kctna.htm

Once you have been alerted to the need for training, you must determine what specific type of training is needed. An employee might be able to tell you him- or herself. You can use a survey to determine explicit needs or use a focus group. You can simply watch and draw your own conclusions.

When you have determined that training is necessary, specify training goals. What explicit changes or results do you expect the training to achieve? These goals should be clear to both you and the employee. For example, the new service assistant at a Kinko's Copy Centre is expected to be able to 1. use all photocopying equipment, 2. enlarge and shrink copies, 3. send and receive domestic and international faxes, 4. operate the passport photo machine, 5. operate and answer technical questions about the Macintosh computer rentals, 6. answer all technical questions regarding photo processing and differences in paper quality, and 7. operate the cash register and make change. These goals then guide the design of the training program and can be used after the program is complete to assess its effectiveness.

ALLOCATING TRAINING RESPONSIBILITIES

Like Catalino, as supervisor you are responsible for ensuring that all those who report to you are adequately trained. Since you'll eventually be judged on the performance of the people who work for you, it is in your best interest to do so.

This doesn't mean, however, that you must necessarily conduct all the training yourself. Exactly what role you play in training your employees will generally depend on the size of your organization, your training budget, and your own training skills. The larger your organization, the more likely it is that there will be a separate training department or training specialists in the human resources group. As you'll see, they can provide valuable support resources and may perform some centralized training functions. Additionally, the size of your departmental training budget will have a large bearing on your role. The more generous the budget, the more you can look to specialists outside your department for assistance. Finally, supervisors vary in their abilities to conduct effective training sessions. The higher your skills, the more of the actual training you can do yourself.

In addition to yourself, there are three other training resources you should consider (see Figure 8-1). As previously noted, where available, you should consult with your firm's *in-house training specialists*. They can help you identify training needs, design specific programs for your employees, provide advice on teaching methods, and assist you in assessing the effectiveness of your training efforts. In most large organizations, these in-house specialists will also conduct centralized training on general

- *You* can provide training for people in your department
- *In-house training specialists* are often available in large organizations
- *Outside trainers* can be hired to provide specialized expertise
- *Your employees* often are capable of training their peers

FIGURE 8-1

Where to look for training resources

issues affecting all employees. For instance, specialists may provide organization-wide training on issues such as company history and policies, employee benefits, basic business economics, math and literacy skills, time management, and interpersonal skills. Job-specific training is then typically left to the responsibility of departmental supervisors.

In small organizations or in cases where very specialized expertise is required, supervisors will rely on *outside trainers*. Outsiders, for instance, may be the best source for teaching your people about the implications of new legislation or for improving their communication skills.

Last, but not least, don't forget the potential of your employees to train their peers. You may want to delegate some training activities to skilled and experienced employees. If you do so, remember that just because employees can do their own job well, it is no assurance that they can teach others. Just as the best athletes don't always make the best coaches, the best workers don't always make the best trainers. The experienced employee must not only know the job, but also know how to train others. So if you use employees as trainers, make sure that they have been properly prepared for these added responsibilities. You may wish to enhance their skills by having them participate in "train-the-trainer" learning.

Langevin offers extensive "train-the-trainer" workshops
www.langevin.com

DESIGNING THE PROPER TRAINING PROGRAM: UNDERSTANDING HOW PEOPLE LEARN

You're developing a training program for your department. You want the program to be effective. That is, you want to create a learning experience that results in changing employees so it improves their ability to perform their jobs. Toward this end, you should understand how people learn. An understanding of learning principles can help you to structure effective training experiences.

LEARNING GUIDELINES

The following suggestions highlight what we know about how people learn.[1]

LEARNING IS ENHANCED WHEN THE LEARNER IS MOTIVATED

Merely exposing an employee to a learning experience is no guarantee that learning will take place. The employee must be motivated to learn. This is best achieved by linking the learning experience to one or more employee goals. Show the employee how he or she can benefit from the training, for example, how completion of the course will lead to higher pay, promotion opportunities, heightened departmental status, increased protection against layoffs, or other benefits.

LEARNING REQUIRES FEEDBACK

Feedback on results is necessary so learners can correct mistakes. Only by getting information about how they're doing can they compare results against goals and correct any deviations. Feedback is best when it is immediate rather than delayed: the sooner a learner has some knowledge of how well he or she is performing, the easier it is to correct deficiencies.

REINFORCEMENT INCREASES THE LIKELIHOOD THAT A LEARNED BEHAVIOUR WILL BE REPEATED

Behaviours that are rewarded tend to be repeated and sustained. For instance, if employees are verbally praised when they have properly performed a task, they are likely to continue doing the task this way and be motivated to strive toward performing better work. Frequent reinforcement is powerful when learning. On the other hand, punishment tends to only temporarily suppress behaviour. Moreover, punishment merely tells someone what they're doing wrong; it doesn't convey the right way to do something.

PRACTICE INCREASES A LEARNER'S PERFORMANCE

When learners actually practise what they have read or seen, they gain confidence and are less likely to make errors or forget what they have learned. Active involvement through practice should therefore be made part of any learning experience.

There are basically two ways an employee can practise a job. One is to practise the whole job at once. The other is to break the job into parts and practise each part independently. Which way is best? It depends on the type of job being done. It appears that if the job is narrowly defined and relatively simple—for example, stocking shelves in a grocery store—practice should cover the whole job. If the job is complicated—for example, tracking space satellites—it is better to practise the parts of the job independently.

LEARNING BEGINS RAPIDLY, THEN LEVELS OFF

Learning rates can be expressed as a curve that usually begins gradually and is followed by a steep rise, then increases at a decreasing rate until a plateau is reached. Learning is very fast near the beginning, but then levels off as opportunities for improvement are reduced.

The **learning curve** concept can be illustrated by observing individuals in training to run a kilometre. At first, their time improves rapidly as they get into shape. Then, as their conditioning develops, their improvement reaches a plateau. Obviously, knocking one minute off a seven-minute kilometre is a lot easier than knocking one minute off a five-minute kilometre. If you have ever learned word processing, you may have had an experience that somewhat follows the pattern shown in Figure 8-2.

Notice the shape of the curve in Figure 8-2. During the first three months, the rate of increase is slow as the subject learns the technique and becomes familiar with the keyboard. During the next three months, learning accelerates as the subject works on developing speed. After six months, learning slows as progress evolves into refinement of technique.

> Learning curve
> Learning begins gradually, followed by a steep rise, then increases at a decreasing rate until a plateau is reached.

LEARNING MUST BE TRANSFERABLE TO THE JOB

It doesn't make much sense to perfect a skill in the classroom and then find that you can't successfully transfer it to the job. Therefore training should be designed for transferability.

This means that the learning environment should simulate the work situation as closely as possible. In cases where learning is done on the job —such as when a senior employee spends a week with a new worker, showing the new employee specifically what to do and watching as he or she perfects the skill—the transferability requirement is not a relevant issue. Neither is it much of a problem where the off-site simulation is

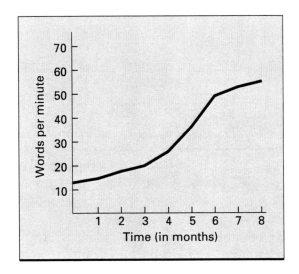

FIGURE 8-2

Learning curve for keyboarding

incredibly realistic—as is the case with today's sophisticated flight simulators used to train pilots. Transferability becomes a problem when the learning environment is considerably unlike that of the actual work situation. If a medical surgeon's training was made up completely of reading books and attending lectures on anatomy and physiology, you'd rightly question whether the surgeon could transfer that knowledge to actually operating on a real patient. This explains why surgical training includes a large segment of actual practice and several years of internship—it ensures transferability of surgical skills.

DESIGNING TRAINING PROGRAMS

The previous section provides insights into how to structure training experiences for your employees. It tells us that you should provide motivation by tying the learning experience into the employee's goals. Employees should have the opportunity to perfect their skills. They should receive feedback on how well the training is progressing, as well as praise and other rewards for each step of progress. And if the training takes place off the job, the employees should have some opportunity to transfer to the job what has been learned, either through actual on-the-job practice or through practice in a highly realistic, simulated job environment.

TRAINING METHODS

Training employees in an economy of constant change has challenged supervisors to react faster and more creatively in preparing employees to perform other jobs. Supervisors are looking for newer, faster, and more effective ways to keep their staff trained to meet the challenges of an increasingly customer-driven market. In this section we'll briefly review various on-the-job and off-the-job training methods and then show that the choice of training methods should reflect the type of problem that needs fixing.

ON-THE-JOB TRAINING

On-the-job training
Training that places
employees in actual
work situations.

Most training takes place on the job. This is because it's easy to do and gives the impression of being low in cost. **On-the-job training** places employees in actual work situations and makes them appear to be immediately productive. It is learning by doing. For jobs that either are difficult to simulate or can be learned quickly by watching and doing, on-the-job training makes sense.

One of the drawbacks of on-the-job training can be low productivity while employees develop their skills. Another drawback can be the errors made by the trainees while they learn. However, when the damage the trainees can do is minimal, where training facilities and personnel are limited or costly, and where it is desirable for the employees to learn the job under normal working conditions, the benefits of on-the-job training frequently offset its drawbacks.

SIMULATION TRAINING

C.A.E. Electronics of Montreal designed a $15 million computer simulator of a "virtual flying experience" to train Boeing 777 pilots (see Figure 8-3). The simulator gives its novice pilots a wild run—mimicking 35 airports, complete with the roar of engines, bumps from turbulent air, snow, birds hitting the windshield, heavy traffic, and warning lights. While the simulator's price tag might seem steep, it costs only $500 per hour to run, a fraction of the $14 000 an hour it costs to fly the real thing.[2]

CAE
www.cae.ca

APPRENTICESHIPS

People seeking to enter skilled trades—to become, for example, plumbers, electricians, or ironworkers—are often required to undergo **apprenticeships** before they are accepted to expert status. Typically, this apprenticeship period lasts from one to five years. For instance, a cosmetician's apprenticeship is two years, a bricklayer's is three years, machinists and printers spend four years, and a patternmaker's apprenticeship requires five years.

Apprenticeship programs put the trainee under the guidance of a master worker (see Figure 8-4). The argument for apprenticeships is that the required job knowledge and skills are so complex as to rule out anything less than a period of time where the trainee understudies a skilled master.

Apprenticeship
A program covering a period of time—typically one to five years—when an individual is considered to be training to learn a skill.

FIGURE 8-3

Pilot flight-training simulators improve the transferability of training from the classroom to the job.

FIGURE 8-4

At Corning, apprentices learn on the job but also in the classroom. Most training is done by ordinary employees. This is consistent with the company's goal of preparing workers in their new roles as teachers, coaches, and leaders.

One disadvantage of apprenticeships is that they are designed solely around the skills of a specific trade; they are not tailored to the needs of a specific organization. So when hired, apprentices may have to be retrained to an organization's specific job requirements. The other disadvantage is that apprenticeships are at odds with the current trend toward cross-training and teamwork. Today's employees need versatility. They need to be able to move quickly between a number of jobs as situations change. Apprenticeships grew out of a time when one learned a specific skilled trade and then practised it for a lifetime. Today's jobs often require a broader range of skills that must be continually updated.

COACHING

Coaching
Day-to-day, hands-on process of helping employees recognize opportunities to improve their work performance.

One of the most significant changes in the supervisor's job over the past few years has been the increased importance placed on coaching employees. **Coaching** is a day-to-day, hands-on process of helping employees recognize opportunities to improve their work performance. A coach analyzes the employee's performance; provides insight as to how that performance can be improved; and offers the leadership, motivation, and supportive climate to help the employee achieve that improvement. In From Concepts to Skills, at the end of this chapter, we'll carefully describe the specifics involved in developing effective coaching skills.

Like training, coaching is a big part of Catalino Misenas's job as sales manager at Russell Food Equipment in British Columbia. "New reps have to give me daily sales reports. I ask them what they did when they went to a particular restaurant. What was the purpose of their visit? What questions did they ask? I ask them questions to get them thinking. What did the kitchen look like? The floor? The rack? Were the dishes sorted? I need the rep to be thinking about what the restaurant could use that they might not realize."

Catalino's description of his coaching illustrates a highlight of effective coaching—the coach asks lots of questions. This may seem odd since the coach is the "expert." However, the questions are important in leading the employee to "think" along the lines of the expert and solve problems later on his or her own. Building a Supervisory Skill describes the coaching skill of using questions to probe logical consequences.

Building a Supervisory Skill

ASKING LOGICAL CONSEQUENCE QUESTIONS AS PART OF COACHING

ABOUT THE SKILL

Asking logical consequence questions refers to asking employees questions to probe the results of specific actions. The purpose is to help employees become more aware of the impact of their actions or of potential actions and to therefore choose their actions more carefully.

For example, an employee says to you, "I don't think I'll have that report done until Monday. It's only going to be a couple of days late." You know there would be grave repercussions to this delay and are tempted to say something sarcastic to that effect. Instead, you respond, "How do you think Peter will feel about that since his work is dependent on your results?" or "How will Sandy be able to make her presentation on Monday to the client without the report with her or without being able to read it and prepare?"

STEPS IN PRACTISING THIS SKILL

Look for an opportunity to ask logical consequence questions. This could be when you and the employee are discussing an error already made, or the employee is discussing what he or she plans to do, or there are a variety of options for the employee to choose from in taking action and you want the employee to think carefully through the choices and their impact. Refrain from asking the question "why," as in "Why did you do it that way?" Although it is a question and it probes their thinking, it tends to put people on the defensive.

Instead of "why," focus on specific consequences through "What happened?" or "What do you think will happen...?". Explore the impact of an action on the customer, coworkers who are linked to the task, equipment, the work environment, the organization, or anything else pertinent to the professional handling of a situation.

Ask for alternative actions. For example, "How else could you have done this?" or "What other options do you see in tackling this potential issue?" and pursue the logical consequences of those actions as well.

You may need to actually give pertinent information if it is apparent that an employee is unaware of an important consequence. For example, he or she may not be aware that "fixing" a machine a certain way may get it working in the short term but damages it in the long run. Or the employee may not be aware that if an ad is not placed in your publication for a customer by a certain date, it will be useless, you will not be able to run that ad, and you may lose that customer's future business.

TRY IT YOURSELF

Consider the circumstances in which an employee may say each of the following to you, their supervisor, and create a question in response to the employee that would get him or her thinking about the impact of their action.

"Thanks for the phone message. I'm not going to phone him back, though. He is so difficult to deal with and if I just leave him alone for a while, maybe he'll cool off."

"I know you want me to make the training session longer but if we cut out the question-and-answer section, which usually takes at least an hour, then we can save a lot of time and some training costs."

MENTORING

Mentoring
Senior employees tutor, coach, counsel, and guide less experienced associates.

Most work groups foster a buddy system where more experienced employees informally show recent hires new skills and help them out when they have problems. **Mentoring** formalizes the buddy system. In formal mentoring programs, senior employees are assigned junior protégés to whom they lend the benefit of their experience. Mentors are tutors, coaches, counsellors, and guides to less experienced associates.

Not every experienced or high-performing employee makes an effective mentor. Successful mentors are good teachers. They can present ideas clearly, listen well, and empathize with the problems of their protégés. In some cases, supervisors will become formal mentors to one or more of the people who work for them. However, this is not typically a good idea. It can create morale problems among other employees who perceive that protégés are getting favoured treatment. The best mentors for operative employees are other operative employees in their department or work group.

JOB ROTATION

Job rotation is an excellent way to broaden employees' perspectives and turn specialists into generalists. It allows employees to increase their experience and absorb new skills.

Job rotation can take one of two forms: planned or situational. *Planned rotation* describes a formal program of sequential moves. For instance, an accountant at Xerox may spend six months working in the tax area, then six months in cost analysis, then six months on auditing activities, and so forth. Japanese companies have relied extensively on job rotation to build a labour force of generalists who can perform a wide range of company functions on a variety of teams and have a network of contacts throughout the organization. *Situational rotation* is more informal—employees are moved to different jobs when their current one is no longer challenging, or in order to meet the needs of work scheduling. Many supervisors use the summer months, when employees typically take vacations, as an opportunity to broaden their staff's skills by situationally rotating people into and out of different jobs to cover for those on vacation.

While job rotation fits well with today's increased need for employee flexibility and cross-training, it comes with some serious drawbacks. Initial productivity often suffers when an employee moves into a new job. And an extensive job-rotation program can result in a vast number of employees situated in positions where their job knowledge is very limited. The organization must therefore be equipped to deal with the day-to-day problems that result when inexperienced personnel perform new tasks. That usually means supervisors must be readily available to help with problems.

Job rotation
Moving employees horizontally to broaden their skills, knowledge, or abilities; turning specialists into generalists.

OFF-THE-JOB TRAINING

Chrysler contracted training for 3000 employees in communications, group motivation and stress management through Sheridan College, a community college in southwestern Ontario. Training sessions were held outside of scheduled production shifts, beginning at 6:00 in the morning or 7:00 in the evening. This training partnership allowed Chrysler to use the expertise of college professors who designed and tailored the **off-the-job training** program directly to the company's needs.

Off-the-job training
Training that takes place outside the direct work area.

1. Supervisors should train their own employees. True or false?
2. Which of the following is true of learning?
   a. Learning requires feedback.
   b. Learning begins slowly, then speeds up and continues to accelerate.
   c. Learning is enhanced by the use of punishment.
   d. All of the above.
3. List advantages and disadvantages of training on the job.
4. "Moving employees horizontally to broaden their skills, knowledge or abilities" describes:
   a. mentoring
   b. job rotation
   c. apprenticeship
   d. simulation training

VESTIBULE TRAINING

Vestibule training
Employees learn their jobs on the equipment they will be using, but away from the actual work floor.

In **vestibule training**, employees learn their jobs on the equipment they will be using, but the training is conducted away from the actual work floor. Many large retail chains train cashiers on their new computer cash registers—which are much more complex because they control inventory and perform other functions in addition to ringing up orders—in specially created vestibule labs that simulate the actual checkout-counter environment. While expensive, vestibule training allows employees to get a feel for doing tasks without real-world interferences such as noise, distractions, and time pressures. Additionally, it minimizes the problem of transferring learning to the job, because vestibule training uses the same equipment the trainee will use on the job.

SEMINARS, CONFERENCES, AND LONGER-TERM EDUCATION

Giving employees the opportunity to participate in seminars and conferences is an effective way of conveying specific information such as corporate policies, job procedures, business economic data, and industry trends. The presentations tend to rely on a mixed bag of techniques, for example, lectures, videos, demonstrations, case studies, role-plays, and group exercises. They are widely used when orienting large groups of new employees. Organizations also rely on seminars and conferences as ways of keeping professional employees up to date in their fields. Professional development budgets typically plan for some employees to attend professional conferences or workshops.

Many companies support employees seeking further education through universities and community colleges, some to the extent of helping pay tuition fees or providing educational leave. For example, Statistics Canada provides for educational leave for its employees when appropriate conditions are met.

Training Available for Employees at Statistics Canada
http://resapp.gc.ca/eng/ rescentr/fulltx/trainde4. htm#8

PROGRAMMED INSTRUCTION

A popular self-paced instructional method is called **programmed instruction**. Trainees are exposed to a small block of information and then tested immediately to see if the material has been understood. When trainees answer correctly, they move on to another block of information. Incorrect answers require repeating the cycle.

Programmed instruction can be in the form of manuals, teaching machines, or video displays. But they all have a common characteristic: they condense material to be learned into highly organized, logical sequences, which require the trainee to respond.

A good illustration of programmed learning is the tutorial programs that often accompany the purchase of computer software. The tutorial walks the user through the software application, giving the individual opportunities to experiment with the various functions the program can perform.

Programmed instruction Individuals learn a small block of information and are then tested immediately to see if the material has been understood.

OUTSIDE READING

It's so basic that it's often overlooked: providing reading material for employees to review in their nonworking hours. Supervisors, for example, can request and purchase subscriptions to job-relevant periodicals and have them mailed to employees' homes. Or, more typically, books, journals, and magazines are provided in rest areas, lunch rooms, and other places where employees may informally gather.

INDUSTRIAL SECTOR TRAINING

In a unique partnership between management and union, a certificate program was developed to cooperatively address training needs within the independent automotive parts manufacturing industry in Canada. The partners, the Automotive Parts Manufacturers' Association (management) and the Canadian Auto Workers Union, must both approve the content

www.capma.com
www.caw.ca

and instruction methods. The ultimate aim is to deliver effective long-term training in an integrated curriculum that focuses on communication, industry, and technology. The program relies heavily on the use of peer trainers—production workers recruited from industry. The trainers work at gaining mutual respect for the agendas of management, labour, employers, and workers with an orientation towards the auto parts manufacturing sector. The certificate informational brochure states:

> Management representatives see the value of this process in increased willingness and ability of their employees to participate in changes occurring at their workplace. Labour representatives see its value in increased empowerment of their members to play a leading role in making and implementing decisions about workplace change. Both agree, however, that the title of the program—"Opening Doors"—expresses its essential purpose.[3]

On-line Learning
www.mapnp.org/library/
trng_dev/methods/
on_line.htm

Training at HSBC
www.hsbc.ca/english/
careers/training_and_
development.asp

Training at Lockheed Martin Canada
www.lockheedmartin.
com/canada/train_and_
develop.htm

E-learning
Employees use network technology to gain access to training materials, to "experts," and to other learners.

Distance learning
Learning that occurs when the student is remote from the teacher.

WEB-BASED LEARNING AND DISTANCE LEARNING

Also known as on-line learning or *e-learning*, web-based learning uses network technology to give employees access to training materials, to "experts," and to interaction with other learners.

Distance learning refers to learning that occurs when the student is remote from the "teacher." This could take the form, for example, of correspondence courses or web-based courses. HSBC Bank Canada offers distance learning opportunities to employees. Lockheed Martin Canada offers both web-based training and other forms of distance learning. These courses have the advantage of allowing the employee to engage in the learning at a time that is convenient and relevant. They can learn it when the knowledge is especially useful, a kind of "Just-in-Time" training. It is also handy for employees who travel a lot, whose schedules are unpredictable, and whose development needs are unusual.

MATCHING TRAINING PROGRAMS TO OBJECTIVES

Supervisors shouldn't select training methods arbitrarily. Each method has certain strengths and weaknesses. A good deal of the success of any training or development program can be attributed to properly selecting a method that fits your objective.

Most skill deficiencies fall into one of three categories: technical, decision-making, or interpersonal. *Technical deficiencies* address the ability to use the tools, equipment, processes, and techniques needed to perform a job. *Decision-making deficiencies* encompass the abilities to identify problems, develop alternatives, analyze and evaluate alternatives, and arrive at effective solutions. *Interpersonal deficiencies* are concerned with abilities to work and communicate with others. In addition, learning in each of these categories may be from a cognitive or experiential perspective. **Cognitive learning** relies on mental processes. When you learn by reading, watching, or thinking, you're engaged in cognitive learning. When training focuses on actually practising, experiencing, or doing something, then you're engaged in **experiential learning**. As we noted earlier in the chapter, surgical training relies both on cognitive concepts and experiential practice.

Cognitive learning
Learning that occurs via mental processes such as reading, watching, and thinking.

Experiential learning
Learning that relies on practising, experiencing, or doing something.

On-the-job training methods are either experiential or a combination of cognitive and experiential learning. These are the preferred methods for learning technical skills and for practising interpersonal skills. Vestibule training, while off-the-job, requires learning by doing. It is an excellent means of dealing with technical deficiencies. Programmed learning can be either cognitive or experiential. For example, when you read about computers, it's cognitive. When you practise what you've learned, it's experiential. Seminars and conferences can likewise be designed along either perspective. Lecturing, for instance, relies on cognitive processes for learning. Role-plays, on the other hand, incorporate learning by doing. Outside reading is an example of a purely cognitive learning activity.

When you want to merely know about something, cognitive learning methods are most effective. If you want to understand what a business plan is, or the pros and cons of putting your department on flexible work hours, or the proper steps to take in disciplining an employee, cognitive learning methods work well. However, if you want to actually write a business plan, or learn to implement flexible work hours, or practise disciplining, you should focus on experiential techniques.

Before you choose a training method, ask yourself what it is you want your trainee to learn (see Figure 8-5). What specifically is the skill deficiency? Then design a training program that will most effectively facilitate the learning of that skill.

- *Technical.* Encompasses the ability to use tools, equipment, processes, and techniques.

- *Decision making.* Encompasses the ability to identify problems, develop alternatives, analyze and evaluate alternatives, and arrive at effective solutions.

- *Interpersonal.* Encompasses the ability to work and communicate with others.

FIGURE 8-5

Categories of skill deficiencies

EVALUATING TRAINING EFFECTIVENESS

It's relatively easy to offer a new training program. But training must be cost-effective. You won't know if it's cost-effective unless you evaluate the training that's taking place. You must be able to show that the benefits gained from the training outweigh the costs of providing the learning experience. The only way to do this is to analyze the outcomes training may have generated.

Is there a way in which training programs are typically evaluated? Frequently, the following scenario takes place. Several individuals—usually representatives from the training department and a group of workers—are asked to critique a recently completed training program. If the comments are generally positive, the program receives a favourable evaluation. Based on that evaluation, the program continues, until something occurs that causes it to be changed or eliminated.

The accuracy of these reactions, however, is questionable. The participants' opinions are often heavily influenced by factors that have little to do with actual training effectiveness—factors such as difficulty, entertainment value, or the personality of the instructor. Obviously, that's not the type of evaluation we're referring to. Rather, you must be certain that employee performance improves. Accordingly, training programs must be evaluated on some performance-based measures. This can be achieved by evaluating how well employees perform their jobs after they have received training, or the differences found between pre- and post-training performance.

HOW IS EMPLOYEE DEVELOPMENT DIFFERENT FROM EMPLOYEE TRAINING?

Employee development Preparation of employees for future positions that require higher-level skills, knowledge, or abilities.

In many organizations, the terms *training* and *development* are used synonymously. In many respects, that may be correct. But employee development is different. Whereas employee training focuses its attention on the skills needed to do one's current job, **employee development** is more future-oriented. That is, it deals with preparing employees for future positions that require higher-level skills, knowledge, or abilities—like the analytical, human, conceptual, political, and specialized skills needed by all supervisors, which we introduced in Chapter 1. Although the methods of delivering employee development programs are similar to training methods, they focus more heavily on employees' personal growth.

It is important to consider one critical component of employee development in today's organizations. All employees, no matter what their level, can be developed. Historically, development was reserved for supervisory personnel, and those aspiring to be such. Although there's no question that development still must include preparing these individuals, the processes of downsizing and empowering have shown us that nonsupervisory personnel need such skills as planning, organizing, leading, and controlling, too. For instance, the use of work teams, workers' greater opportunity to participate in decision making, and the greater emphasis on customer service and quality have all led to development being "pushed" down in the organization. Like training, development efforts must also be evaluated to ensure that the organization is getting its money's worth.

CURRENT ISSUES IN TRAINING AND DEVELOPMENT

Informal discussions with practising supervisors reveal that, in addition to basic job skills, two other issues are high on their list of training needs. One is *diversity training*. Work groups are increasingly made up of individuals of mixed gender and diverse ethnic backgrounds. Employees need training to help them learn to accept people who are different from themselves and to become aware of the advantages diversity can bring to a work group. The other issue is *customer service training*.

DIVERSITY TRAINING

While some organizations rely on outside consultants to provide **diversity training**, others are doing it in-house with their own employees (see Figure 8-6). The Royal Bank has designed an orientation program for all employees on the issues facing people with disabilities. BCTel offers training to its employees on the Chinese and South Asian cultures to help employees better serve their customers from these cultures. BCTel also offers a managing human rights workshop to create greater awareness of discrimination and harassment and what employees can do about it.

Diversity training Training aimed at creating greater awareness of the issues that arise in a staff of varied background and characteristics, encouraging acceptance and appreciation of that variety, and helping employees learn how to accommodate and work with people of diverse backgrounds.

Royal Bank's employee orientation on issues facing people with disabilities
www.neilsquire.ca/news/archiv20.htm

BCTel training on Chinese culture
info.load-otea.hrdc-drhc.gc.ca/~weeweb/autochen.htm#Chinese

BCTel training on South Asian culture
info.load-otea.hrdc-drhc.gc.ca/~weeweb/autochen.htm#asians

HRDC workshop on Recruitment and Retention of Aboriginal Employees
info.load-otea.hrdc-drhc.gc.ca/~weeweb/autochen.htm#retention

Public Service Commission course on Managing Diversity in the Workplace
info.load-otea.hrdc-drhc.gc.ca/~weeweb/autochen.htm#diversity

FIGURE 8-6

This informal, small group training session focuses on increasing diversity awareness among participants

Besides going to private consulting companies for help in offering diversity training, some government organizations also offer resources. For example, HRDC's Equity Advisory Services offers a workshop on recruitment and retention of Aboriginal employees to national organizations, companies, and associations. The Public Service Commission of Canada offers courses on managing diversity in the workplace and preventing harassment in the workplace, to managers and supervisors in both the public and private sectors.

These courses typically aim at creating greater awareness of diversity issues through education, creating greater acceptance of diverse employees, and assisting employees in taking specific action to accommodate and work with diverse people, whether employees or customers.

THE SHIFT TO CUSTOMER ORIENTATION

The example described above, of BCTel providing training to its employees so they can better understand and work with Chinese and South Asian customers, links the focus on diversity training with a second major focus—customer service. As the Canadian economic base becomes more focused on sales and service, supervisors will be challenged to instil a different orientation to customer satisfaction in employees who are accustomed to process-driven jobs. As we look at recent advertising themes in our market, companies are pushing the truth of "the customer is always right!" And companies such as Wal-Mart and Nissan, with proven records of price and quality satisfaction for their clients, have been making their mark on the Canadian market.

The Bank of Nova Scotia tackled the issue of promoting this new orientation among its employees, changing from an audit-driven focus to an emphasis on sales and service. The bank developed in-branch training for mass delivery across its distribution system, including pre-packaged training units and accompanying videos. Account manager Leigh Enlund says, "In reality, the focus needs to be on motivating employees to accept the switch to a sales and service orientation." She estimated that it would take two to three years before the real commitment to a sales orientation is achieved.

Scotiabank
www.scotiabank.ca/

5. Trainees who pace their own instruction, learning a small block of information (usually from a computer or manual), getting tested immediately, and then moving on to the next block of information, are learning by which technique?
   a. vestibule training
   a. sector training
   c. programmed instruction
   d. simulation training

6. Getting several participants to critique a recently completed training program is an effective way to evaluate the training. True or false?

7. Which one of the following statements best reflects the difference between employee training and employee development?
   a. Employee training primarily involves off-the-job training methods whereas employee development tends to use on-the-job methods.
   b. Training focuses on potential employees whereas employee development focuses on current employees.
   c. Employee training focuses on the skills needed for current jobs whereas employee development focuses on the skills needed for future postions.
   d. Employee training and development mean the same thing.

8. Explain why diversity training is offered.

COACHING

Assessing Yourself: What is Effective Coaching?

For each of the following statements, answer either True (T) or False (F).

AN EFFECTIVE COACH SHOULD:

1.	Tell employees the right way to do a job.	T	F
2.	Suspend judgment and evaluation.	T	T
3.	Be a role model.	T	F
4.	Provide long-term career planning.	T	F
5.	Use a collaborative style.	T	F
6.	Never use threats.	T	F
7.	Respect an employee's individuality.	T	F
8.	Focus on getting each employee's performance up to a minimum standard.	T	F
9.	Dismiss mistakes.	T	F
10.	Delegate responsibility for coaching outcomes to the employee.	T	F

SCORING KEY

Give yourself one point for each correct answer: 1. F; 2. T; 3. T; 4. F; 5. T; 6. T; 7. T; 8. F; 9. F; and 10. F. Scores of eight or above indicate you have quite a bit of valid knowledge about coaching.

SKILL BASICS

Effective supervisors have learned how to coach their employees. That is, through coaching you help your employees to improve their performance.

Is coaching synonymous with counselling? Both deal with day-to-day issues rather than the long term. But they're different. Coaching deals with ability issues. As a coach, you provide instruction, guidance, advice, and encouragement to help employees improve their job performance. Counselling, by contrast, deals with personal problems. When employee attitudes or personality are the problem, you need to provide counselling.

Another important dimension of coaching is that it requires you to suspend judgement and evaluation. Supervisors, in the normal routine of carrying out their jobs, regularly express judgements about performance in relation to previously established goals. As a coach, you focus on accepting employees the way they are and helping them to make continual improvement toward the goal of developing to their full potential.

There are three general skills that supervisors should exhibit if they are to help their employees generate breakthroughs in performance.[4] The following reviews these general skills and the specific behaviours associated with each.

1. **Ability to analyze ways of improving an employee's performance and capabilities.**

   a. Observe your employee's behaviour on a day-to-day basis.

   b. Ask questions of the employee: Tell me about how you handled this situation. What other approach could you have used?

   c. Show genuine interest in the person as an individual, not merely as an employee. Respect his or her individuality. The insight you have into the employee's uniqueness is more important than any technical expertise you can provide about improving job performance.

   d. Listen to the employee. You can't understand the world from an employee's perspective unless you listen.

2. **Ability to create a supportive climate.** It's the coach's responsibility to reduce barriers to development and facilitate a climate that encourages performance improvement.

   a. Create a climate that contributes to a free and open exchange of ideas.

   b. Offer help and assistance. Give guidance and advice when asked

   c. Encourage your employees. Be positive and upbeat. Don't use threats.

   d. Focus on mistakes as learning opportunities. Change implies risk and employees must not feel that mistakes will be punished. When failure occurs, ask: "What did we learn that can help us in the future?"

   e. Reduce obstacles. What factors do you control that, if changed, would help the employee to improve his or her job performance?

f. Express to the employee the value of his or her contribution to the department's goals.

g. Take personal responsibility for the outcome, but don't rob employees of their full responsibility. Validate the employees' efforts when they succeed, and point to what was missing when they fail. Never blame the employees for poor results.

3. **Ability to influence employees to change their behaviour.** The ultimate test of coaching effectiveness is whether an employee's performance improves. But this is not a static concept. We are concerned with ongoing growth and development.

a. Encourage continual improvement. Recognize and reward small improvements and treat coaching as helping employees to continually work toward improvement. There are no absolute upper limits to an employee's job performance.

b. Use a collaborative style. Employees will be more responsive to accepting change if they participate in identifying and choosing among improvement ideas.

c. Break difficult tasks down into simpler ones. By breaking down more complex jobs into a series of tasks of increasing difficulty, discouraged employees are more likely to experience success. Achieving success on simpler tasks encourages them to take on more difficult ones.

d. Model the qualities you expect from your employees. If you want openness, dedication, commitment, and responsibility from your employees, you must demonstrate these qualities yourself. Your employees will look to you as a role model, so make sure your deeds match your words.

APPLYING YOUR SKILLS

Read the following scenario. Depending on the instructions given, be prepared to either write a three- or four-page report or discuss in class how you would handle Todd Corsetti based on the coaching skills in this chapter.

SITUATION

You work for a large mortgage brokering company that has 30 offices located in western Canada. You're the supervisor of the Edmonton office and have seven mortgage brokers, an assistant, and a secretary reporting to you. Your business entails helping home buyers find mortgages and acting as a link between lenders and borrowers in getting loans approved and processed.

Todd Corsetti is one of your brokers. He has been in the office for two and a half years. Before that, he sold commercial real estate. You've been in your Edmonton job for 14 months, prior to which you supervised a smaller office for the same company.

You have not been pleased with Todd's job performance, so you decided to review his personnel file. His first six-month review stated: "Todd is enthusiastic. He is a bit disorganized but willing to learn. Seems to have good potential." After a year, his previous supervisor had written, "Todd seems to be losing interest. Seems frequently disorganized. Often rude to clients. Did not mention these problems to him. Hope he'll improve. His long-term potential now much more in question."

You have not spent much time with Todd. Your offices are far apart. But probably the real reason is that he's not a person who's easy to talk to and you have little in common. When you took this job, you decided that you'd wait some time before tackling any problems to make sure you had a good grasp of the people and the situation.

But Todd's problems have become too visible to ignore. He is consistently missing his quarterly sales projections. Based on mortgages processed, he is your lowest performer. In addition, his reports are constantly late. After reviewing last month's performance reports, you made an appointment yesterday to meet him today at 9:00 a.m. But he wasn't in his office when you arrived for that appointment. You waited 15 minutes and gave up. Your secretary tells you that Todd regularly comes in late for work in the morning and takes extra long coffee breaks. Last week, Valerie Oletta, who has the office next to Todd's, complained to you that Todd's behaviour was demoralizing her and some of the other brokers.

You don't want to fire Todd. It wouldn't be easy to find a replacement. Moreover, he has a lot of contacts with new-home builders, which brings in a number of borrowers to your office. In fact, maybe 60 per cent of the business generated by your entire office comes from builders who have personal ties to Todd. If Todd were to leave your company and go to a competitor, he'd probably be able to convince the builders to take their business somewhere else.

DISCUSSION

Using the three general skills in coaching employees, detail a plan of action that you, as Todd's supervisor, might follow in a coaching seminar.

SUMMARY

This summary is organized by the Learning Objectives.

1. Training is defined as a learning experience that results in a relatively permanent change in an individual that improves his or her ability to perform on the job.

2. Signs that suggest employee training may be necessary include the entry of a new employee, the introduction of new equipment or processes, an increase in the number of employee errors, an increase in the number of questions employees ask, an increase in complaints by customers or coworkers, a rise in the number of accidents, or a drop in individual or group productivity.

3. The use of reinforcement encourages the repetition of a behaviour. When a new behaviour is exhibited, it can be sustained by use of reinforcement.

4. The learning curve describes the speed with which learning occurs over time. Learning is very fast near the beginning, which means the curve is steep. Then learning levels off as opportunities for improvement lessen.

5. Four on-the-job training methods are apprenticeship, coaching, mentoring, and job rotation.

6. Four off-the-job training methods are vestibule training, seminars and conferences, programmed instruction, and outside reading.

7. Three skill deficiency categories are technical, decision-making, and interpersonal.

8. Evaluating training effectiveness is an important tool to ensure that training dollars are spent on programs that positively influence employee job performance. Rigorous evaluation can help determine if training makes any difference and whether the improvement justifies the cost.

9. Diversity training is aimed at creating greater awareness of the issues that arise in a staff of varied background and characteristics, encouraging acceptance and appreciation of that variety, and helping employees learn how to accommodate and work with people of diverse backgrounds.

10. Through questioning an employee about what they have done or plan to do, alternative actions, and the impact of the various actions, a coach can encourage the employee to think through and carefully choose future actions based on their results.

UNDERSTANDING THE BASICS

KEY TERMS AND CONCEPTS

Apprenticeship
Coaching
Cognitive learning
Distance learning
Diversity training
E-learning
Employee development
Experiential learning

Job rotation
Learning curve
Mentoring
Off-the-job training
On-the-job training
Programmed instruction
Training
Vestibule training

REVIEWING YOUR KNOWLEDGE

1. Why is training important?
2. When might training not be the solution to ineffective job performance?
3. What is the supervisor's responsibility regarding training?
4. How can you use learning principles to make training more effective?
5. Discuss this statement in terms of designing a training program: "I hear and I forget. I see and I remember. I do and I understand."
6. What are the advantages of on-the-job training? Off-the-job training?
7. What's the best approach for evaluating training? Why?
8. Is it possible to teach people to get along better with each other? Explain.

ANSWERS TO THE POP QUIZZES

1. **False.** Whether the supervisor is involved in training depends on training budget, time, the supervisor's training skills, the size of the organization, and the availability of other training resources.

2. **a. Learning requires feedback.** Learners must be aware of how effective their performance is in order to correct mistakes and focus on improving.

3. Advantages of training on the job include ease, transferability to job, and apparent low cost. Disadvantages include low productivity during training and the costs incurred by errors.

4. **b. job rotation**

5. **c. programmed instruction**

6. **False.** Their critiques are subjective and may be unrelated to actual changes in performance, which must be the focus in evaluating the training.

7. **c. Employee training focuses on the skills needed for current jobs whereas employee development focuses on the skills needed for future positions.**

8. Diversity training is aimed at creating a more tolerant and productive workforce. The workforce is increasingly diverse and it is felt that training can help people better accept and appreciate this diversity.

CASE 8.A

Whose Job Is Employee Development?

Shivani is frustrated. She feels that she should have been promoted long ago. When she confronted her supervisor about it recently, her supervisor said she was highly valued in her current position but suggested that she could take some management or leadership courses. This feels like a "brush-off" to Shivani. Neither of the two people promoted from Shivani's department in her five years at the company had taken this kind of training. And who has time for it anyway? She works such long hours that she has little enough time for her family. And why should she pay for it if there's no guarantee that it will end up in a promotion?

If Shivani worked for Allied Signal Aerospace, the response from her supervisor would have been very different. Allied Signal managers are provided with a development actions resource guide that offers specific ideas for developing employees. The ideas are clustered under the 11 key attributes and behaviours on which all employees are appraised. Had she worked for Allied Signal, Shivani would have received specific feedback on any skill deficiencies long ago and several discussions on development opportunities would have occurred. In those discussions, Shivani and her supervisor would have examined various ways of developing her skills and together created a specific plan.

For example, let's assume that Shivani needs improvement on the "Bias for Action" performance dimension. This may have held her back from consideration for promotion. The supervisor and Shivani would have referred to Allied's development actions resource guide and found many suggestions to consider, including the following:

- Chair a task force on a pressing problem.

- Manage a dissatisfied customer and troubleshoot a performance or quality problem.
- Plan and run an off-site meeting, conference, or event.
- Serve at a community agency for a year.
- Benchmark a competitor's practices and present a report on recommendations for change at your organization.

Shivani and her supervisor would have chosen one or more ideas appropriate to her circumstances and planned the specific goals, deadlines, and evaluation points.

RESPONDING TO THIS CASE

1. Explain the probable impact of Allied Signal having developed this resource guide and linked it to the performance appraisal process. Illustrate by predicting what would happen to Shivani at Allied Signal as opposed to her employer.
2. Explain how Allied Signal's approach to development influences the supervisor's job.
3. Shivani has been employed in the same position for five years. Explain the role that development can play for an employee like Shivani.

CASE 8.B

Training on the Run

Janis, a finance supervisor at a large manufacturing company, believes that keeping up on your skills is tough, whether you're a regular employee or a supervisor. This is especially true in technical areas. Her organization is implementing several new leading-edge software systems that affect her area. This is complicated by the fact that her VP is always suggesting other changes. As soon as he hears the buzz about some new trend, it's "Let's do it." Janis and her staff are expected to become instant experts and implement this "flavour of the month." This is stressful because Janis must jump in and implement as she's learning about something.

When Janis was hired as supervisor, the finance department had been previously decimated by downsizing and early retirements. She was expected to rebuild the team, plus deal with all these software changes. In recruiting and hiring, Janis found it difficult to find candidates with the appropriate software proficiency, so she chose people with the potential to learn. They knew the finance side well and were comfortable in other programs. She knew that, with the right training and support, they would rise to the challenge. But there was no way she could send each one away for a month to learn the new software. And she couldn't expect them to be immediate experts. So, instead, she spaced out the courses for the individuals. First, they would become involved in a process, such as payroll, and then they would attend a course

relating software to that function. This improved their learning experience. Janis calls it "just-in-time learning" and claims it works well. The employees are focused and motivated in the course and describe the experience of a "light bulb" flashing in their head when they make a crucial link in the training.

RESPONDING TO THIS CASE

1. Janis's VP appears to have an interesting view on training needs analysis. Comment.
2. What is wrong with the VP's approach to introducing change and the required training that goes with it?
3. What training method does Janis appear to be using for the software training and why? What other methods might be appropriate for this training? What would be the advantages and disadvantages of each?
4. How might Janis evaluate the effectiveness of the software training?

PART FOUR

STIMULATING INDIVIDUAL AND GROUP PERFORMANCE

9. MOTIVATING YOUR EMPLOYEES

10. PROVIDING LEADERSHIP

11. COMMUNICATING EFFECTIVELY

9

MOTIVATING YOUR EMPLOYEES

LEARNING OBJECTIVES

After reading this chapter, you should be able to:

1. Define *motivation*.
2. Identify and define five personality characteristics relevant to understanding the behaviour of employees at work.
3. Explain the elements and the focus of the three early theories of motivation.
4. Identify the characteristics that stimulate the achievement drive in high achievers.
5. Explain how reinforcement is related to motivation.
6. Describe the role that equity can play in motivation.
7. Identify the three relationships in expectancy theory that determine an individual's level of effort.
8. List those actions a supervisor can take to maximize employee motivation.
9. Contrast the challenges in motivating low-pay service workers versus professional employees.

CHAPTER OUTLINE

PERFORMING EFFECTIVELY

WHAT IS MOTIVATION?

UNDERSTANDING INDIVIDUAL DIFFERENCES
    How Can an Understanding of Personality Help You Be a More Effective Supervisor?

EARLY APPROACHES TO MOTIVATION
    Focus on Needs
    Focus on the Nature of People
    Focus on Satisfaction and Dissatisfaction
    Pop Quiz

CONTEMPORARY THEORIES OF MOTIVATION
    Focus on Achievement
    Focus on Reinforcement
    Focus on Equity
    Focus on Goals
    Focus on Expectancies

APPLYING MOTIVATION CONCEPTS
    Be Clear in Communicating What Is Expected
    Recognize Individual Differences
    Match People to Jobs
    Set Challenging Goals
    Encourage Participation
    Individualize Rewards
    Give Recognition
    Link Rewards to Performance
    Dealing with a Difficult Issue
    Check for Equity
    Don't Ignore Money!

CHALLENGES FOR MOTIVATING TODAY'S EMPLOYEES
    Motivating a Diversified Workforce
    Supervision in Action: Motivating a Diverse Workforce

Motivating Low-Pay Service Workers
Motivating Professionals
Should Employees Be Paid for Performance or Time on the Job?
How Can Employee Stock Ownership Plans Affect Motivation?
Pop Quiz

FROM CONCEPTS TO SKILLS: DESIGNING MOTIVATING JOBS
    Assessing Yourself: Is Enrichment for You?
    Skill Basics
    Practising the Skill
    Applying Your Skills

UNDERSTANDING THE BASICS
    Summary
    Key Terms and Concepts
    Reviewing Your Knowledge
    Answers to the Pop Quizzes

PERFORMING YOUR JOB
    Case 9.A: Just Keep on Trucking
    Case 9.B: Finding the Pleasure in Number-Crunching

Marlene Roy is the supervisor of the labour market information unit of HRDC (Human Resources Development Canada) in Winnipeg, Manitoba. Like the four professional staff who report to her, she researches and writes reports analysing the labour market. Their research produces occupational profiles, describing the duties, licensing requirements, working conditions, prevailing wages, training available, and current demand for a particular occupation. The information is used both internally, by project officers, employment insurance officers and policy makers, and externally by provincial employment counsellors, school guidance counsellors and anyone looking for work.

All Marlene's staff members are independent and competent professionals with long tenure. They sound like an ideal group to supervise, where motivation is not an issue; however, it could be. They have not been recognized financially with a pay increase in over 10 years. The work is complex and demanding, priorities continually change, and the workload is heavy. Last year, when Marlene wanted to give her employees an engraved pen in recognition of their work, she had to "rant and rave" to get approval for even that small reward.

The constant heavy workload can get discouraging if employees don't feel appreciated. Therefore, Marlene works hard to create a motivating work environment.

"I ensure that the staff know that the work they do is important. I pass on to them any positive feedback we receive. I recognize individual performance with specific praise, for example, 'I like the way you did "X" in this report.' Sometimes I bring in a box of chocolates. We have the luxury of being able to control our work to a great extent so when management imposes a change on us, we discuss together how we can adapt it and make it workable. I try hard to match the work to the person and give them challenging work. Some are keen on numbers and prefer to focus on the statistics; others prefer to look at the implications of the statistics. I consider people's workload as well as interests when I am delegating work and I try to be fair."

Marlene knows of other organizations that recognize strong performance with wage increases, bonuses, and gifts, and provide "perks" to employees such as a fitness centre, daycare centre, discounts on products and services, and flexible working hours. Like most supervisors, however, Marlene does not have a "reward" budget and is confined to no-cost motivational initiatives. Yet Marlene knows the importance of motivation and does her best to provide motivating conditions for her staff.

In this chapter, we will examine just what these motivating conditions are.

WHAT IS MOTIVATION?

First, what do we mean by the term *motivation*? **Motivation** is the willingness to do something and is conditioned by this action's ability to satisfy some need for the individual. A **need**, in our terminology, means a physiological or psychological deficiency that makes certain outcomes seem attractive.

An unsatisfied need creates tension, which sets off a drive to satisfy that need. The greater the tension, the greater the drive or effort that will be required to reduce that tension. So when we see employees working hard at some activity, we can conclude that they're driven by a desire to satisfy one or more needs that they value.

Effort is not the only interesting consequence of high motivation. Motivation also influences the selection of an activity, persistence in the face of difficulties, and the performance standards the employee expects to achieve.

Motivation
The willingness to do some action. It is conditioned by this action's ability to satisfy some need for the individual.

Need
A physiological or psychological deficiency that makes certain outcomes seem attractive.

UNDERSTANDING INDIVIDUAL DIFFERENCES

An error that new supervisors commonly make is to assume that other people are like them and motivated by the same things. If they're ambitious, they think others are also ambitious. If they place a high value on spending evenings and weekends with their family, they assume that others feel the same way. Big mistake! People are different. What's important to me is not necessarily important to you. Not everybody, for instance, is driven by the desire for money. Yet a lot of supervisors believe a bonus or the opportunity for a pay increase should make every employee want to work harder. If you're going to be successful in motivating people, you have to begin by accepting and trying to understand individual differences. And you have to be willing to treat different people differently.

To make our point, let's look at personality. Most of us know people who are loud and aggressive. We know others who are quiet and passive. A number of personality characteristics have been singled out as having relevance to understanding the behaviour and motivation of employees at work. These include locus of control, Machiavellianism, self-esteem, self-monitoring, and risk propensity.

Some people believe that they are masters of their own fate. Other people see themselves as pawns of fate, believing that what happens to them in their lives is due to luck or chance. **Locus of control** in the first case is internal; these people believe they control their destiny. Because of this, they thrive on autonomy and flexibility in their job and will respond enthusiastically to an enriched job design (see From Concepts to Skills at the end of the chapter). Those who see their life controlled by outsiders have an external locus of control. Studies tell us that employees who rate

Locus of control
The degree to which people believe they are masters of their own fate.

high in externality are less satisfied with their jobs, more alienated from the work setting, and less involved in their jobs than are internals. For instance, employees with an external locus of control may be less enthusiastic about their jobs because they believe that they have little personal influence on the outcome of their performance appraisals. If they receive a poor appraisal, they're apt to blame it on their supervisor's prejudice, their coworkers, or other events outside their control. As a supervisor, you may need to adjust your style according to locus of control, backing off and giving more freedom to the internal locus of control person and creating much more structure for the person with an external locus of control.

Machiavellianism
The degree to which an individual is manipulative and believes ends can justify means.

The characteristic of **Machiavellianism** (Mach) is named after Niccolo Machiavelli, who wrote in the sixteenth century on how to gain and manipulate power. An individual exhibiting strong Machiavellian tendencies is manipulative and believes ends can justify means. Some might even see these people as ruthless. High Machs tend to be motivated on jobs where there are few rules to confine them, jobs that require bargaining (such as labour negotiator), or where there are substantial rewards for winning (as in commissioned sales). But they can get frustrated in jobs where there are specific rules that must be followed or where rewards are based more on using the proper means rather than on the achievement of outcomes.

Self-esteem
The degree to which individuals like or dislike themselves.

People differ in the degree to which they like or dislike themselves. This trait is called **self-esteem**. Studies confirm that people high in self-esteem (SE) believe that they possess more of the ability they need in order to succeed at work. But the most significant finding on self-esteem is that low-SEs are more susceptible to external influence than are high-SEs. Low-SEs are dependent on receiving positive evaluations from others. As a result, they are more likely to seek approval from others and more prone to conform to the beliefs and behaviours of those they respect than are high-SEs. An employee with low self-esteem will greatly appreciate supportive conditions from his or her supervisor and will likely respond well to praise and recognition. The employee with high self-esteem will also appreciate recognition but will likely expect much more challenge from the job, and an opportunity to participate in decisions.

Self-monitoring
A personality trait that measures an individual's ability to adjust his or her behaviour to external, situational factors.

Some individuals are very adaptable and can easily adjust their behaviour to changing situations. Others are rigid and inflexible. The personality trait that captures this difference is called **self-monitoring**. Individuals high in self-monitoring show considerable adaptability in adjusting their behaviour to external situational factors. They are highly sensitive to external cues and can behave differently in different situations. High self-monitors are capable of presenting striking contradictions between their public personas and their private selves. Low self-monitors can't disguise themselves this way. They tend to display their true feelings and beliefs in every situation. The evidence tells us that high self-monitors tend to pay closer attention to the behaviour of others and are more capable of conforming than are low self-monitors. Additionally, because high self-monitors are flexible, they adjust better than low self-monitors to job situations that require individuals to play multiple roles in their work groups.

People differ in their willingness to take chances. Individuals with a high **risk propensity** make more rapid decisions and use less information in making their choices than low risk-propensity individuals. Not surprisingly, high-risk seekers tend to prefer, and are more satisfied in, jobs such as stockbroker or firefighter on an oil platform.

Risk propensity
The degree to which people are willing to take chances.

How Can an Understanding of Personality Help You Be a More Effective Supervisor?

The major value of understanding personality differences probably lies in selection. You are likely to have higher performing and more satisfied employees if consideration is given to matching personality types with compatible jobs. In addition, there may be other benefits. By recognizing that people approach problem solving, decision making, and job interactions differently, you can better understand why, for instance, an employee is uncomfortable making quick decisions or insists on gathering as much information as possible before addressing a problem. You can also anticipate that individuals with an external locus of control may be less satisfied with their jobs than "internals," and also that they may be less willing to accept responsibility for their actions.

Understanding personality differences can also help delegate more appropriately; adjust supervisory style, for example, being more or less structuring depending on the employee's locus of control; and understand which rewards may be particularly appreciated by an employee.

EARLY APPROACHES TO MOTIVATION

Once we accept individual differences, we begin to understand why there is no single motivator that applies to all employees. Because people are complex, any attempt to explain their motivations will also tend to be complex. We see this in the number of approaches that have been taken in developing theories of employee motivation. In the following pages, we'll review the most popular of these approaches.

Focus on Needs

The most elementary approach to motivation was developed by Abraham Maslow.[1] He identified a set of basic needs which, he argued, were common to all individuals; and he said individuals should be evaluated in terms of the degree to which these needs are fulfilled. According to Maslow's **hierarchy of needs theory**, a satisfied need no longer creates tension and therefore doesn't motivate. The key to motivation then, according to Maslow, is to determine where an individual is located on the needs hierarchy and focus motivation efforts at the point where needs become essentially unfulfilled.

Hierarchy of needs theory
There is a hierarchy of five needs—physiological, safety, social, esteem, and self-actualization. As each need is sequentially satisfied, the next need becomes dominant.

Maslow proposed that within every human being there exists a hierarchy of five needs. These needs are:

1. **Physiological**—includes hunger, thirst, shelter, sex, and other bodily needs.
2. **Safety**—includes security and protection from physical and emotional harm.
3. **Social**—includes affection, a sense of belonging, acceptance, and friendship.
4. **Esteem**—includes internal factors such as self-respect, autonomy, and achievement; and external factors such as status, recognition, and attention.
5. **Self-actualization**—the drive to become what one is capable of becoming; includes growth, achieving one's potential, and self-fulfillment.

As each of these needs becomes substantially satisfied, the next need becomes dominant. In terms of Figure 9-1, the individual moves up the hierarchy. From the standpoint of motivation, the theory would say that although no need is ever fully gratified, a substantially satisfied need no longer motivates.

A number of studies to test the validity of Maslow's theory have been made over the years and don't give strong support to the universality of his hierarchy of needs. So, while this theory has been around for a long time and is certainly well known, it is probably not an effective guide for helping you motivate your employees.

An interesting variation of Maslow's theory has arisen in **ERG theory**, in which Maslow's five levels are reduced to three—existence, relatedness, and growth needs. A further departure from Maslow's ideas is ERG's frustration-regression hypothesis. This hypothesis suggests that if a motivating need is frustrated in its fulfillment, a person will regress to the next

ERG Theory
ERG theory of motivation reduces Maslow's hierarchy to three—existence, relatedness and growth needs—and adds a frustration-regression hypothesis, the idea that people frustrated in their attempt to fulfill an unfulfilled need will regress to a lower need's fulfillment.

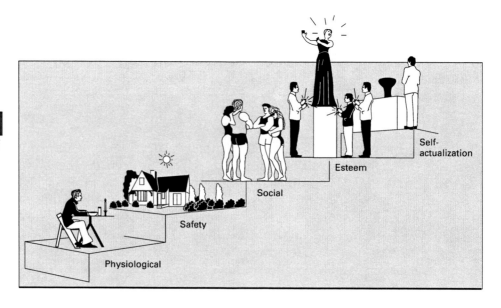

FIGURE 9-1

Maslow's Hierarchy of Needs. (*Source:* By permission of the Modular Project of Organizational Behavior and Instructional Communications Centre. McGill University, Montreal, Canada.)

highest need and emphasize the fulfillment of that need. For example, consider a person who truly wishes for a much more challenging job but nevertheless must take a mundane and boring job because of dire financial needs and the lack of available work. If that person has fulfilled his existence and relatedness needs, and therefore is at the stage of seeking growth satisfaction, he will not beat his head against the wall in frustration but will realistically seek what pleasure and motivation he can through the friendships and social aspect of his work. He may turn to activities outside of work to fulfill his growth needs.

FOCUS ON THE NATURE OF PEOPLE

Some supervisors believe their employees are hard working, committed, and responsible. Other supervisors view their employees as essentially lazy, irresponsible, and lacking ambition. This observation led Douglas McGregor to propose his **Theory X–Theory Y** view of human nature and motivation.[2]

McGregor argued that a supervisor's view of the nature of human beings is based on a certain grouping of assumptions, and that supervisors tend to mould their behaviour toward subordinates according to these assumptions.

Under Theory X, the four assumptions held by supervisors are:

1. Employees inherently dislike work and, whenever possible, will attempt to avoid it.
2. Since employees dislike work, they must be coerced, controlled, or threatened with punishment to achieve desired goals.
3. Employees will shirk responsibility and seek formal direction whenever possible.
4. Most workers place security above all other factors associated with work, and will display little ambition.

Theory X–Theory Y
Two diametrically opposed views of human nature. Theory X assumes people are essentially lazy, irresponsible, and lacking ambition; Theory Y assumes people are hard working, committed, and responsible.

In contrast to these negative views toward the nature of human beings, McGregor listed four other assumptions that he called Theory Y:

1. Employees can view work as being as natural as rest or play.
2. Employees will exercise self-direction and self-control if they are committed to the objectives.
3. The average person can learn to accept, even seek, responsibility.
4. The ability to make good decisions is widely dispersed throughout the population, and not necessarily the sole province of those in management.

What are the motivational implications of Theory X–Theory Y? McGregor argued that Theory Y assumptions were more valid than those of Theory X. As a result, he proposed ideas such as participation in decision making, responsible and challenging jobs, and good group relations as approaches that would maximize an employee's job motivation.

Unfortunately, there is no evidence to confirm that either set of assumptions is valid, or that acceptance of Theory Y assumptions and altering one's actions accordingly will lead to more motivated workers. As will become evident later in this chapter, either Theory X or Theory Y assumptions may be appropriate in a particular situation.

FOCUS ON SATISFACTION AND DISSATISFACTION

"First, describe situations in which you felt exceptionally good about your job. Second, describe situations in which you felt exceptionally bad about your job." Beginning in the late 1950s, Frederick Herzberg asked these two questions of a number of workers. He then tabulated and categorized their responses. What he found was that the replies people gave when they felt good about their jobs were significantly different from the replies given when they felt bad. As shown in Figure 9-2, certain characteristics tend to be consistently related to job satisfaction (when they felt "good"), and others to job dissatisfaction (when they felt "bad"). Intrinsic factors such as achievement, recognition, the work itself, responsibility, and advancement seemed to be related to job satisfaction. When those questioned felt good about their work, they tended to attribute these characteristics to themselves. On the other hand, when they were dissatisfied, they tended to cite external factors, such as company policy and administration, supervision, interpersonal relations, and working conditions.

Motivation-hygiene theory
Intrinsic factors are related to job satisfaction, while extrinsic factors are associated with dissatisfaction.

Herzberg took these results and formulated what he called **motivation-hygiene theory**.[3] He said the responses suggest that the opposite of satisfaction is not dissatisfaction, as was traditionally believed. Removing dissatisfying characteristics from a job does not necessarily make the job satisfying. Herzberg proposed that his findings indicate the existence of a dual continuum: the opposite of "Satisfaction" is "No Satisfaction," and the opposite of "Dissatisfaction" is "No Dissatisfaction" (see Figure 9-3).

According to Herzberg, the factors leading to job satisfaction are separate and distinct from those that lead to job dissatisfaction. Therefore, supervisors who seek to eliminate factors that can create job dissatisfaction may bring about peace, but not necessarily motivation. They will be placating their employees rather than motivating them. As a result, such characteristics as company policy and administration, supervision, interpersonal relations, working conditions, and salary have been characterized by Herzberg as hygiene factors. When they're adequate, people will not be dissatisfied; however, neither will they be satisfied. If we want to motivate people on their jobs, Herzberg suggests emphasizing achievement, recognition, the work itself, responsibility, and growth. These motivating factors are the characteristics that people find intrinsically rewarding.

The motivation-hygiene theory is important because it was the primary initiating force encouraging managers, beginning in the 1960s, to redesign jobs in order to make them more intrinsically interesting and challenging for employees. However, we should point out that the theory is concerned with job satisfaction rather than directly with motivation. That is, it seeks to predict what factors contribute to job satisfaction and dissatisfaction. A large body of research allows us to say, rather definitively, that satisfied workers are not necessarily motivated or productive workers.[4] For example, high job satisfaction tends to result in reduced absenteeism and turnover, but the effect of satisfaction on productivity is minimal. So motivation-hygiene theory should be considered a more valuable guide to an employee's level of job satisfaction than to his or her level of motivation.

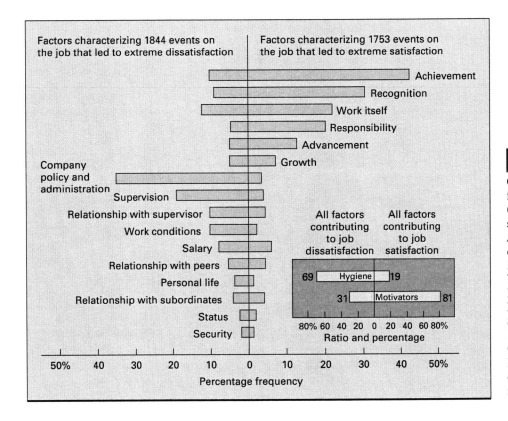

FIGURE 9-2

Comparison of satisfiers and dissatisfiers. (Reprinted by permission of *Harvard Business Review*. An exhibit from "One More Time: How Do You Motivate Employees?" by Frederick Herzberg. September/October 1987. Copyright ©1987 by the President and Fellows of Harvard College; all rights reserved.)

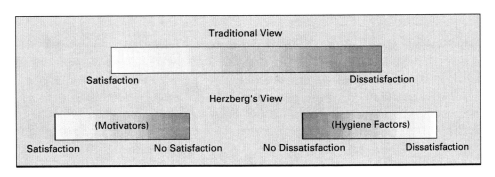

FIGURE 9-3

Contrasting views of satisfaction–dissatisfaction

1. The motto "Let each become all he/she is capable of being" best illustrates:
   a. the expectancy theory of motivation
   b. the relationship between needs and tension
   c. self-actualization needs
   d. Theory Y
2. Describe how needs affect the motivation process.
3. Theory X is basically a positive view of employees, assuming that they are creative, while Theory Y is a negative view of human nature, assuming that employees dislike work. True or False?
4. Motivation-hygiene theory factors that eliminate dissatisfaction are called:
   a. motivators
   b. social needs
   c. eliminators
   d. none of the above

CONTEMPORARY THEORIES OF MOTIVATION

While the previous theories are well known, they unfortunately have not held up well under close examination. However, all is not lost. Some contemporary theories have one thing in common: each has a reasonable degree of valid supporting documentation. The following theories represent the current "state-of-the-art" explanations of employee motivation.

FOCUS ON ACHIEVEMENT

Need for achievement
The need to do things better or more efficiently than they have been done before.

Some people have a compelling drive to succeed, but are striving for personal achievement rather than the rewards of success. They have a desire to do something better or more efficiently than it has been done before. This drive is the **need for achievement**. Those people with a high need for achievement (nAch) are intrinsically motivated.[5] As you'll see, when high achievers are placed into jobs that stimulate their achievement drive, they are self-motivated and require little of a supervisor's time or energy.

High achievers differentiate themselves from others by their desire to do things better. They seek situations where they can attain personal responsibility for finding solutions to problems, where they can receive rapid and unambiguous feedback on their performance so they can tell easily whether they are improving or not, and where they can set moderately challenging goals (see Figure 9-4). High achievers are not gamblers; they dislike succeeding by chance. They prefer the challenge of working at a problem and accepting the personal responsibility for success or failure, rather than leaving the outcome to chance or the actions of others. They avoid what they perceive to be very easy or very difficult tasks.

High achievers perform best when they perceive their probability of success as being 0.5; that is, when they estimate that they have a 50/50 chance of success. They dislike gambling with high odds because they get no achievement satisfaction from accidental success. Similarly, they dislike low odds (high probability of success) because then there is no challenge to their skills. They like to set goals that require them to stretch themselves a little. When there is an approximately equal chance of success or failure, there is the optimum opportunity to experience feelings of accomplishment and satisfaction from their efforts.

What proportion of the workforce is made up of high achievers? In developed countries, the answer appears to be between 10 and 20 per cent. The percentage is considerably lower though in Third World countries. The reason is that the cultures of developed countries tend to socialize more people toward striving for personal achievement.

Based on an extensive amount of achievement research, we can draw three reasonably well-supported conclusions. First, individuals with a high *nAch* prefer job situations with personal responsibility, feedback, and an intermediate degree of risk. When these characteristics are prevalent, high achievers will be strongly motivated. The evidence consistently demonstrates, for instance, that high achievers are successful in entrepreneurial activities such as running their own businesses as well as in many sales positions.

Second, a high need to achieve does not necessarily lead to being a good supervisor or manager, especially in large organizations. High *nAch*

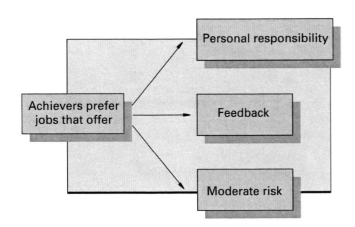

FIGURE 9-4

Matching achievers and jobs

salespeople do not necessarily make good sales supervisors, and the good manager in a large organization does not typically have a high need to achieve. The reason seems to be that high achievers want to do things themselves rather than lead others toward accomplishments.

Lastly, employees have been successfully trained to stimulate their achievement need. If a job calls for a high achiever, you can select a person with a high *nAch* or develop your own candidate through achievement training. Achievement training focuses on teaching people to act, talk, and think like high achievers by having them write stories emphasizing achievement, play simulation games that stimulate feelings of achievement, meet with successful entrepreneurs, and learn how to develop specific and challenging goals.

David McClelland, the person who instigated most of the research on need for achievement, also suggests two other learned needs that vary in degree in people and can influence their motivation. These are need for affiliation (*nAffil*) and need for power (*nPow*). A person with a high *nAffil* will thrive in a social work atmosphere and in group projects where cooperation is expected, but will probably dislike a competitive atmosphere. Those high in *nPow* enjoy exerting influence and will enjoy positions and situations that give them the opportunity to do so.

FOCUS ON REINFORCEMENT

In Chapter 8, in our discussion of learning principles, we said that reinforcement increases the likelihood that a learned behaviour will be repeated. The concept of reinforcement also has application as an approach to motivation.

Reinforcement theory
People will exert higher levels of effort in tasks that are reinforced.

Reinforcement theory states that people will exert higher levels of effort in tasks that are reinforced. A reinforcer is any consequence that, when immediately following a response, increases the probability that the behaviour will be repeated. This would include piece-rate pay plans where workers are paid a fixed sum for each unit of production completed, prizes given to employees for achieving perfect attendance, and compliments to employees when they do something nice for a customer.

The current popularity of pay-for-performance programs in organizations is clearly a direct response to the logic of reinforcement theory. Instead of compensating people on the basis of, for example, seniority, paying workers for performance outcomes increases their effort because the higher their performance, the larger their compensation. But in its pure form, reinforcement theory totally ignores the inner state of an individual and concentrates solely on what happens to a person when he or she takes some action. It's hard to believe that feelings, attitudes, expectations, and similar cognitive variables have no impact on behaviour, but that's what reinforcement theory proposes. Our conclusion is that you should recognize that reinforcement undoubtedly has an important influence on motivation but it is not the only influence.

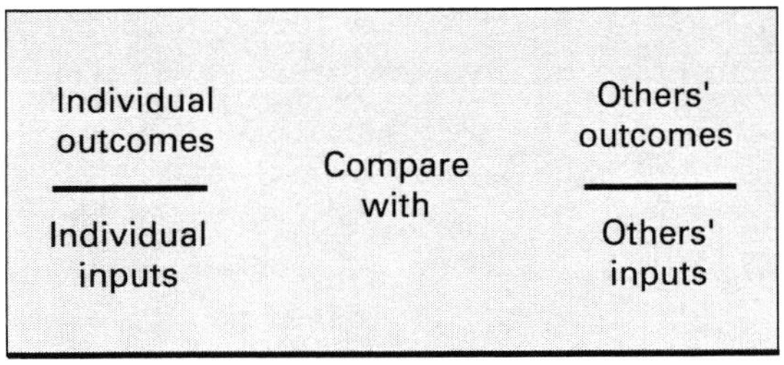

FIGURE 9-5

Equity theory

FOCUS ON EQUITY

Your company just hired someone new to work in your department, doing the same job as you are doing. That person is about the same age as you, with almost identical educational qualifications and experience. The company is paying you $3500 a month (which you consider very competitive). How would you feel if you found out that the company is paying the new person—whose credentials are not one bit better than yours—$4000 a month? You'd probably be upset and angry. You'd probably think it wasn't fair. You're now likely to think you're underpaid. And you might direct your anger into actions such as reducing your work effort, taking longer coffee breaks, or taking extra days off by calling in "sick."

Your reactions illustrate the role that equity plays in motivation. People make comparisons of their job inputs and outcomes relative to others, and inequities have a strong bearing on the degree of effort that employees exert.[6]

Equity theory (see Figure 9-5) states that employees perceive what they can get from a job situation (outcomes) in relation to what they put into it (inputs), and then compare their input/outcome ratio with the input/outcome ratio of others. If they perceive their ratio to be equal to the relevant others with whom they compare themselves, a state of equity is said to exist. They feel their situation is fair, and that justice prevails. If the ratios are unequal, inequity exists; that is, the employees tend to view themselves as underrewarded or overrewarded. When inequities occur, employees will attempt to correct them.

Equity theory recognizes that individuals are concerned not only with the absolute amount of rewards they receive for their efforts, but also with the relationship of this amount to what others receive. They make judgements based on the relationship between their inputs and outcomes and the inputs and outcomes of others. Inputs such as effort, experience, education, and competence can be compared to outcomes such as salary levels, raises, recognition, and other factors. When people perceive an imbalance in their input/outcome ratio relative to others, tension is created. This tension provides the basis for motivation, as people strive for what they perceive as equity and fairness.

Equity theory
Employees perceive what they get from a job situation (outcomes) in relation to what they put into it (inputs), then compare their input-outcome ratio with the input-outcome ratio of others; and then respond so as to eliminate any inequities.

There is substantial evidence to confirm the equity thesis: Employee motivation is influenced significantly by relative rewards as well as by absolute rewards. It helps to explain why, particularly when employees perceive themselves as underrewarded (we all seem to be pretty good at rationalizing being overrewarded), they may reduce their work effort, produce lower quality work, sabotage the system, skip work days, or even resign.

All of this points to the importance of a supervisor keeping perceived equity in mind when rewarding employees. This suggests that there is a fine balancing act between recognizing individual differences and rewarding accordingly, yet still being seen as fair.

FOCUS ON GOALS

Goal setting
Setting specific and measurable performance targets is motivating.

Goal setting was introduced as a planning tool in Chapter 2. However, it is also a powerful motivational tool. Edwin Locke's research suggests that the simple fact of having a specific goal, with no reward attached to its accomplishment, is highly motivating. In field experiments, employees who were given specific performance targets consistently outperformed others who were simply told to do their best. This is not surprising in that we enjoy having a sense of direction and purpose in our actions. Having a measurable goal also sets you up for feedback and recognition as well as giving you a better idea of exactly what "exceptional" performance is.

FOCUS ON EXPECTANCIES

Expectancy theory
The strength of a tendency to act depends on the strength of an expectation that the act will be followed by a given outcome and on the attractiveness of that outcome to the individual.

The final perspective we'll present is an integrative approach to motivation. It focuses on expectations. Specifically, **expectancy theory** argues that individuals analyze three relationships: effort-performance, performance-rewards, and rewards-personal goals. Their level of effort depends on the strengths of their expectations that these relationships can be achieved.[7] According to expectancy theory, an employee will be motivated to exert a high level of effort when he or she believes that effort will lead to a good performance; that a good performance will lead to organizational rewards like a bonus, a salary increase, or a promotion; and that the rewards will satisfy the employee's personal goals. The theory is illustrated in Figure 9-6.

Expectancy theory has proven to provide a powerful explanation of employee motivation. It helps explain why many workers aren't motivated on their jobs and merely do the minimum necessary to get by. This can be made clearer if we look at the theory's three relationships in a little more detail. We'll present them as questions that, if supervisors want to maximize employee motivation, need to be answered affirmatively by those employees.

1. **If I give maximum effort, will I achieve an excellent performance?** The answer may be no, because the employee has not been fully trained or there are insufficient resources and time to do the job well or there are obstacles preventing excellent performance.

2. **If I achieve an excellent performance, will it be recognized by my supervisor**, for example, in my performance evaluation? For many employees, the answer is no. Why? The supervisor may only give negative feedback on a day-to-day basis. Or the company's performance appraisal system may be poorly designed—assessing traits, for example, rather than behaviours—making it difficult or impossible for the employee to achieve a strong evaluation. Still another possibility is that the employee, rightly or wrongly, perceives that her supervisor doesn't like her. As a result, she expects to get a poor appraisal regardless of her level of performance. These examples suggest that one possible source of low employee motivation is the employee's belief that no matter how hard she works, the likelihood of getting a good performance appraisal is low.

3. **If my performance is noticed and I get a good performance appraisal, will it lead to organizational rewards?** Many employees see the performance-reward relationship in their job as weak. The reason is that organizations reward many things besides just performance. For example, when pay is allocated to employees based on factors such as seniority, being cooperative, or "kissing up" to the boss, employees are likely to see the performance-reward relationship as being weak and demotivating.

4. **If I'm rewarded, is the reward one that I find personally attractive?** The employee works hard in hope of getting a promotion, but gets a pay raise instead. Or the employee wants a more interesting and challenging job, but receives only a few words of praise. Unfortunately, many supervisors are limited in the rewards they can distribute. This makes it difficult to tailor rewards to individual employees. Still other supervisors incorrectly assume that all employees want the same thing, thus overlooking the motivational effects of differentiating rewards. In either case, employee motivation is submaximized.

FIGURE 9-6

Expectancy theory

APPLYING MOTIVATION CONCEPTS

We've presented a number of approaches to motivation in this chapter. If you're a supervisor, concerned with motivating your employees, how do you apply the various concepts introduced? While there is no simple, all-encompassing set of guidelines, the following suggestions provide valuable insight.

BE CLEAR IN COMMUNICATING WHAT IS EXPECTED

Recall two specific assignments you have received from instructors in the past. One was absolutely clear—as you read it, you knew exactly what you must do, what standard would achieve an "A," when it was due, what format was expected, how long it should be, and what resources were available and where. The other assignment was not clear—as you read it, you felt your heart sinking because you were confused as to what the instructor wished you to do and you didn't know where to start. These two situations are sometimes replicated in work circumstances. The outcome is predictable—when you are absolutely clear on expectations, the reaction is to jump right in and get going on it. When you are confused as to what you are supposed to do, the result is hesitation, procrastination, and anxiety.

When you are in the position of communicating expectations to employees, remember the school assignment analogy and ensure that you communicate clearly every aspect of your assignment. Describe it in various ways. Ask the employee to recap your points or demonstrate to you so you know your instructions were clear. Encourage questions, recognizing that many people are reluctant to ask questions and risk appearing ignorant.

RECOGNIZE INDIVIDUAL DIFFERENCES

If there is one thing we've learned over the years, it's that employees are not homogeneous. People have different needs. While you may be driven by the need for recognition, I may be far more concerned with satisfying my desire for security. And we identified earlier in the chapter that a minority of employees have a high need for achievement. But if one or more of the people working for you are high achievers, make sure you design their jobs so as to provide them with the personal responsibility, feedback, and intermediate degree of risk that is most likely to provide them with motivation. Your job as a supervisor includes learning to recognize the dominant needs of each of your employees. Susan Mocsan of Brewer's Retail in Ontario notes, "The key is everyone is motivated by different things so you need to know what they need and how often. For example, more work and challenge, or a pat on the back and a thank-you. And you need to find creative ways to motivate when there are things you can't do, for example, if someone is at the top of their salary range yet want more money, I could send them to Los Angeles to a Peoplesoft conference. You have to get to know your staff personally so you understand when they are having down times and know not to push them then. Some like you joking around with them but not on a bad day. You have to read them."

MATCH PEOPLE TO JOBS

At the beginning of the chapter, you read about Marlene Roy at the Labour Market Information unit of HRDC in Winnipeg. One of her considerations in motivating her employees is giving them the kind of work they enjoy. There is abundant evidence to support the idea that motivational benefits accrue from carefully matching people to jobs. Some people prefer routine work with repetitive tasks, while others need constant new challenges to keep them interested. Many people enjoy being part of a team, while others do their best work when they're isolated from other people and able to do their jobs independently. Since jobs differ in terms of autonomy, the variety of tasks to be done, the range of skills they demand, and the like, you should try to match employees to jobs that best fit with their capabilities and personal preferences. Matching with capabilities is important in that success in performance leads to a sense of achievement and pride. This then motivates employees to work even harder.

SET CHALLENGING GOALS

We talked in Chapter 2 about the importance of goals. In that discussion, we showed how challenging goals can be a source of motivation. When people accept and are committed to a set of specific and difficult goals, they will work hard to achieve them. Locke's research, described earlier in the chapter, clearly indicates the power of goals in influencing employee behaviour. Based on that earlier evidence, we suggest that you sit down with each of your employees and jointly set tangible, verifiable, and measurable goals for a specific time period; and then create a mechanism by which these employees will receive ongoing feedback on their progress toward achieving these goals. If done properly, this goal-setting process should act to motivate employees. Daniel Quondam of Com Dev Wireless in Moncton says, "If you don't give people targets they don't know what to strive for. If you do, they will care more, they will flag problems, and the target becomes a personal goal, not just a company goal."

ENCOURAGE PARTICIPATION

"Listen to your people as they have experience and ideas that you don't. Also, the simple act of listening to their input often ensures they become more interested and involved in the job. For example, we were building a road and needed good quality rock for it. Talking it over with the cat operator, who had run cat longer than I had been alive, I suggested hauling rock in from an ore shovel with good material. His suggestion was to cut the rock from a bank immediately beside it. This saved 25 percent of the time to do the job and didn't interrupt the ore flow to the crushers," says Rod Guild, senior foreman at the Highland Valley Copper mine in BC.

Participation is empowering. It allows people to take ownership of decisions. Examples of decisions in which employees might participate include setting work goals, choosing their own benefit packages, and selecting preferred work schedules and assignments. Participation, of course, should be the option of the employee. No one should feel compelled to participate in decision making. While participation is associated with increasing employee commitment and motivation, consistent with our earlier discussion of individual differences, some people may prefer to waive their rights to participate in decisions that affect them. Those preferences should be heeded. If you ask for participation, make sure the involvement is real and not just a token request. Otherwise you may create cynicism and a resistance to getting involved in the future.

INDIVIDUALIZE REWARDS

Since employees have differing needs, what acts as a reinforcer for one may not work for another. You should use your knowledge of individual differences to customize the rewards over which you have control. Some of the more obvious rewards that supervisors allocate include pay, job assignments, work hours, and the opportunity to participate in goal setting and decision making (see Dealing with a Difficult Issue). The difficulty here may be in ensuring that rewards that are different are still perceived to be equal.

GIVE RECOGNITION

FIGURE 9-7

Rod Guild

Again, some words from Rod Guild about motivating employees: "Follow up on the work they've done. Often it seems supervisors just give instructions and think that is all that is required. Checking on the job part way through shows you are interested and allows mistakes to be corrected before it is too late. Following up at the end of the job allows you to give positive reinforcement. For example, when I first started looking after the equipment operators, one operator—not the most ambitious in the world —took it upon himself to build a rock road over a soft mud dump. At the end of the shift when I climbed up on his cat, he looked apprehensive, wondering what I was doing. When I thanked him for doing such a good job, especially without being asked, he visibly relaxed and was very enthusiastic. From then on he showed far more initiative and interest.

I really believe that if the supervisor doesn't show an interest he has no right to expect the worker to show one."

In many jobs, it is difficult to measure degrees of success or failure because there's no bottom-line figure or hard data directly related to performance. People working in such jobs may have difficulty feeling a sense of achievement or progress, so the supervisor, who is one of the few people aware of their efforts, is an important source of recognition.

Library staff members respond well to recognition and the Mississauga library system has recently created a team to look at ways of providing this. Anne Murphy, a library branch manager in Mississauga, describes the "no-cost do-it-now" rewards she uses for recognition. "I may e-mail another manager about a staff member of theirs who came to help us at a busy time. Sometimes I give a thank you note, or put forth someone's name for a committee because I know they would like to get involved. We have recognition as a standing item on our regular staff meeting agenda. Anyone at the meeting is invited to use that time to recognize a particular person or group of people whose recent contributions have been notable."

LINK REWARDS TO PERFORMANCE

In both reinforcement theory and expectancy theory, motivation is maximized when supervisors make rewards contingent on performance. To reward factors other than performance will only act to reinforce and encourage those other factors. Key rewards such as pay increases and promotions should be allocated for the attainment of the employee's specific goals. To maximize the impact of the reward contingencies, supervisors should look for ways to increase the visibility of rewards. Publicizing performance bonuses and allocating annual salary increases in a lump sum (rather than spreading them out over the entire year) are examples of actions that will make rewards more visible and potentially more motivating.

Tom Heighway, the sales manager at Ceridian's Halifax branch, has had success motivating nonsales people—service and implementation staff—to contribute to sales. These people are all salaried, unlike the salespeople, and typically are not expected to bring in sales. However, all of these employees deal with clients extensively and are in a position to get leads for future sales. Tom encouraged them to ask clients for the name of a company that may need Ceridian's services and then rewarded leads with bonuses. Last summer there was a sales contest for the most new leads and all 30 branch members, both sales and nonsales, were eligible to win the barbecue-related prizes that were awarded each month. This resulted in *all* branch members working together in sales in an integrated manner.

Unfortunately, sometimes supervisors unwittingly reward poor performance or low motivation and must deal with the consequences (see Dealing with a Difficult Issue).

REWARDING THE WRONG BEHAVIOUR

"The squeaky wheel gets the oil." The squeaky wheel at work may not be the best performer, but because this person is much more vocal in his or her demands or complaints, the supervisor gives more attention and help to this person. Meanwhile, the other staff member who simply goes about his or her job competently with no complaint is ignored. How will this person react if he or she sees the supervisor giving a lot of attention to the poorer performer and trying to please the person? At the same time, the supervisor may be making the situation worse by giving the competent worker much more work, or the harder tasks, or the more unpleasant ones. This is because the supervisor knows the job will get done well and in time, and the employee will probably not complain. It appears, though, that the good worker is being punished by being given more work whereas the slow or poor worker is allowed to slack off.

Have you seen this happen? What were the consequences? How do you think the supervisor *should* handle a worker who is very loud in his or her demands? How can a supervisor ensure that the quiet, competent worker is not ignored?

CHECK FOR EQUITY

Rewards or outcomes should be perceived by employees as equalling the inputs they give. At a simplistic level, this should mean that experience, abilities, effort, and other obvious inputs should explain differences in pay, responsibility, and other obvious outcomes. The problem, however, is complicated by the fact that there are dozens of inputs and outcomes, and that employee groups place different degrees of importance on them. This suggests that one person's equity is another's inequity, so an ideal reward system should probably weight inputs differently in order to arrive at the proper rewards for each job. In many cases, communication of rewards can reduce perceived inequities in employees' minds. As a supervisor, it can help to announce who is being rewarded and why.

DON'T IGNORE MONEY!

Our last suggestion may seem incredibly obvious. But it's easy to get so caught up in setting goals or providing opportunities for participation that you can forget that money is a major reason why most people work. So the allocation of performance-based wage increases, piece-work bonuses, and other pay incentives are important in determining employee motivation. Maybe the best case for not overlooking money as a motivator is a review of 80 studies evaluating motivational methods and their impacts on employee productivity.[8] Goal setting alone produced, on average, a 16 per cent increase in productivity; efforts to redesign jobs in order to make them more interesting and challenging yielded 8 to 16 per cent increases; employee participation in decision making produced a median increase of less than 1 per cent; while monetary incentives led to an average increase of 30 per cent.

CHALLENGES FOR MOTIVATING TODAY'S EMPLOYEES

Today's supervisors have challenges in motivating their employees that their counterparts of 30 or 40 years ago didn't have. This is most evident when we look at some of the fastest growing employee subgroups.

MOTIVATING A DIVERSIFIED WORKFORCE

Don Connelly (not his real name) supervises four workers in a government office located in Toronto that deals with the public all the time. One employee is Colombian, another Chinese, one is African-Canadian, and the fourth is Jamaican. Two are male and two are female. Their skills in written and spoken English vary widely as does their motivation to improve these skills. They have different ideas about punctuality and what constitutes a full day's work. Don feels vulnerable as a white male in this supervisory situation. To him, it seems he is constantly being monitored for any inkling of racism or sexism in his actions or words. The supervisory job alone is tough enough to handle without this extra complication. Like many managers, he says it's impossible to please everyone no matter how hard he tries.

Diversity has become the norm in organizations. You are likely to supervise departments that include women and men, ethnic minorities, immigrants, people with physical disabilities, seniors, and others from diverse groups. This diversity presents a number of motivation challenges. For instance, diverse group members often have different needs and expectations. If you're going to maximize motivation, you must be able to understand and respond to this diversity (see Supervision in Action).

The key word to guide you should be flexibility. Be ready to design work schedules, benefits, physical work settings, and the like to reflect your employees' varied needs. This might include offering childcare, flexible work hours, and job sharing for employees with family responsibilities. You might offer flexible leave policies for immigrants who want to return occasionally to their homelands. Or consider allowing employees who are attending school to be able to vary their work schedules from semester to semester.

Motivating a Diverse Workforce

The flexibility required to motivate a diverse workforce includes being aware of cultural differences. The theories of motivation we have identified were developed largely by North American psychologists and validated by studying North American workers. Therefore, these theories need to be modified for different cultures.[9]

For instance, the self-interest concept is consistent with capitalism and the extremely high value placed on oneself in countries such as Canada and the United States. Because almost all the motivation theories presented in this chapter are based on the self-interest motive, they should also be applicable to employees in such countries as Great Britain and Australia, where capitalism and self-interest are highly valued. In more collective-oriented nations, such as Venezuela, Singapore, Japan, and Mexico, the individual's loyalty to the organization or society takes precedence over his or her self-interest. Employees in collective-oriented cultures are likely therefore to be more receptive to team-based job design, group goals, and group-performance evaluations. Reliance on the fear of being fired in such cultures is likely to be less effective, even if the laws in these countries allow managers to fire employees.

The need-for-achievement concept provides another example of a motivation theory with a North American bias. The view that a high need for achievement acts as an internal motivator presupposes the existence of two cultural characteristics: a willingness to accept a moderate degree of risk and a concern with performance. However, results of several recent studies among employees in countries outside North America indicate that some aspects of motivation theory are transferable.[10] For instance, motivational techniques presented earlier in this chapter were shown to be effective in changing performance-related behaviours of Russian textile mill workers. However, we shouldn't assume that motivation concepts are universally applicable. The technique of recognizing and embarrassing the worst sales clerks by giving them awards—used by a large department store in Xian, China—may be effective in China.[11] But an action that humiliates employees isn't likely to work in North America or Western Europe.

MOTIVATING LOW-PAY SERVICE WORKERS

You're supervising counter workers at McDonald's, clerks at Blockbuster Video, orderlies in a hospital, or a building maintenance crew. These examples represent some of the fastest-growing job categories. Such jobs represent a challenge: how do you motivate people in low-paying jobs that offer limited opportunities for advancement? In contrast to low-skill, blue-collar manufacturing jobs that paid $10 to $15 an hour in the 1960s, today's low-skill service jobs are paying $7 or $8 an hour—barely enough to satisfy basic needs and far from allowing the worker to move into the middle class.

So what can you do? Pay might be increased a bit, but significantly higher basic wages can't be passed on to consumers. The public isn't ready yet for the $10 Big Mac. So what you're left with are options such as offering job flexibility and variety, providing recognition, and capitalizing on the role of social support. Give employees flexibility in choosing their work hours. Increase variety by allowing them to change tasks and rotate among jobs. And build group cohesiveness, support, and commitment by encouraging employees to be part of a winning team.

FIGURE 9-8

Colin Kirby spent the summer supervising fifteen students painting campus buildings. What motivated them? Colin made their duties clear, pitched in and helped, used humour and challenges; plus they got a bonus for finishing the job.

MOTIVATING PROFESSIONALS

How do you motivate the professional librarian, civil engineer, registered nurse, or lawyer? How do you get the most effort from the C.A. at Price Waterhouse, the software programmer at Corel, or the Calgary Flames hockey player earning $1 million a year?

Professional employees provide a unique challenge in terms of motivation. Money, in an absolute sense, does not tend to be high on their needs list. They tend to be sensitive to the design of their jobs. And they're more likely to attach their identity to their profession than to the organization that employs them.

Since professionals tend to be relatively well paid, money is more likely to be an issue of equity than of absolute amount. Many professionals are equity sensitive; they are likely to compare their salary, job assignments, benefit packages, office furnishings, and the like with those of their colleagues and associates. A $5000 bonus tends to carry significantly more weight to a $25 000-a-year blue-collar worker than to a $75 000-a-year professional.

Professionals tend to place a high value on job factors such as autonomy, personal growth, recognition, and challenging work. Their motivation is closely tied to the degree to which their job satisfies these needs. Much of the discussion that follows on designing motivating jobs is particularly relevant to professionals.

Finally, one characteristic that typically differentiates professional employees from others is that professionals put their allegiance to their

FIGURE 9-9

When asked about motivation issues, Heather Cook (manager of Halton Region Children's Assessment and Treatment Centres) said of the psychologists and social workers, "We deal more with the other end of the continuum. People tend to take on too much; they push themselves because it's hard to say no to urgent, difficult cases."

field of expertise ahead of their allegiance to the organization. A corporate lawyer who works for MacMillan Bloedel will tend to see his or her identity as being more closely tied to the legal profession than to MacMillan Bloedel. This presents a challenge to supervisors, because the rewards offered outside the organization often take precedence over those from within. For example, recognition by professional peers through articles in newsletters, awards, appointment to important committees, or election to a high-ranking office within the professional organization can be powerful motivators to the professional employee. Unfortunately, the typical supervisor has little influence over these outside sources of rewards.

SHOULD EMPLOYEES BE PAID FOR PERFORMANCE OR FOR TIME ON THE JOB?

What's in it for me? That's a question every person consciously or subconsciously asks before engaging in any form of behaviour. Our knowledge of motivation tells us that people do what they do to satisfy some need. Before they do anything, therefore, they look for a payoff or reward. Although there may be many different rewards offered by organizations, most of us are concerned with earning an amount of money that allows us to satisfy our needs and wants. Because pay, as one type of reward, is an important variable in motivation, we need to look at how we can use pay to motivate high levels of employee performance. This principle explains the intent and logic behind pay-for-performance programs.

Pay-for-performance **programs** are compensation plans that pay employees on the basis of some performance measure.[12] Piece-rate plans, gainsharing, wage incentive plans, profit sharing, and lump sum bonuses are examples of pay-for-performance programs.[13] What differentiates these forms of pay from more traditional compensation plans is that instead of paying an employee for time on the job, pay is adjusted to reflect some measures of performance. These performance measures might include such things as individual productivity, team or work group productivity, departmental productivity, or the overall organization's profits for a given period.

Performance-based compensation is probably most compatible with expectancy theory. That is, employees should perceive a strong relationship between their performance and the rewards they receive if motivation is to be maximized. If rewards are allocated solely on nonperformance factors—such as seniority, job title, or across-the-board cost-of-living raises—then employees are likely to reduce their efforts.[14]

Pay-for-performance programs are gaining in popularity in organizations. Their growing popularity can be explained in terms of both motivation and cost control. From a motivation perspective, making some or all of a worker's pay conditional on performance measures focuses his or her attention and effort on that measure, then reinforces the continuation of

Pay-for-performance programs
Compensation plans that pay employees on the basis of some performance measure.

that effort with rewards. However, if the employee, team, or organization's performance declines, so too does the reward.[15] Thus, there's an incentive to keep efforts and motivation strong. For instance, employees at Hallmark Cards, Inc. have up to 10 per cent of their pay at risk. Depending on their productivity on such performance measures as customer satisfaction, retail sales, and profits, employees turn that 10 per cent into rewards as high as 25 per cent.[16] However, failure to reach the performance measures can result in the forfeiture of the 10 per cent of salary placed at risk. Companies such as Saturn, Hewlett-Packard, and DuPont use similar formulas in which employee compensation is composed of base and reward pay.[17] On the cost-savings side, performance-based bonuses and other incentive rewards avoid the fixed expense of permanent—and often annual—salary increases. The bonuses do not accrue to base salary, which means that the amount is not compounded in future years. As a result, they save the company money!

Hallmark
www.hallmark.com
hpclweb.external.
hp.com

HOW CAN EMPLOYEE STOCK OWNERSHIP PLANS AFFECT MOTIVATION?

Many companies are using employee stock ownership plans for improving and motivating employee performance. An employee stock ownership plan (ESOP) is a compensation program in which employees become part owners of the organization by receiving stock as a performance incentive. Millions of employees in such companies as British Petroleum, Avis, and Starbucks participate in ESOPs.[18] Also, many ESOPs allow employees to purchase additional stocks at attractive, below-market prices. Under an ESOP, employees are often motivated to give more effort because they are owners who will share in any gains and losses. The fruits of their labours are no longer just going into the pockets of some unknown owners—the employees are the owners!

Do ESOPs positively affect productivity and employee satisfaction? The answer appears to be yes. The research on ESOPs indicates that they increase employee satisfaction and frequently result in higher performance.[19] However, other studies showed that productivity in organizations with ESOPs does increase, but the impact is greater the longer the ESOP has been in existence.[20] You shouldn't expect immediate increases in employee motivation and productivity if an ESOP is implemented. But over time, employee productivity and satisfaction should increase.

POP QUIZ

5. The degree to which an individual believes that working at a particular level will generate a desired outcome is defined by the expectancy theory as:
   a. attractiveness
   b. performance–reward linkage
   c. effort–performance linkage
   d. value

6. Describe the motivational implications of equity theory.

7. The primary motivational effect of ESOPs comes from the fact that employees become part owners of the organization by receiving stock as a performance incentive. True or False?

8. The key to motivating today's diversified work force lies in
   a. creativity
   b. goal-setting
   c. support
   d. flexibility

DESIGNING MOTIVATING JOBS

ASSESSING YOURSELF: IS ENRICHMENT FOR YOU?

People differ in what they like and dislike in their jobs. Following are 12 pairs of jobs. For each pair, indicate which job you would prefer. Assume that everything else about the jobs is the same—pay attention only to the characteristics actually listed for each pair of jobs. If you would prefer the job in the left column (Column A), indicate how much you prefer it by putting a check mark in a blank to the left of the Neutral point. If you prefer the job in the right-hand column (Column B), check one of the blanks to the right of Neutral. Check the Neutral blank only if you find the two jobs equally attractive or unattractive. Try to use the Neutral blank rarely.

COLUMN A		**COLUMN B**

1. A job that offers little or no challenge

STRONGLY PREFER A — NEUTRAL — STRONGLY PREFER B

A job that requires you to be completely isolated from coworkers

2. A job that pays very well

STRONGLY PREFER A — NEUTRAL — STRONGLY PREFER B

A job that allows considerable opportunity to be creative and innovative

3. A job that often requires you to make important decisions

STRONGLY PREFER A — NEUTRAL — STRONGLY PREFER B

A job in which there are many pleasant people to work with

4. A job with little security in a somewhat unstable organization

STRONGLY PREFER A — NEUTRAL — STRONGLY PREFER B

A job in which you have little or no opportunity to participate in decisions that affect your work

5. A job in which greater responsibility is given to those who do the best work

STRONGLY PREFER A — NEUTRAL — STRONGLY PREFER B

A job in which greater responsibility is given to loyal employees who have the most seniority

6. A job with a supervisor who sometimes is highly critical

STRONGLY PREFER A — NEUTRAL — STRONGLY PREFER B

A job that does not require you to use much of your talent

7. A very routine job

STRONGLY PREFER A — NEUTRAL — STRONGLY PREFER B

A job in which your coworkers are not very friendly

8. A job with a supervisor who respects you and treats you fairly

STRONGLY PREFER A — NEUTRAL — STRONGLY PREFER B

A job that provides constant opportunities for you to learn new and interesting things

9. A job that gives you a real chance to develop yourself personally

STRONGLY PREFER A — NEUTRAL — STRONGLY PREFER B

A job with excellent vacations and fringe benefits

10. A job in which there is a real chance you could be laid off

STRONGLY PREFER A — NEUTRAL — STRONGLY PREFER B

A job with very little chance to do challenging work

11. A job with little freedom and independence to do your work in the way you think best

STRONGLY PREFER A — NEUTRAL — STRONGLY PREFER B

A job with poor working conditions

12. A job with very satisfying teamwork

STRONGLY PREFER A — NEUTRAL — STRONGLY PREFER B

A job that allows you to use your skills and abilities to the fullest extent

Table source: J. R. Hackman and G. R. Oldham (1974), *The Job Diagnostic Survey: The Instrument for the Diagnosis of Jobs and the Evaluation of Job Redesign Projects*. Technical Report No. 4. New Haven, Conn.: Yale University, Department of Administrative Sciences. With permission.

SCORING DIRECTIONS

This 12-item questionnaire taps into the degree to which you have a strong versus weak desire to obtain growth satisfaction from your work.

Each item on the questionnaire yields a score from 1 to 7 (that is, "Strongly prefer A" scores 1; "Neutral" scores 4; and "Strongly prefer B" scores 7). To obtain the score for your individual growth-need, average the twelve items as follows:

> #1, #2, #7, #8, #11, #12 (direct scoring)
> #3, #4, #5, #6, #9, #10 (reverse scoring)

Average scores for typical respondents are close to the midpoint of 4.0. High scores suggest that you will respond to an enriched job because you have a high growth need. Low scores suggest that you wouldn't find enriched jobs satisfying or motivating.

SKILL BASICS

One of the more important factors that influence an employee's motivational level is the structure of his or her work. Is there a lot of variety or is the job repetitive? Is the work closely supervised? Does the job allow the employee discretion? The answers to questions like these will have a major impact on the motivational potential of the job and hence the level of productivity an employee can expect to achieve.

Job design
The way that tasks are combined to form complete jobs.

We use the term **job design** to refer to the way that tasks are combined to form complete jobs. Some jobs are routine because the tasks are standardized and repetitive; others are nonroutine. Some require a large number of varied and diverse skills; others are narrow in scope. Some jobs constrain the employee by requiring him or her to follow very precise procedures; others allow employees substantial freedom in how they do their work. The point is that jobs differ in the way tasks are combined, and these different combinations create a variety of job designs.

What are the key characteristics that define a job? There are five, and together they comprise the core dimensions of any job:

1. **Skill variety:** The degree to which the job requires a variety of different activities, enabling the worker to use a number of different skills and talents.

2. **Task identity:** The degree to which the job requires completion of a whole and identifiable piece of work.

3. **Task significance:** The degree to which the job has a substantial impact on the lives or work of other people.

4. **Autonomy:** The degree to which the job provides substantial freedom, independence, and discretion to the individual in scheduling the work and in determining the procedures to be used in carrying it out.

5. **Feedback:** The degree to which carrying out the work activities required by the job results in the individual obtaining direct and clear information about the effectiveness of his or her performance.

Figure 9-10 offers examples of job activities that rate high and low for each characteristic.

When these five characteristics are all present in a job, the job becomes enriched and potentially motivating. Notice that we said potentially motivating. Whether that potential is actualized is largely dependent on the employee's growth-need strength (refer back to Assessing Yourself exercise at the beginning of this section). Individuals with a high growth need are more likely to be motivated in enriched jobs than their counterparts with a low growth need.

Job enrichment increases the degree to which a worker controls the planning, execution, and evaluation of his or her work. An enriched job organizes tasks so as to allow the worker to perform a complete activity, increases the employee's freedom and independence, increases responsibility, and provides feedback, so an individual will be able to assess and correct his or her own performance.

PRACTISING THE SKILL

So what can you do, as a supervisor, to enrich your employees' jobs and increase their motivation? We can suggest five specific actions (see Figure 9-11):

1. **Combine tasks.** Supervisors should seek to take existing and fractionalized tasks and put them back together to form a new and larger module of work. This increases skill variety and task identity.

Skill variety
The degree to which the job requires a variety of different activities so the worker can use a number of different skills and talents.

Task identity
The degree to which the job requires completion of a whole and identifiable piece of work.

Task significance
The degree to which the job has a substantial impact on the lives or work of other people.

Autonomy
The degree to which the job provides substantial freedom, independence, and discretion to the individual in scheduling the work and in determining the procedures to be used in carrying it out.

Feedback
The degree to which carrying out the work activities required by the job results in the individual obtaining direct and clear information about the effectiveness of his or her performance.

Job enrichment
Increasing the degree to which a worker controls the planning, execution, and evaluation of his or her work.

Skill Variety
    High variety   An owner-operator of a garage who does electrical repair, rebuilds engines, does body work, and interacts with customers
    Low variety   A body shop worker who sprays paint eight hours a day

Task Identity
    High identity   A cabinet maker who designs a piece of furniture, selects the wood, builds the object, and finishes it to perfection
    Low identity   A worker in a furniture factory who operates a lathe solely to make table legs

Task Significance
    High significance   Nursing the sick in a hospital intensive care unit
    Low significance   Sweeping hospital floors

Autonomy
    High autonomy   A telephone installer who schedules his or her own work for the day, makes visits without supervision, and decides on the most effective techniques for a particular installation
    Low autonomy   A telephone operator who must handle calls as they come according to a routine, highly specified procedure

Feedback
    High feedback   An electronics factory worker who assembles a radio and then tests it to determine if it operates properly
    Low feedback   An electronics factory worker who assembles a radio and then routes it to a quality control inspector who tests its proper operation and makes needed adjustments

FIGURE 9-10

Examples of high and low job characteristics Source: G. Johns, *Organizational Behavior: Understanding Life at Work*, 3rd ed. (New York: Harper Collins, 1992), p. 216. With permission.

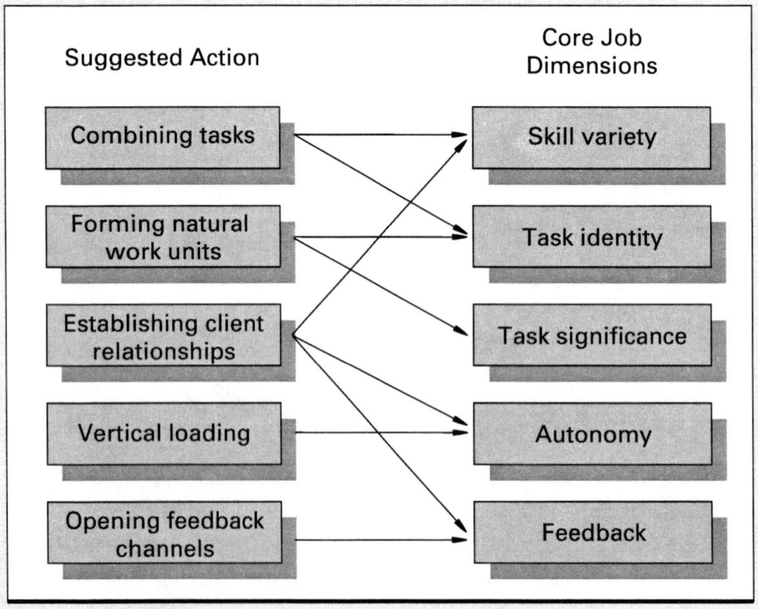

FIGURE 9-11

Guidelines for enriching a job. (Source: *Improving Life at Work* by J. R. Hackman and J. L. Suttle. Copyright ©1977 by Scott, Foresman and Company. Reprinted by permission.)

2. **Create natural work units.** The creation of natural work units means that the tasks an employee does form an identifiable and meaningful whole. This increases employee ownership of the work and improves the likelihood that employees will view their work as meaningful and important rather than as irrelevant and boring.

3. **Establish client relationships.** The client is the user of the product or service that the employee works on. Wherever possible, supervisors should try to establish direct relationships between workers and their clients. This increases skill variety, autonomy, and feedback for the employee.

4. **Expand jobs vertically.** Vertical expansion refers to giving employees responsibilities and control that were formerly reserved for supervisors and other managers. For example, let employees set work schedules, have a hand in budgeting, select work methods, check quality, and decide how to solve problems.

5. **Open feedback channels.** By increasing feedback, employees not only learn how well they are performing their jobs, but also whether their performance is improving, deteriorating, or remaining at a constant level. Ideally, this feedback about performance should be received directly as the employee does the job, rather than from the supervisor on an occasional basis.

The suggestions we've offered in this section refer to the design of individual jobs. But don't forget that we can also design jobs around work teams: in Chapter 5, we discussed how teams can enrich jobs at the group level, and how they can increase motivation and productivity.

APPLYING YOUR SKILLS

Assume you are the owner of a sports equipment store. Your store specializes in hockey and baseball equipment and makes a good proportion of its money from being the official supplier to local leagues. Several part-time people work for you, all students, and all very athletically inclined. This is ideal as they can speak knowledgeably about the equipment. You're very pleased with the current group of students working for you but are afraid you may lose them. They are all bright young people, attending the local college or university, and they need money. Yet you cannot pay them much, as in all retail positions, because your margins are low. You are contemplating the idea of job design as one way to encourage them to stay through their years at school. Maybe, if they feel they are learning and growing, are interested in the work and challenged by it, they will choose to stay rather than leave for more money elsewhere. Therefore you have written down all the tasks you do and they do. You will then consider how tasks could be reallocated or shared to provide more motivation for your part-time student staff.

Manager's tasks
- Handling banking matters
- Ordering stock
- Visiting manufacturers
- Dealing with team representatives for jersey orders and other special orders
- Preparing displays
- Scheduling of staff
- Training of new staff
- Providing customer service
- Dealing with customers when problems arise
- Dealing with customers with special orders
- Overseeing store maintenance
- Paying bills
- Researching new products

Clerks' tasks
- Providing customer service
- Performing store maintenance
- Pricing
- Taking inventory

Your task is to:
Redesign the clerks' jobs in order to make them more motivational.

1. Explain how your proposed changes will alter the core dimensions of the clerks' jobs.

2. Identify how these changes are likely to affect your job as the owner/manager.

3. Explain how you could determine the probable growth-need strength of these students to see if an enriched job would, in fact, be motivational for them.

You have 30 minutes to complete this task.

SUMMARY

This summary is organized by the Learning Objectives.

1. Motivation is the willingness to do something and is conditioned by this action's ability to satisfy some need for the individual.

2. Five personality characteristics relevant to understanding the behaviour and motivation of employees are: 1. locus of control—the degree to which people believe they are masters of their own fate; 2. Machiavellianism—the degree to which an individual is manipulative and believes ends can justify means; 3. self-esteem—an individual's degree of liking or disliking for himself or herself; 4. self-monitoring— an individual's ability to adjust his or her behaviour to external, situational factors; and 5. risk propensity—the degree of an individual's willingness to take chances.

3. Maslow focused on the self. His hierarchy of needs proposes that there are five needs (physiological, safety, social, esteem, and self-actualization) and as each need is sequentially satisfied, the next need becomes the dominant motivating force.

   Theory X–Theory Y proposes two views of human nature, then argues that employees are essentially hard working, committed, and responsible. Therefore, to maximize motivation, employees should be allowed to participate in decision making and be given responsible and challenging jobs; and supervisors should strive to achieve good group relations among employees.

   According to the motivation-hygiene theory, if you want to motivate employees, you must emphasize achievement, recognition, the work itself, responsibility, and growth, These are the characteristics that people find intrinsically rewarding.

4. High achievers prefer jobs that give them personal responsibility for finding solutions to problems, where they can receive rapid and unambiguous feedback on their performance, and where they can set moderately challenging goals.

5. Reinforcement theory proposes that people will exert high levels of effort in tasks that are reinforced.

6. People don't only look at absolute rewards they receive from their job. They also look at relative rewards. A focus on equity deals with this fact.

7. The three relationships in expectancy theory that determine an individual's level of effort are effort-performance, performance-rewards, and rewards-personal goals.

8. To maximize employee motivation, supervisors should set clear expectations, recognize individual differences, match people to jobs,

set challenging goals, encourage participation, individualize rewards, give recognition, link rewards to performance, check for equity, and not ignore money.

9. Low-pay service workers suffer both from essentially permanent low pay and limited promotional opportunities. They are most likely to respond to job flexibility and variety, recognition, and social support. In contrast, money is relevant to professionals mostly from an equity perspective. Professionals prefer enriched jobs. Additionally, their loyalty to their profession typically overrides their loyalty to their employer.

KEY TERMS AND CONCEPTS

Autonomy	Motivation-hygiene theory
ERG Theory	Need
Equity theory	Need for achievement
Expectancy theory	Pay-for-performance programs
Goal setting	Reinforcement theory
Hierarchy of needs theory	Risk propensity
Locus of control	Self-esteem
Machiavellianism	Self-monitoring
Motivation	Theory X–Theory Y

REVIEWING YOUR KNOWLEDGE

1. How does an unsatisfied need create motivation?
2. Contrast behavioural predictions between people with an internal versus an external locus of control.
3. Contrast behavioural predictions between high and low self-monitors.
4. Compare the assumptions of Theory X with Theory Y.
5. What is the importance of the dual-continuum in the motivation-hygiene theory?
6. What does a supervisor need to do to motivate a high achiever?
7. Describe expectancy theory.
8. What motivational challenges does a diversified workforce create for supervisors?
9. What are the five core dimensions in a job?
10. What is job enrichment?

ANSWERS TO THE POP QUIZZES

1. **c. self-actualization needs.** Self-actualization in Maslow's theory means reaching one's full potential. "Being all you can be" reflects this attainment, and thus, the self-actualization needs.

2. Motivation is the willingness to exert high levels of effort in order to satisfy some individual need. The motivation process begins with an unsatisfied need, which creates tension and drives an individual to search for goals that, if attained, will satisfy the need and reduce the tension.

3. **False.** It's just the reverse. Theory X reflects the negative view of human nature, assuming that they dislike work. Theory Y, on the other hand, is basically a positive view of employees, assuming that they are creative.

4. **d. none of the above.** Motivation-hygiene theory factors that eliminate dissatisfaction are called **hygiene factors**.

5. **c. effort-performance linkage.** The degree to which an individual believes that working at a particular level will generate a desired outcome reflects the effort that individual must expend in order to perform successfully.

6. In equity theory, individuals compare their job's inputs-outcomes ratio to those of colleagues and other relevant individuals. If they perceive that they are underrewarded, their work motivation declines. When individuals perceive that they are overrewarded, they may be motivated to work harder in order to justify their pay.

7. **True.** ESOPs enable employees to receive incentives that are directly tied to their performance. Because they are "part owners," this incentive creates a motivational effect.

8. **d. flexibility.** Employees from diverse cultures have differing needs. To be able to motivate them, and meet their needs, supervisors must be flexible in their dealings with their workers.

CASE 9.A

Just Keep on Trucking

You have met Susan Mocsan, the manager of HRIS and payroll at Ontario's Brewer's Retail, several times before in this book. She describes two motivational challenges. The first is dealing with a subordinate lacking in self-confidence: "Constant attention helps but I'm not available to do that all the time. So, at the beginning of an assignment, I sat down and talked through what was expected, got her to walk through the steps with me, and I helped her to write down a plan. Later, in following up with her on how things were going, I could pull out the plan and together we could check items off the list—it feels good to cross off completed items. We discussed how things were going and I offered her help where it was needed. Each time I gave her an assignment, I would give her a little more to do and then point out afterwards what she had achieved."

The second challenge is dealing with the drain on motivation created when a project is cancelled after substantial effort has already gone into it: "Once we worked Friday night and all day Saturday until 2:30 a.m. to meet a project deadline. Then it was cancelled, which was terribly demoralizing. We decided to celebrate the good work we did do so we went to lunch and the company paid for it. And we kept the work on the shelf because it is likely that someday we will need it."

RESPONDING TO THIS CASE

1. What motivational techniques is Susan using in the case of the unconfident employee? Explain why they worked.
2. What motivational techniques is she using in the case of the cancelled project? Explain

why they dealt positively with the demoralizing effect of the cancellation.
3. Explain how you think Susan keeps herself motivated to handle situations like these, particularly in handling the cancellation setback, which must have been as devastating to her as it was to her staff.

CASE 9.B

Finding the Pleasure in Number-Crunching

Imagine being a junior accountant working for a company that audits the financial statements of its clients. Your job is precise and serious. You work two weeks at one company, then three weeks at another, and so on. At each company you are working with a different group of accountants from your company, under the supervision of a different senior accountant. What would keep you motivated to do an excellent job and enjoy it?

Zahid Fazal, of Ernst & Young's Montreal office, is a senior accountant who supervises staff accountants in exactly these circumstances. Motivation is something he is very aware of. "You must always work with your colleagues as a team. When you approach a deadline and there is a lot of work, a team must work together rather than impose it all on one individual. Team work, proper guidance, and continuous cooperation effectively leads to motivation.

You also must treat your staff well, respect their thoughts, and listen to them. Just because I'm a senior doesn't mean I'm always right. I'll always listen to an intermediate or junior accountant on why they did [something] a certain way."

Zahid also believes strongly in using humour, given the nature of the job. "We joke around a lot, throwing comments back and forth. But our joking is appropriate, taking into consideration the workload, the team members, and the nature of the mandate."

RESPONDING TO THIS CASE

1. Why would the junior accountant's job pose potential motivational challenges? What might be the consequences if an accountant is feeling unmotivated?

2. What motivational techniques is Zahid using? Also consider what you learned about Zahid in Chapters 2 and 3 in answering this question.

3. Would an accounting education have trained Zahid in these motivational techniques? If not, where did he acquire them? If these skills are important to a supervising accountant and not part of the accounting education, how might Ernst & Young make it more likely that any supervisor in their company is skilled at motivating a team of auditors?

10 PROVIDING LEADERSHIP

LEARNING OBJECTIVES

After reading this chapter, you should be able to:

1. Define *leadership*.
2. Describe traits generally associated with leadership.
3. Identify traits associated with charismatic leadership.
4. Contrast task-centred and people-centred styles of leadership.
5. Identify and describe three types of participative leadership styles.
6. Explain situational leadership.
7. Explain the differences in how men and women lead.

CHAPTER OUTLINE

PERFORMING EFFECTIVELY

WHAT IS LEADERSHIP?
  Leaders and Supervisors
  Sometimes "No" Leader is Okay
  Dealing with a Difficult Issue: Influencing without Power
  Are You Born to Lead?
  Traits of Successful Leaders
  What Is This Thing Called Charisma?

HOW DO YOU BECOME A LEADER?
  Technical Skills
  Conceptual Skills
  Networking Skills
  Human Relations Skills

LEADERSHIP BEHAVIOURS AND STYLES
  Task-Centred Behaviours
  People-Centred Behaviours
  What Behaviour Should You Exhibit?

EFFECTIVE LEADERSHIP
  Pop Quiz
  Key Situational Models of Leadership
  Applying Situational Leadership

CONTEMPORARY LEADERSHIP ROLES
  Credibility and Trust
  Supervision in Action: National Culture Could Affect Your Leadership Style
  Playing Favourites
  Building a Supervisory Skill: Building Trust
  Leading through Empowerment

LEADERSHIP ISSUES TODAY
  Do Men and Women Lead Differently?
  Transactional and Transformational Leaders
  Something to Think About
  Pop Quiz

FROM CONCEPTS TO SKILLS: PROJECTING CHARISMA
  Assessing Yourself: Do You Self-Monitor?
  Skill Basics
  Applying Your Skills

UNDERSTANDING THE BASICS
  Summary
  Key Terms and Concepts
  Reviewing Your Knowledge
  Answers to the Pop Quizzes

PERFORMING YOUR JOB
  Case 10.A: This Boss Isn't Bossy
  Case 10.B: Leading the Virtual Team

SaskTel Home Page
www.sasktel.com

When an employee is promoted into a supervisory or management position at SaskTel, he or she is expected to go through three modules of management training. The company takes this so seriously that part of a supervisor's performance pay is based on whether he or she has completed this curriculum. You may find this interesting—why was the person promoted if SaskTel was not confident in his or her leadership abilities? Effective performance in one role does not guarantee effectiveness in another role—particularly one demanding different skills. So, although the person showed promise of effective leadership, SaskTel boosts the odds of this person thriving in a leadership role by providing relevant training.

What does this management training comprise? The first module, called Building a Foundation, teaches the new supervisors what SaskTel considers important and what is expected of managers. They review the collective agreement and the various aspects of dealing with a union in terms of handling grievances and negotiating. Budgeting is also covered. Another module, Managing the Business, examines bottom-line process improvements. The module that is considered by far the most critical module by Susan Pander, the HR manager, is Leading the People. "People who are promoted usually have the technical skills but it's dealing with people that is the challenge. The people issues are the most challenging ones." So the training addresses the people issues that are likely to arise and prepares new managers to deal with them. It also focuses on the difference between leadership and management, and examines what a leader is.

This training is based on an interesting premise, that is, that effective leaders can be created. This is in contrast to those people who believe that a true leader is born, not created. The SaskTel training not only believes that leadership skills can be developed, but also falls in line with the situational leadership models that assert that there is no one best way of leading. Instead, leadership behaviours must alter in response to the needs of the situation.

All of these leadership concepts will be covered in this chapter.

Leadership
The ability to influence others to act in a particular way through direction, encouragement, sensitivity, consideration, and support.

WHAT IS LEADERSHIP?

Leadership is the ability you demonstrate when you influence others to act in a particular way. Through direction, encouragement, sensitivity, consideration, and support, you inspire your followers to accept challenges and achieve goals that may be viewed as difficult to achieve. As a leader, you're also someone who sees and can get the best out of others - helping them develop a sense of persona and professional accomplishment. Being a leader means building commitment to goal attainment among those being led, as well as a strong desire for them to continue to follow your leadership.

When you think of leaders, you may often view them as those individuals who are in charge of others. These people would include yourself, as an authority over your employees; your boss; and anyone else who holds a position of power over you—like your professor in this class. Obviously, through a variety of actions, you and the other leaders have the ability to influence. Yet, leadership frequently goes beyond formal positions. In fact, sometimes this person of power is not around, yet leadership may still exist (see Dealing with a Difficult Issue). Let's look at this pair of issues.

LEADERS AND SUPERVISORS

Let's begin by clarifying the distinction between those who supervise others and those we call leaders. The two are frequently used as if they mean the same thing, but they do not.

Those who supervise others are appointed by the organization. They have legitimate power that allows them to reward and punish their employees. Their ability to influence employees is based on the formal authority inherent in their positions. In contrast, *leaders* influence others to perform *beyond* the actions dictated by formal authority. They may emerge from within a group as an informal leader. A supervisor who is also a leader gains this influence not from his or her position but through actions and characteristics that earn others' respect.

Should all those who supervise others be leaders? Conversely, should all leaders be individuals who formally direct the activities of others? Because no one yet has been able to demonstrate through research or logical argument that leadership ability is a hindrance to those who supervise, we can state that anyone who supervises employees should ideally be a leader. However, not all leaders necessarily have capabilities in other supervisory functions, and thus not all should have formal authority. Therefore when we refer to a leader in this chapter, we will be talking about anyone who is able to influence others.

INFLUENCING WITHOUT POWER

Leadership is about your influence over others—especially in those instances where you don't have formal authority over them—and the "power" you wield. The use or misuse of power can generate ethical questions about right and wrong. For instance, consider the following scenario.

Your boss has been dissatisfied with the way one of your supervisors is handling a project. She has reassigned the project to you, but your colleague hasn't been told of this action. You've been told to work with this colleague to find out what he's already done, discuss any other necessary information that he might have, and to prepare a project report by the end of next month.

Your colleague is not giving you the information you need to even start, much less complete, the project. He finds your questions unusual. After all, it's his project, and he doesn't have time to stop and talk to you. That would delay him more—and jeopardize the success of his department. However, without this information, you won't be able to meet your deadline either. If that happens, you both may lose.

Do you see any problem in talking to your colleague and telling him the reason you're getting involved? How can you influence him in gaining his cooperation? What would you do in this situation?

SOMETIMES "NO" LEADER IS OKAY

Given that as a supervisor you should ideally be a leader, we might expect you to exhibit leadership ability. But that may not be the case. Although you have the formal authority to oversee employee activities, your leadership skills may be lacking. While that may not be the best of situations, can your employees survive if you provide little or no leadership? The answer is *yes*. In fact, leadership may not always be important. Many research studies have concluded that, in many situations, a leader's behaviour may be irrelevant to goal attainment. That is, certain individual, job, and organizational factors can act as "substitutes for leadership." As a result, the "person in charge" has little influence on others.[1]

Employee characteristics such as experience, skill levels and training, "professional" orientation, or the need for autonomy, can neutralize the effect of leadership. These characteristics can replace the need for a leader's support. The drive to succeed in these cases comes from within, so no external stimulus is needed. Similarly, jobs that are well defined and routine require less leadership influence. In this case, employees know exactly what is expected and how it is to be done. In such cases, it generally doesn't take an inspirational leader to enforce compliance. Also, in jobs that are intrinsically satisfying, employees may have less need to be influenced, because the job itself provides the influence to excel. Finally, organizational characteristics such as explicit and formalized goals, rigid rules and procedures, or cohesive work groups can act in the place of formal leadership. In fact, the existence of self-managed teams is based on the assumption that they can thrive with no leader appointed to make them do what they should. Effective self-managed teams tend to have many of the characteristics noted in this paragraph.

Although the previous paragraph cites instances where leadership may be irrelevant, don't take this to mean that your leadership is not important in today's world of work. Rather, recognize that these "substitutions" for leadership are the exceptions. In most organizations, leadership is critical for organizational survival. That's why we will spend the rest of this chapter looking at what makes a good leader, and at the kinds of things a good leader does.

ARE YOU BORN TO LEAD?

Ask the average person what comes to mind when he or she thinks of leadership. You're likely to get a list of qualities such as intelligence, charm, decisiveness, enthusiasm, strength, bravery, integrity, and self-confidence. In fact, these are probably some of the same characteristics you may have listed yourself. The responses that we get, in essence, represent **leadership traits**. The search for traits or characteristics that separate leaders from nonleaders dominated the early research efforts in the study of leadership. The old expression that royalty had "blue blood" illustrates the long-standing belief that leaders were biologically different from the rest of us.

Is it possible to isolate one or more traits in individuals who are generally acknowledged to be able to influence others—people such as Jean Chrétien, Nelson Mandela, or Mother Teresa—that nonleaders do not possess? You may agree that these individuals meet the fundamental

Leadership traits Qualities such as intelligence, charm, decisiveness, enthusiasm, strength, bravery, integrity, and self-confidence.

definition of a leader, but they represent individuals with widely varying characteristics. If the concept of leadership traits was to prove valid, there would have to be identifiable characteristics that all leaders are born with.

TRAITS OF SUCCESSFUL LEADERS

Research efforts at isolating specific traits resulted in a number of dead ends. Attempts failed to identify a set of traits that would always differentiate leaders from followers and effective leaders from ineffective leaders. Perhaps it was a bit optimistic to believe that a set of consistent and unique personality traits could apply across the board to all effective leaders - in such widely diverse organizations as Grant MacEwan Community College, The Hospital for Sick Children, Schneider National Carriers Ltd., and Toyota.

Attempts to identify traits consistently associated with those who are successful in influencing others has been more promising. For example, six traits on which leaders are seen to differ from nonleaders include drive, the desire to influence others, honesty and moral character, self-confidence, intelligence, and relevant knowledge (see Figure 10-1).[2]

A person's *drive* reflects his or her desire to exert a high level of effort to complete a task. This type of individual often has a strong need to achieve and excel in what they do. Ambitious, this leader demonstrates high energy levels in his or her endless persistence in all activities. Furthermore, a person with drive frequently shows a willingness to take initiative. Leaders have a *clear desire to influence others*. Often, this desire to lead is viewed as a willingness to accept responsibility for a variety of tasks (see Figure 10-2). A leader is also someone who builds trusting

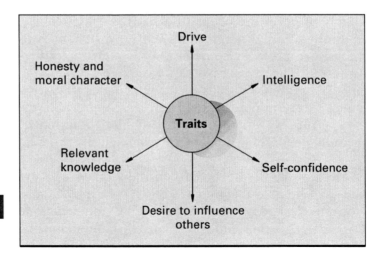

FIGURE 10-1

Six traits of effective leaders

FIGURE 10-2

What traits characterize supervisory leaders? Research has identified six: drive, the desire to lead, honesty and integrity, self-confidence, intelligence, and job-related knowledge.

relationships with those he or she influences. This is done by being truthful and by showing a high consistency between spoken words and actions. In other words, people are more apt to be influenced by someone whom they view as *honest and having high moral character*.

A person who leads is also someone who shows *self-confidence*, and thus is able to convince others of the correctness of goals and decisions. It has been shown that employees prefer to be influenced by individuals who are free of self-doubt. In other words, they are influenced more by a supervisor who has a strong belief as opposed to one who frequently wavers on decisions. Influencing others requires a level of *intelligence*, too. To successfully influence others, one needs to be able to gather, synthesize, and interpret a lot of information. The leader must also be able to create a vision (a plan), communicate it in such a way that others understand it, solve problems, and make good decisions (see Figure 10-3). Many of these "intelligence" requirements derive from education and experience. Finally, an effective leader is someone who has a high degree of *relevant knowledge* about the department and the unit's employees. This in-depth knowledge assists the supervisor in making well-informed decisions, as well as understanding the implications those decisions have on others in the department.

FIGURE 10-3

"Whether it's a house or a satellite you're constructing, you have to be able to visualize what it is you want at the end and how you're going to get there," says Joe Sferrazza, a man who has built both. "As a manager, you have to know your stuff, have an eye out for costs all the time, be confident, optimistic, and have a good relationship with your subordinates."

What Is This Thing Called Charisma?

What do people as diverse as the late Prime Minister Pierre Trudeau, dancer Karen Kain, and TV personality Don Cherry have in common? They all have something in their personality construct called charisma. Charisma is a magnetism that, among other things, inspires followers to go the "extra mile" to reach goals that are perceived as difficult or unpopular. Being charismatic, however, is not attributed to a single factor. It too evolves from one's possession of several characteristics.[3]

Charismatic leader An individual with a compelling vision or sense of purpose, an ability to communicate that vision in clear terms that followers can understand, a demonstrated consistency and focus in pursuit of his or her vision, and an understanding of his or her own strengths.

Over the past two decades, several authors have attempted to identify the personal characteristics associated with the **charismatic leader**. Some of the earlier writings focused on such attributes as confidence level, dominance, and strong convictions in one's beliefs.[4] More charismatic dimensions were added when Warren Bennis, after studying 90 highly effective and successful leaders, found they had four common competencies. These were the individual's compelling vision or sense of purpose; an ability to communicate that vision in clear terms that their followers could readily understand; a demonstrated consistency and focus in the pursuit of their vision; and an understanding of their own strengths.[5]

The most recent and comprehensive analysis has been completed by two researchers from McGill University.[6] Among their conclusions (see Figure 10-4), they propose that charismatic leaders have an idealized goal that they want to achieve, and are able to communicate it to others in a way that they can understand. That goal, however, is something quite different from the "status quo." It's a better "state" for the future, something that will significantly improve the present situation. Of course, the charismatic leader has a strong personal commitment to achieving that goal. This leadership trait also includes behaving in a way that is viewed as unconventional, or at best, out of the ordinary. A charismatic leader often does things that come as a surprise to the followers.

A charismatic leader is also assertive and self-confident. As previously noted, it is not surprising that a charismatic leader would have these traits. The individual's personal conviction and ability to convince others that he or she is leading them in the right direction provide followers with a sense that the leader knows best.

In Chapter 9, we introduced the personality dimension called self-monitoring. As you'll recall, we described high self-monitors as individuals who can easily adjust their behaviour to different situations. They can read verbal and nonverbal social cues and alter their behaviour accordingly. This ability to be a "good actor" has been found to be associated with charismatic leadership. Because high self-monitors can accurately read a situation, understand the feelings of employees, and then exhibit behaviours that match employees' expectations, they tend to emerge as effective and charismatic supervisors.[7]

Finally, a charismatic leader is often perceived as an agent of radical change. His or her refusal to be satisfied with the status quo means that

FIGURE 10-4

Key characteristics of charismatic leaders (*Source*: Conger, Jay A. and Kanungo, Rabindra N., "Behavioral Dimensions of Charasmatic Leadership," adaptation as submitted of Table 1, p. 91. In J. A. Conger, R. N. Kanungo, and Associates, *Charasmatic Leadership: The Elusive Factor in Organizational Effectiveness.* Copyright 1988 Jossey-Bass Inc., Publishers.)

1. **Idealized goal.** Charismatic leaders have vision that proposes a future better than the status quo. The greater the disparity between this idealized goal and the status quo, the more likely that followers will attribute extraordinary vision to the leader.

2. **Ability to help others understand the goal.** They are able to clarify and state the vision in terms that are understandable to others. This explanation demonstrates an understanding of the followers' needs, and acts as a motivating force.

3. **Strong convictions about their goal.** Charismatic leaders are perceived as being strongly committed, and willing to take on high personal risk, incur high costs, and engage in self-sacrifice to achieve their vision.

4. **Behaviour that is unconventional.** They engage in behaviour that is perceived as being novel, out of the ordinary, and counter to norms. When successful, these behaviours evoke surprise and admiration in followers.

5. **Assertive and self-confident.** Charismatic leaders have complete confidence in their judgment and ability.

6. **High self-monitoring.** They can easily adjust their behaviour to different situations.

7. **Appearance as a change agent.** They are perceived as agents of radical change rather than as caretakers of the status quo.

everything is open to change. In the end, his or her vision, conviction, and unconventional nature of doing things leads to an admiration by the followers—and success for the charismatic leader.

What can be said about the charismatic leader's effect on his or her followers? There is increasing belief that there is a strong link between charismatic leadership and high performance and satisfaction among followers.[8] That is, people working for charismatic leaders are motivated to exert extra work effort and, because they like their leader, express greater satisfaction.

HOW DO YOU BECOME A LEADER?

Although traits of successful leaders have been identified over the years, these traits alone do not adequately explain leadership effectiveness.

If they were an adequate explanation, then leaders could be identified right from birth. But while you may have been the natural line leader in kindergarten—exhibiting your influencing abilities at an early age—true leadership requires more than such traits. The problem with focusing solely on traits is that it ignores the skills leaders must have, as well as the behaviours they must demonstrate in a variety of situations. Fortunately, skills and behaviours are both learned! Therefore, it is more correct to say that leaders are made than born.

Whether or not you currently hold a formal position of authority over others, you can be in a position where you are able to influence others. Becoming a leader, however, requires certain skills (as well as possessing many of the traits described above). These are technical, conceptual, networking, and human relations skills. You're probably thinking you've heard these before. If you are, congratulations. You're paying close attention. Some of these are the competencies that effective supervisors need—as we discussed in Chapter 1. Because of their importance to leadership, let's look at them again—this time with an eye on leadership!

TECHNICAL SKILLS

It's a rare occurrence when you can influence others even though you have absolutely no idea of what they are doing. Although people may respect you as a person, when it comes to influencing them, they would like to believe you have the experience to make recommendations. This experience generally comes from your technical skills.

Technical skills are those tools, procedures, and techniques that are unique to your specialized situation. You need to "master" your job in your attempt to be viewed as a source of help—the "expert." Others generally won't come to you unless they need assistance. It's often the exceptions that they can't—or are ill equipped to—handle. That's when they'll look to you for guidance. By having the technical skills, you're able to assist. But imagine if you didn't. You'd constantly have to ask someone else for the information. When you got it, you might be unable to adequately explain it to your employee who has requested it. At some point, employees may simply go around you, and talk directly to the "source" of the technical information. When that happens, you've lost some of your influence!

You can't overemphasize the importance of the technical skills related to your job. Those seen as being "in the know" do influence others, so if you want "followers" to have confidence in your advice and the direction you give, they've got to perceive you as a technically competent supervisor.

CONCEPTUAL SKILLS

Conceptual skills are your mental ability to coordinate a variety of interests and activities. Having conceptual skills means having the ability to think in the abstract, analyze lots of information, and make connections between the data. Earlier, we described an effective leader as someone who could create a vision. In order to do this, you must be able to think critically and conceptualize how a situation *could be*, as well as understanding how it presently *is*.

Thinking conceptually is not as easy as you may believe. You must look at the "big picture." Too many times, we get caught up in the daily grind, focusing our attention on the minute details. Not that focusing on the details isn't important—without it, little may be accomplished. But setting long-term directions requires you to think about the future. It requires you to deal with uncertainty and the risk of the unknown. To be a good leader, then, you must be able to make some sense out of this chaos and envision what could be.

NETWORKING SKILLS

Networking skills are your ability to socialize and interact with outsiders —those not associated with your unit. It's understood that as a leader, you cannot do everything by yourself. Therefore, you need to know where to go to get the things your followers need. This may mean "fighting" for more resources or establishing relationships outside your area that will provide some benefit to your followers. Networking, if you're making the connection, means having good political skills. That's a point that shouldn't be overlooked.

Your employees will often look to you to provide them what they need to do an excellent job. If they can depend on you for giving them the tools (or "running the interference" they need), then you'll once again inspire a level of confidence in them. They are also likely to respond better if they know you're willing to fight for them.

HUMAN RELATIONS SKILLS

Human relations skills focus on your ability to work with, understand, and motivate those around you. As you've been reading this book, you'll notice that these skills have been highlighted. Good human relations skills require you to be able to effectively communicate—and especially to communicate your vision—with your employees and those outside your unit. They also involve listening to what others have to say. A good leader is not a "know it all," but rather someone who freely accepts and encourages involvement from his or her followers.

Human relations skills are those "people skills" that are frequently mentioned in today's discussion of effective supervision. They lie in the coaching, the facilitating, and supporting of others around you;[9] in understanding yourself, and being confident in your abilities; in your honesty in dealing with others and the values you live by; in your confidence in knowing that by helping others succeed—and letting them get the credit—you're doing the right thing for them, the organization, and yourself.

If you fail as a leader, it most likely won't be because you lack technical skills. Rather, it's more likely that your followers, as well as others, have lost respect for you because of your lack of human relations skills. If that ever happens, your ability to influence others will be seriously impaired.

LEADERSHIP BEHAVIOURS AND STYLES

One of the interesting aspects of leadership is that its defining traits and skills are difficult for followers to detect. As a result, they define your leadership by the behaviours they see in you. As the adage goes, "actions speak louder than words." It's what you do that matters. Therefore, you need to understand leadership behaviours.

The inability to explain leadership solely in terms of traits and skills has led researchers to look at the behaviours and styles that specific leaders exhibit (see Figure 10-5). Researchers wondered whether there was something unique in the behaviour of effective leaders, and the style in which they practised their "craft." For example, do leaders tend to be more participative than autocratic?

A number of studies looked at behavioural styles. The most comprehensive of the behavioural theories resulted from research that began at Ohio State University in the late 1940s.[10] This study (as well as others) sought to identify independent dimensions of leader behaviour. Beginning with more than 1000 dimensions, they eventually narrowed the list down to two categories that accounted for most of the leadership behaviour described by employees. These are best identified as task-centred and employee-centred behaviours.[11]

TASK-CENTRED BEHAVIOURS

Task-centred leader
An individual with a strong tendency to emphasize the technical or task aspects of a job.

A **task-centred leader** is an individual who has a strong tendency to emphasize the technical or task aspects of the job. This individual's major concern is ensuring that employees know precisely what is expected of them and providing any guidance necessary for goals to be met. Employees, as viewed by this leader, are a means to an end. That is, in order to achieve goals, employees have to do their jobs. As long as they do what is expected, this leader is happy.

Calling such a production-oriented person a leader may be something of a misnomer. This individual may not lead in the classic sense, but simply ensures compliance with stated rules, regulations, and production goals. In motivational terms, a production-oriented leader is someone who frequently exhibits a Theory X orientation (see Chapter 9) or an autocratic/authoritarian leadership style.

An **autocratic leader** is someone who can best be described as a taskmaster. This individual leaves no doubt as to who's in charge and who has the authority and power in the group. He or she makes all the decisions affecting the group and tells others what to do. This telling frequently happens in the form of orders—mandates that are expected to be followed. Failure to obey these orders usually results in some negative reinforcement at the hands of the authoritarian leader

Autocratic leadership is clearly inappropriate in today's organizations —right? Well, maybe not. There are leaders in all types of organizations— including business, government, and the military—who have found the autocratic style to work best.

PEOPLE-CENTRED BEHAVIOURS

A **people-centred leader** is a person who emphasizes interpersonal relations with those he or she leads. This leader takes a personal interest in the needs of employees, and is concerned for employees' welfare. Interactions between this leader and his or her employees are characterized as trusting, friendly, and supportive. Furthermore, this leader is very sensitive to the concerns and feelings of employees. From a motivational point of view, a people-centred leader is one who exhibits more Theory Y orientations. As a result, this individual often exhibits a participative (or democratic) leadership style.

A participative leadership style is one where input from followers is actively sought for many of the activities in the organization. This means that establishing plans, solving problems, and making decisions is not done solely by the supervisor. Instead, the entire work group participates. The only question that really remains is who has the final say. That is, participative leadership can be viewed from two perspectives. First is one where the leader seeks input, hears the concerns and issues of the followers, but makes the final decision him- or herself. In this capacity, the leader is using the input as an information-seeking exercise. We call this **consultative-participative leadership**. On the other hand, a participative leader may allow the followers to have a say in what's decided. Here, decisions are made truly by the group. This is referred to as **democratic-participative leadership**.

There is one other behavioural leadership style beyond participative leadership. This is often referred to as free-reigning leadership. A **free-reign** (or laissez-faire) **leader** is someone who gives employees total autonomy to make the decisions that will affect them. After overall objectives and general guidelines have been established, employees are free to establish their own plans for achieving their goals. This is not meant to imply that there's a lack of leadership. Rather, it implies that the leader is removed from the day-to-day activities of the employees—but is always available to deal with the exceptions.

Autocratic leader
A task master who leaves no doubt as to who is in charge and has authority and power in the group.

People-centred leader
An individual who emphasizes interpersonal relations with those he or she leads.

Consultative-participative leadership
The leadership style of an individual who seeks input, hears the concerns and issues of the followers, but makes the final decision himself or herself, using input as an information-seeking exercise.

Democratic-participative leadership
A leadership style that allows followers to have a say in what is decided.

Free-reign leader
An individual who gives employees total autonomy to make decisions that will affect them.

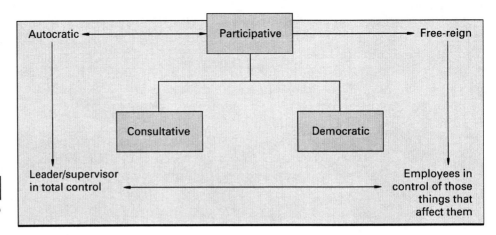

FIGURE 10-5

Supervisory leadership
behaviours

WHAT BEHAVIOUR SHOULD YOU EXHIBIT?

In today's organizations, many employees appear to prefer to work for a supervisor with a people-centred leadership style. However, just because this style appears "friendlier" to employees, we cannot make a sweeping generalization that a people-centred leadership style will make you a more effective supervisor. There has actually been very little success in identifying consistent relationships between patterns of leadership behaviour and successful organizational performance. In some cases, people-centred styles generate both high productivity and high follower satisfaction. However, in others, followers are happy, but productivity suffers. What is sometimes overlooked in trying to determine the superiority of one style over the other is the plethora of the situational factors that influence effective leadership.

EFFECTIVE LEADERSHIP

It became increasingly clear to those studying leadership that predicting leadership success involves something more complex than isolating a few traits or preferable behaviours. The failure to find answers led to a new focus on situational influences. The relationship between leadership style and effectiveness suggested that under condition a, style X would be appropriate, whereas style Y would be more suitable for condition b, and style Z for condition c. But what were the conditions a, b, c, and so forth? It was one thing to say that leadership effectiveness depends on the situation and another to be able to isolate those situational conditions. The key to many of these situational theories was their inclusion of followers in the leadership equation.

POP QUIZ

Are You Comprehending What You're Reading?

1. Which one of the following statements about leadership is false?
   a. Sometimes formal leadership is irrelevant.
   b. All supervisors should be leaders.
   c. Leadership is the ability to influence others.
   d. All leaders should be supervisors.
2. Summarize the conclusions of trait theories of leadership.
3. A supervisor who gets input from his or her staff but makes the decision him- or herself would be classified as a democratic-participative leader. True or false?
4. Which one of the following characteristics is not associated with a supervisor who is regarded as a charismatic leader?
   a. Unconvential behaviour
   b. A future vision of the organization
   c. A strong commitment to the status quo
   d. An agent of radical change

KEY SITUATIONAL MODELS OF LEADERSHIP

Some approaches to isolating key situational variables have proven more successful than others and, as a result, have gained wider recognition.[12] The first comprehensive model, developed by Fred Fiedler, proposed that effective leadership is a function of a proper match between the leader's style of interaction with followers and the degree to which the situation gives control and influence to the leader.[13] According to Fiedler, a leader's style can be identified based on how the leader describes an individual whom he or she least enjoys working with. When a leader describes this person in favourable terms, it indicates that the leader is interested in good relationships. Accordingly, that leader's style would tend to be more people-centred. On the other hand, describing this least-preferred individual in unfavourable terms indicates more of a task-centred style. Fiedler believed that an individual's style is fixed. Using three situational factors (leader-member relations, the degree of structure in the task, the degree of formal position power), he identified eight situations where either the task- or people-centred styles would work best. That is, these situational factors would dictate which leadership style would be more effective (see Figure 10-6). Essentially, his research indicated that a task-centred approach is superior in highly unfavourable situations, where decisive action is respected, and in highly favourable situations, where the leader is so well established that he or she need not worry about the relationship aspect and can simply focus on getting the job done. On the other hand, a people-centred style is more successful in situations of intermediate favourability.

One of the more respected approaches to situational leadership was developed by Robert House. It is called the **path-goal theory** of leadership.[14] The basis of this model is that it's the leader's job to assist his or her followers in attaining their goals. This is done by providing the necessary direction and/or support to ensure that their goals are compatible with the overall objectives of the group or organization. The leader clarifies the path by which employees may get from where they are to a point where they will have achieved their goals—assisting them also by reducing potential roadblocks and pitfalls.

A few examples will illustrate how you can use the path-goal approach. If your employees have considerable experience and perceive themselves to have the ability to do their jobs, they don't need task-centred leadership. They know how to do their work, so people-centred leadership is appropriate. In contrast, new employees, those lacking confidence in their abilities, or those who are insecure will appreciate the help provided through task-centred leadership. Similarly, when an employee's job is unstructured and ambiguous, a task approach to leadership is appreciated. But if the employee has clear job goals, structured tasks, and a supportive work group that provides assistance, task-centred leadership will be seen at best as redundant and maybe even as overbearing and controlling.

Path-goal theory
The leader's job is to assist followers in overcoming obstacles in the way of attaining the goals by promoting the proper leadership style.

Situational Factors	I	II	III	IV	V	VI	VII	VIII
Respect for Followers	Good	Good	Good	Good	Poor	Poor	Poor	Poor
Structured Jobs	High	High	Low	Low	High	High	Low	Low
Influence Over Employment Process	Strong	Weak	Strong	Weak	Strong	Weak	Strong	Weak
Preferred Leader Behaviour	Task Centred	Task Centred	Task Centred	People Centred	People Centred	People Centred	Task Centred	Task Centred

FIGURE 10-6
Fiedler's leadership findings

In summary, path-goal theory demonstrates that employees are likely to be most productive and satisfied when their supervisor compensates for things lacking in either the employee or the work setting. However, the supervisor who spends time explaining tasks when those tasks are already clear or when the employee has the ability and experience to handle them without interference is likely to be ineffective. The employee will view this behaviour as redundant or even insulting. The fundamental issue, then, is to adjust your style to the needs of your employees.

APPLYING SITUATIONAL LEADERSHIP

Another situational model of leadership was proposed by Paul Hersey and Kenneth Blanchard. Called simply **situational leadership**, its emphasis is on adjusting leadership style to reflect employees' needs.[15]

First, situational leadership places much attention on what is called the **readiness** or maturity of employees. Readiness or maturity in this context reflects how able and willing an employee is to do a job. Hersey and Blanchard have identified four stages of follower readiness. These are:

R1: An employee is both unable and unwilling to do a job.
R2: An employee is unable to do the job, but willing to perform the necessary tasks.
R3: An employee is able to do the job, but unwilling to be told by a leader what to do.
R4: An employee is both able and willing to do the job.

Note that unwillingness is not the same unwillingness that you would associate with an employee being insubordinate. Rather, it's an unwillingness that stems from the individual's lack of confidence and competence to do a job. You'll see how this works in a moment.

A second component of the model focuses on what you do as a leader, specifically your communication. Task behaviour can be seen as one-way communication—*from* you *to* the employee. Relationship behaviour, on the other hand, reflects two-way communication—between you and the employee. Given that high and low degrees of each of these two behaviours can exist, Hersey and Blanchard identified four specific leadership styles based on the maturity of the follower. Let's see how this model works by going through an example of a new employee in your department, and her first day on the job (see Figure 10-7).

When this employee first arrives at work, she is anxious. She's uncertain about what she is getting into and how to handle the job responsibilities. You feel that the employment process worked well in properly matching her to the job and orienting her to the organization. Now it's time for her to start the job she was hired to do. Imagine if at this point you just assigned a list of tasks for her to complete and walked away. She would probably have some difficulty. Why? Because at this time, she's not ready (R1). It's doubtful she even knows the right questions to ask.

Situational leadership
A leadership model that emphasizes adjusting the leader's communication style to the readiness or maturity of the subordinates.

Readiness
How willing and able an employee is to do a job.

Communications between you and the employee, at this point, need to be one-way: you need to tell her what to do and give her specific directions on how to do it. According to situational leadership, at this stage you are using a *telling* style of leadership.

But this new employee won't stay at R1 forever. After having been provided with ample directions and becoming more familiar with the job, she's moving to stage R2. At the R2 stage of work development, the employee is becoming more involved in her job, but she still lacks some ability. She's not yet fully trained. She's asking questions about things she may not fully understand. She may question why certain things have to be done as you have asked. Accordingly, you may need to *sell* this employee on some of your ideas to get her to accept them. At this point, high degrees of both one-way and two-way communication are happening simultaneously.

At some later point (R3), this employee has become the expert on her job. She knows her duties better than anyone else, and she's beginning to put her special mark on things. You no longer need to tell her what to do, but the reality is, you still need to be involved in what she's doing. She has not quite reached the point where you can feel comfortable leaving her totally alone. That's not an insult—it's just that you recognize that this employee still has some developing to do. Accordingly, you will best deal with this situation by being supportive of her and not being overly task-centred. Hersey and Blanchard refer to this as a *participating* style of leadership.

Finally, this employee has fully developed. She has your trust and can carry out her duties with little, if any, direction (R4). In this situation, she basically needs to be left alone. At this *delegating* stage of leadership, you simply assign the tasks and let her do her job. You now know—based on your appraisal of her performance—that she can and will get the job done. If she needs help, you're always available to deal with the exceptions.

An important aspect of situational leadership is that an employee can be in all four quadrants at the same time. To lead properly, you must be able to exhibit the correct leadership style given what each employee needs. If a seasoned employee generally at stage R4 gets a new assignment, you cannot assume that he or she will necessarily be at R4 for the new tasks. In fact, the employee may need to be clearly directed in these new tasks—and that implies a telling style of leadership. If that doesn't occur, problems may arise. On the other hand, if an employee who has been at R4 for some time gets additional assignments that require a telling style, problems will arise if that individual is treated like an R1 employee on *all* aspects of his or her job. If, all of a sudden, the employee is being told how to do what he or she has been doing for many months or years, it can have the effect of implying that you perceive the employee as not doing the job properly. The point is, you need to demonstrate a leadership style that's consistent at all times with your employees' abilities (see Supervision in Action).

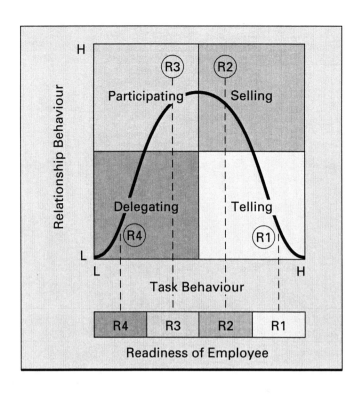

FIGURE 10-7
Situational leadership

CONTEMPORARY LEADERSHIP ROLES

Let's turn our attention to some important issues that every effective supervisor today is, and will continue to be, concerned about. Specifically, how do you build credibility and trust with your employees and how can you become a more empowering supervisor?

CREDIBILITY AND TRUST

Followers want leaders who are credible and whom they can trust. But what do these terms—credibility and trust—really mean?

The most dominant component of **credibility** is honesty. In addition, credible supervisors have been found to be competent and inspiring. By inspiring, we mean that they are able to effectively communicate their confidence and enthusiasm to their employees. So employees judge their supervisors' credibility in terms of their honesty, competence, and ability to inspire.

Trust is so closely linked with the concept of credibility that the two terms are frequently used interchangeably. We define trust as belief in the integrity, character, and ability of a leader. When employees trust their supervisor, they're willing to be vulnerable to their supervisor's actions

Credibility
Supervisory qualities of honesty, competence, and the ability to inspire.

Trust
The belief in the integrity, character, and ability of a leader.

National Culture Could Affect Your Leadership Style

One general conclusion that surfaces from learning about leadership is that you shouldn't use any single leadership style in every case. Instead, you should adjust your style to the situation. Although not mentioned specifically in any of the theories we've presented, national culture is clearly an important situational variable in determining which leadership style will be most effective for you.

National culture affects leadership by way of your employees. You cannot choose your leadership styles at will. Rather, you are constrained by the cultural conditions your employees come to expect.[16] For example, an autocratic leadership style is more compatible with cultures where power is unequal, such as those found in Arabic, Far Eastern, and Latin countries. This cultural "power" ranking should be a good indicator of employees' willingness to accept participative leadership. Participation is likely to be most effective in cultures where power is more equally distributed—such as those in Norway, Finland, Denmark, and Sweden.

It's important to remember that most leadership theories were developed by North American researchers using North American subjects. Canada, the United States, and the Scandinavian countries all rate below average on the "power" criterion. This fact may help explain why our theories tend to favour more participative and empowering styles of leadership. Accordingly, you need to consider national culture as yet another contingency variable in determining your most effective leadership style.

because they're confident that their rights and interests won't be abused.[17] Recent evidence has identified five dimensions that underlie the concept of trust.[18] These are integrity, competence, consistency, loyalty, and openness (see Figure 10-8).

• Integrity:	Honesty and truthfulness
• Competence:	Technical and interpersonal knowledge and skills
• Consistency:	Reliability, predictability, and good judgment in handling situations
• Loyalty:	Willingness to protect and save face for a person
• Openness:	Willingness to share ideas and information freely

FIGURE 10-8

Five dimensions of trust. *Source:* Modified and reproduced with permission of authors and publishers from Schindler, P. L., & Thomas, C. C., "The Structure of Interpersonal Trust in the Workplace," *Psychological Reports*, 1993, 73, pp. 563–73. © Psychological Reports 1993

WHY ARE CREDIBILITY AND TRUST IMPORTANT?

The top rating of honesty as an identifying characteristic of admired supervisors indicates the importance of credibility and trust to leadership effectiveness.[19] This has probably always been true. However, recent changes in the workplace have reignited interest and concern with supervisors building trust.

The trend toward empowering employees and creating work teams has reduced or removed many of the traditional control mechanisms used to monitor employees.[20] For instance, employees are increasingly free to schedule their own work, evaluate their own performance, and in some cases even make their own team hiring decisions. Therefore, trust becomes critical. Employees have to trust supervisors to treat them fairly and supervisors have to trust employees to conscientiously fulfill their responsibilities.

Supervisors are increasingly having to lead others who are not in their direct line of authority—members of project teams, individuals who work for suppliers, customers, and people who represent other organizations through such arrangements as corporate partnerships. These situations don't allow supervisors to fall back on their formal positions to enact compliance. Many of the relationships, in fact, are dynamic. The ability to quickly develop trust may be crucial to the success of such relationships.

How can you build trust? We've listed several suggestions in Building a Supervisory Skill.

PLAYING FAVOURITES

You might think that a sure way to undermine employees' trust in you would be to be seen as someone who plays favourites. In many cases you'd be right. But many supervisors, it appears, do in a sense play favourites, in that they don't treat all their employees in the same manner.[21]

BUILDING TRUST

ABOUT THE SKILL

Given the importance trust plays in the leadership role today, supervisors should actively seek to build trust among their employees. Here are some suggestions for achieving that goal.[22]

PRACTISING THE SKILL

1. **Practise openness.** Mistrust comes as much from what people don't know as from what they do know. Openness leads to confidence and trust. Keep people informed, make the criteria on how decisions are made overt and clear, explain the rationale for your decisions, be candid about problems, and fully disclose relevant information.
2. **Be fair.** Before making decisions or taking actions, consider how others will perceive them in terms of objectivity and fairness. Give credit where it's due, be objective and impartial in performance appraisals, and pay attention to equity perceptions when you distribute rewards.
3. **Speak your feelings.** Supervisors who convey only hard facts come across as cold and distant. If you share your feelings, others will see you as real and human. They'll know who you are and their respect for you will increase.
4. **Tell the truth.** Because honesty is critical to credibility, you must be perceived as someone who tells the truth. Employees are more tolerant of learning something they "don't want to hear" than of finding of out that their leader lied to them.
5. **Show consistency.** Employees want predictability. Mistrust comes from not knowing what to expect. Take the time to think about your values and beliefs. Then let them consistently guide your decisions. When you know your central purpose, your actions will follow accordingly, and you'll project a consistency that earns trust.
6. **Fulfill your promises.** Trust requires that employees believe you're dependable. So you need to ensure that you keep your word. Promises made must be promises kept.
7. **Maintain confidences.** You trust those whom you believe to be discreet and whom you can rely on. Employees feel the same way. If they make themselves vulnerable by telling you something in confidence, they need to feel assured that you won't discuss it with others or betray that confidence. If employees perceive you as someone who leaks personal confidences or someone who can't be depended on, you won't be perceived as trustworthy.
8. **Demonstrate confidence.** Develop the admiration and respect of others by demonstrating technical and professional ability. Pay particular attention to developing and displaying your communication, negotiation, and other interpersonal skills.

You're likely to have favourite employees who make up your "in" group. You'll have a special relationship with this small group. You'll trust them, give them a lot of your attention, and often give them special privileges. Not surprisingly, they'll perceive themselves as having preferred status. Be aware that this creation of a favoured in-group can undermine your credibility, especially among those employees outside this group.

Be cautious of this tendency to create favourites in your department. You're human, so you'll naturally find some employees you feel closer to and with whom you want to be more open. What you need to think through is whether you want this favouritism to show. When this favoured-employee status is granted to someone based on nonperformance criteria—for example, you share similar interests or common personality traits—it is likely to lessen your leadership effectiveness. However, favouritism may have a place when it falls on those employees who are high performers. In such cases, you are rewarding a behaviour you want to reinforce. But always be careful when you follow this practice. Unless performance measures are objective and widely visible, you may be seen as arbitrary and unfair.

LEADING THROUGH EMPOWERMENT

Several times in different sections of this book, we've stated that supervisors are increasingly leading by empowering their employees. Millions of individual employees and teams of employees are making key operating decisions that directly affect their work. They are developing budgets, scheduling workloads, controlling inventories, solving quality problems, evaluating their own performance, and so on—activities that until very recently were viewed exclusively as part of the supervisor's job.

The increased use of empowerment is being driven by two forces. The first is the need for quick decisions by those people who are most knowledgeable about the issues. If organizations are to successfully compete in a dynamic global village, they have to be able to make decisions and implement changes quickly. That requires, at times, moving decision making to the employee level. The second force is the reality that the downsizing and restructuring of organizations left many supervisors with considerably larger spans of control than they had before. In order to cope with the demands of an increased workload, supervisors have to empower their people. As a result, they are sharing power and responsibility with their employees.[23] This means their role is to show trust, provide vision, remove performance-blocking barriers, offer encouragement, and motivate and coach employees.[24]

Does this wholesale support of shared leadership appear strange given the attention paid earlier to contingency theories of leadership? If it doesn't, it should. Why? Because empowerment proponents are essentially advocating a noncontingent approach to leadership. That means they claim that empowerment will work anywhere. Such being the case, directive, task-oriented, autocratic leadership is out.

The problem with this kind of thinking is that the current empower-ment movement ignores the conditions that facilitate successful shared leadership and the extent to which leadership can be shared. Because of factors such as downsizing, which results in the need for higher-level employee skills, commitment of organizations to continuous training, implementation of continuous improvement programs, and introduction of self-managed teams, the need for shared leadership is certainly increasing. But that is not true in all situations, and blanket acceptance of empowerment or any universal approach to leadership is inconsistent with the best and most current evidence we have on the subject.

LEADERSHIP ISSUES TODAY

We'll finish this chapter by looking at two current debates about leader-ship. These are 1. the issue of differing leadership styles between men and women, and 2. the movement from transactional to transformation-al leadership.

Do Men and Women Lead Differently?

Are there differences in leadership styles based on gender? Are men more effective leaders or does that honour belong to women? Just asking these questions is certain to evoke emotions on both sides of the debate. Before we attempt to respond to them, let's set down one important fact: the bottom line is that the two sexes are more alike than different in terms of the way they lead.[25] Much of this similarity is based on the fact that lead-ers, irrespective of gender, perform similar activities in influencing others. That's their job, and both sexes do it equally well. This is similar to what can be said of nurses. Although the stereotypical nurse is a woman, men are equally effective—and successful—in this career choice.

However, there are notable differences between men and women as leaders. The most common difference lies in leadership style. Women tend to lead more with a democratic style. This implies that they encour-age participation of their followers and are willing to share their position-al power with others. In addition, women tend to influence others best through their "charisma, expertise, contacts, and interpersonal skills."[26] Men, on the other hand, tend to use a task-centred leadership style. Their directing of activities and reliance on their positional power to control the organization's activities tend to dominate the way they influence others. And yet even this difference is blurred, because other things being equal, when a woman leads in a traditionally male-dominated job (like that of a police officer), she too tends to lead in a manner that is more task-centred.[27]

SOMETHING TO THINK ABOUT
•AND TO PROMOTE CLASS DISCUSSION•

Go to the library and find two or three recent articles that discuss the issue of gender differences in leadership. Summarize these articles. Then, respond to the following: Do you believe that in today's organizations, both "masculine" and "feminine" approaches to leadership are equally important? Discuss. Also, explain how the specific situation one faces may affect one's leadership style.

Further compounding this issue is the changing role of supervisors in today's organizations. With more emphasis on teams, employee involvement, and interpersonal skills, democratic leadership styles are more in demand. Supervisors need to be more sensitive to their employees' needs, be more open in their communication, and build more trusting relationships. Ironically, many of these are behaviours that women have typically grown up developing.

Women are still not accepted as leaders as readily as men and must be prepared to deal with this, preferably with a sense of humour. Della Tardif, as the corporate credit manager at IPSCO in Regina, found that being a woman in management was a challenge. For example, she got a call from a customer who wanted to "talk with the f---ing credit manager, not his secretary." She replied calmly, "I am the f---ing credit manager. If you'd like to speak with my assistant who is male, that's fine. But I do have to approve his decisions." The customer apologized and dealt cooperatively with her.

TRANSACTIONAL AND TRANSFORMATIONAL LEADERS

The second issue is the interest in differentiating transformational leaders from transactional leaders.[28] As you'll see, because transformational leaders are also charismatic, there is some overlap between this topic and the preceding discussion on charismatic traits.

Most of the leadership models address **transactional leaders**. These leaders guide or motivate their employees in the direction of established goals by clarifying role and task requirements. There is another type of leader who inspires followers to transcend their own self-interest for the good of the organization. This type of leader is capable of having a profound and extraordinary effect on his or her followers. They are called

Transactional leaders Leaders who guide or motivate their employees in the direction of established goals by clarifying role and task requirements.

Transformational leaders
Leaders who inspire followers to transcend self-interest for the good of the organization and who are capable of having a profound and extraordinary effect on their followers.

transformational leaders. They pay attention to the concerns and developmental needs of employees; they change employees' awareness of issues by helping them to look at old problems in new ways; and they are able to excite, arouse, and inspire followers to put out extra effort to achieve group goals.

Transactional and transformational supervision should not be viewed as opposing approaches to getting things done.[29] Rather, transformational supervision is built on top of transactional supervision. Transformational supervision produces levels of employee effort and performance that go beyond what would occur with a transactional approach alone. Moreover, transformational supervision is more than charisma. "The purely charismatic [leader] may want employees to adopt the charismatic's world view and go no further. The transformational supervisor will attempt to instill in employees the ability to question not only established views but eventually those established by the leader."[30]

The evidence supporting the superiority of transformational supervision over the transactional variety is overwhelmingly impressive. In summary, it indicates that transformational supervision leads to lower turnover rates, higher productivity, and higher employee satisfaction.[31]

Are You Comprehending
What You're Reading?

5. According to the theory of situational leadership, when an employee is both unable and unwilling to perform the duties of his or her job, which supervisory leadership style would work best?
   a. delegating
   b. telling
   c. selling
   d. participating
6. Describe how credibility and trust affect leadership.
7. Empowering supervisors share power and responsibility with their employees. True or false?
8. Which one of the following statements about gender differences in leadership is correct?
   a. There are no differences in leadership based on gender.
   b. Women leaders have a tendency to lead using a directive leadership style.
   c. Men have a tendency to use a leadership style that encourages participation of their followers.
   d. None of the above statements about gender differences is correct.

NETWORKING: HAVING CONVERSATIONS WITH PEOPLE YOU DO NOT KNOW WELL

ASSESSING YOURSELF: HOW WELL CAN YOU CONNECT WITH NEW PEOPLE?

Indicate the degree to which you think the following statements are true or false by circling the appropriate number; for example, if a statement is always true, you would circle the 5 next to that statement.

5 = Always true
4 = Generally true
3 = Somewhat true, but with exceptions
2 = Somewhat false, but with exceptions
1 = Generally false
0 = Always false

1. In social situations, I approach people I have never met and introduce myself.	5	4	3	2	1	0
2. In work situations, if I am around new people, I wait for them to introduce themselves or others to introduce us to each other; I wouldn't approach them.	5	4	3	2	1	0
3. I know how to start a conversation with a person I have never met before.	5	4	3	2	1	0
4. Once I have started a conversation with a new person, I can effectively keep the conversation going.	5	4	3	2	1	0
5. I believe that only extraverted people can effectively network, making connections with people they do not know.	5	4	3	2	1	0
6. The opening line one uses in starting a conversation is critical in determining the effectiveness of the conversation.	5	4	3	2	1	0
7. One cannot "prepare" for a conversation when meeting a new person.	5	4	3	2	1	0
8. You can tell when you approach a new person whether the person is willing to be approached.	5	4	3	2	1	0

9. Starting a conversation with a new
   person means taking a bit of a risk.   5   4   3   2   1   0

10. The trick to making a conversation
    work is focusing on making the other
    person feel comfortable.   5   4   3   2   1   0

SCORING DIRECTIONS

This questionnaire measures your awareness of what it takes to start conversations with new people and your willingness to do so. To obtain your total score, add up the numbers circled, except reverse scores for questions 2, 5, 6, and 7. On those, a circled 5 becomes a 0, 4 becomes 1, and so forth.

The lower your score, the less comfortable you are in starting conversations with new people, probably because you are not familiar with the steps you can take to do so effectively. The higher the score, the more comfortable you are at this important networking skill, probably because you know how to do it.

SKILL BASICS

Being able to connect on a personal level with other people at work will make a big difference to your success. You will appear more trustworthy and you will be more visible. Conversational skills can help you turn business circumstances into an opportunity to establish strong relationships that will help you in the future, whether the relationship is with a customer, a subordinate, or a boss. You will develop business friendships and, all things being equal, people like to do business with their friends.

Approaching a Person. You must take the risk to initiate contact rather than wait for the other person to approach you. You do not have to be an extrovert to do this. Approach someone who is standing or sitting by him or herself. Provide eye contact first—if the person responds, rather than looking away, he or she is approachable. Smile and introduce yourself, for example, "Hi, I'm Cynthia Rall; this is my first time at this conference." The other person will likely pick up on your cue, model your lead, and give you material for continuing the conversation. Note that we decide as someone approaches whether we're willing to be approached so it doesn't matter if you have the perfect opening line.

Starting a Conversation. The focus in starting and sustaining a conversation must be on making the other person comfortable. If you do this, you take the pressure off yourself as the focus and provide a relaxing situation for the other person. You can start with a statement, for example, "It's hot in this room," or, "I didn't expect so many people to show up at this," but people will not always pick up on your cue so you need to follow up with an open-ended question. Some sample open-ended questions are: "How was the traffic for you on the way here?" "What got you into marketing/teaching/whatever?" "How did you get involved in ...?"

Preparing for a Conversation. This is not only possible but advisable if you know you will be meeting new people and are unsure of what to talk about with them. Make yourself think beforehand of several things to discuss, just in case the conversation lags, for example, something going on in the community, something on the news today, or something about the situation you have in common.

During the conversation, learn the other person's name; don't rush through introductions to get to the business at hand. Concentrate on his or her name and repeat it out loud at least once after hearing it. Keep on digging; pick up on what the person has said. For example, "How was your day?" "Busy." "What's a busy day like for you?" Use information available to you; you will get cues from appearance—for example, you see a diploma on the wall and ask "What made you choose U.B.C.?"; behaviour—for example, you notice that the person is left-handed and ask about the challenges of using the right-handed equipment at the company; or the occasion—for example, all the people are connected to the same event so you ask "What brought you here?"

Listening is an essential part of a good conversation and it does not mean not talking. Use eye contact, nodding, and body language to show you're interested and "tuned in." Contribute to the conversation, encouraging the person to continue, by saying, for example, "Oh, I see," "What happened then?" Use paraphrasing to clarify and let the person know you heard him or her. This means recapping what the person just said in your own words. For example, "It sounds like you're really disappointed that the project has been shelved temporarily."

Small talk and starting conversations with new people is not easy for most people but it becomes easier with practice. Consider every conversation to be an opportunity. Conversation is what connects us to others and makes people feel good about being with us.

APPLYING YOUR SKILLS

Have conversations with three new people. These could be three people you've never met before or people you know or have met but have simply never had a conversation with before, such as a boss, customer, teacher, coworker, or another student.

Write up a report covering the following points:

For each conversation, describe
- why you chose this person
- how you prepared
- how you started the conversation
- how you sustained the conversation
- what you felt before/during/after the conversation
- your analysis of why it did or did not go well

After discussing the conversations individually, consider them as a whole and discuss what you learned from doing this, and explain why being able to "do small talk" effectively would be a useful skill for someone in your career, or future career. Give specific circumstances where this skill would be helpful.

SUMMARY

This summary is organized by the Learning Objectives.

1. Leadership is the ability to influence others.
2. Six traits have been found that distinguish leaders differ from non-leaders: drive, the desire to influence others, honesty and moral character, self-confidence, intelligence, and relevant knowledge. Yet possession of these traits is no guarantee of leadership because situational factors are also important.
3. Charisma is a magnetism that inspires employees to reach goals that are perceived as difficult or unpopular. Charismatic leaders are self-confident, possess a vision of a better future, have a strong belief in that vision, engage in unconventional behaviours, have a high degree of self-monitoring, and are perceived as agents of radical change.
4. Task-centred leadership behaviours focus on the technical or task aspects of a job. People-centred leadership behaviours focus on interpersonal relations among the employees.
5. The three types of participative leadership styles are consultative (seeking input from employees); democratic (giving employees a role in making decisions); and free-reign (giving employees total autonomy to make the decisions that affect them).
6. Situational leadership involves adjusting one's leadership style to the readiness level of the employee for a given set of tasks. Given an employee's ability and willingness to do a specific job, a situational leader will use one of four leadership styles—telling, selling, participating, or delegating.
7. While there are some differences, men and women are more alike than different in how they lead. The differences that do exist lie in leadership styles. Women tend to rely on charisma, expertise, and interpersonal skills to influence others. Men, on the other hand, tend to use positional power to direct and control organizational activities.

KEY TERMS AND CONCEPTS

Autocratic leader

Charismatic leader

Consultative-participative
    leadership

Credibility

Democratic-participative
    leadership

Free-reign leader

Leadership

Leadership traits

Path-goal theory

People-centred leader

Readiness

Situational leadership

Task-centred leader

Transactional leaders

Transformational leaders

Trust

REVIEWING YOUR KNOWLEDGE

1. "All supervisors should be leaders but not all leaders should be supervisors." Do you agree or disagree? Support your position.
2. How is intelligence related to leadership?
3. What is charismatic leadership? Why might high self-monitors be more effective leaders? Discuss.
4. What is the difference between a task-centred and a people-centred supervisor? Which one do you believe employees would prefer to work for? Why? Which one would you prefer to work for? Explain.
5. Compare and contrast consultative, democratic, and free-reign styles of participative leadership.
6. How can supervisors be both flexible and consistent in their leadership styles? Aren't these contradictory? Explain.
7. How could a professor apply situational leadership with students in a classroom setting?
8. If leaders play favourites, is it good or bad for their department's performance? Discuss.
9. "Given the emphasis on caring for employees, women may be more effective supervisors." Do you agree or disagree? Support your position.

ANSWERS TO THE POP QUIZZES

1. **d. All leaders should be supervisors.** Leaders do not have to be supervisors, nor serve in any supervisory capacity whatsoever.

2. Six traits have been found on which leaders differ from nonleaders—drive, the desire to lead, honesty and integrity, self-confidence, intelligence, and job-relevant knowledge. Yet possession of these traits is no guarantee of leadership because situational factors must also be considered.

3. **False.** A supervisor who gets input from his or her staff but makes the decision himself or herself would be classified as a consultative-participative leader.

4. **c. A strong commitment to the status quo.** A strong commitment to the status quo. A charismatic supervisor does what is necessary to make changes to move his or her department/organization forward. In doing so, this individual looks beyond the current state of events—the status quo.

5. **b. telling.** The unwillingness and inability to do the job reflects an employee in the R1 stage of readiness. Therefore the telling style of supervisory leadership would be best used.

6. Credibility and trust do influence leadership effectiveness. If employees do not view their supervisor as being honest, competent, consistent, loyal, open, and having the ability to inspire them, they may not have a strong sense of unity—nor a commitment to their jobs or the organization.

7. **True.** Empowering supervisors share power and responsibility with their employees. That's one of the basic concepts of empowering supervisors.

8. **d. None of the above statements about gender differences is correct.** Although men and women do, in some cases, demonstrate similar leadership styles, they are different in their style orientation. Women tend to use a leadership style that encourages participation of their followers. Men, on the other hand, tend to lead using a directive leadership style.

CASE 10.A

This Boss Isn't Bossy

Krista Harris is the regional director of CBC Radio for the Maritimes. She is responsible for the six radio stations in Charlottetown, Halifax, Sydney, Moncton, Fredericton and Saint John. Krista's background is unusual for someone in this business. She started out as a chartered accountant but found it unfulfilling so, after two years, moved on. After a series of various jobs in which she developed her management skills, Krista found herself at the CBC. She attributes it to "being in the right place at the right time."

Because Krista did not come from a traditional journalistic background, she feels it has been important to earn credibility and respect with her employees. How has she done this? "By showing how much I rely on their [her subordinates'] good judgement. I'm always learning and watching, and will admit when I don't know something. I don't expect myself to be a technical expert, and I don't pretend to be. That takes the pressure off me."

Krista loves working with people and with teams. "I'm always so amazed by what can be accomplished by teamwork and motivated people. I set broad parameters for people and then let them decide on the specifics. I allow risk and some failures, and I don't get upset over failure." Earlier, in Chapter 4, you read about how Krista works with her station leaders at the beginning of each program season to set objectives. There are always clear areas or principles to work on through the regional objectives. However, Krista also asks the station leaders to meet with their staff to jointly discuss potential objectives before they meet with her.

"I have a weekly conference call on Tuesday at 2 [p.m.] with the station leaders where I tell them what's happening nationally and they tell me what's happening locally. I visit the stations strategically—when there's an important issue or a special show. During these visits, I make time to speak with individuals. We hold regional meetings twice a year where we all meet in Halifax to discuss ideas for regional programming. All stations contribute to—and later broadcast—the two or three regional specials we do each year—the last one was on poverty in the Maritimes. I ask the station managers to poll their people for ideas for the specials.

"It's been a challenge to build a sense of teamwork among the stations. They were separated into three teams previously, and were used to operating independently. I think they first saw the amalgamation as interference and micromanagement. Now, it feels like there's a greater sense of region. My focus is on fostering this even more, and on community outreach and innovation in our broadcasting. The radio service has come through a period of uncertainty but now things are stable. It's a challenge to get people to start thinking differently and be innovative.

"When we have our regional meetings, we set the agenda together—here are my ideas, what would you like to add? I always start meetings with a temperature check—what's going on in, for example, Moncton, what's going well and not. I find this is a good way to start because often we discover common themes and concerns.

"Sometimes, in meetings, I have to drone on as I have to explain a new initiative. But I try not to talk much in meetings but to be a facilitator, and make the discussion as open as possible. No idea is too small or too silly.

"I run a tight meeting. People can get on a certain topic and turn it into a gripe session—I allocate time so no one takes over a meeting. Although, if something is important, I allow the topic to run over.

"At meetings I try to build in time for people to talk among themselves when I'm not there. For example, giving them a half-hour to discuss common issues when I'm not there. Usually the meeting is really constructive when I return.

"Communication is the most important thing to me. I give everyone as much information as possible as soon as I can. I try my darnedest not to give surprises. I expect my staff to contact me regularly by e-mail or phone to keep me in touch, including sharing good news with me."

RESPONDING TO THIS CASE

1. Krista describes her landing in a CBC management position as "being in the right place at the right time." Her success there suggests it was a matter of skill, not luck. Evaluate the leadership skills shown by Krista in this case—what skills does she bring to her position that do not depend on a background in journalism or broadcasting?

2. Explain whether you think Krista uses a "female" style of leadership.

3. Use one of the leadership theories to explain Krista's leadership style and its appropriateness for her situation.

4. Relate the components of building trust— from Building a Supervisory Skill—to Krista's leadership style.

5. Explain the importance of the half-hour Krista schedules into the biannual regional meetings for the station leaders to discuss common issues in her absence. Why is this an effective tool and what does it accomplish?

FIGURE 10-9

Krista Harris

CASE 10.B

Leading the Virtual Team

Earlier in the text, you met Carolyn Moore, the HR technology team user support team leader at NCR in Waterloo. She supervises the work of four other people, each of whom provides support to a regional grouping of NCR managers. Because NCR is an international organization, Carolyn's team members are located in the United Kingdom, the United States, Australia, and Germany. They are there to help HR managers use the human resources information system to get the employee information they need, which is sensitive to the unique aspects of their location such as data privacy laws.

Carolyn also has a second leadership role as the team leader for a major project—adding new functionality to the current HRIS in order to support NCR needs. This team of 25 people includes the user support group but also technical experts and subject matter experts. Their mandate is to develop customizations to the Peoplesoft HRIS that will allow NCR to have global HR processes rather than each region doing things differently. This means that all NCR offices worldwide will use common processes. For example, they will use the same functions and parameters to describe what an employee in a particular position does. As a result, they will be able to consolidate and analyze aggregate information.

Developing these global procedures is not easy, as currently the various countries have a mix of locally unique processes, legal restrictions, and globally common practices in place. For example, the European data privacy laws are much more stringent than American ones, German companies must return resumes to applicants not hired for a position, and the storage and movement of electronic Japanese data must be done separately from English, German, and French data because of the uniqueness of the Japanese characters in their written language.

Carolyn "meets" weekly with the whole project team to discuss progress on the plan through a conference call. Because of NCR's rigorous expectations, she must document and track the project carefully and get approval before undertaking any new steps which require additional funding or resource allocation. Team members must be proactive and innovative in determining ways to utilize the system to support the business needs. This project is unprecedented in that one globally defined HRIS for use by all NCR countries has never existed before. As a result, Carolyn and her team have a project where the needs analysis is critical—they could not know upfront just what the HRIS customization would require or how technically challenging it would be. Their project was difficult to plan out in detail and will be constantly revised as new information and demands emerge. Consequently, effective communication among the dispersed members of the virtual team is paramount.

As well as communicating by phone, which is complicated by the many time zones covered, Carolyn deals with many issues by e-mail. She regularly travels to Dayton, Ohio, home to NCR world headquarters, to meet with subteams. Her manager is based in England but she sees him in Dayton every few months. All team members meet together face-to-face once a year for their annual kick-off meeting, where objectives are defined. This year they will spend two weeks in Dayton testing the system together.

Carolyn is particularly proud of the kick-off meeting she organized to start the project, and for good reason. She had to facilitate all three days, yet she was new as the team leader, had not met many of the team members before, and was performing in front of her manager for the first time. Carolyn worked for a full month to plan and put together all the meeting elements. She wanted to ensure that they accomplished what was needed to launch this high-profile project and also to put her stake in the ground as a leader, gaining the respect of the team. One of the things Carolyn wanted to do with the team was a team building exercise. She hired a consultant who spent two hours one evening discussing virtual teams and issues related to communication style and methods. Together the team discussed the pitfalls of a virtual team and what they needed to be aware of to be able to communicate effectively with each other, with others in the organization, and with their "customers."

RESPONDING TO THIS CASE

1. In Chapter 1, you read about Susan Mocsan at Brewer's Retail. Like Carolyn, Susan was charged with creating an HRIS that effectively met the needs of all management at her organization. Yet, unlike Carolyn, Susan could walk from her office to the offices of company managers and the other people with whom she networked to gain information and support for her project. Given the dispersion of NCR's people and offices, how could Carolyn use her networking and "politicking" skills to assist her team? Or will she not need to do so?

2. All of Carolyn's team members came from other roles in the company onto this project team. They are expected to work with all parts and levels of the company in different countries and different cultures. What demands would these facts put on Carolyn as their team leader?

3. What skills would Carolyn have needed to design and run the three-day project kick-off meeting? Explain in detail what she would have had to do and what skills contributed to their successful completion.

11

COMMUNICATING EFFECTIVELY

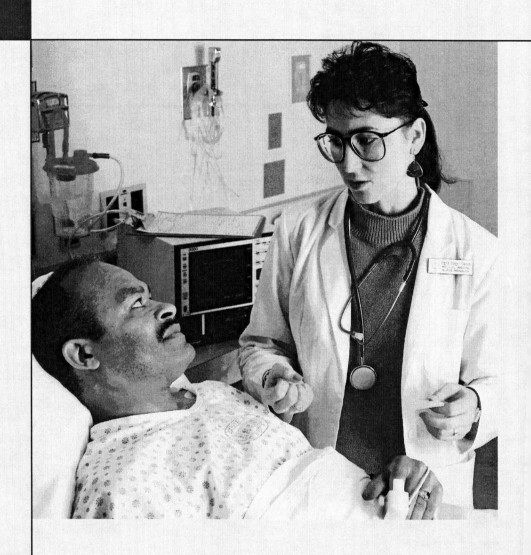

LEARNING OBJECTIVES

After reading this chapter, you should be able to:

1. Define communication.
2. Contrast formal and informal communication.
3. Explain how electronic communications affect the supervisor's job.
4. List barriers to effective communication.
5. Describe techniques for overcoming communication barriers.
6. List the essential requirements for active listening.
7. Explain what behaviours are necessary for providing effective feedback.

CHAPTER OUTLINE

PERFORMING EFFECTIVELY

WHAT IS COMMUNICATION?

METHODS OF COMMUNICATION
 Oral Communication
 Written Communication
 Electronic Communication
 Something to Think About
 Something to Think About
 Nonverbal Communication
 The Grapevine

THE SUPERVISOR'S DAY-TO-DAY COMMUNICATION

BARRIERS TO EFFECTIVE COMMUNICATION
 Language
 Poor Listening Habits
 Lack of Feedback
 Differences in Perception
 Role Requirements
 Choice of Information Medium
 Lack of Honesty
 Dealing with a Difficult Issue: Should You Tell the Whole Truth?
 Emotions

IMPROVING YOUR COMMUNICATION EFFECTIVENESS
 Think First!
 Constrain Emotions
 Learn to Listen
 Tailor Language to the Receiver
 Match Words and Actions
 Supervision in Action: Communication Differences in a Global Village
 Utilize Feedback
 Participate in Assertiveness Training
 Building a Supervisory Skill: Confronting
 Pop Quiz

THE IMPORTANCE OF FEEDBACK SKILLS
 What's the Difference Between Positive and Negative Feedback?
 How Do You Give Effective Feedback?

FROM CONCEPTS TO SKILLS: ACTIVE LISTENING
 Assessing Yourself: Do You Listen Actively?
 Skill Basics
 Applying Your Skills
 Pop Quiz

UNDERSTANDING THE BASICS
 Summary
 Key Terms and Concepts
 Reviewing Your Knowledge
 Answers to the Pop Quizzes

PERFORMING YOUR JOB
 Case 11.A: Tricia Mah
 Case 11.B: Communicating Across Distances

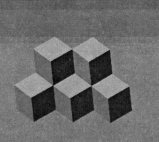

"Growing" a customer service call centre in Moncton for Imperial Oil has been a challenge for Stacy Goodale, especially since she is located in Toronto. As the HR Project Coordinator for the call centre, her responsibility has been to design the jobs, decide on the skill sets needed, do the recruiting, develop and execute the training, and develop an approach for measuring proficiencies. Stacy's team of subordinates has varied in size between four and six with the movement of contract workers in and out of the team.

As with all supervisors, Stacy recognizes communication is a major aspect of her job. "When I started as a supervisor, my biggest challenge was communication—giving feedback, providing clear expectations, delegating work. I was learning to operate in a new role, as a manager of a project and of people, and trying to articulate a vision and provide work direction to my staff at the same time. And I didn't know how to be sure another person really understood my expectations. Because staff on this project are located across the country, we talk on the phone and e-mail a lot. However, I use face-to-face communication or phone, not e-mail, in anything to do with staffing or with any contentious issues. I'm a better listener face-to-face and I believe I get a better sense of how others are reacting when I can see their body language and facial expressions.

"Negative feedback is tough. There's a tendency to want to do the job myself if something has not been done the way I wanted. But I have learned to work with them, discussing how we can take what they have done and build on it.

"I deal with thirty to forty e-mails a day. To make life easier, I use the trick of getting all my carbon copy (i.e. FYI) e-mails stored in a separate folder so I can look at them later. I know then which e-mails to focus on because they need responses directly from me.

"Another important aspect of communication is in dealing with management. When I'm presenting ideas, I need to know when to be aggressive and push my ideas and when not to. I have to know my audience, what they're interested in, what I need them for, and what is or is not in my control so I can focus on the right things."

All supervisors need strong communication skills. Like Stacy, they are involved in frequent communication with employees, peers, their immediate manager, customers, people in other departments and others in order to get their department's objectives accomplished. The communication can be face-to-face, by e-mail, phone, memo, or formal report. Regardless of the form, the wrong words, the wrong tone, or an insensitivity to the audience can have dire consequences. Communication skills alone don't make an effective manager but ineffective communication skills can lead to a continuous stream of problems for the supervisor.

WHAT IS COMMUNICATION?

Communication is the transference and understanding of meaning. Perfect communication, if such a thing were possible, would exist when a transmitted thought or idea was perceived by the receiver exactly as it was envisioned by the sender.

Good communication *does not* mean "agreement." If someone disagrees with us, many of us assume the person just didn't fully understand our position. In other words, many of us define good communication as having someone accept our views. But I can understand very clearly what you mean and not agree with what you say. In fact, when a supervisor concludes that a lack of communication must exist because a conflict between two of her employees has continued for a prolonged time, a closer examination often reveals that there is plenty of effective communication going on. Each person fully understands the other's position. The problem is one of erroneously equating effective communication with agreement.

Communication
The transference and understanding of meaning.

METHODS OF COMMUNICATION

Supervisors participate in two types of communication. One is **formal communication**. It addresses task-related issues and tends to follow the organization's authority chain. When supervisors give orders to an employee, provide advice to a team in their department, are offered suggestions by employees, interact with other supervisors on a project, or respond to a request made by their boss, they are engaged in formal communication. The other type is **informal communication**. This type of communication moves in any direction, skips authority levels, and is as likely to satisfy social needs as it is to facilitate task accomplishments.

Supervisors engage in formal communication through speech, written documents, electronic media, and nonverbal behaviour. Informal communication takes place on the **grapevine**.

Formal communication
Addresses task-related issues and tends to follow the organization's authority chain.

Informal communication
Moves in any direction and is as likely to satisfy social needs as to facilitate task accomplishments.

Grapevine
The means by which informal communication takes place.

ORAL COMMUNICATION

Supervisors rely heavily on oral communication. They meet one-on-one with an employee, give a speech to their department, engage in a problem-solving session with a group of employees, or talk on the phone to a disgruntled customer.

What are the advantages of oral communication? You can transmit information quickly through the spoken word, and oral communications include a nonverbal component that can enhance the message. A phone call, for instance, conveys not only words but also tone and mood. A one-on-one meeting further includes gestures and facial expressions. Additionally, today's supervisors are becoming increasingly aware that not only are oral communications an effective means for quickly conveying information, but they also have positive symbolic value. In contrast to a memo or e-mail message, the spoken word is more personal. It conveys more intimacy and caring. As a result, some of the best supervisors rely extensively on oral communication even when the use of written or electronic channels would seem to be as effective. They have found, through experience, that reliance on oral communication tends to build trust with employees and creates a climate of openness and support (see Something to Think About). "I try to talk to as many people as possible personally, whether they are senior or junior to me. I have an open-door policy and I get back to everyone who contacts me. It's much easier to discuss opposing points of view when you know the person, see them face-to-face, and have a history of treating them with respect," says Lenny Jackson, manager of TV Production Services for CBC Halifax.

WRITTEN COMMUNICATION

When your message is intended to be official, when it has long-term implications, and when it is highly complex, you'll want to convey it in written form. Introducing a new departmental procedure, for instance, should be conveyed in writing so there will be a permanent record to which all employees can refer. Providing a written summary to employees following performance reviews is a good idea because it helps reduce misunderstandings and creates a formal record of what was discussed. Departmental reports that contain lots of detailed numbers and facts are best conveyed in writing because of their complexity.

The fact that written communications provide better documentation than the spoken word is both a plus and a minus. On the plus side, written documents provide a reliable "paper trail" for decisions or actions that are later called into question. They also reduce ambiguity for recipients. But on the negative side, obsessive concern with documenting everything in writing leads to risk avoidance, decision paralysis, and creation of a highly politicized work environment. At the extreme, task accomplishment becomes subordinated to "covering your rear" and ensuring that no one person is held responsible for any questionable decision.

ELECTRONIC COMMUNICATION

Computers and digitalization are dramatically increasing a supervisor's communication options. Today, you can rely on a number of sophisticated electronic media to carry your communications. These include electronic mail (e-mail), intranets, electronic paging, cellular telephones,

Do men and women communicate in the same way? The answer is "not always." The differences in communication styles between men and women may lead to some interesting insights. When men talk, they tend to do so to emphasize status and independence; whereas women tend to use communications to create connections and intimacy. For instance, men frequently complain that women talk too much about their problems. Women, however, criticize men for not listening. What's happening is that when a man hears a woman talking about a problem, he frequently asserts his desire for independence and control by providing solutions. Many women, in contrast, view conversing about a problem as a means to promote closeness. The woman presents the problem to gain support and connection—not to get the male's advice.

Some research suggests that men are more likely to boast, and less likely to apologize, or to seek help when they need it. Women are more likely to be indirect in their requests, and men more blunt and direct, which can lead to women sometimes being viewed as manipulative and sneaky, and men as insensitive.

Because effective communication between the sexes is important to all supervisors for meeting departmental goals, how can you manage the differences in communication style? Preventing gender differences from becoming persistent barriers to effective communication requires acceptance, understanding, and a commitment to adaptive communication across gender lines. Both men and women need to acknowledge that there are differences in communication styles, that one style isn't better than the other, and that it takes real effort to "talk" with each other successfully.

What do you think? Do men and women really communicate differently? How would the apparent "women's" style of communication potentially affect their success in business?

video conferencing, modem-based transmissions, and other forms of network-related communications.

Supervisors are increasingly using many of these technological advances. E-mail (see Something to Think About on page 426) and voice mail allow people to transmit messages 24 hours a day. Even though you're away from your office, others can still leave messages for you to review on your return. And for important and complex communiques, a permanent record of e-mail messages can be obtained by printing out a

THE PROS AND CONS OF E-MAIL

"Because it's so fast and efficient, we use e-mail a lot," says Tammy Abel, the student placement coordinator who supervises all four Student Employment Centres in Winnipeg. "But it's not necessarily the most effective, and it can easily lead to overload."

"E-mail is an effective business tool that can go very wrong. To pass on an attached report, fine. But to try to discuss an issue—no, it can mess things up. You need to hear the tone, see the expression. Phone is better, face-to-face best," adds Susan Mocsan of Brewer's Retail. "Sometimes people say something in an e-mail that they would never say in person—somehow feeling anonymous."

Tammy and Susan's comments bring up the pros and cons. E-mail allows easy transmission of documents and transfer of straightforward information. It is quick and can contact as many people as you want simultaneously. On the other hand, it has led to a far greater stream of information for most supervisors, not all of it useful or desirable. It has led to discipline issues—to be discussed later in the chapter on discipline. When used inappropriately, it can cause miscommunication and greater problems.

How do you decide when it is appropriate to use e-mail versus another form of communication? What skills are required in using e-mail effectively? How can a supervisor coach a subordinate in the appropriate use of e-mail? How do you feel about your company reading your e-mails—do you feel they are company property or yours?

hard copy. Cellular phones are dramatically changing the role of the telephone as a communication device. In the past, telephone numbers were attached to physical locations. Now, with cellular technology, the phone number attaches to the individual. As such, supervisors can be in constant contact with department members, other supervisors, and key members of the management team, regardless of where they are physically located. Network-related communications allow supervisors to monitor the work of employees whose jobs are done on computers, to participate in electronic meetings, and to communicate with suppliers and customers on interorganizational networks.

FIGURE 11-1
Words, either written
or spoken, don't have
to exist for meaning to
be transferred. This
sign tells you plenty.

NONVERBAL COMMUNICATION

Some of the most meaningful communications aren't spoken, written, or transmitted on a computer. These are **nonverbal communications** (see Figure 11-1). A loud siren or a red light at an intersection tells you something without words. When a supervisor is conducting a training session, he doesn't need words to tell him that people are bored when eyes become glassy. Similarly, he can tell in an instant by his boss's body language and verbal intonations whether she's angry, upbeat, anxious, or distracted.

Nonverbal communications Communication that sends messages without words.

Body language refers to gestures, facial configurations, and other movements of the body. A snarled face, for example, says something different from a smile. Hand motions, facial expressions, and other gestures can communicate emotions or temperaments such as aggression, fear, shyness, arrogance, joy, and anger.

Body language Gestures, facial configurations, and other movements of the body.

Verbal intonation refers to the emphasis someone gives to words or phrases. To illustrate how intonations can change the meaning of a message, consider the employee who asks a colleague a question. The colleague replies, "What do you mean by that?" The employee's reaction will vary, depending on the tone of the colleague's response. A soft, smooth tone creates a different meaning from one that is abrasive and puts a strong emphasis on the last word. Most of us would view the first intonation as coming from someone who sincerely sought clarification, whereas the second suggests that the person is being aggressive or defensive.

Verbal intonations The emphasis someone gives to words or phrases.

The fact that every oral communication also has a nonverbal message cannot be overemphasized. Why? Because the nonverbal component is likely to carry the greatest impact. One study found that 55 percent of an oral message is derived from facial expression and physical posture, 38 percent from verbal intonations, and only 7 percent from the actual words used.[1] Most of us know that animals respond to the way we say something rather than the content of what we say. Apparently, people aren't much different.

THE GRAPEVINE

The grapevine is active in almost all organizations. In fact, studies typically find that the grapevine is the means of communication by which most operative employees first hear about important changes introduced by management. It rates ahead of supervisors, official memoranda, and other formal sources.

Is the information that flows along the grapevine accurate? The evidence indicates that about 75 percent of what is carried is accurate.[2] But what conditions foster an active grapevine? What gets the rumour mill rolling?

It is frequently assumed that rumours start because they make titillating gossip. Such is rarely the case. Rumours have at least four purposes:

- to structure and reduce anxiety;
- to make sense of limited or fragmented information;
- to serve as a vehicle to organize group members, and possibly outsiders, into coalitions; and
- to signal a sender's status (I'm an insider and you're not) or power (I have the power to make you into an insider).

Studies have found that rumours emerge as a response to situations that are *important* to us, where there is *ambiguity*, and under conditions that arouse *anxiety*. Work situations frequently contain these three elements, which explains why rumours flourish in organizations. The secrecy and competition that typically prevail in large organizations—around such issues as the appointment of new bosses, the relocation of offices, the realignment of work assignments, and layoffs—create conditions that encourage and sustain rumours on the grapevine. A rumour will persist either until the wants and expectations creating the uncertainty underlying the rumour are fulfilled or the anxiety is reduced.

What can we conclude from this discussion? Certainly, the grapevine is an important part of any group or organization's communication system and is well worth understanding. Moreover, it's never going to be eliminated, so supervisors should use it in beneficial ways.

Given that only a small set of employees typically passes information to more than one other person, supervisors can analyze grapevine information and predict its flow. Certain messages are likely to follow predictable patterns (see Figure 11-2). Supervisors might even consider using

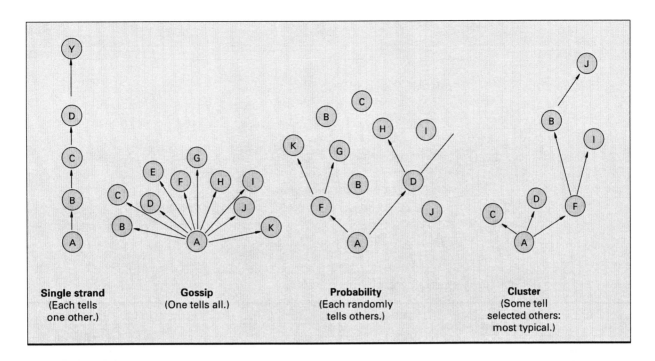

Single strand	Gossip	Probability	Cluster
(Each tells one other.)	(One tells all.)	(Each randomly tells others.)	(Some tell selected others: most typical.)

FIGURE 11-2

Grapevine patterns. (*Source:* John W. Newstrom and Keith Davis, *Organizational Behavior: Human Behavior at Work*, 9th ed., New York: McGraw Hill, 1993, p. 445. Reproduced with permission.)

the grapevine informally to transmit information to specific individuals by planting messages with key people who are active on the grapevine and are likely to find a given message worthy of passing on.

Supervisors should not lose sight of the grapevine's value for identifying issues that employees consider important and that create anxiety among them. It acts as both a filter and a feedback mechanism, picking up issues that employees consider relevant, and planting messages that employees want passed on to upper management. For instance, the grapevine can tap employee concerns (see Figure 11-3). If the grapevine is abuzz with a rumour of a mass layoff, and if you know the rumour is totally false, the message still has meaning. It reflects the fears and concerns of employees, and hence should not be ignored.

THE SUPERVISOR'S DAY-TO-DAY COMMUNICATION

Chapter 2, Supervisory Planning and Time Management, described the value of planning. It was suggested that supervisors schedule their time in order to minimize interruptions and block out segments of time to focus on high-priority activities. In practice, this is very hard to do. Diaries and observations of supervisory activities reveal three interesting findings that relate to communication.[3]

1. **Supervisors are busy.** The typical supervisor's day is made up of hundreds of separate incidents. Instead of planning their days in great detail, supervisors are often forced to react to events and people on the spur of the moment.
2. **Supervisory work is fragmented.** Interruptions are frequent in supervisory work, allowing little time to be devoted to any single activity. Tasks are completed quickly.
3. **Supervisors rely on oral communication.** Supervisors spend most of their time communicating verbally on the telephone, in meetings, or in one-on-one personal contacts.

Taken together, these findings remind us that a supervisor's day-to-day communications are made up of literally dozens of brief encounters punctuated by constant interruptions. At any given moment, a supervisor might be reading correspondence, involved in a phone conversation, responding to an e-mail message, participating in a formal or informal meeting, taking an observational tour, or cornered in a hallway by his or her immediate manager or by an employee with a question. The effective supervisor learns to differentiate important messages from the unimportant ones and not to let the constant disruptions deter him or her from the pursuit of paramount goals.

BARRIERS TO EFFECTIVE COMMUNICATION

As noted earlier, the goal of perfect communication is to transmit a thought or idea from a sender to a receiver so that it is perceived by the receiver exactly as it was envisioned by the sender. That goal is almost never achieved because of distortions and other barriers (see Figure 11-4). In this section, we will describe some of the more serious barriers that hinder effective communication. In the following section, we'll offer some suggestions for how to overcome these barriers.

FIGURE 11-3

Information that is shared is often fodder for the workplace grapevine.

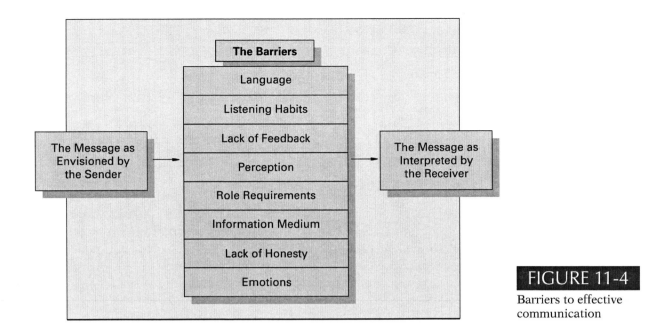

FIGURE 11-4

Barriers to effective communication

LANGUAGE

Words means different things to different people. Age, education, and cultural background are three of the more obvious variables that influence the language people use and the definitions they give to words. In an organization, employees usually come from diverse backgrounds. Furthermore, horizontal differentiation creates specialists who develop their own jargon or technical language. In large organizations, members are often widely dispersed geographically, and those in each locale will use terms and phrases that are unique to their area. Vertical differentiation can also cause language problems. For instance, differences in the meaning of words such as incentives and quotas occur at different levels of management. Top managers often speak about the need for *incentives* and *quotas*, yet these terms have been found to imply manipulation and create resentment among supervisors.

The point is that while you and I may both speak the same language (English), our use of that language is far from uniform. A knowledge of how each of us modifies the language would minimize communication difficulties. The problem is that you don't know how your various employees, peers, superiors, customers, and others with whom you interact have modified the language. Senders tend to assume that the words and terms they use mean the same to the receiver as they to do them. This, of course, is often incorrect, and thus creates communication difficulties.

POOR LISTENING HABITS

Most of us hear but we always don't listen! Hearing is merely picking up sound vibrations. Listening is making sense out of what we hear. That is, listening requires that you pay attention, interpret, and remember what is being said.

Most of us are pretty poor listeners. At this point, it suffices to say that if you don't have good listening skills, you're not going to get the full message as the sender meant to convey it. For example, there are common flaws that many of us share regarding listening. We get distracted and end up hearing only parts of a message. Instead of listening for meaning, we listen to determine whether we agree or disagree with what's being said—selective perception. We begin thinking about our response to what's being said rather than listening for the complete message. Each of these flaws in our listening habits contributes to messages being received differently from the way the sender intended.

LACK OF FEEDBACK

Effective communication means the transference and *understanding* of meaning. But how do you know if someone has received your message and comprehended it in the way that you meant? The answer is: Use feedback. When a supervisor requests that each member of her staff submit a specific report, receipt of the report is feedback. When your instructor tests you on the material in this book, he gets feedback on your understanding of the text material and his lectures.

When a sender fails to use feedback, he or she never knows if the message has been received as intended. So lack of feedback creates the potential for inaccuracies and distortions.

FIGURE 11-5

What do you see— an old woman or a young girl?

DIFFERENCES IN PERCEPTION

Our attitudes, interests, past experiences, and expectations determine how we organize and interpret our surroundings. This explains how we can look at the same things and perceive them differently (see Figure 11-5). In the communication process, the receiver selectively sees and hears messages based on his or her background and personal characteristics. The receiver also projects his or her interests and expectations into communications when interpreting them. Since senders and receivers of communications each bring their own set of perceptual biases, the messages they seek to transfer are often subject to distortions.

ROLE REQUIREMENTS

People in organizations play **roles**. They engage in behaviour patterns that go with the position they occupy in the organization (see Figure 11-6). Managerial jobs, for instance, come with role identities. Managers know they are supposed to be loyal to, and defend, their boss and the organization. Union leaders' roles typically require loyalty to union goals such as improving employee security. Marketing roles demand efforts to increase sales, while the roles of people working in the credit department emphasize minimizing losses from bad debts.

With the differing role requirements of different members come communication barriers. Each role comes with its own jargon that sets the role apart from others. Additionally, fulfilling role requirements often requires individuals to selectively interpret events. They hear and see the world in a way that is consistent with their role requirements. The result is that people in different roles often have difficulty communicating with each other. Marketing people say they want to "increase sales." So, too, do the people in credit. The difference is that the marketing people want to sell everything to anybody, while credit only wants to sell to those who are creditworthy. Labour and management representatives have difficulty negotiating because their roles encompass very different language and interests. Many of the internal communication breakdowns in organizations are merely individuals enacting behaviours consistent with the roles they are playing.

Roles
Behaviour patterns that go with the position one occupies in the organization.

CHOICE OF INFORMATION MEDIUM

The amount of information transmitted in a face-to-face conversation is considerably greater than that received from a flyer posted on a bulletin board. The former offers multiple information cues (words, posture, facial expressions, gestures, intonation), immediate feedback, and the

FIGURE 11-6

Union-management negotiations, such as those between Ford and the Canadian Auto Workers, require the parties to play roles.

Richness of information
The amount of information a medium is capable of transmitting.

personal touch of "being there," all of which the flyer lacks. This reminds us that media differ in the **richness of information** they transmit. Figure 11-7 illustrates the hierarchy of information richness. The higher a medium rates in richness, the more information it is capable of transmitting.

Generally speaking, the more ambiguous and complicated the message, the more the sender should rely on a rich communication medium. For example, as a supervisor, if you want to share with your employees a major new product line that your company will be introducing—and which will affect everyone in your department—your communication is more likely to be effective in a face-to-face departmental meeting than through use of a memo. Why? Because this message is likely to initiate apprehension among employees and require clarification. In contrast, a modest change in tomorrow's departmental production schedule can be effectively communicated in a memo. Unfortunately, people in organizations don't always match the medium to the message, and thereby create communication problems.

LACK OF HONESTY

A colleague asks you what you think of the ideas he suggested in the recent team meeting in which you both participated. You personally think his suggestions were weak. But you don't tell him that. Rather, you compliment his ideas and say how much they contributed to the final results.

A good deal of what passes as "poor communication" is nothing other than individuals purposely avoiding honesty and openness (see Dealing with a Difficult Issue). To avoid confrontations and hurting others' feelings, some organizational members engage in practices such as conveying ambiguous messages, saying what they think others want to hear, or cutting off communication altogether.

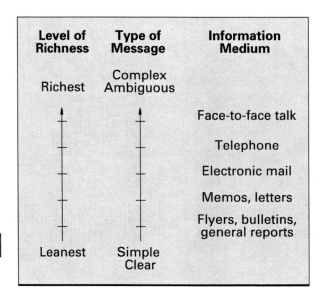

FIGURE 11-7

Hierarchy of information richness

SHOULD YOU TELL THE WHOLE TRUTH?

Effective communications in both your personal life and work life is built on the expectation that appropriate and accurate information is being given. In any communications encounter, people should be afforded the respect and dignity of being given complete and factual information. Under what circumstances, then, is it appropriate to withhold information from someone?

One instance that calls for discretion in conveying information is when the issue of confidentiality is involved. The decision to withhold confidential information is sometimes a must—especially at work. Take a situation where one of your employees has just been diagnosed with a treatable form of cancer. He's confided in you about the status of his health. He's also asked you not to say a word to anyone because he considers his health to be a personal matter.

Over the next few months, your employee is absent frequently, especially during his radiation treatments. Because of the circumstances surrounding his illness, you do not feel his absences are a major problem. In part, that's because some of his duties involve direct computer work, which he can do while at home and forward electronically to the appropriate people. You've also discreetly divided the rest of his work among other employees in your work unit. Your employees, though, are wondering what is wrong. Many have come to you to you to find out. You simply, and politely, decline to discuss the issue about this employee with his coworkers. However, a number of them think that you're giving him preferential treatment, and they are ready to go to your boss to complain. You know that if they only knew what was going on, they'd understand, but you can't reveal the reason for his absence. On the other hand, if some individuals begin to make trouble for you or for this employee, it could create more problems for him. That's something he doesn't need right now in his life.

Is it ever appropriate to withhold or filter information in an organization? Should you tell your other employees the whole story? What do you think? Would your views change if this employee had a contagious disease and was working in close contact with his coworkers?

Some people run from confrontation. They want everyone to like them. As such, they avoid communicating any messages they think might be displeasing to the receiver. What they end up doing is increasing tension and further hindering effective communication.

EMOTIONS

How the receiver feels at the time of receipt of a message will influence how he or she interprets it. A message received negatively when you're angry or distraught is likely to be interpreted differently when you're in a neutral disposition. Extreme emotions such as jubilation or depression are most likely to hinder effective communication. In such instances, we are most prone to disregard our rational and objective thinking processes and to substitute emotional judgements. These are also the times we're most likely to use inflammatory language that we later regret.

IMPROVING YOUR COMMUNICATION EFFECTIVENESS

A few of the barriers we've described are part of organizational life and will never be fully eliminated. Perceptual and role differences, for example, should be recognized as barriers but should not be considered easy to correct. However, most barriers to effective communication can be overcome. The following suggestions provide you with some guidance.

THINK FIRST!

"Think before you speak!" That cliché can be expanded to include all forms of communication. Before you speak or write, ask yourself: What message am I trying to convey? Then ask: How can I organize and present my message so that it will achieve the desired outcome?

Most of us follow the "think first" rule when writing a message. The formal and deliberate process of writing encourages thinking through what we want to say and how best to say it. The concept of "working on a draft" implies that the written document will be edited and revised. But few of us give anywhere near the same attention to our verbal communications. That's a mistake. Before you speak, make sure you know what you want to say. Then present your message in a logical and organized fashion so it will be clear and understood by your receiver.

CONSTRAIN EMOTIONS

It would be naive to assume that supervisors always communicate in a fully rational manner. Yet we know that emotions can severely cloud and distort the transference of meaning. If you as a supervisor are emotionally upset over an issue, you are more likely to misconstrue incoming messages and fail to clearly and accurately express outgoing messages.

What can you do? The simplest answer is to pause and wait until you have regained composure. Count to 10. Talk to yourself to get you through a situation without losing control. For example, "Keep cool. You know that if you snap you'll appear unprofessional and make the situation even worse."

LEARN TO LISTEN

We stated earlier that most of us are poor listeners. But that doesn't mean we can't improve our listening skills. There are specific behaviours that have been found to be related to effective listening. We present those skills in the From Concepts to Skills section at the end of this chapter.

TAILOR LANGUAGE TO THE RECEIVER

Since language can be a barrier, supervisors should choose words and structure their messages in ways that will make them clear and understandable to the receiver. The supervisor needs to simplify his or her language and consider the audience to whom the message is directed, so the language will be tailored to the receivers (see Figure 11-8). Remember that effective communication is achieved when a message is both received and *understood* (see Supervision in Action). Understanding is improved in many cases by simplifying the language used. This means, for example, that a nursing supervisor should always try to communicate in clear and easily understood terms, and that the language used in messages to a patient should be purposely different from that used with the medical staff. Jargon can facilitate understanding when used with those who know what it means, but it can cause innumerable problems when used outside that group.

MATCH WORDS AND ACTIONS

If actions speak louder than words, then it's important to watch your actions to make sure they align with and reinforce the words that go along with them. As a supervisor, you must ensure your verbal and nonverbal communication match. Otherwise, your words will not be trusted. When you must discipline someone, don't smile to soften the blow—you'll seem like a hypocrite. When you give positive feedback, use an enthusiast voice. If you are aware that you show little expression in your face, consider compensating through animation in your voice. You may be misinterpreted if you don't look like you really mean what you are saying.

As a supervisor, your employees will look at your behaviour as a model. If your verbal comments are backed up by your actions, you will gain credibility and build trust. If, on the other hand, you say one thing and do another, your employees will ignore what you say and model themselves on what you do. At the extreme, people stop listening because they no longer believe your words have credibility. Incidentally, this is a problem that often plagues politicians.

FIGURE 11-8

Supervising a group of animators at Nelvana in Toronto, Brian Lemay sometimes used cartoon memos to get his message across—a vivid example of tailoring the message to the audience.

Communication Differences in a Global Village

It's important to recognize that communication isn't conducted in the same way around the world.[4] For example, contrast countries that place a high value on individualism (such as Canada) with countries where the emphasis is on collectivism (such as Japan).[5]

Owing to the emphasis on the individual in countries such as Canada, communication patterns are individual-oriented and rather clearly spelled out. For instance, North American supervisors rely heavily on memoranda, announcements, position papers, and other formal types of communication to stake out their positions in the organization. They also often hoard secret information in an attempt to promote their own advancement and as a way of inducing their employees to accept decisions and plans. For their own protection, lower-level employees also engage in this practice.

In collectivist countries such as Japan, there is more interaction for its own sake and a more informal manner of interpersonal contact. The Japanese manager, in contrast to Canadian managers, will engage in extensive verbal consultation over an issue first and will draw up a formal document later, only to outline the agreement that was made. Face-to-face communication is encouraged. Additionally, open communication is an inherent part of the Japanese work setting. Work spaces are open and crowded with individuals at different levels in the work hierarchy. In contrast, Canadian organizations emphasize authority, hierarchy, and formal lines of communication.

UTILIZE FEEDBACK

Many communication problems can be directly attributed to misunderstandings and inaccuracies. These problems are less likely to occur if the supervisor uses feedback. This feedback can be verbal or nonverbal.

If a supervisor asks a receiver, "Did you understand what I said?" the response represents feedback. But feedback should include more than yes and no answers. And if the person claims to understand, that answer is often not true because the person is too embarrassed to admit not understanding. The supervisor can ask a set of questions about a message in order to determine whether the message was received as intended. Better yet, the supervisor can ask the receiver to restate the message in his or her own words. If the supervisor then hears what was intended, understanding and accuracy should be enhanced. Colleen Murphy of the City of Brampton will ask a subordinate, "What do you think I just said?" in order to check understanding. She checks because she often finds misinterpretation.

Feedback does not have to be conveyed in words. The sales supervisor who sends his staff a directive, in which he describes a new monthly sales report that all sales personnel will need to complete, receives feedback if some of the salespeople fail to turn in the new report. This feedback suggests that he needs to clarify further the initial directive. Similarly, when you give a speech to a group of people, you watch their eyes and look for other nonverbal clues to tell you whether they are getting your message. This may explain why television performers on comedy shows prefer to tape their programs in front of a live audience. Immediate laughter and applause, or their absence, convey to the performer whether the message is getting across as intended.

A supervisor must focus not only on ensuring that others understand his or her messages but also that the supervisor him- or herself is also "getting the message" sent by others. Paraphrasing is an effective way to do this. This means that the listener expresses in his or her own words what he or she understood the speaker to have said. This can be even more effective if the listener also includes a reflection of feeling, as this demonstrates how "tuned in" to the total message the listener is. For example, if a subordinate says in a subdued voice, "Look, send someone else on this training. I'm too old to learn this high tech stuff," the supervisor could reply, "You seem apprehensive about this training—as if it's not worth even trying." The subordinate is more likely to open up and discuss his or her concerns than if the supervisor replies, "So you want me to send someone else instead."

PARTICIPATE IN ASSERTIVENESS TRAINING

Many people have no trouble asserting themselves. Being open and honest comes naturally to them. Some, in fact, are too assertive. They cross over the line to become aggressive and abrasive. Other individuals suffer from a constant fear of upsetting others and fall back on avoidance or ambiguous communication, when what they need is to be open and assertive. Such people would benefit from participation in assertiveness training. An effective supervisor needn't always be assertive, but should be capable of being so when it's needed.

Assertiveness training is designed to make people more open and self-expressive. Assertive people confront issues in a straightforward manner. They say what they mean, but without being rude or thoughtless.

Individuals who take assertiveness training learn verbal and nonverbal behaviours that enhance their ability to communicate openly and unambiguously. These behaviours include direct and unambiguous language; the use of "I" statements and cooperative "we" statements; a strong, steady, audible voice; good eye contact; facial expressions matched to the message; an appropriately serious tone; and a comfortable but firm posture.

One communication skill that is part of assertiveness and is very useful is confrontation. This skill is explained in Building a Supervisory Skill.

Assertiveness training
Training designed to make people more open and self-expressive.

Building a Supervisory Skill

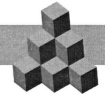

CONFRONTING

ABOUT THE SKILL

Confronting refers to the pointing out of discrepancies in attitudes, thoughts, or behaviours in the other person. It is giving feedback in a factual, non-judgemental way. The purpose is to help the other person look at a situation more realistically and accurately.

For example, you ask a subordinate, "How are things going with this new position?" The person responds, "Well, things are going very well. I, you know, feel like I fit in and it's, uh, going to be okay. I haven't got to know the others yet but, uh, that's okay. And I have no problem with the actual job duties. Yeah, fine." All this is said in a flat monotone.

Examples of nonconfronting ways in which you could respond include "Sounds like things are better for you"—which is a paraphrase but is not "tuned in"—or "I've had similar situations where things were hard at the beginning and later got better." Neither statement gets at the real issue, which is that the person is for some reason feeling uncomfortable.

An example of an *ineffective* confronting response would be "You're lying."

Effective confronting responses include, "You say things are okay but your voice and expression suggest that's not totally true," or "On the one hand, you say you fit in, but on the other hand, you say you haven't got to know the others yet." The objective is to point out a discrepancy in a non-aggressive way to encourage the person to be honest and explore the real issue further.

Confronting
Pointing out discrepancies in attitudes, thoughts or behaviours in another person in a non-judgemental way.

Steps in Practising the Skill

1. **Notice the discrepancy.** There are different types of discrepancies. It could be a discrepancy between words and action, for example, a subordinate says that he or she will get something done on time but actually hands it in two days late. Or it could be mixed emotions, such as when a subordinate is both excited and apprehensive about a possible transfer.

2. **Consider how to word your feedback, pointing out the discrepancy.** A common way to help you get started is to think in terms of "On the one hand... but on the other hand..."

3. **Calmly express the conflicting variables.** Identify the two confronting aspects, describing them in a factual way, with no judgement attached. For example, "You told me that you were having no problems with the report, yet you still have not completed it and it was due two days ago."

4. **Stay silent and let the person respond.** The person may feel somewhat awkward about your feedback, and not respond immediately. Don't try to make it easy for him or her by jumping in with an explanation. Let the person think and respond in his or her own time.

5. **Calmly follow up on the response with pertinent facts and implications.** Continue the conversation in a problem-solving way, remaining constructive and refraining from any accusations. If the person simply denies the truth you have presented, the person may not be prepared to deal with it yet. It may be useful to drop the issue for the moment and follow up later when he or she has thought about it.

Try It Yourself

Consider the appropriate confronting response in the following situations:

a) "Yeah, I know it's important and needs to get done. Just give me some time. I have other things that need to get done first. I know I promised it to you for this week but there's just no way. I hate to disappoint you; I know how critical this is for you. I'll get it done as soon as possible."

b) "I really enjoyed your training session. It was full of useful information and was fun at the same time." You are surprised. The entire training session, she sat watching you without a trace of interest or reaction on her face, and never asked a question or volunteered an answer.

c) "I really want to work on that project. Can you get me on that committee?" The subordinate who says this to you annoyed the team members on his last project by not pulling his weight. You discussed this issue with him in a recent performance review. He has not shown any particular initiative since that discussion.

d) Your manager says to you, "Thanks for doing such a great job. I really appreciate your contribution to this. I don't know what we'd do without you." Meanwhile, you are aware that you received the lowest performance bonus of all the supervisors.

POP QUIZ

Are You Comprehending What You're Reading?

1. Good communication does not require:
   a. transference
   b. agreement
   c. understanding
   d. meaning
2. What value can a grapevine offer to a supervisor?
3. The advantage of oral communication is that it creates an accurate and permanent record of the communication that took place. True or false?
4. Communication is distorted when:
   a. body language and verbal intonation are used
   b. e-mail, which lacks feedback opportunities, is used
   c. body language and the words spoken are not aligned
   d. the information is complex

THE IMPORTANCE OF FEEDBACK SKILLS

Ask a supervisor about the feedback he or she gives to employees, and you're likely to get a qualified answer. If the feedback is positive, it's likely to be given promptly and enthusiastically. Negative feedback is often treated very differently. Like most of us, supervisors don't particularly enjoy communicating bad news. They fear offending or having to deal with the receiver's defensiveness. The result is that negative feedback is often avoided, delayed, or substantially distorted.[6] The purposes of this section are to show you the importance of providing both positive and negative feedback and to identify specific techniques to help make your feedback more effective.

WHAT'S THE DIFFERENCE BETWEEN POSITIVE AND NEGATIVE FEEDBACK?

We stated that supervisors treat positive and negative feedback differently. So, too, do receivers. You need to understand this fact and adjust your feedback style accordingly.

Positive feedback is more readily and accurately perceived than negative feedback. Furthermore, while positive feedback is almost always accepted, you can expect negative feedback to meet resistance. Why? The logical answer appears to be that people want to hear good news and block out the rest. Positive feedback fits what most people wish to hear and already believe about themselves.

Does this mean, then, that you should avoid giving negative feedback? No, what it means is that you need to be aware of potential resistance and learn to use negative feedback in situations in which it's most likely to be accepted.[7] That is, negative feedback should be used when it's supported by hard data—numbers, specific examples, and the like.

HOW DO YOU GIVE EFFECTIVE FEEDBACK?

There are six specific suggestions that we can make to help you become more effective in providing feedback, which we will discuss below.

FOCUS ON SPECIFIC BEHAVIOURS

Feedback should be specific rather than general. Avoid such statements as "You have a bad attitude" or "I'm really impressed with the good job you did." They're vague and, while they provide information, they don't tell the receiver enough to correct the "bad attitude" or on what basis you concluded that a "good job" has been done so the person knows what behaviours to repeat.

KEEP FEEDBACK IMPERSONAL

Feedback, particularly the negative kind, should be descriptive rather than judgemental or evaluative. No matter how upset you are, keep the feedback focused on job-related behaviours and never criticize someone personally because of an inappropriate action. Telling people they're incompetent, lazy, or the like is almost always counterproductive. It provokes such an emotional reaction that the performance deviation itself is apt to be overlooked. When you're criticizing, remember that you're censuring job-related behaviour, not the person. You might be tempted to tell someone he or she is rude and insensitive (which might just be true); however, that's hardly impersonal. It's better to say something more specific like, "You've interrupted me three times with questions that weren't urgent when you knew I was talking long distance to a customer in Brazil."

KEEP FEEDBACK GOAL-ORIENTED

Feedback should not be given primarily to "unload" on another person. If you have to say something negative, make sure it's directed toward the receiver's goals. Ask yourself whom the feedback is supposed to help. If the answer is essentially you—"I've got something I just want to get off my chest"—bite your tongue and hold the comment. Such feedback undermines your credibility and lessens the meaning and influence of future feedback sessions.

MAKE FEEDBACK WELL TIMED

Feedback is most meaningful to a receiver when there is a very short interval between his or her behaviour and the receipt of feedback about that behaviour. For example, a new employee who makes a mistake is more likely to respond to suggestions for improving right after the mistake or at the end of the work day—rather than during a performance review session six months later. If you have to spend time recreating a situation and refreshing someone's memory of it, the feedback you're providing is likely to be ineffective.[8] Moreover, if you're particularly concerned with changing behaviour, delays in providing timely feedback on the undesirable actions lessens the likelihood that the feedback will be effective in bringing about the desired change. Of course, making feedback prompt merely for promptness' sake can backfire if you have insufficient information or if you're emotionally upset. In such instances, "well timed" might be better defined as "somewhat delayed."

ENSURE UNDERSTANDING

Is your feedback concise and complete enough that the receiver clearly and fully understands your communication? Remember, every successful communication requires both transference and understanding of meaning.

If feedback is to be effective, you need to ensure that the receiver understands it. Consistent with our discussion of listening techniques, you should have the receiver rephrase the content of your feedback to find out whether it fully captured the meaning you intended.

DIRECT NEGATIVE FEEDBACK

Negative feedback should be directed toward behaviour the receiver can do something about. There's little value in reminding a person of some shortcoming over which he or she has no control. For instance, to criticize an employee who's late for work because she forgot to set her alarm clock would be valid. To take her to task for being late for work when the subway she takes to work every day had a power failure, stranding her for 90 minutes, would be pointless. There's nothing she could have done to correct what happened—short of finding a different means of travel, which may be unrealistic.

In addition, when negative feedback is given concerning something that the receiver can control, it might be a good idea to indicate specifically what can be done to improve the situation. This takes some of the sting out of the criticism and offers guidance to employees who understand the problem, but don't know how to resolve it.

ACTIVE LISTENING

This chapter has repeatedly noted that most of us suffer from poor listening skills. Listening is difficult and often more tiring than talking. It demands intellectual effort and concentration. The average person speaks at a rate of about 150 words per minute, whereas we have the capacity to listen at the rate of over 1000 words per minute. The difference leaves idle time for the brain and opportunities for the mind to wander.

This section is designed to help you correct and improve your listening habits.

ASSESSING YOURSELF: DO YOU LISTEN ACTIVELY?

For each of the following questions, select the answer that best describes your listening habits.

	Usually	Sometimes	Seldom
1. I maintain eye contact with the speaker.	❑	❑	❑
2. I determine whether a speaker's ideas are worthwhile solely by his or her appearance and delivery.	❑	❑	❑
3. I try to align my thoughts and feelings with those of the speaker.	❑	❑	❑
4. I listen for specific facts rather than for "the big picture."	❑	❑	❑
5. I listen for both factual content and the underlying emotion.	❑	❑	❑
6. I ask questions for clarification and understanding.	❑	❑	❑
7. I withhold judgment of what the speaker is saying until he or she is finished.	❑	❑	❑
8. I make a conscious effort to evaluate the logic and consistency of what is being said.	❑	❑	❑
9. While listening, I think about what I'm going to say as soon as I have my chance.	❑	❑	❑
10. I try to have the last word.	❑	❑	❑

SCORING KEY AND INTERPRETATION

For questions 1, 3, 5, 6, 7, and 8, give yourself three points for Usually, two points for Sometimes, and one point for Seldom. For questions 2, 4, 9, and 10, give yourself three points for Seldom, two points for Sometimes, and one point for Usually.

Total up your points. A score of 27 or higher means that you're a good listener. A score of 22 to 26 suggests you have some listening deficiencies. A score below 22 indicates that you have developed a number of bad listening habits.

SKILL BASICS

Passive listening
Absorbing information as it is literally transmitted.

Active listening
Listening with intensity, empathy, acceptance, and a willingness to take responsibility for completeness.

Effective listening is active rather than passive. In **passive listening**, you are much like a tape recorder. You absorb the information given. If the speaker provides you with a clear message and makes his or her delivery interesting enough to keep your attention, you'll probably get most of what the speaker is trying to communicate. But **active listening** requires you to understand the communication from the speaker's point of view.

There are four essential requirements for active listening. You need to listen with

1. intensity,
2. empathy,
3. acceptance, and
4. a willingness to take responsibility for completeness.

Because listening presents the opportunity for the mind to wander, the active listener concentrates intensely on what the speaker is saying and tunes out thousands of miscellaneous thoughts (work deadlines, money, personal problems) that create distractions. What do active listeners do with their idle brain time? Summarize and integrate what has been said! They put each new bit of information into the context of what has preceded it.

Empathy requires you to put yourself in the speaker's shoes. Try to understand what the speaker wants to communicate rather than what you want to understand. Notice that empathy demands from you both knowledge of the speaker and flexibility. Suspend your own thoughts and feelings and adjust what you see and feel to your speaker's world. In that way, you increase the likelihood that you will interpret the message being spoken in the way the speaker intended.

An active listener demonstrates acceptance. He or she listens objectively without judging content. This is no easy task. It is natural to be distracted by the content of what a speaker says, especially when we disagree with it. When we hear something we disagree with, we begin formulating mental arguments to counter what is being said. Of course, in doing so, we miss the rest of the message. The challenge for the active listener is to absorb what is being said and to withhold judgement on content until the speaker is finished.

The final ingredient of active listening is taking responsibility for completeness. That is, the listener does whatever is necessary to get the full intended meaning from the speaker's communication.

The following guide summarizes 14 specific techniques to use for effective listening.

1. **Be motivated.** If a listener is unwilling to exert the effort to hear and understand, no amount of additional advice is likely to improve listening effectiveness. As we previously noted, active listening is hard work. So your first step toward becoming an effective listener is a willingness to make the effort.

2. **Make eye contact.** How do you feel when somebody doesn't look at you when you're speaking? If you're like most people, you're likely to interpret this as aloofness or lack of interest. It's ironic that while "you listen with your ears, people judge whether you are listening by looking at your eyes." Making eye contact with the speaker focuses your attention, reduces the likelihood that will become distracted, and encourages the speaker.

3. **Show interest.** The effective listener shows interest in what is being said. How? Through nonverbal signals. Affirmative head nods and appropriate facial expressions, when added to good eye contact, convey to the speaker that you're listening. Verbal signals —comments such as "I see," "Yes," and "I know what you mean"— offer even more direct evidence that you are listening. Leaning slightly forward in your seat suggests interest, whereas leaning back suggests the opposite.

4. **Avoid distracting actions.** The other side of showing interest is avoiding actions that suggest your mind is somewhere else. When listening, don't look at your watch, shuffle papers, play with your pencil, or engage in similar distractions. They make the speaker feel you're bored or uninterested. Maybe more importantly, they indicate that you aren't fully attentive and may be missing part of the message that they want to convey.

5. **Empathize.** We said the active listener tries to understand what the speaker sees and feels by putting herself in his shoes. Don't pro-

ject your own needs and intentions onto the speaker. When you do so, you're likely to hear what you want to hear. So ask yourself: Who is this speaker and where is he coming from? What are his attitudes, interests, experiences, needs, and expectations?

6. **Take in the whole picture.** The effective listener interprets feelings and emotions as well as factual content. If you listen to words alone and ignore other vocal cues and nonverbal signals, you will miss a wealth of subtle messages. To test this point, read the script of a play. Then go and see that play live in a theatre. The characters and the message take on a much richer meaning when you see the play acted on stage.

7. **Ask questions.** The critical listener analyzes what he or she hears and asks questions. This behaviour provides clarification, ensures understanding, and assures the speaker that you're listening.

8. **Paraphrase.** Paraphrasing means restating what the speaker has said in your own words. The effective listener uses phrases like: "What I hear you saying is…" or "Do you mean…?" Why rephrase what's already been said? Two reasons! First, it's an excellent control device with which to check whether you're listening carefully. You can't paraphrase accurately if your mind is wandering or if you're thinking about what you're going to say next. Second, it's a control for accuracy. By rephrasing what the speaker has said in your own words and feeding it back to the speaker, you verify the accuracy of your understanding.

9. **Don't interrupt.** Let the speaker complete his or her thought before you try to respond. Don't try to second-guess where the speaker's thoughts are going. When the speaker is finished, you'll know it!

10. **Integrate what's being said.** Use your spare time while listening to better understand the speaker's ideas. Instead of treating each new piece of information as an independent entity, put the pieces together. Treat each part of the message as if it were an additional piece of a puzzle. By the time the speaker is done, instead of having 10 unrelated bits of information, you'll have 10 integrated pieces of information that form a comprehensive message. If you don't, you should ask the questions that will fill in the blanks.

11. **Don't overtalk.** Most of us would rather speak our own ideas than listen to what someone else says. Too many of us listen only

because it's the price we have to pay to get people to let us talk. While talking may be more fun and silence may be uncomfortable, you can't talk and listen at the same time. The good listener recognizes this fact and doesn't overtalk.

12. **Confront your biases.** Evaluate the source of the message. Notice such things as the speaker's credibility, appearance, vocabulary, and speech mannerisms. But don't let them distract you. For instance, all of us have "red flag" words that prick our attention or cause us to draw premature conclusions. Examples might include terms such as *racist, gay, chauvinist, conservative, liberal, feminist*, or *blue collar*. Use information about the speaker to improve your understanding of what he or she has to say, but don't let your biases distort the message.

13. **Make smooth transitions between speaker and listener roles.** In most work situations, you're continually shifting back and forth between the roles of speaker and listener. The effective listener makes transitions smoothly from speaker to listener and back to speaker. From a listening perspective, this means concentrating on what a speaker has to say and practising not thinking about what you're going to say as soon as you get your chance.

14. **Be natural.** An effective listener develops a style that is natural and authentic. Don't try to become a compulsive listener. If you exaggerate eye contact, facial expressions, the asking of questions, showing of interest, and the like, you'll lose credibility.

A good listener is not a manipulator. Use moderation and develop listening techniques that are effective and fit well with your interpersonal style.

APPLYING YOUR SKILLS

This is a role play to practise listening skills. Break into groups of three. One person will be the observer. He or she will evaluate the two other role players and provide feedback on their listening skills using the 14 points listed above.

Choose one of the following role-plays to enact and decide who will play each character.

Why Lose the Good and Keep the Bad An employee has come to speak to his supervisor. This employee is frustrated that a friend who has been a contract worker at the plant is being laid off after 18 months of excellent work. Meanwhile, other full-time employees who are much less competent than this contract employee are keeping their jobs. It does not seem fair that this is how good work is rewarded. It also seems like a stupid decision from the point of view of the company and its productivity. The supervisor needs to work with this person to have him understand that if contract employees remain too long with the company, then they are considered full-time by the government and incur additional expenses for the company (such as benefits). The company does not want to increase its full-time staff. It wants to cover additional work with the flexibility of contract workers.

What Should I Do? One supervisor has approached another supervisor for advice on dealing with a subordinate. He believes that one of his subordinates has been stealing from the company. Several pieces of the new computer equipment have disappeared; the supervisor has heard this employee, named Peter, make cracks about the great new equipment he has at home, and he makes no secret that in his previous position at the company, he was allowed to "borrow" software packages, books, and audiovisual equipment. But the supervisor has no proof of the theft; it is simply a suspicion. He is aware that Peter is a close friend of an executive at the firm and if the supervisor makes a wrong move in handling this, it could mean big trouble.

Can We Work Something Out? An employee is approaching her supervisor to discuss her needs for accommodation at work. One of her parents is critically ill and the other is not in strong health. She needs to spend a lot of time with them helping them cope with daily issues such as shopping, cleaning their house, and accompanying them to medical appointments. Plus, she has her own life to lead. It's a very stressful time in her life. Her employer has been good to her in the past and she is hoping they will continue to be so. She would like them to allow her to work flexible hours and she may need to take a leave of absence. The supervisor has never dealt with a situation like this. The two role players will need to decide what kind of job the employee does.

After each person has read the appropriate roles, begin the exercise. You have up to 15 minutes. When completed, the observer should provide feedback to both of the role players on how well they listened to each other.

Are You Comprehending
What You're Reading?

5. What should active listeners do with idle brain time?
   a. summarize and integrate what has been said
   b. organize their schedules for the next few hours
   c. plan how to ask questions of the speaker
   d. rest and prepare to receive future communication
6. Identify the six elements of giving feedback.
7. Empathy in communications means you listen objectively without judging content. True or false?
8. The greatest value of feedback is that it:
   a. forces the sender to think twice about what is communicated
   b. allows for further discussions between the sender and receiver
   c. is not necessary in written communication because the message is tangible and verifiable
   d. improves communication by reducing the chance of misunderstandings

SUMMARY

This summary is organized by the Learning Objectives.

1. Communication is the transference and understanding of meaning.
2. Formal communication addresses task-related issues and tends to follow the organization's authority chain. Informal communication moves in any direction, skips authority levels, and is as likely to satisfy social needs as it is to facilitate task accomplishments.
3. Electronic communications allow supervisors to transmit messages 24 hours a day and stay in constant contact with department members, other supervisors, and key members of the management team regardless of where they are physically located. Networks also allow supervisors to participate in electronic meetings and interact with key people outside the organization.
4. Barriers to effective communication include language differences, poor listening habits, lack of feedback, differences in perception, role requirements, poor choice of information medium, lack of honesty, and emotion.
5. Techniques for overcoming communication barriers include thinking through what you want to say before communicating, constraining emotions, learning to listen, tailoring language to the receiver, matching words and actions, utilizing feedback, and participating in assertiveness training.
6. The essential requirements for active listening are: 1. intensity, 2. empathy, 3. acceptance, and 4. a willingness to take responsibility for completeness.
7. Behaviours that are necessary for providing effective feedback include focusing on specific behaviours; keeping feedback impersonal, goal-oriented, and well-timed; ensuring understanding; and directing negative feedback toward behaviour that the recipient can control.

UNDERSTANDING THE BASICS

KEY TERMS AND CONCEPTS

Active listening
Assertiveness training
Body language
Communication
Confronting
Formal communication
Grapevine

Informal communication
Nonverbal communication
Passive listening
Richness of information
Roles
Verbal intonation

REVIEWING YOUR KNOWLEDGE

1. "Everything a supervisor does involves communicating." Build an argument to support this statement.
2. Why isn't agreement necessarily a part of good communication?
3. When is a written communication superior to an oral one?
4. "Do what I say, not what I do." Analyze this phrase in terms of supervisors being effective communicators.
5. How can nonverbal messages be powerful communicators?
6. What are the purposes of rumours?
7. Can supervisors control the grapevine? Discuss.
8. Given all the barriers to communication, how is it possible for any two people in an organization to accurately transfer information?
9. "A supervisor should always select the information medium that rates highest in information richness." Do you agree or disagree? Discuss.
10. Why is active listening so difficult for many people to accomplish?

UNDERSTANDING THE BASICS

ANSWERS TO THE POP QUIZZES

1. **b. agreement.** Good communication involves transference of meaning—which enables understanding between the parties. It does not require agreement. In fact, two individuals can be in complete agreement, yet still not be communicating

2. The grapevine can indicate to a supervisor that employees perceive certain problems in the organization. Although the grapevine may not be totally accurate, information flowing through the grapevine can be valuable to a supervisor.

3. **False.** The advantage of oral communication is that it creates a chance for timely feedback. An advantage of written communications is that it creates an accurate and permanent record of the communication that took place.

4. **c. body language and the words spoken are not aligned.** Effective communications requires that body language and intonation be aligned. Otherwise, they send mixed signals and create a barrier to effective communications.

5. **a. summarize and integrate what has been said.** This response is one of the basic elements of active listening.

6. The six elements of giving feedback are: 1. focus on specific behaviours; 2. keep feedback impersonal; 3. keep feedback goal-oriented; 4. make feedback well timed; 5. ensure understanding; and 6. direct negative feedback toward behaviour that the receiver can control.

7. **False.** Empathy in the communications process means trying to understand what the speaker wants to communicate rather than what you want to understand.

8. **d. improves communication by reducing the chance of misunderstandings.** Reducing the chance of misunderstandings—thus helping the transference of meaning—is the foundation of effective feedback.

PERFORMING YOUR JOB

CASE 11.A

Tricia Mah

"The first thing I do every morning is a walk-about," explains Tricia Mah, the director of support services for an intermediate-care nursing home in Vancouver. During this walkabout, she speaks with every staff member in the areas she supervises—food services, housekeeping, laundry, and maintenance. "I greet them. I ask them how things are and how they're feeling. At the moment, I'm a little worried about the older staff while so much construction is going on. During the walkabout, I give reminders of food safety, for example, checking that they have washed their hands, and I give feedback on anything pertinent so they know my expectations."

Tricia doesn't then retreat to her office for the rest of the day, despite the administrative demands of her job. She chats with staff during lunch duties and in the afternoon when new staff arrive. "The front-line staff members know their job a lot better than I do. I tell them this. And I'll say, "I can look with my eyes and see if the system is working but you need to tell me if my eyes are wide open or half shut."

The construction that Tricia mentioned comes with an extensive expansion of the facility, growing from 90 beds to over 150 beds. All Tricia's systems had to change because of the expansion. The success of her changes have been linked with Tricia's use of communication. "I had nine unionized staff members moved here from other places. Most were in their late fifties and early sixties and brought over 20 years' seniority with them so this affected the other staff, too. I got the established staff ready for the integration by asking them to consider how it must feel for these workers to be uprooted by this, and I asked for their help in making these "new" staff members welcome. With the new staff members, I interviewed each one to get to know them and I tell them regularly how they're doing.

"The expansion meant everyone had new positions. To prepare them, I told them before-

hand in staff meetings what was happening and why. I find that lack of information can lead to rumours and anxiety.

"In creating the new systems I asked for employee input, for example, on timelines. I asked for their feedback once we implemented new systems and they knew I was open to adjusting things.

"Change is hard for all and some had a struggle with it. When we were implementing the changes, I pulled all the 'old-timers' into my office individually to say I was looking to them to be the leaders and I wanted to get to the core concerns. It worked—they got involved and I thanked them for their help."

RESPONDING TO THIS CASE

1. Why does Tricia rely so much on oral communication in her job? Consider the different communication situations she describes and decide whether the communication medium she chose was appropriate.
2. How does Tricia attempt to avoid communications getting distorted by the typical "barriers"? What potential communication barriers were created with the influx of the nine employees from another facility?

CASE 11.B

Communicating Across Distances

Carolyn Moore has three clocks on her desk, each showing a different time zone. She refers to them frequently in her contact with team members in the United Kingdom, Australia, and Germany. As you read earlier, Carolyn is both the team leader of the five-person international HRIS user-support group at NCR, and the project leader of the team that decides new functionality for the Human Resource Technology.

CHAPTER 11   COMMUNICATING EFFECTIVELY

451

Consequently, she is regularly in touch with technical staff, functional specialists, and managers throughout NCR worldwide.

How does Carolyn manage communications with this wide variety of dispersed people? She has many mechanisms to do so. Every Monday at 7 a.m. EST, Carolyn has a conference call with the whole project team. She also has weekly conference calls with smaller subteams. There is a predefined list of topics for each meeting, for example, technical updates on projects, deadlines and risks. All meetings have minutes recorded and team members take turns doing this task. The minutes are posted on a shared network drive so anyone can examine them later. Carolyn reports that running these meetings is a challenge. "When you have 15 or 20 people on a conference call and only 1.5 hours to cover everything, you need to know how to ask questions, when to move on, and when to give an issue to one or two people to investigate between calls."

Another forum for communication is resource board meetings. This is like a steering committee to which Carolyn must present work-to-date at each phase of the project. Then the board decides whether to further support the project.

At the beginning of each year, there's a formal kick-off meeting where all the technical and business people meet together in person for several days to discuss project requirements and plans.

In terms of more spontaneous communication, e-mail is popular because often there is a need that could be addressed by a variety of people. "For example, someone will ask for ideas in dealing with an error they have come across, or they'll ask if anyone remembers something in particular. There's a lot of banter that brings others into the environment. Because so many of us travel a lot, e-mail is the best way to get hold of people.

"Since this is an ongoing project, we spend a lot of time reviewing material and giving input. I'll send a draft out and ask for feedback, using the technology to track revisions; for example, the eight people reviewing a document will each use a different colour in [Microsoft] Word to make their changes."

"We work with people from so many language backgrounds that we often get e-mail from someone who has poor English. We must ask many questions to ensure we understand their needs or their input. If five or six people are on a conference call, people will interpret for one another all the time."

Dealing with performance issues from a distance calls for exceptional communication skills. For example, Carolyn may have a manager call or e-mail her about one of her user-support team, thousands of kilometres away, who has too many things on his plate and is failing to fulfill requests in a timely manner. Carolyn needs to follow up on the phone with the employee. Doing this takes tact and compassion because, if the employee is remote, the person may feel that needed resources aren't there to help him or her do the job, or that he or she can't refuse any request because no one else is available to deal with it. When Carolyn first had to deal with a performance issue involving a remote subordinate, she sought advice from other managers and found they couldn't really help—she had to "wing it" on her own to learn what would work.

RESPONDING TO THIS CASE

1. One manager refers to remote employees sometimes having a "bunker mentality." She was referring to the tendency for employees located far away from headquarters organizational support to feel that they really are "on their own." There is a defensiveness, feeling that others don't understand their position and can't really imagine what they must deal with. How can and does Carolyn use communication to avoid the development of this "bunker mentality"?

2. Apply the rules of effective feedback to Carolyn's unique circumstance of having to deal with performance issues over the phone with far-distant subordinates.

3. Consider the different audiences with whom Carolyn communicates and how she will need to adjust her communication style and content for those audiences.

P A R T F I V E

COPING WITH WORKPLACE DYNAMICS

12. MANAGING CONFLICT AND POLITICS

13. MANAGING CHANGE AND STRESS

14. DISCIPLINING EMPLOYEES

15. THE SUPERVISOR'S ROLE IN EMPLOYEE RELATIONS

12

MANAGING CONFLICT AND POLITICS

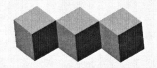

LEARNING OBJECTIVES

After reading this chapter, you should be able to:

1. Define conflict.
2. Identify the three general sources of conflict.
3. List the five basic techniques for resolving conflict.
4. Describe how a supervisor could stimulate conflict.
5. Define politicking.
6. Explain the existence of politics in organizations.
7. Describe the situational factors that determine political options.
8. List specific guidelines for developing and improving political skills.
9. Contrast distributive and integrative bargaining.

CHAPTER OUTLINE

PERFORMING EFFECTIVELY

WHAT IS CONFLICT?

ARE ALL CONFLICTS BAD?

SOURCES OF CONFLICT
  Communication Differences
  Structural Differentiation
  Personal Differences

TECHNIQUES FOR MANAGING CONFLICT
  Resolution Techniques
  Building a Supervisory Skill
  Which Conflicts Should You Tackle?
  Choosing the Appropriate Resolution Technique
  Assessing Yourself: Your Preferred Conflict-Handling Style
  Stimulation Techniques
  Pop Quiz

UNDERSTANDING ORGANIZATIONAL POLITICS
  What Is Politics?
  Why Is There Politics in Organizations?

THE ETHICS OF "PLAYING POLITICS"

ASSESSING THE POLITICAL LANDSCAPE
  Your Organization's Culture
  The Power of Others
  Your Power
  Building a Supervisory Skill: Becoming Politically Smart
  Something to Think About

FROM CONCEPTS TO SKILLS: NEGOTIATION
  Assessing Yourself: Do You Understand What It Takes to Be an Effective Negotiator?
  Skill Basics
  Applying Your Skills
  Pop Quiz

UNDERSTANDING THE BASICS
  Summary
  Key Terms and Concepts
  Reviewing Your Knowledge
  Answers to the Pop Quizzes

PERFORMING YOUR JOB
  Case 12.A: Was the Knife a Joke?
  Case 12.B: Joe and Catalino Deal with Angry Clients

Marlene Roy is the supervisor of the Manitoba HRDC Labour Market Information Unit in Winnipeg. She recalls a situation where she knew there was something wrong within her group of employees, but did not know what it was. "Then an employee told me that there was resentment because the full-time (FT) employees were covering for the part-time (PT) people when they were off. It was perceived that the FTs had the bulk of the work yet were treated the same by the organization. Once I knew this, I could be receptive to the innuendo and confront it. I spoke with the staff and explained the situation. I, myself, am not FT, working four days a week. I told them I make less than they do and here are the benefits the PT people don't get..."

The situation Marlene describes draws together many typical elements in a conflict. The conflict is based on a misperception or miscommunication. The conflict simmers unspoken, influencing atmosphere and behaviour, until it is finally brought out in the open. Resentful employees don't approach the supervisor because they feel she is party to the "unfair" situation. However, once the issue is discussed and the misperceptions clarified, the conflict and the tension disappear.

Not all conflicts are so easily resolved. Marlene says, "There are different styles in doing things and people need to accept that but they sometimes don't. I know I need to accept that some people may simply not like each other, but it's hard to stay out of it."

Dealing with conflict is a part of every supervisor's job. Those who learn how to manage conflict properly are likely to reap significant benefits. For instance, one study of a group of managers looked at 25 skill and personality factors to determine which, if any, were related to managerial success (defined in terms of ratings by one's boss, salary increases, and promotions).[1] Of the 25 measures, only one—the ability to handle conflict—was positively related to managerial success.

In this chapter, we'll define conflict, explore what brings it about, and examine the various ways supervisors can handle it. Then we'll discuss organizational politics—why understanding politics is important for all supervisors and how you can make politics work for you.

WHAT IS CONFLICT?

Conflict is a process in which one party consciously interferes in the goal-achievement of another party. This interference can be between a supervisor and a member of his or her department, between two employees within a department, between a supervisor and his or her boss, or involve interdepartmental parties, such as two supervisors in separate departments. Conflicts with customers are also often handled by supervisors. The opening story about Marlene Roy demonstrated a conflict between part-time and full-time employees, and between the full-time employees and the supervisor, who was part-time herself.

Conflict
A process in which one party consciously interferes in the goal-achievement efforts of another party.

ARE ALL CONFLICTS BAD?

Most of us have grown up with the idea that all conflicts are bad. We were told not to argue with our parents or teachers, to get along with our brothers and sisters, and that countries spent billions of dollars on military outlays to preserve peace. But conflicts aren't *all* bad, especially in organizations.[2]

Conflict is a natural phenomenon of organizational life. It can't be completely eliminated. Why? For the following reasons:

1. Organizational members have different goals.
2. There are scarce resources, such as budget allocations, which various people want and are willing to fight over.
3. People in organizations don't all see things alike, as a result of their diverse backgrounds, education, experiences, and interests.

However, the existence of conflict in organizations has a positive side. It stimulates creativity, innovation, and change. And only through change can an organization adapt and survive (see Figure 12-1). For instance, a positive level of conflict in an organization supports disagreements, the open questioning of others, and challenging the status quo. If organizations were completely devoid of conflict, they would become apathetic, stagnant, and unresponsive to change.

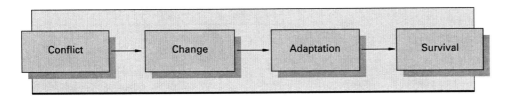

FIGURE 12-1
The positive role of conflict

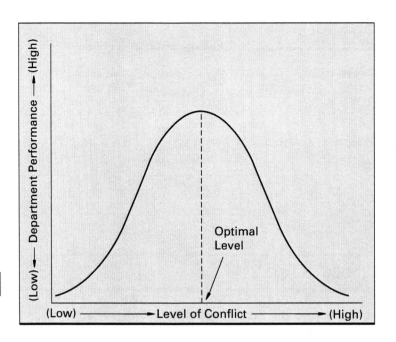

FIGURE 12-2

Conflict and depart-
ment performance

Supervisors should consider conflict as having an upside as well as a downside. They should encourage enough conflict to keep their departments viable, self-critical, and creative. Of course, too much conflict is bad and should be reduced. The supervisor's goal should be to have enough conflict in the department to keep the unit responsive and innovative, but not so much as to hinder departmental performance (see Figure 12-2).

SOURCES OF CONFLICT

Conflicts don't pop out of thin air. They have causes. These causes can be separated into three general categories: communication differences, structural differences, and personal differences.

COMMUNICATION DIFFERENCES

Communication differences encompass those conflicts arising from misunderstandings and different meanings attached to words, from someone not having needed communication passed on to them, or from an overload of information that makes it difficult to know what is important.

One of the major myths that most of us carry around with us is that poor communication is the only reason for conflicts—"If we could just communicate with each other, we could eliminate our differences." Poor communication is certainly not the source of all conflicts, though there is considerable evidence to suggest that problems in the communication process act to hinder collaboration and stimulate misunderstanding.

STRUCTURAL DIFFERENTIATION

As explained earlier in this book, organizations are horizontally and vertically differentiated. Management divides up tasks, groups common tasks into departments, and establishes rules and regulations to facilitate standardized practices between departments.

This structural differentiation often causes conflicts. Individuals disagree over goals, decision alternatives, performance criteria, and resource allocations. These conflicts, however, are not due to poor communication or personal animosities. Rather, they are rooted in the structure of the organization itself. The "goodies" that people want—budgets, promotions, pay increases, additional staff, office space, influence over decision—are scarce resources that must be divided up. The creation of horizontal units (departments) and vertical levels (the management hierarchy) brings about efficiencies through specialization and coordination, but at the same time produces the potential for structural conflicts. People tend to see their needs as paramount and may be unaware or uncaring of the needs of others in the organization.

PERSONAL DIFFERENCES

The third source of conflict is personal differences. These include value systems and personality characteristics that account for individual idiosyncrasies and differences.

For example: Your values emphasize acquiring material possessions, while mine focus on developing close family ties. An employee in your department thinks salary increases should be based on seniority. You think the criterion should be job performance. These value differences stimulate conflicts. Similarly, the chemistry between some people makes it hard for them to work together. Factors such as background, education, experience, and training mould each individual into a unique personality. Some personality types are attracted to each other, while some types are like oil and water—they just don't mix. The result is that some people may be perceived by others as abrasive, hard to work with, untrustworthy, or strange. This creates interpersonal conflicts.

Institute for Conflict Analysis and Resolution
http://www.gmu.edu/departments/ICAR/

Mediation Training Institute International
http://mediationworks.com/mti/

Program on Negotiation
http://www.law.harvard.edu/Programs/PON/

TECHNIQUES FOR MANAGING CONFLICT

As a supervisor, you want to have the optimum level of conflict in your department. That means you need to manage it. You'll want to *resolve* conflict when it is too high and disrupts your department's performance.

Conflict management The application of resolution and stimulation techniques to achieve the optimum level of departmental conflict.

You'll want to *stimulate* conflict when it's too low. So **conflict management** is defined as the application of resolution and stimulation techniques to achieve the optimum level of departmental conflict.

RESOLUTION TECHNIQUES

What options are available to eliminate or reduce conflicts? You have five basic approaches or techniques to resolving conflict: avoidance, accommodation, force, compromise, and collaboration. As shown in Figure 12-3, they differ in terms of the emphasis they place on concern for others versus concern for oneself. Each technique has particular strengths and weaknesses, and no single technique is ideal for every situation. You should consider each technique as a tool in your conflict management tool chest. While you may be better at using some tools than others, the skilled supervisor knows what each tool can do and when it is likely to be most effective.

AVOIDANCE

Avoidance The desire to withdraw from or suppress a conflict.

Sometimes **avoidance** is the best solution—just withdrawing from the conflict or ignoring its existence. When would that be? When the conflict is trivial, when emotions are running high and time can help cool things down, or when the potential disruption from a more assertive action outweighs the benefits of resolution. The thing to be concerned about with this approach is that some supervisors believe that they can run away from all conflicts. These conflict avoiders are often very poor supervisors. They frustrate their employees and usually lose their respect. For

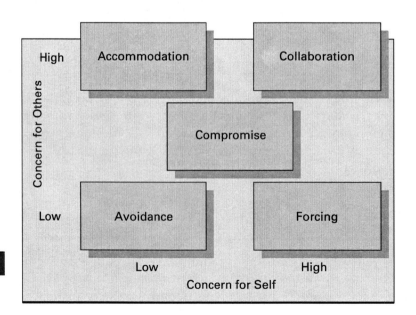

example, such a supervisor may fail to confront an employee who is not doing his work adequately or is breaking rules. The lack of action can anger the other employees. There *are* times when the best action is no action, but that shouldn't be the way you respond to every conflict.

ACCOMMODATION

The goal of **accommodation** is to maintain harmonious relationships by placing another's needs and concerns above your own. You might, for example, yield to another person's position on an issue or try to defuse a conflict by focusing on points of agreement. This approach is most viable when the issue under dispute isn't important to you or when you want to build up "credits" for possible later issues.

Accommodation
The willingness of one party in a conflict to place the opponent's interests above his or her own.

FORCING

With **forcing**, you attempt to satisfy your own needs at the expense of the other party. In organizations, this is most often illustrated by supervisors and managers using their formal authority to resolve a dispute. The use of physical threats, intimidation, majority-rule voting, or stubborn refusal to give in on your position are other examples of force. Force works well 1. when you need a quick resolution, 2. on important issues where unpopular actions must be taken, and 3. where commitment by others to your solution is not critical. However, force can damage morale, and cause resistance and a future lack of cooperation.

Forcing
The desire to satisfy your own needs at the expense of the other party.

COMPROMISE

A **compromise** approach requires each party to give up something of value. This is typically the approach taken by management and unions in negotiating a new labour contract. Supervisors often use compromise to deal with interpersonal conflicts. For instance, a supervisor in a small printing company wanted one of his employees to come in over a weekend to finish an important project. The employee didn't want to spend his whole weekend at work. After considerable discussion, they arrived at a compromise solution: the employee would come in on Saturday only, the supervisor would also come in and help out, and the employee would receive eight hours of overtime pay plus the following Friday off.

Compromise
A situation in which each party to a conflict is willing to give up something of value.

When should a supervisor look to compromise as an option? When conflicting parties are about equal in power, when it is desirable to achieve a temporary solution to a complex issue, or when time pressures demand an expedient solution.

COLLABORATION

The ultimate win-win solution is **collaboration**. All parties to the conflict seek to satisfy their interests. This technique is typically characterized by open and honest discussion among the parties, intensive listening in order

Collaboration
A situation where the parties to a conflict each desire to satisfy fully the concerns of all parties.

to understand differences and identify areas of mutual agreement, and careful deliberation over a full range of alternatives in order to find a solution that is advantageous to all. When is collaboration the best conflict approach? When time pressures are minimal, when all parties seriously want a solution, and when the issue is too important to be compromised. A discussion of the skills used in collaborating is presented in Building a Supervisory Skill.

Building a Supervisory Skill

HANDLING CONFLICT THROUGH A ROLE-REVERSAL TECHNIQUE

ABOUT THE SKILL

You approach a conflict from the belief that the best way to solve a conflict is to understand the other person's position. Using this technique, you are much more likely to gain two goals in a conflict—a solution acceptable to both, and a healthy relationship between the two. You may assume, after reading the description below, that the technique would take a long time and therefore not gain the third goal in many conflicts—a timely solution. However, ironically, because it is respectful, future-oriented, and constructive, it often takes less time than an approach that arouses strong emotions.

STEPS IN PRACTISING THE SKILL

1. **Use paraphrasing.** After the other person has spoken, paraphrase the main points before you go on to explain your viewpoint. This means you summarize what they have just said in your own words. By doing this, you force yourself to concentrate on the other person and listen to his or her points, you can clarify any misunderstanding, and you immediately gain greater credibility from the speaker, who knows you really are listening. Note that it is not effective to simply say, "I see" or "I understand how you feel." You may think that is true, but the other person will not believe you and you have not proven with your words that you really do understand.

2. **Stay calm.** You are a professional. This means you control your emotions. Losing your temper or crying will not win respect. Staying calm despite obvious tension in the situation and perhaps some goading from the other person *will gain you respect*.

3. **Focus on the issue, not the other person.** If you stick to the issue without bringing in anything personal about the other person, emotions are more likely to stay under control, and the conversation is more likely to stay constructive.

4. **Concentrate on what can be done in the future to resolve the problem rather than looking for blame.** Blaming arouses emotions and is usually a waste of time. Focusing on resolving the issue presents an opportunity for both parties to contribute positively to the discussion.

5. **Assume the other person means well.** Few people are intentionally malicious. Usually, a conflict has happened despite the genuinely well-meaning efforts of those involved. It is safer to assume that this has happened in a particular situation—until proven otherwise.

6. **Protect your own interests.** You still want a solution that works for you, but you don't want to sacrifice the relationship in order to get it.

WHICH CONFLICTS SHOULD YOU TACKLE?

Not every conflict justifies your attention. Some might not be worth the effort; others might be unmanageable. While avoidance might appear to be a "cop-out," it can sometimes be the most appropriate response. You can improve your overall management effectiveness, and your conflict management skills in particular, by avoiding trivial conflicts. Choose your battles judiciously, saving your efforts for the ones that count.

Regardless of our desires, reality tells us that some conflicts are unmanageable.[3] When antagonisms are deeply rooted, when one or both parties wish to prolong a conflict, or when emotions run so high that constructive interaction is impossible, your efforts to manage the conflict are unlikely to meet with much success. Don't be lured into the naive belief that a good supervisor can resolve every conflict effectively. Some aren't worth the effort. Some are outside your realm of influence. Still others may be functional and, as such, are best left alone. Those you choose to handle, you need to know how to handle in the best way possible.

CHOOSING THE APPROPRIATE RESOLUTION TECHNIQUE

Now that you're familiar with your options, how should you proceed if you find you have a conflict that needs resolving?

Start by considering your *preferred conflict-handling style* (see Assessing Yourself: Your Preferred Conflict-Handling Style). Each of us has a basic approach to handling conflict with which we feel most comfortable. Do you try to postpone dealing with conflicts, hoping they'll go away (avoidance)? Do you prefer soothing the other party's feelings so the disagreement doesn't damage your relationship (accommodation)? Are you stubborn and determined to get your way (forcing)? Do you look for middle-ground solutions (compromise)? Or do you prefer to sit down and discuss differences in order to find a solution that will make everybody happy (collaboration)?

Everyone has a basic resolution approach that reflects his or her personality. You should understand what yours is. But most people aren't held prisoner by that approach. They're flexible and can use different approaches if they need to. Unfortunately, some people are extremely rigid and incapable of adjusting their styles. These people are at a severe disadvantage because they can't use all the resolution options. You should know your basic resolution style and try to show flexibility in using others. However, keep in mind that when push comes to shove, most of us fall back on our basic approach because it's the one we know best and feel most comfortable with.

The next thing you should look is what you want to achieve. The best solution is closely intertwined with your definition of best. Three goals dominate the preceding discussion of resolution approaches: the *importance* of the conflict, concern over maintaining long-term *interpersonal relations*, and the *speed* with which you need to resolve the conflict. All other things held constant, if the issue is critical to your unit's success,

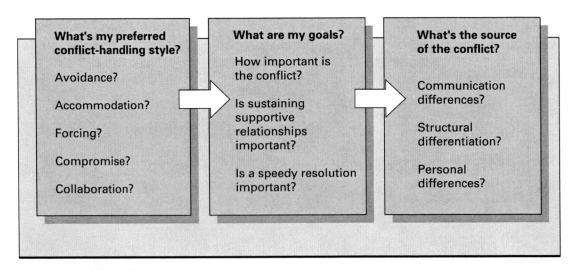

FIGURE 12-4

Choosing the appropriate resolution technique

Your Preferred Conflict-Handling Style

Instructions: Indicate how often you do the following—by checking *seldom, sometimes,* or *usually*—when you differ with someone.

	Seldom	Sometimes	Usually
1. I explore our differences, not backing down, but not imposing my view either.	❏	❏	❏
2. I disagree openly, then invite more discussion about our differences.	❏	❏	❏
3. I look for a mutually satisfactory solution.	❏	❏	❏
4. Rather than let the other person make a decision without my input, I make sure I am heard and also that I hear out the other person.	❏	❏	❏
5. I agree to a middle ground rather than look for a completely satisfying solution.	❏	❏	❏
6. I admit I am half wrong rather than explore our differences.	❏	❏	❏
7. I have a reputation for meeting a person halfway.	❏	❏	❏
8. I expect to get out about half of what I really want to say.	❏	❏	❏
9. I give in totally rather than try to change another's opinion.	❏	❏	❏
10. I put aside any controversial aspects of an issue.	❏	❏	❏
11. I agree early on, rather than argue about a point.	❏	❏	❏
12. I give in as soon as the other party gets emotional about an issue.	❏	❏	❏

	Seldom	Sometimes	Usually
13. I try to win the other person over.	❏	❏	❏
14. I work to come out victorious, no matter what.	❏	❏	❏
15. I never back away from a good argument.	❏	❏	❏
16. I would rather win than end up compromising.	❏	❏	❏

SCORING

Total your choices as follows: give yourself five points for "Usually," three points for "sometimes," and one point for "seldom." Then total them for each set of statements grouped as follows:

Set A:	Items 13–16	Set B:	Items 9–12
Set C:	Items 5–8	Set D:	Items 1–4.

WHAT THE ASSESSMENT MEANS

Treat each set separately. A score of 17 or above on any set is considered high; scores of 12–16 are moderately high; scores of 8–11 are moderately low; and scores of 7 or less are considered low. Sets A, B, C, and D represent different conflict-resolution strategies.

A = Forcing: I win, you lose
B = Accommodation: I lose, you win
C = Compromise: Both you and I win some and lose some
D = Collaboration: Both you and I win

Everyone has a basic underlying conflict-handling style. Your highest scoring set(s) in this exercise indicates the strategy or strategies you rely on most.

*A suggestion: Get someone who knows you well to complete this questionnaire, describing how **you** handle conflicts. That person's evaluation of you may not match yours and the differences may be enlightening.*

collaboration is preferred. If sustaining supportive relationships is important, the best approaches, in order of preference, are accommodation, collaboration, compromise, and avoidance. If it's crucial to resolve the conflict as quickly as possible, then force, accommodation, and compromise—in that order—are preferred.

Lastly, you need to consider the *source of the conflict*. The resolution technique that works best depends, to a large degree, on the cause of the conflict. Communication-based conflicts revolve around misinformation and misunderstandings. Such conflicts lend themselves to collaboration. In contrast, conflicts based on personal differences arise out of disparities between the parties' values and personalities. Such conflicts are most susceptible to avoidance because these differences are often deeply entrenched. When supervisors have to resolve conflicts rooted in personal differences, they frequently rely on force—not so much because it placates the parties, but because it works! The third category, structural conflicts, offers opportunities to use most of the conflict approaches.

This process of blending your personal style, your goals, and the source of the conflict should result in identifying the approach or set of approaches most likely to be effective for you in any specific conflict.

STIMULATION TECHNIQUES

What about the other side of conflict management—situations that require supervisors to stimulate conflict? The notion of stimulating conflict is often difficult to accept. For almost all of us, the term conflict has a negative connotation, and the idea of purposely creating conflict seems to be counter to good supervisory practices. Few of us personally enjoy being in conflict situations. Yet there are situations where an increase in conflict is constructive. Figure 12-5 provides a set of questions that can help you to determine whether a situation might justify conflict stimulation. An affirmative answer to one or more of the questions suggests that an increase in conflict might help your unit's performance.

We know a lot more about resolving conflict than about stimulating it. However, the following are some suggestions you might want to consider if you find your department is in need of an increased level of conflict.

USE COMMUNICATION

Politicians are well known for using communication to stimulate conflict. Senior officials float trial balloons by "planting" possible decisions with the media through the infamous "reliable source" route. For example, a policy draft is "leaked" to determine public support. However, if the media or the public do not support the intent of the policy, some high-level official will invariably come forward and make a formal statement such as, "At no time was this policy under consideration."

FIGURE 12-5

Is conflict stimulation needed? An affirmative answer to any or all of these questions suggests that it may be. (*Source:* Adapted from Stephen P. Robbins, "'Conflict Management' and 'Conflict Resolution' Are Not Synonymous Terms," *California Management Review*, Winter 1978, p. 71.)

1. Are you surrounded by "yes people"?

2. Are subordinates afraid to admit ignorance and uncertainties to you?

3. Do you and department members concentrate so hard on reaching a compromise that you lose sight of key values, long-term objectives, or the organization's welfare?

4. Do you believe that it is in your best interest to maintain the impression of peace and cooperation in your unit, regardless of the price?

5. Is there an excessive concern in your department not to hurt the feelings of others?

6. Do people in your department believe that popularity is more important for obtaining rewards than competence and high performance?

7. Is your department unduly enamoured of obtaining consensus for all decisions?

8. Do employees show unusually high resistance to change?

9. Is there a lack of new ideas?

10. Is there an unusually low level of employee turnover?

You can use rumours and ambiguous messages to stimulate conflict in your department. Information that some employees might be transferred, that serious budget cuts are coming, or that a layoff is possible can reduce apathy, stimulate new ideas, and force re-evaluation—all positive outcomes as a result of increased conflict.

BRING IN OUTSIDERS

A widely used method for shaking up a stagnant department is to bring in —either by hiring from outside or by internal transfer—individuals whose backgrounds, values, attitudes, or personalities differ from those of present members. One of the major benefits of the diversity movement (encouraging the hiring and promotion of people who are different) is that it can stimulate constructive conflict and improve an organization's performance.

RESTRUCTURE THE DEPARTMENT

We know that structural variables are a source of conflict. It is therefore only logical that supervisors look to structure as a conflict stimulation device. Centralizing decisions, realigning work groups, and increasing formalization are examples of structural devices that disrupt the status quo and act to increase conflict levels.

APPOINT A DEVIL'S ADVOCATE

A devil's advocate is a person who intentionally presents arguments that run counter to those proposed by the majority or against current practices. He or she plays the role of the critic, even to the point of arguing against positions with which he or she actually agrees.

A devil's advocate acts as a check against groupthink and practices that have no better justification than "that's the way we've always done it around here." When thoughtfully listened to, the advocate can improve the quality of group decision making. On the other hand, others in the group often view advocates as time-wasters; appointment of an advocate is almost certain to delay any decision process.

> Devil's advocate
> A person who purposely presents arguments that run counter to those proposed by the majority or against current practices.

A WORD OF CAUTION

Even though there are situations in which departmental performance can be enhanced through conflict stimulation, it may not be in your best career interests to use stimulation techniques.

If your organizational culture or your immediate superior view any kind of conflict in your department as a negative reflection on your supervisory performance, think twice before stimulating conflict or even allowing low levels of conflict to exist. Where upper management believes that all conflicts are bad, it's not uncommon for lower-level managers and supervisors to be evaluated on how peaceful and harmonious conditions are in their department. While a conflict-free climate tends to create stagnant and apathetic organizations, and eventually lower performance, it is important for your survival to adopt a conflict-management style that's compatible with your organization. In some cases, that might mean using only resolution techniques.

1. Which one of the following situations best suggests the need for a manager to stimulate conflict?
   a. when a supervisor is surrounded by "yes people"
   b. when employees in a department lack specific expertise
   c. when the work unit is peaceful and cooperative
   d. when creativity and innovation are present
2. Describe why all conflict cannot be completely eliminated in organizations.
3. The ultimate win-win conflict resolution technique is accommodation, which seeks to satisfy each party's interests. True or False?
4. A person who purposely presents arguments that run counter to those proposed by the majority or against current practices is called a(n) _____ .
   a. conflict stimulator
   b. devil's advocate
   c. external consultant
   d. all of the above

   .

UNDERSTANDING ORGANIZATIONAL POLITICS

"If your organization's senior management views all conflicts as bad, don't use conflict stimulation techniques, even if they improve your department's performance." This summary of the previous paragraph acknowledges the political nature of organizations. You're not always rewarded for doing the right things. In the real world of organizations, the good guys don't always win. Demonstrating openness, trust, objectivity, support, and similar humane qualities in relationships with others doesn't always lead to improved supervisory performance. There will be times when, to get things done or to protect your interests against the manoeuvering of others, you'll have to engage in politicking. Effective supervisors understand the political nature of organizations and adjust their actions accordingly.

WHAT IS POLITICS?

Politics relates to who gets what, when, and how. **Politicking** is the actions you can take to influence, or attempt to influence, the distribution of advantages and disadvantages within your organization. Some examples of political behaviour include creating friendly relationships with others in key organizational positions, withholding key information from decision makers, whistle-blowing, spreading rumours, leaking confidential information about organizational activities to the media, exchanging favours with others in the organization for mutual benefit, and lobbying on behalf of or against a particular individual or decision alternative.

One of the most interesting insights about politics is that what constitutes a political action is almost entirely a judgement call. Like beauty, politics is in the eye of the beholder (see Figure 12-6). A behaviour that one person labels "organizational politics" is very likely to be characterized as an instance of "effective management" by another. This doesn't mean that effective management is necessarily political, though in some cases it might be. Rather, a person's reference point determines what he or she classifies as organizational politics. Take a look at the contrasting labels in Figure 12-6 that are used to describe the same activities.

Politicking
The actions you can take to influence, or attempt to influence, the distribution of advantages and disadvantages within your organization.

POLITICAL LABEL		EFFECTIVE MANAGEMENT LABEL
1. Blaming others	or	Fixing responsibility
2. Kissing up	or	Developing working relationships
3. Apple-polishing	or	Demonstrating loyalty
4. Passing the buck	or	Delegating authority
5. Covering your rear	or	Documenting decisions
6. Creating conflict	or	Encouraging change and innovation
7. Forming coalitions	or	Facilitating teamwork
8. Whistleblowing	or	Improving efficiency
9. Nitpicking	or	Meticulous attention to detail
10. Scheming	or	Planning ahead

FIGURE 12-6

Is it politics or effective management? You make the call!

WHY IS THERE POLITICS IN ORGANIZATIONS?

Can you conceive of an organization that is free of politics? It's possible but most unlikely.

Organizations are made up of individuals and groups with different values, goals, and interests. This sets up the potential for conflict over resources. Departmental budgets, space allocations, project responsibilities, and salary adjustments are just a few examples of the resources about whose allocation organizational members will disagree.

Resources in organizations are limited, which often turns potential conflict into real conflict. If resources were abundant, then all the various interests within the organization could satisfy their goals. But, because they're limited, not everyone's interests can be provided for. Further, gains by one individual or group are often perceived, accurately or not, as being at the expense of others within the organization. These forces create competition among members for the organization's limited resources.

Maybe the most important factor leading to politics within organizations is the realization that most of the "facts" that are used to allocate the limited resources are open to interpretation. What, for instance, is "good" performance? What's a "good" job? What's an "adequate" improvement? When there is an obvious difference in skill and experience levels between employees, a promotion decision is straightforward. But what if you have to choose between employees with highly similar skill and experience? Then other factors—less objective ones—come into play: attitude, potential, ability to handle stress, and so on. Most managerial decisions in organizations involve tough decisions like these. It is in this large and ambiguous middle ground of organizational life—where the facts *don't* speak for themselves—that politics takes place.

Finally, because most decisions have to be made in a climate of ambiguity—where facts are rarely fully objective, and thus are open to interpretation—people within the organization will use whatever influence they can to taint the facts to support their goals and interests. That, of course, creates motivation for the activities we call politicking.

THE ETHICS OF "PLAYING POLITICS"

Not all political actions are necessarily unethical. To help guide you in differentiating ethical from unethical politicking, there are some questions you should consider (see Figure 12-7, which illustrates a decision tree to guide ethical actions). The three questions are illustrated by the following examples.

The first question you need to answer addresses self-interest versus organizational goals. Ethical actions are consistent with the organization's goals. Spreading untrue rumours about the safety of a new product introduced by your company, in order to make that product's design

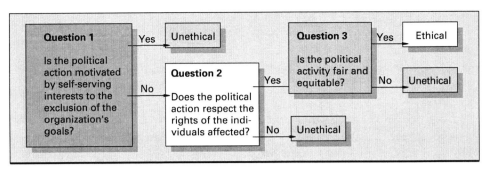

FIGURE 12-7

Is a political action
ethical?

group look bad, is unethical. However, there may be nothing unethical if you, as a department head, exchange favours with your division's purchasing manager, in order to get a critical contract processed quickly.

The second question is concerned with the rights of other parties. If you went down to the mail room during your lunch hour and read through the mail directed to the purchasing manager with the intent of "getting something on him" so he'd expedite your contract, you'd be acting unethically. You would have violated the purchasing manager's right to privacy.

The final question you need to address relates to whether the political activity conforms to standards of equity and justice. If you inflate the performance evaluation of a favoured employee and deflate the evaluation of a disfavoured employee, and then use these evaluations to justify giving the former a big raise and nothing to the latter, you have treated the disfavoured employee unfairly.

ASSESSING THE POLITICAL LANDSCAPE

Before you consider your political options in any situation, you need to evaluate that situation. The key situational factors are your organization's culture, the power of others, and your own power.

YOUR ORGANIZATION'S CULTURE

The place to begin is an assessment of your organization's culture, to determine which behaviours are desirable and which aren't.

Every organization has a system of shared meaning called its **culture**. This culture is a set of unwritten norms that members of the organization accept and understand, and that guide their actions. For example, some organizations' cultures encourage risk taking, accept conflicts and disagreements, allow employees a great deal of autonomy, and reward members according to performance criteria. But there are cultures that differ by 180 degrees: they punish risk taking, seek harmony and cooperation at any price, minimize opportunities for employees to show initiative, and allocate rewards to people according to such criteria as seniority, effort, or loyalty.

Culture
A system of shared
meaning.

The point is that every organization's culture is somewhat different, and if a political strategy is to succeed, it must be compatible with the culture.

Diane McArthur of ServiceOntario finds her networking strengths particularly important in helping her subordinates now that their project has moved from the Ministry of Transportation (MTO) to the auspices of the Ministry of Consumer and Corporate Commercial Relations (MCCR). Whereas the MTO was filled with engineers and had a methodical, rule-based culture, the MCCR is very small, not dominated by any one profession, and has a more organic culture. In the MCCR, actions succeed on the basis of relationships as much as rules or structures. This shift was a challenge for Diane's staff because, although very connected with each other, they did not know people in the new ministry. They needed multiple points of contact to get their jobs done and it was not obvious what they were or how to find out. Diane's skill in getting to know people has turned out to be important in the MCCR. She picks up information and gets to know people. Consequently, she can link her project people with the appropriate people in the ministry.

THE POWER OF OTHERS

People are either powerful or they're not, right? Wrong! On some issues, a person may be very powerful. Yet that same person may be relatively powerless on other issues. What you need to do, therefore, is determine which individuals or groups will be powerful in a given situation.

Some people will have influence as a result of their formal position in the organization. So that is probably the best place to begin your power assessment. What decision or issue do you want to influence? Who has formal authority to affect that issue? The answer to that question is only the beginning. After determining who has formal authority, consider others—individuals, coalitions, or departments—who may have a vested interest in the decision's outcome. Who might gain or lose as a result of one choice being selected over another? This helps to identify the power players—those motivated to engage in politicking. It also pinpoints your likely adversaries.

Now you need to specifically assess the power of each player or group of players. In addition to each one's formal authority, evaluate the resources each controls and his or her location in the organization. The control of scarce and important resources is a source of power in organizations. Control and access to key information, expert knowledge, and possession of special skills are examples of resources that may be scarce and important to the organization; hence, they become potential means of influencing organizational decisions. In addition, being in the right place in the organization can be a source of power. This explains, for example, the frequent power of secretaries. They are often in the direct flow of key information and control the access of others to their bosses.

Assess your boss's influence in any power analysis. What is his or her position on the issue under concern? For, against, or neutral? If it's for or against, how intense is your boss's stand? What is your boss's power status in the organization—strong or weak? Answers to these questions can help you assess whether the support or opposition of your boss will be relevant.

YOUR POWER

After looking at others' power, assess your own power base. What is your personal power? What power does your supervisory position in the organization provide? Where do you stand relative to others who hold power?

Your power can come from several sources. If you've got a charismatic personality, for instance, you can exert power because others will want to know your position on issues, your arguments will often be persuasive, and your position is likely to carry considerable weight in others' decisions. Another frequent source of power for supervisors is access to important information that others in the organization need.

Building a Supervisory Skill

BECOMING POLITICALLY SMART

ABOUT THE SKILL

Although there are few clear-cut ways to avoid getting involved in office politics, here are some suggestions that we offer to help you become more politically smart. These recommendations, however, are not designed to teach you how to take advantage of someone else or of a given situation. Rather, they are intended to help you develop a personal profile, which can assist you if you find yourself in a political situation.

STEPS IN PRACTISING THE SKILL

1. **Frame arguments in terms of organizational goals.** Effective politicking requires covering up self-interest. No matter that your objective is self-serving; all the arguments you marshal in support of it must be framed in terms of the benefits that will accrue to the organization. People whose actions appear to blatantly further their own interests at the expense of the organization's are almost universally denounced, are likely to lose influence, and often suffer the ultimate penalty of being expelled from the organization.

2. **Portray the proper image.** What others think about you is important to your political success. You need to understand the organization's culture and act accordingly. Accept and demonstrate the values, norms, and behaviours that the organization wants. Doing so shows that you know what is important for organizational survival. Portraying the proper image also increases the likelihood that when you do raise an issue, others may give it more legitimacy. An "outcast" who's always complaining rarely gets an audience—even if he or she is right.

3. **Gain control of organizational resources.** The control of organizational resources that are scarce and important is a source of power. Knowledge and expertise are particularly effective resources to control. They make you more valuable to the organization, and therefore more likely to gain security, advancement, and a receptive audience for your ideas.

4. **Make yourself appear indispensable.** Since we're dealing with appearances rather than objective facts, you can enhance your power by appearing to be indispensable. That is, you don't have to *really* be indispensable, as long as key people in the organization believe that you are. If the prime decision makers believe there is no ready substitute for what you are giving the organization, they are likely to go to great lengths to ensure that your desires are satisfied. How do you make yourself appear indispensable? The most effective means is to develop expertise (through experience, contacts, secret techniques, and natural talents) that is perceived as critical to the organization's operations and that key decision makers believe no one else possesses to the extent that you do.

5. **Be visible.** Because the evaluation of supervisory effectiveness has a substantial subjective component, it is important that your boss and those in power in the organization be made aware of your contribution. If you are fortunate enough to have responsibilities that bring your accomplishments to the attention of others, it may not be necessary to take direct measures to increase your visibility. But your department may handle activities that are low in visibility, or your specific contribution may be indistinguishable because you're part of a team endeavour. In such cases—without creating the image of a braggart—you'll want to call attention to yourself by giving progress reports to your boss and others, being seen at social functions, being active in your professional associations, developing powerful allies who speak positively about your accomplishments, and similar tactics. Of course, the skilled politician actively and successfully lobbies to get those projects that will increase his or her visibility.

6. **Find a mentor.** Nothing helps you avoid land mines better than someone who knows where the land mines are. Getting them to navigate your path makes things so much safer. In organizations, this navigator is called a mentor. A mentor is someone who is usually a more experienced and more senior member of the organization. The mentor is usually already part of the "power" group, and his or her role is to be your support system. Mentors are also people who can vouch for you in the organization. They often are able to get you exposure to the power-brokers in the organization, and provide you advice on how to effectively manoeuvre through the system. From a political point of view, a mentor can act as a sounding-board for you, providing vital suggestions and feedback on how to survive and succeed.

7. **Develop powerful allies.** It helps to have powerful people in your camp. In addition to a mentor, you can cultivate contacts with potentially influential people above you and among other supervisors. They can provide you with important information that may not be available through normal channels. Additionally, there will be times when decisions will be made by those with the greatest support. Sometimes—though not always—there is strength in numbers. Having powerful allies can provide you with a coalition of support if and when you need it.

8. **Avoid tarnished individuals.** In almost every organization, there are fringe members whose status is questionable. Their performance and/or loyalty is under close scrutiny. Such individuals, while they are under the microscope, are "tainted." Carefully keep your distance from them. We all tend to judge others by the company they keep. Given the reality that effectiveness has a large subjective component, your own effectiveness might be called into question if you are perceived as being too closely associated with tainted people.

9. **Support your boss.** Your immediate future is in the hands of your current boss. Since he or she evaluates your performance, you will typically want to do whatever is necessary to have your boss on your side. You should make every effort to help your boss succeed and look good. Provide support if he or she is under siege and spend the time to find out what criteria will be used to assess your effectiveness. Don't undermine your boss. Don't speak negatively of him or her to others. If the individual is competent, visible, and in possession of a power base, she or he is likely to be on the way up in the organization. By being perceived as supportive, you increase the likelihood that you will be pulled along.

Gaining political power and building a power base in an organization is often fostered with the help of a mentor. In the past, however, most of those who were "supported" by an experienced, senior member of the organization often shared something in common. That is, they were usually male and white. But what about women and people of colour? What opportunities lie ahead for them to find and gain this support?

Finding or getting a mentor is rarely easy. In fact, more often than not, you are approached by the other person. What can serve as the "attraction" to bring the two of you together? In the past, it was something a potential mentor saw in you—which was often something they saw in themselves years ago. But how can a male properly relate to a female or vice versa? How can individuals from different races or national origins identify with each other when there's no foundation of commonality between them? Unquestionably, these can be major issues—many of which we've highlighted in previous chapters. Organizations are attempting to bridge this gap. Many recognize that leaving it up to nature just won't work so they establish a formal program that encourages senior members to take junior members under their wing. Even when such programs exist, other problems still may arise. For example, is the male supervisor mentoring a younger female employee exhibiting appropriate mentoring behaviour, or is she getting special treatment because she's a woman? If the two of them develop a close, personal work relationship is there a risk of them crossing the line into sexual harassment?

Despite the potential difficulties diversity offers for mentoring, the fact remains that each of us needs this support. Therefore, if someone doesn't approach you, you must make every effort to find a mentor yourself. In either case, being mentored requires work on your part. That effort will only be magnified when your mentor is someone who has personal attributes different from yours.

What do you think about this diversity issue?

NEGOTIATION

As a supervisor, your success in resolving conflict and playing politics will be influenced by your negotiating skills. We know that lawyers and car salespeople spend a lot of time negotiating, but so do supervisors. They have to negotiate salaries for incoming employees, bargain over budgets, work out differences with associates, and resolve conflicts with subordinates. This section will help you to improve your negotiating skills.

ASSESSING YOURSELF: DO YOU UNDERSTAND WHAT IT TAKES TO BE AN EFFECTIVE NEGOTIATOR?

For each of the following statements, indicate your degree of agreement or disagreement by circling one of the five responses.

SA = Strongly agree
A = Agree
U = Undecided
D = Disagree
SD = Strongly disagree

1. I believe everything is negotiable.	SA	A	U	D	SD
2. In every negotiation, someone wins and someone loses.	SA	A	U	D	SD
3. I try to get as much information as possible about the other party prior to negotiation.	SA	A	U	D	SD
4. The other party's initial offer shapes my negotiating strategy.	SA	A	U	D	SD
5. I try to open negotiations with a positive action such as offering a small concession.	SA	A	U	D	SD
6. I build an image of success by focusing on winning as much as possible in every bargaining situation.	SA	A	U	D	SD

SCORING DIRECTIONS AND KEY

For questions 1, 3, and 5, give yourself five points for SA, four points for A, three points for U, two points for D, and one point for SD. For questions 2, 4, and 5, reverse the scoring; that is, give yourself one point for SA, two points for A, and so forth.

A score of 25 or above suggests you have a basic understanding of how to be an effective negotiator. Scores of 19 to 24 indicate you have room for improvement. Those who scored 18 or less should find the following discussion and exercise very valuable in improving their overall supervisory effectiveness.

SKILL BASICS

Negotiation
A process in which two or more parties exchange goods or services and attempt to agree upon the exchange rate for them.

What is **negotiation**? It's a process in which two or more parties exchange goods or services and attempt to agree upon the exchange rate for them. For our purposes, we'll also use the term interchangeably with bargaining.

BARGAINING STRATEGIES

There are two general approaches to negotiation: *distributive bargaining* and *integrative bargaining*.

Distributive bargaining
Zero-sum negotiations where any gain by one is at the expense of the other.

You see a used car advertised for sale in the newspaper. It appears to be just what you're looking for. You go out to see the car. It's great and you want it. The owner tells you the asking price. You don't want to pay that much. The two of you then negotiate over the price. The negotiating process you are engaging in is called **distributive bargaining**. Its most distinctive feature is that it operates under zero-sum conditions. That is, any gain I make is at your expense, and vice versa. Every dollar you can get the seller to cut from the car's price is a dollar you save. Conversely, every dollar more he or she can get from you comes at your expense. Thus the essence of distributive bargaining is negotiating over who gets what share of a fixed pie.

Probably the most widely cited example of distributive bargaining is in labour-management negotiations over wages and benefits (see Chapter 15). Typically, labour's representatives come to the bargaining table determined to get as much as they can from management. Because every cent more that labour negotiates increases management's costs, each party bargains aggressively and often treats the other as an opponent who must be defeated.

Figure 12-8 depicts the distributive bargaining strategy. Parties A and B represent the two negotiators. Each has a target point that defines what he or she would like to achieve. Each also has a resistance point, which marks the lowest outcome that is acceptable—the point below which he or she would break off negotiations rather than accept a less favourable settlement. The area between their resistance points is the settlement range. As long as there is some overlap in their aspiration ranges, there exists a settlement area where each one's aspirations can be met.

When engaged in distributive bargaining, your tactics should focus on trying to get your opponent to agree to your specific target point or to get as close to it as possible. Examples of such tactics are persuading your opponent of the impossibility of getting to his or her target point and the advisability of accepting a settlement near yours; arguing that your target is fair, while your opponent's isn't; and attempting to get your opponent to feel emotionally generous toward you and thus to accept an outcome close to your target point.

Now let's look at **integrative bargaining**. Assume a sales representative for a women's sportswear manufacturer has just closed a $15 000 order from a small clothing retailer. The sales rep calls in the order to her firm's credit department. She is told that the firm can't approve credit to this customer because of a past slow-pay record. The next day, the sales rep and the firm's credit supervisor meet to discuss the problem. The sales rep doesn't want to lose the business. Neither does the credit super-

Integrative bargaining
Bargaining under the assumption that there is at least one settlement option that can create a win-win solution.

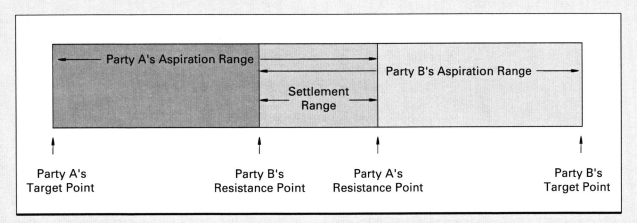

FIGURE 12-8
Staking out the bargaining zone

visor, but he also doesn't want to get stuck with an uncollectable debt. The two openly review their options. After considerable discussion, they agree on a solution that meets both their needs: the credit supervisor will approve the sale, but the clothing store's owner will provide a bank guarantee that will assure payment if the bill isn't paid within 60 days.

The sales-credit negotiation is an example of **integrative bargaining**. In contrast to distributive bargaining, integrative problem solving operates under the assumption that there is at least one settlement that can create a win-win solution.

In general, integrative bargaining is preferable to distributive bargaining. Why? Because the former builds long-term relationships and facilitates working together in the future. It bonds negotiators and allows each to leave the bargaining table feeling that he or she has achieved a victory. Distributive bargaining, on the other hand, leaves one party a loser. It tends to build animosities and deepen divisions between people who have to work together on an ongoing basis.

Why, then, don't we see more integrative bargaining in organizations? The answer lies in the conditions necessary for this type of negotiation to succeed. These conditions include openness with information and frankness between parties; sensitivity on the part of each party to the other's needs; the ability to trust one another; and a willingness by both parties to maintain flexibility. Because many organizational cultures and interpersonal relationships are not characterized by openness, trust, and flexibility, it isn't surprising that negotiations often take on a win-at-any-cost dynamic.

BECOMING AN EFFECTIVE NEGOTIATOR

The essence of effective negotiation can be summarized in the following six guidelines.

1. **Consider the other party's situation.** Acquire as much information as you can about your opponent's interests and goals. What is his or her strategy? This information will help you understand your opponent's behaviour, predict his or her responses to your offers, and frame solutions in terms of his or her interests. Additionally, when you can anticipate your opponent's position, you are better equipped to counter his or her arguments with the facts and figures that support your position.

2. **Have a concrete strategy.** Treat negotiation like a chess match. Expert chess players have a strategy. They know ahead of time how they will respond to any given situation. How strong is your situation

and how important is the issue? Are you willing to split differences to achieve an early solution? If the issue is very important to you, is your position strong enough to let you play hardball and show little or no willingness to compromise? These are questions you should address before you begin bargaining.

3. **Begin with a positive overture.** Studies on negotiation show that concessions tend to be reciprocated and lead to agreements. As a result, begin bargaining with a positive overture—perhaps a small concession—and then reciprocate your opponent's concessions.

4. **Address problems, not personalities.** Concentrate on the negotiation issues, not on the personal characteristics of your opponent. When negotiations get tough, avoid the tendency to attack your opponent. It's your opponent's ideas or position that you disagree with, not him or her personally. Separate the people from the problem, and don't personalize differences.

5. **Pay little attention to initial offers.** Treat an initial offer as merely a point of departure. Everyone has to have an initial position. These initial offers tend to be extreme and idealistic. Treat them as such.

6. **Emphasize win-win solutions.** Bargainers often assume that their gain must come at the expense of the other party. As noted with integrative bargaining, that needn't be the case. There are often win-win solutions. But assuming a zero-sum game means missed opportunities for trade-offs that could benefit both sides. So if conditions are supportive, look for an integrative solution. Frame options in terms of your opponent's interests and look for solutions that can allow your opponent, as well as yourself, to declare a victory.

APPLYING YOUR SKILLS

Break into groups of three. You will each take on one of the roles described below and attempt to negotiate a solution as to where you will reinvest your company's money. You are three partners in a training firm that specializes in providing experiential events for corporate training, customized "gaming," outdoor challenges for team building—such as high-ropes challenges and Outward Bound-like events. Your four-year-old business has "taken off" recently. Your staff has grown to 10 in the last year (all trainers on contract, however; none are partners like you three). The company has opened offices in Burlington, Vancouver, and Edmonton. Previously the three of you basically worked out of your homes.

Canadian companies similar to those described in the exercise can be researched at their home pages
www.deltasynergy.com
www.eaglesflight.com

You are meeting with your two partners to discuss how you should use the recent profit from the company. You have all agreed to reinvest the money in the growing company but you have not discussed how best to do so.

Person 1 Your feelings are that you need to lure in a really top trainer/marketer to be a partner in the firm. The three of you are spread too thin now that you are offering your services across Canada and even taking on some international contracts. You need another major player who's good at getting and keeping new clients (so can handle the sales end of the business) and can also be an effective facilitator in many of your training activities. This "double duty" is exactly what the three of you have been doing so successfully for four years. But, as the old adage goes: Be careful of what you wish, as your wish may come true. And your business's success has meant no time for any of you other than work. It's now time to share the load.

If you did take on a new partner, his or her deal would be the same as for the rest of you—he or she would be paid based on the work he or she brings in as well as a straight salary for facilitation work. But you'll need money to recruit the right person, to provide training, and to set up the requisite office. Also, you think you need to offer the right person a decent base salary to start with for some security. The candidates you're thinking of will need to be lured away from some pretty good money at their present employer.

Your company's success depends on the people within it. As the company grows, you think it critical to grow the right "talent" along with it.

Person 2 Your feelings are that you need to hire some support staff. You are a company of trainers who are constantly on the move and you have no "secretaries" or support people to staff the offices. You make do with voicemail at the offices, and the partners are responsible for picking up and distributing messages. This has caused some problems because the partners are often too busy to regularly collect calls and respond to them. Delays have caused some problems with customers. The offices really exist simply for a mailing address and a place to hold meetings when clients prefer to meet at your company's premises rather than their own. There is no live person at any of the offices on a continuous basis.

You think that a live presence is needed in each office to create a professional image, answer the phone, respond to questions when possible, ensure the right partner or contract trainer is informed in a timely manner, and also handle administrative details such as invoices and report production.

Person 3 You believe that the company needs to become much more technologically sophisticated. Money needs to be spent on purchasing good computer equipment and software, Internet access, e-mail for all members of the firm, and creating and supporting a website for the company. Right now your company is not "wired" and you think it is pitiful that the partners are still producing their materials on their own personal PCs, which are all outdated. In fact, the partners don't even use the same software and are limited in their skills. All of them could benefit from some basic training on common computer software.

The clients you deal with tend to be quite progressive in their communication systems and they are typically surprised that you don't have e-mail or a website. You think it's beginning to look bad for a company that is supposed to be so "leading edge" in the training field.

5. Which one of the following is not an example of political behaviour that exists in an organization?
   a. leaking confidential information about organizational activities to the media
   b. using informal communications channels to expedite important messages
   c. whistleblowing
   d. withholding key information from decision makers
6. What situational factors lead to office politics?
7. The most distinctive feature of distributive bargaining is that it operates under zero-sum conditions. True or false?
8. The process in which two or more parties who have different preferences must make a joint decision to come to an agreement is called _____.
   a. delegation
   b. empowerment
   c. conflict-handling
   d. none of the above

UNDERSTANDING THE BASICS

SUMMARY

This summary is organized by the Learning Objectives.

1. Conflict is a process in which one party consciously interferes in the goal-achievement efforts of another party.
2. Conflicts generally come from one of three sources: communication differences, structural differences, or personal differences.
3. The five basic techniques for resolving conflict are avoidance, accommodation, force, compromise, and collaboration.
4. A supervisor could stimulate conflict by communicating ambiguous messages, bringing in outsiders with different backgrounds or personalities, restructuring the department, or appointing a devil's advocate.
5. Politicking is the actions you can take to influence, or attempt to influence, the distribution of advantages and disadvantages within your department.
6. Politics exist in organizations because individuals have different values, goals, and interests; because organizational resources are limited; because the criteria for allocating the limited resources are ambiguous; and because individuals seek influence so they can shape the criteria to support their goals and interests.
7. The situational factors that determine political options are 1. your organization's culture, 2. the power of others, and 3. your own power.
8. To develop and improve your political skills, you should frame arguments in terms of organizational goals; develop the right image; gain control of organizational resources; make yourself appear indispensable; be visible; get a mentor; develop powerful allies; avoid "tainted" members; and support your boss.
9. Distributive bargaining creates a win-lose situation because the object of negotiation is treated as fixed in amount. Integrative bargaining treats available resources as variable, and hence creates the potential for win-win solutions.

UNDERSTANDING THE BASICS

KEY TERMS AND CONCEPTS

Accommodation
Avoidance
Collaboration
Compromise
Conflict
Conflict management
Culture

Devil's advocate
Distributive bargaining
Forcing
Integrative bargaining
Negotiation
Politicking

REVIEWING YOUR KNOWLEDGE

1. How can conflict benefit an organization?
2. How can an organization's structure create conflict?
3. What is conflict management?
4. When should you avoid conflict? When should you seek compromise?
5. What is a devil's advocate? How does an advocate affect conflict in a department?
6. Can an organization be free of politics? Explain.
7. Is it unethical to "play politics"?
8. How do you assess another person's power in an organization?
9. Why does effective politicking require covering up self-interest?
10. How can increased visibility enhance a person's power?

ANSWERS TO THE POP QUIZZES

1. **a. when a supervisor is surrounded by "yes people."** This is one of the situations listed in Figure 12-6, indicating a need to stimulate conflict. Response b) indicates a need for training. Responses c) and d) are preferred unit characteristics.

2. All conflict cannot be completely eliminated in organizations because it is a natural phenomenon of organizational life. That's because 1. organizational members have different goals; 2. there are scarce resources, like budget allocations, which various people want and are willing to fight over; and 3. people in organizations don't all see things alike as a result of their diverse backgrounds, education, experiences, and interests.

3. **False.** The ultimate win-win conflict resolution technique, which seeks to satisfy each party's interests, is **collaboration**.

4. **b. devil's advocate.** This is the definition of the actions of a devil's advocate.

5. **b. using informal communications channels to expedite important messages.** This choice was not identified as an example of political behaviour. The other responses were examples.

6. Situational factors leading to office politics include individuals with different backgrounds and values, conflict over limited resources, and the realization that most of the "facts" that are used to allocate the limited resources are open to interpretation.

7. **True.** The most distinctive feature of distributive bargaining is that it operates under zero-sum conditions. That is, any gain one makes is at the expense of the other person, and vice versa.

8. **d. none of the above.** The process in which two or more parties who have different preferences must make a joint decision to come to an agreement is called **negotiation**.

CASE 12.A

Was the Knife a Joke?*

Kendall is a business student at a community college. She missed classes this morning because she was at the local police station reporting an incident. Several days ago, a coworker at her part-time job in the shipping department of a large manufacturing company threatened her with a knife. It took Kendall a while to get up the nerve to report the incident to the police, but her supervisor and her family kept pushing her to do it. Kendall did not want to make a fuss. After all, the guy got fired so she wouldn't see him anymore. And the company is making sure she never leaves the building alone, always being accompanied to her car. Now that she has reported it, though, she feels relieved.

When Kendall thinks of it, she's still not sure whether he was joking. He had always teased her, but the teasing had gradually become worse. He started making cracks about stalking her and how he knew the car she drove—he had been watching her. When he pulled out the knife and pushed it against her stomach, he said, "Hey, you're not scared, are you?" Kendall had tried to ignore him up to that point but here she drew the line. She immediately reported the incident to her supervisor who, recognizing the seriousness of the situation, took her to the human resources office. An investigation into the incident confirmed Kendall's report and her "attacker" was fired

RESPONDING TO THIS CASE

1. Why did the supervisor take Kendall to the HR office to have the HR staff deal with this? What if you were the supervisor in this situation and the company was smaller and had no HR department— what would you do then?

2. The inappropriate "teasing" continued for a long time before the knife incident. Comment on Kendall choosing avoidance as her way of dealing with it. Was this right? What other ways could she have dealt with it? What could a supervisor have done to prevent this kind of behaviour in the first place, or to encourage employees not to "ignore" it until it got this bad?

3. Consider specific examples of unacceptable behaviour you have observed in employees in your own experiences. How did the supervisor react? What was the result of the supervisor's actions? How could the circumstances have been handled better? Share these examples with others and discuss.

*This is based on a true story, with the name and some details changed.

CASE 12.B

Joe and Catalino Deal with Angry Clients

Supervisors of front-line service employees are often drawn into dealing with customer/employee interactions that have gone wrong. The supervisor is in the unenviable position of trying to win over an angry customer plus avoid humiliating the employee, who likely did his or her best to handle the situation in the first place. Catalino Misenas, sales manager at Russell Food Equipment in Vancouver, and Joe Puiia, supervisor at the HRDC office in Summerside, PEI, describe their experiences.

"When I deal with an angry client, I find that often all they really need is attention and having someone listen to them. I get them away from the open office into a quiet place. I might say, 'Gee, I don't blame you for being upset. Please tell me what happened.' Then I do some creative fact-finding and allow them to vent. There are a lot of grey areas in policies and regulations, like who is eligible to join a skills development program. So I explain the policies and programs, and I spend a lot of time in definitions, for example, defining strict eligibility," says Joe Puiia.

Catalino's approach is similar. "I thrive on the goal of making an upset customer my best customer. I really listen to what the customer is saying. I repeat what he says and probe what the concern is. Once I've listened and grasped it, I can deal with it. I know I have to deal with a problem right away. For example, I learned that a customer was upset about a whipped-cream dispenser not being delivered—there had been a misunderstanding between the customer and the sales rep. I called her myself and apologized for the error, saying we would rectify the situation immediately. She was happy."

RESPONDING TO THIS CASE

1. What principles and techniques of conflict management are evident in their handling of these customer conflicts?

2. How can a supervisor both satisfy the customer yet treat the employee who dealt with the customer as a competent professional? Consider the supervisors you have seen in this type of situation—how successful were they, and what was the impact?

3. Suppose a supervisor pacifies a customer by incorrectly blaming the employee, saying the employee was out of line and had no right to say what he or she did. Is this unethical? Under what grounds?

4. How can the skills Catalino and Joe illustrate above in dealing with customers also be potentially useful to them in dealing with the internal politics of their organizations?

13 MANAGING CHANGE AND STRESS

LEARNING OBJECTIVES

After reading this chapter, you should be able to:

1. Contrast the old and contemporary views of change.
2. Identify the forces for change in today's organizations.
3. Explain why people resist change.
4. Identify ways supervisors can reduce resistance to change.
5. Define stress.
6. Explain what brings about employee stress.
7. Contrast Type A and Type B behaviour.

CHAPTER OUTLINE

PERFORMING EFFECTIVELY

FORCES FOR CHANGE
New Technologies
Environmental Dynamics
Internal Forces
Dealing with a Difficult Issue
Assessing Yourself: How Ready Are You for Coping with Work-Related Change?
Can You Serve as a Change Agent?

CHANGING PERSPECTIVES ON CHANGE
The Old View of Change
The Contemporary View of Change

RESISTANCE TO CHANGE
Habit
Threat to Job or Income
Fear of the Unknown
Selective Perception
Threat to Expertise
Threat to Established Power Relationships
Threat to Interpersonal Relationships
Pop Quiz

REDUCING RESISTANCE TO CHANGE
Build Trust
Open Channels of Communication
Involve Employees
Provide Incentives
Something to Think About

WORK STRESS
What Is Stress?
Sources of Work Stress
Assessing Yourself
The Symptoms of Stress

Companies Take Action on Stress

FROM CONCEPTS TO SKILLS: STRESS REDUCTION
Assessing Yourself: How Well Can You Identify Stressful Events?
Skill Basics
Applying Your Skills
Pop Quiz

UNDERSTANDING THE BASICS
Summary
Key Terms and Concepts
Reviewing Your Knowledge
Answers to the Pop Quizzes

PERFORMING YOUR JOB
Case 13.A: The Changes Never Stop
Case 13.B: "New" is Exciting but Stressful

Daniel Quondam is the operations manager for Com Dev Wireless' facility in Moncton where components for cellular phones are made. Handling change is a fact of life for Daniel, whether the change is planned or unplanned.

In the realm of planned change, the plant recently altered its manufacturing philosophy, making it into a "visual" factory. Previously, you could not see from one end of the shop to the other and there was a lack of organization, plus a low level of control on work in progress. Over one weekend, the entire floor was transformed by being opened up. Now it is possible to see where a product is and its status—a light goes on to alert staff when a product is down.

Part of Daniel's job was to help the staff adapt to the change. Employees now have a standardized and paperless workspace with no clutter, where they can easily find their tools. However, they resented no longer being able to have a family photo by them. Daniel explained to them why the changes were made and how they would benefit from working smarter, not harder. Working within the new system, they've now experienced its success and benefits.

Of more immediate impact on Daniel and his staff are the unplanned changes with which they must regularly cope. There are two main sources—sudden increases in orders and unpredicted downtime. Cellular phones are in hot demand right now. Daniel has to develop work schedules based on customer forecasts of sales. When those forecasts suddenly "ramp up," Daniel must respond, despite it not fitting his schedule. Yet increasing production depends on having the needed labour, so Daniel has been working with two temporary-help agencies in Moncton to bring in the required labour quickly. This also puts demands on him to ensure that those people are adequately trained.

When the pressure is on to meet these heightened customer demands, it is particularly frustrating to have to deal with unexpected downtime from technical problems. Downtime can't be planned, although Com Dev uses systems to try to detect imminent problems. In the case of downtime, it is critical for Daniel to have key people around to deal with the problem and minimize the downtime.

How does Daniel cope with the stresses of managing these circumstances? "We have a great staff. We share the stress, each understanding his or her responsibility. We succeed or fail as a team."

Daniel's job, like most supervisory positions, has change built right into it. No two days are the same. As a result, managing the change effectively and dealing with the accompanying stress are critical skills for a supervisor. In this chapter, we will examine the typical sources of change, the way people react to change, and how supervisors and organizations can ease the change experience for all. Then stress will be addressed—what it is and what can be done about it.

FORCES FOR CHANGE

NEW TECHNOLOGIES

Fax machines, e-mail, and computers are technological changes that have affected many jobs. If you talk to supervisors at Canada Post, they'll tell you how automated readers and sorters have changed the jobs of those responsible for sorting the mail. Take a look at today's automobile assembly lines. Thousands of jobs on these assembly lines have been replaced with automated robots. Few jobs today have not been directly affected by technological change.

The introduction of new equipment, tools, methods, automated machinery, and computerization allows employees and supervisors to do their jobs better and faster. We can expect that technological changes will continue to modify the way work is done. Most importantly, because these technological changes tend to be focused at the operating level, supervisors will have the primary responsibility for introducing and managing these change efforts.

ENVIRONMENTAL DYNAMICS

Changes that occur outside the organization can affect supervisors. These changes include new government regulations, changing social and political trends, new tax laws, changes in labour market conditions, and new strategies taken by competitors. For example, when human rights legislation was passed, many supervisors had to fill out additional reports, modify historical hiring criteria, and participate in the redesign of physical facilities to reduce barriers for people with disabilities. Similarly, the trend toward supervisors having wider spans of control has been largely driven by global competition and the need for organizations to cut costs.

The recent implementation of equal pay for work of equal value by SaskTel was prompted by government mandate and has had an impact on many in the organization (see Dealing with a Difficult Issue).

INTERNAL FORCES

In addition to technological and environmental factors, internal forces can stimulate the need for change. These internal forces include changes in the organization's overall strategy (like Com Dev Wireless' shift in manufacturing philosophy in Moncton) reorganizations, changes in the composition of the workforce, introduction of new equipment, and the need to modify employee attitudes.

An organization's workforce is rarely static. Its composition changes in terms of age, education, gender, and ethnicity. The increasing number of women and minorities in the workforce has required many supervisors to become more sensitive to diversity and to change some of their previous practices. The introduction of new equipment represents another internal force for change. Employees may have their jobs redesigned, need to undergo training to operate the new equipment, or be required to establish new interaction patterns within their formal work group. Employee attitudes, such as increased job dissatisfaction, may lead to increased absenteeism, more voluntary resignations, and even strikes. Such events will, in turn, often lead to changes in supervisory practices.

Dealing with a Difficult Issue

LIVING WITH EQUAL PAY FOR WORK OF EQUAL VALUE

SaskTel recently implemented equal pay for work of equal value (EPWEV). This means that all positions have been examined and rated so that different jobs could be compared on the same base criteria. Then inequities in pay could be corrected. The rationale for EPWEV has been the need to address the low pay of undervalued positions traditionally occupied by women. As a result of the EPWEV process at SaskTel, supervisors are now hearing complaints from some employees who feel they have been treated unfairly by the EPWEV process, even after exhausting the appeal process.

Not all SaskTel supervisors agree with the concept of EPWEV. Some think that their own staff should have been rated higher by the process. Yet supervisors are expected to support and implement management decisions.

How should a supervisor react in this situation when an employee complains of the pay decision in his or her case? What should a supervisor do when the organization makes a major change with which he or she disagrees?

Assessing Yourself

HOW READY ARE YOU FOR COPING WITH WORK-RELATED CHANGE?

Instructions: Listed below are some statements a supervisor made about working in a large, successful corporation. If your job had these characteristics, how would you react to them? After each statement are five letters, A to E. Circle the letter that best describes how you think you would react according to the following scale:

A I would enjoy this very much; it's completely acceptable.
B This would be enjoyable and acceptable most of the time.
C I'd have no reaction to this feature one way or another,
   or it would be about equal parts enjoyable and unpleasant.
D This feature would be somewhat unpleasant for me.
E This feature would be very unpleasant for me.

1. I regularly spend 30 to 40 per cent
   of my time in meetings.   A   B   C   D   E

2. Eighteen months ago, my job did not exist,
   and I have been essentially inventing it as
   I go along.   A   B   C   D   E

3. The responsibilities I either assume or am
   assigned consistently exceed the authority
   I have for discharging them.   A   B   C   D   E

4. At any given moment in my job, I have on
   the average about a dozen phone calls to be
   returned.   A   B   C   D   E

5. There seems to be very little relationship
   in my job between the quality of my
   performance and my actual pay and
   benefits.   A   B   C   D   E

6. About two weeks a year of formal
   supervisory training is needed in my job
   just to stay current.   A   B   C   D   E

7. Because we have very effective equal employment opportunity (EEO) in my company and because it is thoroughly multinational, my job consistently brings me into close working contact at a professional level with people of many races, ethnic groups, and nationalities and of both sexes. A   B   C   D   E

8. There is no objective way to measure my effectiveness. A   B   C   D   E

9. I report to three different bosses for different aspects of my job, and each has an equal say in my performance appraisal. A   B   C   D   E

10. On average, about a third of my time is spent dealing with unexpected emergencies that force all scheduled work to be postponed. A   B   C   D   E

11. When I have to have a meeting of the people who report to me, it takes my secretary most of a day to find a time when we are all available, and even then, I have yet to have a meeting where everyone is present for the entire meeting. A   B   C   D   E

12. The college degree I earned in preparation for this type of work is now obsolete, and I probably should go back for another degree. A   B   C   D   E

13. My job requires that I absorb 100–200 pages per week of technical materials. A   B   C   D   E

14. I am out of town overnight at least one night per week. A   B   C   D   E

15. My department is so interdependent with several other departments in the company that all distinctions about which departments are responsible for which tasks are quite arbitrary. A   B   C   D   E

16. I will probably get a promotion in about a year to a job in another department that has most of these same characteristics.

    A   B   C   D   E

17. During the period of my employment here, either the entire company or the department I worked in has been reorganized every year or so.

    A   B   C   D   E

18. While there are several possible promotions I can see ahead of me, I have no real career path in an objective sense.

    A   B   C   D   E

19. While there are several possible promotions I can see ahead of me, I think I have no realistic chance of getting to the top levels of the company.

    A   B   C   D   E

20. While I have many ideas about how to make things work better, I have no direct influence on either the business policies or the personnel policies that govern my department.

    A   B   C   D   E

21. My company has recently put in an "assessment centre" where I and all other supervisors will be required to go through an extensive battery of psychological tests to assess our potential.

    A   B   C   D   E

22. My company is a defendant in an antitrust suit, and if the case comes to trial, I will probably have to testify about some decisions that were made a few years ago.

    A   B   C   D   E

23. Advanced computer and other electronic office technology is continually being introduced into my division, necessitating constant learning on my part.

    A   B   C   D   E

24. The computer terminal and screen I have in my office can be monitored in my bosses' offices without my knowledge.

    A   B   C   D   E

SCORING

Give yourself four points for each A, three points for each B, two points for each C, one point for each D, and no points for each E. Compute your total, and divide that score by 24. Round your answer to one decimal place.

WHAT THE ASSESSMENT MEANS

While the results of this assessment are not intended to be more than suggestive, the higher your score, the more comfortable you appear to be with change. The test's author suggests analyzing scores as if they were grade point averages. In this way, a 4.0 average is an "A," a 2.0 is a "C," and scores below 1.0 "flunk." Using replies from nearly 500 students and individuals new to supervisory positions, the range of scores was found to be relatively narrow: between 1.0 and 2.2. The average score was between 1.5 and 1.6—a D+/C− sort of grade!

Source: Peter B. Vail, *Managing as a Performing Art: New Ideas for a World of Chaotic Change,* Exhibit 1, pp. 8–9. © 1989 Jossey-Bass, Inc., Publishers.

Can You Serve as a Change Agent?

Changes within an organization need a catalyst. People who act as catalysts and assume the responsibility for overseeing the change process are called **change agents**.

Any supervisor can be a change agent. The change agent can also be a nonmanager—for example, an internal staff specialist or outside consultant whose expertise is in change implementation. For major systemwide changes, company officials will often hire outside consultants to provide advice and assistance. Because they are from the outside, they often can offer an objective perspective usually lacking in insiders. However, outside consultants may be at a disadvantage because they have an inadequate understanding of the organization's history, culture, operating procedures, and personnel. Outside consultants are also prone to initiate more drastic changes than insiders—which can be either a benefit or a disadvantage—because they do not have to live with the repercussions of the change after it is implemented. In contrast, supervisors who act as change agents may be more thoughtful—and possibly more cautious—because they must live with the consequences of their actions.

Change agents
People who act as catalysts and assume the responsibility for overseeing the change process.

CHANGING PERSPECTIVES ON CHANGE

Supervisors historically treated the management of change as a periodic activity with a distinct beginning and end. A problem surfaced that required a change. That change would then be introduced, and the situation would return to a state of equilibrium. This perspective on change is no longer very accurate. Today's supervisor is increasingly finding that change is a constant. It has no distinct beginning or end. Supervisors are having to learn to manage in a world of continuous change.

THE OLD VIEW OF CHANGE

The old view of change is best illustrated in the classic three-step model of the **change process**[1] (See Figure 13-1).

Change process
Unfreezing the status quo, changing to a new state, and refreezing the new change to make it permanent.

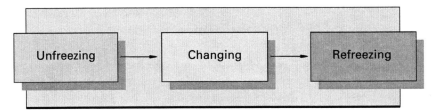

FIGURE 13-1
The three step change process

According to this model, successful change requires unfreezing the status quo, changing to a new state, and refreezing the new change to make it permanent. The status quo can be considered an equilibrium state. To move from this equilibrium, unfreezing is necessary. It can be achieved in one of three ways:

1. The driving forces that direct behaviour away from the status quo can be increased.
2. The restraining forces that hinder movement from the existing equilibrium can be decreased.
3. The two approaches can be combined.

Once unfreezing has been accomplished, the change itself can be implemented. However, the mere introduction of change does not ensure that it will take hold. The new situation therefore needs to be *refrozen* so that it can be sustained over time. Unless this last step is attended to, there is a very strong chance that the change will be short-lived and that employees will revert to the previous equilibrium state. The objective of refreezing, then, is to stabilize the new situation by balancing the driving and restraining forces.

Note how this three-step process treats change as a break in the organization's equilibrium state. The status quo has been disturbed and change is necessary to establish a new equilibrium state. This view might have been appropriate to the relatively calm environment that most organizations faced in the 1950s, 1960s, and early 1970s. But this model does not describe the world in which current supervisors must manage. However, the model *is* useful in emphasizing the importance of follow-up to ensure that a new change is absorbed appropriately.

THE CONTEMPORARY VIEW OF CHANGE

The contemporary view of change takes into consideration that environments are both uncertain and dynamic. To get a feeling for what directing change might be like when you have to continually manoeuvre in uninterrupted rapids, consider going on a ski trip and facing the following scenario: The ski slopes that are open vary in length and difficulty. Unfortunately, when you start a "run," you don't know what the ski course will be. It might be a simple course, or one that is very challenging. Furthermore, you've planned your ski vacation assuming that the slopes will be open. After all, it's January—and that is prime ski time at the resort. But the course does not always open. As if that were not bad enough, on some days the slopes are closed for no apparent reason at all. Oh yes, and one more thing—lift ticket prices can change dramatically on the hour. And there is no apparent pattern to the price fluctuations.

To succeed under these conditions, you would have to be incredibly flexible and be able to respond quickly to every changing condition. Those who were too slow or too structured would have difficulty—and clearly no fun!

A growing number of supervisors are coming to accept that their job is much like what one might face on such a ski vacation. The stability and predictability of the traditional view of change may not exist. Disruptions in the status quo are not occasional and temporary, and followed by a return to "calm waters." Many of today's supervisors never get out of the rapids. They face constant change. These supervisors are being forced to play a game they've never played before, which is governed by rules that are created as the game progresses.[2]

RESISTANCE TO CHANGE

One of the most well-documented findings in the study of people at work is that individuals resist change. As one person once put it, "Most people hate any change that doesn't jingle in their pockets."

Resistance to change surfaces in many forms. It can be overt, implicit, immediate, or deferred. It is easiest for supervisors to deal with resistance when it is overt and immediate. For instance, a change is proposed and employees quickly respond by voicing complaints, engaging in a work slowdown, threatening to go on strike, or the like. The greater challenge is managing resistance that is implicit or deferred. Implicit resistance efforts are more subtle, for example, loss of loyalty to the organization, loss of motivation to work, increased errors or mistakes, increased absenteeism due to "sickness," and hence more difficult to recognize. Similarly, deferred actions cloud the link between the source of the resistance and the reaction to it. A change may produce what appears to be only a minimal reaction at the time it is initiated, but then resistance surfaces weeks, months, or even years later. A single change that in and of itself might have little impact can become the straw that breaks the camel's back. Reactions to change can build up and then explode in some response that seems totally out of proportion to the particular change action it follows. The resistance, of course, has merely been deferred and stockpiled. What surfaces is a response to an accumulation of previous changes.

So why do people resist change? There are a number of reasons (see Figure 13-2).

Reasons for Resistance
www.smartbiz.com/sbs/
arts/pod1.htm

HABIT

As human beings, we're creatures of habit. Life is complex enough; we don't need to consider the full range of options for the hundreds of decisions we have to make every day. To cope with this complexity, we all rely on habits or programmed responses. But when confronted with change, our programmed responses are no longer appropriate. So when your department is moved to a new office building across town, it means your employees are

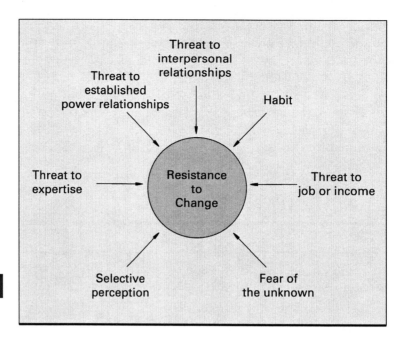

FIGURE 13-2

Why employees resist change

likely to have to change many habits: waking up 10 minutes earlier, taking a new route to work, finding a new parking place, adjusting to the new office layout, developing a new lunch-time routine, and so on.

THREAT TO JOB OR INCOME

Employees fear any change they think may reduce their job security or income. New labour-saving equipment, for instance, may be interpreted as the forerunner of layoffs. People are also often threatened by changes in job tasks or established work routines if they are fearful that they won't be able to perform them successfully. This is particularly threatening where pay is closely tied to productivity.

FEAR OF THE UNKNOWN

Human beings don't like ambiguity. But changes substitute ambiguity and uncertainty for the known. If the introduction of a desktop publishing system by a small book publisher means that editorial staff will have to learn to do their entire jobs on computers, some of these people may fear that they will be unable to learn the intricacies of the system. They may, therefore, develop a negative attitude toward working with desktop publishing or behave dysfunctionally—complaining, purposely working slowly, undermining department morale—if required to use the system.

FIGURE 13-3
Labour-saving equipment, like assembly-line robots, have replaced thousands of workers in automobile plants. Many auto workers fear changes because they're afraid their jobs might be eliminated.

SELECTIVE PERCEPTION

Individuals shape the world through their perceptions. Once they have created this world, it resists change. So individuals are guilty of selectively processing what they see and hear in order to keep their perceptions intact. They often hear what they want to hear. They ignore information that challenges the world they've created. For example, book editors faced with the introduction of desktop publishing may ignore the arguments their supervisors make in explaining why the new equipment has been purchased or what potential benefits the change will provide them.

THREAT TO EXPERTISE

Changes in organizational policies and practices may threaten the expertise of specialized groups and departments. The introduction of decentralized personal computers, which allow supervisors and managers access to information directly from a company's mainframe, is an example of a change that was strongly resisted by many information systems departments in the early 1980s. Why? Because decentralized end-user computing was a threat to the specialized skills held by those in the centralized information systems departments.

THREAT TO ESTABLISHED POWER RELATIONSHIPS

Any redistribution of decision-making authority can threaten existing power relationships within an organization. Efforts by top management to empower operating employees or introduce self-managed work teams have frequently been met by resistance from supervisors who are threatened by a loss of power.

THREAT TO INTERPERSONAL RELATIONSHIPS

Work is more than a means to earn a living. The interpersonal relationships that are part of a person's job often play an important role in satisfying the individual's social needs. We look forward to going to work to interact with coworkers and make friends. Change can be a threat to those relationships. Reorganizations, transfers, and restructuring of work layouts change the people that employees work with, report to, and regularly interact with. Since such changes are often seen as threats, they tend to be resisted.

POP QUIZ

Are You Comprehending What You're Reading?

1. A person who acts as a catalyst and assumes responsibility for overseeing the change process is called:
   a. a change agent
   b. a supervisor
   c. a change broker
   d. a transformer
2. Give some examples of planned change and unplanned change with which a supervisor may have to deal.
3. The correct order of the traditional view of change is unfreezing—refreezing—changing. True or false?
4. The contemporary view of change:
   a. is of little use to most organizations today
   b. is consistent with dynamic environmental forces
   c. involves unfreezing, change, and refreezing
   d. encourages individualism

REDUCING RESISTANCE TO CHANGE

The resistance we've described to change can be overcome. We offer four specific techniques:

1. Build trust.
2. Open channels of communication.
3. Involve employees.
4. Provide incentives.

Resistance is most likely to be eliminated when supervisors implement all four of the techniques. The techniques are discussed below.

BUILD TRUST

If employees trust and have confidence in you, they're less likely to be threatened by changes you propose.

Trust takes a long time to develop. It's also very fragile; it can be destroyed easily. What can you do to build trust? Be fair and impartial. Be consistent and predictable in your decisions and in the way you treat your employees. Develop a reputation for making good on your promises, both explicit and implied. Be supportive. Employees trust supervisors who offer praise, are good listeners, exhibit confidence in their people, and protect their interests. Finally, be candid and honest. Your people should believe that you'll tell them the truth.

OPEN CHANNELS OF COMMUNICATION

Resistance can often be reduced by communicating with employees to help them see the logic of a change.

When employees receive the full facts and any misunderstandings are cleared up, resistance often fades. A longitudinal study of a work reorganization found that employees who felt they were well informed about the change were much more open to the change when it occurred than were those who felt less informed.[3] Opening communication channels, however, will only be effective when there is a climate of trust and where the organization is truly concerned with the welfare of its employees. In a hospital implementing empowerment among nurses, different nurses heard the management message differently depending on how much they trusted management. Those who trusted management were more likely to believe the reasons management gave for the empowerment. Those who did not trust management were more likely to be suspicious of the real reasons behind their decision.[4]

Improved communication is particularly effective in reducing threats created by ambiguity. For instance, when the grapevine is active with rumours of cutbacks and layoffs, honest and open communication of the true facts can be a calming force. Even if the news is bad, a clear message often wins points and opens people to accepting change. When communication is ambiguous and people are threatened, they often contrive scenarios that are considerably worse than the actual "bad news."

INVOLVE EMPLOYEES

Many organizations are asking employees to participate in planning major change programs. Why? It's difficult for individuals to resist a change decision in which they have participated. So solicit employee input early in the change process. When employees have been involved in a change from its beginning, they will usually actively support the change. No one wants to oppose something that he or she helped develop.

PROVIDE INCENTIVES

FIGURE 13-4

Graham Van Brunt, director of plant operations at Churchill Falls Labrador Corp.

Newfoundland and Labrador Hydro
http://www.nlh.nf.ca/

How to Overcome Resistance to Change
www.smartbiz.com/sbs/arts/pos7.htm

Our last suggestion is to make sure that people see how supporting a change is in their best interests. What's the source of their resistance? What do you control that might overcome that resistance? Are they afraid they won't be able to do a new task? Provide them with new-skills training. Or maybe provide a short paid leave of absence so they'll have time to rethink their fears, calm down, and come to the realization that their concerns are unfounded. Similarly, layoffs can become opportunities for those who remain. Jobs can be redesigned to provide new challenges and responsibilities. A pay increase, a new title, flexible work hours, or increased job autonomy are additional examples of incentives that can help reduce resistance.

Graham Van Brunt, director of plant operations and maintenance at Churchill Falls Labrador Corp., a huge hydro facility, knows the value of preparing people for change through training. "When we put in new equipment, like a new relay or a new annunciating system, a substantial part of our expense is in training, to make sure employees understand and can operate the new equipment. We typically do a pilot where consultants train key personnel on site in one localized area. Then we use those employees to train others in the organization." Graham's approach must be successful as "there is little, if any, resistance to the technology. In fact, most embrace it and the new knowledge. We get people demanding to get training they hear others are getting. For example, we got new governor systems to keep the machines running in synch and at the right speed. Theoretical training was given to the technicians but not to the operators. The operators asked to get the theoretical training, too."

Change at the Churchill Falls hydro facility in recent years has included a major reorganization. This required much more adaptation than working with new equipment (see Something to Think About).

SAME PLACE, NEW JOB

Over a year ago, Churchill Falls Labrador Corp. (CFLC) switched to activity-based budgeting. As a result, management responsibilities were drastically altered to align with activities. Graham Van Brunt describes the changes. "For example, whereas before a superintendent would look after all welders and equipment in an area—tools, labour, generator—now the labour and assets are split. For example, one superintendent looks after the people, and another will manage the generator. The latter, therefore, does not have to worry about training, absenteeism, or employee relations. He must try to get the work done well and inexpensively; this means he could go to the labour manager for staff, but he could also go outside the organization and arrange for the work to be done by someone locally. The decision would rest on factors like cost, professionalism, reaction, the big-picture impact on the company.

"Some employees loved the change. Others hated it—one said 'It feels like someone kicked me in the stomach.' It would be nice if we had a brand-new company to start with instead of going from old to new. It's tough when you tell someone you're no longer looking after this equipment as you have for the past 20 years. Now, you'll be looking after people, and it will be five times as many as before. There's a fear of the unknown.

"Even now, we're still riding the bumps of that change. Some areas were hard to define and we are still dealing with some 'grey' areas."

The changes described seem to make each supervisor's area of responsibility operate like a mini business unit. The mindset to handle this seems very different from the mindset of a supervisor who is part of a hierarchy in a large corporation. Why would CFLC undertake this change? What supervisory skills would be needed to adjust to this change? What preparation could CFLC give the supervisors to be able to cope with the shift?

WORK STRESS

A 1998 study by Statistics Canada shows:

- roughly 25 per cent of Canadians between the ages of 25 and 44 describe themselves as severely time-stressed;

- 30 per cent view themselves as workaholics;

- more than 50 per cent believe they are not spending enough time with family and friends.[5]

Statscan statistics on time stress in Canadians
http://www.statcan.ca/ Daily/English/991109/ d991109a.htm

CBC site on stress
www.cbc.ca/news/ indepth/stress/

Work stress is a problem. A recent survey of North American workers found that 46 per cent felt their jobs were highly stressful and 34 per cent reported that the stress was so bad they were thinking of quitting. High-stress jobs include air traffic controllers, police officers, fire fighters, emergency-room physicians, and assembly-line workers. But employees in all types of jobs are reporting increased stress levels. And change seems to be a major contributor to this increase in stress levels. In addition, the uncertain environment characterized by takeovers, mergers, restructurings, forced retirements, and mass layoffs has created a large number of employees who are overworked and stressed out. Therefore, stress is an issue that all supervisors need to pay attention to.

What Is Stress?

Stress
An adaptive response resulting from any environmental action, situation, or event that places excessive psychological and/or physical demands on a person.

The formal definition of **stress** is complex: an adaptive response resulting from any environmental action, situation, or event that places excessive psychological and/or physical demands on a person. Essentially, the adaptive response we typically associate with stress includes things such as tension, anxiety, or a rush of adrenaline. The demands refer to the potential loss of something that a person desires; for instance, respect, his or her job, or a promotion.

Two conditions are necessary for a potentially stressful situation to create actual stress for a person. There must be uncertainty over the outcome and the outcome must be important. Stress is highest for those who don't know whether they will win or lose and lowest for those who think that winning or losing is a certainty. But importance is also critical. If winning or losing is an unimportant outcome, there is no stress. If keeping your job doesn't hold any importance to you, you have no reason to feel stress over having to undergo a performance review. Athletes typically experience greater stress during championship competition because there is increased importance placed on the outcome.

Keep in mind that stress, like conflict, isn't all bad. While it's typically discussed in a negative context, stress has positive value. Consider the times when you have been under major performance deadlines and it has pushed you to do your best work, for example, writing a paper for a school assignment the night before its due date. For many employees, the high demands associated with stress create the adrenaline kick they depend on to accomplish high quantities of work and to meet ambitious deadlines.

Sources of Work Stress

Work-related stress is brought about by both organizational and individual factors. As shown in Figure 13-5, these in turn are influenced by individual differences. That is, not all people in similar situations experience similar levels of stress.

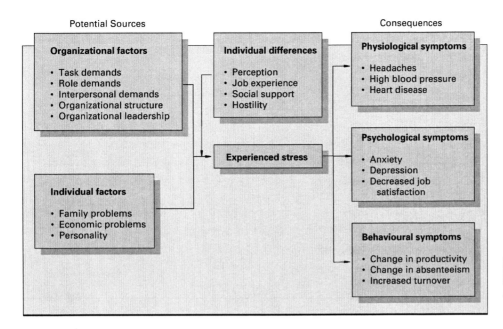

Organizational factors

- Task demands
- Role demands
- Interpersonal demands
- Organizational structure
- Organizational leadership

Individual differences

- Perception
- Job experience
- Social support
- Hostility

Consequences

Physiological symptoms

- Headaches
- High blood pressure
- Heart disease

Experienced stress

Psychological symptoms

- Anxiety
- Depression
- Decreased job satisfaction

Individual factors

- Family problems
- Economic problems
- Personality

Behavioural symptoms

- Change in productivity
- Change in absenteeism
- Increased turnover

FIGURE 13-5

A closer look at stress

ORGANIZATIONAL FACTORS

There is no shortage of factors within the organization that can cause stress. Pressures to avoid errors or complete tasks in a limited time period, a demanding supervisor, and unpleasant coworkers are a few examples. The discussion that follows organizes stress factors into five categories: task, role, and interpersonal demands; organizational structure; and organizational leadership.

Task demands are factors related to an employee's job. They include the design of the job (autonomy, task variety, degree of automation), working conditions, and the physical work layout. Assembly lines can put pressure on people when the line's speed is perceived as excessive. The more interdependence between a person's tasks and the tasks of others, the more potential stress there is. Autonomy, on the other hand, tends to lessen stress. Jobs where temperatures, noise, or other working conditions are dangerous or undesirable can increase anxiety. So, too, can working in an overcrowded room or in a location where interruptions are constant.

Role demands relate to pressures placed on an employee as a function of the particular role he or she plays in the organization. **Role conflicts** create expectations that may be hard to reconcile or satisfy. Supervisors often experience role conflict through the "intermediary" position they occupy, expected to be an advocate for both management and employees. **Role overload** is experienced when the employee is expected to do more than time permits. **Role ambiguity** is created when role expectations are not clearly understood and the employee is unsure of what he or she is to do.

Role conflicts
Situations in which individuals are confronted by divergent role expectations.

Role overload
Situations where an employee is expected to do more than time permits.

Role ambiguity
Situation where role expectations are not clearly understood and the employee is not sure what he or she is to do.

Interpersonal demands are pressures created by other employees. Lack of social support from colleagues and poor interpersonal relationships can cause considerable stress, especially among employees with a high social need.

Organizational structure can increase stress. Excessive rules and an employee's lack of opportunity to participate in decisions that affect him or her are examples of structural variables that might be potential sources of stress.

Organizational leadership represents the managerial style of the organization's senior executives. Some chief executive officers create a culture characterized by tension, fear, and anxiety. They establish unrealistic pressures to perform in the short run, impose excessively tight controls, and routinely fire employees who don't measure up. This style of leadership flows down through the organization to affect all employees.

INDIVIDUAL FACTORS

The typical employee works about 40 hours a week. The experiences and problems that people encounter in the remaining nonwork hours each week can spill over to the job. Our other category, then, encompasses factors in the employee's personal life. Primarily, these factors are *family issues, personal economic problems*, and *inherent personality characteristics*.

Surveys consistently show that people hold family and personal relationships dear. Marital difficulties, the breaking off of a relationship, discipline troubles with children, and relatives with serious illnesses are examples of relationship problems that create stress for employees and that aren't left at the front door when they leave for work.

Economic problems created by individuals overextending their financial resources are another set of personal troubles that can create stress for employees and distract their attention from their work. Regardless of income level (people who earn $80 000 a year seem to have as much trouble handling their finances as those who earn $18 000), some people are poor money managers or have material desires that always seem to exceed their earning capacity.

Recent studies have found that stress symptoms reported prior to beginning a job don't change much from those reported nine months later. This has led to the conclusion that some people may have an inherent tendency to accentuate negative aspects of the world in general. If true, then a significant individual factor influencing stress is a person's basic disposition. That is, stress symptoms expressed on the job may actually originate in the person's personality (see Something to Think About).

Stress factors are additive. A fact that tends to be overlooked when stress factors are reviewed individually is that stress is an additive phenomenon. Stress builds up. Each new and persistent stressor adds to an individual's stress level. A single stressor may seem relatively unimportant in and of itself, but if it is added to an already high level of stress, it can be "the straw that breaks the camel's back."

HOW MUCH STRESS IN YOUR LIFE?

Below are 20 statements. Use the following scale in responding to each statement:

    4 = all the time
    3 = often
    2 = sometimes
    1 = never

1. I'm exhausted by daily demands at work, college, and home.   4   3   2   1

2. My stress is caused by outside forces beyond my control.   4   3   2   1

3. I'm trapped by circumstances that I just have to live with.   4   3   2   1

4. No matter how hard I work to stay on top of my schedule, I can't get caught up.   4   3   2   1

5. I have financial obligations that I can't seem to meet.   4   3   2   1

6. I dislike my work, but I can't take the risk of making a career change (or if not working: I dislike college, but can't take the risk of dropping out).   4   3   2   1

7. I'm dissatisfied with my personal relationships.   4   3   2   1

8. I feel responsible for the happiness of people around me.   4   3   2   1

9. I'm embarrassed to ask for help.   4   3   2   1

10. I don't know what I want out of life.   4   3   2   1

11. I'm disappointed that I have not achieved what I had hoped for.   4   3   2   1

12. No matter how much success I have, I feel empty.   4   3   2   1

13. If the people around me were more competent, I would feel happier.   4   3   2   1

14. People let me down.   4   3   2   1

15. I stew in my anger rather than express it.   4   3   2   1

16. I become enraged and resentful when I am hurt.   4   3   2   1

17. I can't take criticism.	4	3	2	1
18. I'm afraid I'll lose my job (or fail school).	4	3	2	1
19. I don't see the value of expressing sadness or grief.	4	3	2	1
20. I don't trust that things will work out.	4	3	2	1

SCORING

After rating each statement, total your score for the 20 items. Scores of 20-29 indicate a high degree of control, self-esteem, and low stress levels. Scores of 30-49 suggest that your occasional negative self-talk causes you to feel anxious in stressful situations, thus causing moderate levels of stress. Scores of 50-69 indicate a relatively high level of stress. This might indicate you feel trapped. Scores of 70 or more indicate very high stress levels—indicating life has become one crisis and struggle after another for you.

Using this questionnaire as a guide, describe the kinds of things that are causing stress in your life. How are you handling this stress? Do you feel successful? Why or why not? For those who have low stress, what tips could you offer to others for coping with the stress?

Source: *From Stress to Strength*, by R. S. Eliot, M.D. ©1994 by Robert S. Eliot, M.D. Used by permission of Bantam Books, a division of Bantam Doubleday Dell Publishing Group, Inc.

INDIVIDUAL DIFFERENCES

Some people thrive on stressful situations, while others are overwhelmed by them. What is it that differentiates people in terms of their ability to handle stress? Four individual difference factors have been found to be important: perception, experience, social support, and hostility.

One person's fear that he'll lose his job because his company is laying off personnel may be perceived by another as an opportunity to get a large severance allowance and start his own business. Similarly, what one employee perceives as an efficient and challenging work environment may be viewed as threatening and demanding by others. So stress potential doesn't lie in objective conditions. Rather, it lies in an employee's *perception* and interpretation of those conditions. The same situation may be perceived as a challenge by one, but as a burden by another. Those who report challenge-related work stress have higher job satisfaction than those who report hindrance-related work stress.[6]

Experience is said to be a great teacher. It can also be a great stress-reducer. Think back to your first date or your first few days in college. For most of us, the uncertainty and newness of these situations created stress. But as we gained experience, that stress disappeared or at least significantly decreased. The same phenomenon seems to apply to work situations. Why? One explanation is the process of selective withdrawal. Voluntary turnover is more likely among people who experience more stress. Therefore, people who remain with the organization longer are those with more stress-resistant traits, or those who are more resistant to the stress characteristics of their organization. A second explanation is that people eventually develop coping mechanisms to deal with stress. Because this takes time, senior members of the organization are more likely to be fully adapted and experience less stress.

There is increasing evidence that *social support*—collegial relationships with coworkers and supervisors—can buffer the impact of stress. The logic underlying this conclusion is that social support acts as a palliative, lessening the negative effects of even high-stress jobs.

You may have heard of Type A behaviour being used to explain who would be affected by stress. **Type A behaviour** is characterized by feelings of a chronic sense of time urgency and by an excessive competitive drive. Type As try to do more and more in less and less time. The opposite of Type A is **Type B behaviour**. Type Bs never suffer from time urgency or impatience. Until quite recently, it was believed that Type As were more likely to experience stress on and off the job. A closer analysis of the evidence, however, has produced new conclusions. It has been found that only the hostility and anger associated with some Type A behaviour is actually associated with the negative effects of stress. The chronically angry, suspicious, and distrustful person is the one at risk of stressing out.

Type A behaviour
Aggressive behaviour in a chronic, incessant struggle to achieve more and more in less and less time.

Type B behaviour
The behaviour of a person who is rarely harried by the desire to obtain a wildly increasing number of things or participate in an endlessly growing series of events in an ever-decreasing amount of time.

THE SYMPTOMS OF STRESS

What signs indicate that an employee's stress level might be too high? There are three general ways that stress reveals itself. These include physiological, psychological, and behavioural symptoms.

Most of the early interest over stress focused heavily on health-related or *physiological* concerns. This was attributed to the realization that high stress levels result in changes in metabolism, increased heart and breathing rates, increased blood pressure, headaches, and increased risk of heart attacks. Because detecting many of these symptoms requires the skills of trained medical personnel, their immediate and direct relevance to supervisors is negligible.

Of greater importance to supervisors are psychological and behavioural symptoms of stress. These are things that can be witnessed in the person. The *psychological* symptoms can be seen as increased tension and anxiety, boredom, or procrastination—which can all lead to productivity decreases. So too, can the *behaviourally related* symptoms—changes in eating habits, increased smoking or substance consumption, rapid speech, or sleep disorders. The astute supervisor, upon witnessing such symptoms, does what he or she can to assist the employee in reducing stress levels.

COMPANIES TAKE ACTION ON STRESS

With the annual cost of stress in Canadian companies exceeding $12 billion, Canadian companies are implementing a variety of stress-reducing options including flextime (49 per cent of employers), job sharing (19 per cent), and part-time prorated benefits (30 per cent). These companies are responding to the needs of a very different workforce in which:

- 62 per cent of all husband-and-wife families have both spouses working
- 66 per cent of all women with children under 16 work outside the home
- 16 per cent of workers report that they care for elderly members of their family

Much of the stress in the Canadian workforce seems to be centred on the new generation of working parents. This group is vulnerable to work/family stress caused by raising their families and caring for elder family members, with no adult family member at home full-time to take on these tasks as their major responsibility. Companies are beginning to look at options to give greater flexibility in handling both work and personal responsibilities.

For example, the Bank of Montreal has implemented a number of policies to help its employees deal with stress. Policies include family emergency days; unpaid leaves of up to two years for personal reasons; flexible work options; telecommuting; condensed work weeks; and child care and elder-care referral services.

Although many firms have recognized the need to address work/family stress, Hal Morgan of Work/Family Directions says that widespread support for work/family programs is a gradual process. Ambitious programs remain few and far between. In many cases, employers have adopted some benefits, but have resisted the global rethink of their employee policies that's necessary for real change to occur.

STRESS REDUCTION

If employee stress levels are too high in your department, is there anything you can do? The answer is a resounding yes. In this section, we'll review some of your options.

ASSESSING YOURSELF: HOW WELL CAN YOU IDENTIFY STRESSFUL EVENTS?

Which life events typically create the greatest stress? To test your knowledge, rank-order the following 12 events from the most stressful (rank number 1) to least stressful (number 12). Note that positive events can cause stress as well as negative ones.

		Rank
1.	Divorce	_____
2.	Being fired at work	_____
3.	Minor violation of the law such as receiving a traffic ticket	_____
4.	Changing to a different line of work	_____
5.	Death of a spouse	_____
6.	Outstanding personal achievement	_____
7.	Major changes in working hours or conditions	_____
8.	Foreclosure on a mortgage or loan	_____
9.	Gaining a new family member through birth, adoption, or a relative moving in	_____
10.	Major personal injury or illness	_____
11.	Major change in responsibilities at work such as a promotion, demotion, or lateral transfer	_____
12.	Marriage	_____

Source: Based on T.H. Holmes and R.H. Rahe, "The Social Readjustment Scale," *Journal of Psychosomatic Research*, 11 (1967), p. 216.

SCORING DIRECTIONS AND KEY

To find out how you did, transpose your ranking numbers to Column A below. The numbers in Column B represent the correct ranking (from most to least stressful). Now subtract Column B from Column A for each event and put that number in Column C. In Column D, calculate the square of the difference you calculated in Column C e.g., $3^2=9$).

Event	Column A	Column B	Column C	Column D
1	___	5	___	___
2	___	1	___	___
3	___	10	___	___
4	___	12	___	___
5	___	2	___	___
6	___	9	___	___
7	___	4	___	___
8	___	8	___	___
9	___	11	___	___
10	___	6	___	___
11	___	7	___	___
12	___	3	___	___

Total ___ ÷ 12 = _____

Sum up the total of Column D and divide by 12. The result is a measure of variation. The lower the number, the better you are at identifying the stressfulness of various events. An excellent variation score would be 10 or less.

SKILL BASICS

Low-to-moderate levels of employee stress may not require your attention. The reason, as we noted earlier in the chapter, is that such levels of stress can be functional and can lead to higher employee performance. But high levels of stress, or even low levels sustained over long periods of time, can lead to reduced employee performance and thus require supervisory action.

While a limited amount of stress may benefit an employee's performance, don't expect employees to see it that way. From the individual's standpoint, even low levels of stress are likely to be perceived as undesirable. It's not unlikely, therefore, that you and your employees will differ on what constitutes an acceptable level of stress on the job. What you may consider a positive stimulus that keeps the adrenaline running may be seen as excessive pressure by your employees. Keep this in mind as we discuss techniques for reducing stress.

SELECT EMPLOYEES WITH THE SPECIFIC JOB IN MIND

While certain jobs are more stressful than others, we know that individuals differ in their response to stress situations. Selection and placement decisions should take these facts into consideration. Match personalities to the demands of the job. And remember that, especially in stressful jobs, experienced individuals are likely to adapt better and perform their jobs more effectively.

CLARIFY EXPECTATIONS

Employees are more motivated and less stressed when they clearly understand what is expected of them. The use of goals can also reduce stress. Specific goals that employees believe are attainable reduce the stress caused by unrealistic expectations. Additionally, goal feedback reduces uncertainties as to actual job performance. The result is less employee frustration, role ambiguity, and stress.

ENCOURAGE TIME MANAGEMENT

As discussed in Chapter 2, many people manage their time poorly. However, the well-organized employee can often accomplish twice as much as the person who is poorly organized. The understanding and use of basic time-management principles can help individuals better cope with job demands.

REDESIGN JOBS TO ALIGN WITH INDIVIDUAL PREFERENCES

Redesigning jobs to give employees more responsibility, meaningful work, autonomy, and increased feedback can reduce stress because these factors give the employee greater control over work activities and lessen dependence on others. Of course, not all employees want enriched jobs. The right job redesign for some employees might then be less responsibility and increased division of labour. If individuals prefer structure and routine, standardizing the job should also reduce uncertainties and stress levels.

LET EMPLOYEES PARTICIPATE IN DECISION MAKING

Role stress is detrimental to a large extent because employees feel uncertain about goals, expectations, how they'll be evaluated, and the like. By giving employees a voice in those decisions that directly affect their job performance, you can increase employee control and reduce this role stress.

Research has shown that inviting employees to participate in any change process can result in reduced resistance to the change and a greater sense of control over the change, meaning lower stress.[7]

PROVIDE SOCIAL SUPPORT

Having friends, family, or colleagues to talk to provides an outlet when stress levels become excessive. Helping employees expand their social support networks can be a means to reduce tension. Having someone else to hear a problem can provide a more objective perspective on a given situation. Interestingly, the value of social support in lessening stress may be an important, but rarely mentioned, advantage provided by work teams.

INCREASE FORMAL COMMUNICATION

Increasing formal communication with employees reduces uncertainty by lessening role ambiguity and role conflict. When employees think they're being kept "in the dark," stress levels rise. When you provide "the light," stress should decline.

GIVE POSITIVE FEEDBACK

Self-efficacy
Belief in one's ability to tackle events successfully.

Self-efficacy has a role to play in moderating reaction to stressful events. Research with over 2000 U.S. Army soldiers demonstrated that belief in one's ability to tackle events successfully, or self-efficacy, was linked to much less psychological and physical strain experienced by those soldiers when confronted with work-related stressors, such as long hours and work overload.[8]

A supervisor can influence an employee's perception of efficacy through a solid training base and a consistent support system, but also through giving positive feedback. An employee whose supervisor openly and frequently acknowledges the employee's skills and strengths, rather than focusing most on weaknesses, is much more likely to feel confidence in his or her capabilities.

ENCOURAGE EMPLOYEES TO EXERCISE AND RELAX

Noncompetitive physical exercise such as aerobics, race walking, jogging, swimming, and riding a bicycle have long been recommended by physicians as a way to deal with excessive stress levels. These forms of exercise increase heart capacity, lower at-rest heart rate, provide a mental diversion from work pressures, and offer a means to "let off steam."

Employees can also be encouraged to practice relaxation techniques such as meditation, hypnosis, and biofeedback. Fifteen or twenty minutes a day of deep relaxation releases tension and provides a person with a pronounced sense of peacefulness.

Some organizations offer wellness programs that focus on the employees' total physical and mental condition. For example, they typically provide workshops to help people quit smoking, control alcohol use, lose weight, and eat better. If your organization offers such programs, encourage your employees to participate.

SET AN EXAMPLE—LOOK AT STRESSFUL SITUATIONS AS CHALLENGES

If you curse when unexpected changes happen or appear frustrated with overload or new demands, employees will take their cue from you. If, on the other hand, you treat stressful events with a sense of humour, as one more interesting challenge to face in an interesting job, that interpretation will rub off on others.

APPLYING YOUR SKILLS

Complete the following questionnaire by circling one number in each line across. To what extent does each of the following sentences fit as a description of you?

	Very true	Quite true	Some-what true	Not very true	Not at all true
1. I "roll with the punches" when problems come up.	1	2	3	4	5
2. I spend almost all of my time thinking about my work.	5	4	3	2	1
3. I treat other people as individuals and care about their feelings and opinions.	1	2	3	4	5
4. I recognize and accept my own limitations and assets.	1	2	3	4	5
5. There are quite a few people I could describe as "good friends."	1	2	3	4	5

	Very true	Quite true	Some-what true	Not very true	Not at all true
6. I enjoy using my skills and abilities both on and off the job.	1	2	3	4	5
7. I get bored easily.	5	4	3	2	1
8. I enjoy meeting and talking with people who have different ways of thinking about the world.	1	2	3	4	5
9. Often in my job I "bite off more than I can chew."	5	4	3	2	1
10. I'm usually very active on weekends with projects or recreation.	1	2	3	4	5
11. I prefer working with people who are very much like myself.	5	4	3	2	1
12. I work primarily because I have to survive, not necessarily because I enjoy what I do.	5	4	3	2	1
13. I believe I have a realistic picture of my personal strengths and weakness.	1	2	3	4	5
14. Often I get into arguments with people who don't think my way.	5	4	3	2	1
15. Often I have trouble getting much done on my job.	5	4	3	2	1
16. I'm interested in a lot of different topics.	1	2	3	4	5
17. I get upset when things don't go my way.	5	4	3	2	1
18. Often I'm not sure how I stand on a controversial topic.	5	4	3	2	1
19. I'm usually able to find a way around anything that blocks me from an important goal.	1	2	3	4	5
20. I often disagree with my boss or others at work.	5	4	3	2	1

SCORING AND INTERPRETATION

The author of this questionnaire believes that people who cope with stress effectively have five characteristics.

1. They know themselves well and accept their own strengths and weaknesses.

2. They have a variety of interests off the job, and they are not total "workaholics."
3. They exhibit a variety of reactions to stress, rather than always getting a headache or always becoming depressed.
4. They are accepting of others who have values or styles different from their own.
5. They are active and productive both on and off the job.

Add together the numbers you circled for the four questions contained in each of the five coping scales.

Coping scale	Add together your responses to these questions	Your score (write in)
Knows self	4, 9, 13, 18	_____
Many interests	2, 5, 7, 16	_____
Variety of reactions	1, 11, 17, 19	_____
Accepts other's values	3, 8, 14, 20	_____
Active and productive	6, 10, 12, 15	_____

Then, add the five scores together for your overall total score: _____

Scores on each of the five areas can vary between 5 and 20. Scores of 12 or above suggest that it might perhaps be useful to direct more attention to the area.

The overall total score can range between 20 and 100. Scores of 60 or more may suggest some general difficulty in coping on the dimensions covered.

Source: McLean, A. A. *Work Stress* (Reading, MA: Addison-Wesley, 1979), pp. 126–27. Copyright © 1976 by Management Decision Systems, Inc. Reprinted by permission.

GROUP INTERACTION

Break into groups of three or four. Compare your scale and total scores. Discuss what you might be able to do if your score is high.

Have the two people in each group with the highest score and lowest score enact a role-play. The person with the lowest score is the supervisor; the person with the highest is the employee. Assume that the supervisor has concluded that the employee seems to be acting strangely recently on his or her job. You think high stress may be part of the problem. Conduct a counselling session with the employee to discuss what you (the supervisor) might do to help the employee reduce his or her stress level.

5. For potential stress to become actual stress, which two conditions must exist?
   a. uncertainty and importance
   b. people and organizations
   c. certainty and importance
   d. uncertainty and risk
6. What are the three symptoms of stress? Which one is least important to detect in those one supervises?
7. Role conflict refers to a situation where jobs are ill-defined. True or false?
8. Indicate which of the following statements is true:
   a. The use of goals can reduce stress.
   b. Enriched jobs will always reduce stress.
   c. Letting employees participate in decisions that affect their performance will give them more control and, therefore, more stress.
   d. Increasing formal communication will create more stress through overwhelming people with information.

UNDERSTANDING THE BASICS

SUMMARY

This summary is organized by the Learning Objectives.

1. The old view of change treats change as a break in the organization's equilibrium state. Change is initiated and then stabilized at a new equilibrium. The contemporary view of change is that it is constant. Disequilibria is the natural state.
2. The forces for change in today's organization include new technologies (e.g., automation, computerization, e-mail and voicemail); environmental dynamics (e.g., new government regulations, changing labour market, increased competition); and internal forces (e.g., reorganizations, change in strategy, new equipment introduced).
3. People resist change out of habit, fear of the unknown, selective perception, or if they perceive the change as a threat to their job, income, expertise, established power relationships, or interpersonal relationships.
4. Supervisors can reduce resistance by building trust, opening channels of communication, involving employees in the change decisions, and by providing incentives to employees for accepting change.
5. Stress is an adaptive response resulting from any environmental action, situation, or event that places excessive psychological and/or physical demands on a person.
6. Stress comes from organizational factors such as task and role demands, interpersonal demands, and structural variables; it can also be caused by individual factors such as family problems, economic problems, and personality variables.
7. Type A behaviour is characterized by a chronic sense of time urgency and an excessive competitive drive. Type B behaviour is the opposite —characterized by an absence of time urgency or impatience.

KEY TERMS AND CONCEPTS

Change agents   Self-efficacy

Change process   Stress

Role ambiguity   Type A behaviour

Role conflict   Type B behaviour

Role overload

REVIEWING YOUR KNOWLEDGE

1. Give several examples of environmental forces that might affect supervisors and require changes in a department.
2. Describe the three-step model of the change process.
3. What signals or cues might tell you that an employee is resistant to a change you're planning to implement?
4. What is selective perception and how is it related to change resistance?
5. How does building trust lessen change resistance?
6. Why should supervisors be concerned with an employee's work-related stress?
7. Does stress increase or decrease when a person becomes a supervisor? Explain.
8. Is all stress bad? Discuss.
9. How can supervisors reduce employee stress?
10. Do supervisors have the right to inquire about, or try to help employees deal with, stresses that result from factors outside the job? Discuss.

ANSWERS TO THE POP QUIZZES

1. **a. a change agent.**
2. Planned change examples: replacing equipment, increasing or decreasing the staff, introducing a new procedure or rule, employee training.

   Unplanned change examples: employee absenteeism, customer order cancelled at last minute, machine breakdown, late shipment from supplier.
3. **False.** The correct order of the traditional view of change is unfreezing—changing—refreezing.
4. **b. is consistent with dynamic environmental forces.** The rapidly changing environmental forces often create a chaotic work environment, one similar to "shooting the rapids."
5. **a. uncertainty and importance.** These two elements are critical in creating stressful situations.
6. There are three general ways that stress reveals itself. These include physiological, psychological, and behavioural symptoms. Because detecting such things as changes in metabolism, increased heart and breathing rates, increased blood pressure, headaches, and increased risk of heart attacks requires the skills of trained medical personnel, the immediate and direct relevance of physiological stress symptoms to supervisors is negligible.
7. **False.** Role conflict refers to a situation where role expectations are hard to reconcile or satisfy.
8. **a. The use of goals can reduce stress.** Through the process of setting goals, the employee better understands expectations, reducing ambiguity and frustration.

CASE 13.A

The Changes Never Stop

Three and a half years ago, Kerri Reid joined Cedara Software Corp., a Mississauga-based high tech company that provides medical imaging software technology and custom imaging technology development to multinational healthcare solution providers. As is typical in the dynamic, rapid-growth high tech sector, Cedara has gone through several organizational restructurings since Kerri joined the company. As Director, Staffing, Learning and Employee Communications, Kerri has been involved in facilitating and supporting organizational change. Each restructuring is designed to address the different business issues involved and accommodate the magnitude of the change. Kerri describes how a recent one was handled:

"At various stages of planning and implementation, input and/or assistance were solicited from individuals representing different functions and different levels in the organization. Discretion and confidentiality were of utmost importance to ensure the integrity of the process. By involving the right people with specific knowledge and specific expertise at the right time, Cedara was able to develop a plan that was appropriate for the organization and the employees.

"When the reorganization was rolled out, we first met with the department that was being most affected by the change. Interestingly, a Vice President whose position was being eliminated as a result of the organization requested the opportunity to be part of the communications team announcing the changes to his group. He joined the meetings and helped explain what was happening and why.

"The reorganization involved a department being divided into two separate groups to support two business units rather than the function being a shared service. Part of any well-planned reorganization includes a comprehensive implementation and communications strategy. In this case, the department most affected by the change met as a whole with the communications team to learn about the reorganization. The two newly-formed teams then met with their respective managers to receive more detail about the reorganization and resulting transition plans. Cedara senior executives met with the entire management team to explain the new organizational model and the change drivers. Cedara managers were tasked with rolling out the communications to their staff. In addition to in-person meetings held on the day of the announcement, there were subsequent meetings throughout the week and beyond with teams and individuals to communicate more detail, provide clarification, and respond to questions. E-mail communications from members of the senior executive to employees were deployed as a follow-up means of communication.

"We'll soon learn how things are going in the new structure. We hold quarterly status meetings hosted by members of the executive where we invite all staff—over 400—to receive updates, interpret quarterly results, and address key business issues.

"To further support communications in the organization, a number of strategies are incorporated such as management forums, departmental meetings, and breakfast meetings with the CEO and staff members."

Cedara Home Page
www.cedara.com

RESPONDING TO THIS CASE

1. What change management techniques did Cedara use to reduce resistance?

2, Cedara is a "high-tech" company. "High-tech" industries experience more change than most. Do you think the people who choose to work in "high-tech" organizations are simply much better at handling change than other workers? Do you think they find change less stressful? Explain.

3. Why would an executive outplaced by a reorganization volunteer to help rollout the change with the remaining managers?

CASE 13.B

"New" Is Exciting But Stressful

Anne Murphy is the branch manager of the Frank McKechnie Library in Mississauga, a new library combined with a recreation facility. Although it opened in June 2000, Anne started work on the new branch 18 months earlier. She was responsible for ordering all the materials and hiring all 27 staff members, most of whom transferred from other branches. The full-time staff members spent many months before opening processing all the new items, which numbered 80 000. So, even though the staff members were hired for an eventual customer service function, they spent almost all of their first year on the job in a support service or technical service function. They grew accustomed to working from 8:30 a.m. to 4:30 p.m., with no evening or weekend work. It was a quiet, structured atmosphere. All employees met weekly for an hour in a staff meeting.

"It was a major shift going from 'behind the scenes' to public when the library opened. Even though we opened for a few shifts before official opening, no one was prepared for the chaos of opening. Five thousand people showed up. It was pandemonium and excitement."

The noise levels haven't subsided much since then as the facility is enjoying heavy use by the community. Now staff must take their turns working weekend and evening shifts, and there is never a time when all employees can attend a meeting at the same time. There is so much new to deal with now that, as well as the biweekly staff meetings, whose minutes are given to those who can't attend, mini-meetings are held before opening each morning. Anne herself is scheduled on the desk for some shifts, including at least one evening a week, and filling in when the library is shortstaffed.

RESPONDING TO THIS CASE

1. List all the changes that the employees working at the library have been through. And Anne, as their supervisor?
2. Which changes are likely to be stressful and why? Which changes are likely to be much less stressful and why?
3. Apply the "change process" model to this circumstance to this change. What, in particular, will Anne need to do to "refreeze" the new changes?
4. Anne is the prime change agent in this situation. What skills did she need in this role?

14 DISCIPLINING EMPLOYEES

LEARNING OBJECTIVES

After reading this chapter, you should be able to:

1. Define *discipline*.
2. Identify the four most common types of discipline problems.
3. List the typical steps in progressive discipline.
4. Explain the "hot stove" rule.
5. Describe the role of extenuating circumstances in applying discipline.
6. Explain the three legal dismissal situations.
7. Describe how a collective bargaining agreement affects the disciplining of unionized employees.

CHAPTER OUTLINE

PERFORMING EFFECTIVELY

WHAT IS DISCIPLINE?

TYPES OF DISCIPLINE PROBLEMS
Attendance
On-the-Job Behaviours
Dishonesty
Something to Think About
Outside Activities

DISCIPLINE ISN'T ALWAYS THE SOLUTION

BASIC TENETS OF DISCIPLINE
Lay the Groundwork
Make Discipline Progressive
Follow the "Hot Stove" Rule
Pop Quiz

FACTORS TO CONSIDER IN DISCIPLINING

DISCIPLINE AND THE LAW
Unionization
Pop Quiz

FROM CONCEPTS TO SKILLS: DISCIPLINING
Assessing Yourself: Are You Effective at Disciplining?
Skill Basics
Applying Your Skills

UNDERSTANDING THE BASICS
Summary
Key Terms and Concepts
Reviewing Your Knowledge
Answers to the Pop Quizzes

PERFORMING YOUR JOB
Case 14.A: Dealing with the Poor Performer Who Has Political Connections
Case 14.B: Discipline in a Union Setting

Rob Mastrotto is the inserts finishing team leader in the molds division of Husky Injection Molding Systems in Bolton, Ontario. You've read about Rob earlier in the text and the time, energy, and compassion he devotes to his team. But what happens if one of his team members doesn't hold up his or her side of the employment relationship?

"We abide by an honour code here. There's an open cash box in the cafeteria. No one punches cards. People leave their wallets on their desk sometimes." Rob works hard to ensure expectations are clear, everyone knows what is unacceptable, and there is a lot of feedback, on positive as well as negative performance. When people fail to live up to the trust shown them by the company, for example, by dishonestly entering their hours or leaving their shift without permission, Rob is "heavy on disciplining."

In dealing with discipline situations, Rob explains, "I'm acting as the company's agent but I'm also dealing with my own conscience." He believes that if guidelines, expectations, and consequences have been laid out, and each employee is both aware and capable of meeting them, then the employee deserves the consequences.

WHAT IS DISCIPLINE?

Discipline
Actions taken by supervisors to enforce an organization's standards and regulations.

What specifically do we mean when we use the term **discipline** in the workplace? It refers to actions taken by a supervisor to enforce the organization's standards and regulations. It generally follows a typical sequence of four steps: verbal warning, written warning, suspension, and dismissal (see Figure 14-1).

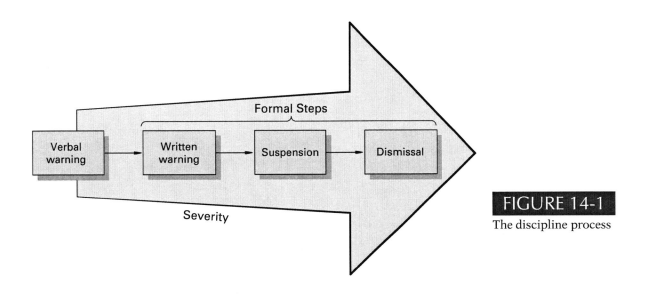

Formal Steps

Verbal warning → Written warning → Suspension → Dismissal

Severity

FIGURE 14-1

The discipline process

The mildest form of discipline is the **verbal warning**. A verbal warning is a temporary record of a reprimand, which is placed in the supervisor's file. This verbal warning typically states the purpose, date, and outcome of the feedback session with you. If the verbal warning is effective, no further disciplinary action is needed. However, if an employee fails to improve his or her performance, he or she will encounter more severe action—the written warning. The **written warning** is the first formal stage of the disciplinary procedure. This is because the written warning becomes part of an employee's official personnel file. In all other ways, however, the written warning is similar to the verbal warning. That is, the employee is advised in private of the violation, its effects, and potential consequences of future violations. Also, after a period of time if no further disciplinary problems arise, the warning is removed from the file.

A **suspension** or time off without pay may be the next disciplinary step, usually taken only if the prior two steps have not achieved the desired results—although exceptions do exist where suspension may be given without any prior verbal or written warning if the infraction is of a serious nature. Why would you suspend an employee? One reason is that a short lay-off, without pay, is potentially a rude awakening. It may convince the employee that you are serious, and may help him or her to fully understand and accept responsibility for following the organization's rules.

Your ultimate disciplinary punishment is terminating employment. While **dismissal** is often used for the most serious offences, it may be the only feasible alternative if your employee's behaviour seriously interferes with a department or the organization's operation.

Verbal warning
A temporary record of a reprimand, which is placed in the supervisor's file.

Written warning
The first formal stage of the disciplinary procedure; the warning becomes part of an employee's official personnel file.

Suspension
Time off without pay; this step is usually taken only if neither verbal nor written warnings have achieved desired results.

Dismissal
Termination of employment.

While many organizations may follow the process described above, recognize that it may be bypassed if an employee's behaviour is extreme. For example, stealing, or attacking another employee with intent to inflict serious harm, may result in immediate suspension or dismissal. Regardless of any action taken, however, discipline should be fair and consistent. That is, the punishment an employee receives should be appropriate to what he or she did, and others doing the same thing should be disciplined in a like manner.

TYPES OF DISCIPLINE PROBLEMS

With very little difficulty, we could list several dozen or more infractions that supervisors might believe require disciplinary action. For simplicity's sake, we have classified the more frequent violations into four categories: attendance, on-the-job behaviours, dishonesty, and outside activities.

ATTENDANCE

The most common disciplinary problems facing supervisors undoubtedly involve attendance. For instance, in a study of 200 organizations, 60 per cent of which employed over 1000 workers, absenteeism, tardiness, abuse of sick leave, and other aspects of attendance were rated as the foremost problems by 79 per cent of the respondents.[1] Importantly, attendance problems appear to be even more widespread than those related to productivity (carelessness in doing work, neglect of duty, and not following established procedures).

ON-THE-JOB BEHAVIOURS

This blanket label includes insubordination, horseplay, fighting, gambling, failure to use safety devices, carelessness, alcohol and drug abuse, and inappropriate use of e-mail (see Something to Think About).

DISHONESTY

Although it is not one of the more widespread employee problems confronting a supervisor, dishonesty has traditionally resulted in the most severe disciplinary actions. One study found that 90 per cent of surveyed organizations would discharge an employee for theft, even if it was only a first offence. Similarly, 88 per cent would discharge employees who were found to have falsified information on their employment applications.[2] These findings reflect the strong cultural norm against dishonesty in North America.

IMPROPER E-MAIL USE

In 1996 an Imperial Oil employee lost his job for misconduct involving sending racist and sexist e-mails on his computer at work.[3] The employee was aware of Imperial Oil's clear policy specifying that its e-mail system was to be used for business purposes only. The dismissal was upheld on appeal.

Six Canada Customs and Revenue Agency (formerly known as Revenue Canada) employees were given two-day suspensions for using the e-mail system to pass on offensive material. All government departments have been alerted to catch unauthorized use of its computers, partly because of the 1996 case where a civilian scientist working for the defence department was sentenced for downloading more than 20 000 images of child pornography and storing them in his office.[4]

Catching employees using the e-mail system improperly involves monitoring e-mail. This offends some people who believe that it is an invasion of privacy. When this has been contested, it has been lost. For example, in 1994 a B.C. arbitrator upheld the dismissal of a claims adjuster on the basis of initiating and engaging in offensive and insubordinate e-mail communication with coworkers over an extended period. The union argued that the e-mails were private but the arbitrator rejected this, asserting that the employer's e-mail system was not intended to be used for private, non-business-related communication. As it was the employer's property and to be used for business purposes only, there was not an expectation of personal privacy for employees.[5]

Disciplining for improper e-mail use is not easy, however. Dismissals have been overturned on the basis that there was no policy regarding e-mail use in the company, or there was no proof that the policy was known by the employee.[6] As with other disciplinary situations, there is a legal expectation that employees will be informed of what is considered unacceptable behaviour and the consequences for engaging in this behaviour. If they have not been informed, the policy is ambiguous, or it has not been applied consistently, then one must begin at the bottom of the progressive discipline ladder. It appears that all organizations are advised to create an e-mail policy to protect themselves.

How does one decide what is "improper" use of e-mail? Is it reasonable for a company to forbid use of e-mail for all non-business communications? What is an appropriate level of punishment if someone is caught?

Decision of Board of Referees re Imperial Oil dismissal
http://aix1.uottawa.ca/~geist/Bhamre.html

Ottawa Citizen article re suspension of Revenue Canada employees
www.ottawacitizen.com/national/990729/2661118.html

Ontario law firm devoted to labour and employment law
http://www.emond-harnden.com/apr00/camo.html

OpenDocument, Developing an E-Mail Policy for the Workplace
http://www.rdcounsel.com/RussDuMu/articles.nsf/

Article on "developing law of cyberspace in workplace in Canada," Quebec, U.S.
www.lapros.qc.ca/puba/cyber_work.html

OUTSIDE ACTIVITIES

Our final problem category covers activities that employees engage in outside of work, but which either affect their on-the-job performance or generally reflect negatively on the organization's image. Included here are unauthorized strike activity, outside criminal activities, and working for a competing organization.

DISCIPLINE ISN'T ALWAYS THE SOLUTION

Just because you have a problem with an employee, don't assume that discipline is the automatic answer. Before you consider disciplining an employee, be sure that the employee has both the ability and the influence to correct his or her behaviour.

If an employee doesn't have the ability—that is, he or she *can't* perform—disciplinary action is not the answer. Similarly, if there are external factors beyond the employee's control that block goal attainment—for example, inadequate equipment, disruptive colleagues, or excessive noise —discipline doesn't make much sense. If an employee *can* perform but won't, then disciplinary action is called for. However, ability problems should be responded to with solutions such as skill training, on-the-job coaching, job redesign, or a job transfer. Serious personal problems that interfere with work performance are typically best met with professional counselling or a medical referral. And, of course, if there are external obstacles in the employee's way, you should act to remove them. The point is that if the cause of an employee's problem is outside his or her control, then discipline is not the answer.

BASIC TENETS OF DISCIPLINE

Based on decades of experience, supervisors have learned what works best when administering discipline. In this section, we'll review some of the lessons learned. We'll present the basic groundwork that needs to be laid prior to any punitive action, the importance of making discipline progressive, and how the "hot stove" rule can guide your actions

LAY THE GROUNDWORK

Any disciplinary action you take should be perceived as fair and reasonable. This increases the likelihood that the employee will change his or her behaviour to align with the organization's standards, and also prevents unnecessary legal entanglements. The foundation of a fair and reasonable disciplinary climate is created by ensuring that employees are given adequate advance notice of disciplining rules and that a proper investigation precedes any action.

ADVANCE NOTICE

Employees have a right to know what is expected of them and the probable consequences should they fail to meet those expectations. They should also understand just how serious different types of offences are. This information can be communicated in employee handbooks, company newsletters, posted rules, or labour contracts. The fact that CP Rail had a message informing users about unauthorized use of the company's e-mail whenever users logged on was instrumental in upholding a dismissal for improper e-mail use.[7] It is always preferable to have these expectations in writing. This provides protection for you, the organization, and your employees.

PROPER INVESTIGATION

Fair treatment of employees demands that a proper investigation precede any decision. Employees should be treated as innocent until proven guilty. And importantly, no judgement should occur before all the relevant facts have been gathered.

As the employee's supervisor, you will typically be responsible for conducting the investigation. However, if the problem includes an interpersonal conflict between you and the employee, a neutral third party should be chosen to conduct the investigation.

The investigation should focus not only on the event that might lead to discipline but also on any related matters. This is important because these related concerns may reveal mitigating factors that will need to be considered. And, of course, the employee must be notified of the offence with which he or she is being charged so that a defence can be prepared. Remember, you have an obligation to listen objectively to the employee's interpretation and explanation of the offence. A fair and objective investigation will include identification and interviewing of any witnesses and documentation of all evidence that is uncovered.

Failure to conduct a full and impartial investigation can carry high costs. A good employee may be unjustly punished, the trust of other employees may be severely jeopardized, and you may place your organization under possible risk for financial damages should the employee file a suit.

MAKE DISCIPLINE PROGRESSIVE

Punishment should be applied in steps. That is, penalties should get progressively stronger if or when an offence is repeated. As outlined at the start of this chapter, progressive disciplinary action typically begins with a verbal warning, and then proceeds through written reprimands, suspension, and finally, in the most serious cases, dismissal (see Figure 14-1).

The logic underlying **progressive discipline** is twofold. First, stronger penalties for repeated offences discourage repetition. Second, progressive discipline is consistent with court and arbitration rulings that mitigating factors (such as length of service, past performance record, or ambiguous organizational policies) be considered when taking disciplinary action.

Progressive discipline
Penalties are made progressively stronger if, or when, an offence is repeated.

FOLLOW THE "HOT STOVE" RULE

"Hot stove" rule
Principles that can guide disciplining; the action should be immediate, offer advance warning, be consistent, and impartial.

The **"hot stove" rule** is a frequently cited set of principles that can guide you in effectively disciplining an employee.[8] The name comes from the similarities between touching a hot stove and administering discipline.

Both are painful, but the analogy goes further. When you touch a hot stove, you get an immediate response: the burn you receive is instantaneous, leaving no doubt in your mind about the cause and the effect. You have ample warning: you know in advance what happens if you touch a red-hot stove. Further, the result is consistent: every time you touch a hot stove, you get the same response—you get burned. Finally, the result is impartial. Regardless of who you are, if you touch a hot stove, you will be burned. The analogy with discipline should be apparent, but let's briefly expand on each of these four points because they are central tenets in developing your disciplining skills.

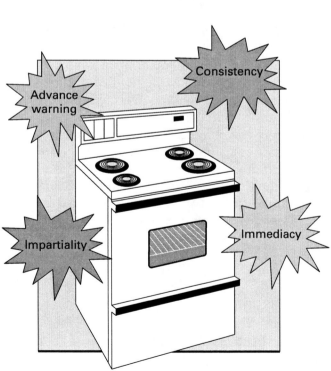

FIGURE 14-2

The "hot stove" rule

IMMEDIACY

The impact of a disciplinary action will be reduced as the time between the infraction and the penalty's implementation lengthens. The more quickly the discipline follows the offence, the more likely it is that the employee will associate the discipline with the offence rather than with you as the imposer of the discipline. Of course, the immediacy requirement should not result in undue haste. Fair and objective treatment should not be compromised for expediency.

ADVANCE WARNING

As we noted earlier, you have an obligation to give advance warning before initiating formal disciplinary action. This means the employee must be aware of the organization's rules and accept its standards of behaviour. Disciplinary action is more likely to be interpreted as fair by employees when they have received clear warning that a given violation will lead to discipline and when they know what that discipline will be.

CONSISTENCY

Fair treatment of employees demands that disciplinary action be consistent. If you enforce rule violations in an inconsistent manner, the rules will lose their impact. Morale will decline and employees will question your competence. Productivity will suffer as a result of employee insecurity and anxiety. Your employees will want to know the limits of permissible behaviour and they will look to your actions for guidance. If Hans is reprimanded today for an action he took last week, at which time nothing was said, these limits become blurry. Similarly, if Pooja and Nitu are both goofing around at their desks and only Pooja is reprimanded, Nitu is likely to question the fairness of the action. The point, then, is that discipline should be consistent. This need not result in treating everyone exactly alike, because that would mean ignoring mitigating circumstances. But it does put the responsibility on you to clearly justify disciplinary actions that may appear inconsistent to employees.

IMPARTIALITY

The last guideline that flows from the "hot stove" rule is to keep the discipline impartial. Penalties should be connected with a given violation, not with the personality of the violator. That is, discipline should be directed at what the employee has done, not at the employee. As a supervisor, you should make it clear that you are avoiding personal judgements about the employee's character. You are penalizing the rule violation, not the individual. And all employees committing the violation can be expected to be penalized. Further, once the penalty has been imposed, you must make every effort to forget the incident. You should attempt to treat the employee in the same manner you did prior to the infraction.

1. The first formal step in the discipline process is _____ .
   a. verbal warning
   b. written warning
   c. suspension
   d. dismissal
2. What is the purpose of suspension in the disciplinary process?
3. There are circumstances in which an employee's behaviour justifies immediate suspension or dismissal, bypassing the normal sequence of discipline. True or false?
4. Which one of the following statements would not indicate a need for discipline?
   a. attendance problems
   b. insubordination
   c. inability to do the job
   d. illegal strike activity

FACTORS TO CONSIDER IN DISCIPLINING

Defining what is "reasonable in relation to the offence" is one of the most challenging aspects of the discipline process. Why? Because infractions vary greatly in terms of severity. Suspending an employee is considerably more stringent than issuing a verbal warning. Similarly, the decision to fire someone—the organizational equivalent of the death penalty—is dramatically more punitive than a two-week suspension without pay. If you fail to recognize relevant extenuating factors and make the proper adjustments in the severity of penalties, you risk having your action perceived as being unfair. The following factors (summarized in Figure 14-3) should be taken into consideration when applying discipline:

1. **Seriousness of the problem.** How severe is the problem? Dishonesty, for example, is usually considered a more serious infraction than reporting to work 20 minutes late.

- Seriousness of the problem

- Duration of the problem

- Frequency and nature of the problem

- Employee's work history

- Extenuating circumstances

- Degree of warning

- History of the organization's discipline practices

- Implications for other employees

- Upper-management support

FIGURE 14-3

Relevant factors
determining the
severity of penalties

2. **Duration of the problem.** Have there been other discipline problems with this employee, and if so, over how long a time span? A first occurrence is usually viewed differently from a third or fourth offence.

3. **Frequency and nature of the problem.** Is the current problem part of an emerging or continuing pattern of discipline infractions? Continual infractions may require a different type of discipline from that applied to isolated instances of misconduct.

4. **Employee's work history.** How long has the employee worked for the organization, and what has been the quality of his or her performance? For many violations, the punishment will be less severe for those who have developed a strong track record.

5. **Extenuating circumstances.** Are there extenuating factors, such as influences outside the employee's control, that lessen the severity of the infraction? The employee who missed the plane for an important meeting because his wife went into labour with their first child is likely to have his violation assessed more leniently than would his peer who missed the same plane because he overslept.

6. **Degree of warning.** To what extent has the employee been previously warned about the offence? Did he or she know and understand the rule that was broken? As we have noted several times previously, discipline severity should reflect the degree of knowledge the violator holds of the organization's standards of acceptable behaviour. In addition, an organization that has formalized written rules governing employee conduct is more justified in aggressively enforcing violations than is an organization whose rules are informal or vague.

7. **History of the organization's discipline practices.** How have similar infractions been dealt with in the past within your department? Within the entire organization? Equitable treatment of employees must take into consideration precedents within the unit where the infraction occurs, as well as previous disciplinary actions taken in other units within the organization.

8. **Implications for other employees.** What impact will the discipline selected have on other workers in the unit? There is little point in taking a certain action against an employee if it will have a major dysfunctional effect on others within the unit. The result may be to convert a narrow and single disciplinary problem into a severe supervisory headache. Conversely, failure to impose discipline where it's justified can reduce departmental morale, undermine your credibility, and lessen employee concern for obeying the rules. For instance, more than 40 per cent of respondents to a survey felt their managers were too lenient with poor performers, which generated resentment among hard-working employees.[9]

9. **Upper-management support.** If a disciplined employee decides to appeal the case to a higher level of management, will you have reasonable evidence to justify your decision? If you have the data to support your action, can you count on your superiors backing you up? Your disciplinary actions aren't likely to carry much weight if violators believe that they can get your decision overridden.

DISCIPLINE AND THE LAW

Making a mistake when disciplining an employee can have very serious repercussions for an organization. As a result, most large organizations have specific procedures that supervisors are required to follow. Supervisors typically are provided training in how to handle the discipline process. Moreover, they are encouraged to work closely with staff specialists in the human resources department.

Most large corporations have specific rules to follow, including documentation and progressive steps, in cases that might lead to eventual dismissal. As a supervisor, it is your responsibility to defend your disciplinary actions. Proper documentation is the best protection against employees who claim, "I never knew there was any problem," or, "I was treated unfairly." In addition, you will want to obey **due process** when taking any disciplinary action. This includes:

Due process
Assuming an employee is innocent until proved otherwise; giving the employee the right to be heard; and invoking disciplinary action that is reasonable in relation to the offence involved.

1. a presumption of innocence until reasonable proof of an employee's role in an offence is substantiated;
2. the right of the employee to be heard, and in some cases to be represented by another person; and
3. discipline that is reasonable in relation to the offence involved.

Does the threat of legal action then prevent companies from letting employees go? Certainly not. In Canada, there are three basic ways to dismiss employees.

DISMISSAL WITH JUST CAUSE

These cases involve employees with documented offences such as disobedience of a lawful and reasonable order, gross negligence, or criminal activities. The supervisor must have documented proof of such offences.

DISMISSAL WITH REASONABLE NOTICE

An employee can be discharged, even if performance is entirely satisfactory, as long as reasonable notice is given. Provincial Employment Standards Acts and the federal Labour Code define the minimum notice periods. Since these regulations change frequently, supervisors need to take care to keep abreast of the legislative updates.

DISMISSAL WITH REASONABLE COMPENSATION

Again, a satisfactory employee might be let go immediately, with reasonable compensation in lieu of notice. Provincial and federal acts again outline the conditions of minimum compensation.

UNIONIZATION

What if your employees are unionized and are protected by a collective bargaining agreement? How does this affect the disciplinary process?

Where employees belong to a union, there will be a *collective bargaining agreement*. This agreement, among other things, will outline rules governing the behaviour of union members. It will also identify disciplinary procedures and clarify the steps members are to follow if they believe that they are receiving arbitrary or unfair treatment.

The collective bargaining agreement will typically define what represents a rule violation and what penalties are applicable. Keep in mind that the more serious actions - suspension or dismissal of an employee— usually can be expected to be vigorously opposed by both the employee and the union.

Most collective bargaining agreements

1. stipulate that employees can only be disciplined for "just cause";
2. provide a grievance procedure; and
3. afford opportunities for third-party review if employees believe they have been wronged.

Disciplining unionized employees, therefore, tends to be a more quasi-legal undertaking than disciplining nonunion employees. The bargaining contract, the existence of a grievance procedure, the right to have differences evaluated and resolved by a third party, and the whole quasi-legal labour-management relationship all act to reduce your authority as a supervisor in taking disciplinary action.

Union leaders tend to argue in favour of resolution of problems rather than discipline, except in the case of criminal actions by employees. Depending on the maturity of the workplace relationship, the union can play a role in helping to solve the problem. Many unions view discipline as a draconian system that represses the workers, and if coupled with a lean operating philosophy, discipline measures often come down hard on absenteeism. A real problem can develop if legitimate time off is challenged. Increased pressure is felt by all workers because those at work are expected to produce despite a workforce depleted by absent employees. Union members would prefer to look at resolving the bigger issue of what causes absenteeism than face discipline for days away from work.

POP QUIZ

Are You Comprehending What You're Reading?

5. Which one of the following is not a recommended guideline in administering discipline?
   a. Make it immediate
   b. Make it progressive
   c. Make it corrective
   d. Make it visible
6. What are the two keys to the groundwork of the discipline process?
7. It is sometimes necessary to discipline an employee in public—especially when that employee's inappropriate actions were witnessed by other employees in the department. True or False?
8. In Canada, the following are all bases for dismissal, except:
   a. dismissal with reasonable compensation.
   b. dismissal with reasonable notice.
   c. dismissal with just cause.
   d. dismissal with guaranteed rights.

DISCIPLINING

Let's translate what you've learned about disciplining into specific skills you can apply on the job. As we've done throughout this book, we'll begin by testing your current basic skill level.

ASSESSING YOURSELF: ARE YOU EFFECTIVE AT DISCIPLINING?

For each of the following statements, select the answer that best describes you. Remember to respond as you have behaved or would behave, not as you think you should behave. If you have no supervisory experience, answer the statements assuming you were a supervisor.

WHEN DISCIPLINING AN EMPLOYEE:	Usually	Sometimes	Seldom
1. I provide ample warning before taking formal action.	❑	❑	❑
2. I wait for a pattern of infractions before calling it to the employee's attention.	❑	❑	❑
3. Even after repeated offences, I prefer informal discussion about correcting the problem rather than formal disciplinary action.	❑	❑	❑
4. I delay confronting the employee about an infraction until his or her next performance-appraisal review.	❑	❑	❑
5. In discussing an infraction with the employee, my style and tone are serious.	❑	❑	❑
6. I explicitly seek to allow the employee to explain his or her position.	❑	❑	❑
7. I remain impartial in allocating punishment.	❑	❑	❑
8. I allocate stronger penalties for repeated offences.	❑	❑	❑

SCORING KEY AND INTERPRETATION

For questions 1, 5, 6, 7, and 8, give yourself three points for Usually, two points for Sometimes, and one point for Seldom.

For questions 2, 3, and 4, give yourself three points for Seldom, two points for Sometimes, and one point for Usually.

Total up your points. A score of 22 points or higher indicates excellent skills at disciplining. Scores in the 19 to 21 range suggest some deficiencies. Scores below nineteen indicate considerable room for improvement.

SKILL BASICS

The following dozen principles should guide you when you have to discipline an employee.

1. **Before you accuse anyone, do your homework.** What happened? If you didn't personally see the infraction, investigate and verify any accusations made by others. Was it completely the employee's fault? If not, who or what else was involved? Did the employee know and understand the rule or regulation that was broken? Document the facts: date, time, place, individuals involved, mitigating circumstances, and the like.

2. **Provide ample warning.** Before you take formal action, be sure you've provided the employee with reasonable previous warnings and that those warnings have been documented. Ask yourself: if challenged, will my action be defensible? Did I provide ample warning to the employee before taking formal action? It's very likely that applying stiffer punitive actions later on will be judged as unjust by the employee, an arbitrator, and the courts if it is determined that these punitive actions could not be readily anticipated by the employee. New supervisors, whose predecessors were lax on discipline, often move quickly to tighten discipline practices. Their frequent mistake is failing to provide adequate notice to employees of this change. In these cases, employees have a good basis for claiming arbitrary and discriminatory practices.

   The preliminary warning should typically be informal and of the verbal variety. That is, you point out the rule violation, the problem that this infraction has caused, what the correct behaviour should be, and the specific consequences if the infraction is repeated.

   It's a good idea to make a temporary record of this oral reprimand and place it in the employee's file. Once the employee has corrected the problem, the record of the reprimand can be removed.

Of course, if this warning is ineffective, you have documentation of your warning.

3. **Act in a timely fashion.** When you become aware of an infraction and it has been supported by your investigation, do something and do it quickly. Delay weakens the link between actions and consequences, sends the wrong message to others, undermines your credibility with your subordinates, creates doubt that any action will be taken, and invites repetition of the problem.

4. **Conduct the discipline session in private.** Praise employees in public but keep punishment private. Your objective is not to humiliate the violator. Public reprimands embarrass an employee and are unlikely to produce the change in behaviour you desire.

5. **Adopt a calm and serious tone.** Many interpersonal situations are facilitated by a loose, informal, and relaxed manner on the part of a supervisor. The idea in such situations is to put the employee at ease. Administering discipline is not one of those situations. Avoid anger or other emotional responses, and convey your comments in a calm and serious tone. But do not try to lessen the tension by cracking jokes or making small talk. Such actions are only likely to confuse the employee because they send out conflicting signals.

6. **Be specific about the problem.** When you sit down with the employee, indicate that you have documentation and be specific about the problem. Define the violation in exact terms instead of just citing company regulations or the union contract. Explain why the behaviour can't be continued by showing how it specifically affects the employee's job performance, the unit's effectiveness, and the employee's coworkers.

7. **Keep it impersonal.** Criticism should be focused on the employee's behaviour rather than on the individual personally. For instance, if an employee has been late for work several times, point out how this behaviour has increased the workload of others or has lowered departmental morale. Don't criticize the person for being thoughtless or irresponsible.

8. **Get the employee's side of the story.** Regardless of what your investigation has revealed, due process demands that you give the employee the opportunity to explain his or her position. From the employee's perspective, what happened? Why did it happen? What was his or her perception of the rules, regulations, and circumstances? If there are significant discrepancies between your version of the violation and the employee's, you may need to do more investigating. Of course, you'll want to document your employee's response for the record.

   Keep an open mind and use your active listening skills. It is possible that your initial information on the violation was biased or in error. Additionally, there might be extenuating circumstances of which you were unaware. The point is that you should not merely go through the motions to meet "due process" requirements; rather, you should solicit the employee's explanation to ensure that you have all the relevant facts.

9. **Keep control of the discussion.** In most interpersonal exchanges with employees, you want to encourage open dialogue. You want to give up control and create a climate of communication between equals. This won't work in administering discipline. Why? Violators are prone to use any leverage to put you on the defensive. In other words, if you don't take control, they will. Disciplining, by definition, is an authority-based act. You are enforcing the organization's standards and regulations. So take control. Ask the employee for his or her side of the story. Get the facts. But don't let the employee interrupt you or divert you from your objective.

10. **Agree on how mistakes can be prevented next time.**
    Disciplining should include guidance and direction for correcting the problem. Let the employee state what he or she plans to do in the future to ensure that the violation isn't repeated. For serious violations, have the employee draft a step-by-step plan to change the problem behaviour. Then set a timetable, with follow-up meetings in which progress can be evaluated. If the employee is genuinely unable to develop a satisfactory solution to the problem, you may be called upon to become a counsellor. You might need to help the employee understand the problem, identify courses of corrective action, assess the advantages and disadvantages of each, and plan a specific strategy for improving the situation. When the root of the problem is personal (relationships, children, financial, or the like) or has considerable emotional content, you may need to direct the employee to a professional counsellor.

11. **Select progressive disciplinary action and consider mitigating circumstances.** Choose a punishment that is appropriate to the crime. For the typical minor infraction, begin with a verbal warning, and then progress up the disciplinary chain. For more serious violations (for example, stealing, falsification of records, sabotage, gross insubordination, selling drugs at the work site, or attacking another employee with the intent to do serious harm) stronger punishments are justified from the outset. The punishment you select should be viewed as fair and consistent. But once you've arrived at your decision, tell the employee what the action will be, your reasons for taking it, and when it will be carried out.

12. **Fully document the disciplinary session.** To complete your disciplinary action, make sure that your ongoing documentation (what occurred, the results of your investigation, your initial warnings, the employee's explanation and responses, the discipline decision, and the consequences of further misconduct) is complete and accurate. This full documentation should be made part of the employee's permanent file. In addition, it's a good idea to give the employee a formal letter that highlights what was resolved during your discussion, specifics about the punishment, future expectations, and what actions you are prepared to take if the behaviour isn't corrected or the violation is repeated.

APPLYING YOUR SKILLS

Divide into groups of three or four and take turns being the observer and the two role players in the following four role-plays. Only read your role-play when it is your turn. The "supervisor" in each role-play is expected to handle the disciplinary situation using the guidelines described in the chapter.

1. WHAT A MESS!

BRIEFING FOR THE SUPERVISOR

You feel you must speak to one of your subordinates about her untidy work area. It is important that tools be put back where they belong, that only current projects be in the work area, and that nothing be misplaced such that it could cause a hazard (e.g., someone tripping over it). This

one employee is excellent at her job and you have no complaint with the quantity and quality of her work. But you are not pleased with how she keeps her work area. It is so messy that you suspect it slows her down looking for things and you are concerned about hazards. You have tried to make her aware of it with jokes but it obviously has not worked so you've decided you must have a meeting with her and make it official.

BRIEFING FOR THE SUBORDINATE

Your boss has asked to speak with you. It sounds serious. Usually the supervisor is a friendly person who jokes around but there was no joking this time. You don't know what it is about. You are a strong member of the supervisor's team, producing very good work, both in terms of speed and accuracy. You don't think there can be any complaint about your work. Occasionally you are a few minutes late getting back from break, and you're not the most organized person around. Your work area is not in good shape but you know where everything is. And it's just the way you work. Even your supervisor has made cracks about it. No, maybe it's about you not going out of your way to help the new guy. He's a pain, asking too many questions and not listening to the answers. Who knows what the supervisor wants? You'll just have to wait and see.

2. TIME IS MONEY

BRIEFING FOR THE SUPERVISOR

You have decided to speak to one of your subordinates about her very loose interpretation of the work schedule. This person has been arriving a few minutes late all week and leaving a few minutes early each shift. Normally, you don't even watch out for the exact moment your staff start and stop. After all, they're all reliable, good workers. And there hasn't been a problem recently with any of them. But one of the other workers made a comment about how this particular subordinate must be getting promoted to management because she seems to set her own clock. So you watched more closely and indeed this subordinate is taking advantage and working close to half an hour less than she should be. It is setting a bad example and needs to stop.

This person is normally one of your best workers. You don't know this person well because she is a very quiet, private person.

BRIEFING FOR THE SUBORDINATE

Your supervisor has asked to speak with you. You hope it is not a problem because you have enough to deal with these days. One of your children is very sick and, although your mother is staying at your home to help out, you are very concerned about your child and you know it's really too much for your mother. Plus, you have to take your child to various specialists' appointments and your mother can't drive. So you have been cutting time at work, coming in a little late and leaving a little early. You don't feel guilty because you have been taking a short lunch to make up some of the time. Plus, you've always been a very reliable worker. This is only a temporary problem, you hope.

You are not keen on discussing this matter with your supervisor as you consider it a private affair. It is up to you how much you will reveal.

3. FACE IT, IT'S OVER

BRIEFING FOR THE SUPERVISOR

One of your subordinates, a young woman, has just complained to you about another worker who also reports to you. She reported that he had grabbed her behind some packing boxes and tried to kiss her. She and he had previously dated but had parted over a year ago and, since then, she has become engaged to someone else. She has made it absolutely clear that she wants no personal relationship beyond work. She says he won't face that and she expects you to make sure he treats her with respect.

You are aware of their former relationship and you are also aware that he was very unhappy when they broke up. He hasn't dated since. You have asked him to come speak with you.

BRIEFING FOR THE SUBORDINATE

Your supervisor has just asked to speak with you. You aren't sure but you think it's about your former girlfriend since you just saw her leave the supervisor's office (you both work in the same company under the same supervisor). You did a stupid thing this morning. You ran into her accidentally in a packing area and decided on the spur of the moment to take advantage of the privacy. You grabbed her and tried to kiss her. She pulled away and left, telling you in no uncertain terms what she thought of you. The two of you split up over a year ago and she is now engaged to someone else. But you know her new relationship is a mistake and you really want her to give you another chance. It was not the best approach to take, you realize. Well, you hope your supervisor stays out of the situation because it is none of his business.

4. No, It's Not Private

BRIEFING FOR THE SUPERVISOR

You have just received some interesting information from a computer consultant who was hired by the company to set up some new policies and practices linked to the new programs. As part of his job, he does occasional audits of computer use by company personnel. He came to you to show you how one of your subordinates has been using his e-mail. This subordinate has been receiving and sending pornographic material, as well as receiving and sending a variety of jokes, some fairly mild, many seriously inappropriate. At the moment there is no policy regarding using e-mail for personal use. But, regardless, this is certainly using company property and time in an unacceptable way. You are shocked at this and must deal with the situation immediately. You have called the employee to your office.

BRIEFING FOR THE (male) SUBORDINATE

Your supervisor has just asked to speak with you. You don't know what it's about but you have a sick feeling in your stomach. You just saw the company's computer consultant leave the supervisor's office and you know that the consultant has been doing occasional audits of how company personnel are using the computer. You were praying he wouldn't check up on you. You do quite a bit of work on the computer but you also use it for a bit of fun. You have a group of friends who pass around material by e-mail. Some dirty jokes, a few pictures. Nothing too obscene. But the company may not be too happy about it.

SUMMARY

This summary is organized by the chapter Learning Objectives.

1. Discipline refers to actions taken to enforce the organization's rules and standards.
2. The most common disciplinary problems facing supervisors relate to attendance issues such as absenteeism, tardiness, and abuse of sick leaves. The other major types of discipline problems are on-the-job behaviours (including insubordination and substance abuse), dishonesty, and outside activities that affect on-the-job performance or reflect poorly on the organization.
3. The typical steps in progressive discipline are: 1. a verbal warning, 2. written reprimands, 3. suspension, 4. dismissal.
4. The "hot stove" rule states that discipline should be administered in the same way that people are burned by a hot stove. The response should be immediate; there should be a warning; the result should be consistent; and the result should be impartial.
5. Fairness demands that extenuating circumstances be considered before applying negative discipline. Factors such as the duration of the problem, the employee's work history, and past discipline practices in the organization are all legitimate factors that can influence the degree of disciplinary action.
6. The three methods of dismissal permitted by law are dismissal with just cause, dismissal with reasonable notice, and dismissal with reasonable compensation.
7. In disciplining unionized employees, the bargaining contract, the existence of a grievance procedure, the right to have differences evaluated and resolved by a third party, and the entire quasi-legal labour-management relationship all act to reduce a supervisor's range of discretion.

KEY TERMS AND CONCEPTS

Discipline
Dismissal
Due process
"Hot stove" rule

Progressive discipline
Suspension
Verbal warning
Written warning

REVIEWING YOUR KNOWLEDGE

1. "A good supervisor will never have to use discipline." Do you agree or disagree with this statement? Discuss.
2. Is punishment consistent with 1. having confidence in employees, 2. team work, and 3. empowerment? Discuss.
3. Why is it common for an organization to immediately dismiss a high-performing employee who lied about his educational qualifications on his application but take less harsh action against an average employee who misses a day of work to go fishing? Is this fair?
4. Why isn't discipline always the solution?
5. If you see a violation of an organizational rule by one of your employees with your own eyes, do you still need to investigate? Discuss.
6. Why is it so important to document, in writing, any disciplinary action you take against an employee?
7. What authority, if any, do you think human resource departments should have over a supervisor's disciplinary practices?
8. What should you do to follow due process when taking disciplinary action?

ANSWERS TO THE POP QUIZZES

1. **b. written warning.** This is the first formal step of the discipline process because it is the first step in which a record of the discipline is placed in the employee's personnel file. The first step of the discipline process, the verbal warning, results in documentation that is informally kept in the supervisor's file on the employee.

2. The purpose of a suspension—a short lay-off, typically without pay—is to create a rude awakening for the employee. It is designed to convince the employee that the supervisor is serious about the action being taken. Furthermore, it is designed to help the employee fully understand and accept responsibility for following the organization's rules.

3. **True.** Examples are stealing and attack with intent to seriously harm another employee.

4. **c. inability to do the job.** Lack of ability to do the job is not the same thing as a lack of desire to do it. Inability to do a job is best dealt with through training—not discipline.

5. **d. make it visible.** All discipline should be handled privately. It's a matter of respecting the individual, even though disciplinary action is taking place.

6. The keys to the discipline process are that the process be perceived as being both fair and reasonable.

7. **False.** All discipline should be conducted in private. The fact that the inappropriate behaviours were witnessed by other employees does not give the supervisor the freedom to discipline in public.

8. **d. dismissal with guaranteed rights.** The three acceptable approaches to dismissing employees are dismissal with just cause, dismissal with reasonable notice and dismissal with reasonable compensation.

CASE 14.A

Dealing with the Poor Performer Who Has Political Connections

"I had concerns about him even at the beginning but we needed to hire five part-time employees and there weren't a lot of applicants."

Anne Murphy, branch manager of a Mississauga library, went on to explain how her suspicions were confirmed and how she dealt with it.

"At the interview, he said he was available for any days, any hours. Then, when I phoned him back, it turned out he was not so available in that two evenings were impossible. We ended up hiring him anyway.

"He left early one day. Then he came in 15 minutes late the next shift and didn't speak to me about it. I confronted him privately, saying we needed to talk. He retorted that 15 minutes was no big deal, he just wouldn't take a break; he always did this at his other job. I responded by talking about the expectations of this job. I knew the other staff had noticed that he wasn't pulling his weight. I also knew he had important political connections through his family and had got away with similar behaviour in another job. But it was important to deal with him. I wouldn't not have had that conversation about expectations and consequences. He chose to go back to his old position. And I never got any flak."

RESPONDING TO THIS CASE

1. Why was Anne successful in handling this?

2. Why is it important to deal with poor performers early on?

3. The employee in this case seemed to enjoy a certain "immunity" from discipline and normal expectations in his other job. Other than family connections, what else can seem to give someone this kind of immunity? Why was Anne able to ignore this "immunity"? What is the impact on other employees if one seems to be treated as an exception?

4. Was Anne wrong to hire him when she had doubts?

CASE 14.B

Discipline in a Union Setting

In his many years of supervising in a unionized environment, Rod Guild has never had any grievances or problems regarding his handling of a disciplinary situation. Yet he has handled many situations of improper employee behaviour. What is his secret?

"I'm consistent. And I'm meticulous—I document everything. I document conversations under a person's name. I pay attention to what people do, I'm consistent in what I expect, and I deal with them in a nonthreatening way. I spend time and influence them in small steps. I start low key, assuming it's a problem of ability, not attitude. If the person does not come around after coaching and training, I start progressive discipline.

"I would advise a supervisor to document everything you can; do not assume it is trivial. I believe this is more important in a union environment because anything you do may be vigorously contested. As an example, I repeatedly spoke to a driller who was quitting too early. After several times, I asked him how many times I had told him this already. He figured a couple of times, so I pulled out my diary and showed him the dates and times. This really got his attention, especially when I told him that the next time we would be talking with the shop steward."

Rod is a senior foreman at Highland Valley Copper in B.C. A second "disciplinary" incident further illustrates Rod's style. "We used to have a female truck-driver. She was well liked but some guys took liberties. One night, when she came to work in a hockey jersey, one of them said, 'Is that hockey—or hooker?' I wasn't there but the incident was reported to me by someone else. In fact, when I investigated it, the woman involved didn't want it to be a big deal. I spoke to the guy who did it, told him his remark was inappropriate, and next time she may not be so forgiving. He said the remark didn't mean anything. I reminded him of a previous time when he had had problems with someone calling him names. As far as I know, he never made another inappropriate remark to the woman."

RESPONDING TO THIS CASE

1. Why would Rod give so many "reminders" before becoming "official" in his discipline?
2. Which disciplinary principles does Rod follow? Why has his approach to disciplining stood up well in a unionized environment?

15 THE SUPERVISOR'S ROLE IN EMPLOYEE RELATIONS

LEARNING OBJECTIVES

After reading this chapter, you should be able to:

1. Describe the current status of labour unions in Canada.
2. Explain the appeal of unions to employees.
3. Identify the legislation pertinent to employee relations.
4. Identify the primary purpose of collective bargaining.
5. Describe the supervisor's role in labour matters.
6. Discuss who a union steward is and what a supervisor's relations with this person should be.
7. Describe the steps for handling a grievance.

CHAPTER OUTLINE

PERFORMING EFFECTIVELY

WHAT IS EMPLOYEE RELATIONS?

A BASIC QUESTION: WHY WOULD EMPLOYEES JOIN A UNION?

LABOUR LEGISLATION YOU NEED TO KNOW ABOUT
    Federal and Provincial Labour Relations Acts
    The Charter of Rights and Freedoms

FROM CONFLICT TO COOPERATION

AN OVERVIEW OF THE COLLECTIVE BARGAINING PROCESS
    Pop Quiz
    Organization and Certification
    OK, The Union Won— What Now?
    Preparation for Negotiation
    Negotiation
    Contract Administration

THE SUPERVISOR'S ROLE IN LABOUR MATTERS
    Organizing Drives
    Negotiation
    Contract Administration
    Relations with the Union Steward
    When an Impasse is Reached

FROM CONCEPTS TO SKILLS: HANDLING GRIEVANCES
    Assessing Yourself: Are You an Effective Grievance-Handler?
    Skill Basics
    Applying Your Skills
    Pop Quiz

UNDERSTANDING THE BASICS
    Summary
    Key Terms and Concepts
    Reviewing Your Knowledge
    Answers to the Pop Quizzes

PERFORMING YOUR JOB
    Case 15.A: Three Different Supervisory Views on Unions
    Case 15.B: Making a Union Unnecessary

FIGURE 15-1

Graham Van Brunt

FIGURE 15-2

Rod Guild

Graham Van Brunt is the director of plant operations and maintenance at Churchill Falls Labrador Corporation (CFLC), a gigantic hydro facility located in Labrador. Churchill Falls is a company town—the community consists entirely of CFLC employees and their families. Employees are also unionized, however, which has interesting implications. "We went through a labour strike last year and you never want to do that in a small town. It is important to keep the union happy. You do that by working with them as closely as possible. Some management people don't like the union at their elbows watching them but that's the old way of thinking. I've seen things work much better if we keep the union involved. For example, now we have joint programs, like the safety program, to which both the union and management are committed.

"In day-to-day operations, there's nothing wrong with sitting down with the union and listening to what they have to say about the business. Keep them close. Keep the lines of communication open. Explain why you're making the decisions you're making. In most cases, it doesn't hurt to tell them what you're thinking. It saves a lot of grief in the long run."

Graham's emphasis on open communications is echoed by many other supervisors in unionized settings. The focus also appears to be on changing the labour/management relationship to a less adversarial and more cooperative one.

This change is illustrated by the relationship that Rod Guild, a mine foreman, has with his unionized workers. As you've read in previous chapters, he concentrates on maintaining respectful, positive relationships with the mine workers. Fairness and consistency are of prime importance to him. As a result, in 20 years in a unionized environment, he has had no problems. However, there are still frustrations for him. "Because of the union's emphasis on seniority, people don't always get the job on merit. Someone may move into a job because it pays better, and it's easier, but they are not interested in the job itself. As a result, I have to spend more time training and coaching. There is a general union protectionism that caters to the lowest common denominator. The standards must protect everyone and, since not everyone works at the same level or has the same motivation, the standards are low—essentially simply relying on passing probation and then seniority is the deciding factor."

As Rod describes, supervising unionized workers is different from supervising nonunionized employees. In this chapter, we'll discuss why employees join unions, review the key labour laws you need to know about, and then consider the role that supervisors play in labour matters.

WHAT IS EMPLOYEE RELATIONS?

Employee relations includes all the activities within a company that involve dealing with a union and its members. But what's a **union**? It's an organization that represents workers and seeks to protect their interests through collective bargaining.

In Canada, union membership comprises 32.2 per cent of the workforce. Membership varies greatly by industry and by sector—the public sector has 69.9 per cent unionization whereas the private sector has 18.9 per cent of its workforce unionized. The pattern of current membership also varies widely according to region:

Newfoundland	39.2% (the highest in Canada)
Quebec	36.1%
British Columbia	35%
Ontario	27.3%
Alberta	21.1% (the lowest in Canada)[1]

Union membership in the major industrialized countries, as a percentage of the civilian workforce, has been declining for many years. A number of factors have contributed to this decline. The economic sectors where union strength has traditionally been greatest—particularly blue-collar manufacturing jobs in the automobile, steel, rubber, and chemical industries—have significantly cut their North American workforces. Many of these jobs have been eliminated through automation or exported to countries with lower labour costs. The growth in the labour force since the late 1960s has been among women, professionals, government employees, and service workers—groups that have been more resistant to labour's effort to organize them. And, of course, unions have suffered directly as a result of their own success. Labour union growth in the 1930s and 1940s was largely a result of responding to the depressed status of the working class. But as unions succeeded in raising wages and improving working conditions, the reasons for their very existence became less obvious.

However, in many key industries, for instance, mining, construction, railways, and trucking, most workers are unionized. Most importantly, we can't overlook the **spillover effect**. Successes made by unions at the negotiating table spill over to influence the wages, working conditions, and terms of employment for workers who are not unionized (particularly in the same industry).

A BASIC QUESTION: WHY WOULD EMPLOYEES JOIN A UNION?

What do employees seek to gain when they join a union? The answer to this question varies with the individual and the union context, but the following captures the most common reasons.

Employee relations
All activities within a company that involve dealing with a union and its members.

Union
An organization that represents workers and seeks to protect their interests through collective bargaining.

Spillover effect
Successes made by unions at the negotiating table influence the wages, working conditions, and terms of employment for workers who are not unionized.

Canadian Labour Congress
www.clc-ctc.ca/

Ontario Federation of Labour
www.ofl-fto.on.ca/

HIGHER WAGES AND BENEFITS

There's power in numbers. As a result, unions are often able to obtain higher wages and benefit packages for their members than these employees would be able to negotiate individually. One or two employees walking off the job over a wage dispute is unlikely to significantly affect most businesses, but hundreds of workers going out on strike can temporarily disrupt or even close down a company. Additionally, professional bargainers employed by the union may be able to negotiate more skilfully than any individual could do on his or her own behalf.

GREATER JOB SECURITY

Unions provide members with a sense of independence from management's power to arbitrarily hire, promote, or fire. The collective bargaining contract will stipulate rules that apply to all members, thus providing fairer and more uniform treatment.

INCREASED OPPORTUNITIES TO INFLUENCE WORK RULES

Where a union exists, workers are provided with an opportunity to participate in determining the conditions under which they work, and an effective channel through which they can protest conditions they believe are unfair. Therefore, a union not only represents the worker but also provides rules that define channels through which complaints and concerns of workers can be registered. Grievance procedures and rights to third-party arbitration of disputes are examples of practices that are frequently defined and regulated as a result of union efforts.

COMPULSORY MEMBERSHIP

Union shop
A workplace where employees must join the union.

Agency shop
A workplace where employees do not have to join the union but must pay union dues if they want to keep their jobs.

Many labour agreements require that individuals must join the union (such a workplace is referred to as a **union shop**) or at least pay dues (an **agency shop**) if they want to keep their jobs. These requirements are typically imposed by the unions themselves on free riders (employees who gain the benefits of union membership without paying fees and dues).

UNHAPPINESS WITH A SUPERVISOR

Setting aside the other reasons why employees join a union, there appears to be one common factor—you, the supervisor. If employees are upset with the way you handle problems or the way you disciplined one of their co-workers, they are likely to seek help from a union. In fact, research has shown that when employees vote to unionize, it's often a vote against their immediate supervisor rather than a vote in support of a particular union.

LABOUR LEGISLATION YOU NEED TO KNOW ABOUT

Supervisors don't need to be labour lawyers to deal with legal issues surrounding union-management relations. But there are some basic laws with which you need to be familiar.

In Canada, there are three legislative areas that deal with the relationships among employees, unions and employers: the federal Labour Relations Act, provincial Labour Relations Acts, and the federal Charter of Rights and Freedoms. Again, as with other legislation, the jurisdiction will be largely determined by the nature of the company.

FEDERAL AND PROVINCIAL LABOUR RELATIONS ACTS

The labour relations acts set out the responsibilities and rights of employees and their unions, generally outlining the following issues:

- rules for starting a union
- rules for joining a union
- supporting or not supporting a union
- collective bargaining procedures
- administration of collective agreements
- unfair labour practices

These acts specifically prohibit employers from:

1. interfering with, restraining, or coercing employees in the exercise of the rights to join unions and bargain collectively
2. dominating or interfering with the formation or administration of any labour organization
3. discriminating against anyone because of union activity
4. discharging or otherwise discriminating against any employee because he or she filed charges or gave testimony under the act
5. refusing to bargain collectively with the representatives chosen by the employees

These acts also prohibit union actions that may not be in the best interests of the employees. Specifically, a union may not:

1. force an employee to bargain through it if the union is not the bargaining agent
2. participate or interfere with the administration of the company
3. attempt, at the workplace or during working hours, to persuade an employee to become a union member, except with the employer's consent

Ontario Labour Relations Board Guide to the Labour Relations Act
http://employers.gc.ca/

Newfoundland Labour Relations Act
www.gov.nf.ca/

Canada Labour Code
http://laws.justice.gc.ca/en/L-2/index.html

4. expel or suspend an employee from the union by applying union membership rules in a discriminatory manner
5. penalize a member for filing a complaint or testifying pursuant to the code

Each jurisdiction has a labour relations board that regulates the actions of both unions and companies, playing a role in settling disputes in contract administration and collective bargaining.

THE CHARTER OF RIGHTS AND FREEDOMS

The Charter of Rights and Freedoms, passed by the federal government in 1982, also influences the relationship between employees and their union representative. Any action that contravenes an individual's fundamental freedom can be challenged. For example, fundamental freedoms include freedom of religion; freedom of expression; freedom of association; freedom of peaceful assembly; and freedom of thought, belief and opinion. By joining a union, an employee does not surrender these fundamental freedoms guaranteed by the charter.

FROM CONFLICT TO COOPERATION

Historically, the relationship between labour and management was built on conflict. The interests of management and labour were seen as basically at odds; each treated the other as the enemy.

But times have changed. Management has become increasingly aware that successful efforts to increase productivity, improve quality, and lower costs require employee involvement and commitment. And labour unions have come to recognize that they can help their members more by cooperating with management than by fighting them.

Ironically, current labour laws, passed in an era of mistrust and antagonism between management and labour, have become barriers to these parties putting their differences aside and becoming cooperative partners.

AN OVERVIEW OF THE COLLECTIVE BARGAINING PROCESS

As a supervisor, you won't typically be directly involved in the collective bargaining process. You will, however, be affected by the process and outcome. The next section will describe things you can and cannot legally do

Are You Comprehending What You're Reading?

1. Which one of the following is not a reason for an individual to join a union?
   a. better wages and benefits
   b. good supervision
   c. compulsory union membership
   d. ability to influence work rules
2. Explain the spillover effect.
3. A union organizer's best weapon for convincing workers to join a union is poor supervision. True or false?
4. Rules for starting a union and for joining a union, collective bargaining procedures and unfair labour practices are set out in:
   a. the federal and provincial labour relations acts.
   b. the Charter of Rights and Freedoms.
   c. municipal bylaws.
   d. all of the above.

during the period when a union is attempting to organize employees in your company; it will also show how you play a major part in the administration of the final union contract. So you need a basic understanding of collective bargaining.

Collective bargaining is a process for negotiating a union contract and for administrating the contract after it has been negotiated (see Figure 15-3). The following discussion briefly summarizes how the process typically flows in the private sector.

ORGANIZATION AND CERTIFICATION

Efforts to organize a group of employees may begin when employee representatives ask union officials to visit the employees' organization and solicit members or when the union itself initiates a membership drive. Either way, the law requires that a union must secure signed authorization cards from a specified percentage of the employees it

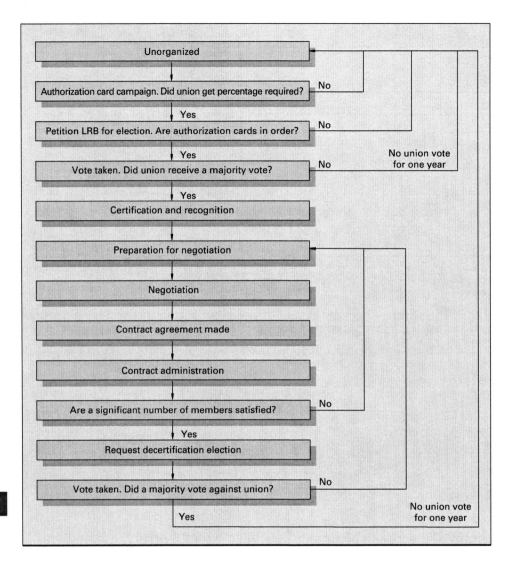

FIGURE 15-3

The collective bargaining process

desires to represent. If the percentage goal is achieved, either the union or management will file a petition with the Labour Relations Board (LRB), requesting a representation election. The percentage of employees needed to hold an election varies from a low of 35 per cent in Quebec to a high of 40 per cent in Ontario.

When the LRB receives the required number of authorization cards, it evaluates them, verifies that legal requirements have been satisfied, and then clarifies the appropriate **bargaining unit**; that is, it identifies which employees the union will represent if it wins the election.

A secret-ballot election is usually called within 25 days after the LRB receives the authorization cards. If the union gets a majority in this election, the LRB certifies the union and recognizes it as the exclusive bargaining representative for all employees within the specified

Bargaining unit
Identifies which employees the union will represent if it wins an election.

bargaining unit. Should the union fail to get a majority, another election cannot be held for one year.

Occasionally, employees become dissatisfied with a certified union. In such instances, employees may request a decertification election by the LRB. If a majority of the members vote for decertification, the union is out. However, recognize two things about decertification. First, most contracts forbid it during the contract's term. Second, union members cannot decertify today and bring in another union tomorrow. In most cases, at least one year must transpire between votes.

Ok, the Union Won—What Now?

After a union has been certified—meaning it won the election and was successful in organizing a group of workers—the collective bargaining process commences. **Collective bargaining** is a process for negotiating a union contract and for administering the contract after it has been negotiated. It includes preparing to negotiate, the actual contract negotiations, and administering the contract after it has been ratified.

The people who do the negotiating for both the union and the company are referred to as the negotiations teams. The company's representatives will often depend on the size of the organization. In a small firm, for instance, bargaining is probably done by the president—and probably some other staff the president feels are necessary participants. In larger organizations, there is usually an industrial relations expert. In such cases, you can expect the company to be represented by the senior official for industrial relations, other company executives, and company lawyers—with support provided by legal and economic specialists in wage and salary administration, labour law, benefits, and so forth.

On the union side, you typically can expect to see a bargaining team made up of an officer of the local union, local shop stewards, and some representation from the union. Again, as with the company, representation is modified to reflect the size of the bargaining unit. If negotiations involve a contract that will cover many employees at company locations throughout Canada, the team will be dominated by several union officers, with a strong supporting cast of economic and legal experts employed by the union. In a small firm or for local negotiations covering special issues at the plant level for a nationwide organization, bargaining representatives for the union might be the local officers and a few specially elected committee members.

Collective bargaining
A process for negotiating a union contract and for administrating the contract after it has been negotiated. It includes preparing to negotiate, the actual contract negotiations, and administering the contract after it has been ratified.

Preparation for Negotiation

Once a union has been certified, management will begin preparing for negotiations. It will gather information on the economy, copies of recently negotiated contracts between other unions and employers, cost-of-living data, labour market statistics, and similar external factors. It will also gather internal information on complaints and accident records, employee performance reports, and overtime figures.

This information will tell management their organization's current labour-performance status, what similar organizations are doing, and what it can anticipate from the economy in the near term. Management then uses these data to determine what it can expect to achieve in the negotiation. What can it expect the union to ask for? What is management prepared to give?

NEGOTIATION

Negotiation customarily begins when the union delivers a list of demands to management. These are typically ambitious in order to create room for trading in the later stages of negotiation. Not surprisingly, management's initial response may be to counter by offering little more than the terms of the previous contract or, in an increasing number of cases, to even propose reductions in current wages, benefits, and previously agreed-to conditions.

These introductory proposals usually initiate a period of long and intense bargaining. Compromises are made, and after an oral agreement is achieved, it is converted into a written contract. Finally, negotiation concludes with the union's representatives submitting the contract to its members for ratification.

CONTRACT ADMINISTRATION

Once a contract is agreed upon and ratified, it must be administered. The way in which it will be administered is specified in the contract itself.

Probably the most important element of contract administration—particularly in terms of the supervisor's job—has to do with the spelling out of a procedure for handling contractual disputes. Almost all collective bargaining agreements contain formal procedures for resolving grievances over the interpretation and application of the contract.

THE SUPERVISOR'S ROLE IN LABOUR MATTERS

Now let's turn our attention to the various demands placed on supervisors as a result of labour-management relations.

ORGANIZING DRIVES

If your employees aren't currently unionized, you may experience a union organizing drive. If that happens, be very careful about what you say and do. For example, the law is clear in stating that you can't threaten or intimidate employees in order to get them to vote against the union.

Because supervisors are the closest level of management to the workers, you represent the best source of information about intentions and actions. So pay attention. If you see that union-organizing activities are taking place among employees, report your observations to your boss or to the human resources department. Early detection can allow your company to plan a proper response.

Figure 15-4 provides a list of guidelines to lessen the likelihood that you'll break the law or hinder your company's response to the union's organizing effort. You are free to express your views and opinions about unions to your employees. But the law forbids you from interfering in your employee's right to choose a union to represent them. And because the line is often vague about where your free speech becomes interference, you must be cautious.

- If your employees ask for your opinion on unionization, respond in a neutral manner. For example, "I really have no position on the issue. Do what you think is best."

- You can prohibit union organizing activities in your workplace during work hours only if they interfere with work operations.

- You can prohibit outside union organizers from distributing union information in the workplace.

- Employees have the right to distribute union information to other employees during break and lunch periods.

- Don't question employees publicly or privately about union-organizing activities. For example, "Are you planning to go to that union rally this weekend?" But if an employee freely tells you about the activities, you may listen.

- Don't spy on employees' union activities, for example, by standing in the lunchroom to see who is distributing pro-union literature.

- Don't make any threats or promises that are related to the possibility of unionization. For example, "If this union effort succeeds, upper management is seriously thinking about closing down this plant. But if it's defeated, they plan to push through an immediate wage increase."

- Don't discriminate against any employee who is involved in the unionization effort.

- Be on the lookout for efforts by the union to coerce employees to join its ranks. This is illegal. If you see this occurring, report it to your boss or the human resources department. Your company may want to file a complaint against the union with the LRB.

FIGURE 15-4

Supervisory guidelines during a union organizing drive

NEGOTIATION

Supervisors typically play a minor part in the actual negotiation of the contract. Basic responsibility for this activity lies with specialists in the human resource department and top management.

The supervisor's role during the negotiation period tends to be limited to that of a resource person. You may be called upon to provide your organization's negotiators with departmental information on past problems with work-shift schedules, seniority rights, transfers, discipline, or ambiguous terminology in the current contract. This suggests that it's important for you to keep careful records of labour problems you experience during the current contract period so that these problems can be addressed during the next contract negotiation.

CONTRACT ADMINISTRATION

Once a formal agreement is in place, you must manage your department within the framework established by that contract. This means that you must fully understand all the "fine print" in the contract—and you need to make sure departmental members have the contract information, too.

Large and small organizations alike will hold supervisory training sessions and meetings to help you understand the contract and to clarify new provisions. You'll be given a copy of the agreement to study, an opportunity to get questions answered, and procedures to follow when problems arise.

Why do organizations place so much emphasis on ensuring that supervisors know and understand the contract? Because supervisors are the primary link between management and the employees. For the typical unionized employee, the supervisor is his or her sole contact with management. What supervisors say and do, then, largely determines the labour-management climate in the organization. If you misinterpret a contract provision, treat an employee unfairly, or engage in a similar contract violation, the consequences for you and the company might be immediate, or they might be postponed until the next negotiation. The union's representatives will keep track of these incidents and they'll use them to help win concessions in the next contract.

Keep in mind that working under a labour contract and supervising unionized employees does not take away your rights to make decisions or manage your people. What it does is spell out limitations to your authority and establish procedures for employees to challenge any action you take that they see as a violation of the labour agreement. So, for instance, you can still assign work schedules, make job transfers, and discipline problem employees—but you must do so within the framework defined in the labour contract.

Remember, too, that the labour contract is a bilateral agreement. It also specifies responsibilities for employees, and procedures you can take when employees fail to comply with provisions in the contract. So the labour agreement constrains employees as well as management.

Depending on the relationship that has been built between the supervisor and workers, a looser interpretation of the contract can lead to agreement in solving day-to-day problems.

RELATIONS WITH THE UNION STEWARD

The **union steward** in your department is essentially to the union what you are to the company. Just as you're there to protect the rights of management, he or she is an employee who is the elected representative of the employees in your work unit, and is there to protect the rights of the union members.

What authority does a union steward have in running your department? Very little to none! The steward cannot tell you or any employee what to do. The only authority stewards have is to give advice. They can offer advice to you and employees as to their understanding of how the contract limits your actions.

Just because union stewards have limited formal authority doesn't mean they can't be troublesome. Poor relations with your steward are likely to result in increased challenges to your actions and increased grievance filings. So getting along with your union steward tends to make your life at work a lot more pleasant.

The role of steward comes with certain expectations from employees. The steward is their representative. He or she is elected to protect their rights. You have to expect the steward's loyalties to lie with the union members. That doesn't mean, however, that you can't attempt to minimize hostilities with your steward. The best means for developing a cooperative relationship is to show respect for the steward and to keep him or her informed of problems you're having and of any changes that will affect the people in your department. A good supervisor-steward relationship can allow problems to be resolved quickly in the department and avoid the stress and cost associated with a lengthy dispute.

> **Union steward**
> An employee who is the elected representative of the employees in a work unit, and is there to protect the rights of the union members.

WHEN AN IMPASSE IS REACHED

Sometimes representatives of management and labour cannot reach an agreement on a new contract. When this happens, the union may choose to call a **strike**. In a strike, employees leave their jobs and refuse to come to work until a contract has been signed. Realize, too, that there's a company equivalent to a strike. It's called a **lockout**. That is when management denies unionized employees access to their jobs.

Historically, the strike was a potent weapon. By withholding labour, the union could impose financial hardships on an employer. However, beginning in the early 1980s, strikes began to lose much of their potency.

> **Strike**
> A situation in which employees leave their jobs and refuse to come to work until a contract has been signed.
>
> **Lockout**
> A company action equivalent to a strike; occurs when management denies unionized employees access to their jobs.

For one thing, public sentiment supporting their use by unions has declined. As well, employers in some provinces are allowed to hire replacement workers during a strike, which tends to nullify the impact. Replacement workers are currently banned in Quebec, British Columbia, and Ontario.

When labour and management cannot reach a satisfactory agreement themselves, they may need the assistance of an objective third-party individual. This assistance comes in the form of conciliation and mediation, fact-finding, or interest arbitration.

Conciliation and **mediation** are two very closely related impasse resolution techniques. Both are techniques whereby a neutral third party attempts to get labour and management to resolve their differences. Under conciliation, the role of the third party is to keep the negotiations ongoing. In other words, this individual is a go-between—advocating a voluntary means through which both sides can continue negotiating. Mediation goes one step further. The mediator attempts to pull together the common ground that exists and make settlement recommendations for overcoming the barriers that exist between the two sides. A mediator's suggestions, however, are only advisory. That means that the suggestions are not binding on either party.

Fact-finding is a technique whereby a neutral third-party individual conducts a hearing to gather evidence from both labour and management. The fact-finder then renders a decision as to how he or she views an appropriate settlement. Similar to mediation, the fact-finder's recommendations are only suggestions—they, too, are not binding on either party.

The final impasse resolution technique is called **interest arbitration**. Under interest arbitration, generally a panel of three individuals—one neutral and one each from the union and management—hears testimony from both sides. After the hearing, the panel renders a decision on how to settle the current contract negotiation dispute. If all three members of the panel are unanimous in their decision, that decision may be binding on both parties. Interest arbitration is found more frequently in public-sector collective bargaining; its use in private-sector labour disputes is rare.

There is little you can do to directly resolve a strike. However, if your employees go out on strike, you may be called upon to assume an increased number of nonsupervisory tasks in order to keep the business going. Or if management decides to replace striking workers, you will have to train and orient the new employees.

A more troublesome situation for supervisors is the **wildcat strike**. This is an illegal strike where employees refuse to work during the term of a binding contract. Such strikes can be brought about by a number of factors, but they usually involve ambiguities in the current contract. For instance, employee concerns over management's right to contract out some assembly work has resulted in wildcat strikes at several electronic-component manufacturers. The key point to remember is that wildcat strikes are illegal. Grievance procedures exist precisely to settle such dif-

Conciliation
An impasse-resolution technique in which a third party acts as a go-between with the aim of keeping negotiations ongoing.

Mediation
An impasse-resolution technique in which a mediator attempts to pull together the common ground that exists and make settlement recommendations for overcoming the barriers that exist between the two sides in a conflict.

Fact-finding
A technique whereby a neutral third-party individual conducts a hearing to gather evidence from both labour and management.

Interest arbitration
Arbitration in which a panel of three individuals hears testimony from both sides and renders a decision on how to settle the current contract negotiation dispute.

Wildcat strike
An illegal strike where employees refuse to work during the term of a binding contract, often due to ambiguities in the current contract.

ferences. Should you find yourself in the middle of a wildcat strike, Figure 15-5 provides you with some guidelines to follow.

When the Canada Labour Relations Board ruled that Royal Oak Mines in Yellowknife had acted in bad faith, the final chapter in one of Canada's most bitter labour disputes was written.

The management of Royal Oak Mines was ruled to have encouraged a union raid, with the apparent aim of getting a rival union to take over. This would have eliminated the need to negotiate with the original union, which had been a tough adversary. The Board ruled that negotiations were to resume with the original union. In this famous case, the relationship between Royal Oak and the union deteriorated to the point that nine men (strikebreakers) were killed while working the mine. A union member who was out on strike was charged in their deaths.

- Stay on the job.
- Notify higher management by telephone or messenger.
- Carefully record the events as they happen.
- Pay strict attention to who the leaders are and record their behaviour.
- Record any lack of action by union officials.
- Report all information as fully and as soon as possible to higher management.
- Encourage employees to go back to work.
- Ask union officials to instruct employees to go back to work.
- Don't discuss the cause of the strike.
- Don't make any agreements or say anything that might imply permission to leave work.
- Make it clear that management will discuss the issue when all of the employees are back at work.

FIGURE 15-5

Supervisory guidelines for handling wildcat strikes. (*Source:* L. W. Rue and L. L. Byars, *Supervision: Key Link to Productivity*, 4th ed., Homewood, IL: Richard D. Irwin, 1993, p. 325. With permission.)

HANDLING GRIEVANCES

We've used the term grievance at several points in this chapter to refer to a dispute. But how does a supervisor go about handling a grievance? Of all the activities that supervisors of unionized employees get involved in, none are more important than the handling of grievances. In this section, we'll help you develop your grievance-handling skills.

ASSESSING YOURSELF: ARE YOU AN EFFECTIVE GRIEVANCE-HANDLER?

Answer each of the following questions as you have or would behave, not as you think you *should* behave.

	Strongly Agree	Agree	Undecided	Disagree	Strongly Disagree
1. If an employee has a grievance, the first thing I do is review the relevant clause in the union contract.	❏	❏	❏	❏	❏
2. As soon as an employee informs me of a grievance, to avoid escalation I specifically provide him or her with management's side of the story.	❏	❏	❏	❏	❏
3. If I'm unsure about wording or an interpretation in the contract, I contact a labour specialist in the organization for counsel.	❏	❏	❏	❏	❏
4. I make sure I get all the facts pertinent to the dispute, regardless of how much time it may take.	❏	❏	❏	❏	❏
5. I avoid letting personalities or personal preferences influence my decision on a grievance.	❏	❏	❏	❏	❏
6. If a grievance has merit, I assume I have the authority to take immediate corrective action.	❏	❏	❏	❏	❏
7. I keep comprehensive records on every grievance in expectation that my decision will be appealed.	❏	❏	❏	❏	❏

SCORING DIRECTIONS AND KEY

For questions 3, 5, and 7, give yourself five points for Strongly Agree, four points for Agree, three points for Undecided, two points for Disagree, and one point for Strongly Disagree. For questions 1, 2, 4, and 6, reverse the scoring (for example, one point for Strongly Agree). Add up your total score. The range will be between 7 and 35. Scores of 30 and above indicate good grievance-handling skills. Scores of 25 to 29 indicate room for improvement. Scores of less than 25 suggest a strong need to work on these skills.

SKILL BASICS

Almost all collective bargaining agreements contain formal procedures to be used in resolving disputes surrounding the interpretation and application of the contract. These procedures are typically designed to resolve disputes as quickly as possible and at the lowest level in the organization. Whenever possible, then, the supervisor is encouraged to resolve employee grievances without involving upper levels of management and senior union officials.

Consistent with this belief that grievances should be handled at the lowest level possible in the organization, the typical grievance procedure looks like Figure 15-6. An employee's first efforts should be directed at attempting to resolve the complaint with his or her immediate supervisor.

If dissatisfied with the supervisor's response, the grievance typically escalates through the following stages: the supervisor and union steward discuss the complaint; the supervisor and a labour specialist from the human resources department discuss the complaint with the chief union steward or union grievance committee; the facilities manager and the labour specialist meet with the union grievance committee; the organization's top management meet with the union grievance committee and a representative of the national union to try to work out a solution. If the grievance still cannot be resolved, the dispute will be referred to an impartial third-party **arbitrator** who will hear the case and make a ruling. In practice, 98 percent of all collective bargaining agreements provide for arbitration as the final step in an impasse. Grievance arbitration usually focuses on one of two issues—contract interpretation and discipline and discharge. The party claiming that the contract language has been improperly interpreted has the burden of going forward in presenting its case. In discipline and discharge cases, because the action was initiated

Arbitrator
An impartial third party who hears grievances and makes rulings on them.

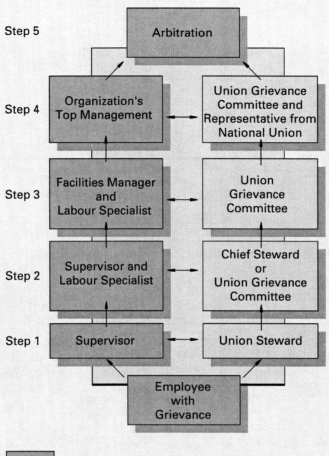

Step 5 — Arbitration

Step 4 — Organization's Top Management — Union Grievance Committee and Representative from National Union

Step 3 — Facilities Manager and Labour Specialist — Union Grievance Committee

Step 2 — Supervisor and Labour Specialist — Chief Steward or Union Grievance Committee

Step 1 — Supervisor — Union Steward

Employee with Grievance

FIGURE 15-6

Typical grievance procedure

☐ Management representatives

☐ Union representatives

by the company, the company officials have the burden of showing that they had just cause. As for who pays the arbitrator, it's often dependent on who's raising the issue. More often, though, the labour agreement will stipulate who pays, or how the costs of arbitration will be divided.

The previous steps describe the overall grievance procedure. But our concern is in building supervisory skills. So we need to address a more specific question: how should you, as a supervisor, respond if an employee or union steward presents a formal grievance? We suggest you do the following:

1. **Listen to the employee's complaint.** Don't be defensive and don't take the complaint personally. Employees regularly have grievances and you're the first contact point in the process that represents the organization.

   - Calmly listen to the employee's complaint. Keep an open mind.
   - Very importantly at this stage, don't argue with the employee. What you want to do is gain understanding.
   - Using your active listening skills will help you better understand the employee's complaint. Additionally, hostilities and tensions are likely to become subdued as you honestly demonstrate your willingness to understand the grievance.
   - Ask questions to make sure you get to the real problem. Is the employee complaining about unfair allocation of overtime when the real issue is that the employee is having serious personal financial problems and was counting on lots of overtime to help pay bills? You want to make sure you fully understand the details of the grievance and what specific provision of the labour contract the employee believes is involved.

2. **Investigate to get the facts.** You want to separate facts from opinions. Are the facts, as presented by the employee, complete and factual? Interview any key people who may be able to verify the employee's claims. Review all pertinent documents. Go over the clauses in the labour contract that apply to the employee's complaint. If you're unsure about the contract's language or how a relevant clause should be interpreted, get counsel from a labour specialist in your human resources department.

3. **Make your decision and explain it clearly.** You need to complete your investigation promptly so you can reach your decision in a relatively short period of time. Why? Because most labour agreements specify a definite time period within which a grievance must be answered.

   - If you determine that the grievance is unfounded, verbally give the employee and union steward your interpretation. Be sure to back up your decision with specific reasons for denying the grievance, citing evidence from your investigation and/or language from the contract. You should then follow up the verbal answer with a written response.
   - If the grievance has merit, provide a written response to the employee and union steward stating this fact. Additionally, you

should describe the corrective action you plan to take. But before you write this response, be sure that your remedy is consistent with established practices, doesn't set any new precedents, and is within your authority. When in doubt, get approval from your boss or a manager in human resources. You should be very careful about making individual exceptions to past practices. This might seem like an easy way to make the grievance disappear, but you could end up setting a precedent that might seriously hurt the organization in future contract negotiations or in future arbitration decisions.

4. **Keep records and documents.** It's important to document everything you do relating to a grievance. Remember that the labour agreement is a binding, legal contract. As such, formality is important. You have to follow the language of the contract. To protect yourself and the organization against charges that you have not followed the contract as intended, you must keep all the records that you've accumulated on every grievance.

5. **Be prepared for appeals.** If you rule against the employee, you should expect the employee or the union steward to appeal your decision to a higher level. Be prepared to be questioned by union officials and various labour specialists from your organization's human resource group. Don't let this shake you. And don't let an employee or union representative's threat of appeal influence your decision.

The grievance procedure is essentially a formal appeals system. It is designed to protect an employee's rights. Your judgement may be overruled at a higher level. But that's OK. If you've followed the contract's procedures, made your decision in good faith, and carefully documented your actions, you've correctly fulfilled your obligations in the grievance procedure.

PREVENTING GRIEVANCES

"Keep your nose clean. If you are going to be at an employee's machine, make sure you have a valid reason for doing it. You have to watch how you deal with reprimands. You must follow the book. For example, you must go by the progressive discipline procedure and not play favourites with anyone," says Tina Payton, prepress supervisor at Robinson-Blackmore, a printing company in St. John's, Newfoundland.

"Treat employees fairly. Make the limits clear. And recognize that you'll never make everyone happy," comments Larry Bowzeylo, Operations Integration Manager for Suncor in Fort McMurray, Alberta.

"If you follow the appropriate steps in disciplining someone, the union can't do anything. And if you treat people with respect and integrity, so they know you're fair and won't backstab anybody, you'll be fine," adds Paula Aylward, a shift manager at Cavendish Farms in PEI.

"Be very honest and forthright with the shop steward. Let them know if there's a concern. For example, if there's an incident where I have to speak to the cook about yelling and swearing, I will invite the shop steward to be there, even though it is not necessary. Be fair and make sure everyone understands what's on the table. Show respect regardless of what's happening. Be diplomatic; people can get heated and emotional," says Tricia Mah, director of support services at a large Vancouver nursing home.

APPLYING YOUR SKILLS

Break the class into groups of three. This role-play requires one person to play the role of the supervisor (Alex), another the role of the employee (Pat), and the third will play the union steward (C.J.).

All players should read the following scenario and the excerpt from the union's contract. Then you are to role-play a meeting in Alex's office. This role play should take no more than 15 minutes.

SCENARIO

The head of security guards has recently been focusing attention on the possession of drugs at the company's workplace. One morning last week, the guard suspected the possession of a controlled substance by an employee, Pat Davis. The guard, noticing Pat placing a bag in his/her personal locker, searched the locker for drugs. The guard found a variety of pills, some of which he thought were non-prescription amphetamines.

As Pat was leaving work for the day, the security guard stopped him/her and asked Pat to empty the contents of the bag. Pat was not told why the request was being made. Pat refused to honour the request, stormed out the door, and left the company premises. Pat was informed the next morning that he/she was being terminated for refusing to obey the legitimate order of a plant security guard.

Alex has just gone into a meeting with Pat and C.J. Alex wishes to enforce management's decision to terminate Pat, and justify the reason for it. C.J. and Pat, on the other hand, claim this action is a violation of the contract.

RELEVANT CONTRACT LANGUAGE

The following is extracted from the union-management contract.

An employee who fails to maintain proper standards of conduct at all times, or who violates any of the following rules, shall subject him- or herself to disciplinary action:

Rule 4. Bringing illegal substances or intoxicating liquors onto company premises, using or possessing these on company property, or reporting to work under the influence is strictly prohibited.

Rule 11. Refusal to follow supervisory orders, or in any way act insubordinate to any management agent, is strictly prohibited.

5. Which one of the following is not part of the collective bargaining process?
   a. interpretation of a written agreement
   b. negotiation of a written agreement
   c. approval of a written agreement by the LRB
   d. administration of a written agreement

6. Bargaining in good faith means that the company and labour union must negotiate until they've reached an agreement acceptable to both parties. True or false?

7. Explain what is meant by the terms conciliation, mediation, and fact-finding. When are any of the three used?

8. The procedure used in resolving disputes surrounding the interpretation and application of the contract is called _____.
   a. the grievance procedure
   b. interest arbitration
   c. a strike or a lockout
   d. none of the above

UNDERSTANDING THE BASICS

SUMMARY

This summary is organized by the Learning Objectives.

1. Union membership has been gradually declining but still remains high in the public sector. But this decline should not be interpreted as implying that labour union influence is low. Labour unions still represent the majority of workers in many key industries. Additionally, wages and benefits won by labour unions typically spill over to influence the wages and benefits of nonunionized employees.

2. Unions are appealing to employees because their power offers the promise of higher wages and benefits, greater job security, and increased opportunities to influence work rules.

3. The federal Canada Labour Code and provincial labour relations acts provide guidelines for both companies and unions. The Charter of Rights and Freedoms further protects all individual rights of every Canadian.

4. The primary purpose of collective bargaining is to negotiate a union contract and spell out the terms for administering that contract.

5. The supervisor plays a very important role in contract administration. He or she needs to know the details of the contract in order to interpret it and carry out its procedures. What supervisors say and do largely determines the labour-management climate in the organization.

6. A union steward is the elected representative of the employees in a work unit and is there to protect the rights of union members. Ideally, the relationship between the union steward and supervisor should be a cooperative one. The supervisor should share information regarding changes coming in the unit and keep the steward informed regarding any problems, for example, having given verbal warnings to an employee repeatedly regarding lateness.

7. The steps involved in handling a grievance are: 1. listen to the employee's complaint; 2. investigate to get the facts; 3. make your decision and explain it clearly; 4. keep records and documents; and 5. be prepared for appeals.

UNDERSTANDING THE BASICS

KEY TERMS AND CONCEPTS

Agency shop

Arbitrator

Bargaining unit

Collective bargaining

Conciliation

Employee relations

Fact-finding

Interest arbitration

Lockout

Mediation

Spillover effect

Strike

Union

Union shop

Union steward

Wildcat strike

REVIEWING YOUR KNOWLEDGE

1. What might explain the decline in union membership over the past 40 years?
2. Contrast agency and union shops.
3. How are labour issues influenced by legislation?
4. Describe the supervisor's role in the collective bargaining process.
5. "An employer might not want to stifle a union organizing effort. In fact, an employer might want to encourage his employees to join a union." Do you agree or disagree with this statement? Discuss.
6. What is collective bargaining?
7. What is the purpose of a grievance procedure? Describe the typical steps in the grievance process.
8. "You can predict strikes. Union administrators have to call a strike every now and then just to demonstrate to their membership that they're fighting hard for them." Do you agree or disagree with this statement? Explain.
9. How would the existence of a union and a collective bargaining contract affect a) employee recruitment and selection, b) compensation, and c) discipline?

 UNDERSTANDING THE BASICS

ANSWERS TO THE POP QUIZZES

1. **b. good supervision.** Where supervision and supervisory practices are "good," there's less likely a chance for a successful union organizing campaign.
2. The conditions negotiated by unionized workers influence the wages and terms of employment of nonunionized workers.
3. **True.** As in question 1, where supervision is good, the likelihood of having a union is low; where supervisory practices are poor, a union is likely to be encouraged to represent the workers.
4. **a. the federal and provincial labour relations acts.**
5. **c. approval of a written agreement by the LRB.** The LRB does not approve labour-management agreements. Final approval of a contract is the province of the rank-and-file members who are to ratify a contract before it is binding.
6. **False.** Bargaining in good faith means the company and labour union must negotiate in an attempt to reach an agreement acceptable to both parties. Reaching an agreement is not guaranteed, however.
7. Conciliation, mediation, and fact-finding are three impasse-resolution techniques. Conciliation and mediation involve a neutral third party who attempts to get labour and management to resolve their differences. Fact-finding is a technique whereby a neutral third-party individual conducts a hearing to gather evidence from both labour and management. The fact-finder then renders a decision as to how he or she views an appropriate settlement. Suggestions from all three techniques, however, are not binding on either party.
8. **a. the grievance procedure.** This is the definition of the process used in labour-management relationships to resolve disputes surrounding the interpretation and application of the contract.

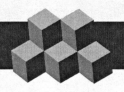

CASE 15.A

Three Different Supervisory Views on Unions

Bill Kaine is the manager of health and safety at Skyjack Inc. in Guelph, Ontario. Although Skyjack is not unionized, Bill's previous employer was unionized. Bill's comment on the impact of unionization? "To me, it is irrelevant whether there is a union or not. In order to ensure that health and safety concerns are addressed, you must have labour support anyway."

Tricia Mah, the director of support services at an intermediate-care nursing home in Vancouver, feels a greater impact from the hospital employees' union on her position. "They can be quite militant. It depends on who is in the local executive positions. If they are militant, every single thing a union member does is questioned. And my actions, too, can be questioned. For example, if I pick up a glass, is that acceptable? This can be stressful and make it hard for us all to relax and work as a team."

Anne Murphy, the Mississauga library branch manager, has yet another view. "I don't really think about it within the library. We work as a team. I don't hear, 'You can't do that or I'll go to the union.' The union does ensure fairness, for example, getting schedules posted two weeks in advance, and making sure that the job application process is appropriate. I'm a supporter of the union."

RESPONDING TO THIS CASE

1. Speculate on why the experiences of the three supervisors have been so different regarding unions. To what do you attribute it?
2. Link your speculations in #1 to your experience with unions or the experiences of those close to you. Is there such a thing as a "good" union and a "bad" union? Describe an ideal union from your perspective.
3. Do you believe that certain types of individuals—both supervisory and operative personnel -are attracted to work in either a unionized company or a nonunionized company? Explain.

CASE 15.B

Making a Union Unnecessary

You are a supervisor at a chicken processing plant. It started out small but the owners are ambitious and energetic and the company is rapidly growing. You and the others on the management team are concerned about preventing unionization at the plant. There has been some talk among the employees about organizing, and the increase in the size of the workforce at the plant makes it a likely target for a union drive. There are many unionized companies in the area.

Employees are paid competitive wages but the jobs are not exciting. The place is kept very clean and the newly hired HR manager is ensuring that all appropriate health and safety precautions and procedures are followed. The benefit package is meagre, as the company has been reinvesting heavily in its growth. The jobs are unskilled yet it is a challenge to recruit all the staff needed because the unemployment rate is low in the region.

RESPONDING TO THIS CASE

1. Why do you and the other managers fear unionization? What specific consequences do you fear?
2. What would attract the employees to a union? What benefits would they anticipate?
3. How could you and/or the other managers find out what issues employees have, both immediately and on an ongoing basis, in order to resolve these issues and create a more positive relationship?
4. The plant workers have relatively low education whereas the supervisors and managers, including you, have a college or university education. How can this create a division? How can this division be bridged? What can the company do to integrate these two quite different "types" of employees? What can the individual supervisors and managers do to create a relationship that feels to the employees like a partnership, rather than a hierarchical and authoritarian relationship?

Chapter 1

[1] Allen I. Kraut et al., "The Role of the Manager: What's Really Important in Different Management Jobs," *Academy of Management Executive* (November 1989), pp. 286-93.

[2] This section is based on Linda A. Hill, *Becoming a Manager: Mastery of a New Identity* (Boston: Harvard Business School Press, 1992).

[3] Robert L. Katz, "Skills of an Effective Administrator," *Harvard Business Review* (September/October 1974), pp. 90-102.

[4] Daniel Goleman, *Working with Emotional Intelligence* (NY: Bantam Books, 1998), p. 318.

[5] D. Farrell and J. C. Petersen, "Patterns of Political Behavior in Organizations," *Academy of Management Review* (July 1982), p. 405.

[6] R. E. Boyatzis, *The Competent Manager: A Model for Effective Performance* (New York: John Wiley & Sons, 1982), p. 33.

[7] Based on John W. Newstrom and Keith Davis, *Organizational Behavior: Human Behavior at Work*, 9th ed. (New York: McGraw-Hill, 1993), p. 239.

[8] See Richard E. Crandall, *First-Line Supervisors: Tomorrow's Professionals*, Personnel (November 1988), pp. 24-31.

[9] T. Roberts, "Who are the high-tech Home Workers?" *Inc. Technology*, 1994, p. 31.

[10] Geert Hofstede, *Culture's Consequences: International Differences in Workplace Values* (Gage Publications, 1997).

[11] Hofstede called this last dimension masculinity/femininity. We've changed it because of the sexist connotation of the choice of terms.

[12] Adapted from C. M. Solomon, "Managing the Baby Busters," *Personnel Journal* (March 1992), p. 56.

[13] See, for example, S. Ratan, "Why Busters Hate Boomers," *Fortune* (October 4, 1993), pp. 56-70.

[14] L. Thornburg, "The Age Wave Hits: What Older Workers Want and Need," *HRMagazine* (February 1995), pp. 43-44.

[15] "Office Hours," *Fortune* (November 5, 1990), p. 184.

Chapter 2

[1] H. Mintzberg, *The Rise and Fall of Strategic Planning* (New York: Free Press, 1994).

[2] Ibid.

[3] K. Rebello and P. Burrows, The Fall of an American Icon, *Business Week*, February 5, 1996, pp. 34-42.

[4] D. Miller, "The Architecture of Simplicity," *Academy of Management Review*, January 1993, pp. 116-138.

[5] Cited in Harold E. Fearon and others, *Fundamentals of Production/Operations Management*, 3rd ed. (St. Paul, MN: West Publishing, 1986), p. 97.

Chapter 3

[1] This list is based on James J. Semrodek, Jr., "Nine Steps to Cost Control," *Supervisory Management*, April 1976, pp. 29-32.

[2] S. Lam, C. Hui and K.S. Law, "Organizational Citizenship Behavior: Comparing Perspectives of Supervisors and Subordinates Across Four International Samples," *Journal of Applied Psychology*, 1999, Vol. 84, No. 4, pp. 594-601.

[3] Cited in G. Bylinsky, "How Companies Spy on Employees," *Fortune*, November 4, 1991, pp. 131-40.

[4] Cited in Archie B. Carroll, "In Search of the Moral Manager," *Business Horizons*, March/April 1987, p. 7.

Chapter 4

[1] Alan J. Rowe, James D. Boulgarides, and Michael R. McGrath, *Managerial Decision Making, Modules in Management Series* (Chicago, IL: SRA, 1984), pp. 18-22.

[2] Saul W. Gellerman, Why "Good" Managers Make Bad Ethical Choices, *Harvard Business Review*, July/August 1986, p. 89.

[3] Adapted from Laura L. Nash, Ethics Without the Sermon, *Harvard Business Review*, November/December 1981, p. 81.

[4] See William M. Bulkeley, "Computizing" Dull Meetings Is Touted as an Antidote to the Mouth that Bored, *The Wall Street Journal*, January 28, 1992, p. 1.

[5] R. Richards et al., "Assessing Everyday Creativity: Characteristics of the Lifetime Creativity Scales and Validation with Three Large Samples," *Journal of Personality and Social Psychology*, March 1988, pp. 476-85.

[6] Adapted from J. Calano and J Salzman, "Ten Ways to Fire up Your Creativity," *Working Woman* (July 1989), pp. 94-95.

Chapter 5

[1] Henry Mintzberg, *Structure in Fives: Designing Effective Organizations* (Englewood Cliffs, NJ: Prentice-Hall, Inc., 1983), p. 157.

[2] A Master Class of Radical Change, *Fortune* (December 13, 1993), p. 83.

[3] Ibid, p. 88.

[4] Jon R. Katzenbach and Douglas K. Smith, *The Wisdom of Teams* (Boston, MA: Harvard Business School Press, 1993), pp. 43-64.

[5] J. Mathieu, T. Heffner, G. Goodwin, E. Salas, J. Cannon Bowers, The Influence of Shared Mental Models on Team Process and Performance, *Journal of Applied Psychology*, April 2000, pp. 273-283.

[6] See James A. Shepperd, "Productivity Loss in Performance Groups: A Motivation Analysis," *Psychological Bulletin*, January 1993, pp. 67-81.

[7] Fernando Bartolome, "Nobody Trusts the Boss Completely—Now What?" *Harvard Business Review*, March/April 1989, pp. 135-42.

[8] K. Dirks, "The Effects of Interpersonal Trust on Work Group Performance," *Journal of Applied Psychology*, June 1999, pp. 445-455.

[9] P. Tesluk and J. Mathieu, "Overcoming Roadblocks to

Effectiveness: Incorporating Management of Performance Barriers into Models of Work Group Effectiveness," *Journal of Applied Psychology*, 1999, Vol. 84, No. 2, pp. 200-217.

[10]This questionnaire is adapted from L. Steinmetz and R. Todd, *First Line Management*, 4th ed. (Homewood, IL: Irwin, 1986), pp. 64-67. With permission.

Chapter 6

[1]Lyle Spencer and Signe Spencer, *Competence at Work: Models for Superior Performance*, (John Wiley, 1993).

[2]G. A. Neuman and J. Wright, "Team Effectiveness: Beyond Skills and Cognitive Ability," *Journal of Applied Psychology*, 1999, Vol. 84, No. 3, pp. 376-389.

[3]Allan Halcrow, "Employees Are Your Best Recruiters," *Personnel Journal*, November 1988, pp. 42-49.

[4]Wayne F. Cascio, *Applied Psychology in Personnel Management*, 4th ed. (Englewood Cliffs, NJ: Prentice Hall, 1991), p. 265.

[5]John B. Miner, *Industrial and Organizational Psychology* (New York: McGraw-Hill, 1991), pp. 504-11.

[6]Walter C. Borman and Glenn L. Hallman, "Observation Accuracy for Assessors of Work Sample Performance: Consistency Across Task and Individual Differences Correlates," *Journal of Applied Psychology*, February 1991, pp. 11-18.

[7]See Robert L. Dipboye, *Selection Interviews: Process Perspectives* (Cincinnati: South-Western, 1992), Chapter 2.

[8]Irwin L. Goldstein, "The Application Blank: How Honest Are the Responses?" *Journal of Applied Psychology*, October 1971, pp. 491-92.

[9]Cited in "If You Can't Say Something Nice," *Wall Street Journal*, March 4, 1988, p. 25.

[10]T. Janz, L. Hellervik and D. Gilmore, *Behavior Description Interviewing* (Allyn & Bacon, 1986).

[11]See, for example, S. L. Premack and J. P. Wanous, "A Meta-Analysis of Realistic Job Preview Experiments", *Journal of Applied Psychology*, November 1985, pp. 706-20.

Chapter 7

[1]Laura Ramsay, "Time to Examine the Exam: Mostly Everyone Dreads a Performance Appraisal... And for Good Reason," *National Post*, October 18, 1999.

[2]W. Smith, K. V. Harrington and J. Houghton, "Predictors of Performance Appraisal Discomfort," *Public Personnel Management*, March 22, 2000, p. 21.

[3]Gary P. Latham and Kenneth N. Wexley, *Increasing Productivity Through Performance Appraisal* (Reading, MA: Addison-Wesley, 1981), p. 80.

[4]Peter M. Blau, *The Dynamics of Bureaucracy*, rev. ed. (Chicago, IL: University of Chicago Press, 1963).

[5]See, for example, Michael J. Kavanagh, "Evaluating Performance," in K. M. Rowland and G. R. Ferris, eds., *Personnel Management* (Boston: Allyn & Bacon, 1982), pp. 187-126.

[6]K. R. Murphy and V. A Pardaffy, "Bias in Behaviorally Anchored Rating Scales: Global or Scale Specific," *Journal of Applied Psychology*, April 1989, pp. 343-46; and M. J. Piotrowski, J. L. Barnes-Farrell, and F. H. Esris, "Behaviorally Anchored Bias: A Replication and Extension of Murphy and Constans," *Journal of Applied Psychology*, October 1988, pp. 827-28.

[7]R. Mayer and J. Davis, "The Effect of the Performance Appraisal System on Trust for Management: A Field Quasi-Experiment," *Journal of Applied Psychology*, February 1999, pp. 123-136.

[8]J. Conway, Distinguishing Contextual Performance from Ask Performance for Managerial Jobs, *Journal of Applied Psychology*, February 1999, pp. 3-13.

[9]H. John Bernardin, "The Effects of Rater Training on Leniency and Halo Errors in Student Rating of Instructors," *Journal of Applied Psychology*, October 1975, pp. 550-55.

[10]L. O'Brien, "Improving Performance Appraisal Interviews," *Supply Management*, May 4, 2000, pp. 36-37.

[11]W. Bridges, "The End of the Job," Fortune, September 19, 1984, p. 64.

[12]This discussion is based on Scott A. Snell and Kenneth N. Wexley, "How to Make Your Performance Appraisals More Effective," *Personnel Administrator*, April 1985, pp. 117-118.

[13]J. Wisinski, "A Logical Approach to a Difficult Employee," *HR Focus*, January 1992, p. 9.

[14]G. D. Cook, Employee Counseling Session, *Supervision*, August 1989, p. 3.

[15]Norman R. F. Maier, *The Appraisal Interview: Three Basic Approaches* (La Jolla, CA: University Associates, 1976).

[16]"How Do I Love Me? Let Me Count the Ways," *Psychology Today*, May 1980, p. 16.

[17]Ronald J. Burke, R. J. Weitzel, and T. Weir, "Characteristics of Effective Employee Performance Review and Development Interviews: Replication and Extension," *Personnel Psychology*, Winter 1978, pp. 903-19.

[18]Latham and Wexley, *Increasing Productivity through Performance Appraisal*, (Reading, MA: Addison-Wesley, 1981), p. 151.

Chapter 8

[1]This is based on Albert Bandura, *Social Learning Theory* (Englewood Cliffs, N.J.: Prentice Hall, Inc., 1977).

[2]*Toronto Star*, June 2, 1994.

[3]Auto Parts Certificate, Automotive Parts Sectoral Training Council, Jeffry Piker, Educational Consultant.

[4]Charles D. Orth, Harry E. Wilkinson, and Robert C. Benfari, "The Manager's Role as Coach and Mentor," *Organizational Dynamics*, Spring 1987, p. 67.

Chapter 9

[1]Abraham Maslow, *Motivation and Personality* (New York: Harper and Row, 1954).

[2]Douglas McGregor, *The Human Side of Enterprise* (New York: McGraw-Hill, 1960).

[3]Frederick Herzberg, B. Mausner, and B. Snyderman, *The Motivation to Work* (New York: John Wiley and Sons, 1959).

[4]See Raymond A. Katzell, Donna E. Thompson, and Richard A. Guzzo, *How Job Satisfaction and Job Performance Are and Are Not Linked*, in C. J. Cranny, Patricia Cain Smith, and Eugene F. Stone, Job Satisfaction (New York: Lexington Books, 1992), pp. 195-217.

[5]David C. McClelland, *The Achieving Society* (New York: Van Nostrand Reinhold, 1961).

[6]J. Stacey Adams, "Inequity in Social Exchanges," in L. Berkowitz (ed.), *Advances in Experimental Social Psychology*, Vol. 2 (New York: Academic Press, 1965), pp. 267-300.

[7]Victor H. Vroom, *Work and Motivation* (New York: John Wiley, 1964).

[8]Edwin A. Locke et al., "The Relative Effectiveness of Four Methods of Motivating Employee Performance," in K. D. Duncan, M. M. Gruneberg, and D. Wallis, eds., *Changes in Working Life*

(London: John Wiley, Ltd., 1980), pp. 363-83.

[9]G. Hofstede, "Motivation, Leadership, and Organizations: Do American Theories Apply Abroad?" *Organizational Dynamics*, Summer 1980, p. 55.

[10]D. H. B. Walsh, F. Luthens, and S. M. Sommer, "Organizational Behavior Modification Goes to Russia: Replicating an Experimental Analysis Across Cultures and Tasks," *Journal of Organizational Behavior Management*, Fall 1993, pp. 15-35; and J. R. Baum et al., "Nationality and Work Role Interactions: A Cultural Contrast of Israel and U.S. Entrepreneurs' Versus Managers' Needs," *Journal of Business Venturing*, November 1993, pp. 499-512.

[11]A. Ignatius, "Now If Ms. Wong Insults a Customer, She Gets an Award," *Wall Street Journal*, January 24, 1989, p. A-1.

[12]A.M. Dickinson and K.L. Gillette, "A Comparison of the Effects on Productivity: Piece-Rate Pay Versus Base Pay Plus Incentives," *Journal of Organizational Behavior Management*, Spring 1994, pp. 3-82.

[13]See, for example, D. Fenn, "Compensation: Bonuses That Make Sense," *Inc.*, March 1996, p. 95.

[14]G. Grib and S. O'Donnell, "Pay Plans that Reward Employee Achievement," *HRMagazine*, July 1995, pp. 49-50.

[15]"Compensation: Sales Managers as Team Players," *Inc.*, August 1994, p. 102.

[16]D. Fenn, "Compensation: Goal-Driven Incentives," Inc., August 1996, p. 91; M.A. Verespej, "More Value for Compensation," *Industry Week*, June 17, 1996, p. 20.

[17]S. Overman, "Saturn Teams Working and Profiting," *HRMagazine*, March 1995, p. 72.

[18]K. Capell, "Options for Everyone," *Business Week*, July 22, 1996, pp. 80-88.

[19]See, for example, T. R. Stenhouse, "The Long and the Short of Gainsharing," *Academy of Management Executive*, Vol. 9, No. 1 (1995), pp. 77-78.

[20]S. A. Lee, "ESOP is a Powerful Tool to Align Employees with Corporate Goals," *Pension World*, April 1994, pp. 40-42.

Chapter 10

[1]For example, see J. P. Howell, D. E. Bowen, P. W. Dorfman, S. Kerr, and P. M. Podsakoff, "Substitutes for Leadership: Effective Alternatives to Ineffective Leadership," *Organizational Dynamics*, Summer 1990, pp. 21-38.

[2]S. A. Kirkpatrick and E. A. Locke, "Leadership: Do Traits Matter?" *Academy of Management Executive*, May 1991, pp. 48-60.

[3]See, for example, Patricia Sellers, "What Exactly Is Charisma?" *Fortune*, January 15, 1996, pp. 68-75.

[4]R. J. House, "A 1976 Theory of Charismatic Leadership," in J. G. Hunt and L. L. Larson, eds., *Leadership: The Cutting Edge* (Carbondale, IL: Southern Illinois University Press, 1977), pp. 189-207.

[5]W. Bennis, "The 4 Competencies of Leadership," *Training and Development Journal*, August 1984, pp. 15-19; see also Marshall Loeb, "Where Leaders Come From," *Fortune*, September 19, 1994, p. 241.

[6]J. C. Conger and R. N. Kanungo, "Behavioural Dimensions of Charismatic Leadership," in J. A. Conger, R. N. Kanungo and Associates, *Charismatic Leadership* (San Francisco, CA: Jossey-Bass, 1988), p. 79.

[7]G. H. Dobbins et al., "The Role of Self-Monitoring and Gender on Leader Emergence: A Laboratory and Field Study," *Journal of Management*, September 1990, pp. 609-18.

[8]R. J. House, J. Woycke, and E. M. Fodor, "Charismatic and Noncharismatic Leaders: Differences in Behavior and Effectiveness," in Conger and Kanungo, *Charismatic Leadership*, pp. 103-104.

[9]See, for example, S. Camminiti, "What Team Leaders Need to Know," *Fortune*, February 20, 1995, pp. 93-100.

[10]R. M. Stogdill and A. E. Coons, eds., *Leader Behavior: Its Description and Measurement*, Research Monograph No. 88 (Columbus, OH: Ohio State University, Bureau of Business Research, 1951).

[11]Ibid.; and R. Kahn and D. Katz, "Leadership Practices in Relation to Productivity and Morale," in D. Cartwright and A. Zander, eds., *Group Dynamics: Research and Theory*, 2nd ed. (Elmsford, NY: Row, Paterson, 1960).

[12]For a good review of the Fielder Contingency Model, Path-Goal Theory, and Leader-Participation Model, see S. P. Robbins and D. A. De Cenzo, *Fundamentals of Management* (Englewood Cliffs, NJ: Prentice-Hall, Inc., 1995), pp. 300-306.

[13]F. E. Fiedler, *A Theory of Leadership Effectiveness* (New York: McGraw-Hill, 1967).

[14]R. J. House and T. R. Mitchell, "Path-Goal Theory of Leadership," *Journal of Contemporary Business*, Autumn 1974, pp. 81-97.

[15]P. Hersey and K. H. Blanchard, *Management of Organizational Behavior: Utilizing Human Resources*, 5th ed. (Englewood Cliffs, NJ: Prentice-Hall, Inc., 1988). For those who wish to look at both sides of the debate on the validity of situational leadership, you are encouraged to read W. R. Norris and R. P Vecchio, "Situational Leadership Theory: A Replication," *Group and Organization Management*, September 1992, pp. 331-42; and W. Blank, J. R. Weitzel, and S. G. Green, "A Test of the Situational Leadership Theory, *Personnel Psychology*, Autumn 1990, pp. 579 - 97.

[16]G. Hofstede, "Motivation, Leadership, and Organization: Do American Theories Apply Abroad?" *Organizational Dynamics* (Summer 1980), p. 57; and A. Ede, "Leadership and Decision Making: Management Styles and Culture," *Journal of Managerial Psychology* (July 1992), pp. 28-31.

[17]Based on L. T. Hosmer, "Trust: The Connecting Link Between Organizational Theory and Philosophical Ethics," *Academy of Management Review*, April 1995, p. 393; and R. C. Mayer, J. H. Davis, and F. D. Shoorman, "An Integrative Model of Organizational Trust," *Academy of Management Review*, July 1995, p. 712.

[18]P. L. Schindler and C. C. Thomas, "The Structure of Interpersonal Trust in the Workplace," *Psychological Reports*, October 1993, pp. 563 - 73.

[19]T. A. Stewart, "The Nine Dilemmas Leaders Face," *Fortune*, March 18, 1996, p. 113.

[20]See, for example, W. H. Miller, "Leadership at a Crossroads," *Industry Week*, August 19, 1996, pp. 43-44.

[21]D. Duchon, S. G. Green, and T. D. Taylor, "Vertical Dyad Linkage: A Longitudinal Assessment of Antecedents, Measures, and Consequences," *Journal of Applied Psychology*, February 1986, pp. 56-60.

[22]This skills box is based on F. Bartolome, "Nobody Trusts the Boss Completely—Now What?" *Harvard Business Review*, March/April 1989, pp. 35-142; and J. K. Butler, Jr., "Toward Understanding and Measuring Conditions of Trust: Evolution of a Condition of Trust Inventory," *Journal of Management*, September 1991, pp. 643-63.

[23]L. Holpp, "Applied Empowerment," *Training*, February 1994, pp. 39-44.

[24]See, for example, R. Wellins and J. Worklan, "The Philadelphia Story," *Training*, March 1994, pp. 93-100.

[25]G. N. Powell, *Women and Men in Management*, 2nd ed. (Thousand Oaks, CA: Sage, 1993).

[26]S. P. Robbins. *Organizational Behavior: Concepts, Controversies, and Applications*, 7th ed. (Englewood Cliffs, NJ: Prentice-Hall, Inc., 1996), p. 441.

[27]Ibid.

[28]B. M. Bass, "From Transactional to Transformational Leadership: Learning to Share the Vision," *Organizational Dynamics*, Winter 1990, pp. 19-31.

[29]See, for example, J. Seitzer and B. M. Bass, "Transformational Leadership: Beyond Initiation and Consideration," *Journal of Management*, December 1990, pp. 693-703.

[30]B. J. Avolio and B. M. Bass, Transformational Leadership: Charisma and Beyond, working paper, School of Management, State University of New York, Binghamton (1995), p. 14.

[31]Deborah Fine, *Talking from 9 to 5*, (NY: William Morrow and Company, Inc., 1994).

Chapter 11

[1]Albert Mehrabian, "Communication Without Words," *Psychology Today*, September 1968, pp. 53-55.

[2]Keith Davis, cited in R. Rowan, "Where Did That Rumor Come From?" *Fortune*, August 13, 1979, p. 134.

[3]See, for example, Morgan W. McCall, Jr., Ann M. Morrison, and Robert L. Hannan, "Studies of Managerial Work: Results and Methods," Technical Report No. 9 (Greensboro, NC: Center for Creative Leadership, 1978), pp. 7-9; and Fred Luthans and Janet K. Larsen, "How Managers Really Communicate," *Human Relations*, February 1986, pp. 161-78.

[4]See, for example, L. K. Larkey, "Toward a Theory of Communicative Interactions in Culturally Diverse Workgroups," *Academy of Management Review*, June 1996, pp. 463-91; R. V. Lindahl, "Automation Breaks the Language Barrier," *HRMagazine*, March 1996, pp. 79-82; D. Lindorff, "In Beijing the Long March Is Just Starting," *Business Week*, February 12, 1996, p. 68; and L. Miller, "Two Aspects of Japanese and American Coworker Interaction:

Giving Instructions and Creating Rapport," *Journal of Applied Behavioral Science*, June 1995, pp. 141-61.

[5]Based on S. D. Saleh, "Relational Orientation and Organizational Functioning: A Cross-Cultural Perspective," *Canadian Journal of Administrative Sciences*, September 1987, pp. 276-93.

[6]C. Fisher, "Transmission of Positive and Negative Feedback to Subordinates," *Journal of Applied Psychology*, October 1979, pp. 433-540.

[7]F. Bartolome, "Teaching About Whether to Give Negative Feedback," *The Organizational Behavior Teaching Review*, Vol. 9, No. 2, 1986-1987, pp. 95-104.

[8]K. S. Verderber and R. F. Verderber, *Inter-Act: Using Interpersonal Communication Skills*, 4th ed. (Belmont, CA: Wadsworth, 1986).

Chapter 12

[1]J. Graves, "Successful Management and Organizational Muggings," in J. Papp, ed., *New Directions in Human Resource Management* (Englewood Cliffs, N.J.: Prentice-Hall Inc., 1978).

[2]See Stephen P. Robbins, *Managing Organizational Conflict: A Nontraditional Approach* (Englewood Cliffs, N.J.: Prentice-Hall Inc., 1974).

[3]L. Greenhalgh, "Managing Conflict," *Sloan Management Review*, Summer 1986, pp. 45-51.

Chapter 13

[1]Kurt Lewin, *Field Theory in Social Science* (New York: Harper & Row, 1951).

[2]See, for instance, T. Peters, *Thriving on Chaos* (New York: Alfred A. Knopf, 1987).

[3]C. Wanberg and J. Banas, "Predictors and Outcomes of Openness to Changes in a Reorganizing Workplace," *Journal of Applied Psychology*, February 2000, pp. 132-142.

[4]D. N. Rousseau and S. A. Tijoriwala, "What's a Good Reason to Change? Motivated Reasoning and Social Accounts in Promoting Organizational Change," *Journal of Applied Psychology*, 1999, Vol. 84, No. 4, pp. 514- 528.

[5]Statscan, "General Social Survey: Time Use," *The Daily*, November 9, 1999.

[6]M. Cavanaugh, W. Boswell, M. Roehling and J. Boudreau, "An Empirical Examination of Self-Reported Work Stress Among U.S. Managers," *Journal of Applied Psychology*, February 2000, pp. 65-74.

[7]Wanberg and Banas, op. cit.

[8]S. Jex and P. Bliese, "Efficacy Beliefs as a Moderator of the Impact of Work-Related Stressors: A Multi-Level Study," *Journal of Applied Psychology*, June 1999, pp. 349 to 361.

Chapter 14

[1]Employee Conduct and Discipline, Personnel Policies Forum, Survey No. 102 (Washington, D.C.: Bureau of National Affairs, August 1973).

[2]Employee Conduct and Discipline, Personnel Policies Forum, Survey No. 102 (Washington, D.C.: Bureau of National Affairs, August 1973).

[3]CUB42012A

[4]Jake Rupert, "Public Servants Suspended for E-mailing Jokes," *The Ottawa Citizen*, July 29, 1999.

[5]T. S. Cohen, "Is Somebody Monitoring Your E-mail at Work?" *Education Leader*, May 1998.

[6]C. Deehy, Franchising and the Use of Cyberspace in the Workplace, www.lapros.qc/puba/cyber_work.html

[7]C. Deehy, op. cit.

[8]Douglas McGregor, "Hot Stove Rules of Discipline," in George Strauss and Leonard Sayles, eds., *Personnel: The Human Problems of Management* (Englewood Cliffs, N.J.: Prentice-Hall Inc., 1967).

[9]A study by the Wyatt Company cited in *Boardroom Reports*, April 1, 1989, p. 2.

Chapter 15

[1]This section is based on D.A. De Cenzo and S. P. Robbins, *Human Resource Management*, 5th ed. (New York: John Wiley & Sons, Inc., 1996), pp. 494-97.

Absenteeism Failure to report to work.

Accept errors Accepting those candidates who subsequently perform poorly on the job.

Accommodation The willingness of one party in a conflict to place the opponent's interests above his or her own.

Accountability Holding a person to performing an assignment in a satisfactory manner.

Active listening Listening with intensity, empathy, acceptance, and a willingness to take responsibility for completeness.

Activities Time or resources required to progress from one event to another on a PERT chart.

Agency shop Work setting in which employees do not have to join the union but they must pay union dues if they want to keep their jobs.

Agenda A written statement of a meeting's purpose, who will be in attendance, and the issues that will be discussed.

Apprenticeships A program covering a period of time—typically from one to five years—when an individual is considered to be training to learn a skill.

Arbitrator An impartial third party who hears grievances and makes rulings on them.

Assertiveness training Training designed to make people more open and self-expressive.

Assignable causes Nonchance variations.

Attitudes Evaluative statements or judgments concerning objects, people, or events.

Attribute charts Charts that measure a product characteristic in terms of whether it is good or bad.

Authority The managerial right to give orders and expect the orders to be obeyed.

Authority after discussion Decision making by a group leader after weighing group members' decisions.

Autocratic leader A task master who leaves no doubt as to who's in charge, and who has the authority and power in the group.

Autonomy The degree to which the job provides substantial freedom, independence, and discretion to the individual in scheduling the work and in determining the procedures to be used in carrying it out.

Avoidance The desire to withdraw from or suppress a conflict.

Baby-boomers The largest group in the workforce; they are regarded as the career climbers—at the right place at the right time. Mature workers view them as unrealistic in their views and workaholics.

Baby-busters A group of workers less committed, less rule-bound, and more into self-gratification, with an intolerance of baby-boomers and their attitudes. They are viewed as selfish and not willing to play by the rules.

Bargaining unit Identifies which employees the union will represent if it wins an election.

Behaviour-based interviewing Probing the applicant for specific narrative details of actual events in their past in order to predict their probable behaviour on the job for which they are applying.

Behaviourally anchored rating scales (BARS) A performance appraisal technique in which an evaluator rates employees on specific job behaviours derived from performance dimensions.

Benchmarking The continuous process of measuring products and practices against the toughest competition and those companies recognized as world-class leaders.

Body language Gestures, facial configurations, and other movements of the body.

Bottom-up budgeting Budgeting in which budget requests are prepared by those who implement them and are then sent to higher levels of management for approval.

Brainstorming An idea-generation process that specifically encourages any and all alternatives while withholding any criticism of those alternatives.

Budgets Numerical plans.

Cause and effect diagrams Diagrams used to speculate on potential effects of taking an action, grouping the effects according to common categories.

Central limit theorem A sampling distribution approaches normality as the size of the sample increases.

Central tendency error A reluctance by an evaluator to use the extremes of the appraising scale.

Centralized authority Decision making carried out by top management.

Chance causes Variations caused by randomness in the process.

Change agents People who act as catalysts and assume the responsibility for overseeing the change process.

Change process Unfreezing the status quo, changing to a new state, and refreezing the new change to make it permanent.

Charismatic leadership An attribution made of individuals with self-confidence, vision, the ability to articulate the vision, strong convictions in the vision, novel or unconventional behaviour, and the perception that they are agents of radical change.

Checklist A performance appraisal technique where an evaluator uses a list of behavioural descriptions and checks off those behaviours that apply to the employee.

Coaching Day-to-day, hands-on process of helping employees recognize opportunities to improve their work performance.

Code of ethics A formal document that states an organization's primary values and the ethical rules it expects employees to follow.

Cognitive learning Occurs via mental processes such as reading, watching, and thinking.

Cohesiveness The degree to which members are attracted to each other and are motivated to stay in the group.

Collaboration A situation where the parties to a conflict each desire to satisfy fully the concerns of all parties.

Collective bargaining A process for negotiating a union contract and for administrating the contract after it has been negotiated.

Communication The transference and understanding of meaning.

Compromise A situation in which each party to a conflict is willing to give up something of value.

Conceptual competence The mental ability to analyze and diagnose complex situations.

Conciliation An impasse-resolution technique that states that the role of the third party is to keep the negotiations ongoing and to act as a go-between.

Concurrent controls Controls that are enacted while an activity is in progress.

Conflict A process in which one party consciously interferes in the goal-achievement efforts of another party.

Conflict management The application of resolution and stimulation techniques to achieve the optimum level of departmental conflict.

Confronting Pointing out discrepancies in attitudes, thoughts or behaviours in another person in a non-judgmental way.

Consensus Agreement to support a decision by all members of a group.

Consultative participative leadership The leadership style of an individual who seeks input, hears the concerns and issues of the followers, but makes the final decision him- or herself, using input as an information-seeking exercise.

Control by exception Strategic control devices should call attention only to exceptions from standard.

Control charts Charts that show plotting of results over a period of time, with statistically determined upper and lower limits.

Control process Establishing performance indicators, establishing performance standards, measuring actual performance, comparing actual performance with planned performance, and taking corrective action where needed.

Controlling Monitoring activities to ensure that objectives are being met as planned and correcting any significant deviations.

Corrective control Provides feedback, after an activity is finished, to prevent any future deviations.

Counselling Discussion of a problem (usually one with emotional content) with an employee in order to resolve the problem or, at a minimum, help the employee to cope with it better.

Counselling process The five steps that describe how a counselling session should be conducted.

Credibility Supervisor qualities of honesty, competence, and the ability to inspire.

Critical incidents A performance appraisal technique in which an evaluator lists key behaviours that separate effective from ineffective job performance.

Critical path The longest sequence of events and activities in a PERT chart.

Cross-functional teams Managers and employees from different levels and different parts of the organization form teams to solve problems.

Culture A system of shared meaning.

Customer Everyone internally or externally who interacts with the organization's product or service.

Customer departmentalization Grouping activities on the basis of common customers.

Data Raw, unanalyzed facts.

Decentralized authority Top management pushes decision making down to lower levels.

Decision trees A diagrammatic technique for analyzing decisions by assigning probabilities to various outcomes and calculating payoffs for each.

Decision-making process The seven steps to making rational decisions.

Delegation A four-step process of allocating duties, delegating authority, assigning responsibility, and creating accountability.

Delphi technique A group decision technique where members act independently but need not be physically present for discussion.

Democratic participative leadership A leadership style that allows followers to have a say in what's decided.

Departmentalization Grouping departments based on work functions, product or service, target customer or client, geographic territory, or the process used to turn inputs into outputs.

Devils advocate A person who purposely presents arguments that run counter to those proposed by the majority or against current practices.

Discipline Actions taken by a supervisor to enforce the organization's rules and standards.

Discretionary time The portion of a supervisor's time that is under his or her control.

Dismissal Termination of one's employment.

Distributive bargaining Zero-sum negotiations, where any gain by one is at the expense of the other.

Diversity training Training aimed at creating a greater awareness of the issues that arise in a staff of varied background and characteristics, encouraging acceptance and appreciation of that variety, and helping employees learn how to accommodate and work with people of diverse background.

Division of labour The breakdown of jobs into narrow, repetitive tasks.

Downsizing A reduction in the workforce and reshaping of operations to create "lean and mean" organizations. The goals of organizational downsizing are greater efficiency and reduced costs.

Due process Assuming an employee is innocent until proved otherwise; giving the employee the right to be heard; and invoking disciplinary action that is reasonable in relation to the offence involved.

85-15 rule Eighty-five per cent of what goes wrong is due to the system, while 15 per cent is attributed to the employees who operate the system.

Effectiveness Doing a task right; goal attainment.

Efficiency Doing a task right; also refers to the relationship between inputs and outputs.

Electronic meeting A group of individuals make decisions by communicating anonymously on computer terminals.

Emergent leaders Leaders who arise out of a group but who have no formal authority in the organization.

Emotional intelligence A set of skills including self-awareness, self-regulation, motivation, empathy, and social skills that correlate highly with effectiveness at work.

Employee Assistance Programs (EAPs) Programs designed to act as a first stop for individuals seeking psychiatric or substance-abuse help, with the goal of getting productive employees back on the job as swiftly as possible.

Employee counselling An emphasis on encouraging training and development efforts in a situation in which employee unwillingness or inability to perform his or her job satisfactorily is either voluntary or involuntary.

Employee development Preparation of employees for future positions that require higher-level skills, knowledge, or abilities.

Employee relations All activities within a company that involve dealing with a union and its members.

Employee stock ownership plan (ESOP) A compensation program that allows employees to become part owners of an organization by receiving stock as a performance incentive.

Employee training Changing skills, knowledge, attitudes, or behaviour of employees. Determination of training needs is made by supervisors.

Empowered work teams The primary working units in a TQM program who have hands-on involvement in process improvement.

Empowerment Increasing an employee's involvement in making decisions and taking responsibility for work outcomes.

End-users Individuals who take responsibility for accessing and analyzing information they need on their personal computers.

Equity theory Employees perceive what they get from a job situation (outcomes) in relation to what they put into it (inputs), and then compare their input-outcome ratio with the input-outcome ratio of others; then respond so as to eliminate any inequities.

ERG theory of motivation Reduces Maslow's hierarchy to three—existence, relatedness and growth needs—and adds a frustration-regression hypothesis, the idea that people frustrated in their attempt to fulfill an unfulfilled need will regress to a lower need's fulfillment.

Ethical dilemmas Situations requiring one to define right and wrong conduct.

Ethics Rules or principles that define right and wrong conduct.

Events End points on a PERT chart that represent the completion of major activities.

Expectancy theory The strength of a tendency to act depends on the strength of an expectation that the act will be followed by a given outcome and on the attractiveness of that outcome to the individual.

Expected value analysis Calculating the expected value of a particular alternative by weighting its possible outcomes by the probability of achieving the alternative, then summing up the totals derived from the weighting process.

Experiential learning Relies on practising, experiencing, or doing something.

Expert A person with special skill or knowledge in a particular field.

Extrinsic feedback Performance feedback provided by an outside source.

Fact-finding A technique whereby a neutral third-party individual conducts a hearing to gather evidence from both labour and management.

Feedback The degree to which carrying out the work activities required by the job results in the individual obtaining direct and clear information about the effectiveness of his or her performance.

Fiedler's contingency theory A leadership theory; proposes that effectiveness depends upon a proper match between a leader's style of interacting with subordinates and the degree to which the situation gives control and influence to the leader.

First-level managers Supervisors.

Flow charts Visual representations of the sequence of events for a particular process.

Forcing The desire to satisfy your own needs at the expense of the other party.

Formal communication Addresses task-related issues and tends to follow the organization's authority chain.

Formal group A work group where objectives and work assignments are defined by management.

Free-reign leader An individual who gives employees total autonomy to make decisions that will affect them.

Functional authority Rights over individuals outside one's own direct areas of responsibility.

Functional departmentalization Grouping activities by functions performed.

Gantt chart A bar graph, with time on the horizontal axis and activities to be scheduled on the vertical axis, that shows planned and actual activities.

Gap analysis Involves defining the difference between what is actually happening and what you would like to have happening.

Geographic departmentalization Grouping activities on the basis of territory.

Grapevine The means by which informal communication takes place; rumour mill.

Graphic rating scale A performance-appraisal technique in which an evaluator rates a set of performance factors on an incremental scale.

Grievance procedures Procedures designed to resolve disputes as quickly as possible and at the lowest level in the organization.

Group Two or more people who come together to achieve a particular objective.

Group order ranking A performance appraisal approach that groups employees into ordered classifications.

Groupthink Group members withhold different views in order to appear to be in agreement.

Halo error A tendency to rate an individual high or low on all factors due to the impression of a high or low rating on some specific factor.

Hierarchy of needs theory Theory that there is a hierarchy of five needs—physiological, safety, social, esteem, and self-actualization. As each need is sequentially satisfied, the next need becomes dominant.

Histograms Bar charts used to show the frequency with which something occurs.

Horizontal structures Very flat structures used in small businesses as well as giant companies in which job-related activities cut across all parts of the organization.

"Hot stove" rule Principles that can guide disciplining; the action should be immediate, offer advance warning, and be consistent and impartial.

Human resource planning Ensuring that a department has the right personnel, who are capable of completing those tasks that help the department reach its objectives.

Immediate corrective action Action that adjusts something right now and gets things back on track.

Incident rate A measure of the number of injuries, illnesses, or lost workdays as it relates to a common base rate of 100 full-time employees.

Incremental budget A budget that develops out of the previous budget.

Individual ranking A performance appraisal approach that ranks employees in order from highest to lowest.

Informal communication Moves in any direction and is as likely to satisfy social needs as to facilitate task accomplishments.

Informal group Natural formations in the work place that are neither formally structured nor defined by management.

Information Analyzed and processed data.

Integrative bargaining Assumes there is at least one settlement option that can create a win-win solution.

Interest arbitration Arbitration in which a panel of three individuals hears testimony from both sides and renders a decision on how to settle the current contract negotiation dispute.

Intermediate-term plans Plans that cover from one to five years.

Interpersonal competence The ability to work with, understand, and motivate other people, both individually and in groups.

Intrinsic feedback Self-generated feedback on performance provided by the work itself.

Job description A written statement of what a jobholder does, how the job is done, and why it is done.

Job design The way tasks are combined to form complete jobs.

Job enrichment Increasing the degree to which a worker controls the planning, execution, and evaluation of his or her work.

Job rotation Moving employees horizontally to broaden their skills, knowledge, or abilities; turning specialists into generalists.

Job specification The minimum acceptable qualifications an applicant must possess to perform a given job successfully.

Justice view of ethics Decisions that seek fair and impartial distribution of benefits and costs.

Just-in-time (JIT) inventory system A system in which inventory items arrive when they are needed in the production process instead of being stored in stock. See also Kanban.

Kanban In Japanese, a "card" or "sign." Shipped in a container, a kanban is returned to the supplier when the container is opened, initiating the shipment of a second container that arrives just as the first container is emptied.

Leader-member relations The degree of confidence, trust, and respect subordinates have in their leader.

Leadership The ability to influence a group toward the achievement of goals.

Leading Directing and coordinating people.

Learning curve Learning begins with a steep rise, then increases at a decreasing rate until a plateau is reached.

Leniency error The tendency to appraise a set of employees too high (positive) or too low (negative).

Lifelong learning The need to continually upgrade skills through reading, seminars, and formal education.

Line authority The authority that entitles a supervisor to direct the work of his or her direct reports and to make certain decisions without consulting others.

Lockout A company action equivalent to a strike; when management denies unionized employees access to their jobs.

Locus of control The degree to which people believe they are masters of their own fate.

Long-term plans Plans covering more than five years.

Machiavellianism Degree to which an individual is manipulative and believes ends can justify means.

Majority vote Agreement to a decision by at least 51 percent of a group's members.

Management The process of getting things done, effectively and efficiently, through and with others.

Management by objectives (MBO) A system in which subordinates jointly determine specific performance objectives with their superiors, progress toward objectives is periodically reviewed, and on the basis of which rewards are allocated.

Management competencies General categories of skills necessary to successfully perform a managerial job.

Management functions Planning, organizing, leading, and controlling.

Management information system (MIS) A mechanism to provide managers with needed and accurate information on a regular and timely basis.

Management process The four managerial functions of planning, organizing, leading, and controlling.

Marginal analysis Analyzing decisions in terms of their incremental costs.

Matrix A structural design that assigns specialists from functional departments to work on one or more projects that are led by a project manager.

Matrix assessment Sets up a comparison between alternatives based on weighted criteria.

Mature workers A group of workers born prior to 1946 who are security-oriented and have a committed work ethic.

Mediation An impasse-resolution technique where a mediator attempts to pull together the common ground that exists, and makes settlement recommendations for overcoming the barriers that exist between two sides in a conflict.

Mentors Senior employees who tutor, coach, counsel, and guide less experienced associates.

Middle managers All employees below the top-management level who manage other managers.

Minority vote Decision-making power held by a sub-group of a larger group.

Motivation The willingness to do something; is conditioned by this action's ability to satisfy some need for the individual.

Motivation-hygiene theory Intrinsic factors are related to job satisfaction, while extrinsic factors are associated with dissatisfaction.

Need A physiological or psychological deficiency that makes certain outcomes seem attractive.

Need for achievement The need to do things better or more efficiently than they have been done before.

Negative discipline The supervisor identifies employee performance problems and initiates sanctions to correct them.

Negotiation A process in which two or more parties exchange goods or services and attempt to agree upon the exchange rate for them.

Networking Developing contacts (could be in organization, industry, community) for potential use in future.

Nominal group technique A group decision technique in which all members are present but operate independently.

Nonverbal communications Communication that sends messages without words.

Normal distribution Variations are assumed to follow a bell-shaped distribution curve.

Norms Acceptable standards of behaviour within a group that are shared by the group's members.

Off-the-job training Training that takes place outside the direct work area.

On-the-job training Training that places employees in actual work situations.

Operative employees Rank-and-file workers who physically produce an organization's goods and services.

Organization A systematic grouping of people brought together to accomplish some specific purpose.

Organizational culture A shared perception of the organization's values.

Organizing Arranging and grouping jobs, allocating resources, and assigning work in a department so that activities can be accomplished as planned.

Orientation An expansion on information a new employee obtained during the recruitment and selection stages; an attempt to familiarize new employees with the job, the work unit, and the organization as a whole.

Pareto charts Simple bar charts that rank causes of a problem by their quantity over a certain time.

Participative leadership The leadership style of an individual who actively seeks input from followers for many of the activities in the organization.

Passive listening Absorbing information as it is literally transmitted.

Path-goal theory The leader's job is to assist followers in overcoming obstacles in the way of attaining their goals by providing the proper leadership style.

Pay-for-performance programs Compensation plans that pay employees on the basis of some performance measure.

People-centred leaders Emphasize good interpersonal relations.

Performance appraisal An evaluation and development tool. Involves reviewing past performance to identify accomplishments and deficiencies, and creating detailed plans to improve future performance.

PERT chart A technique for scheduling complex projects.

Planning Defining objectives and the means for attaining them.

Policies Broad guidelines for managerial action.

Political competence A supervisor's ability to enhance his or her power, build a power base, and establish the "right" connections in the organization.

Politicking The actions you can take to influence, or attempt to influence, the distribution of advantages and disadvantages within your organization.

Polychronicity The degree to which a person prefers doing two or more things simultaneously.

Position power The degree of influence a leader has over factors such as hiring, firing, discipline, promotions, and salary increases.

Positive discipline A technique that attempts to reinforce the good work behaviours of an employee, while simultaneously emphasizing to the employee the problems created by undesirable performance.

Preventive control Controls that anticipate and prevent undesirable outcomes.

Problem A discrepancy between an existing and a desired state of affairs.

Procedure A series of steps for responding to a recurring problem.

Process departmentalization Grouping activities on the basis of product or customer flow.

Product departmentalization Grouping activities by product line.

Program A single-use set of plans for a specific major undertaking.

Programmed instruction Individuals learn a small block of information and are then tested immediately to see if the material has been understood.

Progressive discipline Action that begins with a verbal warning, and then proceeds through written reprimands, suspension, and finally, in the most serious cases, dismissal.

Quality Defined as what the customer says the term means.

Quality control Identification of mistakes that may have occurred; monitoring quality to ensure that it meets some preestablished standard.

Range of variation The degree of acceptable variation between actual performance and the standard.

Readiness The ability and willingness of an employee to complete a task.

Realistic Job Preview Information given to job applicant during hiring process which includes both positive and negative information about the job and company; it creates realistic expectations.

Recency error The tendency for evaluators to recall and give greater importance to employee job behaviours that have occurred near the end of the performance-measuring period.

Reengineering Radical or quantum change that occurs when most of the work being done in an organization is evaluated, and then altered. Reengineering requires organizational members to rethink what work should be done, how it is to be done, and how to best implement these decisions.

Reinforcement theory People will exert higher levels of effort in tasks that are reinforced.

Reject errors Rejecting candidates who would later perform successfully on the job.

Reliability The ability of a selection device to measure the same thing consistently.

Response time Responding to requests, demands, and problems initiated by others.

Responsibility An obligation to perform assigned activities.

Richness of information A measure of the amount of information that is transmitted based on multiple information cues (words, posture, facial expressions, gestures, intonations), immediate feedback, and the personal touch.

Rights view of ethics Decisions emphasize respecting and protecting the basic rights of individuals.

Risk propensity The degree to which people are willing to take chances.

Role ambiguity A situation where role expectations are not clearly understood and the employee is not sure what he or she is to do.

Role conflicts Situations in which individuals are confronted by divergent role expectations.

Role overload Situations where an employee is expected to do more than time permits.

Roles Behaviour patterns that go with the position one occupies in the organization.

Rule An explicit statement that tells a manager what he or she ought or ought not to do.

Run charts The results of a process plotted over a period of time.

Scatter diagrams Illustrate the relationship between two variables.

Scheduling Determining what activities have to be done, the order they are to be done in, who is to do each, and when they are to be completed.

Self-efficacy Belief in one's ability to tackle events successfully.

Self-esteem The degree to which individuals like or dislike themselves.

Self-monitoring A personality trait that measures an individual's ability to adjust his or her behaviour to external, situational factors. High self-monitors are adaptable in adjusting their behaviour to external situational factors, and are capable of presenting striking contradictions between public personas and private selves. Low self-monitors tend to display their true feelings and beliefs in every situation.

Sexual harassment Sexually suggestive remarks, unwanted touching and sexual advances, requests for sexual favours, and other verbal and physical conduct of a sexual nature.

Short-term plans Plans that are less than one year in length.

Similarity error Giving special consideration when rating others to those qualities that the evaluator perceives in himself or herself.

Simple structure A non-elaborate structure low in complexity, with little formalization, and with authority centralized in a single person; a "flat" organization with only two or three levels.

Single-use plans Detailed courses of action used once or only occasionally.

Situational leadership A leadership model that emphasizes adjusting the leader's communication style to the readiness or maturity of the subordinates.

Skill The ability to demonstrate a system and sequence of behaviour that is functionally related to attainment of a performance goal.

Skill variety The degree to which the job requires a variety of different activities so the worker can use a number of different skills and talents.

Social loafing The tendency of group members to do less than they are capable of individually when their individual contribution is not measured.

Social network analysis A process of graphically mapping social interactions to identify meaningful patterns.

Span of control The number of subordinates a supervisor can direct efficiently and effectively.

Spillover effect Successes made by unions at the negotiating table influence the wages, working conditions, and terms of employment for workers who are not unionized.

Staff authority A limited authority that supports line authority by advising, servicing, and assisting.

Standard deviation A measure of variability in a group of numerical values.

Standing plans Plans used over and over again for recurring activities.

Status A social rank or the importance one has in a group.

Strategic planning Covering the entire organization, it establishes overall goals and positions the organization's products or services against the competition.

Stress An adaptive response resulting from any environmental action, situation, or event that places excessive psychological and/or physical demands on a person.

Strike Employees leave their jobs and refuse to come to work until a contract has been signed.

Supervisors First-level managers who oversee the work of operatives or nonmanagement employees.

Supervisory competencies Conceptual, interpersonal, technical, and political capabilities.

Suspension Time off without pay; this disciplinary step is usually taken only if neither verbal nor written warnings have achieved desired results.

Tactical planning Specific plans on how overall goals are to be achieved.

Task identity The degree to which the job requires completion of a whole and identifiable piece of work.

Task significance The degree to which the job has a substantial impact on the lives or work of other people.

Task structure The degree to which job assignments are structured and procedurized.

Task-centred leaders Leaders who emphasize the technical or task aspects of the employee's job.

Team A workgroup whose members are committed to a common purpose, have a set of specific performance goals, and hold themselves mutually accountable for the team's results.

Team discipline Discipline is imposed by group control rather than supervisory control.

Technical competence The ability to apply specialized knowledge or expertise.

Telecommuting The linking by computer and modem of workers at home with coworkers and management at an office.

Test-retest method Evaluating training effectiveness by giving participants a test before training begins, a test after training is complete, and assessing the difference in test scores.

Theory X–Theory Y Two diametrically-opposed views on human nature. Theory X assumes people are essentially lazy, irresponsible, and lacking ambition; Theory Y assumes people are hard-working, committed, and responsible.

Time management A personal form of scheduling; maximizing the allocation of the use of time.

Top management The highest level of management. Those people responsible for establishing the organization's overall objectives and developing the policies to achieve those objectives.

Top-down budgeting Budgets that are initiated, controlled, and directed by top management.

Total quality management (TQM) A philosophy of management that is driven by the constant attainment of customer satisfaction through the continuous improvement of all organizational processes.

Traditional career path A sequence of management positions with increasing responsibilities; characterized by relative predictability, upward vertical movement, and the organization taking responsibility for employee career development.

Traditional objective setting Objectives are set at the top and then broken down into subgoals for each level in the organization.

Training Learning experience that results in a relatively permanent change in an individual that improves his or her ability to perform on the job.

Traits Specific characteristics held by individuals that allow them to effectively lead others.

Transactional leaders Leaders who guide or motivate their employees in the direction of established goals by clarifying role and task requirements.

Transformational leaders Leaders who inspire followers to transcend self-interests for the good of the organization and who are capable of having a profound and extraordinary effect on their followers.

Trust Team members believe in the integrity, character, and ability of each other.

Type A behaviour Aggressive involvement in a chronic, incessant struggle to achieve more and more in less and less time.

Type B behaviour Rarely harried by the desire to obtain a wildly increasing number of things or participate in an endlessly growing series of events in an ever-decreasing amount of time.

Union An organization that represents workers and seeks to protect their interests through collective bargaining.

Union shop Requires that employees must join the union.

Union steward An employee who is the elected representative of the employees in a work unit, and is there to protect the rights of the union members.

Unity of command The principle that a subordinate should have one and only one superior to whom he or she is directly responsible.

Utilitarian view of ethics Decisions are based solely on the basis of their outcomes; the goal is to provide the greatest good for the greatest number.

Validity The proven relationship that exists between a selection device and some relevant criterion.

Variable charts Measure a characteristic on a continuous scale.

Verbal intonation The emphasis someone gives to words or phrases.

Vestibule training Employees learn their jobs on the equipment they will be using, but away from the actual work floor.

Wellness programs Any type of program that is designed to keep employees healthy, focusing on such things as smoking cessation, weight control, stress management, physical fitness, nutrition education, high blood-pressure control, and so on.

Wildcat strike An illegal strike where employees refuse to work during the term of a binding contract.

Work sampling A selection device in which job applicants are presented with a miniature replica of a job and are asked to perform tasks central to that job.

Workforce diversity The increasing heterogeneity of organizations with the inclusion of different groups.

Work specialization Also known as division of labour. The process of breaking down a job into a number of steps, with each step being completed by a separate individual.

Written essay A performance appraisal technique in which an evaluator writes out a description of an employee's strengths, weaknesses, past performance, and potential and then makes suggestions for improvement.

Written warning The first formal stage of the disciplinary procedure; the warning becomes part of an employee's official personnel file.

Wrongful discharge Improper or unjust termination of an employee.

Zero-base budget A budget that makes no reference to previous appropriations; all items must be justified.

INDEX

A

absolute standards performance measurements, 274-276
  behaviourally-anchored rating scales (BARS), 276
  checklists, 274
  graphic rating scales, 274-276
  written essays, 274
accept errors, 241
accident prevention, 100-101
accommodation, 461
accountability, 210
active listening, 441-446
activities, in PERT chart, 58
advertisements, 235-236
age groupings, 31-33
agency shop, 562
analytic style of decision making, 139
application forms, 242-243
appraisal training, 286
apprenticeship, 315-316
arbitration, 572
arbitrator, 575
assertiveness training, 434-435
assignment of responsibility, 210
attendance problems, 534
authority, 180-183
  and responsibility, 182
  centralized, 182-183
  decentralized, 182-183
  delegation of, 210
  line, 180
  functional, 180-182
  staff, 180
autocratic leader, 389
autonomy, 367
avoidance, 460-461

B

baby-boomers, 31
baby-busters, 31
background investigations, 245
bargaining unit, 566
behavioural control devices, 103
behavioural style of decision making, 139
behavioural symptoms of stress, 515-516

behavioural-based interviewing, 246-248
behavioural-based performance measures, 283-284
behaviourally anchored rating scales (BARS), 276-277
body language, 421
brainstorming, 155
budgeting, 111-116
budgets, 55
  incremental, 112-113
  zero-base, 112-113
  top-down, 113-114
  bottom-up, 113-114
  process of, 114-115
bureaucracy, 192

C

cause-effect (fishbone) diagrams, 135
central tendency error, 281-282
centralized authority, 182-183
challenges of supervisors, 25-35
change, 35, 492-509
  agent, 501
  changing perspectives on, 501-503
  assessing comfort with, 497-500
  forces for, 495-496
  managing, 492-509
  process, 501
  reducing resistance to, 507-509
  resistance to, 503-506
changing expectations of supervisors, 25-28
changing size or restructuring, 28-29
charisma, 384
charismatic leaders, 384-385
Charter of Rights and Freedoms, 564
checklist (in performance appraisal), 274
coach, 27
coaching, 316-318, 328-330
cognitive learning, 323
collaboration, 461-462
collective bargaining, 564-568
  and discipline, 543-544
  definition, 567
collectivism, 32
communication, 415-446
  active listening, 441-446
  and supervisors, 423-424

  barriers to, 424-430
  body language in, 421
  definition, 417
  differences as source of conflict, 458
  differences in cultures, 433
  electronic, 418-420
  gender differences in, 419
  improving, 430-438
  media, 427-428
  methods of, 417-423
competencies, 17-19
  technical, 17
  interpersonal, 17-18
  conceptual, 18
  political, 19
  and managerial level, 19-20
compromise, 461
conceptual competencies, 18
conceptual skills, 386-387
conceptual style of decision making, 139
conciliation, 572
concurrent controls, 92
conflict, 461-491
  benefits, 463-464
  collaboration, 461-462
  compromise, 461
  definition, 457
  resolution of, 460-467
  sources of, 458-459
  stimulation of, 467-469
  techniques for managing, 453-463
confronting, 435-437
consensus, 150
consultative–participative leadership, 389
contract workers, 33-35
contract administration, 568, 570-571
control:
  by exception, 105
  characteristics of effective, 103-105
  charts, 88-90
  concurrent, 92
  control devices and ethics, 110
  corrective, 93
  focus of, 93-103
  negative outcomes of, 105-107
  preventive, 91-92
  types of, 91-93
control process, 83-86

controlling, 9, 92-103
  costs, 93-95
  employee performance, 101-103
  inventories, 95-96
  quality, 96-98
  safety, 98-101
corrective control 93
costs, 93-95
cost categories, 94
cost-reduction programs, 94
counselling employees, 294-298
creative problem solving, 159-165
  characteristics of, 163
  stimulating, 164-165
credibility and leadership, 401
critical incidents, 274
critical path (on PERT chart), 58
cultural variables, 32-33
  individualism vs. collectivism, 32
  power distance, 32
  uncertainty avoidance, 32-33
  quantity vs. quality of life, 32-33
culture, organizational, 473-474
  and politics, 473-478
customer departmentalization, 187

D

decentralized authority, 183
decision:
  by authority after discussion,
    150-151
  by expert, 149
  by minority, 149
  trees, 130-131
decision tools, 129-137
  cause-and-effect diagrams, 135
  decision trees, 130-131
  expected value analysis, 129-130
  gap analysis, 133
  management information systems,
    135-137
  marginal analysis, 132
  matrix assessments, 133-135
decision-making, 122-165
  ethics in, 143-147
  group, 147-151
  process, 125-129
  styles, 138-142
delegation, 208-215
  of authority, 210
  process, 210
delphi technique, 156
democratic-participative leadership,
  349
departmentalization, 184-194
  customer, 187-188
  functional, 185
  geographic, 186-187
  matrix, 189-191

  process, 188-189
  product, 186
designing jobs, 365-370
developing employees, 306-331
  vs. training, 324-325
devils advocate, 469
directive style of decision making, 139
discipline, 530-557
  and dismissal, 533
  and due process, 542
  and suspension, 533
  and the law, 542-544
  and unionization, 543-544
  and verbal warnings, 533
  and written warnings, 533
  basic tenets of, 536-539
  definition, 532
  factors to consider in, 540-542
  hot stove rule, 538
  how to, 545-552
  principles, 545-552
  process, 532
  progressive, 537-538
  types of problems in, 534-536
  when not suitable, 536
discretionary time, 63
dishonesty, and discipline, 534
dismissal, 533
  with just cause, 543
  with reasonable compensation, 543
  with reasonable notice, 543
distance learning, 322
distributive bargaining, 480
diversity, workforce, 31-34
  and motivation, 359-360
  training, 325-326
diversity training, 325-326
division of labour, 176-177
documentation of employee
    performance, 283
downsizing, 28
dual chain of command, 201
due process, 542

E

effectiveness, 8
efficiency, 8
E-learning, 322
electronic communications, 418-420
electronic meetings, 150-151
E-mail, 420
  improper use, 535
emotional intelligence, 18, 35
emotions as barrier to
    communication, 430
empathy, 433-434
employee counselling, 288-292
employee development, 306-331
employee discipline, 531-557

employee referrals, 236-237
employee relations, 558-586
employee selection, 240-248
employee stock ownership plans
    (ESOPS), 363
employee training, 302-331
employment agencies, 237
employment equity, 228-229
empowerment, 208, 399-400
equal employment opportunities,
    225-230
equal pay for work of equal
    value, 496
equity theory, 351-352
ERG theory, 344-345
ethical decision guide, 147
ethical dilemmas, 36
ethics and control, 110
ethics and counselling, 291-292
ethics and decision-making, 143-147
  common rationalizations, 143-144
  three different views, 144-146
events (in PERT charts), 58
expectancy theory, 352-353
expected value analysis, 129-130
experiential learning, 323
expert decision making, 150
extrinsic feedback, 269

F

fact-finding, 572
feedback,
  360 degree, 18, 285
  as job characteristic, 367
  extrinsic, 269
  how to give effective, 438-440
  in communication, 433-434
  in job design, 367
  intrinsic, 269
  lack of, 426
  negative, 438
  positive, 438
  timing, 439
first-level managers, 7
  and relevant competencies, 19-20
fish-bone diagrams, 135
flow charts, 87-89
forcing, 461
formal planning, 50
free-reign leader, 389
functional authority, 180-182
functional departmentalization,
    185-186
functions of management, 7-9

G

Gantt chart, 56-57, 96

Gap analysis, 133
Generation Xers, 31
geographic departmentalization, 186-187
goal-setting, 60-62, 69-73, 352, 355
    in MBO, 62
    self-assessment, 69-70
goals, 60-62
    characteristics of good, 61
grapevine, 422-423
graphic rating scales, 274-278
grievance,
    handling, 574-579
    procedures, 576
    self-assessment in handling, 574-575
group decision making, 147-151
    advantages, 147
    disadvantages, 148
    improving, 155-157
    types of, 149-151
        consensus, 150
        decision by authority after discussion, 150
        decision by expert, 150
        decision by minority vote, 150
        majority vote, 149-150
    when to use, 148-149
group order ranking, 277-278
groupthink, 148
growth, 28-29

H

halo error, 280-281
hierarchy of needs theory, 344
honesty,
    and leadership, 395
    in communications, 428-429
    dismissal for dishonesty, 534
horizontal organizational structures, 193-194
hot stove rule, 538-539
human relation skills, 387-388
human resource department and supervisors, 225
human resource planning, 231-232
human rights legislation, 227-228
hygiene factors, 346

I

individual differences in motivation, 354-355
individual ranking, 278
individualism, 32
industrial sector training, 321-322
inflationary pressures, 282
influencing, and leadership, 378, 380

in-house training specialists, 310
integrative bargaining, 480-482
intelligence, and leadership, 382
interest arbitration, 572
intermediate-term plans, 51
internal search, 235
interpersonal competence, 17-18
interpersonal demands and stress, 512
interviewing, 244-245, 246-248, 253-255
intrinsic feedback, 269
inventory, 95-96
ISO, 97-98
issues in training and development, 474-476

J

job candidates, recruiting, 231-235
job characteristics, 366-367
    autonomy, 367
    feedback, 367
    skill variety, 367
    task identity, 367
    task significance, 367
job descriptions, 296-297
job design 365-370
job enrichment, 367-368
    self-assessment of responsiveness to, 365-366
job rotation, 319
job specifications, 232-233
justice view of ethics, 144-146
just-in-time (JIT) inventory system, 95-96

K

key supervisory skills, 23
key supervisory tasks, 10

L

labour legislation, 563-564
language, as communication barrier, 425
leader,
    autocratic, 389
    becoming a, 385-386
    charismatic, 378-379
    consultative-participative, 389
    democratic-consultative, 390
    free-reign, 389
    lack of, 379-380
    participative, 389
    people-centred, 389
    task-centred, 389

vs. supervisor, 379
leading, 8
leadership, 376-407
    and employee characteristics, 392-393
    and empowerment, 399
    and national culture, 396
    and stress, 512
    behaviours and styles, 388-390
    charismatic, 384-385
        credibility and trust, 395-397
    Fiedler's theory of, 391-392
        in men and women, 400
    path-goal theory of, 386-387
    situational, 393-394
    situational models of, 393-394
    skills of, 370-401
    traits of, 381-383
    transactional, 401-402
    transformational, 401-402
leaders and supervisors, 379
leading function, 8
learning curve, 313
learning guidelines, 312-314
legislation
    human rights, 237-228
    labour, 563-564
    safety, 98-100
leniency error, 280
line authority, 180
listening, active, 441-446
listening, passive, 442
listening habits, as communication barrier, 426
listening skills, 431-434, 441-446
lockout, 571
locus of control, 341-342
logical consequences, 317-318
long-term plans, 51
low-pay service workers, motivating, 361

M

Machiavellianism, 342
majority vote, 143-144
management, 7, 24
    competencies, 17-29
        conceptual, 18
        interpersonal, 17-18
        political, 19
        technical, 17
        variation in demand with level, 19-20
    functions, 7-9
        controlling, 9
        leading, 8
        organizing, 8
        planning, 8
    levels, 6-7

and competencies, 19-20
linking, 51
management by objectives
    (MBO), 62
management information systems,
    135-137
management levels
  and competencies, 19-20
  and planning, 50-51
  linking, 51
managing diversity, 31-34
managing technology, 29-30
marginal analysis, 132
Maslow's hierarchy of needs
    theory, 344
matrix assessments, 133-135
matrix structure, 189-191
mature workers, 31
measurement tools, 86-90
  cause-and-effect diagrams, 86-87
  control charts, 88, 90
  flow charts, 86-89
  scatter diagrams, 88, 90
measuring performance, 84
mediation, 578
medium, choice of, 427-428
meetings, conducting, 152-157
meetings, overcoming obstacles, 154
mentoring, 318
middle managers, 6
minority vote, 150
money as motivator, 358-359
motivation, 340-370
  and employee stock ownership
      plans (ESOPs), 363
  and individual differences/
      personality, 354-355
  and pay-for-performance
      programs, 362-363
  and the design of jobs, 365-370
  applying concepts of, 354-359
  challenges, 359-363
  contemporary theories of, 348-353
    equity theory, 351-352
    expectancy theory, 352-353
    goal setting, 352
    need for achievement, 348-350
    reinforcement theory, 350
  early approaches to, 343-347
    ERG theory, 344-345
    hierarchy of needs theory,
        343-344
    motivation-hygiene theory,
        346-347
    Theory X-Theory Y, 345-346
  of diversified workforce, 359-360
  of low-pay service workers, 361
  of professionals, 361-362
motivation-hygiene theory, 346-347
multiple raters, 285

N

national culture, and leadership
    style, 396
need, 341
need for achievement, 348-350
needs,
  and motivation, 348-350
  assessment for employee training,
      309-310
  in hierarchy of needs theory, 343
negotiation, 479, 567-568, 570
  and supervisors, 570
  becoming more effective in,
      482-483
  distributive bargaining in, 480
  integrative bargaining in, 481
  preparation for, 567-568
  self-assessment of understanding,
      479-480
networking, 387, 404-407
nominal group technique, 155
nonverbal communication, 421-422

O

occupational health and safety
    legislation, 98-100
off-site employees, 30
off-the-job training, 319-322
  industrial sector training, 321-322
  outside reading, 321
  programmed instruction, 321
  seminars, conferences, 320-321
  vestibule training, 320
  web-based learning, distance
      learning, 322
on-the-job behaviours as discipline
    problems, 528
on-the-job training, 314-319
  apprenticeships, 315-316
  coaching, 316-318
  job rotation, 319
  mentoring, 318-319
  simulation training, 315
operative employees, 6, 11
oral communication, 417-418
organization, 5
  characteristics of, 6
organizational culture, 473-476
  and politics, 473-476
organizational politics, 470-478
  inevitability of, 472
  ethics of, 472-473
organizational structure, 175-194
  and stress, 511-512
  customer, 187-188
  functional, 185-186
  geography, 186-187

horizontal, 193-194
  matrix, 189-191
  process, 188-189
  product, 186
  simple, 192
organizing, 8, 175-176
  as a function of management, 8
  basic concepts, 176-183
    centralized vs. decentralized
        authority, 182-183
    division of labour, 176-177
    equating authority and
        responsibility, 182
    line, staff and functional
        authority, 180-182
    span of control, 177-179
    unity of command, 180
  defined, 175-176
orientation, 248-250
outside activities, as discipline
    problems, 536
outside trainers, 311

P

Paraphrasing, 444, 462
Parkinson's Law, 67
participation:
  as motivator, 355-356
  by employee in performance
      reviews, 295
  in change programs to reduce
      resistance, 508
  in goal setting, 70, 71
participative leader, 389
path-goal theory of leadership,
    392-393
pay-for performance programs,
    362-363
people-centred leader, 389
perception differences
  as a source of stress, 514
  as a communication barrier, 426
  between supervisors and
      subordinates, 102
performance appraisal, 264-297
  absolute standards measurements,
      274-276
  criteria, 271-272
    behaviours, 272
    individual task outcomes, 272
    traits, 272
  conducting, 293-299
  documentation, 283
  formal reviews, 265
  hurdles in, 280-282
  improving, 284-286
  informal appraisals, 265
  interview, 293-299

legal issues in, 270
methods of, 273-279
multiple raters in, 276-277
overcoming hurdles, 282-286
potential problems in, 280-282
central tendency errors, 281-282
halo errors, 280-281
inflationary pressures, 282
leniency errors, 280
recency errors, 281
similarity errors, 281
purpose of, 264-265
supervisor's role in, 265-270
team, 286-288
timing, 265
performance-based compensation, 362-363
performance measurement, 84-90
cause and effect diagrams, 85, 86
control charts, 88, 90
flow charts, 86-88
scatter diagrams, 87-88
sources of information, 84
oral reports, 84
personal observation, 84
statistical reports, 84
written reports, 84
what is measured, 93-102
personal differences, as a source of conflict, 459
personality characteristics, and stress, 512
PERT chart, 57-58, 96
activities, 58
critical path, 58
events, 58
physical examinations, and employee selection, 245
physiological symptoms of stress, 515
plans
single-use, 52-54
budgets, 55
programs, 54-55
schedules, 56-58
standing, 52-54
policies, 52-53
procedures, 53-54
rules, 54
planning, 8, 49-62
breadth, 49-51
formal, 50
key guides,
linkages in organizational levels, 51
single-use plans, 54-58
standing plans, 57-58
time frame, 51
playing favourites, 390, 388
policies, 52-53
political competence, 19
assessment, 21-22

politicking, 471
politics, organizational, 470-478
and organizational culture, 473-476
becoming politically smart, 475-477
ethics of, 472-473
why inevitable, 472
polychronicity, 67
potential team, 200
power, 474-475
gaining, 475-476
power distance, 32
preventive control, 91-92
problem-solving and decision-making, 122-165
procedures, 53-54
process departmentalization, 188
process mapping, 87-89
product departmentalization, 186
professionals, motivating, 361-362
programmed instruction, 321
programs, 54-55
pseudoteam, 200
psychological symptoms of stress, 515
pyramid, organizational, 6

Q

quality control, 96-98
quality of life, 32-33
quantity of life, 32-33

R

range of variation, 85
readiness, employee, 393
realistic job preview, 251
recency error, 281
recruiting, 235-340
advertisements, 235-236
casual or unsolicited applicants, 239
employee referrals, 236-237
employment agencies, 237
internal search, 235
professional organizations, 239
schools, colleges, universities, 238
unemployment centres and agencies, 239
referrals, employee, 236-237
reinforcement theory, 350
reject errors, 240
relative standards performance measurements, 277-279
group order ranking, 277
individual ranking, 278
reliability, 241-242
resistance to change, 503-506
overcoming, 507-509

reasons for, 503-506
fear of the unknown, 504
habits, 503
selective perception, 505
threats to job or income, 504
threat to established power relationship, 505
threat to expertise, 505
threat to interpersonal relationships, 506
resistance to controls, 105-106
response time, 63
responsibility, 182
restructuring, 29
rewards, 356-358
checking for equity in, 358
individualizing, 358
linking to performance, 357
richness of information, 428
rights view of ethics, 151
risk analysis, 138-139
risk propensity, 343
role ambiguity, 25, 511
role conflicts, 511
role demands, 511
role overload, 511
role requirements, 427
role-reversal technique, 462-463
rules, 54

S

safety, 98-101
accident prevention, 100-101
occupational health and safety legislation, 98-100
scatter diagrams, 88, 90
scheduling, 56-58
Gantt chart, 56-57
PERT chart, 57-58
selection, 240-248
devices, 242-245
application form, 242
background investigations, 245
interviews, 244-245
performance simulation tests, 244
physical exams, 245
written tests, 242-243
self-assessment,
active listening, 441-442
budgeting, 111
coaching, 328
conducting an appraisal interview, 293
coping with work-related change, 497-500
creativity, 153-157
decision making, 136-138
delegation, 208-209
disciplining, 545-546

goal setting, 68-70
handling conflicts, 465-466
handling grievances, 574-575
identifying stressful events, 517-519
interviewing, 253-254
job enrichment, 365-366
negotiation, 479-480
networking, 404-405
political competence, 21-22
self-confidence, and leadership, 383
self-efficacy, 520
self-esteem, 342
self-evaluations, in performance appraisals, 295-296
self-monitoring, 342
setting goals, 60-62, 69-73
sexual harassment, 229-230
short-term plans, 51
similarity error, 281
simple organizational structure, 192-193
simulation training, 315
single-use plans, 54-58
  budgets, 55
  programs, 54-55
  schedules, 56-58
situational leadership, 393-394
situational models of leadership, 391-394
skill, 23
skill variety, 373
social loafing, 202
span of control, 177-179
specialization, 176-177
spillover effects, 561
staff authority, 180
standing plans, 52-54
  policies, 52-53
  procedures, 53-54
  rules, 54
statistics, 84
strategic human resource planning, 231-232
  current assessment, conducting, 231
  future assessment, 231
  future programs, developing, 232
strategic planning, 49
stress, 509-523
  assessment of quantity, 513-514
  companies' action on, 516
  definition of, 510
  identifying stressful events, 517-518
  reduction, 517-523
  sources of, 510-515
  symptoms of, 515-516
strike, 571

structural differentiation, as source of conflict, 459
supervisors, 7
  and the human resource department, 225
  and the union steward, 571
  as coach, 27
  challenges of being, 25-35
  changing expectations of, 25-28
  competencies of, 17-19
  increased importance of, 26
  pros and cons of being, 14-17
  reengineering and, 33-34
  role ambiguity of, 25
  sources of, 10-12
  surprises in becoming, 12-13
  transition from employee to, 10, 12-14
supervisory competencies, 17-19
  and management level, 19-20
  conceptual, 18
  interpersonal, 17-18
  political, 19
  technical, 17
supervisory skills, 23
supervisory tasks, 10
suspension, 533

T

tactical planning, 49-51
task-centred leadership, 388
task demands and stress, 511
task identity, 317
task significance, 317
teams, 198-205
  characteristics of effective, 200-202
  overcoming obstacles in, 202-205
  potential, 200
  types of, 199-200
  vs. working groups, 199
  why used, 198
team performance appraisals, 286-288
technical,
  competence, 17
  skills, 388
technology, 29-30
telecommuting, 178
Theory X-Theory Y, 345-346
timeliness, and control systems, 106
time management, 63-68
  steps to better, 64-65
top-down vs. bottom-up budgeting, 119-120
top management, 6
  and competencies, 19-20
Total Quality Management (TQM), 96-97

trainers:
  in-house, 310
  outside, 311
training, 308-331
  assessing needs for, 309-310
  allocating responsibilities, 310-311
  designing programs for, 311-314
  evaluating effectiveness of, 324
  issues in, 325-326
  learning guidelines, 312-314
  matching to objectives, 322-323
  methods, 314-322
  off-the-job, 319-322
  on-the-job, 314-319
  versus employee development, 324-325
traits, leadership, 381-383
transactional leaders, 401-402
transformational leaders, 401-402
trust, 395-397
  building, 398
Type A/Type B, 515

U

uncertainty avoidance, 32-33
union, 561
  shop, 562
  steward, 571
  why employees join a, 561-562
unionization and discipline, 543-544
unity of command, 180
utilitarian view of ethics, 144-146

V

validity, 241
verbal intonations, 421
verbal warnings, 533
vestibule training, 320

W

warnings
  verbal, 533
  written, 533
wildcat strike, 572
work sampling, 244
workforce diversity, 31-34
working group, 199-200
workplace safety, 98-101
  accident prevention, 100-101
  occupational health and safety legislation, 98-100
written communication, 417
written warning, 533